THE EMBARRASSMENT OF RICHES

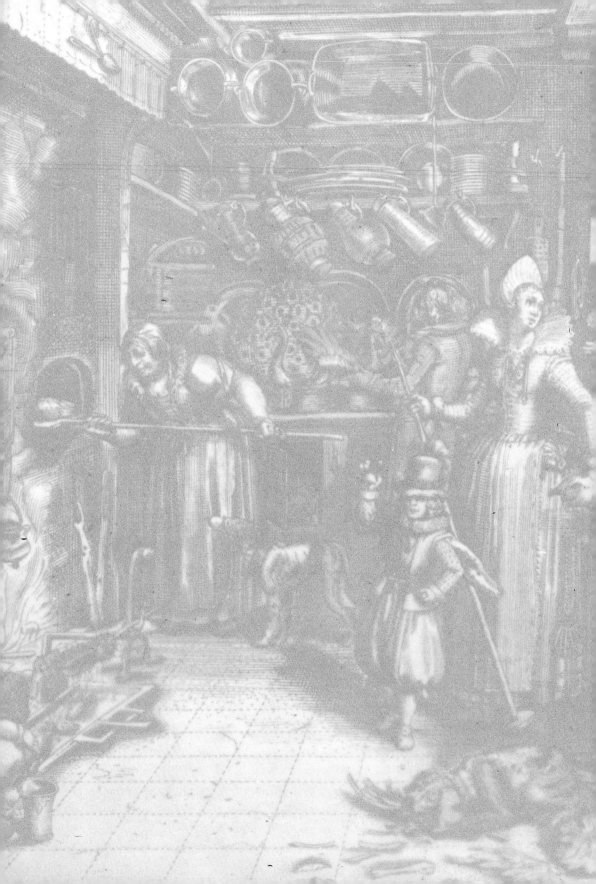

THE

EMBARRASSMENT

OF RICHES

An Interpretation of

Dutch Culture

in the Golden Age

SIMON SCHAMA

FONTANA PRESS

First published in Great Britain
by William Collins Sons and Co Ltd 1987
First published in paperback by Fontana Press 1988
Fontana Press is an imprint of Fontana,
a division of the Collins Publishing Group

Made and printed in the United States of America

Second Printing

For Ginny, with all my heart

"Let those who have abundance remember that they are surrounded with thorns, and let them take great care not to be pricked by them."

John Calvin
Commentary on Genesis
13:5,7

Contents

"I have bin the longer aboutt the discription of this place etts., because there are soe many particularities wherein it differs (and in som excells) allsoe beeing myself somewhat affectionated and enclined to the Manner of the Country."

So wrote the traveler Peter Mundy of his stay in Holland in 1640. I must plead the same excuse but with less exoneration. His account ran to twenty pages, mine to somewhat more. I had not meant the shape of this book to exemplify its thesis: the anxieties of superabundance. And the result is more embarrassing because my own concerns are pretty much the same as Peter Mundy's: the physical and mental bric-a-brac that describe a culture: "dwellings very Costly and Curious, Full of pleasure and home contentment"; as well as pickled whales eyes, catchpenny prints and the Great Tun of Amsterdam. So that when I write of culture I don't mean Culture. There is nothing here about theater or poetry or music, and if there are images in abundance, they are summoned as impressions of mentality, not vessels of Art. What, then, is the Dutch culture offered here? An allegiance that was fashioned as the consequence, not the cause, of freedom, and that was defined by common habits rather than legislated by institutions. It was a manner of sharing a peculiar—very peculiar— space at a particular time, so as to differentiate between a new "us" and an old "them." It formed eventually what Maurice Halbwachs called a "collective memory": the product of the encounter between fresh historical experience and the constraints of geography.

If it is to the inspiration of Halbwachs's social theory that this book owes its point of departure, I have incurred many more pressing debts of gratitude over the long haul of this book's writing. It began as the Erasmus Lectures on the Civilization of the Netherlands in 1978, and I must thank Harvard University for the opportunity to air some very improbable speculations. Since then, many friends and colleagues have been kind enough to comment on their substance and to help me make those rather wild notions a little more respectable. They are certainly not to blame if the whole project remains more eccentric than persuasive. I am especially grateful to Gary and Loekie Schwartz for their friendship, hospitality and enlightenment about things close to the heart of Dutch culture. A number of Dutch art historians have been generous with their time and patience in entertaining my notions, and I hope they will not take it amiss if I thank them for making me feel as much at home in their own discipline as in my own. I want to thank, in particular, Barbara Haeger and Ivan Gaskell, on whom I inflicted many of these preoccupations when they were not much more than hunches, and who helped me think more rigorously about them. Though we have differed on some issues, I owe to Svetlana Alpers a great debt for her constantly stimulating and enriching discussions of Dutch images and her kindness in encouraging my own work. Ann Jensen Adams, Ronni Baer, Christopher Brown, Margaret Carroll, David Freedberg, Egbert Haverkamp-Begemann, Sandra Hindman, Eddy de Jongh, Otto Naumann, Seymour Slive, Peter Sutton and James Welu have all been most kind in sharing their erudition with me and saving me from some of the most egregious blunders in the interpretation of Dutch art. I should also like to thank Benjamin Kaplan and Christopher Wood, whose research on Netherlandish imagery of money helped me to clarify my own speculations on this subject. Frances Gouda has been kind enough to share with me her rich knowledge of Dutch social history and save me from some (not, I fear, all) blunders. Bernard Richards supplied me intriguing cross-cultural references on dirt and cleanliness from English literature.

In the Netherlands, a number of institutions and their custodians were most helpful in providing assistance with prints and rare books. This whole project would have been impossible but for the generosity and thoughtfulness of the late Meyer Elte, antiquariaat extraordinary of The Hague, who placed his knowledge of popular texts and rare books at my disposal. I am also grateful to Mr. Nix of the Atlas van Stolk, Mej. Isabella van Eeghen of the Gemeente Archief, Amsterdam, J. P. Filedt Kok of the Rijksprentenkabinet and the staff of the department of Oude Drukken in the Koninklijke Bibliotheek, The Hague, for their help. At Harvard, Susan Halpern and the staff of the Houghton Library and Ruth Rogers of the Kress Library, Harvard Business School, have responded with invariable courtesy and resourcefulness to my infuriating habits of demanding the impossible at short notice. It has been one of the great pleasures of this research to observe the Kress collection of prints grow from strength to strength.

I wish also to thank Boyd Hill, Richard Unger, Kent Gerard, Ivan Gaskell and Jan de Vries, for placing unpublished material at my disposal. The Guggenheim Fellowship Foundation made possible research on Hollandophobia and patriotism, and the Lewis and Linda Geyser Foundation provided funds for the completion of work on visual and textual sources in the Netherlands. Christopher Michaels provided invaluable help with the hard labor of obtaining photographs and permissions for which I am most grateful.

To Michael Sissons — friend, agent and guardian angel — I owe my survival as an historical writer. Peter Matson has been a generous and wise counsellor. And I am grateful to Helen Fraser at Collins and Carol Brown Janeway at Knopf for neither giving up, nor, on seeing the manuscript, passing out.

A great many friends and colleagues in my discipline have sustained me over the years in what must have seemed an increasingly improbable endeavor. Sir John Plumb encouraged me to extend my early speculations on the cleanliness fetish in Dutch culture into a more deeply considered account of Dutch behavior. Much of what this book has to say springs from his own illuminating approach to the social history of culture. Robert Darnton has listened patiently and has done his best to make clear water out of turbid mud. At various times, T. J. Clark, John Clive, Peter Gay, Aron Rodrigue, Quentin Skinner, Keith Thomas and Emily Rovetch Whitman have all helped me to think more carefully about the implications of cultural generalizations. I am grateful to the members of the Cambridge Seminar in Early Modern History, and especially to David Harris Sacks, for their enlivening historical fellowship over the past five years of our meetings. The Center for European Studies at Harvard has provided me with the finest intellectual and personal company that an historian could ask for. And it is to John Brewer that I owe the greatest debt: for his intellectual energy, critical imagination and all-weather friendship.

All history tends towards autobiographical confession and I suspect that the centrality of household culture presented in this book owes much to my own witness of family pleasures and adventures. My "other" family, the Slotovers, over many years of dear friendship, have supplied such a bounty of domestic happiness as to make some of the beatitudes of seventeenth-century idealism actually plausible. My children, Chloë and Gabriel, have provided me with more insight into the hectic world of childhood than is to be gained from the archives. The joy of my own family history throughout this project is altogether the creation of my beloved wife, Ginny. Even a big book seems a paltry offering for the daily riches of her companionship.

LEXINGTON, MASSACHUSETTS, 1986

THE EMBARRASSMENT OF RICHES

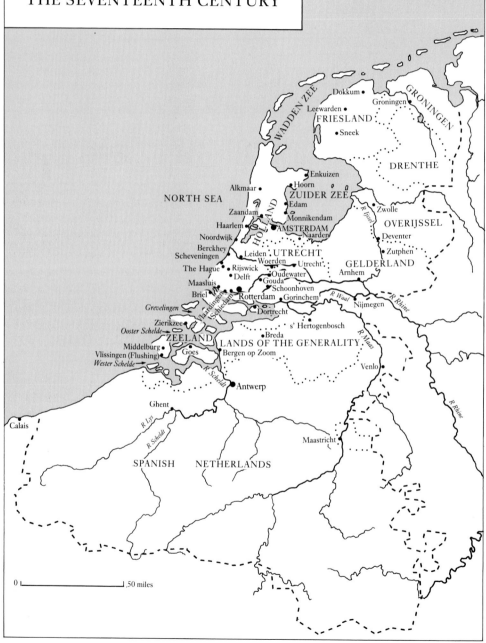

THE NETHERLANDS IN
THE SEVENTEENTH CENTURY

WADDEN ZEE

Dokkum •

Leewarden •   Groningen •   GRONINGEN

FRIESLAND

• Sneek

DRENTHE

• Enkuizen

Alkmaar •   • Hoorn

ZUIDER ZEE

NORTH SEA   • Edam
                   • Monnikendam   Zwolle •
Zaandam •   OVERIJSSEL
Haarlem •   AMSTERDAM
                   • Naarden   Deventer •
Noordwijk •
Berckhey •   Zutphen •
Scheveningen •   Leiden • Woerden   GELDERLAND
The Hague •   • Rijswick • Utrecht   Arnhem •
                   • Delft   Oudewater
Maasluis •   Gouda •
Briel •   Schoonhoven •
                   Rotterdam • Gorinchem   R Waal
                   Vlaardingen Schiedam   Nijmegen R Rhine
Grevelingen •   Dortrecht •
Zierikzee •   • s' Hertogenbosch
Ooster Schelde →   • Breda   R Maas
Middelburg •   ZEELAND LANDS OF THE GENERALITY
Vlissingen (Flushing) • Goes • Bergen op Zoom
Wester Schelde →   Venlo •
                   • Antwerp

Ghent •   R Rhine

Calais •   Maastricht •

R Lys
R Scheldt

SPANISH   NETHERLANDS

HOLLAND
UTRECHT

0 ├─────────────┤ 50 miles

It is the peculiar genius of the Dutch to seem, at the same time, familiar and incomprehensible. Something like this reflection crossed the strenuous mind of Henry James in 1874 as he observed a Dutch housemaid washing the stoop. What ought to have been a banal chore seemed on closer inspection to be a bit odd, even a little compulsive. It was all the odder, since to the casual eye there seemed precious little to expunge. The canal walks were "periodically raked by the broom and the scrubbing brush and religiously manured with soapsuds." But the cleaner any surface seemed the more merciless the scouring it received.

> Where could the speck or two possibly have come from unless produced by spontaneous generation: there are no specks in the road . . . nor on the trees whose trunks are to all appearance carefully sponged every morning. The speck exists evidently only as a sort of mathematical point, capable of extension in the good woman's Batavian brain, and the operation with the copper kettle is, as the metaphysicians would say, purely subjective. It is a necessity, not as regards the house, but as regards her own temperament.[1]

The mysteries of that temperament are the subject of this book of essays. They, too, presuppose that there was more to Dutch behavior than met the casual eye. Together, they attempt to set out the cultural peculiarities of the Dutch in the springtime of their nationality. It is an informal description that says nothing much about institutions or theologies or economic structures. Instead, I have attempted to explore the paradoxes of being Dutch in terms of social beliefs and behavior. So there is a good deal more about pipe smoking and washing the stoop than about the Synod of Dordrecht or the economic origins of the Anglo-Dutch wars. Despite this attention to the commonplace, I have tried to avoid the estrangement between social and political history that belongs more to the historical profession than to historical reality. In the Netherlands (as elsewhere in republican Europe), the two were so intimately related that the ideal of the good family was a miniature of the ideal commonwealth. Above all, I have wanted to discover how the Dutch made themselves up as they went along. What animated their sense of community; what generated their allegiance; what crystallized the set of manners that became recognizably their own?

When I airily refer to the Dutch, the exacting social historian will want me to be more precise. What I really mean, it will be said, is the Dutch elite: that upper crust of the property-owning class who could afford to pass off *their* culture as the national heritage. Some of this is true. What follows is certainly not intended as a history of popular culture if by that is meant the beliefs of the very poor, the illiterate and the vagrant. Documentary attempts to reconstruct the culture of the Dutch underclass are in any case fraught with difficulty, being so heavily dependent on the records of their incrimination. Recent social history in the Netherlands has made an auspicious beginning in this work.[2] But if the culture of this book was not the culture of *all* Dutch men and women, neither was it the property of the very few. It was shared, in large measure, by that very broad stratum of the population between artisans and trading merchants that in England would have been known as "the middling sort"; in Holland the *brede middenstand*. It described a world that was predominantly urban, surprisingly literate for its time; one that nourished a market hungry for prints, engraved histories, poems and polemics. It worked and rested in what, by seventeenth-century standards, was a remarkably stable society. And it was stable in great measure because it was well fed and, most important of all for this overwhelmingly residential culture, decently housed.

This does not mean that what I have to offer may be conveniently classified as bourgeois culture. The argument of the book resists the kind of functionalism that assumes culture to be an outcrop of social class, and that imagines a kind of behavioral segregation in which "elite culture," "popular culture" and "bourgeois culture" arbitrarily inhabit the same space but pass by each other like ships in the night. In the Netherlands, where the contours of class are notoriously difficult to plot, and where culture may not be reduced to an extension of the tax censuses, it makes little sense to make the boundaries between popular and elite too sharp. To whose culture did a Calvinist sermon belong: that of the patrician or the plebeian? Who bought a four-guilder genre painting, or a ten-stuiver print: a scholar or a shopkeeper? Who shared in the cult of patriotic heroes like de Ruyter and Tromp: a merchant or a fisherman? In the same year, 1655, editions of the same work, Jacob Cats's verse marriage

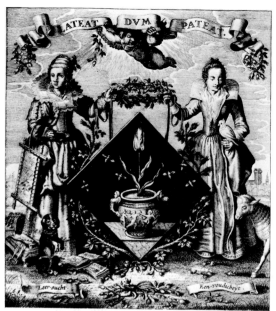

1. Engraved frontispiece of Jacob Cats, *Houwelijck* (Amsterdam, 1655)

2. Woodcut, title page of Jacob Cats, *Houwelijck* (Dordrecht, 1655)

manual, *Houwelijk,* were published in folio with fine engravings for the grand and duodecimo with woodcuts for the humble. Even though the simpler version got its emblems mixed up, assigning "Simplicity" to the puppy and "Aptitude" to the sheep instead of vice versa, the fact of a common text presupposes a reading public not strictly bound by distinctions of class. So that while this is more a history of shapers than of the shaped, I remain unapologetic about the catholicity of its discussion.

My subject is the community of the nation, an entity not supposed to have existed before the French Revolution. But when seventeenth-century writers and preachers speak of their Fatherland, I take them seriously, at least in not supposing the term to be a subterfuge for the interests of class. And an approach that takes patriotism or civism as a unit of cultural community does at least rescue the Netherlands from its ancient stereotype as quintessentially bourgeois. For a long time now, the culture of the Netherlands has languished in this gloomy conceptual dungeon. We are told, in the dancing prose of a recent history, that the Dutch economy was "hegemonic" in its day, and so, inevitably its state "was an essential instrument used by the Dutch bourgeoisie to consolidate an economic hegemony they had won originally in the sphere of production and had then extended to commerce. . . . How," the writer continues, "could there not be a cultural expression of hegemony?"[3] How indeed! Even a historian as expansive and subtle as Huizinga was unable to avoid the deadening cliché that tells us at once too much and not enough.[4] So that when the Dutch have been rescued from quaintness it is to bear witness to the evolving chronicle of European capitalism.[5] Usually they are allotted the role of third-leg baton carrier in the race that took capitalism from medieval merchant venturers through Renaissance banking to the Dutch international staple economy and onwards at a sprint to the finishing line of British industrialization. The questions asked of Dutch history are those of incipience; of might-have-beens. Why did the Dutch act as the commercial incubator but fail to hatch the industrial chicks? (Which is as much to say, why were the Dutch so obstinately themselves?) And all such questions assume, monotonously, that the business of the Dutch was business, and that their politics, religion, even their art somehow all obeyed that iron law. The result is a kind of depressing historical perennialism by which the Dutch, being bourgeois, were whatever the modern mind supposes bourgeois to be. In this social genealogy, the slouch hats on Frans Hals's regents are the lineal ancestors of Daumier's high hats and frock coats. Through that continuity are assumed to run the unmistakable bourgeois addiction to the prosaic, the literal, the frugal—the dispassionate objectification of the world and its reduction of mystery to commodity. It is strange how difficult it is to settle these clichés on a merchant of Venice, but how natural they have appeared in

Holland, as though the alteration from satin to black velour had wrought a kind of social mutation from patrician to bourgeois.

At the center of the Dutch world was a burgher, not a bourgeois. There is a difference, and it is more than a nuance of translation. For the burgher was a citizen first and *homo oeconomicus* second. And the obligations of civism conditioned the opportunities of prosperity. So that if any one obsession linked together their several concerns with family, the fortunes of state, the power of their empire and the condition of their poor, their standing in history and the uncertainties of geography; it was the moral ambiguity of good fortune. Much of what follows in my account turns on the ways they coped with that ambiguity. It is not an original insight, but it is one that has perhaps been left behind in the methodological mud of materialism. Erasmus knew all about it. In his uncharacteristically gentle view of Batavia he wrote:

> If you look at the manners of everyday life, there is no race more open to humanity and kindness or less given to wildness or ferocious behavior. It is a straightforward nature, without treachery or deceit and not prone to any serious vices except, that is, a little given to pleasure, especially to feasting. The reason for this is, I think, the wonderful supply of everything which can tempt one to enjoyment; due partly to the ease of importing goods and partly to the natural fertility of the region . . . intersected as it is by navigable rivers full of fish and abounding in rich pastures. . . . They say that there is no other country which holds so many towns in a small place. . . . if there are few deeply learned scholars, especially in the classics, this may be due to the luxury of life, or it may be that they think more of moral excellence than excellence in scholarship.[6]

Historians are not unlike gold prospectors. When, after years of toil, they finally hit on a precious nugget of evidence, they have a tendency to secrete it away, permitting occasional privileged glimpses while erecting grubstake signs to discourage trespassers. They also like to make much of the unique value of their lucky strike. I am no exception. In trying too hard to suggest the peculiarities of the Dutch world I probably exaggerate its distinctness. I have no doubt at all that those more learned than I in the social history of other seventeenth-century cultures will immediately recognize traits and attitudes that are here shown in their Dutch setting. There is, obviously, a common pool of cultural responses — especially to the Protestant family — from which more than one society drew for its prescriptions. The real particularity of the Dutch world lies not in these individual attitudes or practices, but in the ways in which they became connected in the collective mind. Dutch painters worked with the same pigments as their Italian and Flemish counterparts, but somehow the end result was distinctly different. And it is how that end result came about that concerns me.

For there was something special about the Dutch situation — its fortune and its predicament — that did set it apart from other states and nations in baroque Europe. That something was its precocity. It had become a world empire in two generations; the most formidable economic power stretched across the globe from van Diemen's Land to Novaya Zemlya. But the Dutch were claustrophobic circumnavigators. All that power and stupendous wealth was, in the end, sucked into the cramped space between the Scheldt and the Ems: the swarming *bijenkorf* (beehive) of fewer than two million. The prodigious quality of their success went to their heads, but it also made them a bit queasy. Even their most uninhibited documents of self-congratulation are haunted by the threat of *overvloed,* the surfeit that rose like a cresting flood — a word heavy with warning as well as euphoria. One of the founding patriarchs of Netherlands culture, the humanist Dirck Volkertszoon Coornhert, wrote *The Comedy of the Rich Man,* in which the character Overvloed, in the guise of an abundantly endowed serving maid, but wearing blinkers, contends for the soul of the rich man with Conscience and Scriptural Wisdom ("an old and honorable pastor"). At the outset of the play, Overvloed complains that though she eats succulently, though her "tongue laps" the sweetest wine and she dresses in finery, she remains somehow heartsick and troubled.[7] So perhaps it is no surprise to discover in the Netherlands what de Tocqueville noticed in another precocious cornucopia, nineteenth-century America, namely, "that strange melancholy which often haunts the inhabitants of democratic countries in the midst of their abundance, and the disgust at life which sometimes seizes upon them in the midst of calm and easy circumstances."[8] "Melancholy" and "disgust" may be too much to impute to the temper of the seventeenth-century Dutch burgher, though intimations of mortality — their own and that of their worldly goods — saturated their art. But at the very least, the continuous pricking of conscience on complacency produced the self-consciousness that we think of as embarrassed.

IN WANDERING around the Dutch city, bumping into its cultural furniture, I have strayed a good deal from the straight and narrow of the historical method. Shameless eclecticism has been my only methodological guide. The thieving-magpie approach to other disciplines may seem, superficially, to be newfangled but in fact it is very old-fashioned. It follows on from the precedent of those venerable nineteenth-century compendia of manners and mores (*zeden en gewoonten,* the Dutch call them) that were part folklore, part antiquarian anthology and which for all their methodological innocence remain a rich treasure house of arcane and intricate knowledge. Before them, the eighteenth century had already produced the first great Dutch ethnographies, the product of encyclopedic social exploration. Their authors had the authentic eighteenth-century compulsion to acquire, accumulate and codify information on every kind of physical and social phenomenon in their country. Where some natural scientists made seashells or tropical flora and fauna their specialty, writers such as Kornelis van Alkemade turned to drinking horns, ceremonial goblets, standing salts and the history of native feasts.[9] An even more omnivorous intelligence, the physician le Francq van Berkhey, in his *Natural History of Holland* encompassed an exhaustive account of habitat, with volumes on social custom and costume, literally from the cradle to the grave. From the engraved plates in his volumes it is possible to examine, in detail, the reproductive organs of the cow or the human funeral rites appropriate for different classes of the bereaved.[10]

So that there is nothing especially daring about a working definition of culture drawn from social anthropology. In this well-established tradition I follow the kind of characterization offered by Mary Douglas of cultural bias as "an array of beliefs locked together into relational patterns."[11] In the same essay, however, she cautions that for those beliefs to be considered the matrix of a culture, they should "be treated as part of the [social] action and not separated from it." I have tried to follow this rather Durkheimian command in what is, essentially, a descriptive enterprise that emphasizes social process rather than social structure, habits rather than institutions. Acting upon one another, beliefs and customs together form what Emile Durkheim called "a determinate system that has its own life: . . . the *collective or common conscience* . . . it is by definition diffuse in every reach of society. Nevertheless it has specific conditions that make it a distinct reality."[12]

To see this elusive quarry — the *conscience collectif* — in its proper habitat and in action, rather than prone and eviscerated on the sociologist's dissecting table, I have used visual as well as textual evidence. Even this has a respectable pedigree, for le Francq van Berkhey thought nothing of alluding to still lifes or genre paintings when trying to evoke a particular set of customs or some items of the national diet. To exploit the bottomless riches of Dutch art — not merely panels and canvases, but architecture, sculpture, and the cornucopia of the decorative arts on glass, ceramic, tapestry — seems so natural and so obvious that it is difficult to conceive of any kind of cultural history, even an anthropologically bent one that leaves them out. "What other people," wrote the nineteenth-century critic-politician Théophile Thoré, "has written its history in its art?" Unlike the art of Renaissance Italy, Dutch art, he thought, was so much the record of the here and now, of *"la vie vivante,"* anchored in a specific time and place. It was the record of "the men and the matter, the sentiments and habits, the deeds and gestures of a whole nation."[13] And the quality of social document inherent in much of Dutch art does indeed make it an irresistible source for the cultural historian.

Treating art as a kind of historical evidence, though, has dangers for the unwary. Thoré also supposed it to be "a sort of photography of their great seventeenth century," a phrase that has been used time and again to suggest the kind of descriptive literalism that is supposed to reflect the empirical ethos of the prosaic bourgeois. There are undoubtedly some pictures that record with unmediated naturalism what was in front of the artist's eye. But in another passage Thoré reminded his readers that "nothing is less real than reality in painting. And what is called that depends strictly on a way of seeing."[14] And unless one supposes baskets full of lepers' rattles or cripples' crutches to be typically suspended over Jan Steen's kitchen, it should be obvious that very many Dutch paintings, and even more engraved prints, filter the perception of the eye through the lens of moral sensibility. Even Jacob van Ruisdael, for example, was known to rearrange or invent landscape, most famously in his versions of *The Jewish Cemetery,* to accommodate symbolic rumination.[15] In keeping with these important reservations, then, I have used Dutch art not as a literal record of social experience, but as a document of beliefs. Where imagery is set to text, as in emblem books or the innumerable engraved how-to manuals that flourished in Holland, its meaning is immediately accessible for historical interpretation, and I have made liberal use of it. Where, in genre painting, for example, meaning may be hidden but seems open to iconographic reading through reference to related emblematic imagery, I have borrowed from that scholarly technique with what, I hope, is the respect due for the special qualities inherent in a work of art.

Surprisingly, then, Dutch art invites the cultural historian to probe below the surface of appearances. By illuminating an interior world as much as illustrating an exterior one, it moves back and forth between morals and matter, between the durable and the ephemeral, the concrete and the imaginary, in a way that was peculiarly Netherlandish. And the paradoxes crowd in so thickly that the culture seems almost to be designed as a contrapuntal arrangement. Thoré thought *nature morte* absurdly inappropriate a term for the heaps of fruit, flowers, or fish that in some Dutch pictures sat carefully on white linen, on others tumbled over silver and glass. *Still* life was a misnomer, he wrote, for these things still live; they respire. Life in death; animation in immobility; the illusion of vitality and the reality of inertia: all these polarities seemed deliberately made to rebound off each other. Even allowing for his Catholic bias in favor of the disintegration of the mortal world, Paul Claudel, who wrote with exceptional intelligence and sensitivity on Dutch painting eighty years after Thoré, also noticed this preoccupation with what he called *désagrégation* — a coming apart. Still lifes, he thought, were caught (in the

Dutch) at their *toppunt*: the zenith before the fall; the moment of perfect ripeness before the decay. Militia pieces like *The Night Watch* represented the *désagrégation* of the group; both a setting-off and a coming-apart. So that the animate and inanimate world of the Dutch was seen in a state of organic flux, forever composing, decomposing and recomposing itself. This was what, in a wonderful phrase, Claudel called its *élasticité secrète*; the essential kinetic quality for a country where the very elements of land and water seemed indeterminately separated, and where the immense space of sky was in a state of perpetual alteration. And it was this acute sense of the mutable world that he thought gave the lie to those who supposed the Dutch lived out their existences according to some sort of clodlike bourgeois adhesion to the concrete. Was not the landscape itself, he mused, "a kind of preparation for the sea, a flattening of all relief . . . an anticipation through the grass of the water, so much so that it seems not too much to suggest that the enterprise of Dutch art is like a liquefaction of reality."[16]

That, perhaps *is* too much. But it is a sobering reminder to the cultural historian that the collective image he may try to recover might at best be fugitive and ghostly, like the outline of houses that Proust saw reflected in the Maas at Dordrecht, which trembled into incoherence with every ripple of the evening tide.[17]

Becoming

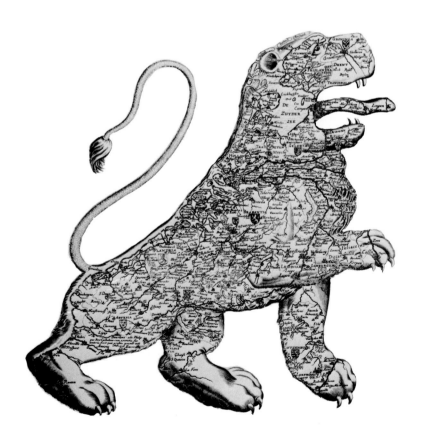

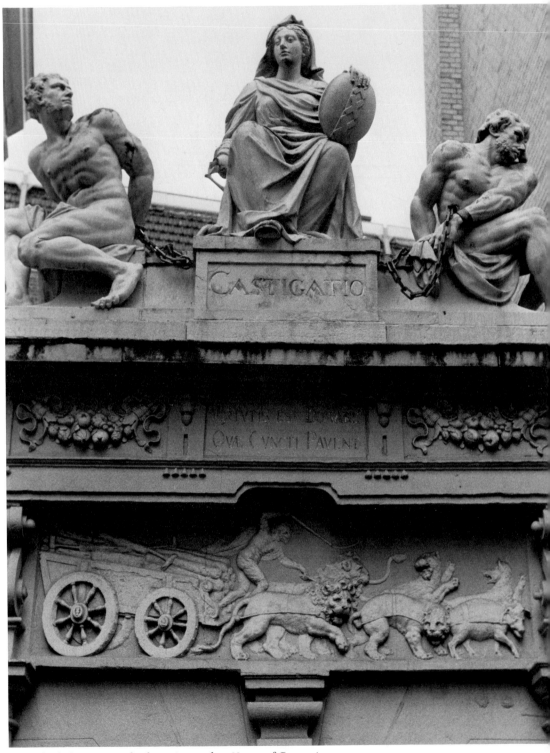

3. Hendrick de Keyser and others. Amsterdam House of Correction, gateway.

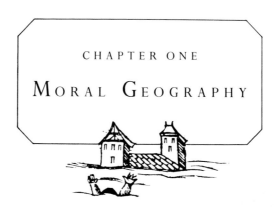

CHAPTER ONE

MORAL GEOGRAPHY

i THE MYSTERY OF THE DROWNING CELL

In high summer, Amsterdam smells of frying oil, shag tobacco and unwashed beer glasses. In narrow streets, where the press of human traffic adds its own pungency, these vapors stand in the air like an aromatic heat mist. Along the Kalverstraat, the ancient and noisy alley that snakes south from the Dam, the swarm of tourists at four in the afternoon coagulates into a single, viscid mass. But in Amsterdam, alleys attract; avenues repel. The Kalverstraat's din and cheerful vulgarity are the authentic Dutch answer to the alienating breadth of a boulevard, a piece of urban bombast that has never worked well in their towns. The same tourists who make for the Champs Elysées or Piccadilly, in Amsterdam instinctively shun the pompous space of the Rokin for the sweaty shove and jostle of the Kalverstraat.

At some points this relentless ant march towards the Rembrandtsplein (once the Botermarkt) is interrupted by cross streets, one of them still called by its medieval name, the Heiligeweg (the Holy Way). It is at this now altogether profane station that, in late July, as the school vacation peters out, small bands of children cut their way across and against the crowds to reach a shady doorway in the Heiligeweg itself. Before the Reformation the street took its name from the several religious foundations that shared the neighborhood with tradesmen's stalls and artisans' shops. The site of the building into which the children disappear, clutching swim fins and gaudy towels, was once the Convent of the Sisters of Saint Clare, the Klarissenklooster. From its lobby, sounds of spacious hooting and whiffs of chlorine confirm it as one of Amsterdam's public swimming pools. And it was here, so travelers reported in the seventeenth century, that men were faced with a stark choice: drown or be Dutch.

After Erasmus, Netherlandish humanism was short on jokes, so that it seems unlikely that the metamorphosis of the drowning cell into the swimming pool would have amused the city fathers. Certainly, there is nothing lighthearted about the sculpture that they placed at the entrance of the house in the Heiligeweg. The forbidding group atop the roof, showing Amsterdam dishing out *CASTIGATIO* (punishment) to heavily manacled and fettered delinquents — a constabular version of Michelangelo's prisoners — was added in the late seventeenth century.[1] The alarming flail she held in her right hand has, quite recently, mysteriously disappeared, as perhaps out of keeping with Amsterdam's present ethos of relaxed liberalism. Farther down, immediately above the keystone of the arch, is a much earlier bas-relief dating from 1607 and carved by Hendrick de Keyser, the greatest of Amsterdam's generation of late Renaissance architects and sculptors. It shows a team of bridled lions and wolves cringing before the charioteer's lash. The accompanying motto, *Virtutis est domare quae cuncti pavent* (It is a virtue to subdue those before whom all go in dread), was taken from *Hercules Furens*[2] by Seneca, a favorite author of the humanist magistrates whose civic mission it advertised. It should come as no surprise, then, to learn that the door in the Heiligeweg once greeted new inmates for the city's first House of Correction: the Tugthuis. A very similar work of penal iconography by de Keyser can still be made out through the sooty masonry of the door on the Oude Zijds Achterburgwal Spinhuis, where, from 1597, "fallen women" — vagrants, whores and thieves — were sent for stiff doses of improvement at loom and wheel. There, too, the upraised arm is reinforced by the edifying motto that de Keyser commissioned from the humanist poet and historian Pieter Corneliszoon Hooft in 1607. "Cry not," the house mother is made to declare as she briskly sets about the impenitent, "for I exact no vengeance for wrong but force you to be good. My hand is stern but my heart is kind."

These grim hostels were founded at the end of the sixteenth century[3] through the recommendations of earlier inspectors for vagabondage. Lodged on the sites of the dissolved religious orders, they signified the change from voluntary ecclesiastical alms to the aggressive social intervention that characterized humanist reform, both Catholic and Protestant.[4] Around the middle of the sixteenth century, magistrates in many of the larger European cities sought to deal with the rapidly increasing hordes of beggars, destitute rural migrants and what they perceived as whole armies of petty criminals by means other than the indiscriminate brutalities — brandings, mutilations, floggings and bloody executions — that constituted traditional punishment and deterrence. The two purposes of economic relief and penal reform united in an ambitious correctional program designed to reform the malefactor as well as punish him for his past sins and crimes. The physician and professor of surgery Dr. Sebastiaan Egbertszoon, who was one of the prime movers in establishing the Amsterdam house, and who saw the reform as a kind of clinical therapy for the delinquent, took it into his head that "to provide a prisoner with the right treatment and prevent his misconduct in the future, it is necessary to consider what causes brought him to prison."[5]

In July 1589, the governing council of Amsterdam, mindful of the inappropriateness of death penalties inflicted on young offenders, announced itself interested in establishing a "house where all vagabonds, evildoers, rascals and the like could be imprisoned." Their counterparts in London had already set up the Bridewell in 1555 for similar ends, but it seems that the Amsterdam magistracy paid little heed to the example, referring instead to an indigenous Dutch tradition of reform. In 1530, Gouda had proposed a House of Chastisement for delinquent youth, and the poet, scholar, engraver and moralist Dirck Volkertszoon Coornhert had written a seminal tract on the matter, the *Boeventucht* (Punishment of Rogues) not long after his own imprisonment by the Spanish regime, and no doubt much preoccupied with questions of fit or unfit penalties.[6] But it was the son of a well-to-do mercantile dynasty, Jan Laurenszoon Spieghel, who responded to the magistrates' brief by suggesting the site at the old Klarissenklooster and setting out in a detailed memorandum his proposals for "the correction and improvement" of the delinquents.

By the standards of the time, Spieghel's scheme was reasonably enlightened. It attempted to balance off the required dosage of corrective discipline with some incentives for rehabilitation through work and moral teaching. He stressed the need to keep the identity of the inmates secret so that when they should be returned to decent society they should suffer no stigma. Diet was to be ample though plain: dark bread, grits, porridges, peas and beans; a little pork or stockfish once or twice a week. It was, at least, to be sufficiently varied that its deprivation for bread and water would seem like punishment. Recreation in the form of ball games and the like was meant to be robust and vigorous. Prisoners who showed any willingness toward reform were to be taught a skilled trade, and only those who remained obstinately slothful forced to do monotonous, harsh labor like rasping wood. And the program for economic rehabilitation was to be completed by a wage commensurate with the measured effort.

In practice, the Amsterdam Tugthuis, which opened its doors on the Heiligeweg in 1595, fell short of Spieghel's idealism. In its earliest days it seems to have attempted to honor his principle of prisoners' anonymity, going so far as to admit them to the house under cover of darkness. But even by the time that Jan van Hout, the poet and town clerk of Leiden, visited the place in 1597–98 with the object of making similar provisions for his city, it had

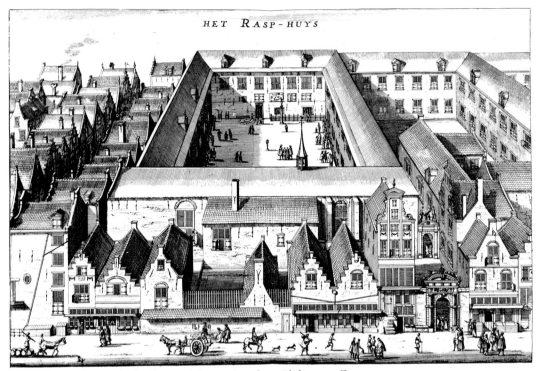

HET RASP-HUYS

4. The Heiligeweg with the House of Correction, from Philips von Zesen,
Beschreibung der Stat Amsterdam (Amsterdam. 1633)

inevitably become a detention center for petty felons rather than a moral
reformatory.[7] Different categories of prisoners were jumbled together without
much thought of providing separate accommodation or work regimes.
Housebreakers, pickpockets and other kinds of professional criminals were
confined together with casual vagrants, beggars and persistent disturbers of the
peace: those who had been convicted of drunken brawls or violent affrays.
The magistrates came to use the house as a standard resort for previous
offenders who had violated earlier terms of banishment or had been undeterred
by floggings. Coornhert's emphasis on juvenile correction was honored, but in
a way that muddied his humanist program of disciplinary pedagogy. Those
adolescents who had committed some dreadful offense against both family and
the law—stealing from their parents or threatening them with violence—
could be committed in the regular way after trial. Subjected to the same work
program as the rest of the inmates, these little criminals could be very young
indeed. In 1620 a thirteen-year-old who had perpetrated manslaughter was
committed "because of his youth," having been symbolically decapitated in

public, with a sword swung over his head, flogged and branded before admission. In 1637 a ten-year-old was confined for theft.[8] But there was also a further category of arbitrarily defined "lawless" offspring, who could be committed by their own parents, and detained at the pleasure of the regents of the house until their families petitioned for release. The costs of these "white-bread children," so called for their privileged diet, were borne by their families. In 1603 a special court to the north of the main building was opened to separate their accommodation from the deleterious effects of mingling with the riffraff of the Tugthuis proper.

Sentencing could be capricious. In 1614 an ordinance against able-bodied begging laid down six weeks as the penalty for first offenders and six months for a recurrence. In practice, confinement could be much longer and was never shorter. In the Utrecht house, modeled on Amsterdam (and where the records are more detailed), the mean average stay during the 1620s was three and a half years. The most vicious offenders could be given a lifetime sentence, and those who had been sent there for "reform" were simply detained at the magistrates' pleasure without limit of time.[9] In Amsterdam, sentences of three, five or even seven years were not uncommon, and lifetime incarceration was the fate of those whom the magistrates deemed too incorrigible or dangerous to be let loose on the community. Every January before the retirement of the incumbent city administration, the sheriff (*schout*) and the bench of nine magistrates (*schepen*) convened a review tribunal at the house, where they could commute or prolong a sentence depending on reports of the inmate's conduct through the year. Not surprisingly, then, the house was fairly crowded for most of the seventeenth century. By 1598 it had 70 inmates, and when Thomas Bowrey visited it in 1698, it had 117.[10]

The humanist worthies who invented these places labored, as they supposed, in the shadow of Erasmus. Magistrates and men of letters, poetizing civic busybodies — figures like Coornhert and Spieghel — could be said to have inherited his restless Christian conscience and his schoolmasterly approach to social iniquity. But they conspicuously lacked his ironic sense of limits. The reformatories were in dead earnest, especially where the work ethic was concerned. The first industry established there was the weaving of "tripe" velveteen, and the commission to teach the willing and able a skilled trade was ostensibly answered by the weaving of such other kinds of coarse textiles as fustian and bombazeen. But the Amsterdam House became famous for a wholly different kind of labor. In 1599 the city granted the overseers of the Tugthuis the monopoly in powdered brazilwood for its dyeworks, and it was colloquially known thereafter as the Rasphuis (Saw-House). For this was the regime that was supposed to turn idlers, spongers, beggars and assorted ne'er-do-wells into industrious responsible members of society. The work was

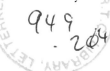

so grueling and the rewards so paltry, though, that the distinction between rehabilitation and punishment must have been lost on those who were bound to it. And since the institution came to depend for its existence on the proceeds of the brazilwood sales, there are some grounds for supposing that means came to dominate ends. For shifts that could last as long as fourteen hours, inmates worked with the twelve-bladed saws to reduce at least forty (and as much as sixty) Amsterdam pounds. In return they were credited with eight and a half stuivers a day, a meager wage that on Saturdays might buy them the treat of a loaf of white bread. If they were capable of working for more than their regular allotment, they could earn a whole guilder for every additional hundred pounds. And the overseers even incorporated the notion of involuntary saving into this wage-incentive system by docking two stuivers each week from each inmate's pay, which went towards a small sum to be given to him on his discharge.[11]

The inmates' salvation was supposed to be spiritual as well as civic and economic. Daily prayers and catechisms led by the *ziekentrooster,* or curate of souls, were of course an obligatory fixture morning and evening, as well as before and after meals. Bible readings and psalm singing were encouraged, and on Sundays there was an obligatory sermon to endure. A "school" of sorts provided instruction from dusk to seven on winter evenings, as well as during spells of "free time" at three in the afternoon. Lessons were of a rudimentary kind, meant to instill the basic tenets of the faith and drawn from anthologies of the sayings of the Apostles and editions of the *Wisdoms of Solomon* (Proverbs, Ecclesiastes and Ecclesiasticus specially published for use in houses of correction). This moral regimen was extended to their casual manners of speech and

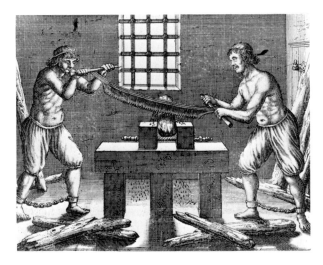

5. Raspers, from von Zesen,
Beschreibung der Stat Amsterdam

demeanor. Nicknames, for example, that thieves and prostitutes rejoiced in, were forbidden, as was the use of their private canting slang, known in Amsterdam as peddlers' French. Privacy of habit or indulgence in the ways of the old vicious community was by definition anathema to the rule of improvement. Cursing, shouting and, above all, smoking were strictly prohibited. The objects of all this intensive moral scrutiny were supposed to be passive, transparent receptacles into which could be poured the pure milk of Christian redemption.

Spieghel had proposed some degree of secrecy and privacy to preserve a modicum of dignity for the "patients" submitted to the care of the house. But in practice the essence of its work was close and unrelenting observation. From their first admission to the house through their early weeks and months, the prisoners were watched to see if any signs of civic life could be discerned struggling to break free from the old crust of vice. After they passed through de Keyser's daunting gateway, new inmates would be taken to a subterranean cell, where they would be kept for a while in dark solitary confinement for initial observation before being visited by one of the overseers, who would acquaint them with the rules. This sharp dose of early corrective "medicine" was also supposed to condition the "patient" better to the regimen that awaited him in the light. And by the 1630s, it was not only the "house father" (Binnenhuisvader) and his warders who watched their charges. For a copper coin, the general public was admitted to watch the inmates at their labors in both the Tugthuis and the female Spinhuis. The houses plainly regarded this as a useful source of revenue, though by the eighteenth century it particularly appalled some visitors (one of whom complained that "they make a dumb show of them like so many brutes"). At carnival (*kermis*) time admission was free, and throngs came to gawk at these unfortunates, and in particular to jeer at the whores in the Spinhuis, so their plight must have been particularly wretched. Thus the original attempt to protect prisoners from public ignominy had been entirely abandoned. Instead, a rival ethic — both humanist and more bleakly Calvinist — held that the shame incurred in exhibition could be the herald of self-improvement. That, at any rate, was the theory.

In any event, the Rasphuis and the Spinhuis became obligatory stops on any tourist itinerary of Amsterdam. Ushered there by burgomasters and magistrates, who were only too eager to show them off as model reformatories, a procession of visitors from England, France, Italy, Germany, Scandinavia and even Hungary all recorded their visits there and published their impressions. Many of them were struck by the formidable system of disciplinary punishments that backed up the house regime. Ranging from deprivation of meat rations through to floggings at the post with "a bull's pistle" (penis) according to one source.[12] On November 13, 1618, no fewer than twenty prisoners (or about a

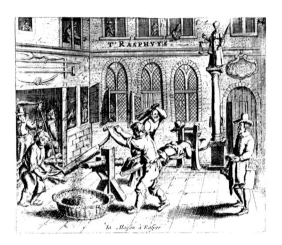

6. Rasphuis discipline, from Johan Pontanus, *Rerum et Urbis Amstelo-damensium Historia* (Amsterdam, 1611)

quarter of the inmates) were whipped in one day for their obstinacy. Worse was the contraption that bent the prisoner across a bench, with his head in a vise, while the birch was applied to the body. As grim as these "correctives" were, a good number of travelers mentioned another punishment for the incorrigibly idle so sinister as to defy credulity. This was the drowning cell or "water house." Jean de Parival's terse reference in 1662 is typical of the laconic — but emphatic — description of this dramatic frightener: "If they do not want to work they are tethered like asses and are put in a cellar that is filled with water so that they must partly empty it by pumping if they do not wish to drown."[13]

It is difficult not to blink in disbelief on reading this. But caravans of tourists from the early to the late seventeenth century all pointed it out in their accounts. The Hungarian schoolmaster Martin Szombor, who was there in 1618, wrote of the "water house used to tame boys who refused to work."[14] Marmaduke Rawdon of York claimed that he had actually seen such a place in 1662, and Edward Brown wrote that his guides had expressly told him of the "large cistern" in which the delinquents were set "placing only a pump by them for relief whereby they are forced to labor for their lives."[15] Others who mention the cell include the Levant merchant Robert Bargrave in 1634, William Aglionby, a Fellow of the Royal Society, in 1671, Maximilien Misson, the French savant, in 1688, who added the detail that it took just a quarter of an hour for the cell to fill were the pump not used, William Montague in 1696, Thomas Bowrey in 1698, Thomas Nugent in the 1730s and even Joseph Marshall, the economics writer, who congratulated the magistrates on so "admirable a contrivance."[16]

For all his sharp-eyed empiricism on so many other aspects of Holland,

Marshall's report of the drowning cell is suspiciously inaccurate. He was led to suppose that "by law" the incorrigibly idle were supposed to drown if they did not use the pump to the best of their ability. Yet at about the same date as his visit in the 1760s, the official historian of Amsterdam, Johan Wagenaar, who gave a thorough account of the punishment of offenders, dismissed the cell as pure hearsay. The most recent historical writing on penal practice has followed that dismissal, though perhaps more emphatically than Wagenaar intended.[17] It is certainly true that travelers' accounts, many (though not all) secondhand, should be offset by the eloquent silence of contemporary Dutch sources, including city descriptions like the *Beschryving der Stat Amsterdam* of 1665 by Tobias van Domselaer and Olfert Dapper that surveyed the city sites in great detail, in both text and engravings.[18]

Was the drowning cell a bizarre fable, a sadistic fantasy, concocted from half-digested gobbets of hearsay? There was, of course, the dark and close cell into which prisoners were confined on admission and to which they returned for spells of solitary confinement when they broke the rules of the house. Domselaer describes that cell as subterranean and "damp." But it seems unlikely that by *vochtig* he meant capable of total submersion. Nor can archival sources of the Tugthuis throw any light on the matter, since they barely survive in fragments for much of the seventeenth century. Yet for all these gaps in our knowledge, the possibility of this cold-blooded experiment in behaviorist persuasion having functioned at some time cannot be altogether dismissed. There is at least one early-seventeenth-century Dutch source, the *History of the Wonderful Miracles . . . in a Place Called the Tucht-huys,* a persiflage published in 1612 sardonically describing "miraculous" transformations wrought in the institution, that gave a detailed account of the cell.

> In the vestibule or entrance to the house there is running water, and beside it, a room with two pumps one on the outside and the other on the inside. The patient was brought thither so that by pumping into the room first as high as his knees, then as high as his waist, and as he was not yet prepared to give his attention to St. Pono [i.e., to the devotion of labor] as high as his armpits, and finally up to his neck when fearing that he would drown, began his devotion to St. Pono and by furious pumping until he had emptied the room when he discovered that his weakness had left him and he had to confess his cure.[19]

For all the satirical relish, there is a topographical specificity in this account that suggests something more than a fiendish joke. And near two centuries later, when Sir John Carr visited the old Rasphuis (a new and much more spacious workhouse had been built in 1694 and a Verbeterhuis, primarily for juveniles), he was expressly shown "a cell in the corner of the yard" that had been used for the water terror. What was equally apparent, though, was that such a device had not been used for many generations, backing up de Blainville's report in 1705 that after one impenitent "scoundrel" had actually preferred to drown than pump, the punishment had been abandoned.[20]

When taken together with the interest shown by the magistrates of Danzig in the house and this device, and their attempt to engineer a modified version of it (with rope and well), there seems more than a shred of possibility that the drowning cell did, for a while at least, carry out its work of salutary intimidation. But supposing it was only a popular and perennially repeated myth, would that obviate its historical importance? Not, at any rate, in the realm of culture, where belief and utterance were as potent social realities as tangible action. This was, after all, a culture saturated in symbolic and ritualized messages. The broadsword of the public executioner swishing over the bowed criminal's head on the scaffold was not idle mummery. And at a time when all manner of gruesome public retribution was taken — slit noses, wheel-broken bodies, bored tongues, even pierced eyes — the notion of the traumatic coercion of the lazy would not have seemed particularly barbaric. So if the story of the drowning cell seemed to the parade of well-to-do travelers entirely of a piece with Amsterdam's other provision for the delinquent, how much more compelling would have been even a rumor to those of the common people that might expect a spell in the house on the Heiligeweg.

As a punitive myth — and still more as an exercise in regulated terror — the drowning cell drew its psychological force from the watery depths of Dutch culture. It was, in effect, an exercise in that sort of pedagogy around which Dutch identity had itself crystallized: moral geography. So that the frightening experience inflicted, *in extremis,* on the "patient" was designed to be an intensive rehearsal of the primal Dutch experience: the struggle to survive rising waters. Was not the heraldic device of Zeeland a lion breasting the waves, its motto, *Luctor et Emergo* — "I fight to emerge"? The ordeal (or its threat) was a traumatic shock, almost akin to some sort of violent electrical convulsion. Shaken down to the elemental essentials, it must have been argued, even the most vicious and abandoned person would respond with the effort and perseverance that would, at last, proclaim him a member of the Dutch community. And not without a didactic point, some of the inmates discharged from the house were sent to work on the Heer Hugowaard polders to the north of Amsterdam, near Alkmaar, where a prototype of an "open" prison was meant to further the simultaneous process of geographical and moral reclamation. And these "patients," once recovered, were meant to recognize the peculiar sort of moral geography that would certify them as Dutch.

To be wet was to be captive, idle and poor. To be dry was to be free, industrious and comfortable. This was the lesson of the drowning cell.

ii   TRIALS BY WATER

Whether fact or fantasy, the premise on which the drowning cell was dreamed up was that survival in the teeth of calamity was the beginning of self-respect: a recovery of identity. To its first generation of patriotic eulogists, Dutchness was often equated with the transformation, under divine guidance, of catastrophe into good fortune, infirmity into strength, water into dry land, mud into gold. This arrogation of a special destiny, marked by suffering and redemption, was not so particular to the Dutch as they imagined. But the uncanny ways in which geography reinforced moral analogy gave their collective self-recognition great immediacy. Those who had come through flood and had survived could hardly miss the differentiating significance of *beproeving,* or ordeal. So the trial of faith by adversity was a formative element of the national culture.

The ordeal of water as a determinant of moral authenticity could, within the same cultural frame, be turned upside down to isolate the self-evidently alien. Any crime so abhorrent that its very perpetration announced the impossibility of Dutchness might be punished by a drowning from which no escape was possible. Before the Reformation, radical heresy was as close to such unnatural practice as could be imagined, and in 1535, twenty-eight men and women were bound in sacks and thrown into the river IJ. After the wonderfully euphemized process of the Protestant "Alteration" in Amsterdam in 1578, it was crimes against the family or the "natural" sexual order that called for extirpation by water. In 1598, a woman was drowned in a water barrel set on the public scaffold for kidnapping and maltreating a child, and in 1641, a mother who had committed infanticide was executed in the same way.[21] In 1730, some of those convicted of sodomy, during a great wave of trials throughout the republic, were duly condemned in the archaic style to be drowned in the IJ with hundred-pound weights about their necks. Those who were actually executed were first strangled so that they were spared the terror of the penalty, but the sentence was read in its full awfulness and in some cases carried out posthumously. An unfortunate minister of the village of Vianen, Emmanuel Valck, who was convicted of the same "unnatural crime," took his own life in prison, but his remains were duly taken by cart and dumped in the sea at Brielle so that the cleansing extirpation might be duly completed.[22]

These alarming spectacles — both the drowning with escape and the drowning without one — were dramatic lessons in the judicial function of disaster in Dutch culture. Just as conspicuous prosperity, in Calvinist ethics, was held to be a presumptive sign of membership of the Elect, so triumph over calamity was a presumptive sign of grace. Associated with this was the allied notion of rescue through providential intervention. That was provided not merely from divine compassion, but as a specific reward for steadfastness to God's law, even on the brink of despair. In 1668 a triumphal anthology of verse and prose entitled *'t Verheerlickt Nederland* (The Glorified Netherlands) included a more somber reminder by the Calvinist writer and preacher Jacobus Lydius of the "forty death years" of the war against Spain: "Truly was the violence of these calamities so great that men could only weigh the suffering as a *test* sent from Heaven . . . [to try] the virtue and steadfastness of this people in burdensome affairs."[23] Fidelity in privation, then, earned deliverance in this world as well as salvation in the next. The same writer later remarked that "when, as on so many occasions, the Netherlands has fallen into the most devilish peril, and has been brought to the utmost extremity, so that all seemed quite lost and without hope; then God has come to our aid with sudden miracles."[24]

Eleventh-hour rescue, the epic counterpart of the ram in the thicket, was a standard feature of many of the chronicles and verse histories that related the eighty years' war against Spain. The descent of the Sea Beggars on Brielle, the siege of Alkmaar, Voorne and Bergen op Zoom, all lent themselves to this dramatic narrative. Later, in the seventeenth century, in 1672, when the republic faced the nightmare of a joint attack by British and French fleets, a "miraculous ebb tide" was said to have delayed the junction of the enemy fleets until they could be engaged and separately defeated by de Ruyter and Cornelis Tromp.[25]

No episode in the early history of Dutch independence seemed to exemplify celestial deliverance as obviously as the relief of Leiden in 1574. From May to September of that year, the Spanish had invested the city in a wide arc from The Hague in the south to the Haarlem Road to the north. Without a garrison of regular troops, only the armed militia, the *schutters,* stiffened a resistance that was gradually succumbing to desperate hunger and disease. Since Haarlem itself had fallen to the Spanish after a long siege, the situation in the center of Holland seemed desperate enough for William of Orange to activate a plan of systematic inundation.[26] On the third and fourth of August, the Ijsseldijk was pierced, and in the following weeks many more of the river defenses were opened, isolating major urban centers like Gouda and Rotterdam. But to help Leiden, the water had to be deep enough to paralyze all Spanish troop movement *and* permit a rebel flotilla to sail almost to the city walls as a relieving force. And it was a formidable storm in mid-September sweeping across the Haarlemmermeer that delivered the city from its ordeal. In vernacular accounts that became popular in the first generation of free Dutch men and

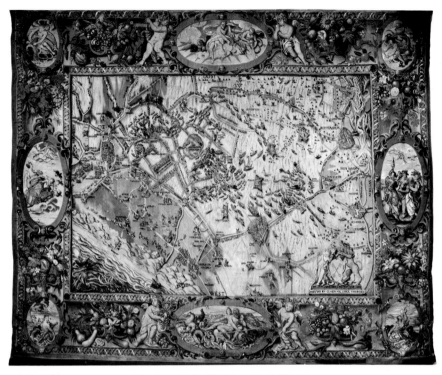

7. J. Lanckaert, tapestry with the relief of Leiden. Stedelijk Museum,
"De Lakenhal," Leiden

women, like the propaganda play of the rhetorician Jacob Duym, the siege of
Leiden was represented as the national epic par excellence, when sea, wind
and polders had fought on the side of the righteous.[27] The local historian
Orlers illustrated his city chronicle with graphic engravings of the beleaguered
citizens, forced to cram their mouths with cats, dogs, grass and roots, and
nursing mothers whose breasts had run dry.[28] Only prayer, psalms and the
self-sacrificing exhortation of the burgomaster van der Werff staved off complete despair. Then, when no more could be endured, God Almighty sent the
great wind from the north to put fear into the hearts of the Midianites (a.k.a.,
Alva's Spanish troops)—who broke camp as the waters rose around them. The
people were thus delivered from their ordeal, their *beproeving,* amidst general
thanksgiving and rejoicing. Thus ran one of the most potent of the founding
scriptures: a witness to providential intervention and godly history. The
chronicle became a patriotic Haggadah complete with a commemorative meal
that in bread and herring—the food of salvation—reenacted the ordeals of
famine and deliverance. It was a reminder, not just of victory over the Spanish,
but of necessary suffering and earned recompense. And there were other times

when the ordeal was invoked to reconsecrate the separateness of their history. In 1830, for example, following the traumatic humiliation of the Belgian revolution, reminders of the peculiar identity of the northern, Protestant Netherlands were urgently needed to comfort national self-esteem. Predictably, then, a rash of history painting depicted over and over again the consolatory epic of Leiden.

Since freedom was an award made for surviving ordeals, it is perhaps not so surprising to discover that the seventeenth-century Dutch had a marked taste for disaster epics. The genre grew naturally out of travel and discovery literature that had always included hair-raising encounters and narrow escapes, actual or imagined. What the Dutch added, and made something of a specialty, were shipwreck tales featuring intrepid nautical heroes. And because of their skill at engraving, and the rapid expansion of a cheap octavo line in popular literature, publishers like Joost Gillis Saeghman and Joost Hartgers were able to produce a whole series of dramatically illustrated briny yarns.[29] Those tales of the deep blended narratives of voyages of exploration—dramatic enough in their own right—with fantastic additions drawn from an ancient repertoire of sea monsters and mutant humanoids. Engraved prints or wood-cuts of ships in remote or terrifying circumstances, trapped in Arctic ice or battered by tropical storms, and of fights with horribly tattooed savages further enriched the genre. Saeghman, who, at the same time as he churned out these epics, produced sophisticated, expensively engraved folio editions for the literary elite and almanacs for everybody, had had an early success with the relatively sober journal of the mariner-explorer Linschoten. Being a shrewd entrepreneur, Saeghman understood the need to create a gallery of heroes and was not above sharp practice if the material was not always to hand. For the frontispiece of the first edition of Linschoten's voyages, for example, he pirated the engraving from (of all things) a work celebrating the campaigns of a Spanish general and printed it up as the Dutch hero.[30]

The prolific genre of timber-shivering, hair-raising voyage literature, then, was always part fact, part fable. Some of the most popular, like Joris van Spilbergen's journal, sailed pretty close to the facts; others, like the diaries of Paulus Olofsz. Rotman (1657), seem to have indulged in more fanciful embroidery of the narrative. Shipwrecks and disasters were in any case common enough for this vital ingredient in the tale to occur without any fabrication, and two best-sellers, *The Unfortunate Voyage of the Ship Batavia* (1647)[31] and Janssen van der Heiden's *Shipwreck off Bengal*, were authentic enough in their maritime drama. The prototype disaster epic, and by far the most popular and enduring, was Willem Ysbrantzoon Bontekoe's journal, *The Memorable Account of the Voyage of the Nieuw Hoorn*, first published by Jan Janszoon Deutel in 1646 in a popular quarto edition.[32] All the ingredients for a great disaster, so laboriously

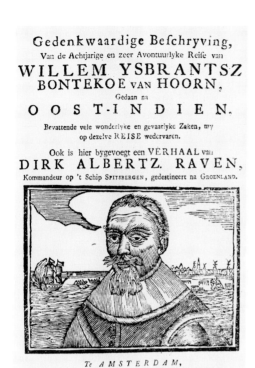

Gedenkwaardige Befchryving,

Van de Achtjarige en zeer Avontuurlyke Reife van

WILLEM YSBRANTSZ BONTEKOE van HOORN,

Gedaan na

O O S T-I N D I E N.

Bevattende vele wonderlyke en gevaarlyke Zaken, my op dezelve R E I S E wedervaren.

Ook is hier bygevoegt een VERHAAL van DIRK ALBERTZ. RAVEN,

Kommandeur op 't Schip SPITSBERGEN, gedestineert na GROENLAND.

Te AMSTERDAM,
By B. KOENE, Boekdrukker in de Boomstraat.

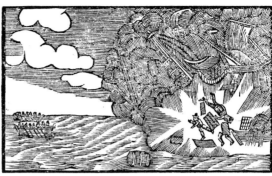

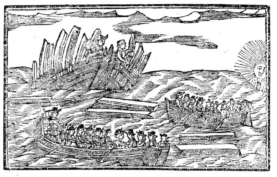

8–10. Anon. woodcuts, from Willem Ysbrantsz. Bontekoe, *Gedenkwaardige Beschryving* (Amsterdam, n.d.)

manufactured in twentieth-century pulp fiction and cinema, were already present in Bontekoe's journal. In the long chronology of this kind of semi-oracular epics it sits halfway between the Argonauts of antiquity and Hollywood's *Poseidon Adventure,* and like them was targeted at an audience that expected good fortune to be struck by retributive calamity from which only the virtuous and heroic might escape. It was all the more spectacular and prophetic because Bontekoe's ship, the *Nieuw Hoorn,* was the seventeenth-century equivalent of a Cunarder or a high-rise hotel, being an East Indiaman of 1,100 Holland tonnes and with a crew and soldiery on board of 206 men. (The average Dutch *fluit* ship was crewed by 6 to 12 men.) Disaster had to be on a correspondingly vast scale; in Bontekoe's tale, it was a fire at sea in the Sunda Straits in the East Indies in November 1619 that caused the dramatic explosion of the powder kegs. The skipper, who is blown high into the sky and then down into the ocean, miraculously survives and is found clinging to a spar. The obligatory ordeal then follows, with the 72 survivors drifting in a small boat. During that rite of passage, the humanist ideal of community and the Calvinist precept of obedience to the divine will are put to stern tests, the temptation of cannibalism being warded off only by the inflexible piety of the godly captain.

> Our distress became every day greater and heavier to bear and the men began to look with such despair, distrust and malevolence at one another almost as if they would devour each other, verily they did speak of it among themselves, deeming fit to eat first the boys and when these were finished, they should draw lots who should be the next one. I was shocked to the depths of my soul at this, from out of the anguish of my soul I prayed to Almighty God that in his Fatherly compassion he would have mercy and not let it come to this; that he would not afflict us beyond endurance knowing the weakness of his creatures. . . . with God's help I dissuaded them, praying for the boys, and said "Men, let us not do this thing. God will deliver us for we cannot be far from land."[33]

Three days of grace are granted before the first boys are to be eaten, and, of course, it is on the third that land is finally sighted. Terrifying melees with murderous natives armed with poisoned spears then ensue, from which the Christian band escapes, much diminished, to be rescued and brought safely to Batavia, where they are received with somewhat understated sympathy by Governor Jan Pieterszoon Coen. ("A great misfortune; it can't be helped. Boy, bring me the golden cup; Here's to you, Captain, Good Luck!" [Swig.])[34]

The Dutch publishers who turned out this sort of epic were the first entrepreneurs of armchair calamity. Bontekoe's text was reprinted eight times in fifty years and seventy times before 1800, making it one of the best-sellers on the Dutch popular market. Publishers catering to this sensational market were resourceful at finding new themes and more exotic locations to quicken jaded curiosity. As their readership tired of tropical shipwrecks and heroes, they came up with skippers-turned-rovers like Claes Campaan, or the astonishing story of multiple murder and debauchery that stained the pages of the story of *The Unfortunate Ship Batavia*.[35] When the tropics were old hat, Frederick Maarten's spectacular voyages to the Arctic kept the market happy with engravings of polar bears, walruses and less identifiable shaggy carnivores.

None of this publishing success could have been accomplished without satisfying some deep craving in the Dutch popular literary market for disaster stories. Part of this addiction was the perennial fascination with danger, lived vicariously, and the need for citizen-heroes in a young republic that had repudiated the imperial aura of the Habsburgs. This was frontier literature, as much as the Wild West stories that fed another young republic's sense of courage, sin and virtue. But like that later genre, it also drew on certain habits of self-description that had already become ingrained in native culture. Just as much as the vernacular history chronicles, the shipwreck epics were parables of a manifest national destiny and followed a standard moral formula in the narrative. (They still do.) Many of them emphasized the *suddenness* of catastrophe, even when fortunes seemed brightest. (It is not a coincidence that Saeghman's other specialty was almanacs that, among other services, indicated the likelihood of astral conjunctions.) The object of retribution (in this case a richly laden cargo ship) is nearly always a symbol of worldly vanity and is often destroyed from within by an act of corruption or moral laxity that invites nemesis. In the case of the *Nieuw Hoorn,* fire occurred when one of the crew took a naked candle to a brandywine cask from which he was to take the crew's grog ration. The "raging inferno" then spread to nearby powder kegs and caused a catastrophic explosion. *The Unfortunate Ship Batavia* is driven on to the reefs of the Houtman Abrolhos Islands the very night its skipper, Ariaen Jacobszoon, had planned mutiny against the fleet commander, Pelsaert.[36]

All of this played on Dutch anxieties about unlooked-for adversity, relentlessly stressed by their preachers who insisted that the more lavish the feast, the more imminent the writing on the wall. The superfatted cargo vessel became an emblem of the fatherland itself, loosely derived from an earlier, quite independent, symbolic repertoire. The medieval commonplace of the ship as mother church, the allegorical parable of the *Narrenschiff,* the Ship of Fools, and the humanist image of the Ship of State were all garbled together to make a composite metaphor for the Dutch community, set adrift on the "great historical ocean," to use another phrase from popular literature. Whether these symbolic connotations were translated into marine imagery is an open, but challenging question. A late sixteenth-century seascape, once thought to be by Bruegel, shows a ship laboring in a roiling sea, along with the proverbial detail of "casting a barrel before a whale" that alluded to the deflection of misfortune by jettisoning worldly goods (Jonah come to the Dogger Bank).[37] The earliest Dutch marine painters, like Hendrik Vroom, may have retained some of the metaphorical imagery of faith tested by trial, and even occasional examples of Willem van de Velde the Younger's work, like *De Windstoot* (The Squall) seem strikingly close in their unnatural illumination to the kinds of engravings that gave scriptural overtones to the Bontekoe saga.

In the *Nieuw Hoorn,* at any rate, the didacticism is straightforward. The vessel itself was controlled not by the skipper, but by a seagoing merchant, Heyn Rol, the shipboard agent of the East India Company appointed to oversee its commercial interests during the voyage. And this provided the useful narrative motif of the ship already dangerously compromised by its sacrifice to money. It was common and necessary for other maritime nations, especially the English, to accuse the Dutch of cutting corners in their shipbuilding specifications (using green timber and the like), in the interests of profit. When Bontekoe watches the *Nieuw Hoorn* sink from his splintered

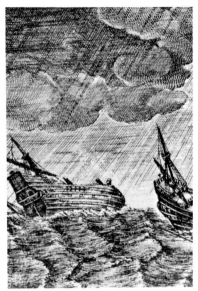

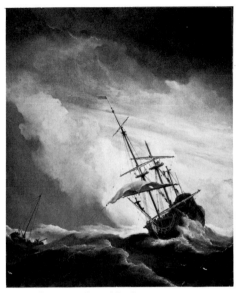

11. Anon. engraving, from Willem
Ysbrantsz. Bontekoe, *Gedenkwaardige
Beschryving* (Amsterdam, n.d.)

12. Willem van de Velde the Younger,
The Gust of Wind. Rijksmuseum, Amsterdam

spar, his exclamation is properly homiletic, dwelling on the set relationship between greed, sin and disaster: "Oh God, how is this fine ship undone, yea, even as Sodom and Gomorrah."[38]

Expiation follows through suffering, and miracles answer forbearance (from eating each other). And in tribulation, of course, the merchant obeys the godly captain who takes on an almost Mosaic quality, imploring the Almighty for guidance in leading his flock to safety. ("Yea, with deep sighs I prayed 'O Lord shew us the way and guide me; yet if Thy wisdom deem it best not to bring me in safety to our Nation, suffer then [if it be Thy will] some of our company to be saved.' ")[39] The importance of this purgatorial phase of the ordeal was presented through both text and the engravings as a sequence of providential intercessions during the "wanderings" at sea. At the time of direst need, Bontekoe wrote, "when we could endure no longer without food, God Almighty sent seagulls to fly over the boat verily as if they desired to be caught, for they flew almost into our very hands."[40] And a few days later, having consumed their boot-toes and [being] reduced to chewing on musket shot and drinking their own urine, a shoal of fishes miraculously burst from the sea and flew into the boat. The likeness to manna and quail in the briny wilderness is not at all accidental. A trial had also to be a rite of passage or, more precisely, a progress, not merely from Europe to the Indies, but from a state of transgression to a state of grace — with the pilgrim in the guise of the skipper. (One of the most popular of all seventeenth-century miscellanies of legends, fables, parables and yarns was the pious schoolmaster Simon de Vries's *Groot Historisch Ocean.*) And in Bontekoe's story, East Indian flying fish and booby birds are appointed agents of divine compassion and signposts on the way to rescue and redemption. In the end, Bontekoe insisted, self-denial, godliness and abstinence (accompanied by psalm-singing led by the captain) prevailed over heathen terror and skeptics' despond.

In these accounts, the reduction of worldly state and goods to a condition of humility and contrition was the precondition of redemption. Set adrift in that "great historical ocean," the little crew, chastened by ordeal, are led by a skipper who is both prince and bishop, leader and pastor: a true godly captain. Consoled and disciplined by his faith (and his rules), they are forced through adversity to be at harmony with one another. Whatever their differences, survival precluded degeneration into a Hobbesian state of animal chaos. So that the most extreme form of brutish self-interest — cannibalism — is represented as the antithesis to *vaderlandsch eenheid* (patriotic unity) invoked by the history chronicles as the ethos of community. Danger, trial and stress, in this view, were supposed to generate the kind of solidarity that was encapsulated in the patriotic motto *Eendracht maakt macht,* "Unity makes might." So it is not surprising to find Jan Deutel, the Hoorn publisher, persuading old Bontekoe, twenty-five years after the wreck, to let his journal be published. For it was not just a patriotic exemplum (though that features prominently in Deutel's prefatory dedication). It was also a parable of Christian community, much as Bunyan's great *Progress,* written at about the same time. "Who shall not greatly marvel," wrote Deutel in his preface, "when reading how a man of that kind

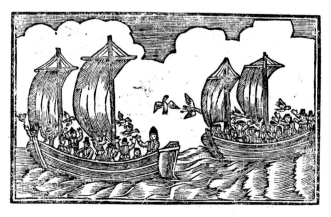

13. Anon. woodcut, Bontekoe, *Gedenkwaardige Beschryving* (Hoorn, 1646)

who come so often to a sudden end—through so much peril and adversity, indeed through dangers in which to hope for any escape appeared to be like despairing, was, by the Lord's mercy brought to a place of safety."[41]

THE NOTION of a communal identity retrieved from the primal flood and made watertight in conditions of peril was not just a matter of heroic metaphor or exemplary allegory. Quite apart from the (now debatable) importance of the inland seas and river barriers in thwarting the conquests of the Spanish armies,[42] it can never be overemphasized that the period between 1550 and 1650, when the political identity of an independent Netherlands nation was being established, was also a time of dramatic physical alteration of its landscape. In both the political and geographical senses, then, this was the formative era of a northern, Dutch, nationhood. In the subsequent historical consciousness of that people, those two processes were inseparably linked together. The nineteenth-century nationalist historian Robert Fruin noted that memories of epic inundations in the late Middle Ages, transmitted to succeeding genera-tions as written and oral folklore—fables, ballads and fairy tales—conditioned the sixteenth-century Dutch to regard themselves as ordained and blessed survivors of the deluge.[43] As one might expect, Calvinist preachers pushed this

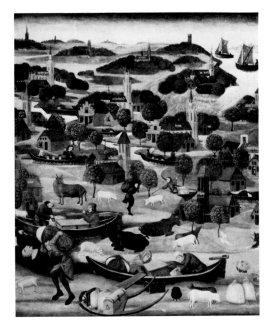

14. Master of the St. Elizabeth's Day Panel, *The St. Elizabeth's Day Flood* 1421. Rijksmuseum, Amsterdam

analogy further. In their rhetoric, the survivors were predestined to inherit; the land was not merely reclaimed but redeemed, and in the process both were morally transformed. So the act of separating dry land from wet was laden with scriptural significance. "The making of new land belongs to God alone," wrote the great sixteenth-century hydraulic engineer Andries Vierlingh, "for He gives to some people the wit and the strength to do it."[44] In other words, the special favor of the Almighty had delegated to the Dutch a kind of license in the act of territorial creation. As a consequence they held a sacred title to their land that precluded intervening allegiance to temporal lords or emperors. Compounded in their determination not to yield to foreign tyrants what had been laboriously wrested from the sea were the *historical* title of ancestral reclamation, the *moral* title awarded to those whose work had created the land and the *scriptural* title that survival against the flood was itself a token of divine ordination. This three-tiered historical self-legitimation helps account for the nationalist intransigence of kindred frontier cultures: the Boer *trekkers* of the South African veldt, the godly settlers of the early American frontier, even the agrarian pioneers of Zionist Palestine. All those groups saw themselves as reincarnations of the biblical Children of Israel, armed with a fresh version of the covenant to Canaan. And that claim to land based on divine allotment was reinforced by the dues owing to their direct labor. Together their title was thought to supersede the temporal claims of legal sovereignty or tenurial residence.[45]

In retrospect, the great inundations of the fourteenth and fifteenth centuries seemed to mark a definite caesura in early Netherlandish history. Economically, they brought to an end the entrepôt role of the Scheldt estuary ports, separating Dordrecht from Geertruidenberg with a wide new arm of the sea, and disrupting the links between southern Holland and thriving Flanders. Zeeland Flanders was itself badly hit by flooding, and a shift in commercial orientation to the north was accelerated by the break. The major disaster occurred on the eighteenth and nineteenth of November 1421, when a violent storm wind from the west simultaneously tore a hole in the sea defenses at Broek and broke the interior dikes at the junction of the Waal and the Maas. On St. Elizabeth's Day, 500 square kilometers were flooded with seawater, right up to Heusden, turning Dordrecht once more into an urban island. Early accounts tell of one hundred thousand deaths and seventy-two villages lost — a maritime apocalypse — but more plausible modern accounts put the figure at ten thousand dead and twenty villages drowned, a dreadful toll in itself. The whole of the fertile and populous Groot Hollandse Waard went under water for good, creating that eerie inland sea, represented in an anonymous panel around 1500, where spires of drowned churches were said to protrude amidst reed beds and the nests of wading birds. Around the east Scheldt fishermen pulled

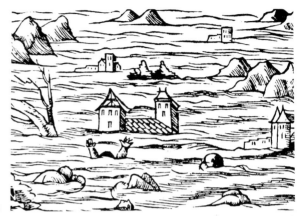

15. Anon. woodcut, "Batavia" from Sebastian Munster, *Cosmographia Universalis* (Basel, 1552)

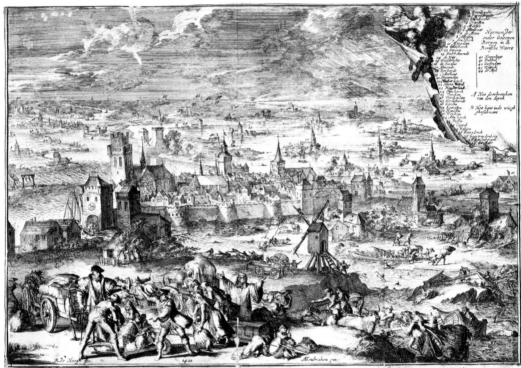

16. Engraving, Romeyn de Hooghe after Arnoud van Houbraken, *The St. Elizabeth's Day Flood*

up skulls and bones along with their catches of shrimp and sprat, and even today boatmen enjoy grim jokes of teeth caught in their trawls and sold to local dentists. Even those hamlets and villages that did survive took generations to recover and were subjected for a long time to boat piracy and plunder raids by the wretched refugees of the flood.[46] It was probably the enduring memory of this inundation that supplied the image of Holland as a drowned land in Sebastian Munster's *Cosmographia universalis* of 1552.[47]

The tidal deluges of the late medieval period occupied the same place in the collective folk memory of south Hollanders and Zeelanders as the visitations of the Black Death in Flanders and Italy. Over two centuries later Romeyn de Hooghe still pictured the St. Elizabeth's Day flood as the primal catastrophe of the Netherlandish nation. The calamities seemed to portend an apocalyptic end to a sinful world, a winnowing of souls, or — an image that meant a great deal to the Dutch — a wiping clean of the slate of iniquity. From that act of awesome retribution, a new and cleaner world was to be reborn, and the Noah analogy was here adapted to suit the Dutch self-image as a nation blessed with infant innocence. It was said, in one of the most popular legends of the sixteenth century, that at the point where the Alblasserwaard dike had withstood one of the onslaughts of storm floods, a cradle was washed ashore. On its roof was a cat, and inside was a baby alive and kicking.[48] Thus the long defense line of dikes and pumping windmills established along the turbulent and frighteningly deep River Lek to prevent further encroachment became known as the Kinderdijk — the child's dike. And the incarnation of national innocence in a diluvian foundling was restated in Theo Rodenburgh's patriotic play, *Batavierse Vryagiespel,* in which another infant is cast onto the waters in his cradle by the military inundations of 1574.

It is sometimes forgotten by political historians that the war for national independence took place at the same time as a particularly fierce phase in the struggle against the sea. The grimness of that latter endeavor made the self-inflicted "patriotic" inundations of 1574 especially poignant. But in many other respects, the two battles were linked in the contemporary mind. Oddly enough, as the climate of politics deteriorated and collapsed in the Netherlands, so did the dikes. There had, of course, been punishing floods well before midcentury, notably in 1502, 1509, 1530, 1532 and 1551–52.[49] But beginning in the 1560s they became particularly calamitous. In 1565, the Diefdyk, longitudinally bisecting the Betuwe region of the lower Rhine between Nijmegen and Rotterdam, had broken, sending water into the repeatedly flooded but fertile Alblasserwaard. But five years later, all these miseries were dwarfed by an immense northwest tempest that swept aside the North Sea defenses on an immense front from Flanders to the Danish coast. The contemporary historian P. C. Hooft wrote feelingly of the scale of the disaster: villagers surprised in their beds, cattle drowned in their stalls, water lapping three feet deep in the church at Scheveningen and along the streets of Dordrecht and Rotterdam. Three thousand souls, he wrote, perished on the Zeeland islands alone, and "not less than a hundred thousand" over the whole extent of the flooded country.[50] But Hooft also unfailingly made the connection between the disturbances of the heavens and those of the state. The Spanish, he commented, supposed that this calamity was a wrathful punishment for the Calvinist blasphemies of image-breaking, while the Protestants held it to be a portent of approaching upheavals.[51]

The flood tides not only functioned in historical chronicle as a metaphor for the ebb and flow of national fortunes; they virtually took on the role of an historical actor—sometimes destroyer, sometimes, as in 1574, deliverer. And if the two processes of resistance—against absolutism and the ocean—were linked together, so were those of national and territorial reclamation. It was noted that the two patriot martyrs, Egmond and Brederode, had also been assiduous in draining lakes and swamps on their estates in the 1540s. And the final repair and drainage of the 1574 floods four years later was greeted as a great public achievement (as indeed it was). Later histories pointed out that the political shape of the Fatherland was being created in the early seventeenth century at the same time that new land was being wrested from the waters. This is not to say that there were not savage floods in this period: on the IJ in 1624 and most spectacularly the collapse of the St. Anthonisdijk in 1651. But they were offset, at least in the official mind, by the appearance of large tracts of lush pasture taken from the sea. The invention of the wind-driven, water-pumping mill, together with massive capital investment, suddenly accelerated the tempo of reclamation. Between 1590 and 1640, some two hundred thousand acres were recovered, over a third from drainage. The most impressive of these projects were concentrated in the Noorderkwartier region north of Amsterdam, where, by 1640, cultivable acreage had increased by forty percent, and its immediate hinterland filled using the labor of three thousand men and a thousand horses. At the inland sea, the engineer Jan Adriaenszoon Leeghwater (Empty Water) deployed a battery of forty-three windmills with a lift of four feet and a system of encircling ring dikes to reclaim 17,500 acres of the richest alluvial soil, both for direct farming and the creation of urban estates for the urban patriciate whose capital had made it possible. The Dutch poet Vondel was sufficiently impressed by the achievement to write a poem on the subject in the sort of lyric hyperbole reserved for military victories.

Together with similar projects on the Purmer (1622), Wormer (1625) and Schermer (1631), the Beemster drainage transformed the domestic economy of north Holland in every sector. Precious additions to both arable and pastoral acreage made it possible to feed not only the exploding population of Amsterdam (31,000 in 1578, 150,000 by 1648) but also its crowded industrial hinterland around the shipyards of the Zaan and the bleaching grounds of Haarlem. The process was to some extent self-replenishing, since the enterprises were largely financed by syndicates of urban capitalists, many of them,

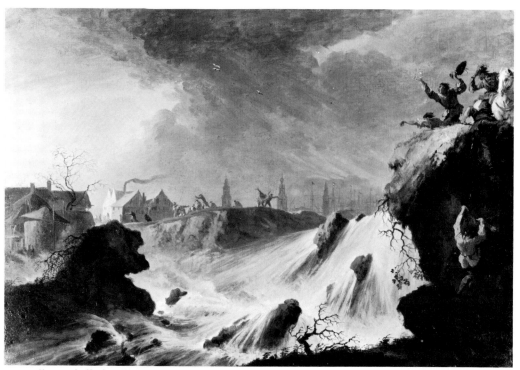

17. Willem Schellinks, *The Collapse of the St. Antonisdyk at Houtewael.* Amsterdams Historisch Museum

like Dirk van Os, a director of the East India Company, based in Amsterdam. Johan Oldenbarneveld, the chief minister of the Republic, personally promoted the Beemster project in 1607–8, and persuaded businessmen to invest nearly a million and a half guilders. By 1612, when the project was completed, the 123 investors recovered rents from the 207 new farms totaling a quarter of a million guilders, or seventeen percent on their outlay.[52] Those who wished to take profit on capital appreciation made a huge killing, and at least some of those profits were plowed back into the mercantile and industrial economy.

The magnitude of these capital gains did not dilute the sense of moral proprietorship that went along with the business of land creation. And there was some historical basis to the geographical roots of republican liberty. For it had been the perennial threat of flood in the already waterlogged lands of Holland, west Utrecht, Flanders, Friesland and Zeeland, which, as early as the eleventh century, had prompted their respective lords (in particular the bishops of Utrecht and the counts of Holland) to offer the inducement of semifree tenurial status to any farmers prepared to colonize and settle the region. The grazing of herds, the settlement of fishing and farming communities, were meant to prevent further encroachment from the sea, and seigneurial lords retained only a tithe right on some produce, modifying even further the conventions of feudalism in the common interest of rural prosperity. Where boats and barges replaced horses and carts, the feudal system was poorly placed to supply the protection or indeed the extortion that underwrote its commands. So that the hardening of feudal hierarchies that took place elsewhere in Europe towards the end of the Middle Ages went by default in the Netherlands. And once labor-extensive stock raising was combined with fishing, market gardening, grain importing and inter-regional river traffic, the domination of the countryside by free farmers and urban mercantile capital became irreversible.

The flood society, then, liberated as well as intimidated. For it dispensed with both the functional need and the historical justification that buttressed social dependence in the rest of the European countryside. If deference to social rules was based on reciprocity for physical safety, it was the dike reeve and the locally elected *heemraadschappen,* the water guardians, rather than any vassal lord, who were in the best position to require it. The autonomy of local communities in respect of taxing themselves to meet hydraulic needs was the territorial basis for their assumptions about the "ascending" nature of political authority, conferred (or at least assented to) from below, rather than devolved from above. From the Middle Ages, the count of Holland shared authority with the local *heemraad* (the title of home council being not insignificant) in administering the essential work of maintenance, repair and extension of the sea defenses. When, in the thirteenth century, these many bodies were amalgamated into larger *hoogheemraadschappen,* they lost none of their practical independence from superior interference. Though the count's man continued to sit along with the councillors, he was customarily appointed from a list of nominees that they presented.[53]

Much of this complicated and peculiar history was patiently explained to the Habsburg emperor Charles V in a famous petition presented by the States of Holland in 1543. Since the fifteenth century it had been recognized that additional taxation was needed for defenses against floods, but the local boards remained wary of this as a pretext for eroding their authority, and, by and large, the rule of the dukes of Burgundy respected this, much as it respected the communal independence of the older towns and provinces. Charles V and his councillors, however, were inclined to a Renaissance model of administrative uniformity that abhorred a profusion of jurisdictions. So that in 1544 the emperor went ahead with organizing a centralized superior body of hydraulic administration, which, however well intentioned, met with immediate resistance, violently expressed in Edam and Assendelft in north Holland. In objecting to imperial nominees as dike reeves, these communities combined highly practical reasoning with more generalized ideological claims. As foreigners, it was asserted, the appointed officials could know nothing of the local *waterstaat* or of the customs and conventions of the communities to which they had been assigned. Andries Vierlingh, the veteran dike master to the princes of Orange, was later to express himself caustically on inexperienced and ignorant place seekers, "the slippers and the tabards" who had been appointed through court favor or relatives in high places, and whose incompetence had literally placed the country in jeopardy.[54] It followed, then, that the appointment of these meddling outsiders was an illegitimate arrogation of local privileges basic to the lives of burghers, and one that had been imposed on them without consultation or assent. The *hoogheemraadschappen* (the governing councils of each of the *waterstaat* regions), it was pointed out, had assumed the *legal* powers to tax and supervise expenditure, so that they were the properly vested executive authority. And it was further implied that it was fiscal ambition, rather than any pretext of concern for efficient hydraulic administration, that had motivated the reform.

A situation already inflamed by religious contention in the mid-sixteenth century was, then, bitterly aggravated by the peculiarly direct relationship between taxes collected for the *waterstaat* in the northern Netherlands and the visibly benign purposes to which they were put. The Burgundian authorities had already placed dikes and dams at public charge in Kenmerland and Friesland in the north, but had been careful not to trespass on local susceptibilities when they did so. While this pre-bureaucratic model of public administration was as perfectly communitarian as one could expect in early modern Europe, it was one that was viable only in small units of government. When engulfed by the ambitions of Renaissance imperial states, it encountered low thresholds of local indignation. Inevitably, the peripatetic officials of the Habsburgs became stigmatized as parasitic intermediaries, usurping the functions of the face-to-face administration preserved in the *hoogheemraadschappen*. However august its credentials, the remote authority on whose behalf they claimed to act was immediately suspected of ulterior motives. The siphoning off of local taxes, especially when they were imposed on local produce or on commercial transactions, for unspecified reasons of state over which the local community had no control was regarded as a conspiracy intended to support unacceptable religious coercion and the foreign army that would be its blunt instrument.

Many of these suspicions were unwarranted. Charles V—many of whose councillors were themselves from the Netherlands—seems to have wanted a centralized regime for the better safeguarding of the sea defenses. But once the seed of suspicion was planted, it proliferated into a thousand ineradicable rumors. No protestation by British governments in the 1760s that stamp and tea duties were to be used for the external defense of the American colonies could dissuade public opinion that they were really part of a plot to subject their freedom to an interfering, arbitrary and *new* despotism. Similarly, in sixteenth-century Holland, these apprehensions had the effect of transforming morally authorized contributions into morally repugnant forced levies. Tax returns from the early seventeenth century show the impositions levied by Dutch authorities to have been far higher than the infamous *Tiende Penning* (Tenth Penny) levied by Philip II's draconian governor, the Duke of Alva. Yet they were accepted without protest, precisely because no suspicion whatever attached to their collection or expenditure.

Right or wrong, the parallelism of the defense against the "tyrant" sea, with the defense against the "tyrant" Spain, was not just a matter of simultaneity. In the minds of those who fought this battle on two fronts, they were causally connected. The appointment of a dike reeve of Holland and West Friesland by William the Silent signified his acceptance, however reluctant, of a *de facto,* if not *de jure,* authority. And in his *Tractaet van Diekgie,* Vierlingh described the struggle with the waters in terms that could have been interchangeable for the war against Spain: "Your foe Oceanus, does not rest nor sleep, either by day or by night, but comes, suddenly, like a roaring lion, seeking to devour the whole land. To have kept your country, then is a great victory."[55] And although Vierlingh died sometime around the formation of the union in 1579, at one point at least he explicitly compares the necessity of a union of means in fighting the waters, the "enemy, against whom Brabant, Holland, Zeeland, Flanders, Henegouwe and Artois together would better resist than one land alone."[56]

The trial by water and the trial by fire were thus directly linked as formative experiences in the creation of Dutch nationhood. The moral analogues of both were repeatedly spelled out in the historical homilies embodied in Vierlingh's and Leeghwater's writings. Vierlingh liked to give the impression of a rough old salt, but in fact he was born into a patrician family, was himself a considerable landowner and quite obviously had enjoyed a rich humanist education. The air of bluff no-nonsense he liked to project did not, for example, preclude him from quoting Cato or Ovid when it seemed appropriate to a discussion of the safety of groins or the digging of ditches. His memoir is full of aphorisms drawn from the standard canon of northern humanism of the generation of Coornhert and Spieghel. So that it is not too much to say that, for all his technical concerns with the details of dike building and maintenance, Vierlingh sets out a humanist philosophy of hydraulics. Reason is preferred to force, for if the waters are met by mere barriers they will repay that *fortse* with interest. Instead, the "persuasion" of streamlining and channel cutting can in effect civilize the waters. The classic humanist virtues of patience, perseverance, resourcefulness and modesty all play a great part in his text, and the *rabauwen en boterriken* (scoundrels and blockheads) who pass for dike masters are denounced for exhibiting the classic vices of ignorance, idleness, pleasure seeking (*gemakzucht*), drink and whoring.[57] To the moral geographer, time must never be squandered but spent usefully (a humanist rather than a Calvinist coinage). Great things may be accomplished through the ingenious use of modest materials supplied by God. "Look at the *dammekens* [small groins]: they are only wattle twigs of willow weighed down with clay, but what benefit they bring at low cost."[58] In the same idiom of humanist pedagogy, Vierlingh saw the waters as wild, natural elements that had to be schooled and trained: bent to the will of civilized man before they could be made benign. The tidal currents and streams, he wrote, were "like green boughs that could be curbed when young," or "like naughty children that must be educated in their infancy."[59] Those that resisted this correction were described as though they were socially delinquent and, to use one of Vierlingh's recurrent terms, had to be *strangled* into nonexistence before they joined forces with other unruly waters to form a hostile and violent force.

Conversely, the paradigm of the Dutch community at its most virtuous and cohesive, was the moment it faced the maximum peril. Vierlingh wrote of this in the language of inspirational communitarianism. "The foe outside must be withstood with our common resources and our common might, for if you yield only slightly the sea will take all." Describing one such emergency, he painted a picture of civic altruism and common purpose that remained the official ideal of the Dutch burgher:

> I saw the danger to the land . . . the gaps in the dikes were jagged and dangerous because much of it had fallen into a deep breach. In the early morning I sent the drummer around to summon every person to work. Those women who had no barrows carried clay in their aprons; others carried it in sacks on their shoulders; others still made bundles of sticks. . . . I managed to collect a large number of people and in the end we succeeded fully in repairing the breach. . . . He who has not seen the anger of old Neptune in his grim wrath and ugliness, should not complain when land is lost.[60]

The virtuous community in danger, moreover, was the opposite of a court at its leisure. It had no room for an aristocracy of manners. Those who put status above duty were, in effect, disqualified from its benefits. Vierlingh was contemptuous of "the slippers, the tabards and the fine fur mantles which have no value at the dikes. They [those who worked against the waters] must be accustomed to hard work from childhood; men who have greased leather boots on their feet and who can stand a rough and harsh climate. In times of storms, wind and hail they must be able to persevere."[61] The antitype to these weatherbeaten republican heroes were men like: "a High Mightiness from The Hague who was so fond of pepper cakes that he was never without them, and who had pea-hen's eggs in his pockets so that he could hatch them out."[62]

Vierlingh and Leeghwater were complementary types in this "hydrographic" culture. The one was an artificer against disaster, a godly captain and tutor of the elements; the other was an engineer of abundance who through the conjunction of virtue and ingenuity could generate prosperity from mud and salt water. Leeghwater, "Jan Wind" to give him his popular nickname, wanted to see the Dutch epic of reclamation consummated in the most ambitious project of all: the drainage of the Harlemmermeer. This huge inland sea, where jet aircraft now land at Schiphol Airport, was some 5 meters deep and 18,000 hectares large. Leeghwater's scheme was positively Egyptian in scale, calling for hundreds of windmills, thousands of laborers and an investment of three and a half million guilders. And although an initial consortium was put together by Anthonie de Hooch, even the most audacious entrepreneurs among the Holland patriciate balked at the risk capital required. The Harlemmermeer had to await the coming of steam power in the nineteenth century before it could be populated with the industrious farms and fat cattle of Leeghwater's vision.

Even without this ultimate accomplishment it is not too much to describe Dutch society as having a diluvian personality, just as archaeologists might describe ancient Nilotic or Gangetic cultures in comparable terms. Its enemies in the seventeenth century were quick to associate this semiaquatic existence with qualities of amphibian baseness — frogs rather than lions — as Oliver Cromwell's propagandists jeered. But one of them, Owen Felltham, who had described the Republic as "an universall quagmire," "the buttock of the world," "a green cheese in a pickle," and who was, therefore, no uncritical admirer, did concede their heroic mastery of the waters. They were, he wrote in 1649, "in some sort Gods, for they set bounds to the Ocean and allow it to come and go as they list."[63] Paradoxically, this ascription of godlike potency would not have been taken as flattery by the Dutch, suggesting as it did inevitable hubris. They were only too well aware that their safety and prosperity were contingent on access to God's bountiful grace and mercy. And that, in turn, demanded obedience to His Commandments. They may be said to have lived within a Christianized diluvian culture in the sense that the behavior of the waters acted as the arbiter of their security and freedom. From whether the flood came as benediction or malediction, victory or nemesis, friend or foe, harbinger or destroyer, they might learn whether they continued to enjoy the protection of the Almighty. That this was the case during the eighty years of the war against Spain was never in doubt, at least to the more emphatically Calvinist chroniclers, preachers and historians. In his contribution to the triumphal anthology *'t Verheerlijckt Nederland,* presented to de Witt in 1668 to mark the happy outcome of the second Anglo-Dutch War, Jacobus Lydius sounded a note that was as much cautionary as self-congratulatory: "When men ask how the Netherlanders, with such little power, could overcome their enemies on land and destroy them at sea and on so many occasions snatch victory from the jaws of defeat . . . then we can only say that this could only have come about through the eternal *covenant* made between God and his children below [*Nederkinderen*]."[64] Likewise, in 1573, William the Silent referred to *"een vaste verbont"*—an unshakable union—made with the King of Kings that self-evidently superseded any earthly allegiance to a mere king of Spain.

More is to be said in the next chapter about the Hebraic analogy, the origins of a national culture in covenant and the exploitation of the Exodus metaphor (from southern fleshpots to northern freedom) in making claims of national birthrights. But it should already be apparent that references in Dutch sermons and tracts to the primal deluge, the *zondvloed,* that ended one world and sealed the new with a covenant, were not fortuitous. Nor were the frequent analogies drawn between the drowning of Pharaoh's hosts in the Red Sea and the waters that rid Leiden of its besiegers. In all these cases, the covenant between God and His Chosen People had destroyed the unrighteous in favor of a new and godly order. In the preface to his treatise on Jewish history, *De Republica Hebraeorum* (1617), Petrus Cunaeus was explicit in connecting the old with the new covenanters: "I offer to your view a commonwealth, the most holy and exemplary in all the world because its author and founder was not mortal but immortal God, . . . that God whose pure veneration and worship you have undertaken and which you now maintain."[65]

To the congregations who flocked to hear the great virtuosi of Calvinist preaching (and who arrived three hours early to be sure of a pew for the great Borstius of Dordrecht),[66] the message that the whole meaning of their national existence was part of a preordained plan that God had for the world must have been simultaneously exhilarating and worrying—just as the preachers intended. To be the instrument by which the haughty and the iniquitous were chastised conferred an awesome sense of historical responsibility. It also helped the Dutch to come to terms with their vulnerable position in Europe and their conspicuously anomalous position as a mercantile republic squeezed between absolutist monarchies. But given the unavoidable fact that, whether they liked it or not, their history was a scroll on which God wrote His providential design, fidelity to the covenant became of paramount importance in sustaining His protection. The Almighty had endowed them with the wit and the will to conquer the waters, and even to turn the waters against their enemies; and He had raised them to great riches and power, the better to proclaim His omnipotence (rather than to liberate them from it in this earthly world). The outward attributes of this wealth, then, had to bear witness to the godly allowance, and imagery within the new Amsterdam Town Hall, completed in the 1660s, took care to allude to Solomon's temple. Ministers who warned against the serpent pride warned the lay magistrates to keep in mind that all the cedars of Lebanon would be of no avail were such edifices to become temples of idolatry.

The fate of Solomon's kingdom was reinforced by other scriptural admonitions in text and image: Belshazzar's feast, the Golden Calf. The message was the same. Were gain and gold to supplant godliness, the new Jerusalem would go the way of the old and follow Nineveh and Babylon into oblivion. Just as they had been raised from the waters, so they would once again be covered by them. In 1653, when the Alblasserwaard was inundated yet again, the plague was raging in the cities and the war against England was going badly, *straf-predikaties* (punishment sermons) were preached throughout Holland. In full spate, Lydius sounded off his jeremiad against the heedless:

> *Sins are come in grievous floods*
> *To lay waste unto the land*
> *Sins are why, with heavy rod*
> *The Lord has armed His hand.*[67]

18. Anon. etching, "Collapse of the Lekkendijk, 1638," from *Staatkundige Historie van Holland* (Amsterdam 1756–82)

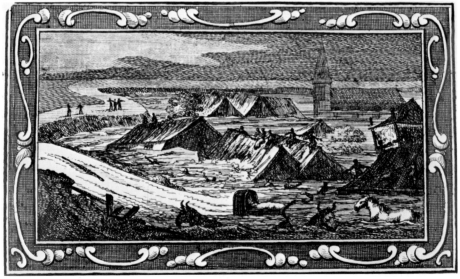

With these rules, it was hard to win. The very success of Dutch society, that material abundance which was the recompense of ordeal, was itself threatening when it reached the point of glut. In Jan Krul's *Wereld-Hatende Nootsaackelijke* (On the Necessity of Other Worldliness) the poet wrote that "an overflow of treasures afflicts the heart and buries the soul in the deepest travail."[68] And a fire on De Rijp in 1655 was ascribed in another devotional work as "an outbreak of God's wrath, a rod of punishment for its inhabitants and for their lust for riches." The playwright Vondel, no Calvinist, warned in similar terms that Amsterdam was "smothered and softened from such an overflow of goods [*stof*]." And in Jan Steen's moving painting of a simple family gracing their meal, there is the homiletic inscription based on Proverbs 30:7-8 pinned to the wall:

> *Three things I wish and nothing more:*
> *Above all else to love my Lord and God*
> No overflow of riches' wealth
> *But to desire what the wisest prayed for:*
> *An honorable life in this vale.*[69]

It was an axiom of Dutch culture that what the flood gave, the flood could take away. So their fear of drowning in destitution and terror was exactly counterbalanced by their fear of drowning in luxury and sin. To defend their

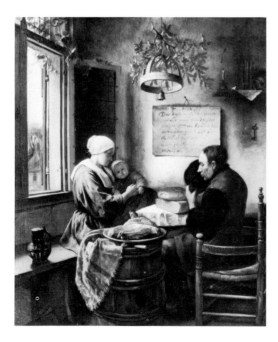

19. Jan Steen, *Grace Before Meat*, 1660. The Lady Ashcombe Collection, Sudeley Castle

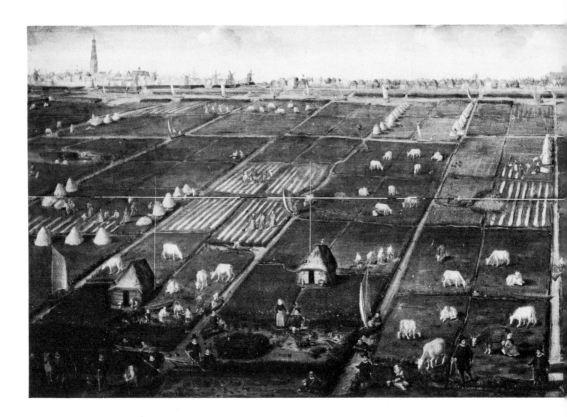

nation's hard-won freedom, even with God's help, demanded the physical resources of strength and power that the waters had provided. But should they begin to wallow in complacency and affluence, they would provoke nemesis, either from the brute elements, or from the covetousness of overbearing neighbors. The arms of Holland bore the device of a lion rampant, guarding a fertile, fenced garden. His sword remained raised, but how to wield it with both dexterity and virtue remained the problem of the lay guardians of the new Israel. Solomon had to remain wise, Josiah pure and Hezekiah repentant — or else the citadel and the temple within it would be razed.

There were no facile solutions to these dilemmas. While Calvinists counseled Christian obedience, their doctrine unhelpfully delegated to lay authorities the responsibility for adjudicating the boundaries between propriety and excess. And many of those magistrates drew on the pre-Calvinist canon of humanist temperance for guidance. The extensive repertoire of rules governing social manners — in respect of diet, drink, dress, relations between the sexes — that came to be thought of as typically Dutch was the product of a particular historical situation. This does not mean that the type of guidance offered in

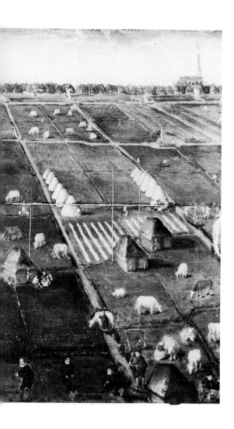

20. Anon., *The Polder Het Grootslag* c. 1595.
Rijksmuseum Zuiderzeemuseum, Enkhuizen,
on loan from the City of Enkhuizen

these areas was their exclusive property. Just as humanism in its social
literature was an international idiom, so there was a successor Calvinist or
Puritan style of counsel that crossed formal frontiers. And even beyond the
confines of Protestant Europe, the same issues of the moral ambiguity of
materialism surfaced in an attempt to patrol manners in the best interest of the
safety of the community. But while the tensions of a capitalism that endeavored
to make itself moral were the same whether in sixteenth-century Venice,
seventeenth-century Amsterdam or eighteenth-century London, the social
forms and vocabularies generated by them were particular to each community.
It can best be summed up as godly patriotism, by definition a general and a
local phenomenon at the same time.

The effort to moralize materialism created special sorts of cultural preoccupations. One that recurs is that of the drama of temptation, so that it is not
surprising to find Potiphar's wife as well as the famished Esau surfacing in both
texts and images of the seventeenth century. But the most profound and
poetic exploration of this torment was neither Calvinist nor Dutch: Goethe's
Faust. Yet in his dying speech, Faust is given a redemptive vision that precisely

rehearses the moral geography of Netherlandish freedom. He conjures up a great scheme of reclamation in which both souls and land would be rescued from the corrupting swamp and the invading flood. By so doing, men were to be made truly free and their freedom would be reaffirmed, not in seductive ease, but through facing perennial danger and ordeal.

> Nur der verdient sich Freiheit
> Der täglich sie erobern muss

Even as Faust carols of a new land made good, "a frontier for the billows of the sea," Mephistopheles assumes the role of tyrannical adversary, the harbinger of deliquescence. For all Faust's belated altruism, Mephisto joins with Neptune, "the old water devil," to break down his barriers and dissolve his flesh into irresistible, unreconstitutable liquefaction. Yet while Mephisto triumphs as the prince of fatal flood, Faust's spirit asserts itself in a terminal passion of purest communitarian virtue: the noblest drowning of all. The new land that he extols is drained of infection and defended against calamity. It is the morality of the Dutch landscape in ecstatic verse:

> I work that millions may possess this space
> If not secure, a free and active race
> Here men and herds, in green and fertile fields
> Will know the joys, that new-won region yields,
> A paradise our closed-in land provides
> Though to its margin rage the blustering tides
> When they eat through in fierce devouring flood
> All swiftly join to make the damage good.   Ay, in this
> Thought I pledge my faith unswerving
> Here wisdom speaks its final word and true
> None is of freedom or life deserving
> Unless he conquers it anew
> With dangers thus begirt, defying fears
> Childhood, youth, age shall strive through strenuous years
> Such busy teeming throngs I long to see
> Standing on freedom's soil, a people free.

> (Solch ein Gewimmel möchte ich sehn
> Auf freiem Grund mit freiem Volke stehn.)[70]

CHAPTER TWO

PATRIOTIC SCRIPTURE

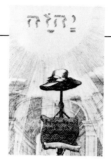

יְהֹוָה

Above all else I thank Him
Who made Holland Jerusalem

JACOBUS LYDIUS
't Verhogde Nederland, 1668

They are the Israelites, passing through the
Red Sea. The waters wall them in and if they set
ope their sluices shall drown up their enemies

OWEN FELLTHAM
A Brief Character of the
Low Countries, 1652

i UNCERTAIN BOUNDARIES

Just who, exactly, did the Dutch think they were?

When a citizen of the Republic consulted the Mirror of the Times, what did he see reflected? What was his image of himself, and his country, set in historical time and geographical space? How sharply were their features defined?

Much depended on station and on generation. Romeyn de Hooghe, as befitted an etcher, historical chronicler and propagandist, had no difficulties

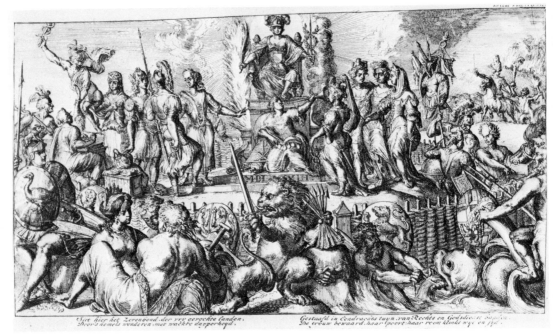

21. Engraving. Romeyn de Hooghe, *The Seven United Provinces*, 1706

with self-definition. In 1706, his *Spiegel van Staat der Vereenigde Nederlanden* (Mirror of the State of the United Netherlands) concluded that the Republic was "far and away the most praiseworthy; the freest and safest [state] that had ever been known."[1] He might have gone further and announced that it was also the richest, but it was in keeping with the national character that he sought to define that he refrained from utterances of sinful pride. The note of confident self-celebration struck in de Hooghe's book was understandable for its time. The Dutch Republic had survived, albeit barely, a war aimed at its dismemberment in 1672, and had had the further satisfaction of witnessing the coalition of its enemies fall apart two years later. Under the captaincy of William III—the object of de Hooghe's most extravagant promotion—the Netherlands had gone on to become the linchpin of an alliance dedicated to opposing the hegemonic ambitions of Louis XIV. So when the Dutch read the history of their own country, the magnitude of its significance was presented as more than purely local. Its fate, they were told, was bound up with mighty global conflicts, wars for the possession of men's souls as well as their lands and taxes. Just as the first generation of the Golden Century invested the struggle against Spain with the global importance of thwarting the Spanish Counter-Reformation, so the last generation saw their own sacrifices of purses and blood as part of the divinely ordained war against Catholic tyranny. If Philip II had played Pharaoh in this eschatology, Louis XIV was cast as Sennacherib to King William's Hezekiah. Daniel Mostaert's *Spieghel der Jeughd of Spaanse Tyrannie* (Mirror for the Young; or, The Spanish Tyranny), through which generations of Dutch schoolchildren learned of the sacred war for freedom in the earlier part of the century, was complemented in 1674 by *De Fransche Tyrannie* (The French Tyranny), repeating many of the same atrocity stories with only the dates and armies changed.[2]

Years of crisis and prolonged military endeavor were likely to imprint on the Dutch mentality an awareness of their symbolic embodiment of the resistance to Catholic absolutism. But this negative identity was matched by a positive synthesis of behavioral traits assembled into a recognizable portrait of themselves. De Hooghe was especially eloquent about what distinguished the Dutch from the other nations of Europe. "The differences between these Lands [and other states] is most singular; glory in other lands reposing in an outward show of flags but here in the manner of thrifty and modest households; elsewhere there is honor in the free spending of money . . . here there is honor in having no debts."[3] The Dutch, in his account, were exceptional in other respects, notably their "strenuous spirit of opposition to a sovereign concentrated in one head"; their respect for commerce rather than nobility; their distaste for superstition "so that in the Seven Lands, sorcerers and miracles; the apparitions of ghosts, spirits and goblins are merely held to be the prattle of women at the spinning wheel."[4] On the other hand, Dutch women were industrious, house-proud and chaste; their menfolk being equally hardworking, frugal in their expenditures and punctilious in honoring contractual obligations. Dueling was anathema in the Fatherland; common riot constrained to a minimum and civil commotion rare, thanks to the blessings of "good governance" (*goede bestier*).

This familiar catalogue of homely virtues more or less conformed to the stock eulogies lavished on the Republic by some (by no means all) foreign commentators. It also ingrained the stereotype of the plain-speaking, soberly dressed, God-fearing burgher, precisely at the historical juncture when it was ceasing to have much relation to social fact. The "age of the periwigs" that stretched before de Hooghe was to be marked by precisely the gradual breakdown of the social and moral consensus that he idealized. Sumptuary extravagance, political ossification and an increasing tempo of tax riots were to characterize the first half of the eighteenth century.[5] Yet the reassuring clichés survived their discrepancies with reality. Nostalgic poetry and, later, in the 1780s, revivalist polemics took the idealized image of the "true" Netherlands as the banner for their grievances against those patricians they accused of betraying it.[6] And the nineteenth-century passion for establishing hallmarks of national differentiation (especially in the aftermath of the disastrous union between the southern and northern Netherlands) revived traditional wisdoms about what made the Dutch Dutch. Passed down through anecdotal lore, popular history, and the corrupt relationship between tourism and self-deprecation, the clichés remain vigorously alive to this day. As any glance at tourist literature attests, fingers remain lodged in the dike, windmills stand guard over lowing herds and the entire country lies low in a posture of immemorial quaintness.

Not all of this is vulgar myth. The windmills *do* stand guard over the lowing herds, and for that matter, candor and caution are two qualities that some Dutch at least suppose to be national traits. But the question at this stage of my argument is not the truth or folly of these very general attributes, but the ways in which they became assembled into a collective self-portrait. Romeyn de Hooghe disposed of the whole problem of *when* the Dutch became Dutch by following much earlier chroniclers in attributing to the Batavians of antiquity most of the characteristics he liked to imagine embodied in his contemporaries. Thus the first dwellers in the bog lands or hol-lands of the nether Rhine exhibited the perseverance, simplicity, hatred of imperial tyranny that was to emerge in their Netherlandish descendants seventeen hundred years later.[7] This imaginary historical continuity was to have great force and endurance, keeping the fable of burghers in bearskins at the back of the popular imagination when it considered its remote national origins.[8] The success of the "Batavian myth" itself signaled the appearance of some sort of early patriotic self-consciousness, and I shall have to return to its chronology and content later in this discussion. But it does not, of itself, answer the difficult question of just when it was that the Dutch began to think of themselves as a separate people.

We may be sure, at any rate, that a strongly developed sense of nationality was the result, not the cause, of the revolt against Spain.[9] In 1609, when the truce that gave the Republic twelve years' respite was signed, it was still far from self-evident where, exactly, the Fatherland lay. Maps that popularly featured the *leo belgicus* superimposed on the Netherlands almost invariably identified it with the seventeen undivided provinces, not the ten of the northern state alone. Even a commonly accepted nomenclature was missing. Dutch chronicle histories that refer repeatedly to *patriotten* are almost studiously vague about the exact definition of the *patria.* "Lands of the United Netherlands" was used in formal treaties and documents to mean the provinces that were signatories to the Union of Utrecht in 1579, but the title was purely formal. Grotius refers more than once to *Republicq,* and *republiek* was common usage by the time of the Peace of Westphalia in 1648, yet misnomers persisted, especially in foreign speech and writing. "The United Provinces" that custom-

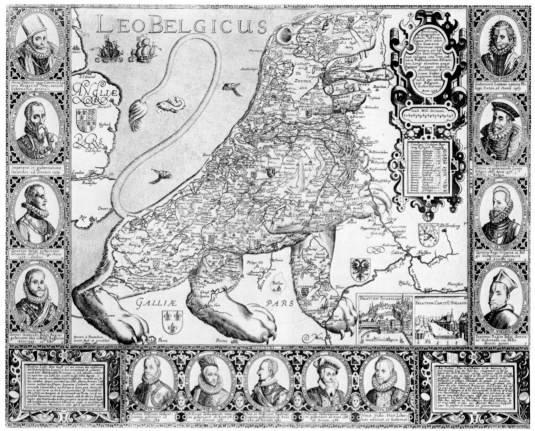

22. Joh. Doetichum, *Map of the Netherlands,* 1598. Rijksprentenkabinet, Amsterdam

arily appears on English maps misleads by implying that what were, in fact, seven virtually sovereign states federated for common defense were provincial dependents of some higher national authority. The French usage of "Low Countries" (*Pays-Bas*) was applied indiscriminately to the Netherlands east and west of the Scheldt and Maas, and the habit of subsuming the entire country within the single province of Holland (however indispensable to its preservation) did most violence of all to accurate description.

In defense of these bewilderingly loose terms, it must be said that the Dutch themselves were deliberately provisional about their own territorial limits, especially in the earlier part of the seventeenth century. Borders were, of course, a prime subject of dispute between contending parties. While never formally renouncing the possibility of a reconquest of Flanders and Brabant, the pragmatic States Party, guided by Oldenbarneveld, was prepared to allow the lines achieved at the truce to harden into a *de facto* frontier. The interests of the vulnerable new nation, it was argued, especially its commerce, would best be served by peace rather than war—a verdict that was by no means concurred with throughout the governing patriciates of the Dutch cities, and especially not in Amsterdam.[10] From intensely divided camps of opinion and a lingering suspicion of Spain's intentions, the militant Calvinists and the military entourage at the Stadholder Maurice's court assembled forces sufficient to dislodge Oldenbarneveld and reverse his policies, in both religion and diplomacy.[11] Thereafter, bellicose assertiveness prevailed, culminating in the renewal of war in 1621, concentrated in precisely those sectors of the south and west that seemed the keys to the "lost" provinces. Many of the most formidable of the Calvinist preachers triumphant in 1618 had themselves come from the south, and to them the thought of abandoning the great cities of the Netherlandish heartland—Antwerp, Leuven and Ghent—to papist idolatry and the hosts of Antichrist was deeply repugnant.

It was only when the interminable campaigning pursued first by Maurice and then by Frederick Henry became mired in protracted sieges and fruitless advances and retreats across minimal areas of territory that this passionate irredentism gradually abated. At the same time, the distinctively Flemish or Brabander character of the southern diaspora was, by the 1630s and 1640s, beginning to melt into a broader, and different, northern Dutch identity. From the middle of the seventeenth century, concern about the south was more likely to be directed against French aggrandizement than profiting from Spanish weakness. On several occasions, beginning in 1635, France had proposed a plan of partition by which the Spanish Netherlands would be divided between itself and the Republic. Even at that early date, when the war with Spain was in progress, the temptation of reunification was offset by the hesitation to have France as an immediate neighbor, and by the prospect of Antwerp's restoration as a rival to Amsterdam. In the 1650s and 1660s, when de Witt attempted to finesse these anxieties by offering to create a quasi-independent "Belgic" republic on the Swiss model, secured by a Franco-Dutch co-protectorate, the scheme still failed to dislodge the traditional objections. Paradoxically, then, Louis XIV was alienated by the refusal of the States General to contemplate an expansion of its own territory into the old heartland of the Netherlands! And this *klein-Nederland* policy was as a result to cost the Republic dear in terms of an ambitious and aggrieved king.[12]

It had taken almost a century, though, before "the Fatherland" became exclusively associated in Dutch minds with the seven provinces and their directly governed territories in Flanders, Brabant and Limburg. Even then, there remained some groups in the population, by no means all Calvinist, who yearned for a "reunion" across the river barriers. Dutch Catholics, who constituted over a third of the population, stood to gain most from such a reunification, not, of course, through force of arms but through some sort of accommodation that might permit mutual and open toleration of faiths in both north and south—a will-o'-the-wisp if ever there was one. Given their existence on sufferance in the Republic, any such feeling had to be discreetly rather than overtly proclaimed. And it may be that Vermeer, who eventually converted to Catholicism, expressed such a nostalgic view of the old Netherlands and its art in his *Allegory of Painting,* the work that, above all others, his widow tried to keep in the family's possession after his death.[13] In the map that appears so prominently above the figure of the painter (once thought to be a self-portrait) the Fatherland is represented, not in its new guise, as the seven provinces of the Republic, but the seventeen of the humanist Renaissance.[14]

The straggling shape of the new country was, then, determined more by fortunes of war and pragmatic considerations of policy, than either natural geography or a self-evidently tribal feeling for blood and soil. The North Sea, of course, was one insuperable natural frontier; and to the east, the River Ems was generally taken to be the border dividing off the "Netherlands" (in whatever configuration) from more authentically low German states such as East Friesland, Bentheim, Münster and Julich. This did not prevent Henry VIII from describing the ill-favored Anne of Cleves as his Flanders mare. Even had the logic of geography been followed in the south and west where the Waal, Maas and Scheldt flowed to the sea, it is hard to imagine what territorial coherence could have been provided by an estuary.

Was the Fatherland, then, as the historian Pieter Geyl believed, where its tongue was spoken?[15] Or what, indeed *was* its native tongue? Flemish, of course, remained the dialect of the "captive" provinces; Frisian dominated in the rural districts of the northern province and Oosterse; a low German dialect, neither Dutch nor *plattdeutsch*, was the spoken and written language of much of Gelderland. Social and cultural distinctions made for further complications. Like most of the rebel nobility whose careers determined the destiny of the new nation, William the Silent spoke and wrote French, the language in which his official justification for revolt, the *Apologie,* was expressed. And in common with their scholarly counterparts across Europe, the humanist circles at Leiden, the university whose foundation in 1575 marked something like a cultural declaration of independence, communicated in Latin. This is not to say that there was no vernacular history or literature early in the career of the Dutch Republic. The greatest of its comic dramatists, Bredero, took special pride in lampooning the pretensions of the Frenchified, the Italianate and Hispanicized and exulted in the robust beauties of Dutch.[16] Bredero's unapologetic delight in Nederduytsch came from his roots in the still flourishing *rederijkers,* the "chambers of rhetoric" that were part drama companies, part schools of oratory and part poetasters. And it was as a *rederijker,* a member of the Amsterdam chamber, "In Liefd Bloeyende," that the humanist writer Hendrik Laurensz. Spieghel published his passionate defense of the virtues of the *moedertaal* (mother-tongue). A spelling book, etymology and grammar all in one, the *Tweesprack van de Nederduitsche Letterkunst* (The Dialogue of Dutch Letters) was, significantly, a collaboration between several hands, all of whom represented the translation north of the flower of Netherlandish culture. It appeared in 1584 under the imprint of Plantijn, the great Antwerp publisher whose house had moved to Leiden to escape Parma's armies, and with an emblematic frontispiece by Hendrick Goltzius, the outstanding genius of the Haarlem school and the pupil of Spieghel's colleague Coornhert, who had himself contributed to the book. In this way, too, it was a product of all the great centers of Netherlandish culture, past and future: Antwerp, Leiden, Haarlem and Amsterdam. Moreover, the work, modest as it was, was not simply a lexicography but took special pride in advertising the distinctive virtues of the Dutch language. It was, Spieghel boasted, "richer than all other tongues known to us"[17] and should be purified from the corruptions of French and the archaisms of Latin. Unlike the ancient tongues, moreover, it was (like the people who spoke it, the text implies) somehow *truer* because closer to nature. By this was meant onomatopoeia that was deemed especially helpful because it assisted understanding along with utterance. Who could possibly speak the word *zucht* and not sigh at the same time, or say the world *trommel* and not sound like the drum it signifies?[18]

The *Tweesprack,* extraordinary though it is, remains unique, so far as I know, as an item in conscious linguistic propaganda in the period of the Revolt. And the urgency of its tone was surely a response to the predicament that the Netherlanders found themselves in in 1585, with the fall of Antwerp to Parma's armies traumatically sundering the old unities of south and north. It was in this period, too, that some histories were translated into the vernacular, though the most famous and enduring of them date from after the truce of 1609. Significantly, it was not until the identity of the new state was much more settled, in the 1620s and 1630s, that a new generation of grammars and dictionaries was produced by scholars like Petrus Montanus and Plempius. At any rate, it seems reasonable to argue that an allegiance shaped by language was the consequence, not the cause, of the war for independence. It was only in 1650 that Vondel could write with revealing satisfaction that the language had come of age, for "our speech is now spoken in the council of state at The Hague and in Amsterdam, the mightiest commercial city in the world, by merchants who exclude all un-Dutch terms."[19]

If borders meandered arbitrarily along shifting fronts of battle, and cultural frontiers petered out into linguistic incoherence, was the early Republic, at least, unified by faith? Here, too, historical reality belies the simplicities of nineteenth-century determinism, according to which the Republic was the political expression of a defiant community of the free and the devout. For in many, if not most, important respects, it is misleading to assume that the Dutch Republic and orthodox Calvinism were interchangeable. Calvinism was certainly the official, and the privileged, denomination, but it never succeeded in becoming *the* state church, still less was it a benchmark of patriotic allegiance. Numbers alone were against any such possibility. One historian of the church has estimated that at the turn of the seventeenth century (in other words when the Republic came into being) no more than ten percent of the population were committed Calvinists.[20] This seems an improbably low estimate, but an upper figure of around fifty-five percent for most of the history of the Republic is not in dispute. This leaves a substantial minority of the population, most of whom would certainly have regarded themselves as belonging to the Fatherland as members of the unreformed Catholic Church, or different (and in many cases hostile) denominations of the Reformation. And even for those who identified themselves as members of the Reformed Church, there was only one predikant (preacher) to every nine hundred of the faithful.[21]

Arithmetic is not everything, of course. It is certainly true that if Calvinists alone could not have made the Republic, the Republic would certainly not have been made without Calvinists. It was their militant iconoclasm in 1566 that first bunched a fist in the face of Counter-Reformation Spain.[22] And contrary to the stock wisdom that theirs was the faith of the common people and petty burghers, resolute Calvinists could be found in strength (especially in the south) among virtually all classes of the population including the nobility. Subsequently, it was during times of desperation (of which there were many) during the Eighty Years' War for independence that the heterodox rallied round the staunchest defenders of the faith, and took courage from the preachers' invocations of the sword of Gideon and the sling of David. When the Spanish armies were literally at the throats of burghers and farmers, it was the unshakeable Calvinist belief in the providentially favored election of the Dutch that fortified the will to survive and resist.[23] But as that immediate physical threat receded and the theaters of war became more remote, in Brabant or in Brazil, so militant Calvinism as the faith of patriotic emergency lost its grip in a country poorly designed for theocratic uniformity. Paradoxically, the same institutional circumstances that gave Calvinism its opportunity also limited its domination. The stubborn localism that made Habsburg centralization impossible was no more encouraging to Calvinist uniformity. In keeping with its pronounced federalism, the thirteenth article of the Union of Utrecht upheld the right of each province to regulate its own religious establishment.[24] A subsequent clarification intervened in that freedom only so far as to preclude Catholicism from suppressing the Reformed religion altogether, but still inclined towards a tolerant, even latitudinarian view of religious practice. So it was not fortuitous that during the whole first century of Dutch freedom, there was but one national synod. And down through the pyramidal structure of the Reformed Church, from provincial synods to the district classes to town church councils, the rule of the clergy was at all times moderated by, and in crucial points obliged to defer to, the government of the laity. Ironically, it was the very doctrine of Calvinism that made life difficult for the clergy. It was required in essential matters (like the solemnization of marriage or the administration of charity) to divest itself of governing authority, and confer it on the magistracy. And it further required that the same pious laity, as elders and deacons, govern and pay for its own personnel. In some centers, like Amsterdam, where a particularly militant clergy was regularly embroiled with a usually tolerant majority of regents, there were even official representatives of the lay power, the "political commissioners" deputed to represent their views before church classes and synods.[25]

In orthodox Calvinist terms, these arrangements assumed a God-pleasing identity of views between clergy and laity in most essentials. And the differences that did arise should not be exaggerated. For the most part there was a considerable degree of harmony between laity and ministry in their joint enterprises. But in the polyglot, metropolitan conditions of a trading republic, such concurrence was by no means automatic or uninterrupted. And laity and clergy could find themselves at odds over the crucial issue of exactly how uniform belief and practice in the Republic should be. The magistracy to whose charge the church itself had confided the tasks of government understood very well that any attempt to create a republic of the orthodox would not result in a unified country, but one that would splinter to pieces. Instead they created a sort of involuntary heterodoxy. Only in 1618, when Oldenbarneveld's truce with Spain was made to seem simultaneously an act of religious and political infirmity, could there have been an attempt to impose the faith militant. This sporadically interrupted Erastianism was of most consequence to the very large Catholic minority, who were obliged to worship in diplomatic privacy, but who were certainly not subjected to any systematic effort at repression. This was not due to any want of vigilance on the part of the church authorities themselves. Synod after synod reiterated bitter complaints at the temerity with which Catholic practices continued, but that very reiteration is, of course, a sure sign that little heed was paid to their recrimination.[26] Even when there seemed opportunities to accompany military by religious conquest, as at 's Hertogenbosch in 1629, the Stadholder himself resisted any kind of organized mission.[27] Nor was Frederick Henry much more determined to root out the more Arminian "Remonstrant" minority against whom his brother Maurice had conducted the coup d'état of 1617–18. At Nijmegen, another key town on the frontier of orthodoxy (and full of Catholics), the Stadholder, who had rights of appointment to the town council, actually restored two important figures, Christoffel Bierman and Johan Biel, who had been evicted in the purges of 1618. While membership of the Reformed Church was a condition of officeholding throughout the Republic, it was made clear that a mere declaration of conformity would suffice for their restoration.[28] And what went for Nijmegen and den Bosch went *a fortiori* for cities like Amsterdam that had embraced the Reformed Church with less than wholehearted devotion. By 1627, not ten years after the purge led by the militant Calvinist Reinier Pauw, his faction had become a weak minority on the council. Anti-Remonstrant riots on Easter Monday in 1626 had, in effect, determined the majority that disorder was too great a price to pay for religious purity. And, with Andries Bicker's elevation to burgomastership in 1627, there was initiated a long period in which social peace was preferred over doctrinal rigor.[29]

That the regents of the Republic, by and large, could afford to take a measured view of the requirements of orthodoxy was in part due to the additional fact that even within the Calvinist fold, serious differences of doctrine and moral guardianship persisted. And the more apparently picayune the issue, the more captious the quarreling could be. Organs, for example, were a great source of contention in the 1630s, when no less a figure than the learned and powerful secretary of Stadholder Frederick Henry, Constantijn Huygens, took it on himself to defend their use.[30] Huygens was himself a virtuoso composer who claimed no fewer than eight hundred works to his credit. But he was also a devout Calvinist who took the greatest pride in his spirituality and who defended the use of organ music on religious grounds alone. The ruling of the Synod of Dordrecht of 1574 that had required their banishment or disuse and forbade their maintenance had, he argued, led to the worst possible situation of their being tolerated as useless ornaments or distractions in church instead of actively contributing to the greater glory of God. Huygens was attacked just as vehemently by a preacher at his own back door in The Hague, Johan Janszoon Calckman, who denounced music as a pagan novelty and who cited Paul's condemnation of Corinthian psalms by way of authority.[31] Faced with this kind of argument between doctrinal purity and devout learning, the church did what it always did in a pinch: left the matter open to local councils to decide for themselves. And in 1638 the Synod of Delft officially gave parishes the right to determine whether or not they wanted to have organ music in church, a decision that in effect awarded the victory to the more lenient view.[32]

Benign incoherence, then, was the working principle in matters of church arbitration. And in other areas where the councils would have liked to have exercised regulation: in Sunday trading; in the persistence of fairs and markets; of "pagan" festivals like St. Nicolas's Day; over personal abominations like the fashion for curled long hair that swept the Republic in the 1640s and gave rise to a great outburst of fulminations from the pulpits, the church accepted a role that was monitorial rather than magisterial. And so long as the magistracy itself professed orthodoxy but practiced heterodoxy, they had no other choice. And in turn, that pragmatism in religion restored much of the old Erastianism to which William the Silent had adhered. It meant, in particular, that alongside the Calvinist majority, minorities of Lutherans, Remonstrants, Mennonites and Jews were not only tolerated but could actually flourish, publish their own sacred and learned texts and even open seminaries.

The institutional diffuseness of the Republic that worked against Calvinism becoming synonymous with the state religion of the Dutch, also undermined other impulses towards national unification. Indeed *national unification* in the case of the Dutch is a contradiction in terms since they had come into being as a nation expressly to avoid becoming a state. Simon Groeneveld, who has written most perceptively on this paradox, goes rather too far, I think, when he claims that "most Netherlanders" would have recognized only their town, neighborhood or province as a home community.[33] But he is absolutely right to emphasize that the Dutch revolt was directed not only at the iniquities of Philip II's religious policy, but against most of the tendencies—fiscal centralization, professional bureaucracy, executive justice, dynastic absolutism, the erosion of urban and seignorial privileges—that characterized the High Renaissance state. To *be* Dutch was to be local, parochial, traditional and customary. It meant insisting that power ascended from the local community to higher authorities only on specific terms and conditions, among which were corporate consent (to military billets and new taxes, for example), the right to recall mandated delegations, and to repudiate unauthorized votes. Especially during the first, long period of military resistance to Spain, from 1570 to 1609, the Dutch were more obviously united by what they commonly abhorred than by what they collectively wished to embrace. Theirs was a politics of contingencies and exigencies that hardened over time into an institutional equilibrium.

This ultrapragmatic view of the forming of republican institutions did not sit well with the nineteenth century's view of immanent nationality. From the American Revolution on, wars for independence were conventionally depicted by their chroniclers as the necessary outcome of some deeply implanted historical incompatibility. New national identities were retrospectively discovered to be incipient within the old allegiance, merely awaiting their liberation. The political acts that led to the sundering of that allegiance are, in that view, demoted from causes to occasions, and the process by which an embryonic identity hatches into new life, characterized as natural. The metaphorical language of biological inevitability was made much of in the Enlightenment, as in the century that followed. It became common, for example, to write of the historical necessity for American freedom in this vein, so that perhaps the most telling word of all in the Declaration of Independence was the first: *When.*

Not surprisingly, then, both John Adams in the 1780s and John Lothrop Motley in the 1840s imposed historicist assumptions about the birth of American freedom on the beginnings of Dutch nationhood. Indeed, they were, in their view, part of a continuously unfolding epic of northern, national liberty.[34] But it was not only Hollandophile foreigners who wrote of the birth of the Dutch Republic in this overdetermined manner. For if fundamentalist Calvinists like Groen van Prinsterer and constitutional liberals like Bakhuizen van den Brink and his pupil Robert Fruin were sharply divided on *what* values had created the new nation, they shared the assumption that it was the inevitable expression of some preexisting Netherlandish ethos. Even Pieter Geyl, who was thought heretical in stressing the geographical arbitrariness of the Republic, did so in the interests of emphasizing the *naturalness* of the larger cultural community of Dutch-speakers, across the Maas and Scheldt.

Historians, of course, like nothing better than to play the tiresome game of generational rebellion. My teacher's orthodoxy shall be my heresy and so I will plant my flag. Perhaps, if the history of the Dutch revolt was once greatly overdetermined, it is now in danger of being so underdetermined as to be merely another of those accidental blips on the surface of the inexorably monotonous historical continuum. (The same fate seems to await all the phenomena that the nineteenth century, for better or worse, thought had shaped their world: the English Civil War, the French Revolution and so on.) But it is fair to say that the mess of complicated uncertainties to which the Dutch revolt has now been reduced by current historiography authentically recovers the anxieties of the contemporaries who lived through it. William the Silent only become the *pater patriae* after his assassination and was deeply ambivalent about the act of rebellion itself. His own office of stadholder, after all, was by definition a stewardship appointed by the king, not the embodiment of some natural leadership answerable only to God. He did, of course, eventually and famously insist on accounting before a "higher" overlordship, but it took a draconian policy on the part of Philip II to push him over the edge. It was only in his (revealingly titled) *Apologie* of 1581 that he referred to himself as "an absolute and free Prince." Alva's regime, the threat it posed to traditional privileges in towns and estates alike, as well as the horrors of the Spanish military, succeeded in rallying to the zealot camp Netherlanders for whom militant Calvinism and rabid iconoclasm had been nearly as distasteful as the Inquisition. To humanist magistrates and noble landowners it was the Spanish crown, and not themselves, that had initiated a radical break with tradition. Until 1789, at least, the legatees of a revolutionary upheaval always invoked the conservation of immemorially prescribed custom and law in justifying resistance to an improperly innovating power. But in the Dutch case, this most cautious, legally minded and conservative argument (expressed, for example, in Grotius's and P. C. Hooft's versions and in Francken's *Deductie*) remained a paramount element in the legitimation of the revolt. It also meant, however, that it was easier to abjure allegiance to Philip II than to decide to whom or what sovereignty should be transferred. During the 1570s, the States had nervously edged towards some sort of sovereignty-claim, so as to be able to provide William with the "high authority" he needed to prosecute the war. And it was a similar military emergency in 1585 that forced them to grasp the nettle again to invest the Earl of Leicester as "Governor-General" under a "protectorship" of Queen Elizabeth I. Implied in the States General's approach was the assumption that the Queen would respect all the local privileges, customs and liberties for which the Dutch had fought. It was this axiomatic abridgment of royal authority that made any close Anglo-Dutch connection impossible. Arguably, it was only when all these "haphazard improvisations" had come to grief that the States General finally openly embraced the sovereign power.[35]

If the Dutch finally espoused independence, they did so with the lowest possible profile. The Union of Utrecht which is conventionally taken to be the "founding document" of the Republic was emphatically not a constitution.[36] It was rather a treaty of common defense between the signatory states, each of which remained sovereign within the federation (*bondgenootschap*) so formed. It made provision for no common institutions of government, the States General being empowered to enact only what had been previously assented to in the separate assemblies of the separate states. Article V did provide for funds necessary to fight the common war, and future Stadholders and Grand Pensionaries (in particular, Simon van Slingelandt at the outset of the eighteenth century) chose to interpret this as a writ for a common system of taxation. Whether or not this was in the mind of those who framed the article is a moot point, but in any event, the interprovincial distribution of whatever global sum was to be raised in a given year was set out in a proportional "quota." Holland, of course, was allotted the lion's share—around fifty-eight to sixty percent—but it was left to the respective provinces to raise funds in whatever manner they saw fit.[37]

Not only were taxes not made uniform throughout the Republic, but coinage, weights and measures further varied widely between province and

province, and occasionally even between town and town. In all these respects
the institutional incoherence of the Republic (which so shocked post-Cartesian
political arithmeticians and state makers in the seventeenth and eighteenth
centuries) was entirely in keeping with its *raison d'être*.

The role allotted to the House of Orange did little to alter this. The office
of Stadholder was in no way comparable with that of the royal dynasties of
baroque Europe, justified by divine unction and armed with absolute power.
However much the princes of Orange rankled under the constraints placed on
their power, only William II made a determined effort to cut loose, by
coalescing the army, the Reformed Church and his faction of Orangist regents
into a formidable Court Party. But his demarche, involving a purge and arrest
of recalcitrant States Party regents in Dordrecht and an armed expedition
against Amsterdam in 1650, ended abruptly with his premature death the same
year. A newly resurgent anti-Orangist group profited from the sudden vacuum
of authority to place even more severe limitations on the Stadholderate and
the dynastic politics which, it claimed, compromised the true interests of the
Republic. In keeping with the decentralization principle, each province had,
in any case, to appoint its own Stadholder, who might not necessarily be the
same prince of Orange, or stem from the dynastic trunk. The Frisian branch,
which succeeded to the Stadholderate of Holland and Zeeland in the eighteenth
century, was, throughout the previous century, quite distinct. Sovereignty, it
was affirmed, lay with the States General, whose bidding the Stadholder was
to do as once he had done the king's. So that not even a late Stuart "king-in-
Parliament" situation prevailed in the Republic. Under the de Witts, the
process of reducing the dynasty to a minor emblem of political insignificance
was taken further by an attempt to make the separation of the Stadholderate
from the captain-generalship and admiral-generalship of the Republic "perpetual."
It was only because of the catastrophic circumstances of 1672 when nearly half
the country succumbed to French invasion, that this policy was reversed,
amidst an irresistible outpouring of Orangist patriotic sentiment. William III
capitalized on this to present himself once again as the living incarnation of
the national will, and around his severe, uncompromising fortitude, the
collapsing nerves of the Dutch made their spectacular rally. Even then,
however, William operated as something less than a king, refraining, after the
first terrible bloodletting in The Hague, from vindictive pursuit of his enemies.

The dynasty did (and does), then, have its patriotic mystique. Its prowess
and charisma is inseparable from the survival of a special and particular Dutch
national identity. Throughout the seventeenth century the imposing sar-
cophagus built by Hendrick de Keyser for the assassinated William the Silent
in the Nieuwe Kerk in Delft became a place of pilgrimage. Under Stadholder
Frederick Henry (1584–1647) and his ambitious wife, Amalia van Solms, there

was a more systematic endeavor to create a court culture in the manner of the Stuarts, to whom the House of Orange had become matrimonially connected. Simple residences at Ter Nieuwburch and Honselaarsdijk were transformed through the classical style then favored in France into elegant small palaces, complete with formal gardens, allegorical statuary and ceilings covered with appropriate history painting announcing the martial prowess and celestially auspicious career of the dynasty.[38] After Frederick Henry's death, the dowager princess had the Oranjezaal at the Huis ten Bosch designed by Pieter Post and decorated as a mausoleum to his memory. Owing a great deal to the style of allegorized history produced by Rubens for James I at Whitehall and Marie de Médicis at the Luxembourg, the Oranjezaal was the most resplendent expression of dynastic aspiration in the Republic. But that, of course, was a contradiction in terms, and the princely palaces remained something of an anomaly in Dutch public life, reserved for the ceremonies of signing treaties, entertaining visiting royalty and sustaining the somewhat ambiguous dynastic politics to which the House of Orange remained committed throughout the seventeenth century. Characteristically, those artists commissioned for the "propaganda" history paintings of the Oranjezaal were either celebrated Flemings like Jacob Jordaens, pupils of Rubens (who had died in 1640) like Pieter Soutman and Theodorus van Thulden, or those Dutch artists who specialized in the grand epic manner and disdained the ignobility of inferior genres: Pieter de Grebber, Adriaan Hanneman, Jan Lievens and Gerrit Honthorst.[39]

There were, of course, no coronations in the Dutch Republic, nor elaborate formal audiences. The Netherlandish version of the royal progress, the *joyeuse entrée,* went back to the Burgundian late Middle Ages, and was periodically revived to greet visiting royalty, and, on occasion, to acclaim a triumphant stadholderian retinue. It was, however, no slavish prostration before a crypto-monarchical conqueror. Built into its ceremonies was a formalized recognition by the visiting magnate of the rights and privileges embodied in town charters and customary law. The symbolic connotation of the triumphal arch, then, had been cunningly reversed from its origins under Augustus, Trajan and Hadrian. Instead of an acceptance of Caesarism, it signified the barrier through which military power passed in order to regain access to — literally — civilized society. In so doing, the victor who once paraded his spoils now accepted the conditions imposed on his "sovereignty." This ritual was respected by royal dignitaries, even in the captive south, where successive Habsburg viceroys in the seventeenth and eighteenth centuries appreciated the need to make tactful concessions to civic amour propre in Brussels, Ghent and Antwerp. The Emperor Joseph II, who treated such antics with contempt as an obscure relic of a dysfunctional past, brought down a violent revolt on himself when he attempted their suppression. In the Dutch Republic, the acclaim that greeted a Stadholder was an even more emphatic resistance to Caesarism. So that in wartime the Stadholder existed in an uneasy capacity, part warlord, part commissioned officer; in peacetime his role was even more presidential-patriarchal, rather than royal-governmental. Whether the House of Orange-Nassau took an active or a passive role in politics, though, it was inconceivable that the Republic should take shape as a mere emanation of the dynasty, much as Muscovy turned into Russia through the formative hegemony of the tsars' hegemony or the Holy Roman Empire in the seventeenth century became dissolved within the proprietary realm of the Habsburg dynasty.

To recapitulate: The independence of the Dutch Republic was uniquely the product of historical contingencies and circumstances — political, religious and military — which in no way predetermined its future character. Nor did it owe its identity to the working out of some iron law of social and economic evolution. Once freed from imperial authority, it was left to make itself up without any of the self-evident markers of territory, tribe, language or dynasty that were customarily held to be the criteria for national self-consciousness. Into the vacuum left by the collapse of monarchy poured the contending (though not mutually exclusive) influences of Calvinism, humanism and commercial pragmatism. By themselves, none of these supplied a ready-made answer to the questions the citizens of the new land needed to ask, to wit: Who are we? Where have we come from? Where do we go from here?

The most extraordinary invention of a country that was to become famous for its ingenuity was its own culture. From ingredients drawn from earlier incarnations, the Dutch created a fresh identity. Its manufacture was in response to what would otherwise have been an unbearably negative legitimation: rebellion against royal authority. Unlike the Venetians, whose historical mythology supplied a pedigree of immemorial antiquity and continuity, the Dutch had committed themselves irrevocably to a "cut" with their actual past, and were now obliged to reinvent it so as to close the wound and make the body politic whole once again. On a more pragmatic level, it was imperative that popular allegiance be mobilized exclusively in favor of the new Fatherland. What was required of a northern Netherlandish culture, then, was that it associate all those living within the frontiers of the new Republic with a fresh common destiny, that it stigmatize the recent past as alien and unclean and rebaptize the future as patriotic and pristine.

This was done by drawing on three kinds of sources. The first reached behind and beyond the immediate past to an imaginary or heavily embellished Dutch antiquity and an equally obscure medieval history. In antiquarian chronicles like the *Divisiekroniek* (written a century before Dutch independence but revised in the seventeenth century for contemporary purposes), the singular qualities of the Dutch nation — their energy, simplicity and passion for liberty — were disclosed in primitive form.

The second source, which complemented the first, was contemporary history, related in erudite tomes written in Latin and in popular chronicles in the vernacular, in illustrated verse and prose epics, in ballads, dramas, commemorative festivals and days of prayer and thanksgiving. Through the imaginative re-enactment and recitation of the (authentically) heroic struggle, future generations of Dutch men and women were to experience, vicariously, the terror and euphoria of the revolt. Their national identity was the crystal residue left from the fire of the historical experience.

Finally, there was association by analogy. Ostensibly, this was the most indirect cultural source of all, yet arguably it became the most compelling way in which the Dutch were drawn together in mutually recognizable community. Two quite different analogies were available, the Batavian and the Israelite, and it is sometimes thought that they were projected at quite different cultural clienteles and by quite different transmitters. It is true that the scriptural idiom came most easily to the lips of preachers, while Tacitus' history of the Batavian rebellion against Rome was cherished by humanist scholars and gentlemen. But in many minds, both learned and vulgar, I am sure, these heroic exempla overlapped and mingled, just as on the walls of the "eighth wonder of the world," the new Amsterdam town hall, there were to be found both Roman and Biblical moralities. Historical chronicle provided reassuring evidence that the stoic virtues of patriotic sacrifice, incorruptibility and magnanimity had always been embodied in Netherlandish culture. But arguably, it was scripture that shone a more radiant light on the spirit of the Dutch future as well as the past. And this was, necessarily, Old Testament scripture. The gospels of the New Testament were self-evidently universal in their import, and ultimately personal in their theme (at least to a Protestant). But the Old Testament was patriotic scripture, the chronicle of a people chosen by God to reveal His light to the world through their history. From their tribulations, victories, captivities, peregrinations and prophecies — related through the printed word of the Bible, the oral culture of the pulpit, the narrative dramatizations of historical theater and the compelling imagery of the print — the Dutch were able to answer those troubling questions about their own identity.

Who were they? They were the new/old Batavians, guardians of the *waare vrijheid* (the true liberty). They were reborn Hebrews, children of the Covenant.

Where had they come from? From slavery and idolatry, through ordeal, to freedom and godliness.

Whither would they go? To reveal God's design for the world through their destiny and to dwell in honor, prosperity and glory, so long as they obeyed His commandments.

ii CHRONICLE

Dutch patriotism was not the cause, but the consequence, of the revolt against Spain. Irrespective of its invention after the fact, however, it rapidly became a powerful focus of allegiance to people who considered themselves fighting for hearth and home. No matter that hearth and home more obviously meant Leiden or Haarlem than some new abstraction of a union, the concept of a common *patria* undoubtedly gave comfort and hope to citizens who might otherwise have felt themselves desperately isolated as well as physically beleaguered. It is not surprising, then, to find that it was in the period of the great sieges of the 1570s that the first signs of a national identity became visible on coins and medals.[40] It was, in fact, the emblem of a siege — a stockaded enclosure defended by a lion rampant — that was transformed from a purely local to a patriotic device in 1573. For according to the eighteenth-century antiquary Kornelis van Alkemade, Count William VI of Holland, following a protracted siege of the fortress town of Hagesteyn in 1406, accepted certain conditions laid down by the defenders concerning their rights and liberties. And in acknowledgment of the compact he issued a new seal showing a fenced enclosure to indicate the constraints on feudal power. In 1573 a medal was struck with the motto *Libertas Patria* showing a maiden wearing the hat of liberty, seated within a fenced enclosure or garden, the Hollandse Tuin.[41]

23–25. Engravings, from Gerard van Loon, *Beschryvinge der Nederlandsche Historiepenningen* ('s Gravenhage, 1723–28)

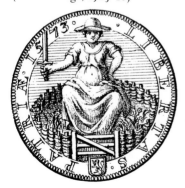 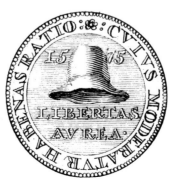 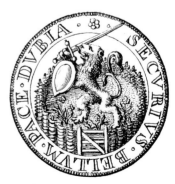

During the 1570s and 1580s, these motifs became the commonplaces of a patriotic iconology. The hat appeared many times, often atop a pike or lance and held by the maid who, in her turn, had become identified with the Hollandse Maagd (Dutch Maid). In 1575, for the first time that I know of, the hat was shown by itself on a medallion with the inscription *Libertas Aurea,* the Golden Freedom. The eighteenth-century medallic historian van Loon explained that the emblem was drawn from Roman sources, both numismatic and literary, and that it alluded to the practice of shaving slaves' heads when they were to be freed and the derived expression, "to be called to the hat," signifying the birth of personal liberty.[42]

On virtually all these devices — on coins, medals, propaganda prints, frontis-

26. Willem Buytewech. *Allegory of the Deceitfulness of Spain and the Liberty and Prosperity of the Republic.* Etching, engraving and drypoint. Collection: David Kiehl, New York

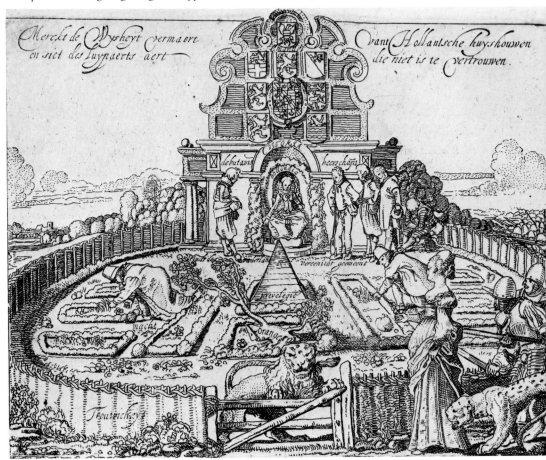

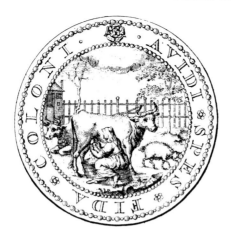

27. Engraving. From van Loon, *Beschryving*

pieces and seals—there were lions: lions rampant holding the martial sword, lions bellicose emerging from the waters as in the seal of Zeeland and the lion of the union itself, clasping in its right paw the seven arrows of the seven confederated provinces. After 1609 it was the party most unhappy about the truce with Spain that used this repertoire of patriotic heraldry most aggressively for its polemics. And in all likelihood the engraving done by Willem Buytewech in 1615 as a satire against the truce was commissioned for an anti-Oldenbarneveld patrician. The enclosure had by now become the verdant and well-stocked garden—the *tuin*—that signified the divinely blessed prosperity of the Netherlands and within the Dutch Maid, both comely and vulnerable, was now enthroned. At the center of the garden is an orange tree with one branch truncated to commemorate the assassinated William the Silent and two flourishing branches representing the Stadholders Maurice and Frederick Henry. At the gate, the lion defends his garden against a two-faced woman who wears a smiling countenance of peace on her outward aspect but the grim visage of the warrior behind and who leads the leopard at the head of a massed troop of soldiers.[43]

Many of these elements of the patriotic iconology were in constant process of invention, embellishment and elaboration. The image of the abundant garden as a metaphor for the nation was itself a striking departure from the heraldic bestiary of the princely states, but even more emphatic was the coinage of the Hollandse kuh, the Dutch cow: fat, fecund and peaceable (and symbolizing both rural and commercial prosperity) as a form of visual self-congratulation.[44] But however novel and imaginative this republican imagery became, it was important, for the purposes of legitimacy, to claim that it was, in fact, of great antiquity. In 1618, following his triumphal entry into Amsterdam, the Stadholder Maurice was accompanied to the city gate at Overtoom by a procession of twenty barges decorated by the Nederduytsche Academie, the inheritor of the Chamber of Rhetoric's guardianship of the native language. In the fourteenth barge was seated a figure representing the Netherlands herself, "dressed according to the old ways of the Land, which once had served true Netherlanders."[45]

In all probability, that costume included slashed flowing sleeves and the long unbelted gown that had come to personify Old Netherlands dress in the immemorial past. And most likely the source for such costume was the most influential of the first generation of history chronicles: the *Cronyke van Hollandt Zeelandt ende Vriesland.* First published in 1517, the *Divisiekroniek,* as it came to be known, had been cobbled together by an Augustinian canon, Cornelius Aurelius, from late medieval folklore and romances, local fables and chronicles as well as a superficial reading of Tacitus' *Germania,* the basic source for the history of the ancient Batavii.[46] However imperfect, the *Divisiekroniek* provided the first chronology of Netherlands history, from antiquity to the sixteenth century, segmented, as its name implied, into an easily understood chapter sequence. Not surprisingly, it had an extraordinarily long life as a school history text, going through fifty-three editions from 1538 to 1802.[47] Even when it was reworked by the Dordrecht antiquary Wouter van Goudhoeven in 1620 to reflect more directly the new circumstances of Holland, van Goudhoeven took good care to preserve its quality as an *"oude chronijcke."*[48]

The popularity and durability of the *Divisiekroniek* lay precisely in its free mingling of fact and fancy, fable and documented history. In its early form it did little to supply a distinctive character to the Dutch past if only because Netherlandish late medieval romances hardly varied from the standard figures of Gallic, Teutonic and Latin lore. Amadis of Gaul, the Knight of the Swan and the flying horse Bayard all rode again in Flemish Burgundian livery alongside more authentically Low Country products like Til Uijlenspiegel and the relentlessly exemplary Griselda the Meek.[49] Local antiquaries, working in towns with genuinely medieval ancestry such as Dordrecht, Haarlem, Utrecht and Middelburg were willing to embroider scanty records with imaginative accounts of their foundation by the inevitable Trojan exile; a branch of the Hungarian Scythians thought to have been ur-Bataves, or even wholly mythical worthies, preferably sired overnight by a visitor from Olympus. Cornelius Aurelius, like his contemporary chronicler of Gelderland, Gerardus Geldenhauer, was especially concerned with identifying the origins of particular place names. And in this tracking, assonance was used to produce pedigrees of ingenious spuriousness. According to one popular fable, singled out for withering ridicule by the Leiden humanist Scriverius, Haarlem was supposed to have been founded by a "Heer Lem" (Baron Lem) and Medemblik by Medea![50] Wouter van Goudhoeven preserved one of the more durable myths:

that the ancient Batavians had taken their name from the fugitive prince Bato, of the tribe of Hermonduren, dwelling in Hercinia—somewhere in the brackish swamps of central Europe.[51] The island in the Rhine where he found refuge then was called Batavia. His brother Salandus, settling farther west, established "Salando" which in turn became Zeeland. And in honor of their late father, Mitellus, its chief town was called Middelburg. That these derivations should have seemed more persuasive than, say, "Sea Land" and "Middle Town" is a tribute to the antiquarian addiction to the esoteric and its aversion to the mundanely self-evident.

The gaping lacuna in the continuum of remote Dutch history was filled by spirited reconstructions. As with the Flemish and Italian communes, a career in the Crusades was considered indispensable in bolstering historical credentials, especially where urban charters were claimed to exist independently of feudal grants. Haarlem cherished its participation in the naval battle of Damiate in Syria, and had the epic painted for its town hall by Cornelis Claesz. van Wieringen around 1630, as well as immortalizing the episode in glass, as its

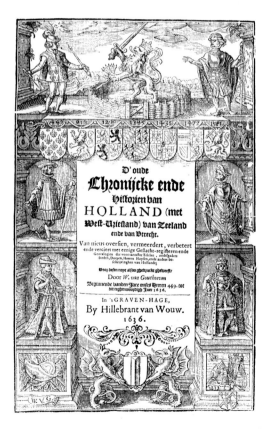

28. Anon. woodcut. Title page, Wouter van Goudhoeven's edition of the *Oude Chronijcke van Holland*, 1636

contribution to the great series of history windows in the Janskerk in Gouda. Leiden made much of its Latin appellation, Lugodunum Batavorum (officially instituted only in 1575), along with pretensions to be recognized as the first capital of the Batavi, Dordrecht of its insular seniority as a medieval trading entrepôt, Alkmaar as the early seat of the counts of Holland. The more distant the pedigree, the better the claim to *echt-Hollands* ancestry. Occasionally, in these half-remembered, half-invented stories, dim figures would float up from the penumbral obscurity of Holland's early medieval past, to be acclaimed the founder of this church and that estate. Saints Willibrord and Swigberd were thought the first apostolic evangelists in Utrecht and Holland, and to have exorcised the wicked King Rathbold of the Frisians, an ordeal that cured his subjects but killed the king. In van Goudhoeven's edition of the *Divisiekroniek,* not only the familiar counts and their families and appendages make an appearance, but subordinate though colorful figures such as the burgrave Jan of Wassenaer, the knights of Assendelft and Wijngaerden, and Vrouwe Jacoba and her duke, Jan van Beyeren. In the popular mind, however, there was nothing to distinguish the scraps and shards of antiquarian lore from the miraculous apparitions, marine deities, swordproof barons and bewitched millers who populated fable histories sung, recited and pictured at fairs and markets.

There was, of course, a rich proverbial literature that had been anthologized

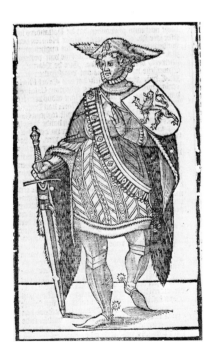

29. *Count Floris the Fat.* From van Goudhoeven, *Oude Chronijcke*

by Flemish scholars in the sixteenth century, and the history of the factional wars between the "cod" and the "fishhook" factions of the Gelders and Brabant nobility in the fourteenth and fifteenth centuries was also chronicled, albeit in a rough and ready manner. But neither of these sources was of much use in establishing a distinctively northern or "Holland" history. Tomb effigies, where they were abundant, as in the great cathedral churches of Dordrecht, Haarlem and Utrecht, were used (with some license) to supply physiognomic sketches of the counts of Holland, illustrated in engravings in Scriverius' history, all the way back to Diederick I in 863. Some established reputations as exemplars of what were deemed to be especially Dutch characteristics. Count William III, for example, was depicted as a Netherlandish Solomon, who on his sickbed summoned sufficient energy to have tried and executed one of his own bailiffs who had been accused of purloining a farmer's cow. Appropriately enough, the subject was painted by Nicolas Jansz. van der Heck expressly for the Chamber of Magistrates in the Alkmaar Town Hall.[52]

All this eclectic dabbling in oral or chronicle sources was much too haphazard for the first nationally minded generation of historians at the end of the sixteenth century. Writing from the scholarly center of Leiden University, they were concerned to create a usable national past based on firmer documentary foundations than folklore and fable. So Lipsius did away with the appealing figure of the errant Prince Bato (though Hooft rescued him as the hero of his play in the 1620s). Scriverius, who styled himself "Your Fatherlands Friend" in the preface to his history, dismissed the tall tales of "Heer Lem" as pure fairy tale. "It is a pure and idle glory," he complained, "which has to be founded on fables alone."[53] Instead, a succession of more austere and critical histories, beginning with the work of the Janus Dousas, father and son, and including contributions from van Leeuwen, Buchelius, and Grotius, stayed close to Tacitus and other dependable Roman sources like Pliny and Strabo to relate the history of the Batavians and their undefeated war against Roman imperial tyranny.[54] Scriverius, who was perhaps the purest of all in his concern for textual authenticity, was, however, adventurous enough to use archaeology — potsherds and ground-plan reconstructions — for his version of Batavian and early medieval history. But it was Janus Dousa the Elder who was the epitome of this new patriotic scholarship, since he was both humanist historian and public servant, emissary to the court of Elizabeth I from the States General and librarian and curator (president-chancellor) of Leiden University. Still more significantly, for the confluence of remote and contemporary history, Dousa was given the responsibility of creating a critical archive of all those charters that might affect the sovereign standing of the towns and provinces of the new union.

This new concern for scholarly authenticity did not, of course, get in the

30. Title page, Petrus Scriverius, *Beschrivinge van Out Batavien* (Amsterdam, 1636)

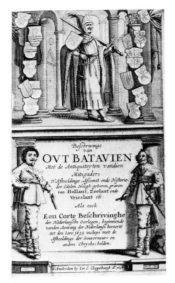

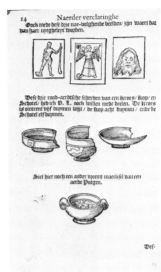

31. Woodcut. From Scriverius, *Beschrivinge van Out Batavien*

way of inventing a classical past that flattered and legitimated the present. Whether they were ostensibly histories of the ancient Batavians like Grotius's *Liber de Antiquitate Republicae Batavicorum* (1610), or whether they dealt with contemporary events like Emmanuel van Meteren's *Belgische ofte Nederlantsche Historien van Onser Tijden* (1605), a view of the Netherlanders was offered in which distinct political and cultural characteristics were retained through the centuries against all tyrants and usurpers. At the same time, theatrical presentations like Rodenburgh's *Trouwen Bataviër* (1609), P. C. Hooft's *Bato* (which represented the founder of the nation as the victim of a tribal court conspiracy, forced to exile himself in the land that became Batavia), and later Joost van Vondel's *De Batavische Gebroeders* all offered epic celebrations of the founding drama as thinly disguised classical history. There is far sparser evidence from the visual arts, both painted and engraved, of the popularity of Batavian historical mythology. While Rembrandt's mutilated masterpiece, *The Conspiracy of Claudius Civilis,* remains the most spectacularly unorthodox version, the visual idiom was first established by Otto van Veen who, in the first decade of the century, painted a series of twelve panels dealing with the Batavian leader's revolt, faithfully following Tacitus' account. The story was told, as in the chronicles, in a series of epic tableaux: the swearing of the confederation in the Schakerbos, the acclamation of Brinio (the second leader), the defeat of the Romans on the Rhine, the betrayal from within and the victory of Cerealis, the Roman general, and finally the honorable reconciliation between Civilis and Cerealis. Throughout, the Batavians, dressed in a

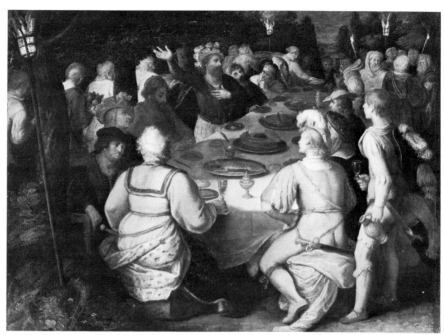

32. Otto van Veen, *The Conspiracy of Claudius Civilis and the Batavians in the Schakerbos*, 1612–13. Rijksmuseum, Amsterdam

combination of high medieval costume and the biblico-classical garb adapted by the Renaissance for history painting, exhibit qualities of bravery, fortitude, vigor and magnanimity.[55] Whether or not the cycle was commissioned, the States General purchased it in 1613 for their assembly chamber at The Hague, precisely at a time when honorable conclusions to conflicts were being mooted. Van Veen's own standing as a patriotic painter, however, ought not to be deduced from this one piece of evidence. He had produced a fine painting of the distribution of bread and herring after the relief of Leiden — one of the standard items in the patriotic canon. But his career went in precisely the opposite direction to the great generation that transplanted itself from south to north, settling in Brussels and working on official commissions at the archducal court of the Habsburg rulers Albert and Isabella.

The printed accounts of Batavian history, especially those in Dutch, had to incorporate certain obligatory features if they were to carry conviction as a proto-national text. First, even if they were intended for semipopular consumption (that is, at the octavo-cum-woodcut level), they had to bear the insignia of humanist scholarship: lavish marginal references to Tacitus, Pliny, Strabo — any classical source making mention of Batavians. Secondly, even when the more inclusive Latin nomenclature of the country was used (as in Grotius's *De Rebus Belgicis*) it was imperative that the Batavians be sharply differentiated from confusingly adjacent peoples such as the Belgae, Gauls, Frisians—all of whom had, at some time, succumbed to the Roman yoke. It was, however, permissible to refer to their alternative name of Caninenfates in describing their geographically indeterminate origins somewhere below the Rhine. Once removed to their oceanic, insular northern fastness, however, Batavians they became and forever remained. In his engagingly blunt manner Scriverius made much of the relation between geography and liberty. "Batavia in the earliest times," he wrote, "was a wild, desolate and uninhabited country."[56] It was precisely the perseverance and industry of the Batavian immigrants that earned them the right to domestic liberty and freedom from interference by outside powers. Within the girdle of their water barriers they could develop according to their own native habits and aptitudes.

From the somewhat meager makings, Grotius put together a version of Batavian history that was at once flattering and instantly recognizable. Not surprisingly they turn out to be hardy, frugal, industrious, pious, brave, hospitable (if a trifle bibulous) and addicted to cleanliness and liberty. Their unconquerable status was acknowledged by their special exemption from tribute payments to Rome, a republican *sine qua non* dear to contemporary Dutchmen.[57] They refused to tolerate any absolute sovereign but governed through periodically convened popular assemblies. Grotius called these the Ordini Batavorum, and in the Dutch translation of his work the word is rendered into *staten*—the term used for the sovereign bodies of the seven provinces. According to van Goudhoeven, the assemblies met every month and were open to any "citizen" to air what grievances he wished. Grotius, Scriverius, Gijsius, Hooft and van Goudhoeven are all very severe with Latin sources describing Brinio or Civilis as king and stressing that any prince or his "council" would have to obtain the assent of the "assembly" before their decisions could be binding.

Grotius even hazards a description of Batavian manners and mores. They drank an ale made of malted corn, and wore loose-fitting, plain-colored garments. Van Goudhoeven goes into more detail, describing the silver clasps that fastened their robes at the throat. Scriverius uses free adaptations of archaeological artifacts to enliven his text, though in so doing the Batavians emerge uncommonly like provincial Romans. According to Grotius, the men allowed their hair and beards to grow freely to distinguish themselves sharply from Romans or the Romanized. The episode in which Claudius Civilis permits his hair to be cut (prior to a reconciliation with Rome) thus had antique as well as Samsonian connotations. It also sparked a fierce debate in 1644 when zealous preachers like Borstius attacked long hair as a filthy pagan habit while humanist historians like Boxhorn defended flowing locks as the practice of heroic ancestry.[58] Batavian women were said to have dyed their hair with henna and their robes with madder (a crop that flourished in seventeenth-century south Holland and Zeeland). Like their Dutch descendants they were renowned for their premarital chastity. (Van Goudhoeven conceded that there were, among the ancient Batavians, women who lived openly with men as a matter of notoriety but by the same token were absolutely prohibited from marriage, "however rich, or young or beautiful they may have been."[59]) Their similarity to contemporaries was further reinforced by Grotius's contention that they retained possession of their marriage portion after the nuptials, and, as widows, had free disposition, an arrangement which was peculiarly Dutch. Children were nursed by their own mothers and were brought up according to a code of family discipline that was morally firm but physically lenient.

This extended exercise in verisimilitude was not without snags. Both the paganism of the Batavians and their service with Roman legions (recorded in all the major Latin histories) sat awkwardly with this group portrait of an indomitable and pious folk. The latter problem was dealt with by having them presented as among the earliest converts of the Christian evangel, and their military service for Rome was explained as the voluntary action of a free ally, not the obligation of a subjugated people. At Rome, it was said, Batavian fighting men, especially their horsemen, were regarded as among the most formidable of the empire's "allies," and neither Claudius nor Caesar would have accomplished his conquest of Britain without them. Civilis himself was conventionally depicted as a veteran who reverted to insurrectionary patriotism when the liberties of his fatherland were threatened by the illegitimate extension of direct imperial rule.

The cumulative effect of these chronicles was to suggest that by the fall of Rome a Batavian nation (the Dutch word *natie* was expressly used) was already in existence. According to this preformation version of national identity, most of the special characteristics by which the Dutch differentiated themselves from other peoples were present in embryonic or incipient form in ancient Batavia. The connection between habitat and polity, between water and liberty, had congealed through habitual custom into prescriptive principle. And the major feature of this historical self-identifying mechanism was the repudiation of absolute lordship. Whatever the subsequent vicissitudes of the medieval period, it was claimed, these essential properties of the Batavians endured. Frisians were pushed back from Holland, Brabanders locked horns with Gelderlanders, but through seven centuries from Count Diederick I to the Emperor Charles V (titled by Scriverius the thirtieth count of Holland), the constraints on sovereignty were sustained by Hollanders and accepted by their

nominal rulers. Hooft, van Meteren, van Goudhoeven, Gijsius and Grotius all
insist that the counts of Holland subscribed to traditional limits on their
sovereignty, and that only with the ambitious dukes of Burgundy in the
fifteenth century was there any sign of an illegitimate concentration of
dynastic power. Grotius was concerned to point out that the authority of the
counts within their own area of jurisdiction was acknowledged by the medieval Holy Roman Emperors as *imperium in imperio,* free from superior arbitration.
By extension, those communal and local sovereignties to which the counts
deferred became true masters in their own house.

Grotius, Hooft and Gijsius all catalogued in detail those restraints on
absolutism they believed intrinsic to the immemorial "Batavian constitution."[60]
Alongside this bald tabulation of the conditions under which the counts
ruled were instances drawn from medieval annals to illustrate their practice.
It was claimed, for example, that the States (a body that Grotius held to be the
direct successor of the Ordini Batavorum of antiquity) should give its assent to
any marriage proposed for a count or sole reigning countess. It was only with
the States' approval, for instance, that Vrouw Ada, the daughter of Count
Diederick VII, was married to the Gelders' Count van Loenen. Accepting this
principle, of course, meant that the States had authority to rule in cases of
disputed or uncertain succession, a residual power that might in some cases
override the claims of primogeniture. Of the two sons of Arnoudt, the third
count, the elder, Sicco, was set aside by the States for the younger, Diederick.
When he in turn died without issue, it was again the States that declared for
the cadet Floris as the next count.[61] Heredity, then, did not make its own
sovereignty, at least not in Holland, an argument which was likely to strike an
ingratiating chord in a country whose sufferings, it was said, had been the
result of fortuitous dynastic matchmaking by Burgundians and Habsburgs.

Likewise, the other indispensable conditions of Batavian rule reflected
contemporary seventeenth-century preoccupations and amounted to a retrospective formulation of criteria for national legitimacy. Grotius's second
condition was that no councillor, fiscal officer, sheriff or bailiff who was not a
native of the Fatherland might be appointed—a principle plainly violated by
the government of Granvelles and Alva. Third, the States were free to assemble,
irrespective of whether they had been summoned by the count. Fourth, no
new taxes, tolls or excises were to be levied without the consent of the States.
Fifth, all acts of war had to be sanctioned by the States, and none might be
waged by the ruler against his own territory. Sixth—and a notable index of
emergent national sensibilities—the counts were obliged to use the Dutch
language in their official correspondence and acts of state. Seventh, the coinage
was to be minted only as the States authorized. Eighth, no part of the realm
was ever to be alienated to "foreigners." Ninth, the States were never to con-

vene outside of Holland and West Friesland. Tenth, tribute or gifts to the count, offered directly or through the appointed stadholder-lieutenant, were expressly prohibited. Eleventh, justice was to be administered only by the regular judiciary. Finally, in the most resounding phrases of Hooft and Grotius: "The old customs and laws shall remain unbreakable. Should the Prince ever take a decision which violates them, no man shall be bound to [obey] that act."[62]

Stated as a self-evident axiom, or an empirical truth, this license for resistance owed much to a body of political thought concerned with the limits of obedience that had been elaborated by generations of humanist and especially Calvinist writers.[63] As with their French and Swiss counterparts, theoretical speculation and historical inquiry sprang from contemporary political exigency. But in the Netherlands, the theoretical and legal aspects receded before the most pressing need to supply a moral warrant for rebellion — a cloak of legitimacy with which to cover the nakedness of abjured allegiance. It was the physical experience of the torments endured during the war that put the stamp of righteousness on the new nation, but the form in which it was expressed could not simply be the outrage of nature, but rather the violation of history. So each item in the "old" Batavian constitution was negatively defined as that principle which Habsburg crimes most demonstrably flouted. And since he was arguing that legitimacy was conferred by precedent, Grotius extended its benefits to cover oligarchy, claiming that local sovereignty had always been exercised by the "most substantial and pious families."[64] This too, he asserted, was a special characteristic of the Bataves. Paradoxically, though, history needed to invoke nature to reinforce its claims. Why respect precedent? asks Grotius rhetorically. Because it is ingrained in us, at birth, to revere our elders, so it is natural for us to defer to laws, customs and usages of ancient authority and prescription.[65]

The "discovery" of a national genealogy, complete with Batavian ethnology and even archaeology, must have been reassuring in a world where to be new was more frightening than invigorating. However much the Calvinist clergy insisted that the Dutch should consider themselves as reborn into a fresh life, cleansed of the filth of idolatry and Romish superstition, it was more comforting to be children sired of an old and fruitful stock than innocent orphans cast before the storm. Yet there was always the residual anxiety (not restricted to preachers) that a belief in national continuity might subvert the patriotic ethos if it should give rise to unwary assumptions about unconditional endurance. In the midst of the war with Spain, of course, there was little cause to fret about complacency. But as the theater of conflict receded from the heartland of Holland in the 1630s and 1640s, the "founding generation" of the Dutch Republic felt it necessary to perpetuate the recollection of its tribulations as a summons to eternal vigilance. Gijsius stated in his *Oorsprong en Voortgang der Neder-Lantsche Beroerten en Ellendicheden* (1616) that he had written his account of contemporary events because "We Netherlanders here in the United Provinces have fought for our freedom with arms, and with arms must we stand fast, even as the stork sleeps with a stone in its claw lest it should fall into too deep a sleep and be devoured by its enemies."[66] As a zealot of church and Fatherland, Gijsius had deep misgivings about the wisdom of the truce arranged by Oldenbarneveld, but even those who were not of the "war party" believed that it was essential to transmit to future generations a vivid sense of the dearness with which their liberty had been bought. Nor was it enough merely to record the events of the revolt and the war as a historical saga. It was incumbent on successor generations to experience the terror and the euphoria, the hatred and the grief, the faith and the rejoicing of the long war, as if they had been firsthand participants and witnesses. Through perennial recall, they would thus enter a sacred community of memory and reaffirm the distinction of their national identity. Willem Baudart believed that what had happened to the Dutch "is too deeply rooted in their hearts for them ever to forget," yet he wrote his history to ensure that it should be "daily remembered what happened to their forefathers, and what may still be expected from ferocious wolves and tyrants."[67] His account, along with many other histories, oral as well as written, verse drama, doggerel poems, historical prints, commemorative ceremonies and engraved utensils and decorative objects all acted as triggers of collective allegiance, much as the Passover Haggadah served the Jews. They reiterated the process by which a nation became simultaneously holy and free, and reminded the Dutch that their freedom was conditional on their holiness.

While the ancient and medieval chronicle histories generally assumed the grave and intricate style appropriate for antiquaries, the contemporary epic histories were written in the more dramatic and urgent vein that suited their didactic purpose. Some, like Grotius's *De Rebus Belgicis,* Gijsius's *Oorsprong en Voortgang* and Scriverius's *Corte historische beschrijvinghe der nederlantsche oorlogen* (Short Historical Description of the Netherlandish Wars), 1639, either flowed naturally from their authors' preoccupations with ancestral legitimacy or were actually appended as sequels bound within the same volume. Others were ostensible continuations—such as Nicolas Clerq's conclusion to van Goudhoeven's chronicle of Old Holland—but were in fact written with much more polemical pungency, and calculated contemporary resonance. Some, like the most celebrated of all the large-scale histories, Pieter Hooft's *Nederlandse Historien* or Emmanuel van Meteren's *Belgische ofte Nederlantsche Historien van Onser Tijden,* combined dramatic narrative with a reasonable integrity of record. Others, as might be expected from their titles—Pieter Borre's *Morgen-Wecker der Vrije Nederlantscher Provintien* (literally, Morning-Waker of the Free Netherlands

Provinces), the 1612 Dordrecht *Martelaar's Boek* (Martyrs' Book) or Harmen Koster's 1614 *Spieghel ter Jeught* (Mirror for the Young), which was reprinted twenty-nine times before 1740, were pugnacious in their propaganda, free with historical scrupulousness and written for the popular end of the market in chronicles.

However varied in style and reliability, the contemporary histories shared certain features that set them off from the antiquarian chronicles. They were concerned to emphasize discontinuity rather than continuity and the inevitability of the rupture with Spain. At the same time, however, they wished to portray the stock heroes of the revolt—Orange, Brederode, Hoorn, and even the Sea Beggars—as painfully forbearing men goaded beyond endurance by Spanish obtuseness and brutality. Hence it was necessary to paint in as stark colors as possible the diabolical excesses perpetrated by the Spanish regime. Gijsius's book, for example, in its quarto edition of 1616, had as its frontispiece engraving the figure of Spain poised to plunge a dagger into the exposed breast of the Dutch Maid—against a background of swinging gibbets, smoldering auto-da-fé and sinister priests. This barbarism and the rebellion it engendered, it was further suggested, arose from a fundamental incompatibility of national temper. And it is striking how axiomatically it is stated that Dutch and Spanish characters were *in any event* too remote for durable reconciliation. Baudart and Scriverius made much of the Spanish fixation with *hoogmoed* —pride or haughtiness—a quality invidiously contrasted with the characteristic Netherlandish virtues of modesty and humility. The one betokened arrogance in the sight of God, it was implied, the other a submission before His will. Aristocratic obsessions and fanatical dogma informed the policies of the Spanish king and his councillors and were wholly out of place in a country which had been shaped by the eminence of *burgerlijk* virtues. And to be a burgher was not, as we might glibly suppose, to be a bourgeois, but to dwell in the ways of Christian civility—the Erasmian way of life. At any rate, it was indifferent or hostile to the feudal preoccupations of war, land and honor it took to be the reigning values of the Spanish court.

The history of the revolt and the war was, then, a working out of these already polarized collective traits, so that what was special to the Netherlands might be extracted from a fortuitously unsuitable framework of allegiance and transferred to one that might be determined by regional character. And the chronicles were written in such a way as to make this separation irreversible through perennial recall of Spanish incivility or, even, inhumanity. Consequently, much of what was related dealt with atrocities committed in the name of the king, described in vivid personal and topographic detail. The more lurid the brutality, the more graphic the account seems to have been a rule of thumb, a vein of writing that owed much to earlier sixteenth-century chronicles of

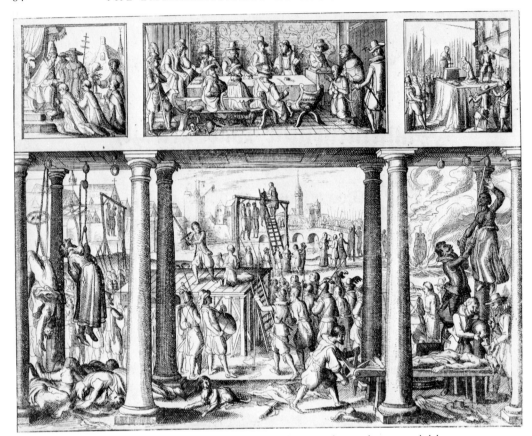

33. Anon., *The Council of Blood,* from *Warachtige Beschrijvinghe . . . vande meer dan onmenschelijke ende Barbarische Tyrannije* (Amsterdam, 1621)

Spanish misdeeds in the Indies, and rival versions of the French wars of religion. Needless to say, the Dominican priest Las Casas' monumental record of horrors perpetrated in the Spanish Empire was translated into Dutch and was lavishly used as the basis for a northern equivalent of the "Black Legend." Jan Evertszoon Cloppenburgh, the writer and publisher, for example, used Las Casas as an introduction to his own history of both the St. Bartholomew's Day Massacre and the war in the Netherlands.[68]

Whether written in the grand manner (Hooft) in folio editions embellished with elaborate copper engravings, or for a more popular readership, using doggerel verse and more primitive prints (Baudart), the contemporary histories all followed a familiar formula. Beginning either with Charles V's journey to the Netherlands in 1549, the accession of Philip II in 1552, or the extension of the Inquisition, the evolving conflict was tied together by a number of "set piece" tableaux. These were written up in expostulatory style and accompanied by engravings that were simultaneously heroic and gruesome, and meant to etch themselves into the collective memory as they were printed on the page. It was an exposition of the macabre melodrama of High Renaissance theater with themselves or their own forefathers as *dramatis personae*. Hooft used the ordeal of his own wife's grandmother at the hands of mutinying Spanish troops in Antwerp to identify the narrator, and by extension the reader, as closely as possible with the victims. And his account of the assault by the soldiers in that city in 1576 is unforgettable, precisely because it combined general description with harrowing detail.

The most memorable martyrology (invariably engraved) concerned a bridal couple assaulted by Spanish mutineers in their own house. The groom is killed and thrown at the feet of his bride, whose mother then dies in her arms. All of Hooft's prodigious poetic and dramatic gifts, for once unrestrained by high

34. *The Spanish Fury at Antwerp,* from Joh. Gijsius, *Oorsrong en Voortgang der Neder-Lantsche Beroerten* (Leiden, 1616)

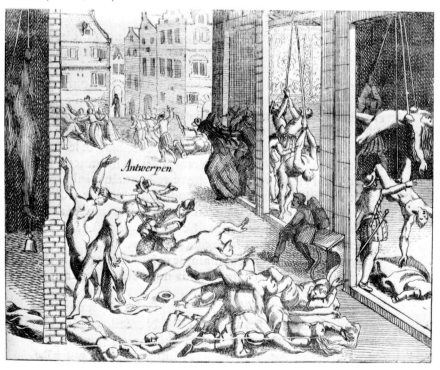

humanist gravity, were brought to bear on passages like these: "This widow, who 'ere had been a wife, let out a pitiful cry, reeled about and threw herself on her mother whose own soul had passed on [lit. "between her lips"]. She was torn from there, by the command of a Spanish captain and dragged to the castle." Her father, who survives these horrors, is himself murdered in flight and his daughter then subjected to physical abuse. "He [the captain] stripped her, [golden] chains, clothing, underthings, everything from top to bottom taken from that pure body," and, having abused her, "hunted her, mother-naked, dripping with the blood of her innumerable wounds, through the city." There she is seized from her last hiding place, finished off by another villain and her corpse thrown into the street to rot.[69] All of Antwerp becomes, in Hooft's grisly panorama, a scene from a Netherlandish apocalypse: "a stage of horror . . . the corpses of men and horses in mountainous heaps . . . the streets dyed with their mingled blood . . . many of the Germans [troops defending the city] lay with legs or heads or shoulders mutilated or missing."[70]

These terrible visions were used expressly to remind future generations that the act of national birth had been a trial and a torment. And while it may have been difficult to engrave on the minds of Dutch children the steps by which the Pacification of Ghent or even the Union of Utrecht was arrived at, the scenes of murder and mayhem were all too memorable. In Gijsius's chronicle, the narrator tells his story as a father instructing his son in patriotic scripture. At the passage where Spanish troops flay men alive and stretch their skins across their regimental drums the son (understandably) interjects, "Father, my hair stands on end to hear you relate such things."[71]

The Spanish Black Legend was, then, at the heart of popular history. But not all of its most vivid tableaux were so bloody. The elaborately terrifying scenes of autos-da-fé in Spain with which so many of the chronicles began were contrasted with the blessed simplicity of Calvinist preachers addressing their flocks beneath the oaks of Flanders and Brabant. There followed a parade of readily recognizable events: the image breaking of 1566–67; the arrival of Granvelle and later Alva and the establishment of the Council of Blood; the arrest and execution of Egmond and Hoorn in 1568; the disaffected wanderings of William of Orange; the Sea Beggars' descent into Brielle; the Spanish advance into south Holland and the sack of Rotterdam; the great sieges of Leiden, Haarlem and Alkmaar; the massacres at Naarden in 1572; the sack of Mechelen (Malines); the disaster at Oudewater in 1575 where the town was set on fire rather than allowing it to fall into Spanish hands; the Spanish fury in Antwerp; the failure of the pacification, and the creation of the unions of Utrecht and Atrecht; the assassination of the Prince at Delft and the ominous reconquests of Parma in the south. Those histories that continued the story into the seventeenth century emphasized the international aspects of the

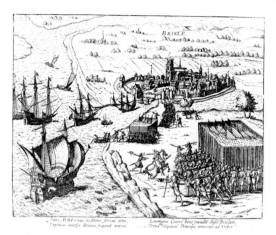

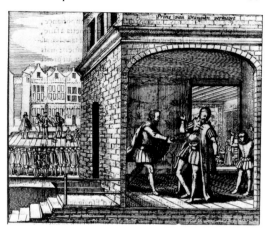

35. Frans Hogenberg (?), *The Descent of the Sea Beggars on Brielle*, 1572. From Gijsius, *Oorsprong*

36. Anon. woodcut. *The assassination of William the Silent*, 1584, from J.E. Cloppenburgh, *Le Miroir de la Tyrannie Espagnole* (Amsterdam, 1620)

conflict as though the outcome of the struggle in the Netherlands would determine the success or defeat of the Counter-Reformation. The captaincies of Leicester and Anjou made way, however, for the more self-celebrating euphoria of Prince Maurice's victories and the spectacular creation of a Dutch empire, east and west, largely at the expense of the Catholic foe.

Within this dramatic continuum it was important to establish heroic or villainous reputations as emphatically as possible. Vignettes engraved after formal portraits helped identify the principal personalities, but the limitations of this style meant that even when the represented figure was as notorious as, say, Granvelle or Philip II, the physiognomy followed the respectful lines of the original commission. Alva, the most infamous figure of all, was occasionally shown trampling vigorously on the necks of heretics, but even this was derived from classical Herculean conventions rather than any polemical attack. Although caricature had been used in the popular libels and broadsheets of both the German Reformation and the French wars of religion,[72] it was not yet a characteristic mode of history illustration in the Netherlands. Instead, generalized versions of specific events in which individual personalities were identified (sometimes by attached captions) served to inculpate or celebrate their role. Dutch martyrology was already established by the first decade of the century. William the Silent's death was represented on countless broadsheets and prints as well as history books, and he himself had been immortalized in one of the stained-glass windows in the Gouda St. Janskerk representing the relief of Leiden, and completed in 1603. Smaller fry were also given a place in the new national pantheon. The "two Batenburgers," Gijsbert and Diederick, were two young nobles from the land province of Gelderland who suffered the same fate in Brussels in 1568 as Egmond and Hoorn, because they had followed the leadership of the "disloyal" nobility. "Sprung from old Bato's stock," as Gijsius's versified eulogy put it, they became known as the most innocent victims of Alva's unslakable bloodthirstiness. Depicted in graphic detail in innumerable versions, their executions became models of the perfect patriotic death. Others were promoted from even dimmer obscurity to the patriotic Valhalla. Jan van Duyvenvorde, the commander of the Leiden garrison, was one, and, better known still, Kenau Hasselaer, the redoubtable matron of Haarlem, who during the siege led the womenfolk of the city to its ramparts, brandishing a formidable arsenal of domestic cutlery, ironmongery and cauldrons of seething liquids to pour on the heads of the assailants.

The courage of ordinary men and women, whose attachment to domestic virtues was in extreme contrast to the unnatural cruelty of their tormentors, was an important feature of these self-consciously patriotic histories. Though there was no shortage of horrific events to record, incidents were chosen that exemplified the Spanish violation of the Netherlandish household (birth, marriage, care for the sick and old) and the fortitude with which the victims attempted to sustain their social bonds in the midst of death and terror. During the long months of the siege of Leiden, Hooft tells us, the milk of nursing mothers ran dry, and many were found dead in the streets, their babies held fast in their arms.[73] At Oudewater in 1575, where a dreadful massacre of

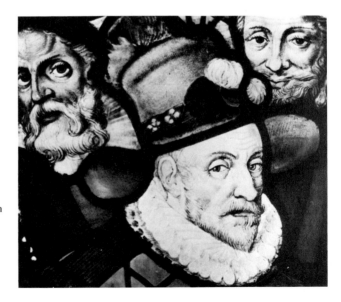

37. William the Silent. Detail from stained glass window, 1609, by Dirck Jansz. Verheyden and Dirck Reiniersz. van Douwe after Isaak Nicolai van Swanenburgh.
St. Janskerk, Gouda

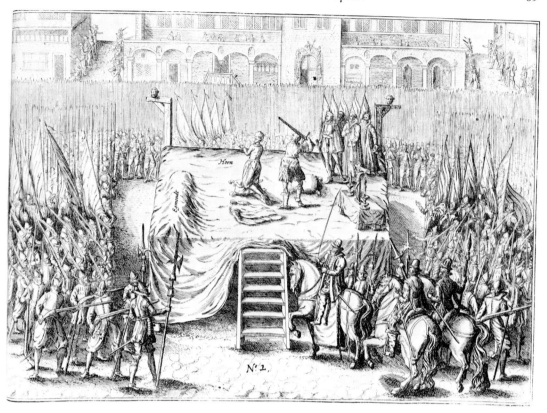

38. *The execution of Egmond and Hoorn.* From *Waarachtige Beschrijvinghe,* 1620

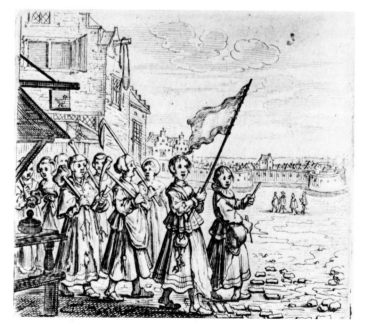

39. Woodcut. Kenau Hasselaer Symons at the siege of Haarlem. From Johan van Beverwijck, *Van de Wtnementheyt des Vrowelicken Geslachts* (Dordrecht, 1643)

the population took place, a pregnant mother was killed along with the fetus, which was slaughtered while still in her womb, an atrocity which then became an obligatory feature of the event's illustration. At Naarden, too, three years earlier, the pregnant Lambertge Claesdogter was raped, killed and thrown in a well, while Margriet Claesdogter, who nursed a six-month-old child, was driven out into the midwinter snows, where she "miraculously" survived to tell her tale in the neighboring town of Heusden.[74] As in Hooft's account of the desecration of the Antwerp wedding, the degree of Spanish barbarism was measured by its indifference to those family and personal bonds that the Dutch held most dear. Even the Batavian chronicles identified compassionate domesticity as a national trait. For in Hooft's translation of Tacitus he emphasized an apparently minor detail—that Claudius Civilis ensured that women and children stood well to the rear of the battle with the Romans—by using a Tempesta/Vaenius engraving as a hymn to family life.

The contrast between Netherlandish regard for family feeling and foreigners' contempt for it could not have been more tellingly made. But in their concern to depict a soldiery bent on tearing out by its roots all that was innocent and peaceful at home, the history chroniclers inevitably embroidered their texts to make them more gripping and atrocious. Nothing the Spanish did, however dreadful, was unusual by the standards of the time, especially in the grim and protracted conditions of siege warfare. Callot's engravings of the *Grandes Misères de la Guerre* and Gelnhausen's *Simplicissimus* tales from the Thirty Years' War provide confirmation that troops and peasants or town dwellers all shared the worst possible expectations of their fate. And even if oral testimony or

40. Anon. woodcut. *Massacre at Naarden.* From Cloppenburgh, *Miroir*

41. Anon. woodcut. *Massacre at Oudewater.* From Cloppenburgh, *Miroir*

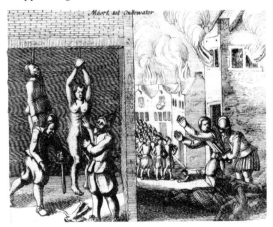

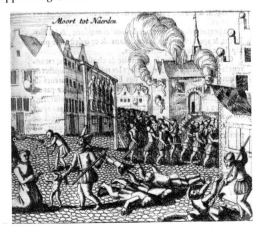

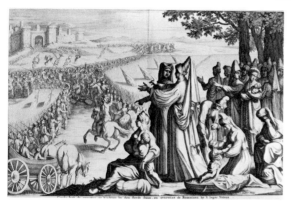

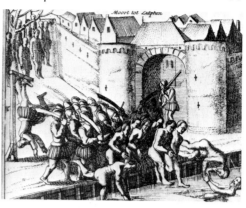

42. Antonio Tempesta, *Claudius Civilis and the Batavian Women and Children,* from P.C. Hooft, *Nederlandse Historien* (Amsterdam, 1642)

43. Anon. woodcut. *Massacre at Zutphen.* From Cloppenburgh, *Miroir*

fly-by-night rumor exaggerated the horrors, there is ample evidence of indiscriminate massacre and routine torture being applied to terrorize civilian populations into absolute submission. For the purpose of generating patriotic solidarity among the Netherlanders, however, the truth or falsehood of these accounts is of less importance than their capacity to create foci of allegiance and sympathy. The habit of specifically identifying the most brutally treated victim lent further credibility to what would otherwise have been general accounts of mayhem and created a special class of heroes and martyrs amidst the ordinary mass of mankind. Gijsbrecht Bont, for example, was a seventy-year-old burgher of Naarden who was first stabbed in the neck then forced to drink his own blood before being dispatched. Violent assault on the old, to whom Dutch culture showed special reverence and tenderness, was another of those "crimes against nature" that served to dehumanize the enemy. At the height of the Naarden massacre, the histories related, Spanish bloodlust expended itself on the helplessly bed-bound like the aged ex-sheriff Cornelis Gijszoon and the linen weaver Arent Lambertszoon. Others who symbolized the public and pastoral charge of the community—two deaf mutes, the inmates of the local hospital (some over eighty) and the beggar Claes Hondslager, were likewise put to the sword.[75] At Malines (Mechelen), in 1572, the nuns who were the soldiers' coreligionists were routinely violated as their convent was pillaged, and at Zutphen in November of the same year, naked men, women and children were driven into the ice-packed river to freeze, drown or asphyxiate.

To seventeenth-century readers of these chronicles, the atrocities were represented not just as "unnatural cruelties" in the Renaissance sense, but as part of an organized campaign of desecration. And it was not merely churches or town halls that were being violated and despoiled but the institutions that were most cherished in the Netherlands: the sanctity of marriage or the veneration of ancestors. The kings of Spain in whose name these infamies were committed thus came to be seen as Behemoth, determined on destroying the bonds that held communities and even families together. To resist him meant arming oneself with faith so as to protect the essential institutions of hearth and home.

In 1621, when the war with Spain was resumed after the brief "twelve years' truce," these raw histories, many of them written by Calvinist preachers, triggered the terror and fortitude without which a further round of "patriotic sacrifice" might not have been so readily forthcoming. Except as the written record of their ordeal there was no need to remind the "exile" generation from the south or the defenders of Haarlem and Alkmaar of the importance of national unity. For the population of the Holland towns in the second quarter of the century enjoying the fruits of an unprecedented prosperity, the war might have come to seem an increasingly peripheral and formal business. Its theater, after all, was no longer the polder meadows and city walls of Haarlem or Dordrecht. Instead, the fight was taken to the high seas of the Atlantic and Indian oceans, or before the garrison towns of Brabant and Limburg. Not that an Amsterdam merchant, however commercially prudent, would have dared suggest relinquishing Maastricht or Breda. But the computation of interest, as much as the burning flame of patriotic zeal, might well determine his support or his coolness towards the prolongation of a particular campaign. There were local communities for whom the war continued to be a disaster, even if it threatened their livelihoods rather than their lives. The herring fisheries of Zeeland and south Holland were easy prey for the privateers operating out of Dunkirk for the Spanish crown. But the high cost of effective convoy protection meant that peace rather than increased force would offer the best chance of relief for their distress.[76] Similarly, the armies of the Republic, even as they became professionalized under Stadholders Maurice and Frederick Henry, came to consist more and more of hired fighting men, and fewer and fewer native-born Netherlanders. Not surprisingly, the army fell under a growing suspicion, in Amsterdam particularly, of prolonging the war in its own interest rather than that of the common good of the Republic. Conversely, that element which historically had represented the direct involvement of the towns in patriotic defense—the city militia companies—were losing martial significance by the 1630s. Their exercises were governed more by considerations of elite display and oligarchical bravura than training as citizens-in-arms, and they looked as much to the dangers of an overmighty Orange dynasty as to the Spanish for their *raison d'être*.

Faced with this backsliding, the inspirational prefaces of the chronicle histories and their formulaic scroll of horrors and heroes served as a summons to patriotic renewal. They not only refreshed hatred of the old enemy, but reminded the easygoing of what clemency they could expect should a new Parma ever cross the river barriers. Other kinds of collective recall galvanized allegiance. Individual towns that had played some memorable role in the war created commemorative rites in order to link their future with an heroic past. At Enkuizen, Monnikendam and Hoorn — fishing ports on the Zuider Zee — a mock naval battle between the Dutch and Spanish fleets was (and still is) reenacted every year, complete with burning hulks and anthems of praise. In Leiden, bread and herrings — the food that had been distributed immediately after the siege was lifted — was symbolically shared around the citizenry every October third, in a kind of historical eucharist. After 1606, Jacob Duym's Orangist propaganda play, *The Siege of Leiden* was regularly performed, with its cast of starving babes-in-arms, fiendish dons watching the waters rise about them and saintlike Burgemeester van der Werff exhorting his people to faith and sacrifice for God and Fatherland.[77] Occasionally, during the seventeenth century, tables would be set up bearing the "food of affliction": rapeseed cakes, rodent meat, boiled hide and gruel from pounded bark that the Leidenaars claimed had been consumed as patriotic rations. Certainly, the great ordeal was kept in mind by the motto on the façade of the Town Hall, *God behoed ons* (The Lord will provide for us), together with a sacramental recitation of the city's delivery from peril. In some towns, like Oudewater, paintings depicting the events of sieges and massacres were hung in prominent places in the council chambers for the public to inspect. But painting was not the chosen medium for the transmission of the patriotic scripture. Its images, by and large, were carried through the graphic arts, and there, for that matter, they were the servants rather than the masters of text. For in this kind of national communion, it was, to begin with, the Word, spoken and read, that turned old Netherlanders into new Dutch.

iii SCRIPTURE

Imagine a paragon of Erasmian virtue: a twelve-year-old Dutch boy, apt, decently Christian and curious to learn his place in the seventeenth-century scheme of things. Antiquarian tomes would have told him that he was a new Batavian, a sprout from an ancient stock. Contemporary histories would have reminded him that he was heir to a generation of martyrs and that the coat of his freedom was soaked in their blood. But his sensibilities were not formed exclusively by the printed text or image. Every Sunday (at least) a cascade of rhetoric would crash down from the pulpit, invoking the destiny of the Hebrews as though the congregation were itself a tribe of Israel. Lines dividing history and scripture dissolved as the meaning of Dutch independence and power was attributed to the providential selection of a new people to be as a light unto the nations.[78] In this Netherlandish addendum to the Old Testament, the United Provinces featured as the new Zion, Philip II as a king of Assyria and William the Silent as a godly captain of Judah. The boy, whom we might call Jacob Isaakszoon, Jacob the son of Isaac, was to understand that he was a Child of Israel, one of the *nederkinderen,* dwelling under the protection of the Almighty for so long as he heeded His commandments. The nation to which he belonged had been delivered from bondage and raised up to prosperity and might through the power of the covenant made with the Lord. Were it to stray from the paths of righteousness it could expect to be humbled as Israel and Judah had been humbled before it. As the boy grew to manhood, his conduct should exemplify acceptance of this covenant, and, accordingly, blessings would be showered upon him.

To a great extent this scriptural exhortation was the common idiom of all Calvinist and Puritan cultures of the early seventeenth century.[79] Abrahams, Isaacs and Jacobs could be found in Rouen, Dundee, Norwich and Basel, as well as Leiden and Zierikzee. The rejection of post-Biblical hagiography as well as the legal authority claimed by the successors of St. Peter in Rome was a central feature of the Reformation, and it invested scripture with commensurately greater status. Among Calvinists and other devotees of the "radical Reformation" the abolition of traditional ritual and the intercession of the clergy and the preference for direct forms of communion further enhanced the importance of scripture in worship. The incessant reading, singing and exegesis that went on in Calvinist churches, schools and homes familiarized the faithful with the most insignificant deeds of patriarchs, judges, kings and prophets, where once they had lingered over the color of a saint's hair or the radiance of his halo. Moreover, the distinction between the wholly sacred nature of the New Testament and the "this worldly" character of the Old Testament, when linked with the Calvinist's obsession with right conduct, meant that the latter was available as a fund of exemplary wisdom and historical truth without any hint of blasphemy. The result of all this was to rescue the Old Testament from its position in Catholic theology as a necessary preface, a "second stage" in the teleology of original sin and eventual redemption, and to restore to the relation between the two books a kind of complementary symmetry. In the world view of Catholics, the exemplary nature of Old Testament stories was overshadowed by the insuperable distinction between Christians and, as it were, incipiently deicidal Jews. In the Calvinist mentality, the eventual Messianic chronicle *could only* be comprehended by the history of the Jews, through whom the Almighty had worked his will.

In practice this meant that the Calvinist sense of their own dwelling in the contemporary world was saturated with scriptural allusion, analogy and example. The epic matter of the Old Testament, after all, seemed particularly relevant to a world perceived as divided into camps of the godly and the heathen where pestilence, fire and famine were the common lot, and where unimaginable atrocities marked the highway to apocalypse. So the bands of the righteous fled to their new Zions, or rebuilt their ravaged Jerusalems, naming their houses, their children and sometimes their institutions for the dwelling places of Israel. The Bible became a source book of analogies for their own contemporary history, as well as an inspirational talisman on the field of battle. Its swarming detail, moreover, allowed for a high degree of specificity to suit all sorts of contingency. If the foe was so evil that extermination was called for, they became the Amalekites whom it was forbidden to spare. If they happened to occupy a piece of territory plainly designated by the Lord for the people of His covenant, then their obstruction was thought of as Canaanite or Midianite. If their sins were so loathsome that they positively invited destruction, they were, of course, Sodomites or, less damnably, Philistines. As for the hosts of God, should they be led by an anointed prince he was generally David, or if facing daunting odds, Hezekiah. If he was a mere general he turned into Joshua, and if reinforcements were depressingly sparse, Gideon was usually invoked—his story bearing the morale-boosting message that victory was likely to go to small battalions, supposing that they combined guile and faith in equal measure.

Given that all these features of the Zion metaphor were present throughout Calvinist Europe, it might seem perverse to argue that in the northern Netherlands they contributed to a sense of *separate* identity. And even if this were shown to be the intention of those who resorted to it, how is it possible to demonstrate its practical effect on allegiance? Might not all this scriptural rhetoric have remained so much frothy fulmination, confined to the drama of stage and pulpit, and wholly irrelevant to the tough, muscular workings of Dutch society? Put another way, can it possibly be argued that the Dutch fascination with the Old Testament colored their own self-perception? And when they saw visions of a bobbing Ark; the Golden Calf in the wilderness; Goliath's dented cranium or Nehemiah's temple arising from the ruins of Jerusalem, how did it affect or modify their behavior?

The answer to both these questions is essentially the same. The type of

scriptural idiom developed in the Netherlands had always been much concerned with the regulation of social manners. This had applied as much
to sixteenth-century Antwerp humanists as to seventeenth-century Leiden
Calvinists. In the formative period of the Dutch Republic's history — between
1580 and 1660 — it contributed to a distinct sense of separate identity insofar
as it meshed with, and reflected, contemporary, mundane circumstances. If
not causal, then, it was self-reinforcing, a language borrowed from myth to
redesign collective perception of reality.

A distinction needs to be drawn between historical fact and contemporary
mentality. The indisputable historical fact that Dutch scriptural rhetoric
could be reproduced with very little variation in Geneva or Prague does not,
of itself, guarantee that Calvinists in all these places subscribed to a common
cause which overrode all other divisions. Indeed the opposite was often the
case. In Holland, zeal to support the plight of besieged brethren in La
Rochelle or the Grisons was confined to money (which was also lent to
non-Calvinists and non-Protestants), and the offer of an asylum in extremity.
There were too many varieties of Protestantism during the Thirty Years' War,
and too many intersecting issues of power, dynasty and territory to encourage
the formation of a solid Calvinist phalanx. The superficial religious affinities
between the Puritan Commonwealth and the Dutch Republic did nothing to
palliate the bitter maritime disputes that produced the first Anglo-Dutch war
in 1651. When Cromwell cited such affinities three years later to justify his
startling proposal for a Godly union of the two republics, he was greeted with
incredulous amazement in The Hague.[80]

Nonetheless, the ways in which English Puritan rhetoric reinforced a
budding patriotism was closer to the Dutch style than in other Calvinist
strongholds where it was used to uphold the supremacy of the Church itself.
This could be most easily managed at the level of cells, conventicles and
consistories where Calvinism was on the defensive within a larger territory, or
wedged between major powers. Embattled enclaves in France, Bohemia or
Hungary might invoke the endurance of Judah, but they remained worried
about the hordes of Medes and Persians at the gates. In this respect, too,
Geneva might be considered an enlarged, geographically fortified conventicle,
rather than a miniature state. Where the whole social organism was larger and
consequently more complex, as in England, the scriptural idiom somehow
had to absorb other, alternatively derived, sources of national allegiance to
recreate a godly patriotism. Given that so much of English (and Scottish)
historical identity was established well before the Reformation, and that it
had blossomed so spectacularly under the eclectic auspices of the Elizabethan
settlement, this was always unlikely, and the Civil War made it completely
impossible. The Puritan Zion-Albion remained confined to the cultural style

of one sect, which attempted to take advantage of the ascendancy of the army to impose it on all the others. And since it has now been shown that the New Model Army was much less homogeneous in its beliefs than was once supposed to be the case, it comes as no surprise that this godly enterprise was doomed from the start.[81] The Restoration liquidated this Anglo-Zionist evangelism with extraordinary rapidity and completeness. Thereafter, it remained the language and idiom of a sect, buried deep below the crust of English culture until it was extruded once more by Blake's hostility to classicism and the first great wave of Romantic-chiliastic fervor.

In the Dutch Republic, the Hebraic self-image functioned much more successfully as a unifying bond than as a divisive dogma. It flowed out of the pulpit and the psalter into the theater and the print shop, diluting Calvinist fundamentalism as it did so, but strengthening its force as a national culture for the very same reason. Indeed it was just because the roots of Netherlandish Hebraism were *not* exclusively Calvinist, but reached back to an earlier and deeper humanist reformation, that it could exert such broad appeal. Those who exploited the scriptural idiom thus included not merely zealous predikants like Borstius and Wittewrongel; humanists like Coornhert, who wrote a contemporary play, *The Comedy of Israel*; crypto-Arminians like Hooft and the passionately patriotic yet ultimately Catholic Vondel. Moreover it was a sign of the versatility and inclusiveness of the idiom that opposing political factions could *both* resort to it to argue their respective positions. This interpenetration with profane history lent Dutch scripturalism its tremendous strength. It was used not in order to swallow up the secular world within the sacred, but rather to attribute to the vagaries of history (with which the Dutch lived, at times, very painfully) the flickering light of providential direction.

This patriotic scripture expressed itself in visual and even musical forms as well as in printed texts. Occasionally, the three came together as in the remarkable history compilation of the Zeelander Adriaan Valerius, the *Neder-Lantsche Gedenck-Clanck* (The Netherlands Anthem of Commemoration).[82] This truly *was* a Dutch Haggadah, being a history of the enslavement and liberation (somewhat slavishly taken from van Meteren's chronicle) in both prose and verse and, more originally, interspersed with songs and dances commemorating salient episodes. The third element was supplied by marvelous history engravings, prominently featuring the *Leo Belgicus,* seen now tortured in "Ducdalf" (a.k.a., Duke of Alva)'s vise, now sporting the lance and hat of freedom or commissioning the Prince of Orange to defend the Fatherland. Valerius was a *rederijker,* a rhetorician, which in the Netherlands made him teacher, preacher and actor rolled into one. Like the author of the 1614 *Spieghel der Jeucht* (Mirror for Youth) who dedicated his work to "the schoolmasters of the Free Netherlands," he meant it as an exercise in dramatic instruction for the young. And the interplay of images and song with the printed word was to make the memorizing of the *Gedenck-Clanck*'s virulently anti-Spanish message itself a kind of patriotic hymnody.

The *Gedenck-Clanck* closes with a special prayer invoking the covenant between God and His people that had become the commonplace of sermons and histories. It was accompanied by an allegorical engraving showing the seven sister-provinces and the princes of Orange-Nassau kneeling before the hat of liberty above which was a banner inscribed with the holy tetragrammaton, an image that had earlier illustrated the beginning of the revolt. The text of the prayer so perfectly exemplifies the union of Biblical analogy and contemporary experience that sanctified the new sense of nation that it merits quotation at length:

Almighty God! Dear, merciful Heavenly Father Thou who art the support of the puny, the comfort of the oppressed, the source and font of all goodness and blessings. We poor sinners acknowledge before you what is merely the truth: that in our own beloved Fatherland we have time and again felt and beheld your all-mighty power and the blessings of your inscrutable wisdom, and have received succor and favor when stricken by ferocious tyrants; even as we were thrown into great poverty and forced to leave our Fatherland, lock and stock, our house, our friends and our trades and so as to escape the bloody claws of our enemies, to go sojourn in strange lands, and, even as from the force of the Spanish Edicts so much blood of the pious has been spilled that together we were reduced to a motley rabble and sunk into the pit of the world, O Lord when all was ill with us You brought us up into a land wherein we were enriched through trade and commerce and have dealt kindly with us, even as you have led the Children of Israel from their Babylonian prison; the waters receded before us and you brought us dry-footed even as the people of yore, with Moses and with Joshua, were brought to their Promised Land. O Lord you have performed wondrous things for us. And when we have not heeded you, you have punished us with hard but Fatherly force so that your visitations have always been meted out as a children's punishment. You have not counted the sins of your people against them but have freed us from the yoke of the Moabites even as it was with Deborah and with Barach whose power went before us in the field and that of stout-hearted Gideon who fought against the violence of the Midianites. So goes it with us, O Lord, as through your goodness so many brave men, Jephthah and Samson and many others have slain the ravening lions, dragons and bears that would have torn us apart. Yea, the courageous and faithful David has been a mirror of piety and steadfastness to us and has not deserted us, and a Solomon [has come] whose wisdom and foresight are above all others. So that, from so many great princes and heroes the Heavenly Light of your godly word shines forth abroad and the Holy Evangel is

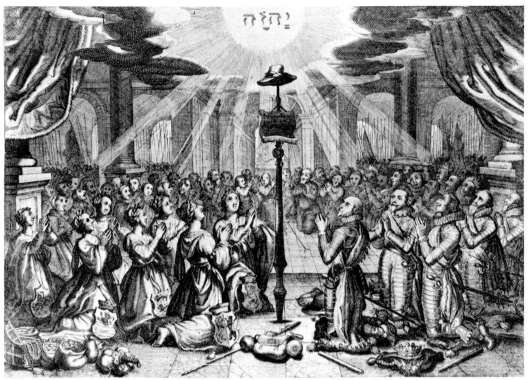

44. Anon. engraving. *Nederlands Dank-Offer.* From Adrianus Valerius, *Nederlantsche gedenckclanck* (Haarlem, 1626)

proclaimed even to the many who lay in idolatry and had drunk from the cup of the Babylonian Whore but who are now brought to the Right Way and dwell here in water-rich lands, flowing with milk and honey and are settled in great walled cities . . . O Lord Your Fatherly blessings and the bounties you have bestowed upon us have been great and prodigious; you have wrought all manner of wondrous things and despite the covetousness of our enemy, have made the golden liberty and olden laws of the Netherlands renowned throughout the world; proof of the covenant of blessings made with [Your] believers, that their seed may establish themselves through the world and with the powerful guidance of your Holy Spirit may increase and multiply.[83]

Just as the text of the prayer drew eclectically on Biblical analogy, historical experience and pious exhortation, the iconography of its engraving is also a free mixture of conventions. The "sorority" of the seven provinces is dressed in classical attire, brows wreathed with the laurels of victory. Beside them are cornucopia, symbols of the treasures that were their just recompense, but instead of the conventional horns of plenty, their riches are more plainly denoted by sacks of coin. The heraldic shields of the respective provinces were, by 1626, the date of the *Gedenck-Clanck*'s publication (and a year after Valerius's own death), familiar conventions and the features of at least the Stadholder-princes would have been immediately recognizable to a lay reader. Likewise in the background, the congregation of Fatherland's believers, kneeling in supplication against a host of waving pikes and banners, are dressed in contemporary clothes to reinforce the immediacy of identification. All of these figures, however, pray before images that are simultaneously classical and pious, humanist and Calvinist: the hat of liberty derived from the award given to freed slaves in the Temple of Feronius in Rome, but itself surmounted by the divine aura, bathing all in its protective radiance with the mystical Yahweh tetragrammaton at its source.

This hodgepodge of contemporary history, archaic allusion, scriptural piety and patriotic anthem has an undeniable raw eloquence. Valerius was a member of the provincial elite in Veere, a second-generation refugee from France who, like so many others, had risen through the war, in his case to be Controller of customs and excise (*convooien en licenten*) at the Zeeland port and, more important, fortification master of the town. He was, in short, a frontline musician and historian whose work was deliberately aimed at a popular audience. Its epic note, struck again and again, was meant to assure the Netherlanders that they were the heroes of the new scripture: the latter-day Maccabees. (Indeed van Reyd's 1644 history explicitly likened the five brothers of the Nassau dynasty to the sons of Mattathias.[84]) Netherlands-Israel, then, was a stirring patriotic commonplace and one, moreover, that did not fade away with the end of the war against Spain. In 1651 the grand pensionary of Holland, Jacob Cats, opened the Great Assembly of the States by apostrophizing them as "Ye Children of Israel" and in 1668 Lydius wrote in one of his eulogies penned in the triumphant year of the Peace of Breda:

> *Above all else I thank him*
> *Whom Holland made Jerusalem*[85]

The Old Testament, of course, had long served as a storehouse of parable and allegory for Renaissance humanists in pursuit of *exempla virtutis*. And in their choice of subjects for history paintings, didactic prints and verse drama, the Dutch often followed Italian, Bohemian and Flemish precedents, especially in associating particular figures with specific moral qualities or flaws. Thus, Elisha, a Renaissance favorite, reappears bedecked in suitably prophetic robes in Ferdinand Bol's painting for the regents of the Amsterdam leper house.[86] Declining the Syrian general Naaman's gifts, he thus upholds the superiority of altruism over worldly gain. Among other stock recurring themes

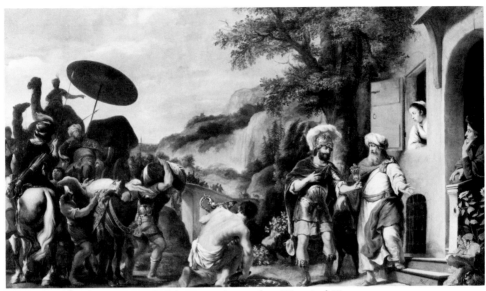

45. Ferdinand Bol, *Naaman and Elisha*, 1661. Amsterdam Historical Museum

46. Jan Steen, *Esther, Ahasuerus and Haman.* The Cleveland Museum of Art. Purchase John L. Severance Fund

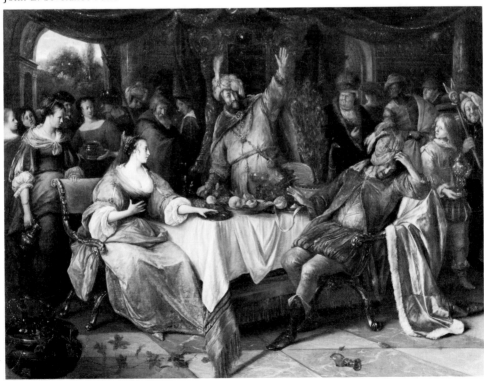

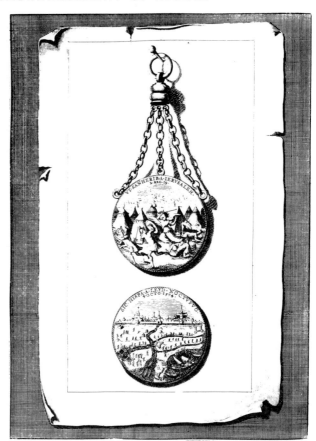

47. The sieges of Jerusalem
and Leiden. Engraving.
From Gerard van Loon,
*Beschryvinge der Nederlandse
Historiepenningen*

were Potiphar's wife spurned by Joseph (lust routed by innocence and resolution), the sufferings of Job and Tobias (fortitude in adversity) and the family sacrifices of Abraham and Jephthah, the first averted through exemplary fidelity to divine command, the second fulfilled as a punishment for fecklessly sworn oaths.[87]

Alongside these war-horses of the Renaissance repertoire there were others that were given a more distinctly local and vernacular accent in their Dutch treatment. Abraham de Koning's dramas of *Esther* (1618) and *Samson* (1619) both made free use of Dutch references and allusions in their connection of the fortunes of old Hebrews and the new Israel. For obvious reasons, the history of Esther, which contrasted the calculated wickedness of a bloodthirsty councillor (Haman/Alva) with the vindication of an innocent patriot hero (Mordecai/Orange) was a perennial favorite. Jacob Revius's *Haman, a Tragedy* (1630), Nicolas Fonteyn's *Esther or the Picture of Obedience* (1638) and

Johannes Serwouter's *Hester or the Deliverance of the Jews* (1659) all pointed up the appealing parallels, with a dramatized portrait of an exemplary marriage into the bargain. Jan Steen, who painted Esther themes at least five times, used a highly theatrical presentation of key scenes which, it has been suggested, owed much to familiarity with the stage versions of the story.[88]

And just as Esther was turned into an heroic *huisvrouw,* both courageous and obedient, so Jerusalem appeared in these scriptural analogies as a Hebrew Leiden or Amsterdam. On one of the best-known medallions, celebrating the relief of Leiden, the Assyrian king Sennacherib is shown fleeing in terror before the guardian angel of Judah at the very gates of Jerusalem.[89] On the reverse was the well-known fate of the Spanish army before Leiden. In Vondel's 1620 verse tragedy, *Hierusalem Verwoest* (Jerusalem Destroyed), the destruction of the Second Temple by Titus and the resistance of the Jews narrated by Josephus was prefaced by a consolatory moral. Though calamity may seem certain, Vondel wrote, "we have had proof here in our united Netherlands for some years now that, with the help of the All Highest, so many perils may, happily, pass us by."[90]

David and Solomon were both taken from the stock of Renaissance biblical heroes for local, patriotic adaptation. Solomon was usually invoked to flatter the wisdom of a government (he appears prominently in the new Amsterdam town hall), rather than an individual. But David was used to personify the struggles of the little nation against brutally superior odds and in that spirit, the Chamber of Rhetoric, Het Boek, duly performed a *tableau vivant* of David with the head of Goliath before the Prince of Orange when he came to Antwerp in 1577.[91] David was also of course the patriot prince himself, reluctant to accept his destiny and then unswervingly courageous. The great anthem, the "Wilhelmus van Nassouwe," attributed to both Coornhert and to William the Silent's prolific propagandist, Philip van Marnix, and which was, significantly, the first recognizable national anthem in European history, has the prince identify himself with David, contending successively against overbearing Philistines and a vindictive king.

> As David had to flee
> Before Saul the tyrant
> So must I sigh
> With many a gentleman[92]

The "Wilhelmus" was popular precisely because its commingling of scripture and historical chronicle faithfully reflected the reassuring self-image of Israel-Holland that the Dutch had adopted as their own heroic identity. The notion of a new chosen people fighting a godly cause beneath the protection of the Lord's banner appears in some of the earliest evidence of a popular patriotic culture. And the fact that this idiom was common to Puritan and Calvinist rhetoric elsewhere does not in the least lessen its force as an early nationalist creed. The historicizing and Gothicizing medievalism common to many nineteenth-century nationalisms did not, after all, weaken its effectiveness as a differentiator. And in the most militant centers of resistance to the Spanish, the seaports of Zeeland and south Holland, the *Geusen-liederen* (the Sea Beggars' songs) kindled patriotic sensibilities by reviling the enemy as idolatrous Philistines and eulogizing William the Silent as the new lion of Judah.[93] This parallelism was reinforced in the decoration of public buildings commissioned during the war years. At Venlo, the town regents had a "siege of Bethel" painted for the town hall as a way of claiming their place in the patriotic martyrology. And in a more spectacular commemoration, two massive stained-glass windows in the St. Janskerk at Gouda deal directly and indirectly, side by side, with the siege of Leiden. The window, presented by Delft and glazed by Dirck Verheyden and Dirck van Douwe, and which incorporates a famous and beautiful portrait of William (see fig. 37) is, in effect, a history chronicle in glass, complete with Boisot's fleet sailing to the rescue. Next to it, Leiden's own window celebrates the same event—and was indeed designed by the same artist, Isaak van Swanenburgh—but does so in the guise of the Syrian king Benhadad's siege of Samaria. It is an extraordinary irony that the same cathedral church contains, among other glories, windows presented half a century earlier by *both* Philip II and William of Orange.

Of all the scriptural analogies for patriotic history, none was more obviously compelling than the Exodus. As Michael Walzer has recently pointed out, the story has been almost perennially used as a metaphor for revolution, but it has also functioned—especially perhaps in the early modern era—as a reference point for godly nationalism. Calvinist writers throughout the sixteenth and seventeenth centuries, not least Cromwell and Milton, could all invoke the Exodus in justification of radical separation from idolatry and the making of a covenant of free people.[94] But while the metaphor was a commonplace, it had a particularly literal relevance for a founding generation of Netherlanders, 150,000 of whom had physically left the fleshpots of the south, crossed formidable water barriers and reached a land of abundance. Persecution, traumatic departure, peregrination, settlement and the defense of the godly nation were not just sermon analogies for those immigrants (most of them of course more devoutly Calvinist than the "old" dwellers of the north); they were the chapters of their own tribal history. It is natural, then, to find the Exodus story everywhere in early modern Dutch culture: in popular songs like the "Nieuw Liedeken van den slach voor Bergen" (The New Song of the Battle of Bergen op Zoom) where the fate of the Spanish army is yet again compared to the Egyptians engulfed in the Red Sea; on precious items for the rich like chased silver plaques, and on simple wall tiles for the humble.[95] On the stage, the meaning of the Exodus for contemporaries was spelled out in the most unequivocal way. Another of the *tableaux vivants* performed for William the Silent at Brussels and at Antwerp by the rhetoricians was, of course, "Moses's Deliverance of the Jews." And in 1612, only three years after the truce with Spain, Vondel wrote his epic *Passcha* (Passover), concluding with a specific "Comparison between the Redemption of the Children of Israel and the Liberation of the United Provinces of the Netherlands." In its heroic coda, Philip II is predictably likened to Pharaoh:

> *The one bowed down Jacob's house with slavery*
> *The other, the Netherlands oppressed with tyranny.*[96]

Vondel's own Mennonite family had participated in the great exodus from Antwerp in 1585 when the city had fallen to Parma. Settling briefly in Cologne, where the future playwright was born in 1587, they came to the Republic in 1596. So that even if Vondel did not have firsthand experience of the uprooting and migration to freedom that was the common lot of the southern exiles, it

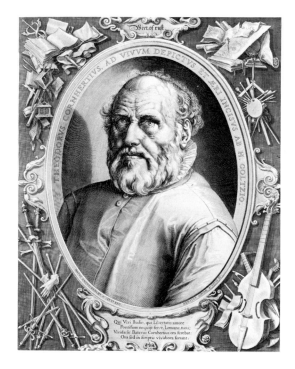

48. Hendrick Goltzius, *Dirck Volkertszoon Coornhert*, 1591. Francis Calley Gray Collection, Fogg Art Museum, Harvard University

must have played a powerful role in his feeling for the history of the Netherlands. And it was that same formative experience of migration that shaped the first authentically Dutch school of artists in Haarlem between 1580 and the 1620s. The group of Mannerists that gathered in that city around the brilliant figures of Goltzius, Cornelis van Haarlem and Karel van Mander had a distinctively southern bias, and in their choice of themes, especially in the graphic arts, often alluded to their own contemporary history. Cornelis, who had been in Antwerp in 1580, was commissioned to provide paintings for the Haarlem Prinsenhof (the residence of the Prince of Orange when staying in the town) and specifically to produce a replacement for a Maarten van Heemskerk panel that had been damaged by the Spanish. This work—the *Massacre of the Innocents*—and a lascivious *Monk and Nun* (the "Haarlem Wonder") must have been directly aimed at contemporary sensibilities.[97]

That Haarlem remained more culturally diverse and spiritually heterodox than Leiden did not lessen its importance as a crucible in which a self-consciously Netherlandish culture was being shaped. Karel van Mander, like the young Vondel, was a Mennonite; Goltzius and Coornhert remained Catho-

49. Hendrick Goltzius, etching and engraving. *Jacques de la Faille,* 1580. Fogg Art Museum, Harvard University

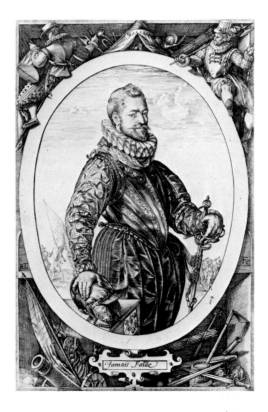

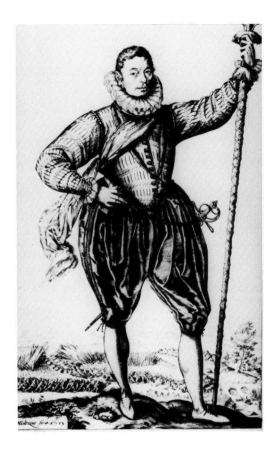

50. Hendrick Goltzius, *The Pike
Bearer,* 1583. New York Public
Library

lics of a humanist persuasion. But however much their stylistic idiosyncrasies
and choice of subjects had in common with "international" mannerism, none
of them was immune from the particular experience of the Dutch revolt.
Coornhert was, in his own person, the living link between the new Dutch
Haarlem and the brilliant Flemish culture of van Heemskerk, Plantijn and
Bruegel.[98] He was also a public man, a magistrate in Haarlem, a prisoner of the
Spanish in 1566 and an exile at Xanten with his young pupil Goltzius before
returning to Holland. And though his own denunciation of Calvinist excesses
as well as Spanish cruelties ensured his eventual estrangement from power, it
would have been strictly inconceivable had Coornhert not thought of himself
as a Netherlands patriot.

The same is surely true for his companion and pupil Goltzius. Some of his
most powerful engravings in the 1570s and 1580s are directly related to the
troubled circumstances of his times, and his own community of emigrants. In
1580, for example, he engraved the portrait of Jacques de la Faille, the
commander of the ninth company of militia at Antwerp, surrounded by martial
attributes, notwithstanding the fact that this was a wedding portrait.[99] And

even though the subject's motto was *jamais faille,* he was forced by Parma's conquest to flee to Haarlem where he established a shipping concern. It was Goltzius, too, who produced the magnificent twelve-sheet series on the tomb and funeral of the Prince of Orange in the year of his assassination and in 1586 another series depicting the counts of Holland for Blyenburgh's chronicle history.[100] And between 1582 and 1587 he engraved a spectacular series of military studies, one a *Pike-Bearer* set against a ferocious infantry battle, and with an inscription that begins:

> *The country's welfare must be defended by the faithful*
> *Who on every side prove that they are true to the fatherland.*[101]

This is not to imply that the Haarlem Mannerists were primarily concerned with historical themes. But they have been often treated as though their only

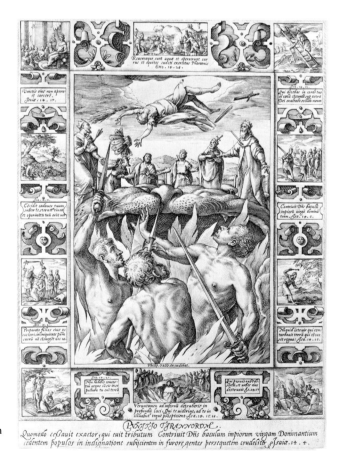

51. Hendrick Goltzius, engraving. *Punitio Tyrannorum,* c. 1578. Metropolitan Museum of Art, New York

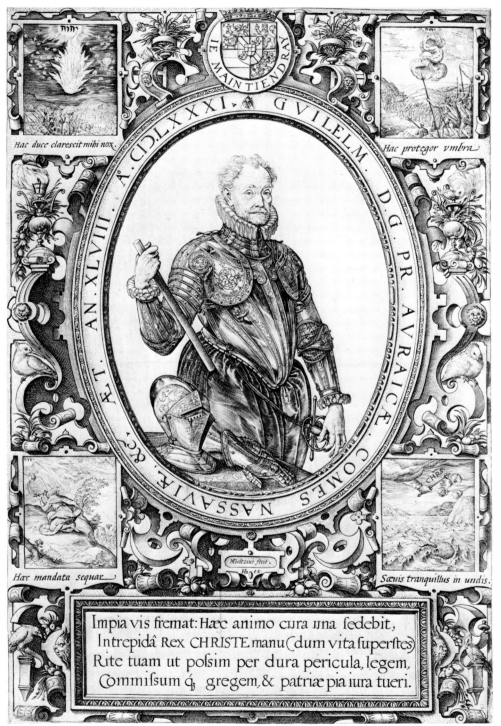

52. Hendrick Goltzius, *William of Orange,* 1581. Fogg Art Museum, Harvard University

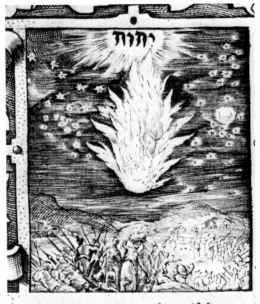

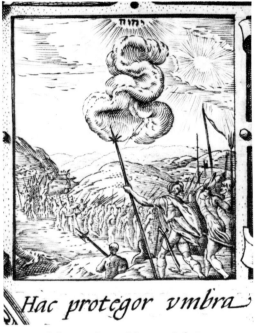

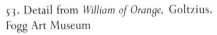

53. Detail from *William of Orange*, Goltzius.
Fogg Art Museum

54. Detail from *William of Orange*, Goltzius.
Fogg Art Museum

interest was the extravagance of their experiments in form. Where content has been considered, it has usually been assumed that their choice of Renaissance heroic and biblical themes responded to purely artistic prompting. At least in the case of the pervasive Exodus themes, this is almost certainly untrue. At least three important engravings by Goltzius of this period explicitly draw on the familiar cross-references of patriotism and scripture. In the *Punishment of Tyranny,* Lucifer falls to earth in the presence of six doomed kings standing at the mouth of hell.[102] And in the top center cartouche, Pharaoh's army is engulfed in the Red Sea, the same motif that is used for the central subject of the closely related *Punishment of Evil*. Lest anyone be in doubt of the direct relevance of the subject to contemporary events, the Holland lion is shown in cartouche at the bottom of the same engraving opposing the savage bear. It should not, then, come as a surprise to find William of Orange depicted in 1581 explicitly in the setting of scenes from the life of Moses: the pillars of cloud and fire, the bestowal of the Ten Commandments on Sinai, and the ultimate proof of divine protection, the passage through the Red Sea.

The evidence of connections between the Exodus story and the patriotic history is not always this unambiguous. It would be delightful to be able to see the stupendous *Moses* of 1583 as in some sense related to Vondel's patriotic leader, or even the ancestor of Bol's and Rembrandt's versions of the mid-seventeenth century. And related episodes of the covenant like the sacrifice of Isaac included in the same print may suggest such a possibility. But it would be as easy to claim a connection with traditional Mosaic iconography like Michelangelo's tomb for Julius II, or the artist's own inclusion of Moses as one of the six prophets of the Annunciation. And other artists produced Exodus scenes with equally tantalizing possibilities. What, for example, are we to make of Cornelis van Haarlem's painting of *The Crossing of the Red Sea?* His figures are costumed according to the fantastic conventions of other Mannerist renderings of the Exodus, in particular those of Joachim Wytewael. But the passage through the sea was a strikingly unusual subject (compared with the brazen serpent or the Golden Calf) and one which the Goltzius engravings suggest had specifically historical undertones. That the appropriation of the Exodus story as a patriotic scripture had become quasi-official, though, is strongly suggested by the window that Isaak Nicolai van Swanenburgh, Leiden's own history painter, had done for the Janskerk at Gouda.[103] At a later date the Utrecht artist Abraham Bloemaert produced an even more suggestive pair of drawings, one of the destruction of Pharaoh in the Red Sea, the other, *The Israelites Purifying Themselves in the Wilderness.* That latter subject seems inexplicable as an obviously dramatic episode from Leviticus, but it is of the

55. Cornelis van Haarlem, *The Israelites Crossing the Red Sea.* The Art Museum, Princeton University

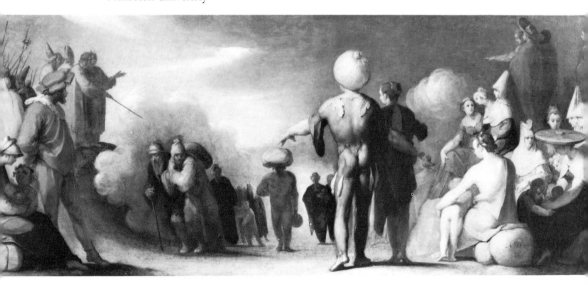

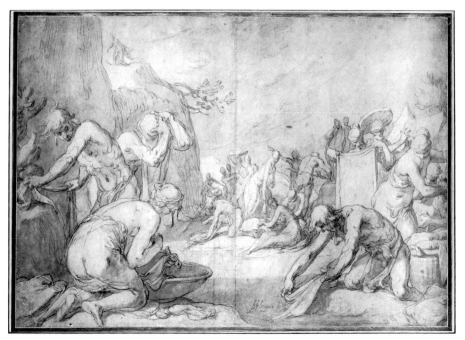

56. Abraham Bloemaert, drawing. *The Ritual Washing of the Israelites,* 1606. National
Gallery of Art, Washington, D.C.

greatest relevance to the Dutch obssession with defilement and purification.
For it was exactly through such a process of ritual cleansing, said the preachers,
that the impurities of the idolatrous and alien past were to be scoured from
the reconsecrated nation.[104]

So the mere fact that Moses had long occupied an important place in
Christian eschatology need not preclude his recruitment in the service of a
more local culture. Like David, Moses had functioned in traditional Catholic
doctrine as a prophetic harbinger of the messianic return, and it was in that
guise that he appears on the tomb of that militant neo-Platonist Julius II. The
Dutch Moses, "ons Moyses" as one pamphlet referred to him in his current
incarnation as William of Orange, retained the heroism of the traditional
Christian stereotype as well as his *keren,* horns of light. But in keeping with the
differentiating role that the Exodus played in what might be called nationalist
(as distinct from universalist) Christianity, he became a separator rather than a
unifier. From an assimilated origin within a host aristocracy, Moses is made to
discover (or rather recover), through the direct word of God, his true identity.
He then transmits this reborn sense of difference to the captive and semi-
assimilated Israelites. He summons them, in effect, to become estranged, to

commit an act of grand departure that means, simultaneously, leaving home and going Home. Having achieved this, his second great mission is to supply them with the content and the boundaries of that new identity in the form of laws and social regulations designed to maintain their separateness. No wonder, then, that Vondel's Moses in *Passcha* sounds sometimes like the first great patriot of the law, the Lands Advocate, Oldenbarneveld, and sometimes like any veteran magistrate, given to upbraiding backsliders and holding forth on the horrors of tyranny and the fickleness of the common multitude. But more obvious than either of these contemporary versions of the lawgiver-statesman was his reincarnation in the *pater patriae,* William, who had also "discovered" his identity while still a loyal member of the imperial nobility, who had also been forced by Pharaonic recalcitrance into violent rebellion, who had also risked his own life for that cause, and who, having delivered his people from bondage, had died within sight of, rather than in secure possession of, the Promised Land.

> *O wondrous fate that joins Moses and Orange*
> *The one fights for the law, the other beats the drum*
> *And with his own arm, frees the Evangelium*
> *The one leads the Hebrews through the Red Sea flood*
> *The other guides his people through a sea . . . of tears and blood.*[105]

In many respects, then, the Dutch (and other Calvinist) versions of the Exodus restored to the scripture much of its original Pentateuchal emphasis. To be sure, this did not necessarily predispose them towards philo-Semitism, as some historians have speculated, since the imagined Hebrews of the Book were closer to archetypal Bataves than to the swarthy, Ladino-speaking Marranos whom they actually encountered on the Sint Anthonis-breestraat in Amsterdam.[106] But this not inconsiderable complication aside, the Exodus epic became for the Dutch what it had been for the Biblical Jews: the legitimation of a great historical rupture, a cut with the past which had made possible the retrospective invention of a collective identity. The historical truth, suggested at the beginning of this chapter, was that that identity had been anything but manifest in the sixteenth century. It had taken a uniquely sorry combination of incompetence, brutality and fanaticism to unite Netherlanders of many persuasions and often faltering resolution behind the banner of Faith, Fatherland and Freedom (not necessarily in that order). Once done, however, those uncertainties were cloaked in a mantle of patriotic mythology in which God's bidding was disclosed just as surely as if it had been announced from the burning bush and hewn in tablets of stone.

It was when individual Dutch men and women tried to discern what exactly it was that those tablets commanded, however, that the scriptural analogy began to lose clarity and coherence. The revelation on Mount Sinai had handily solved the problems of both the authority by which commandments were issued, and the content to which reborn Israelites were required to subscribe. But for their Netherlandish counterparts there was no comparably indisputable source of authority to which all those who thought of themselves as Dutch might axiomatically give assent. There was the civil law of their respective towns or provinces embodied in edicts, but the most zealous of their priests claimed that this was subordinate in all respects to the godly law laid down in synodal decrees. Just as seriously, there were large numbers of patriots outside the congregation of the Reformed Church for whom the institutes of Calvin and the decrees of the Dutch synods were a matter of indifference (at best). As long as the struggle continued against a foe whose obvious beastliness proclaimed the synonymity of ungodliness and unlawfulness, this contention could remain muted. But as the Dutch, in the years following the truce of 1609, turned from abjuration and rebellion to institutional settlement, rival versions of the destination to which the founding exodus had been pointing could no longer be reconciled.

Hebraic patriotism had always contained within itself the possibility of a schism between Israel and Judah. Those humanists—from Coornhert to

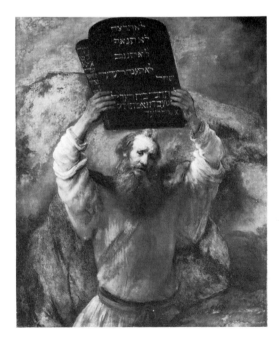

57. Rembrandt van Rijn, *Moses and the Tablets of the Law*, 1659. Gemäldegalerie, Berlin

Grotius—who saw the legitimacy of the revolt resting on toleration, also tended to stress the continuity of customary law, local self-governance and historical prescription. In this respect the unbroken epic of the Bataves, preserved from medieval feudalism and reemerging intact in communal and provincial liberties, served their cause better than a freshly revealed Mosaic law. Conversely, the predikants and Calvinist patricians, for whom the point of the revolt had been the installation of the one godly faith, were more inclined to stress the decisiveness of the conversion of tribe into nation, cleansed, root and branch, body and soul, of earlier "pagan" beliefs.

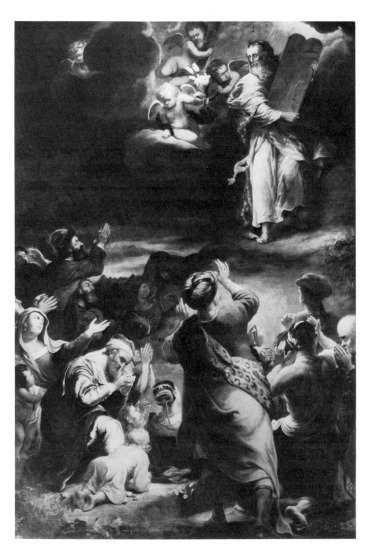

58. Ferdinand Bol, *Moses and the Tablets of the Law.* Royal Palace (formerly Town Hall), Amsterdam

It is, then, all the more extraordinary that the most striking instance of Mosaic iconography, at the heart of Amsterdam's town hall, should have represented, not the ascendancy of the Calvinist zealots, but the polemical ingenuity of their "pliant" (*rekkelijke*) adversaries in the Amsterdam patriciate. Ferdinand Bol's *Moses with the Tablets of Law* (1661–62) is best known to art historians as the stilted and ungainly alternative to what might have been one of Rembrandt's most powerful late history paintings, executed in 1659.[107] Only a fragment of the latter remains, but more than enough to demonstrate that the pupil was no match for his teacher. Bol's work is partly derived, as Albert Blankert has shown, from a Rubens *Assumption of Mary*, and its pretension at baroque monumentalism—a sort of Protestant variation on the grand altar pieces of the south—far outstripped Bol's native ability to deliver. But

59. Gerrit van Berckheyde, *The Dam with the Town Hall, Amsterdam*. Rijksmuseum, Amsterdam

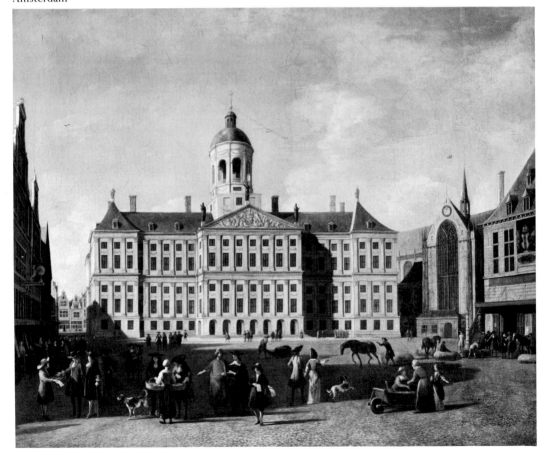

what passes for second-rate may qualify as first-rate historical evidence, and Bol's *Moses,* in all its histrionic glory provides a grandiloquent demonstration of how the Exodus scripture had become a battleground for disputing views of the relationship between church and state.

It was of more than casual significance that Bol's painting resulted from a commission to provide a mantelpiece for the Chamber of Magistrates (Schepenkamer) in van Campen's town hall. Planned since 1643, and accelerated in its execution by the destruction by fire of the old town hall in 1652, the massive new building represented far more than a mere act of urban embellishment or the reconstruction of a seat of administration. In both scale and style it was quite unlike any other town hall in the Netherlands, or for that matter in northern Europe. As much as the ducal palace in Venice, van Campen's formal classicism, and Artus Quellijn's baroque statuary and friezes, were intended to proclaim the imperial ethos of a virtual city-state. By comparison, the modest palaces built for the House of Orange, even the more elaborate additions created by Stadholder Frederick Henry, were mean and dwarfish. The sheer grandeur and august proportions of the building seemed to advertise the disproportionate power exercised by the city and its regents in the affairs of the Republic.[108]

The historical juncture at which the new town hall was built was important. Its foundation stone was laid in 1648, the same year that the Peace of Münster was signed, bringing to an end the eighty-year war with Spain. The peace was intended by the Holland mercantile patriciate to inaugurate a period of mercantile abundance uninterrupted by the fiscal strains of prolonged warfare. As such it displeased the parties within the Republic, especially the ministers of the Reformed Church and the Orangists, who anathematized it as a pact with the Devil. In 1650 the young Stadholder William II took his displeasure with the proposed demobilization of the army so far as to attempt a campaign of armed coercion against Amsterdam and other cities (beginning with the most "senior," Dordrecht), designed to purge the magistracy and replace it with factions prepared to do the Prince's bidding.[109] This was the most serious domestic crisis in the history of the young Republic since the religious commotions that had led to the fall and execution of Oldenbarneveld in 1618, and it was tantamount to a dynastic *coup,* all too reminiscent of the kind of tactics used by William's in-laws, the Stuarts. In the Netherlands it stopped well short of a civil war through a bizarre combination of defensive tactics and providential interventions. Initially, spurred on by the adamant "League of Bickers," Amsterdam prepared its defenses for a siege. The city was spared the need to test its fortitude by the meanderings of the Prince's army, which managed to lose its way in a dense fog. Let off the hook, the more pragmatically minded de Graeff faction in the Amsterdam council promptly offered the eviction of Andries and Cornelis Bicker as the basis for a compromise. That was duly achieved, but any possibility of the Stadholder further strengthening his position through renewed exercises in military intimidation was cut short by his sudden death from smallpox in October 1650.

That fortuitous but crucial event had precluded any long-term change in the balance of power in the Republic. But after their narrow escape, the Amsterdam regents and their counterparts in the other major towns of Holland took advantage of the infancy of William's son to give themselves some insurance against a recurrence of Stadholderian main force. At its most determined, this led to Johan de Witt's attempt to strip the Stadholderate of all but a weakly symbolic presence, but in Amsterdam it was local office with which the patriciate was most immediately concerned. In place of the formal right of the Stadholder to choose magistrates from a double list submitted by the thirty-six-man regency, the regents decided, for the first time, to appoint their own nine-man bench. So that the Chamber of Magistrates, the Schepenkamer, in the town hall, was to be used by a judicial college whose legitimacy rested on the assertion of an autonomous regent sovereignty.

The choice of Exodus chapters 32–35 to symbolize this judicial independence, however, owed more to the part that the church had played in the dispute than to any gloating over the debacle of its dynastic ally. It was, after all, the persistence of crypto-theocratic aspirations on the part of the Reformed Church synods that remained the principal problem. While the death of William II had relieved the States Party and Amsterdam in particular of their most truculent antagonist, the Stadholder's clerical allies continued to press for a strong army, a forceful foreign policy and a godly republic—embodied, for instance, in more stringent censorship and laws against sabbatical profanation. Apart from the practical difficulty of interfering with the clerical hierarchy in the interests of obtaining a more subdued church, so latitudinarian a policy was precluded by the presence *within* the patriciate of a faction committed to the godly cause. From the very beginning of Amsterdam's hesitant and somewhat belated conversion to the Protestant cause in 1578, there had always been a more militantly Calvinist group within the regency urging the council on to greater doctrinal stringency. While that group had generally been a minority among the body of thirty-six regents, they could scarcely be described as an insignificant group, either socially or politically. Some of the richest and most influential of the great patrician families—the Pauws and the Backers—identified themselves with the church polemics against "laxity" and periodically profited from the pressure of external events to impose their will (and their clients) on the rest of the council. That had happened in 1618, and threatened to do so again in the 1640s. While it was highly unlikely that temporary ascendancy could ever be converted into institutionalized domination, the *rekkelijke* majority was prudent enough to offer symbolic (and thus important) concessions to their opponents' public show of piety. When the overall design of the Dam square was under discussion from 1642 onwards, the leading figure of the Calvinist group, Jacob Backer, was appeased by giving the Nieuwe Kerk, rebuilt after a fire in 1645, prominent southern exposure. Abutting on the Dam, it would proclaim through juxtaposition the authority of the church alongside that of the magistracy installed in the town hall. Backer and the ministry, though, were not content with architectural parity. After a heated campaign it was finally agreed to erect an immense tower that would have exceeded the cupola of the Stadhuis by some considerable height and so proclaim the proper submission of earthly to divine power.

Backer's death in 1647 lost the tower its most persistent and formidable advocate on the regency, and the soaring spire was never built. But the plans for the integration of the Nieuwe Kerk into the general configuration of the Dam went ahead. And, if anything, the debacle of the Stadholder's *coup* against Amsterdam in 1650 made the militant clergy more determined to press their cause in the years that followed. Economic depression, a fierce visitation of the plague, and misfortune in the naval war with England provided conditions grim enough for a Calvinist rally. In 1654 Vondel's controversial play *Lucifer* provoked a renewed campaign against profane drama as well as a more active prosecution of cases of "notorious living" that caught, among others, Rembrandt and Hendrikje Stoffels in its net. In 1655, Dr. Tulp, who was both physician and magistrate, succeeded in having an antisumptuary law enacted which reflected clerical as well as humanist alarm at the taste for luxury in the city. It was against this background that the moderate regents, savoring the magnificence of their new town hall, decided to offer an iconographic reproof to theocracy where it most counted: in their seat of law.

In so doing, they reverted unashamedly to the biblical passages used by the Remonstrant minister Uytenbogaert in his ferocious disputes with the Gomarist clergy in the first decades of the century. Cunningly playing on the ultra-Calvinist obsession with scriptural identification, Uytenbogaert had used the Old Testament to insist on the division of governance between lay and spiritual spheres, with the former ultimately responsible for the administration of the commonwealth. It had been Moses, not Aaron, he argued, who had been awarded the godly leadership of the Children of Israel, and after Moses' death, that leadership had passed first to judges and then to kings. The priests and prophets had served as the moral consciences of the state, set apart in a special caste, but never entrusted with the role of government. The mantelpiece painting for the Chamber of the Magistrates was to show the one occasion when government had been placed in the hands of the priests, with demonstrably calamitous consequences. Bol's Moses descends from Mount

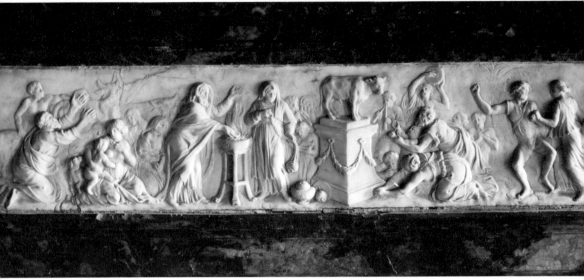

60. Artus Quellijn, marble frieze of the *Worship of the Golden Calf.* Royal Palace (formerly Town Hall), Amsterdam

Sinai with the tablets of the law in his arms, only to witness the scenes of profane iniquity and chaos in the camp of the Israelites. Acknowledging their sins, they kneel before him for forgiveness — the figure in left profile, perhaps dressed so as to embody the contrition of the priestly caste.

This was a neat way of standing on its head much of the clerical polemic against lax government. With Aaron's folly of permitting the Golden Calf understood to be the biblical context, the dissipation and wantonness that the clergy ritually attacked was, by implication, laid at the door of their own unfitness for government. The point was further hammered home by a marble frieze placed beneath the painting in which the full gamut of drunken lechery, mayhem and disorder was vividly portrayed. No doubt happy with this retort to the ministers, like Langelius, who had been responsible for banning his play, and as a Catholic only too keenly aware of the importance of judicial moderation, Vondel had already published a suitable poem in 1659, *On Moses Receiving the Law, in the Chamber of the Magistrates.* Though this may have been intended for the Rembrandt original, Bol's substitute in no way altered its relevance:

> *Hebrew Moses received the Law from God*
> *With which he returns from above to the people*
> *So they become respectful and welcome them with longing.*
> *As the people honor the laws, so shall a Free state stand.*[110]

And in another poem which specifically mentions Bol's painting, Jan Vos further hinted at the special qualities needed for the execution of the law:

> *The Law was given by Moses for all of Israel.*
> *Those who govern the people will need a strong hand.*
> *The laws should strike terror in godless living*
> *Where wise laws are kept; there virtue makes its stand.*[111]

Art historians such as Katherine Fremantle and Albert Blankert who have examined the iconography of the Amsterdam town hall, have generally commented on the oddity of placing a scriptural subject in so prominent a place within what was, overall, a classical decorative scheme. And it is undeniable that the pictorial distribution throughout the many chambers of the building was dominated by appropriate exempla drawn from the literature of antiquity. It was that literature, after all, which distinguished the Latinate humanist education of the patrician elite from the Bible schooling of those they governed. But it is a backhanded compliment to the ubiquitousness of the scriptural idiom that in the most important disputes—and there were none more important than church and state—the oligarchy was ready to borrow the ideological vocabulary of its opponents to win its point.

There is, in any case, no reason to suppose that a resort to the patriotic scripture would have jarred on a humanist sensibility, especially one that paid lip service at least to Calvinism. Aside from the shared assumption that the Dutch were indeed the inheritors of the Hebraic destiny, the midcentury patriciate could agree with the clergy that wantonness, dissipation, luxury, and greed threatened to undo all that the founders of the Republic had built. An ancient moralizing tradition, stretching back at least to Seneca, reinforced rather than subverted these apprehensions. And in the matter of the Golden Calf it is worth noting that the moral drawn from the story by both patricians and preachers was the same. What was at issue, rather, was who was to blame for these lapses, and under whose auspices should they be punished. Who, in other words, had custody of the national morality?

If this issue remained unresolved, there was at least no difficulty in recognizing the ideal Netherlander, by the middle of the seventeenth century. *Deugd, kloekmoedigheid en yver,* virtue, bravery and zeal, were the qualities the Dutch awarded themselves and sought to sustain in the years of their prime. In keeping with a nation sired of David's stock, and obedient to Moses' law, they should combine God-fearing resolution with courage, resourcefulness and a hearty appetite for life, the better to indulge it according to classical canons of moderation and scriptural commandments of prudence. The patriotic scripture, then, the book of a collective identity, was as capacious as it was versatile. By synthesizing the "ancient" seventeen-hundred-year-old history of Batavian freedom with the notion of a national rebirth through ordeal, exodus and redemption, it was able to avoid the kind of moral exclusivism that had brought other countries to civil war in the same period. And it was precisely because external perils and pressures remained so great for most of the century that the national culture, in its formative period, was like an ark, designed to accommodate multifarious species all clinging to the covenanted promise of a collective future, so as to survive against daunting odds.

This made for phenomena which were quite as special in seventeenth-century Europe as the Dutch supposed. Joost van Vondel was just one of a number of distinguished Dutch Catholics whose faith in no way diluted their patriotism. The Amsterdam canal house facades — the epitome of Dutch patrician style — look the way they do largely through the genius of another Catholic, Philips Vingboons. Far from being forced into a mean corner of society, Vingboons was the most celebrated and fashionable architect of the elite at midcentury, the undisputed successor to Hendrick de Keyser. His own faith, moreover, was no bar to his receiving commissions from Catholic and Calvinist clients alike. The creators of what we think of as archetypal Dutch images on canvas often turn out to be equally heterodox in their confessional life. Vermeer's exquisite parlors as well as Steen's rowdy kitchens were both the work of Catholics. Rembrandt came from a family in which the father was a Calvinist and the mother a practicing Catholic. At different times he himself was attracted to Remonstrants, Mennonites, and to highly unorthodox sects like the Collegiants and the Waterlanders whose emphasis on extreme scriptural simplicity appealed to a Christian for whom the Bible was an anthology of human drama. And he was able to paint and etch rabbis, predikants and Mennonite lay preachers with equal conviction and sympathy.

It would be a mistake, then, to align the different elements comprising the national personality with particular religious denominations or social categories, especially a simple classification of Calvinist-scriptural-common people against humanist-Batavian-patrician. These cultural traits cohabited within the same collective ethos just as they could dwell within a single family household or even within the life cycle of an individual. Vondel, after all, began as pious Mennonite and ended as enthusiastic Catholic. The rhetorician Jan Baptist Houwaert did full justice to all these facets of the patriotic personality when he eulogized William the Silent in 1582 as embodying:

> David's compassion, Solomon's prudence
> Cyrus' memory, Tullius' eloquence
> us' steadfastness and Probus' integrity.[112]

And while scripture may have dominated Rembrandt's history painting he was equally at home with the grand classical themes when they struck a chord in the Netherlandish-humanist repertoire. In the same year that he painted the Moses, 1659, he also undertook the major commission of the *Claudius Civilis* for one of the great monumental spaces of the town hall. Similarly, the author of *'t Verheerlijkt Nederland* (The Netherlands Exalted) combined in his eulogy miraculous scripture-history, Ciceronian adages and an exemplary version of the seventeen-hundred-year-old tradition of Batavian freedom.[113]

All these elements could be blended together, as could the iconographic miscellany of the *Nederlantsche Gedenk*, without much concern for consistency. The message was the same, whether expressed in old humanist axioms, dredged up from Seneca, Ovid or Pliny and replenished with Renaissance morality or couched in scriptural prophecy. The meaning of Dutch history was the providential disclosure of a divine plan for the world. God's chosen instrument was the *nederkinderen,* and their feats were, in reality, His miracles, their victories as startling as the sun halted in its tracks over Ai. By any mortal logic, the forty "murder years" should have produced a wasteland. Instead His compatriots dwelt in an earthly paradise that was not only fruitful of itself, but that commanded all the goods of the world in its bulging storehouses. This, it hardly needed saying, was the reward for faithfulness to His covenant. And so long as the people remained steadfast and law-abiding, they would prosper and wax mighty. But "a Republic which has as its foundation godlessness and knavery" is undeserving of praise — indeed undeserving of a future.

In such texts, elation was almost always tempered by circumspection, if not foreboding. In 1668, when *'t Verheerlijkt Nederland* appeared, the Republic seemed to have ample cause for self-congratulation. Its fleet had humiliated the British the previous year, burning their ships in the Medway and seizing the flagship *The Royal Charles* as prize. The Treaty of Breda, which concluded the Anglo-Dutch naval war, had been settled on terms largely favorable to the Netherlands.[114] Through de Witt's formidable tactical skills, the Republic's principal rivals remained divided, and it stood at the center of a complicated skein of diplomatic relationships, which it seemed to be capable of unraveling or tightening at its pleasure. Any complacency on this score was to be traumatically shattered in the "disaster year" of 1672, but even in 1668 it was impossible for the present to be surveyed without obligatory prudential warnings and dire auguries. Once again scripture could be invoked to good effect. If the heroic phase of the country's young history could be related through exodus and conquest, godly captains in succession to Moses — Joshua and Gideon — rulers as brave as David and wise as Solomon, the question then arose as to how this patriotic scripture was to continue. The chapters following Kings I:11 were not auspicious. The Dutch often liked to refer to

Amsterdam as their Jerusalem with the temple of freedom (the town hall) or of purity (the Zuiderkerk) erected therein. But they were only too well aware of the calamities that succeeded Solomon's reign: the division of the kingdoms and their eventual destruction and captivity. Indeed Johan de Witt liked to reinforce his arguments for the abolition of the stadholderate by claiming it would avert such catastrophes. The Israelites had gone wrong, he and polemicists like Pieter de la Court argued, when they had taken a king.[115]

While God would stand guard against enemies from without, the real menace would come from within. And despite conflict over forms of government, which became seriously aggravated in the late 1660s, the danger to which all prophets of doom drew attention was materialism. So the greatest test of *standvastigheid* (steadfastness) which the Lord had laid on His people was, ironically, their own success. The word which recurs over and again in texts ruminating on the nation's destiny is *overvloed,* a drowning surfeit. If the end of gold was to be the Golden Calf, then the covenant would be broken, divine protection withdrawn and the errant people returned to the primal element from which they had been drained. There were other eloquent scriptural reminders sculpted into the decoration of the Amsterdam Town Hall. At the entrance to the Vroedschapzaal, the hall where the full thirty-six regents deliberated, were two cartouches. The first showed Joseph as diviner of Pharaoh's dream, reminding those who relished abundance overmuch that the seven lean years would follow the seven fat. And opposite it, with still more minatory effect, was the figure of Jeremiah, whose lamentations confirmed the worthlessness and ephemerality of worldly power.

Wealth, then, so far from being the reassuring symptom of the predestined Elect, as Weber argued, acted on contemporary consciences as a moral agitator. Without it the Republic would collapse; with it, the Dutch could fall prey to false gods, Mammon and Baal, and engineer their own downfall. What was needed was a set of rules and conventions by which wealth could be absorbed in ways compatible with the godly purposes for which the Republic had been created. Profit was emphatically not one such end, but taxes and philanthropy were, the latter vindicating the humanist belief in the redemptive quality of good works, notwithstanding Calvinism's theological repudiation. There would, however, be no Dutch decalogue, or any kind of moral police appointed to monitor social conduct. In most Dutch towns, the magistracy was loath to permit the church synods the enforcing power they sought, and penalties for erring believers were largely restricted to expressly ecclesiastical forms—exclusion from the communion, and the like. For all this, Dutch society in its prime was hardly the sink of iniquity that the most incensed preachers liked to portray. While there was no formal set of controls regulating social ethics, an extensive array of informal, vernacular and domestic morals acted as the containing membranes of the busy, energetic organism. Some of these had classical origins, some scriptural; many were rooted in ancient Low Country folk fetishes; most were given a dusting of Calvinism for contemporary needs. All had to deal with what was peculiarly a Dutch problem: how to create a moral order *within* a terrestrial paradise.

PART
TWO

DOING AND
NOT DOING

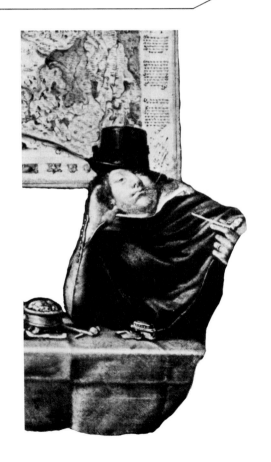

CHAPTER THREE

Feasting, Fasting and Timely Atonement

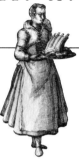

Then, the mariners were afraid and cried every man unto his god, and cast forth the wares that were in the ship into the sea to lighten it of them.

      · · ·

Word came unto the king of Nineveh and he arose from his throne and he laid his robe from him and covered him in sackcloth and sat in ashes.

      · · ·

And he caused it to be proclaimed and published throughout Nineveh by decree of the king and his nobles, saying "Let neither man nor beast, herd nor flock taste any thing."   JONAH 1: v,
3: vi, vii

The seventeenth-century Dutch were perhaps the first to pay for their unprecedented prosperity with their teeth. And we have all been paying the same price ever since.

HARVEY AND SHELDON PECK, orthodontists
Discover, October 1980

*Here lies the landlord of The Lion
Who died in lively hopes of Zion
His son keeps on the business still
Resigned unto the Heavenly will*

Epitaph in Malvern graveyard

*As it was said by men in the Olden Times
that there was a land that flowed with milk and
honey, truly it is in our Holland and here in
Amsterdam that the town overflows with milk
and cheese and butter brought to market every
week. . . . So that truly may it be said that our
Holland overflows with butter, cheese and milk
and that these blessings we receive from the
hands of the Almighty.*

MELCHIOR FOKKENS, *Beschryvinge der
Wijdt-Vermaerde Koop-Stadt Amstelredam,* 1665

*There was a danger that Abram might become
too well pleased with his own good fortune.
Therefore God seasons the sweetness of wealth
with vinegar . . .*

JOHN CALVIN, *Commentary on
Genesis* 13:V, VII

i   WHALES ON THE BEACH; WRITING ON THE WALL

On February 3, 1598, a fifty-four-foot sperm whale beached itself in the sandy shallows at Berckhey, a fishing village between Katwijk and Scheveningen. Lugged ashore with cables, it lay there for four days, feebly twitching its fins and attracting throngs of people whose curiosity had overcome their fear. Before it finally expired, it had begun to decompose. Grotius's account in *De Rebus Belgicus* noted that "as it lay, the Bowels burst out, which so infected the Air thereabouts that many of those who went to see it were cast into Diseases by the stench of it and some died."[1] But the "filthy nauseous savor"[2] was perfumed with profit. Once the state, in the person of an official from the Exchequer (*Rekenkamer*) of the province of Holland, had established its claim, the carcass was put up for public auction. Its price—136 guilders—was a bargain, considering that train oil could be extracted from its blubber and sold to local soap-works and its teeth used for a variety of decorative purposes.

The leviathan died famous as well as useful. Before it was reduced to so much oil and bone, it became the object of intense examination. Its formidably toothed head was presented as a trophy to Jan of Nassau, who was not only a military commander but also a humanist patron.[3] The chronicler Petrus Christiaanszoon Bor made sketches and notes that he incorporated into his patriotic history, and which became the basis for the many subsequent accounts of the stranding, including, in all likelihood, that of Grotius.[4] Learned doctors and divines from Leiden arrived armed with pomanders and measuring rods to inspect its awesome dimensions. The greatest of the Haarlem masters, Hendrick Goltzius, who had made a drawing of a pilot

61. Jacob Matham after Hendrick Goltzius, *Whale Stranded at Berckhey,* 1598. Hart Nautical Collections, M.I.T. Museum, Cambridge, Mass.

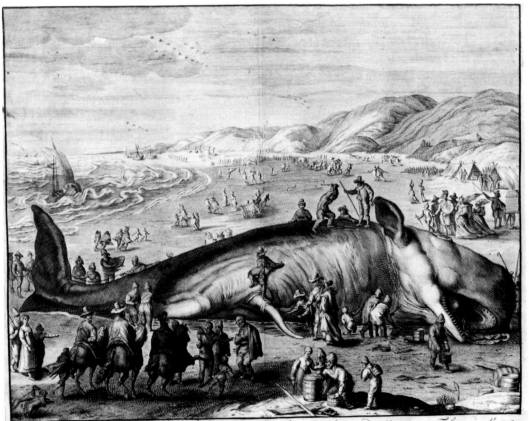

Stranding van een Walvisch van 70. voeten lang, tusschen Katwyk en Schevelingen, in de Maandt van February, A.° 1598.

whale stranded at Zaandvoort in 1594, made a more detailed and splendid drawing that was engraved by his pupil, Jacob Matham.[5] Matham followed Goltzius's famous error in supposing a fin to be the whale's ear, but in other respects, the print was anatomically faithful, and became the prototype for a number of versions.[6] It was used to illustrate Collaert's *Piscium Vivae Icones,* used in reverse for an illustration of another stranding at Ancona in southern Italy in 1601, and in Holland became an obligatory feature of all the great histories of the time, including Hooft's *Nederlandsche Historien* and (retouched by Bernard Picart) Jean Leclerc's magnificent *Histoire des Provinces Unies* at the end of the seventeenth century.

Through these accounts, the sperm whale of Berckhey became a special episode in the natural history of the Republic — as much part of the collective memory as battles and sieges. And as with all such chronicles, both visual and textual reports have much to tell us about the peculiar Dutch relation with fortune, nature and history.

At first sight, Matham's print seems to provide an exemplary instance of their mastery over nature, however imposing its phenomena. It is the absorption of the extraordinary into the ordinary that is so striking, especially when one reflects on Goltzius's Mannerist taste for the fantastic. He has set the huge carcass down on the naturalistically observed dunescape of the North Sea shore, and has peopled the busy scene with the same kind of social repertory that recurs in Avercamp winterscapes or Esaias van de Velde landscapes. The insistence on the mundane — fishermen going about their business, other villagers carrying off the fat in buckets — reduces the magnitude of the event, if not exactly to the level of a commonplace, then at least to measurable dimensions. And if the busyness of the commerce that begins with the ax raised above the head of the figure standing beside the fin is one of the most arresting elements of the scene, the other is surely the work of careful measurement proceeding along the whale's mass. This concern to measure had already been apparent in Goltzius's 1594 sketch, but in the case of the sperm whale there was an object worthier of attention. A line of men surveys the distance along the animal's back from its tail fins while another takes a staff to gauge its penis, which, Bor's text tells us, was "even dead, three feet long."[7] The sexual organs of the larger whales were so awesome that "a yard" (in the English observer's idiom) was preserved in the Leiden anatomy theater along with a copy of Matham's print and other unlikely phenomena such as "the Entrailes of a Man which is made into a Shirt" and (at the other extreme) "a small bone taken from a beaver's penis."[8] Bor's text, while conceding that the whale was "a monstrous ugly beast," is dominated by an inventory of anatomical statistics: eyes, fifteen feet from mouth; under-jaw seven feet long; row of forty-two teeth "white as ivory" and a thirteen-foot tail.[9]

It would be a great mistake, though, to assume that the responses to apparitions of this kind were limited to zoological and commercial arithmetic. Even Bor allows himself the comment that the sighting of the whale occasioned "great uproar and clamor."[10] And the stranding of the whale was a historical event in the fullest sense, an oracular signpost in the flowing continuum between past and future. As such it inevitably had portentous as well as illustrative qualities. In 1577 an earlier stranding had prompted a vernacular verse attached to a print in which the dying animal identifies his origins in Spain, sent to the Netherlands to do ill but confounded, perishing in vile putrefaction.[11] Describing the Berckhey whale, Grotius tellingly divides the response of spectators into two very different moods. The more learned, he wrote in *De Rebus* (translated into Dutch as the *Nederlandse Jaarboeken,* or Netherlands Annals), were most concerned with the reasons for the animal's plight; whether storms had driven it on to the beach. But others, "among the common people," debated its ominous significance, some taking it "as a sign that the Hollanders would triumph over their enemies, others that it was a portent of disaster."[12] And another version of the Berckhey whale that connected it prophetically with the historical drama of the Netherlands was a print combining an image of the animal, a map of the Principality of Cleves occupied in August 1598 by Spanish troops, with an atrocity picture of their conduct in the Cleves towns.[13] The historical episode was thus seen as the fulfillment of the omens announced by the beached whale.

Between 1531 and the end of the seventeenth century there were at least forty occasions when whales landed up on the dune coasts of the Netherlands along a line from the Flemish shore east of Antwerp to Beverwijk just north of Haarlem.[14] Cetologists speculate whether some sort of indeterminate panic might not be responsible for the phenomenon of mass stranding. But errant individual whales are apparently another matter. Recent research has suggested that in muddy, gently sloping shore areas, the delicate echo-sounding system by which whales find their directions goes awry. (Another hypothesis attributes the same effect to an infection or disease.) Sonar pulses are received either omnidirectionally or not at all, resulting, understandably, in navigational confusion. So the North Sea coastline, which corresponds to these specifications, was as treacherous a passage to outsize marine mammals as it was to unpiloted ships. The providential geography that guarded the Fatherland from vengeful galleons also fatally bewildered the migrating bachelor bull whales.

Scientific consideration of this phenomenon was, not surprisingly, limited to rough and ready conjecture, often mostly concerned with storm conditions at sea, as though the whale were some sort of ship without a pilot. But it could hardly escape observation that all of the stranded whales were male, and therefore some early commentators, arguing in a distinctly Renaissance vein, raised the possibility that the hunt for a mate disturbed the animals' behavior. In fact, the bulls seem to have been leaving, rather than seeking, a herd of cows, but scientific information about these matters was as yet very rudimentary. The first texts to rescue the whale from marine demonology were those of the French naturalists, Pierre Belon and Guillaume Rondelet, both published in the 1550s.[15] But even when whales were no longer synonymous with sea monsters, they remained classified as fish until John Ray — and later Linnaeus — classed them with the mammals. Anatomical dissection was also rare, although Leeuwenhoek managed to dissect an eye pickled in brandy brought to him by a whaling captain. And if learned culture was somewhat uncertain about their anatomy and habits, we may be sure that popular culture still regarded their appearance, especially out of their natural element, as an exceptional and ominous event. The business of whaling, which in its heyday at the turn of the eighteenth century would employ nearly fourteen thousand men and 250 large ships, would contribute a great deal to demythologizing the whale, but a century earlier the industry was still in its infancy. It had been only in 1596 that de Rijp, Barendszoon and Heemskerk had seen the huge herds of Greenlanders at Novaya Zemlya while searching for the elusive northeast passage to the Indies. The first Dutch Arctic whaling expedition was fitted out in 1612, and the Company of the North established two years later.

As far as the common reaction to whales is concerned, though, the political and military chronology is more important than the economic history. For while whales were stranded at earlier and later dates, it was between 1570 and 1650 that they made their mark in prints, doggerel verses and moral-polemical broadsides. And this was exactly the formative period when a Dutch culture

62. Esaias van de Velde, *Stranded Whale,* 1617. Kendall Whaling Museum, Sharon, Mass.

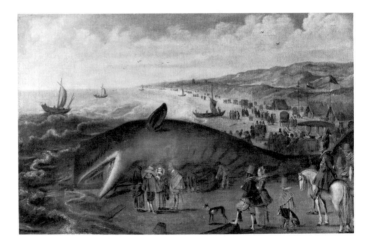

was being shaped by the apprehensions and uncertainties of war and religious conflict. Hence it is not surprising to find the beached whale repeatedly taken as a commentary on national fortunes or an augury of crises ahead. The year of the Berckhey whale, 1598, was a reasonably good one for the fortunes of Maurice's campaign, so that Grotius's report of the popular response to the message of the whale could be both optimistic and pessimistic. But more often the message was interpreted fearfully. An inscription on a print of a whale stranding at Noordwijk added to the list of measurements, "God turn away evil from our beloved Fatherland."[16]

In January 1616 the report of the British ambassador at The Hague, Sir Dudley Carleton, suggested the ways in which the strandings acted as a kind of moral punctuation in contemporaries' anxieties about the stop and start of hostilities: "in the very places and instant time of these tumults they [the whales] cause the most surprise; the rather because it is remembered, that at the first breaking out of these countrey wars there were two of the like bigness driven on shore in the river of the Schelde below Antwerp and at the framing of the truce one were in Holland."[17] The apparitions could be used for commentary on domestic as well as foreign strife (although the two were, at this time, thought to be closely connected). In 1617, a fifty-two-foot whale, cast up a little farther downshore towards Scheveningen, was engraved by Willem Buytewech after a rapid sketch and later painted by Esaias van de Velde.[18] Buytewech was much less prone to associate the whale with allegorical meaning, and his own print is as visually arresting as it is clean of

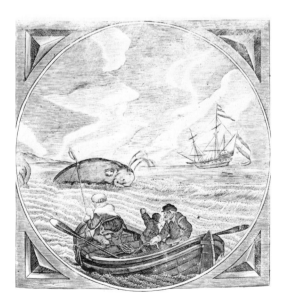

63. Engraving from Jacob Cats, *Emblemata.* Houghton Library, Harvard University

metaphor. But 1617 was also the climactic year in the struggle between
Calvinist militants and their Remonstrant opponents, a dispute in which
foreign policy issues were inextricably linked with theology. In an impression
published by Broer Janszoon, who was also gazetteer to Prince Maurice's army,
the Buytewech whale became a warning dispatched by God against an irresponsible truce and a sinful compromise with the forces of Antichrist.[19]

It would be misleading to suggest a simple chronology by which whale
imagery evolved from moral allusion to dispassionate classification. Whales
entered the moral bestiary through other media, like the emblem book where
Jacob Cats took it as the exemplar of brawn rather than brain. But it is true
that once the Republic's place in Europe seemed more secure, stranded-whale
prints that incorporated some sort of oracular comment became relatively
scarce. Another important factor was the magnitude of the whaling industry
itself. Once the monopoly of the Company of the North had been rescinded in
1641, there was a spectacular expansion. And the naturalistic element in
whaling images came correspondingly to the fore. While there had been some

64. Jan Wierix I, engraving, 1577. Forbes Collection, M.I.T. Museum,
Cambridge, Mass.

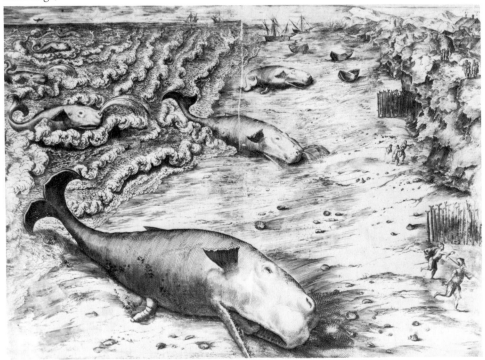

early (and in one example by Cornelis van Wieringen, magnificent) paintings of whaling and trying at Spitzbergen, it was only after the 1660s that marine painters like Abraham Storck and Ludolf Bakhuizen included whaling scenes in their general repertoire.

It is the earlier period, while the stranded whale still figured as a providential messenger, that provides more revealing evidence of some of the tensions in the young national culture. The very first images, from 1577, are the most alarming. Jan Wierix's superb engraving shows a school of thirteen at the shore of ter Heyden, with three beached, and figures running from the scene in panic. In another state, the print included an inscription by Willem Haecht that refers to the disaster as a presage "through which God shows us the perils and distress that have assailed us, and which are still with us." The year 1577 was, of course, critical in the early period of the Dutch revolt, with the Pacification of Ghent, concluded in December 1576, on the point of breaking down under William of Orange's rejection of the government of Don John. The prince entered Brussels that year, but further schism seemed unavoidable.

65. Jan Saenredam, *Whale Stranded at Beverwijk,* engraving, 1602. Hart Nautical Collection, M.I.T. Museum, Cambridge, Mass.

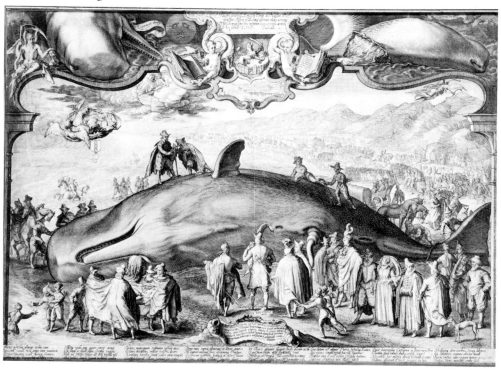

In this difficult climate, the whales, called "monsters" on the print, could be taken as a portent of evil and turned to effective propaganda use by Marnix and the polemicists of patriotic vigilance.

The same connection between portents and contemporary history is present in the most elaborate and grandiose of all the prints, that done by Jan Saenredam of a stranding in December 1601.[20] In some respects, his version repeats the format of the Goltzius/Matham prototype. The dunes at Beverwijk have been realistically represented, together with crowds of figures on the shore and fishing boats bobbing in the middle distance. But the throng has grown into a small army, and, unlike the casual activity seen in the Matham print, it is on the march by horse, carriage and foot toward the massive bulk of the sperm whale. In other words, the theatricality of the occasion has been emphasized by Saenredam's composition and staffage. He has taken care to represent himself in the foreground sketching, and the assiduous penis-measurer has been replaced at the same point along the whale's torso by an aristocratic gathering. Perhaps it was in deference to the loftier tone of the print, its educated audience and the exalted dedicatee — Count Ernst Casimir of Nassau-Dietz, represented prominently in the foreground — that the penis, often commented on as the sign of the beast's loathsomeness, was decently obscured.

Ernst Casimir was not only Stadholder Maurice's nephew, a member of the Friesian branch of the Nassau dynasty (and future Stadholder of Friesland and Groningen), he was, at this juncture, as the inscribed dedication proclaimed, a hero of the free Netherlands, a general of the Dutch army. That alone would make his inclusion in the composition significant. But it is the rich elaborations at the top of the picture proper that make the Saenredam print so rich a commentary. And they all relate, directly or indirectly, to a series of disasters occurring between the end of 1601 and the summer of 1602. That period was grave enough to keep the portent scanners and almanac compilers very busy. The strategically crucial port of Ostend in Flanders was being besieged by Archduke Albert's army, and Italian reinforcements commanded by the formidable Spinola were soon expected. Worse still, there had been reports from Spain that another grand armada of some eighty ships under the margrave of Santa Croce was about to sail for the Netherlands. Under these circumstances it is hardly surprising that the beaching of the Beverwijk whale was seen as an ill omen, or that it was connected with a whole succession of kindred natural calamities, all alluded to in the cartouches. Beneath the only somewhat reassuring figure of the Dutch lion defending the stockaded enclosure, the earth is literally seen in motion, on wheels, blown by the wind (possibly an allusion to the invention of a "wind chariot" by the mathematician Simon Stevin). At left and right respectively the moon and sun are in eclipse. In a third state of the print, a further detail of death shooting arrows at the

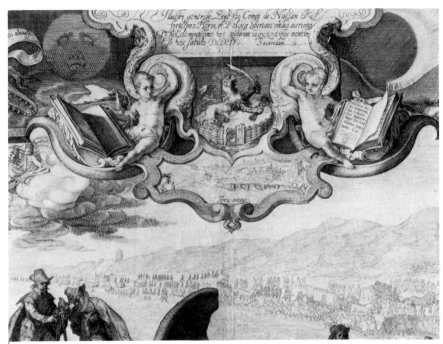

66. Detail, Jan Saenredam, *Whale Stranded at Beverwijk*

Amsterdam Maid was added. While all these details have mistakenly assumed to be generalized pessimistic allegories, they are, in fact, reports.[21] For there had been an eclipse of the sun on Christmas Eve, 1601, four days after the stranding, and an earthquake in Holland, on January 2, 1602. A total eclipse of the moon occurred the following June, and a particularly severe bout of the plague had hit Amsterdam through the midwinter of 1601–2. Not surprisingly, then, the inscribed poem by the historian Theodore Schrevelius refers to the "many calamities and bloodbaths" that follow such events, and specifically to the military setbacks that occurred after the stranding of the Berckhey whale in 1598.

Like so many "disaster prints" of this period, then, the Saenredam functions as both oracle and description, and to insist on its being *either* symbol or fact is to dwell needlessly on a false dichotomy. Dutch prophecies may have scanned heaven and earth for the untoward, but they were rooted firmly in here-and-now concerns. Throughout the seventeenth century, the Republic was never secure enough for even skeptical statesmen and diplomats to do without consulting the omens for their good counsel. This cohabitation of superstition with realpolitik was not, of course, confined to the Netherlands. But given their self-image as children of the covenant, flourishing under the Lord's special protection yet exposed to terrifying hazards were it ever to be withdrawn, the Dutch had a strong interest in ascertaining just how they stood with the Almighty. And it was just because this could *not* be axiomatically deduced from their material well-being, that their forebodings grew whenever some "unnatural" event occurred. So far from calming these anxieties, the consciousness of great wealth swiftly accumulated actually aggravated them. The beached whale was peculiar among a rich array of portents and omens in that it carried in its imposing bulk both associations of riches and reminders of their penitential obliteration. The great leviathans, their sonar scrambled by the North Sea sand, were migrating not only from Atlantic to Arctic, but from the realm of myth and morality to that of matter and commodity, sometimes becoming stranded on the submarine slopes of Dutch cultural contradiction.

This two-way flow of connotation had roots that antedated the founding of a free northern Netherlands. A *Sea Storm,* for a long time attributed to Peter Bruegel the Elder, but now given to Joost de Momper, is early evidence of the

67. Attr. Joost de Momper, *Sea Storm*. Kunsthistorisches Museum, Vienna

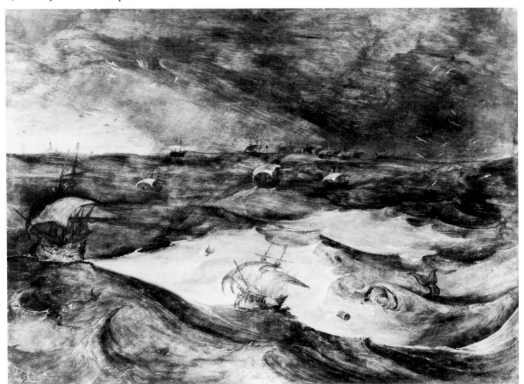

syndrome. In the midst of the tempest near the frail vessel, the artist painted the pink, open maw of a great fish or sea monster. This is not the first time that marine jaws make an appearance in Netherlandish art. In Bruegel's engraving of *The Last Judgment,* for example, the mouth of hell is depicted according to late medieval conventions as that of a great fish. In the famous early print done for Hieronymus Cock, *Big Fish Eat Little Fish,* he used the device of infinite ingestion to illustrate a Flemish proverb satirizing worldly ambition. In both cases, the act of being swallowed is the consequence (or the compounding) of sin. The *Sea Storm* is a variant of these dark themes. Confronted by the mouth of the monster/hell, it has cast a barrel into the waves just as the crew of Jonah's ship jettisoned their cargo to lighten their draught. But as we have seen in an earlier chapter,[22] "casting a barrel before a whale," in the Netherlandish vernacular, also meant deflecting misfortune. And at a secondary level the proverb conveys the sense of propitiation and repentance through the abandonment of worldly goods, a moral that was both perennially Christian and fashionably humanist. It has been suggested that the outbreak of image breaking in 1566–67, described by Philip van Marnix as a "distracting folly," is being alluded to here,[23] but the doctrine of atonement through worldly renunciation seems quite sufficient to account for its appeal to a humanist painter, even if the precise allegorical intention remains somewhat veiled in the marine spray.

There was, of course, another work that dealt with the casting off of worldly vanity, the sinking of the soul into the deep and redemption through atonement, and that was the scripture of Jonah. In a culture thick with the aroma of both sin and fish, the fate of Jonah was likely to make a profound impression. And the fact that it was engraved so many times in the Netherlands from the mid-sixteenth to the mid-seventeenth centuries is striking, given the relative rarity of the subject elsewhere. And where it does figure in Italian art, as on the Sistine ceiling, the "great fish" occupies an incomparably feebler role vis-à-vis the prophet than in northern versions. In fact, the more flamboyant the mannerist treatment, the more appealing the Jonah theme seemed to be, drawings by Maarten de Vos being engraved by the Wierix brothers and Crispijn van de Pas, and those of Dirck Barendszoon reproduced by Jan Sadeler. The most dramatic of all were the drawings of Willem Buytewech engraved by Jan van de Velde II.[24] And evidence of the popularity of the scripture can be found beyond ink and paper: cut into tankards, chased in silver and, most spectacularly, appearing in another of the Janskerk windows by the great master glazier Dirc Crabeth. Appropriately enough, the window was presented by the guild of fishmongers, but it was more than nautical fellowship that gave the Jonah story its local immediacy. No other Old Testament scripture, except possibly the history of Jacob, yokes together human frailty and prophetic destiny with so much exemplary power. The tribulations of a providential mission were a particular preoccupation in the Netherlands, and Jonah's fear, contrition and ire were familiar emotional states to the northern preacher as to his flock.

As a fugitive from his mission, Jonah is the occasion by which the storm-stressed mariners jettison their worldly goods in a futile effort to abate the tempest. Lots cast by divine decree rather than pagan Fortuna (in Dutch, *lot* is the word for fate) determine Jonah's guilt, and he is thrown overboard to sink or swim (*aan zijn lot over*). He has thus become the agent of propitiation, the "barrel cast before the whale" that deflects misfortune from the innocent. The

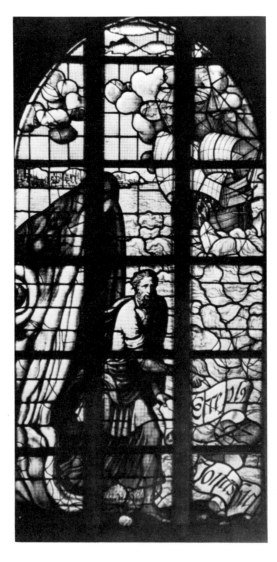

68. Dirc Crabeth, stained glass
window, *Jonah and the Whale*, 1565.
St. Janskerk, Gouda

whale now itself assumes the instrumentality that Jonah had tried to evade, being the means through which he recovers his mission in prayer "out of the belly of hell" towards the sanctity of the unseen temple (Jonah 2:2). Within his mobile purgatory, Jonah travels from sin to redemption, darkness to light and water to dry land. At Nineveh, the role of oracular courier passes back from beast to man as he preaches to the Assyrians of their impending destruction. Thus alerted, the king performs *his* rite of propitiation, donning the garb of mourning and commanding his subjects to express their contrition in a fast. By so doing they succeed in averting catastrophe, much to Jonah's chagrin at the unfulfilled prophecy. The book concludes with the ingenious parable by which the gourd sheltering Jonah becomes the final sacrificial object, and the blasting worm the final providential agent through which the prophet is made to understand the meaning of redemptive atonement.

Perhaps there was a sort of metaphorical compression at work here, with the beached whales of the Netherlands incorporating proverb, prophecy, parable in their disconcerting immensity. Unsummoned (except by God's control of historical pilotage), and thrown up, out of their element, they were exploited by preachers and laymen to convey a version of the Jonah scripture for modern reprobates. In their dreadfulness, they were a potent reminder of the consequences of disobeying the divine law. On the other hand, the clemency extended to Nineveh offered the more comforting moral that salvation *in extremis* might yet be won through acts of sincere penitence.

At the same time that whales were the bearers of bad tidings to the sinful, they were very good news indeed to the merchant capitalist with an eye to fat profits and the nerve to confront high risks. The question was, whether or not the transformation of whales into lucre was precisely the kind of reprehensible thirst for gain likely to bring on another bout of the Jonah syndrome on Berckhey beach? It would be nice to imagine that the whale, in its twin capacities as symbol and commodity, possessed this neatly self-reinforcing property. But what may have disconcerted the pious fisherfolk of the Holland coastal villages may simply have given rise to much rubbing of hands and cracking of knuckles among the Company of the North. And it was in the middle years of the century — when the print tradition of the beached whales seems to have petered out (though the phenomenon continued) — that the whaling industry began its period of spectacular expansion. At the beginning it had been a mysterious and dangerous affair, both to the mariners who embarked upon the Arctic voyages to Spitzbergen and to the capitalists who sank their investment into so perilous and costly a venture.[25] Some of the risks had been moderated by the virtual monopoly enjoyed by the company after its foundation in 1614, and the watchful eye kept on prices of baleen and train oil. By the 1630s, Smerenburg in Greenland had been well established both as base for the harpoon ships and as a seasonal processing location. In 1637 the first domestic tryworks was opened on Marken Island, facing Amsterdam, and five years later the company's monopoly was virtually set aside in favor of a free-for-all by limiting its ventures to twenty per year. As demand expanded it was high-risk traders who took it up in what, by Dutch standards, were huge, labor-intensive ships with crews of seventy to a hundred. Ten whales or more might be caught in a good hunt, bringing back perhaps the equivalent of 300 vats of train. By the later part of the century (1721 being the apex of the industry's fortunes), Dutch whalers had abandoned the overhunted Spitzbergen and Novaya Zemlya schools and voyaged to the Bering and Davis straits, to Baffin Island and the White Sea. Nearly ten thousand men gained their livelihood from the industry in Holland, as a whole quarter of Amsterdam in the northwest of the city became colonized by the rendering works and ware-houses of the trade. The largest of the reservoirs had a capacity for nearly sixteen thousand liters of oil, and along the Brouwersgracht and the lower end of the Keizersgracht, terra cotta plaques inscribed De Walvis or Groenland suggested an unabashed pleasure in advertising the wares within.

It is true that the tryworks, for obvious reasons, were known as *stinkerijen* in the city, but as was so often the case in Amsterdam, the burghers held their noses and patted their purses. Does all this imply a kind of cultural chronol-ogy in which the whale swims out of the realm of myth and proverbial lore into a scriptural portent-bearing element ending up as the raw material of industrial process? It is true that the appearance of *stranded*-whale prints (whether overtly or covertly moralizing) coincided with the more insecure phase of the Republic's history in its "golden century." But it would be too crude to assume that the cosmological overtones of stranded whales were, by the 1660s, buried under mountains of baleen and drowned in vats of train oil. The whale was to enjoy a considerable future as the bearer of nemesis to the haughty in any culture touched by the north European mismatch between conscience and commodity. The Dutch merely transferred their obstinacy and their fretfulness to Nantucket along with their profits when New Englanders assumed domi-nance of the industry in the eighteenth century. Melville, it should surprise no one to learn, had Dutch forebears and was brought up in its Church. Even now, the moral indignation generated over the commercial slaughter of whales is of a different order from concern for other endangered species like the osprey or the tiger. Its bulky innocence—power without guile—seems to act as a prophetic reproof against the capacity of humanity to court hubris.

Undeniably, as whales became more familiar through their incorporation into marine painting, by Abraham Storck, for example, and through prints accompanying popular translations of Friedrich Martens's journeys to the Arctic, so their use as supernatural augurs receded before the preoccupation with scientific classification. But there was no shortage of other natural phenomena to feed the craving for untoward signs and oracles. In 1647, for instance, there was a sudden burst of popular prints illustrating the bizarre history of the Zaandam bull.[26] As with most prints of this kind, which did not use the "cartoon sequence" manner of narrative illustration, the woodcuts and engravings showed all the events of the story as though they were occurring simultaneously, relying on a simple text below to assist in the "reading." The bull, like the whale, is the agent of a providential warning, the occasion for a freak event which betokens an impending calamity. Like the beached whale, too, the Zaandam event takes place not in any mythical setting but in the wholly ordinary location of a country hamlet by the sea. On the 29th of August, 1647, Jacob Egh, the son of a *boer*, was playing with a kite, which succeeded in maddening one of the farmer's bulls. Seeing their son's plight, both his father and mother rushed into the field to divert the animal's attention (calamity deflection once more). The father was — graphically — gored and the mother tossed high into the air, at which point the history leaves the genre

69. Anon. woodcut. Atlas van Stolk, Rotterdam

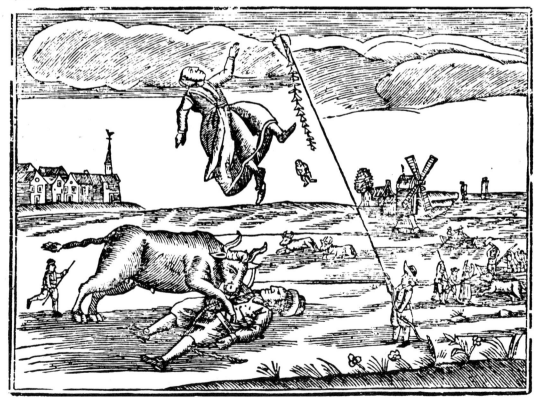

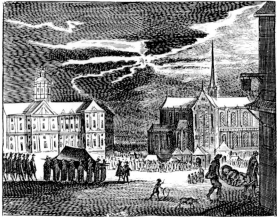
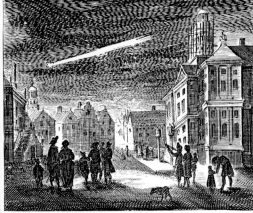

70. Anon., *Afbeeldinge . . . van de Drie
Aenmaerckenswaerdige wonderen in den Jaer
1664 . . . :* "The Pestilence." Koninklijke
Bibliotheek, The Hague

71. "The Comet"

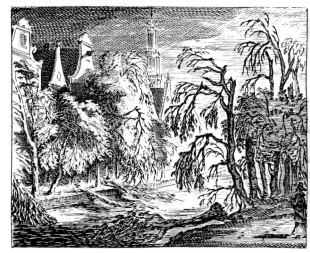

72. "The Fall of the Trees"

of barnyard stories and becomes something more ominous. For Mevrouw Egh, heavily pregnant at the time, delivers her baby in midair, from which it miraculously descends to terrestrial safety. Having done its bit, the bull is, of course, hacked to death by the shore. Mother and father both perish in the onslaught, but the baby survived, was baptized, and lived, albeit briefly, to the following May.

The bizarre story was the subject of a great many prints and reappears as usual in doggerel verse and fulminating sermons. The year, as one might guess, was unusually contentious in that a peace with Spain was under active discussion in the States. For the more zealous Calvinists and Orangists that eventuality was tantamount to another betrayal like the truce of 1609, a compromise with Satan and the sure harbinger of disaster. "I am the rod of

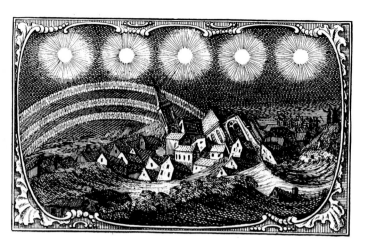

73. Anon., "Appearance of the
Lights at Scheveningen." Atlas
van Stolk, Rotterdam

God" announces one of the captions issuing from the mouth of the Zaandam
bull. On each occasion when the affairs of the Republic became critical — 1608-9,
1617-18, 1647, 1651-55, 1671-72 — the scrutinizing of almanacs and the trembling of the *wigchelrooden,* divining rods, became more frantic. Omens, portents and oracles did not, then, recede from the common culture of the
seventeenth-century Dutch, even if skepticism made headway among the
patrician elite. Even such epigones of humanist learning as Petrus Rabus and
Musschenbroek were devotees of the *wigchelrood* (useful for repelling spooks
as well as making auguries), and, like Newton, found no inconsistency between
scientific curiosity and astrological speculation.

Apart from beached whales and aerial births, there were a multitude of
freaks of nature to feed these anxieties. In 1618, a year of troubles, a brilliant
comet appeared over Holland, prompting Jacob Cats to write fearfully on its
prophetic import.[27] Comets and shooting stars were always occasions for some
consternation and, for preachers, the carefully orchestrated wringing of hands
and knocking of knees. In 1624, Pieter Janszoon Twist had produced his first
Comeet Boeck at Hoorn, allowing the nervous to make their own prognostications,
and the specialized astronomical almanac went into several editions before the
end of the century.[28] In 1664, when plague had struck Amsterdam again, with
the usual stagnation of trade that followed its worst attacks, the sight of a
shooting star was taken as axiomatic confirmation of divine displeasure.
Linked with the sudden death of linden trees on the canal fronts following an
ice storm on December 19-20, it prompted sermons from Jeremiah and Isaiah
and an official fast of penitence and contrition.[29] Other comets had been
observed in 1577, 1651 and 1661 at similar critical junctures and had had the

same disturbing effect. On January 21, 1665, another shooting star, calculated by Dr. Lubincelsus as the 416th following the Great Deluge, was declared to be the direct result of God's wrath "laid on our dear Fatherland for our sins and transgressions."[30] Seamen and fisherfolk—deeply devout and superstitious communities—were especially prone to supernatural visions that took menacing forms. On the 21st of December, 1651 (a comet year, and the first of the war with England), Ewoudt Anszoon Drouwert, a skipper pilot, along with two boatmen twelve miles out from the mouth of the Maas, beheld "at a man's height from the horizon" at nine o'clock in the morning, a full company of cavalry and infantry armed for war coming from the northeast, and swore as much before the sheriff and magistrate of Maassluis.[31] In 1661 a poem was written on "Threatened Netherlands," drawn from a vision vouchsafed to the author "by fire and light over Utrecht." And fires at sea were another favorite "wonder" to be reported, hovering on the horizon, over the spires of drowned churches, or in one case, as early as 1570, as "five bright lights" seen off the coast of Scheveningen as an augury of upheavals to come.[32] So deeply ingrained was this habit of regarding apparently extraterrestrial phenomena as the mark of Jehovah's wrath, that when Pierre Bayle attacked it in a treatise on comets, the incensed clergy persuaded the Rotterdam magistrates to withhold his stipend as a penalty.[33]

The meaning of all these signs and apparitions was self-evident to those who witnessed or imagined they had witnessed them, or who had heard the tale from those who had. Maassluis, the herring fishing port near Rotterdam, published its own almanac-cum-song-and-verse book, *Het Maasluyssche Hoekertje*, which in 1661 could not forbear from greeting the end of Anglo-Dutch hostilities with a mixture of relief and foreboding. The appearance of the inevitable shooting star reinforced the pessimists and prompted a typical hymn in the oracular-penitential mode:

> *O Netherlands will you not turn*
> *From sin and unrighteousness*
> *And walk once more in the ways of God*
> *'Ere He stretch out His hand*
> *Over Netherlanders all*
> *So that sinners shall fall . . .*
>
> *What is heard but swearing and cursing?*
> *What is to be seen but drunkenness and pomp*
> *And daily trafficking in vile gain?*
>
> *A star in the heavens plain*
> *Was seen in the southeast*

With rays, both great and small
What is this if not a sign
That God will punish all our sins?[34]

These arrests of nature, the providential slap in the face at the height of complacent celebration, was, then, a habitual trait in Dutch culture. Jonah was complemented by Belshazzar, the whale by the moving finger, both scriptures tailor-made for preachers perennially agitated by the abominations of luxury, cupidity, lust and drunkenness which had polluted the newborn Fatherland. The text of Daniel, chapter 5, where Belshazzar uses vessels abducted from the temple at Jerusalem by Nebuchadnezzar for the profane purposes of his feast, was used again and again by Borstius and Wittewrongel in their standard fulminations against "the gods of gold and the gods of silver"

74. Rembrandt van Rijn, *Belshazzar's Feast,* 1635. Courtesy of the Trustees, National Gallery, London.

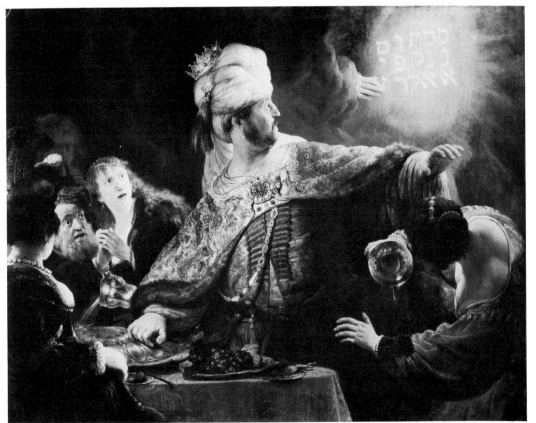

and is probably the scene depicted by Aert de Gelder.[35] But it was his teacher, Rembrandt, who chose the narrative climax for his great history painting, when the king sees the spectral hand inscribing its cryptic message of doom. These moments of nemesis—invariably decoded by venerable and untainted prophets (like Daniel)—were favorite themes for history painters. Even the genre specialist Frans van Mieris, in one of his rare excursions into history painting, chose the ominous moment when King Jereboam's wife visits the aged prophet Ahijah to plead for the health of their stricken son, only to be told of the death and destruction of their house for creating idols for Israel to worship (1 Kings 14). For Israelites, Babylonians and New Hebrews alike the moral was clear. Instead of gluttonous feasting and wanton behavior, fasts of solemn penitence should be decreed. Instead of drowning in their cups, the sinful should wash themselves in tears of remorse; instead of draping themselves in silk they should put on sackcloth and ashes. Were that to be done they might yet be spared the fate set out in MENE MENE TEKEL UPHARSIN. *Nineveh, Not Egypt* was the title of one tract, implying that even at the eleventh hour, respite was available for the truly penitent.[36]

When crises threatened to turn truly apocalyptic, *bededagen* (days of prayer and fasting) were decreed throughout the Republic, and whole congregations prostrated themselves both inside their churches and in the public squares where meetings of hymn and prayer were held. At such moments of catharsis, the Calvinist clergy realized, albeit briefly, their dreams of a contrite and obedient flock. But, by their very nature, such trauma were sporadic and short-lived. At times of more subdued anxiety the Dutch tended rather to resort to habits and conventions that allowed them to enjoy the fruits of their success without choking on its superabundance. Feasts, after all, were deeply embedded in ancient Netherlandish usage, and there were ways to prevent them resembling Belshazzar's nemesis. So it was through the elaboration and prescription of a set of manners that could distinguish between idolatrous gluttony and wholesome nourishment—just as it distinguished between permissible comfort and dangerous luxury—that the Dutch sought to be the masters rather than the victims of their *overvloed*.

ii GRACING THE MEAL

Innkeepers often die popular, and Gerrit van Uyl was no exception. Even by the liberal standards of small-town wakes, his funeral at Sloten in Friesland on

May 21, 1660, was a bumper send-off. According to a contemporary, the procession extended a full fifty-six roods, so it must have included virtually the entire town together with patrons from far and near—with the local vagabond population bringing up the rear. This, then, was a large company—some hundreds of Frisian countryfolk. But even so, van Uyl's estate had seen to it that they were decently catered. The bill of fare included:

        20 oxheads of French and Rhenish wine
        70 half-casks of ale
     1100 pounds of meat "roasted on the Koningsplein"
       550 pounds of sirloin
        28 breasts of veal
        12 whole sheep
        18 great venison in white pastry
       200 pounds of "fricadelle" (mince meat)[37]

together with bread, mustard, cheese, butter and tobacco "in full abundance." No wonder that the beggars staggered off happy.

This was *overvloed* with a vengeance, eccentric rather than typical, an act of valedictory largesse on the part of a genial host who wanted to commend himself to his local version of posterity. The source in which the feast is reported, moreover, is not altogether reliable—being a popular compendium of oddities and caprices. But the Dutch reputation as hearty trenchermen specializing in quantity rather than finesse was not wholly fanciful. Herman Melville, brought up in the austerity of the Dutch Reformed Church, was obviously startled enough by the list of provisions set out in *Den Koopman* (*The Merchant*) for a fleet of 180 Dutch whalers that he too set it out in all its gargantuan immensity: the dietary equivalent of the great white whale:

       400,000 lb of beef
         60,000 lb Friesland pork
       150,000 lb stockfish . . .
         10,800 barrels of beer . . . etc.[38]

And it is more reliably known that in 1703 the deacons of the guild of surgeons at Arnhem—at most seven men—got through, at one sitting, fourteen pounds of beef, eight pounds of veal, six fowl, stuffed cabbages, apples, pears, bread, pretzels, assorted nuts, twenty bottles of red wine, twelve bottles of white wine and coffee.[39]

The Dutch, it was thought by most other European contemporaries, did not pick at their victuals. In caricatures they were almost always depicted as guzzlers and sozzlers, as imposingly broad as they were dauntingly tall. The learned naturalist and indefatigable traveler John Ray was particularly offended by the spectacle of their continual cramming, especially "Dutch men and women . . . almost always eating as they travel, whether by Boat, coach or wagon."[40] And what they ate was crude and substantial: the ubiquitous salad (*sla*), meat stewed in "hotchpots" (*hutsepot*), "boil'd Spinage, minc'd and buttered (sometimes with Currants added) . . . the common people feed[ing] much upon Cabilau [cod] and pickled herrings." Sadly, for Ray, that triumph of English kitchens, the boiled pudding, seemed wholly absent from Dutch tables "either not knowing the goodness of the dish, or not having the skill to make them." Most startling of all was the strange habit in taverns of hung beef swinging from the rafters "which they cut into thin slices and eat with bread and butter laying the slices upon the butter"—the famous *belegde broodje* thus boasting greater antiquity than the sandwich. Even more formidable and copious were Dutch cheeses, yellow discs, red-rind spheres, cumin-studded and "Green cheese said to be colored with the juice of Sheep's dung" all "scraped upon bread buttered and so eaten." No wonder, then, that Ray observed the population to be "for the most part big-boned and gross-bodied," a characterization which congealed into the familiar stereotype of the stolid, heavy, phlegmatic and torpid Dutch, whose pulse was quickened only by the prospects of profit and guzzling.[41]

It was the sheer scale of Dutch banqueting that made even eighteenth-century British visitors (who prided themselves on ample girth and keen appetites) gag. For a moderate company, groaned Joseph Marshall in the 1770s, courses set at table were not of eight or ten dishes but twenty-five or thirty. Should there be the least pretext for a great feast—the birth of a child, the arrival home of a relative or a fleet from the Indies—then all the stays were loosened. "I was present at one of these feasts in Amsterdam," he marveled with the tone of a survivor rather than a celebrant, "where I believe eight tables were four times covered and each course above an *hundred* dishes."[42] So much for Calvinist frugality.

It was notorious, as the "Spectatorial" moralists of the eighteenth century complained, that in what they took to be its periwig decadence, the Republic had succumbed to all manner of vices, among which swinish gluttony was by no means the most reprehensible.[43] But superabundance of food—the glutted kitchen—was an ancient theme in Netherlands culture extending back to the great medieval guild feasts of Flanders and the country *kermissen* (carnivals). Notwithstanding the displeasure of both reforming Catholicism and militant Calvinism, the old ebb and flow of feast and fast was preserved, albeit in manifold variations, in popular habits throughout the period of the Republic. There had been, in any case, a sort of self-adjusting gastric equilibrium built

into the pre-Reformation festive and religious calendar in which the excesses
of carnival feasting were offset by the austere regime of Lent, the two tempers
meeting at Vastenavond, Mardi Gras, after which the ashes of Wednesday
would be scattered on the detritus of its fat predecessor. The contest of
manners — pagan grogging and pious atonement — was painted by Bruegel in
the *Battle of Carnival and Lent*. Carnival sits astride the festive cask, his skewer
packed with trussed capons as he jousts with *magere Lent*, skinny Lent, whose
weapon is the griddle on which reposes the penitential herring. Hans Worst,
Mynheer sausage, was the earthy incarnation of flesh, offal and blood, all
packed tight inside the case of skin, the lord of hibernal warmth and saturnalia,
inaugurated on Martinmas, the eleventh of November in the midst of *slagmaand*,
the slaughter month, when the fatted ox met the knife. He existed in a
dialectical twinship with *pekelhareng*, the briny fool of fish: capricious, mercurial,
mock-solemn, jackanapes-wry. In the same way, the two milieus of the Fat and
the Thin kitchens were locked together in complementary opposition, cut,
etched and engraved by Bruegel and his disciples, like Dirk Hogenburg, Pieter
van der Heiden and Hieronymus Cock over and again.[44] In the seventeenth
century the Dutch inheritors of Bruegel's comic-serious ethos like Jan Steen
and Adriaen van Ostade revived the Fat and Thin kitchens, and it has been
suggested that they find their final metamorphosis in Hogarth's polemical
pairing of the prospering paunches of Beer Street and the emaciated cadavers
of Gin Lane.[45]

    The genre traveled a long way from Bruegel's imaginary *mise en scène* of
church and inn and his visual anthologies of symbol and folklore to Hogarth's

75. Pieter Bruegel the Elder, detail of *The Battle Between Carnival and Lent,* 1559.
Kunsthistorisches Museum, Vienna

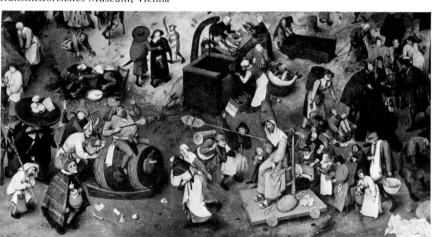

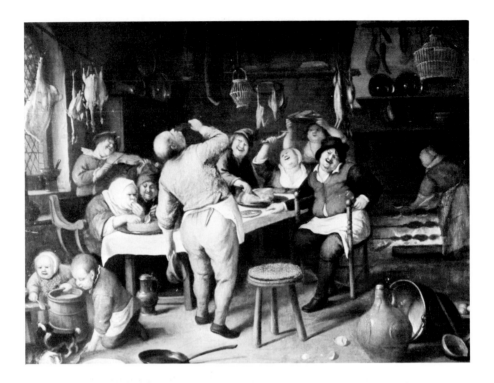

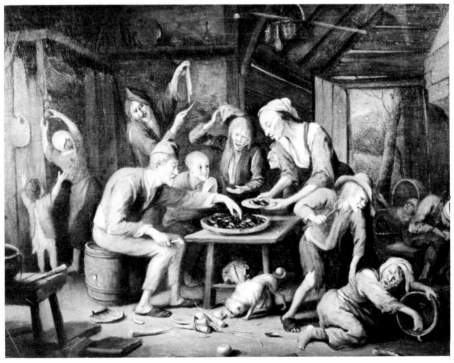

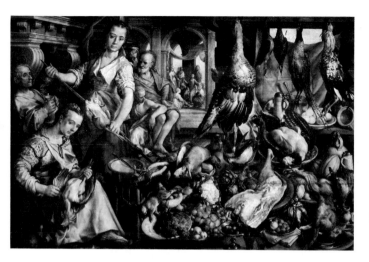

76. Jan Steen, *The Fat Kitchen*.
Cheltenham Art Gallery

77. Jan Steen, *The Thin Kitchen*.
Cheltenham Art Gallery

78. Joachim Beuckelaer, *Christ in
the House of Martha and Mary*, 1566.
Rijksmuseum, Amsterdam

deliberate topographical and social specificity (Beer Street is St. Martin's in the Fields on George II's birthday; Gin Lane the festering alleys of St. Giles). In between, and especially when the "second generation" of humanist painters of both religious and popular themes, like Pieter Aertsen and Joachim Beuckelaer, were producing pictures of kitchen scenes and market stalls, the line between description and prescription was much less sharp. Much of their work inhabits an ambiguous cultural terrain in which humanist moralizing is set in the here-and-now jostle of contemporary life. While Venetian painters like Carpaccio and Paolo Veronese had included a profusion of still-life detail in appropriate subjects like *The Supper at Emmaus* and *Christ in the House of Martha and Mary* (the profanity of which earned Veronese an appearance before the Inquisition), Beuckelaer effectively reversed these priorities through a mannerist treatment that had the ostensible narrative recede into the background while bringing the still life into foreground prominence. Much of that detail continued to convey pious, especially eucharistic, associations, at least in the sixteenth century. But if his mixture of the moral and the merry owed a great deal to the northern humanist absorption with the ethical struggles of everyday life, it also owed as much to the Rabelaisian pleasure of troweling on great heaps of comestible matter. Much of the animation in his paintings comes not just from the raw exuberance of the figures with which they are peopled, but from pyramids of fish slithering over tables, piles of fruit spilling from cornucopia-like baskets or mountains of greenstuff heaped on market stalls.

It is a *topos* that is being described here: a phenomenon of cultural, not material, reality. But the *overvloed* of the Fat kitchen, in all its extravagant visual hyperbole, was nonetheless a recurring theme in Netherlandish culture and one that was never wholly free from the ambiguities of appetite.[46] These ambiguities were flamboyantly set out in a Hendrick de Kempenaer etching after a Vingboons drawing, executed probably in the first decade of the seventeenth century. Set in the kitchen of a Dutch town house, it depicts the preparation of a sumptuous feast. The kitchen is, in fact, bursting at the seams with every conceivable kind of fare. One servant draws a pie from the oven while another sits plucking a bird, half buried alive under game: swans, geese, hare and rabbits. A scullery boy turns birds on the spit while the mistress of the house (identifiable from her keys) clenches a trussed capon in her fist. At the rear a turkey pie is receiving its final decoration. Yet while all this appears like an exercise in drooling Rabelaisian relish, there are, scattered about the composition, unmistakable signs and signals of a more earnest purpose. At the extreme right, a poor man, very possibly Lazarus to the finely appareled master Dives, and at the least, a variation on the theme that was very popular in sixteenth- and early-seventeenth-century Holland. Or perhaps he is *magerman*

79. Hendrick de Kempenaer after David Vinckboons, *Fat Kitchen,* etching. Atlas van Stolk, Rotterdam

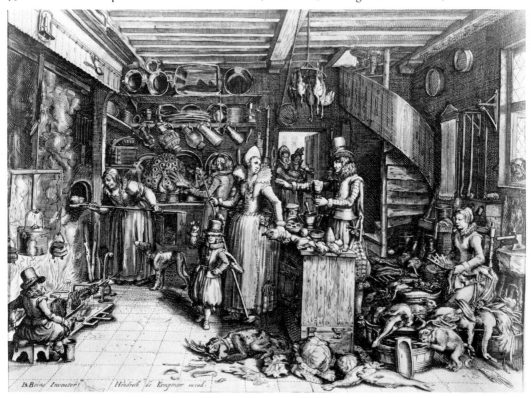

—skinny man—who in Bruegel's pair of prints and Steen's paintings attempts to intrude into the Fat kitchen. Conventional symbols of the transience of earthly pleasures lie strategically placed: the half-spent candle and snuffers at top left, the hatchet in the woodblock at right; the peacock emblem of vanity and worldly pride at rear. In the foreground, the ravages wrought by cat and dog on the food lying almost casually about the floor anticipate their appearance in Dutch genre painting as images of mischief, sensuality, gluttony and greed.

For all this, the etching remains enigmatic. The figure at center who should be most explicit in his remonstrance is nothing of the kind. Is his expression and gesture with the *roemer* one of reproof or blandishment? Is he, dressed in the kind of elaborately ribboned costume satirized by humanists and Calvinists like Huygens, the personification of worldly vanity and idleness, or is he its critic? Is the *roemer* goblet a warning or a temptation?

The print is eloquent, then, not for any resolution of these familiar tensions, but rather for the congested manner of their illustration. Whether its

80. Claes Jansz. Visscher, *Grace Before the Meal.* Engraving, 1609. Rijksprentenkabinet, Amsterdam

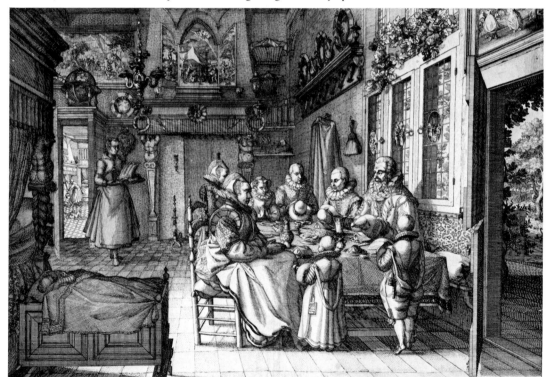

intention is indulgent or censorious (and I lean somewhat to the latter interpretation), its subject is indisputably *surfeit* and its attendant pleasures and perils. As such it stands in the sharpest possible contrast to a Claesz. Jan Visscher engraving of the same period in which a saturnalian, chaotic accumulation of food has been regulated by the grace of a Christian family meal. Instead of the perspiring commotion of the Fat kitchen, the temper of the print is one of the serenity appropriate to the Sabbath meal. Where the de Kempenaer cellar was strewn haphazardly with fish, poultry, and cabbages among which the animals snaffled and rooted, both the parlor in which the Visscher family eats and the kitchen glimpsed through the open door (another device that was to become a convention of genre painting) are exemplary in their order, sobriety and neatness. The maidservant, as decorous as the family she attends, brings the roast, and about the room are biblical pictures celebrating blessed rather than profane meals. Over the doorway, for example, is the painting of the Last Supper, while the windowpane tondo of Abraham visited by the angels links together the theme with its domestic complement: the fruitfulness of the conjugal union. The trailing vines about the doorway that have invaded the house play on this theme of appetites consecrated by Christian lawfulness, for they invoke the verses of Psalm 128:

> For thou shalt eat the labour of thine hands:
> happy shalt thou be, and it shall be well with thee.
> Thy wife shall be as a fruitful vine by the sides of thine house:
> thy children like olive plants round about thy table.
> Behold, that thus shall the man be blessed that feareth the Lord.

Directly above the *pater familias* is a window roundel representing the story of Isaac and Rebecca; he himself holds the soft paternity bonnet as his infant child sleeps in the trundle cot at the side of her parents' bed. It is literally the moment of grace, but it is also the humanist's domestic Arcadia where abundance has been mastered by Christian moderation. The reward for eschewing vicious excess is, literally, plain to see: peace and safety for those dwelling within the tabernacle of the Lord.

The control of *overvloed* through a dam of pious manners became a standard refrain of Dutch family manuals as it already had been in Renaissance Italy and humanist Flanders. The prolific and immensely popular physician-author, Jan van Beverwijck, in his *Schat der Gezontheyt* (Treasure of Health) followed moralists all the way back to Seneca in urging moderation in diet as the best way of avoiding plague, flux, pox, rheum, ague, and insomnia.[47] The standard cookery book designed for households of the middling sort, *De Verstandige Kok of Zorgvuldige Huyshouder* (The Wise Cook or the Painstaking Householder) similarly connected an orderly, regular and balanced dietary regime (fresh meat at least once a week, lots of cheese and bread, nourishing stews and fresh vegetables and salads) with a morally wholesome and thriving family life.[48] Jan Luiken's *Het Leerzaam Huisraad* (The Tutelary Household), a multi-edition best-seller at the end of the seventeenth and beginning of the eighteenth centuries, began its series of fifty piously annotated domestic scenes with the *Tafel.* Luiken supplied both the text and the engravings in his little conduct books, and his evocation of the peaceful family meal, taken with a reunion of old friends, owed something not only to the Visscher prototype but to many other Dutch prescriptive accounts of the ideal meal as a social communion.

> *The table daily all-prepared*
> *With overflow of wholesome fare*
> *Wherever harmony is seated*
> *Along with peace and tranquillity, from there*
> *Is banished hunger and appetite.*[49]

This golden mean, negotiating prudently between privation and excess, was the humanist's ideal, and it affected the first generation of free Dutch in their kitchens, as it did in their wardrobes and their counting houses. It ought not to be confused with the sterner Calvinist commands to abstinence and frugal asceticism, wholly unrealistic as those were in the material circumstances of the Golden Century. Austerity, as the physician Heijman Jacobi

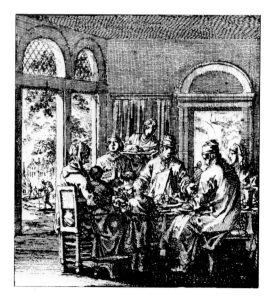

81. Jan Luiken, "De Tafel," from *Het Leerzaam Huisraad* (Amsterdam, 1711)

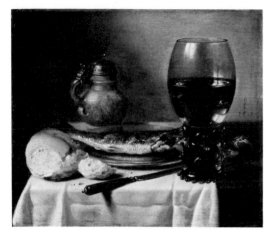

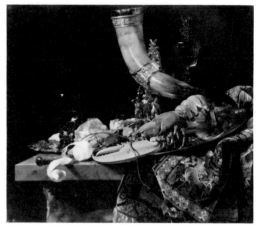

82. Pieter Claesz., *Still Life with Herring, Roemer, and Stone Jug.* Courtesy, Boston Museum of Fine Arts

83. Willem Kalf, *Still Life with Lobster.* Courtesy of the Trustees, National Gallery, London

pointed out, could be as unhealthy as bloat surfeit, the former leading to insomnia and debilitation, the latter to torpor and sluggishness. To be stout but strong, and lead a happy life, he advised plenty of "sweet milk, fresh bread, good mutton and beef, fresh butter and cheese."[50] A healthy moderation, then, presupposed some gratification of appetite, the better to constrain it within wise moral boundaries. What the humanist doctors most admired was the beauty of sustained balance.

Is that the sort of beauty we behold in Dutch still life pictures, especially the *banketjestukken* or breakfast pieces of the 1620s and 1630s that were wholly their invention?[51] Is there a relationship between the artlessness of Dutch cooking, of which so many travelers complained, and the easy transmutation of that plain fare into an object of art? Whatever else may be said of the Haarlem "monochromatic" studies of Pieter Claesz. and Willem Claesz. Heda, they were certainly not exercises in profusion. They testify, rather, to the Dutch ingenuity at creating much from little. The ingredients of a simple meal (not necessarily breakfast): a wedge of cheese, a loaf of bread, a herring, the ubiquitous lemon, a scattering of nuts and fruit, a *roemer* of Rhenish or a tankard of ale — are all assembled with exquisite economy, both of hue and of composition. The *banketjestukken* are as spare and as precise as the later *pronkstilleven* of Willem Kalf and Abraham van Beyeren in the 1650s and 1660s were flamboyant and luxuriant.[52] Kalf's lobsters sit in vermilion brilliance reflecting against silver ewers or Ming dishes; Claesz.'s herrings offer just the merest glint of scaly light to offset the pewter monochrome of their background. Van Beyeren would play with the pellucid quality of glass and the jewel-like depth of wine within it; Heda made hock and *roemer* of the same brown-green transparency. Kalf might set his precious objects on the crimson glow of a Turkish rug; Claesz. and Floris van Schooten generally use starch-white linen on which to place their crust-brown pies and loaves. The monochrome *banketjestukken* are studies in ruminative plainness, to be taken in in the unhurried, contemplative manner of the humanist scholar rather than the cramming sensuousness of the man of fashion, the *pronker.* They are not easily disturbed. In Willem Heda's pictures in particular, the objects are so subtly disposed, their relationship with each other so delicately measured, that the least dislodging collapses the whole. The cunning intrusion of the upturned glass or the casually prostrated flagon acts to reinforce the sense of fragility with which this miraculous equilibrium is sustained.

One ought not to press the analogy between the humanist's regard for balance with the painter's concern for aesthetic harmony too far. It has been said, with good reason, that many of these pieces are also exercises in the "art of describing": as much products of the impulse to map outward anatomy as to disclose interior substance.[53] And it would be perverse to represent them as bromides for the appetite, indifferent to texture, savor and aroma, concerned only with appearance. In their case, the eye is merely the trigger sense that awakens other organs of appetite. And when food is displayed half-eaten, the still lifes go well beyond a visually itemized menu to evoke the experience of eating. The "map" described here is that of the palate, traveling from salt meat of the fish to dense starch of the bread, to the astringency of the lemon and fragrant wash of the Rhenish wine. At their most rigorous, Clara Peeters or Floris van Dyck could exploit the juxtaposition of cheeses of different textures: venerable golden *overjaarige* Gouda sat beside green Texel or younger Edam.[54]

It has been argued, with perhaps more earnestness than sense, that these cheeses are not what they seem. That when they provoke thoughts of a nibble, the beholder ought in fact to be reminded that they symbolize the Transubstantiated Body of Christ.[55] And in the same manner, an over-enthusiastic dedication to unearthing meaning from these compositions has proposed a very formal set of symbolic associations supposedly lodged in different items of food. So that in Nicholas Gillis's *Still Life* of 1611, for example, almonds are made to recall Numbers 17:1–8 where Aaron's rod budded with almond blossoms; strawberries, the essence of perfect righteousness; and, most fancifully, walnuts, the dual nature of Christ, the meat of the nut being flesh and the shell the wooden instrument of the Crucifixion.[56]

Now while the Passion reduced to a walnut makes a good Erasmian joke, it is beyond the remotest possibility that they were so intended by the still life painters. For when still lifes make didactic points, as they certainly do in

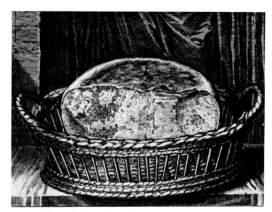

84. Emblem from Johan de Brune, *Emblemata of Sinnewerck* (Amsterdam, 1624)

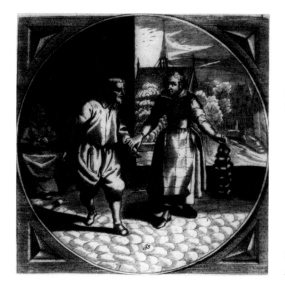

85. Emblem, "Vroeg rijp, vroeg rot," from Roemer Visscher, *Sinnepoppen* (Amsterdam, 1614)

86. "Maagdewapen" from Jacob Cats, *Maechden-plicht* (Middelburg, 1618)

vanitas paintings, for example, the religious connotations are explicit, directly communicated and, above all, make theologically and morally coherent sense. Packing into one composition random associations from the Pentateuch, the Gospels and patristic texts makes no didactic sense at all. As E. de Jongh has aptly put it, "Cheese was rarely consumed on an allegorical level in the seventeenth century."[57]

None of this iconographic overkill means that food could *never* be used in Dutch culture to provoke unworldly reflection, only that there is no evidence that it was the primary intention of still life painters who played with the relationships between the senses of sight, touch and taste. The rich storehouse of Netherlandish proverbs, doggerel wisdoms and emblems had long preferred domestic commonplaces, rather than the classical esoterica of Renaissance emblems, to make their points. And in those works, items of food do indeed operate as moral pointers. Jacob Cats, in *Christelijke Self-Strijt,* used a butter churn to discuss the ambivalence between the body and soul, and his engraver used the perseverance involved in the exercise to make an analogy with the labor of Christian "self-struggle."[58] Another Calvinist moralist, Johan de Brune, in his *Emblemata,* showed a maggoty cheese to invoke, as was customary in these didactic conflations, two morals, one in the *inscriptio* and another in the *subscriptio.*[59] The emblem reads, literally, "Too sharp makes jagged." The primary moral argues against the decay that produced the verminous swarm, but the secondary, more essential point was to warn against the bad ideas produced by soured great minds. Other foods were used in similar fashion. The overblown fruit in Roemer Visscher's *Sinnepoppen* (Dolls for the Spirit) has the self-explanatory legend "early ripe, early rot." In other places, crabs could stand for sidewinding unchristian or irregular upbringing and behavior, oysters for lust, onions for tear-provoking peccadillos and bunches of grapes held by the stem for both premarital chastity and marital fidelity.[60]

If much of this was meant as food for thought, it did not preclude the points being made with as much humor and playfulness as solemnity. Nor did it add up to a rigorously coherent set of domestic ethics, either Calvinist or humanist, but more often a generalized *mengelmoes* (mishmash) of both. Visscher's fruit emblem, after all, was a warning against precocity; the cheese, in one of its aspects, a warning against overripeness and decay. Both, however, succeeded in communicating the stock criticism against immoderation in a deliberately mundane and accessible manner. To swallow these message-bearing foods, the moralists must have hoped, would be to digest lessons along with the fare. *Voedsel,* the Dutch word for victuals, has the same root, *voeden,* to nourish, as the common word for education or upbringing, *opvoeding.*

The new children of Israel, then, as much as the old, were what they ate. Dietary laws were not instituted, but some foods did become invested with generalized moral qualities that the Dutch liked to believe they collectively embodied. Cheese, for example (along with herring), was the great leveler, the universal enjoyment of which dissolved rank within national community. On the other hand, cheese and butter *together* were disapproved of as lactic *overvloed.* An apocryphal story that typically concerns the presumptions of rank against the egalitarian cheese had Prince Maurice and a skipper in a row when the Stadholder presumed to eat cheese and butter together.[61] The contemptuous jokes directed especially by the French and English at the "nation of cheesemongers" could be stood on its head in patriotic lore. Another more famous item of national lore had a Spanish emissary, sometimes said to be

Spinola, observing a group of men eating bread and cheese on a barge, and on being told they were "Their High Mightinesses, the States of Holland," resigning himself to their freedom. And that was just the kind of transparently backhanded self-congratulation in which early Dutch culture abounded. Jacob Westerbaen, who made food poems something of a specialty, contrasted the dilettante, partridge-nibbling Tijs with the honest, cheese-munching Kees, in every sense the salt of the earth:

> *Kees eats only cheese and bread, and says it has strong flavor,*
> *Tijs eats partridges, but they give him no savor.*
> *Kees goes out to work, his appetite's ready and rough,*
> *Tijs is always sated, but never has enough.*
> There is no better sauce than hunger.
> *That's why Kees can taste his cheese*
> *And Tijs can't taste his partridges.*[62]

"Jan Kees" was the common sobriquet for "honest John Goodfellow" (though later used as a term of scorn for bluff obtuseness). Here it is plain that Kees/*kaas* (cheese) stood in direct opposition to the effete patrician/partridge. Equally, the herring was par excellence the patriotic fish, the foundation of the national fortune. It was the object of Westerbaen's verse eulogy *Lof des*

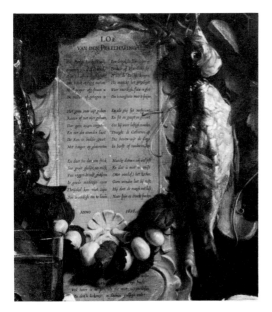

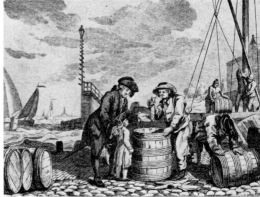

88. Engraving from J.H. Swildens, *Vaderlandsch AB Boek* (Amsterdam, 1781)

87. Joseph de Bray, *Still Life with Poem, "In Praise of the Herring."* Gemäldegalerie, Dresden

Pekelhareng (In Praise of the Pickled Herring), and both poem and fish were brought together in a pictorial encomium by Josephus de Bray.[63] In children's instruction books like Swildens's patriotic ABC from the eighteenth century, the herring was still being held up to small boys as exemplary of how great things (and profits) grew from humble beginnings.[64]

In contrast there were some foods that moralists and especially Calvinist preachers regarded as not only reprehensible but dangerous. Exotic, especially East Indian, spices like cinnamon and mace, with their heady fragrance and pagan origin (unlike homegrown roots and legumes) were to be mistrusted as likely to beguile men away from home cooking and plain morality. Sauces prepared to disguise or dress up honest-to-goodness meat and vegetables were denounced in the same terms used to deplore facial cosmetics and dyed wigs. But the great enemy, a tireless worker for Satan, was sugar. Pouring into the Republic in adequate quantities to reduce the factor cost sufficiently to reach tables of "the middling sort," Brazilian sugar pandered to the already well-established Dutch hankering for confections and delicacies.[65] By the 1640s there were already more than fifty sugar refineries operating in Amsterdam, and traditional favorites like waffles, pancakes and *poffertjes* could be supplemented with dustings of sugar or coatings of caramelized sauces. Cakes and biscuits that had gone unspiced except for the occasional sweetening of honey or, for the rich kitchen, saffron and anise, could now include chips of candied fruit or previously unheard-of combinations of oriental ginger and occidental molasses. The more vigilant predikants took this cult of *lekkerheid*—the craving for sweetness—as a moral menace of frightening proportions. The minister Belcampius lamented:

> Sweetness and excess is today grown so great that were they not ashamed to do so, men would found an Academy to which they would send all cooks and pasty bakers to teach them how to excel in the preparation of sauces, spices, cakes and confections, so that they should taste delicious. . . . Palates have become so demanding nowadays that there is scarcely any sauce that can satisfy them. . . . The men of today would dearly like to hail cooks and other servants of their gluttony with trumpets of honor and crowns of laurel.[66]

Had he but known what Harvey and Sheldon Peck—two museum-going dentists from the United States—discovered, Belcampius might have had the satisfaction of witnessing sweetness paid off with pain. For according to the Pecks' professional inspection of the state of seventeenth-century Dutch teeth and gums, as disclosed by contemporary portraits, the impact of all this sticky stuff on crunching molars was a plague of cavities, an epidemic of decalcification. Rembrandt, they gloomily concluded, "was a dental cripple" doomed to suffer torments more excruciating than any Calvinist pastor could possibly have devised.[67]

The differentiation of food into honest necessities and morally contaminated luxuries suffered the same attrition over time that affected other kinds of self-imposed cultural boundaries. By the time that Kalf and van Beyeren were in their heyday, any inhibitions about exploiting the gorgeousness of fruits, however exotic, or precious metals had given way to the need for ever more rarefied and exquisite decorative effects. Canvases began to glow like jewels, using the play of light on glass and gold; Ming porcelain or mother-of-pearl, for reflections of radiant translucence. The growing popularity of *pronkstilleven* especially with the well-to-do, who could afford their relatively costly prices, did not, however, signal the disappearance of the old "breakfast pieces." Willem Claesz. Heda and Jan Jansz. den Uyl were both followed by their sons and by den Uyl's brother-in-law, Jan Jansz. Treck, who continued to turn out *banketjestukken* well into the 1650s and 1660s.[68] Sometimes the old formula was varied with the addition of fine porcelain dishes, silver rather than pewter ewers or a *berkmeyer* goblet and an elaborate standing salt, but essentially the traditional components—bread, lemons, wine, cheese, oysters and crabs and fish—persisted as did the predominating tones of brown, green and gray. And there were idiosyncratic still life painters, more in the Spanish than the Dutch tradition (though there were many points at which the styles intersected, just as there were personal contacts and visits in both directions),[69] who set large bunches of vegetables against a plain or black ground. There is nothing especially "moral" or even symbolic about Adriaen Coorte's famous *Asparagus* in Cambridge, but it was a common rather than a luxury food, and in the simplicity of its treatment was a far cry from the extravagance of "high finish" flowers and fruits. There were occasions, moreover, when the traditional simplicity of "Fatherlands food" was invoked as a patriotic gesture against the flood tide of unwholesome foreign confections. At a banquet given by an Amsterdam burgomaster in the eighteenth century, the company was treated to courses that corresponded to the history of "Fatherlands" manners. So the first course, served on rude pewter, was mostly fish, bread and ale, while the second (representing the prime years) was meats and fine fruit on porcelain. The surrender of patriotic gastronomy to foreign taste was finally represented by smothering the food in the wine sauces that so provoked pastors and moralists and serving the food on elaborate plate.[70]

It is doubtful whether the guests appreciated this entertainment (or at least its first course). But stigmatizing patrician opulence as alien and symbolic of the distance between rulers and ruled, the tax farmer and the taxed, gathered momentum through the mid-eighteenth century and kindled an increasing number of riots and disturbances.[71] For most of the seventeenth century, though, preachers and moralizing writers made no social distinctions in their attacks on corrupt manners. Their assumption was that abundance was a common, if unevenly distributed patrimony, and that the middling and common people quite as much as the elite needed warning of the dangers of drink and gluttony before they incurred the inevitable wages of sin.

Was that assumption at all reasonable? Were the majority of Dutch bellies as well lined as foreign visitors reported? Did no one go hungry in Holland?

While it would be a mistake to assume that all Dutch cities bathed in a Vermeer-like light of undisturbed tranquillity, it is nonetheless true that, before the 1690s, serious food or excise riots were few and far between. The most recent account of the disturbances that became much more common by the end of the century and into the eighteenth can only find four such riots in Leiden and one in Gouda, both in the dearth year of 1630.[72] There were also disturbances in 1628 and 1662, quite serious in the Brabant town of den Bosch. But for the most part these troubles were localized and sporadic rather than chronic. There were certainly serious years of shortage, particularly at the beginning of the century (1601 was a hard year) and at the end. And during the depression of the 1650s, all sectors of the economy were hit. But none of this substantially alters the impression that Holland was indeed a striking exception in a Europe plagued by constant shortages, the pronounced loss of purchasing power among wage earners, and endemic violence in both town and country. But it has only been with the brilliant research of Jan de Vries on wages and prices that the historian is in a position to test the clichés about a golden age for labor as well as for the well-to-do.[73] De Vries's data, in fact, confirm the observations of all those foreign visitors on the relative prosperity of the work force in the Dutch Republic. Paradoxically, it emerges that *unskilled* labor was always in as good or better a position than its counterpart throughout the century extending from 1580 to 1680, and it was skilled labor that began disadvantaged compared with contemporaries in England, France or the southern Netherlands, but that caught up spectacularly by the middle of the seventeenth century. By 1650–79, a journeyman who would have been earning the equivalent of 16.5 stuivers per day in the southern counties of England (except London) and 15.5 in Cologne, would have earned 27 stuivers in Amsterdam, 25 in Alkmaar and 22 in Arnhem.[74] "It seems undeniable," de Vries concludes, "that real wages rose while they were falling elsewhere in Europe."[75]

Purchasing power, of course, should be measured by costs other than just those of food. And, notoriously, the most unstable element in determining real income was rent, which increased with particular severity in over-crowded industrial towns like Leiden. But the per capita tax burden that emphasized excise duties on basic domestic goods and comestibles, for the first half of the century was exactly compensated by wage rises, and in the third quarter that tax burden actually seems to have fallen. As de Vries points out, it was only in the wake of the ruinously expensive wars against Louis XIV that this situation changed drastically. And along with those changes, predictably, came the first serious wave of riots, in the 1690s.[76]

Even for those who lost their employment through age or sickness, the prolific charitable institutions of the Republic could come to their aid and provide basic foodstuffs to see them through. Not everything was rosy for everyone, of course. Women and girls, who comprised in Leiden something like 30 percent of the labor force, were worked harder for less. A Haarlem bleaching girl in 1610 earned only eight stuivers a day, and in the more crowded industrial towns like Leiden, night piecework was needed to make up a living wage for a household.[77] Nonetheless, the extremes of want and desperation to which the overwhelming majority of the European population were pressed by perennial adversity at this time really do seem to have been absent in the Dutch Republic for much of the golden century.

A great deal of this relatively happy situation was due to Holland's pivotal position in the seventeenth-century grain trade.[78] Growing little herself, the Republic virtually controlled the production of wheat and rye in Poland, East Prussia, Swedish Pomerania and Livonia, by virtue of her dominance over Baltic shipping. Amsterdam, Rotterdam and Middelburg all had massive silo granaries, where the surplus of one year could be stocked to provide against the shortfall of the next. And as a result, prices fluctuated relatively little, with the exception of the 1650s, when the combination of bad harvests in the east and naval wars with both the English and Scandinavian powers interrupted normal supplies. A three-pound loaf of rye bread cost around 4½ stuivers in the middle years of the century. The mean size of households in Holland—the lowest in Europe—has been calculated at 3.75 persons which for the sake of common sense if not demographic precision might be called 4.[79] If we assume that the needs of such a household would be met by two three-pound loaves a day, and that the going rate for skilled artisans—a ship's carpenter in Amsterdam for example—was around 30 stuivers—the proportion of income spent on bread would have been around 30 percent.[80] This left a reasonable but certainly not ample balance for other costs. And the impression given from food historians is that, rather than spend a disproportionate amount on starch alone, the wage earner may well have bought a single loaf and supplemented with the abundant and relatively cheap supplies of vegetables, fish and dairy foods that made up the common diet.

That was itself a virtually unique situation in seventeenth-century Europe, and travelers often commented on the surprising variety of the laboring people's diet. A century later, Diderot was still amazed to see workers in the towns, *boers* in the countryside and fisherfolk eating fresh and cured meat and fish, fresh vegetables and fruit, butter, eggs and cheese, as a matter of weekly routine. Mackerel and red mullet, he was horrified to note, they threw away as unfit for consumption.[81] "The Dutch who are epicures in fish," noted the English traveler Nugent, "are so nice that they buy none [at market] but what are alive. So that if any are dead they are either thrown away or are sold to the poor for a trifle."[82] At Dordrecht, salmon were so prolific that, according to Nugent, "servants used formerly to make a bargain with their master not to be obliged to eat salmon above twice a week."[83] The story was probably apocryphal, but there is no doubt that in the seventeenth as in the eighteenth century, a wide variety of fish, fresh, cured and marinated, formed an essential part in the protein intake of the common people. Fresh soles, plaice, dabs, flounders, haddock, cod and turbot, as well as mussels (considered the most wretched food and featured prominently in "Thin kitchen" paintings), oysters, lobsters, shrimp and crab were cheap and abundant throughout the maritime provinces. And the staples of salted and cured fish ensured that even the most modest households had some fat and protein-based calories in their diet. A pair of bloaters or cured red herring sold for just a *duit,* or an eighth of a stuiver, in the 1650s and fresh "green" or "new Hollands" herring for half a stuiver.

Given the high-yield productivity of the Dutch dairy industry, butter and cheese would also have been within the range of at least skilled artisan families, although some of the very best produce was reserved for export. Sweet-milk cheeses like Gouda sold, in the most expensive years, for around two and a half stuivers an Amsterdam pound, and cumin-studded and green

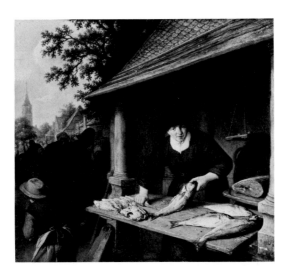

89. Adriaen van Ostade, *The Fishwife,* 1672. Rijksmuseum, Amsterdam

cheeses for rather less.[84] Butter was dearer at five stuivers the pound but still
no luxury, and real aficionados of the breakfast *banket* took pride in offering
several types of butter—Delft, Texel, Goudse—to their guests. A real social
divide, though, existed between households that used butter only for spreading
on bread or soft biscuits and those who could afford to substitute it for lard in
cooking and pastry making. As with bread and cheese, there was an extensive
hierarchy of quality that enabled households to select the foods that best
fitted their means without having to endure the want and the social humiliation of deleting whole staples from the weekly basket. In periodic times of
hardship or unemployment they might have to settle for coarse *semelbrood*
made from buckwheat and grits, but in good times, and for special occasions,
might extend to patrician white wheat bread, or fruit breads studded with
peel and currants. Writers on diet and cookery in the seventeenth century
were, however, shocked to find that in the poorest areas of the countryside, in
Drente and northern Groningen, peasants occasionally descended to making
bread from chestnut meal. Even this, though, was an improvement on the
gruels of acorns, tree bark and grasses that represented the most desperate
attempts to fend off famine in Spain, southern Italy and the Massif Central.

Meat was not wholly out of the question for a Dutch artisan and a regular
part of the diet of a modest burgher, a small shopkeeper. Many urban as well as
rural families invested in an ox or at least a pig in October, and after the
slagmaand in November made full use of it in offal, sausages and cured meat to
see them through the winter. Smoked meat—ham and bacon, preferably on
the fatty side—was a standard item in the weekly regimen, but even fresh meat
was not inconceivable for the household of a skilled worker or guildsman. A
chicken, for example, cost eleven stuivers at market in midcentury Delft, and
a pound of veal just four, representing respectively a third and an eighth of the
skilled artisan's daily wage.[85] Fresh vegetables: onions, white and savoy cabbages,
root crops like parsnips, turnips, beets, carrots and salsify, legumes such as peas,
beans, cucumbers, endive, scallions and leeks—were all cheap and commonplace thanks to the prolific horticulture in which Holland, Zeeland and
Friesland specialized, and the intricate network of canals made marketing cheap
and efficient.[86] There was a charmed circularity about the relationship between
urban consumption and sub- and ex-urban horticulture, with the manure produced from all that stuffing going to fertilize even greater yield ratios in the
fields, that in turn fed larger urban populations, which in turn . . .

Fruit was equally abundant. Orchards in the vicinity of the towns produced
apples, pears, plums and nuts, and it was common for burghers, at any rate, to
add cherries and berries to sweet or sour cream at summer breakfasts. Dried
fruit, especially prunes, raisins and figs, were staple items in Dutch cooking
and were used to flavor meat dishes as well as fruit pies and cakes. Pea and

prune soup was an old favorite, as was roast pork stuffed with prunes, and minced ox tongue and green apple sauce was a great delicacy. Fruit was occasionally the object of suspicion. In 1655 the notion that blue plums, Damsons and black cherries had been responsible for a particularly severe outbreak of the plague (presumably because of their analogous resemblance to buboes) led to their being temporarily banned from market stalls in Holland. The more exotic the item, the more easily such anxieties could be aroused, especially when medical manuals were as much moral tracts as scientific treatises. Reports of beri-beri from the Indies terrified the metropolitan population, and although the pineapple was fairly well known among the elite, having been successfully grown by Paladanus in his garden at Enkhuizen and ripened by Pieter de la Court, its slightly daunting appearance attracted a great deal of hostility. Bontius, for example, argued that it was the carrier of many kinds of gastric and dysenteric infections from the Orient. But part of the appeal of exotic fruits was, of course, precisely their "dangerous" qualities that recommended them to the courageous. Other fruit that had been regarded as luxurious, and priced accordingly — melons, oranges and grapes — became abundant and relatively inexpensive by the last third of the century. Melon juice, indeed, was another, somewhat surprising staple of many Dutch recipes, especially lengthily cooked stews. Asparagus was already a major crop in the south and west of Holland, though globe artichokes (their thistle-like foliage resembling, of course, the pineapple) had a more difficult reception, being denounced by Father Cats as an aphrodisiac, though celebrated by Dr. van Beverwijck as a panacea. When the wife of the the miserable ne'er-do-well in Sweerts's *Ten Diversions of Marriage* becomes pregnant, she develops cravings for, among other delicacies: black cherries, strawberries in wine, black and white plums, peaches and apricots, pineapples, hazelnuts, red and white grapes, almond tarts and whole mountain ranges of marzipan. All these addictions, it was implied, could be satisfied locally, even though they might ruin the husband in the process.[87]

Beverages changed little until later in the century, and then only for social groups well above the level of shopkeepers. Tea, which became familiar in the Republic through Dutch travelers and colonists in the Orient, was first recommended by moral physicians like Johannes van Helmont as a restorative against loss of body fluids from excessive sweating and purges. Dr. Tulp thought that it was the oldest and best herbal beverage known to the world and was good at easing cramps and a stimulant against sluggishness.[88] It remained, however, a panacea strictly for the few during the first half of the century, and even in the 1660s when enough tea was being shipped by the East India Company to send the price plummeting from a hundred guilders a pound to ten, it remained too expensive to replace ale as the drink of the people. Unlike tobacco, which was also much praised for its medicinal properties, tea remained immune from any *odium theologicum*. In fact its most ardent enthusiast, Cornelis Bontekoe, thought that no harm could come of it, however much was drunk. Eight to ten cups a day he thought the minimum for one's health, and fifty to two hundred cups perfectly reasonable.[89] He himself followed his own counsel so literally that in 1696 the *Haagsche Mercurius* reported that tea had so dried his "balsamic sap" that "his joints rattled like castanets."[90] By the early eighteenth century, at any rate, sinking dishes of tea had become sufficiently characteristic to provoke satirical comedies like *de Thezieke Juffers* (the Tea-Sick Misses)[91] and Montesquieu was startled to see a housewife sink thirty cups at a single sitting.[92] In less decorous style it won encomia from popular versifiers in the 1670s:

> Tea that helps our head and heart
> Tea medicates most every part
> Tea rejuvenates the very old
> Tea warms the piss of those who're cold.[93]

Coffee took longer to catch on, even though the writer Blankaart insisted it was the healthiest drink in the world, especially fine for staving off "mouldy joints" and scurvy, and lived up to his claim by drinking no fewer than twelve cups a day. It was not until the early eighteenth century that coffee clubs, for both men and women (though separate), started to spring up in towns like Rotterdam and Amsterdam where modish types would sip it, heavily spiced with cloves, cinnamon and ginger, and sweetened with honey. Milk was readily available of course, but even in the paradise of the cow, physicians differed sharply on the wisdom of drinking it, especially undiluted. Dr. van Beverwijck counseled those who insisted on downing it neat to rinse their mouths out with wine afterwards if they wished to avoid dental decay.[94] At the very least it was likely to be an improvement on the Amsterdam canal water that was drunk by the "common sort" of the city despite its notorious foulness, and the not very successful efforts of the regents to improve its salubrity. Buttermilk and whey were common breakfast beverages, but the drink most generally recommended for both adults and children was beer. Usually this was made from hops and malted barley in various stages of fermentation, much like modern ale. In some domestic variations, though, fruit and herbs could also be used. The *Verstandige Huyshouder* listed at least eighteen types of beer, including those made with marjoram and rosemary, and another with plums, and praised them all as beneficial for young and old alike.[95] A tankard of beer in a tavern cost just half a stuiver in the 1650s, and in casks or stone jugs filled by peripatetic "tappers" and meant for home con-

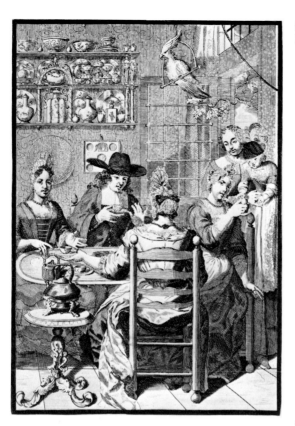

90. Engraving, "De Thee."
Rijksmuseum, Amsterdam

91. Title page, *De Verstandige Huyshouder.* Harvard College Library

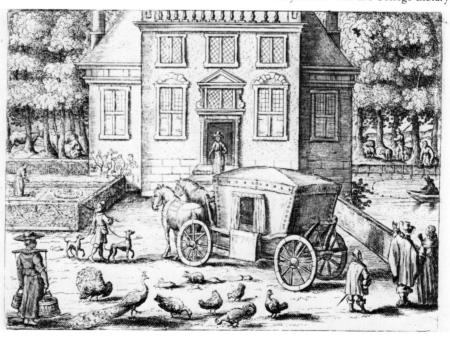

sumption, rather less. On shipboard, barrels of ale were left open for all the crew to enjoy gratis as a prescribed item of their rations.

It seems safe, then, to conclude that the majority of the Dutch population in the seventeenth century enjoyed precisely that ample but not opulent diet that the humanist divines and doctors believed good for the soul as well as the body. The dietary regimen of the Dutch, like the society it fed, did not follow the pyramid shape of most of early modern Europe. The social hierarchy was ovoid or pot-bellied, with an indigent poor at the base consisting of the migrant and vagrant unskilled, seasonal farm workers and artisans in low-paid industries like the Leiden textiles, whom periodic unemployment and wage cutting might well throw on relief. At the top was an affluent patrician aristocracy whose social habits were every bit as extravagant as their counterparts in Venice or Paris. In between, swelling at the middle, was the sprawling entity of the *brede middenstand,* which could include anyone from skilled artisans, members of a guild and earning more than ten stuivers a day, tenant farmers, the sellers and processors of their produce like millers and brewers (Rembrandt's father, a miller, certainly considered himself as belonging to the *burgerij* and attempted to set his son on a professional career via Leiden Latin School), petty professionals like notaries, apothecaries and clerics, all the way up to the magnates of commerce, industry and finance, who would have disdained being classified as aristocrats. It would be naive, of course, to ignore the vast differences of fortune, education and social behavior that separated ranks within this amorphous group. But the fact that they all sat down at more or less the same time to a breakfast consisting of more or less the same ingredients—bread, butter, cheese, fish, pasties, beer and/or buttermilk and whey—suggests a community in which the bonds of shared habit tied together those whom economic conflict would otherwise have sundered.

This was not a dietary democracy, much less a culinary utopia, a sort of Cockaigne of the north. But it was at least a society in which the "unfortunate" poor (as distinct from able-bodied vagrants) were supplied with fare meant to approximate to the diet of the more fortunate rather than stigmatize their wretchedness with a regimen of didactic meanness. Happily, the nineteenth-century utilitarian principle of "least eligibility" with its accompanying terror of the workhouse gruelpot did not yet operate within the homelier culture of Dutch humanism. Not that poorhouse food was exactly festive. Breakfast was a standard two slices of bread with milk or buttermilk. *De noen,* or the midday meal, in the Leiden municipal poorhouse followed a set pattern of vegetable soup and some sort of meat stew, or the occasional fowl, on Sundays and Wednesdays, a porridge of grits, butter and sweet milk on Mondays and Saturdays, green vegetables, bouillon and suet on Tuesdays and Fridays, and rice or barley, mashed vegetables and milk on Thursdays. The evening meal was usually a repeat of breakfast, with some cheese or vegetable mash added, and sick inmates had fresh fruit, soup made with, or accompanied by, white wheaten bread, and, more surprisingly, red wine, as a supplement to their diet.[96]

Another captive population, the students of Leiden University, did somewhat better. Their diet, like that of seamen or military cadets, was laid down by statute, and the statute of 1631 stipulated fairly generous portions of fish and meat. Cheese was generally available at supper along with bread and beer, and breakfast portions specified four ounces of butter and a quarter of a loaf of bread per student. In the week they could expect fresh and smoked fish, hash and ham, while on Sundays both *hutsepot* stew and a roast were offered. Not surprisingly, professors treated themselves more lavishly. The bill for the dozen or so professors of Groningen University for the *two days* of April 24–25, 1664, runs to forty-five guilders and twenty stuivers — nearly half a year's wage for a laboring worker. Their first day's fare alone included a turkey, a jugged hare, a Westphalian ham, a bolt of mutton, veal on the spit, anchovies, bread, butter, mustard and cheese, lemons and twelve tankards of wine.[97]

Perhaps the most dependable instance of what the Dutch meant by a "decent sufficiency" — a diet that avoided the dangerous extremes of the Fat and Thin kitchens — was that of the shipboard galley. Naval fare was carefully regulated according to official notions of the dietary norm, because Dutch vessels were regarded as little republics, floating embodiments of the commonwealth whose flag they flew, subject to the triple authority of its representatives: magisterial/military (the skipper), commercial (the shipboard merchant) and clerical (the marine predikant). And just as the Dutch navy was proud of its reputation for fastidiously spruce and clean vessels, so too it was careful to provide a diet that would compare favorably with the wretched fare to which most seamen were usually condemned, especially over long voyages. Recruitment for naval and colonial vessels was never easy, despite the reputation of the Netherlands as abundant in manpower, and would grow steadily more difficult towards the end of the century.[98] Since the Dutch never resorted to impressment, a generous diet was probably a factor in attracting crews from foreign as well as native maritime populations. Dutch victualing was the counterpart of that most (indeed often the only) alluring appeal of the recruiting officer: *"voici, messieurs, la soupe du régiment."* In 1636 the admiralty of Amsterdam stipulated that every man on board was entitled to half a pound of cheese, half a pound of butter and a five-pound loaf each week, with officers on double rations.[99] By 1654, the exigencies of the first Anglo-Dutch war had highlighted food as an important weapon of war as much as shot or cordage, and the States General embodied the diet provisions into a set of statutory articles that had to be read out to a ship's crew at the beginning of every voyage. The shipboard regimen was, by the standards of the time, as varied as could be expected, given the need to use dried, cured or briny foods. It was also strikingly copious, amounting on average to some 4800 calories a day! The morning meal had the familiar mixture of bread and grits porridge, but the midday meal was less starchy. On Sundays there might be a half pound of smoked ham or a pound of mutton or bully beef with peas. On Monday, Tuesday and Wednesday, the diet revolved around smoked and pickled fish with green or white peas and beans. On Thursdays, each man had a pound of beef or three-quarters of a pound of pork; Friday and Saturday saw a reversion to fish and peas. All of this meant that the larger vessels took on board very substantial quantities of victuals to feed their crews. In 1636, for example, a ship with a hundred crew would have had to carry for *every month* at sea: four hundred fifty pounds of cheese, five tons of meat, four hundred pounds of cured fish, four tons of herring, one and a quarter tons of butter, five and a half tons of dried peas, two and a half tons of dried beans, half a ton of salt, half an oxhead of vinegar, thirty-five tuns of ale in winter (forty-two in summer) and French and Spanish wine for the officers.

The Dutch marine, then, set sail in bottoms heavily ballasted by the staples they were commissioned to protect—those same perennial favorites of the *banketjestuk* artists—fish, butter, cheese, beer and wine. If, through its perishability, bread was missing from long voyages, it was replaced by the formidably long-lived biscuits, baked specifically for shipboard consumption in the villages of the Wormer, north of Amsterdam.[100] The ample provisioning of the fleet thus became an important part of logistics for the admiralties of the Republic and the most successful commanders, Maarten Tromp and de Ruyter, were as much regents as captains: magistrates, stewards and pastors, as concerned with moral and material welfare as with brute force.

For reasons peculiar to shipboard life, the one dish omitted from the naval diet which was common to students, professors and patricians alike—the famous *hutsepot*—was, by midcentury, acquiring the status of a national dish. In the eighteenth century the antiquarian Kornelis van Alkemade invested it with a patriotic mystique when he referred to it as of great antiquity and, "in earlier times named *potvlees* and *pothorst*."[101] The meat and vegetable stew was regarded with some reverence as true *vaderlandse voedsel,* analogous to the identification of "freeborn Englishmen" with barons of beef in the eighteenth century. More than a mere comestible, it was a food that was meant, simultaneously, to reflect the qualities of those who ate it and to reinforce those qualities with its sustenance. If the beefed-up John Bull was supposed to be as virile, ungarnished and bloody (minded) as his chosen food, the Dutch might well have thought of themselves as a hotchpotch commonwealth: rich in variety, harmoniously assorted, hearty, wholesome, sturdy, unpretentious and enduring. Roast beef was the man of action's heroic dish, commingling muscle and blood, energy and power. The great stews of the Netherlands were more to the taste of ruminative humanism: patiently assembled, eclectic in content, moderately spiced, slowly cooked and even more deliberately eaten. They were, however, to be distinguished from a mere *mengelmoes* (mishmash), in which the separate constituents had been reduced to soupy pabulum. That was the pap of slaves and babies. Paradoxically, a somewhat more elaborate variation of the *hutsepot* was commonly assumed in Holland (though with obscure justification) to have been a Spanish dish. *Olipotrigo, olypodrigo* or *olipodraga* consisted of a more flamboyant (dangerously southern?) set of ingredients including capon, lamb, veal fricandelle, rams' testicles, calves' heads, coxcombs, chicory, endive, sausage, marrowbone and, for special occasions, artichokes, asparagus and game, all mixed with four or five egg yolks and reduced with sour wine or vinegar and melted butter.[102] Missing the one ingredient that might have marked it as truly southern—olive oil—it was in fact an unmistakably Netherlandish stew pretending, not very seriously, to be Mediterranean. The purer *hutsepot,* repeated in seventeenth-century cookbooks, was a standard formula that could be varied according to the vegetables in season and the availability of different kinds of meat:

> Take some mutton or beef; wash it clean and chop it fine. Add thereto some greenstuff or parsnips or some stuffed prunes and the juice of lemons or oranges or citron or a pint of strong, clear vinegar. Mix these together, set the pot on a slow fire (for at least three and a half hours); add some ginger and melted butter and you shall have prepared a fine *hutsepot.*[103]

The several treasures of the Dutch economy: agricultural, commercial, and horticultural are all represented in the recipe. Dairy food and meat, and fresh vegetables from Holland, spice from the Indies, citrus from the Levant and wine vinegar from the Mediterranean all came together in the meaty bubble of the *hutsepot.* Copious rather than gluttonous, modest rather than mean, the national stew was the perfect way to sanction abundance without risking retribution for greed. The old alternation between feast and fast, glut and dearth, carnival and Lent was broken by the daily sufficiency that was the peculiar hallmark of the Dutch diet. There were still occasions on which penitential fasts were called, but these were propitiatory responses to exceptional crises (plague, flood, invasion) brought on by the temporary undoing of that moral equilibrium on which the Republic's safety normally rested.

And there were indeed still feasts which need not, moreover, resemble the profanities of Belshazzar. The towns of the Netherlands, north and south, had long been partial to public or semipublic celebrations of either events or institutions associated with their history. Despite the stern admonitions of the clergy, the Reformation made very little inroads into these festive practices, just because the purposes for which they were held were seen as licensed by custom and history, and not by alien, pagan debauch. Some, however, were close to the line. The guild archives at Naarden, for example, complain that "many of the tailors' and drapers' guilds at the time of their assembly [i.e., feast] take the name of God in vain with swearing, cursing and other vile blasphemies."[104] A few of these celebrations were of genuinely remote medieval origin like the feast of the Zwannenbroeders (Confraternity of the Swan) at 's Hertogenbosch where feuds of clan and guild were reconciled as the fellowship tucked into their patron bird. Many more, like the Spyndaghen held in the same city, dated back no further than the Burgundian period, but were given a spurious gloss of antiquity by local historians.[105] In both popular and learned histories, the ancient Batavians, in common with some other Germanic tribes, were depicted as expressing their primitive community in simple but abundant open-air feasts, and many of the modern fraternities purported to uphold those native traditions. Others still, like the annual Leiden commemoration of the relief of 1574, solemnized contemporary as well as ancient history through the medium of the "food of liberty" (bread and herring), shared by all citizens every October third.

All these "legitimate" feasts, however, were marked by a high degree of formality and ceremony, including acts that proclaimed that the point of the assembly was something other than stuffing: Ornate toasts, verses specially commissioned or traditionally handed down from generation to generation, orations and declamations, storytelling of the history of the town or the guild, the chamber of rhetoric or the militia company, even impromptu mummeries and plays, shaped such occasions and gave them a kind of collective benediction. And this heavy emphasis on collective ritual was as true for the humblest gatherings as for the grandest. William Aglionby noted that each of the neighborhood (*wijken*) communities that represented the simplest of all the corporate institutions into which the Republic was divided, had its own Master and Chancellor. These elected officers were responsible, among other duties, for upholding the ordinances and bylaws that attended every feast and solemnly reading them at the beginning. One such set banished children and dogs and forbade both blasphemy *and* any kind of religious discussion on the grounds that it would sow discord where there ought only to be fellowship. And in a similar spirit, anyone striking a fellow was to be evicted and readmitted to the company (these feasts lasting three or four days), only when beseeching its humble pardon for his or her offense.[106]

The inanimate witnesses of these rites and ceremonies were crucial in reinforcing the sense of festive community. Drinking horns, standing salts,

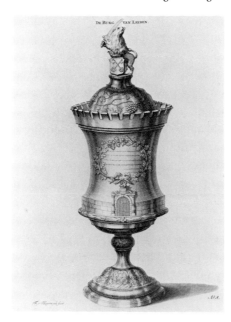

92. Standing salt cellar with "The Castle" of Leiden, from Kornelis van Alkemade, *Nederlandse Displegtigheden* (Rotterdam, 1732)

ewers and basins, glass *roemers,* and *berkmeyer* goblets would be chased, incised and engraved with the arms of the company or town, and in their more elaborate manifestations, with scenes of their history being celebrated. The flamboyant goldsmiths of Utrecht came to specialize in a variation of their history carving that could produce virtually any scene in relief on the inside of a dish or cup.[107] Occasions when feasts were called in honor of some great public occasion, like the relief of Bergen op Zoom in 1622, the entry of Marie de Médicis in 1638 or the Peace of Münster in 1648, were opportunities for aspiring or incumbent grandees to mark their status by the presentation of especially lavish vessels, in silver or gold, suitably inscribed to remind later generations of celebrants of the munificence of their donor.

Often, the content of the dishes was determined by the symbolic associations of the food—some of which were only vaguely recollected by the participants. The fact that a particular dish had been eaten on a specific date through allegedly immemorial time was enough to invest it with a consecrated aura. The goldsmiths' guild at Dordrecht, for example, invariably feasted on ham pasties, roast suckling pig, calf's head, junket, sweet pies, crackers and Cyprus and Burgundy wines. Woe betide the presumptuous cook who dared tamper with the time-honored menu! The Chamber of Musicians at Arnhem dined less sumptuously at the monthly gatherings in which one of their number treated his colleagues, but they too did so according to a standard bill of fare: haddock, leg of mutton, peas, apples, plums (in summer), prunes (in winter), butter, cheese and wine.[108]

The food, however, was more than simply guzzling fuel. Presented with ostentatious pomp, it became a vehicle for the solemnities that bound the celebrants together around the table. Form and protocol were of the utmost importance and not infrequently exhausted the patience of foreign guests. Théophile de Viau, for example, complained poignantly that "all these gentlemen of the Netherlands have so many rules and ceremonies for getting drunk, that I am repelled as much by them as by the sheer excess."[109] But these rites were not laid on for the benefit (or exasperation) of the occasional visitor; they were the mysteries of the burghers' social religion. As such they usually excluded women and children and became as elaborate as the rituals of the old church on which the Republic had turned its back. It mattered terribly, for example, on whom the honors of pouring wine or carving the meat had been conferred at the annual two-day banquets of guildsmen or the *schutter,* militia regiments. Carving became so elaborate an art that reference works like *De Cierlyke Voorsnydinge voor alle Tafelgerechten* (*Fine Carving for All Table Dishes*) (1664) began to appear in editions with special chapters on carving for formal occasions. At the *schuttersmaal* feasts, a high degree of division of labor was rigorously observed. In the company of St. George (Joris) in Haarlem, it was the *provoost,* or second-in-command, who had the privilege of the knife; in the company of St. Adrian it was one of the three regimental captains, while the *provoost* (after 1624 called the *fiscaal*) had charge of the drinking horn.

93. Frans Hals, *The Banquet of the Officers of the St. George Militia of Haarlem,* 1616. Frans Hals Museum, Haarlem

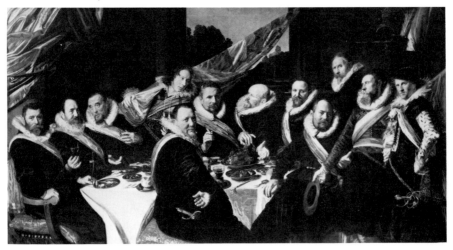

Other rituals, such as the plan of seating and the order of toasts, preserved and even reinforced the pecking order of the hierarchy without subverting its overall fraternity. For all the apparently cavalier spontaneity of the *schutter* banquets in Frans Hals's famous Haarlem series, the eleven officers, as Seymour Slive showed, are arranged according to a punctilious ranking, with the colonel flanked on his right by the *provoost*. Below him (that is, to his left) would be the officers of each of the platoons (orange, white, blue) that made up the company. They were shown with the attributes of the rank, in descending order, the captains (who held tasseled half-pikes or spontoons), lieutenants, sergeants with halberds, and last and least, the young bachelor ensigns, shown standing holding the company banner. It was part of Hals's genius to break up the horizontal relief-disposition that had characterized earlier militia pieces by Frans de Grebber or Ketel by having captains face one another across the table and by introducing variations in depth without sacrificing niceties of rank. Alois Riegl was astute at discerning a peculiarly Dutch concern to balance off fraternity with station, though whether in those respects Amsterdam (with its divisions into "corporalships") was a genuinely more open and "democratic" militia culture than Haarlem is, to say the least, debatable.[110]

However much social and individual differentiation there may have been on these occasions, the equally powerful sense of collective incorporation into an urban brotherhood was expressed by the flamboyant display in which all members (and sometimes even the servants, who were occasionally included in the group portraits) participated. The drinking vessels which appear in the earliest iconic representations of the militia were symbols of that communal fraternity which had engaged to defend the town against the encroachments of feudalism and absolutism. In the sixteenth century those vessels tended to be relatively simple, at least in the northern Netherlands, but prompted by an inventive antiquarianism that tied in the birth of Batavian liberty with the primitive rites of ancient feasts held in the primordial forest, they developed after 1660 into all manner of pseudo-Teutonic drinking horns, lavishly embellished and sometimes inscribed with the names of all present officers or guild masters.[111] Just as Claudius Civilis was said to have sworn his tribal brethren by passing a ritual vessel brimful of wine (some authorities insisted, blood), so the drinking horn was passed from mouth to mouth at the feast to reconsecrate the *schutters'* confederacy. In a similar vein, the great banners of the companies, bearing their arms, and the colors of the town or of the Republic were repeated on the sashes which bound the officers together in their common allegiance.

Initially, of course, the memory of the Haarlem *schutters* who had been thrown into prison following the Spanish capture of the city, and their heroic part in its defense, entitled them to common civic respect. And in honor of that history the city presented the first three barrels of ale for the feast tax-free. But even by the middle of the seventeenth century the flamboyance of the junketing was in marked contrast to military proficiency (and attendance at the drill grounds). The arquebuses from which some of the regiments took their names became more and more antiquated, and the Sunday parades shot at nothing more terrifying than the wooden parrots that had become the special *schutter* sport.[112] Drums and fifes, and above all the spectacular unfurling of banners and ensigns, continued unabated, but they had become a substitute for, rather than the accompaniment of, a serious military role. When the time came for them to participate in the nation's defense in 1672, the inadequacy of their preparation was all too nakedly revealed. This is not to say that their existence — and that of their feasts — was wholly dysfunctional within the culture. On the contrary, like the survival of the Siena *palio* or the Foligno *quintana,* they continued to symbolize the passion for local patriotism and to provide suburban units of allegiance around which different social groups could cohere. On the other hand, the separation of the officer corps — dominated by the patriciate — from the rest of the ranks tended to strengthen rather than weaken the social stratification, which by the 1670s was already being seen as a threat to the Republic's unity. By that time, it became a commonplace to accuse the *schutter* companies of existing for the sake of their routs, rather than the other way about. Once these suspicions were audibly voiced, the mystique by which these collective feasts received the sanction of the community at large could quickly evaporate. Deprived of uplifting associations of local patriotism and citizens' defense, the banquets could all too easily look like pretexts for members of the patrician class to indulge themselves in bouts of gross gluttony while honest citizens scraped along on herring and ale. From being part of the protective consensus by which the Dutch dulled the edges of social conflict, they could contribute to sharpening them. Worse, as a hypocritical counterfeit of a virtuous act they might actually operate as a threat, punishing the innocent along with the guilty. To the perils of the Jonah syndrome, then, one might perhaps add those of the Belshazzar syndrome. And to avoid the unwelcome appearance of writing on the wall, the regents of Dutch towns occasionally instituted sumptuary laws restricting the duration, and more rarely, the size of the banquets.[113]

As one might expect, the Calvinist Church was especially hostile to seasonal or annual feasting, although its ministrations rarely had much effect. It ought to have stood a better chance of suppressing those traditional feasts of the religious calendar which it stigmatized as vile relics of the popish past. But the further down the social scale popular feasting went, the poorer the outlook for a pious crusade of abstinence. Martinmas, or the feast of St. Martin, on November eleventh was a case in point. Its bonfires and the open baskets of nuts and fruit that were shaken over it have suggested a pagan origin, but it was the Bishop of Tours, the apostle of Gaul, who gave his name to the feast. In the Netherlands, as in France, Westphalia and Swabia, St. Martin became the patron saint of many towns, among them Arnhem, Groningen, Middelburg, Sneek, Venlo and, given its central place in the religious life of the country both before and after the Reformation, most significantly, Utrecht. The cult of St. Martin was exactly the sort of folk superstition that the more severe of the Calvinist preachers were determined to extirpate. But the feast was lodged in popular culture in the Low Countries not just as a relic of the hagiographic past, but as part of the dietary and domestic calendar, for it was also the period when the winter pig (or less often ox) was slaughtered and salted. It was the Martinmas goose, however, which supplied the *pièce de résistance* of the November feast, often fattened and force-fed for weeks before, and stuffed to bursting with the last fruits and nuts of the season.[114] At Deventer in Overijssel schoolchildren presented their teacher with a goose as a collective gift in return for which he duly granted them their holiday. In the same town, the learned divine and professor Schookius gravely debated the issue of whether it was compatible with religious orthodoxy to dish up goose to his students for the midday meal. More controversial still was the festive Martinmas liquor, made from a fiery concoction of must, sometimes diluted with wine, mid-November being the season for cellaring new wine. And while the Netherlands did not itself produce any wine, as the center of the staple trade, Dordrecht, for instance, cellared all its French wine at St. Martinmas and produced an appropriate Martini to celebrate.

So deeply buried in popular practice and belief was the feast of St. Martin (among others) that, for all the fire and brimstone threatened by the incensed clergy, there was little chance of removing it from the list of permitted festivities. In 1655, the Synod of Utrecht was still lamenting that "pagan and idolatrous" festivities were being celebrated around the very precincts of the cathedral.[115] Twenty years later the church had virtually resigned itself to periodic denunciations of wantonness without much hope of judicial enforcement. Vastenavond, the three days of feasting prior to Lent which culminated in the carnival of Fat Tuesday, was similarly too deeply embedded in popular custom and dietary lore to uproot by theological dogma. The great outpouring of waffles and pancakes, sausages, ham pies and *vastenavondtaarten* that preceded the grim reckoning of Ash Wednesday's white beans and herring, was a culturally organized memento of the days of feast and famine. By ritualizing the adjacency of glut and austerity at a set time in the calendar and according to strictly observed customs, it was possible to avert an arbitrary visitation of punitive fast.

It is a mistake, though, to reify culture as if it proceeded wholly independently

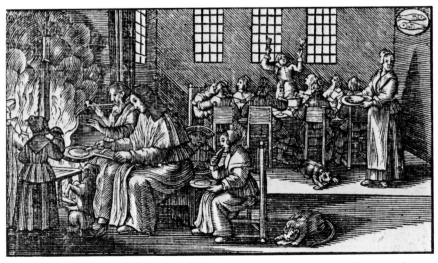

94. Woodcut: "February," from a Dutch almanac for 1664. Atlas van Stolk, Rotterdam

of the social groups that comprised it. In fact, none of these popular festivals would have survived, except as rustic pastimes, had not the ruling caste been persuaded of their moral innocence, if not wholesomeness. Their own sympathetic participation in its rites was a relatively safe way of displaying their union with those whom (on no very strong theoretical grounds) they claimed to govern. In many cases this was not some Machiavellian subterfuge but the authentic expression of a festive community that transcended formal institutions. But whatever the reasons, the church took an extremely dim view of such complaisance, regarding it as a serious dereliction of duty. The Amsterdam minister Petrus Wittewrongel never tired of upbraiding the magistracy for their slackness in suppressing "papist idolatry" and "Baal worship."[116] The feast of St. Nicholas (Sinter Klaas) on December sixth, with its gift-exchanging, the buying and parading of puppets and dolls and cookies set in wooden clogs, gave the zealots particular offense. In some towns they even succeeded briefly in acts of petty suppression, Delft banning gingerbread men in 1607, and Dordrecht briefly doing away with the festival altogether in 1657. In Amsterdam, the clergy had two allies on the regency in Dr. Tulp and Burgermeester Temminck de Vrij, the latter particularly wanting to get rid of the doll sellers' booths on the Vijzeldam. On December 4, 1663, the magistracy finally published a proclamation prohibiting the public sale of dolls as "idolatrous" and imposing a three-guilder fine for violation. Cookies and candles in effigylike forms were equally discouraged. The result was that most alarming form of social disturbance: an insurrection of eleven-year-olds. Bowing to the uproar of children and parents alike, the magistracy let the proclamation go unenforced, and Sinter Klaas commanded his following very much as usual.[117]

Such a breach in the festive calendar could not occur with impunity, and it was bound to be dangerous when the expectations raised by family and local traditions were suddenly confounded by inept demonstrations of official zeal. The family and the neighborhood were, after all, the irreducible primary cells on which the wider community of town or province ultimately rested. Some of the traditional feasts like that of St. Nicholas, the Feast of the Epiphany (Driekoningsavond) on January sixth, White Thursday (prior to Good Friday), or Pentecost Sunday (Pinksterdag) necessarily involved celebration in the home as well as in public. But, of course, there was a whole array of feasts that marked the comings and goings of the family and the neighborhood that expended glut in a such a way as to confer safety rather than danger on the local community. Family feasts celebrated the life cycle of the clan just as calendar feasts and fraternal banquets proclaimed the generational solidarity of the guild, the chamber of rhetoric, and the militia company. Neighborhood feasts, by concentrating celebrations within a particular time span and formal sets of rules, proclaimed the order and safety of the street. And the occasions for banqueting, or for the presentation of gifts to a banquet fund, were, not surprisingly, those that most directly affected the collective life of the social group. So that when a newcomer bought a house in the *wijk*, for example, a sum proportionate to the purchase price was given to the treasurer for entertainment laid on by the neighborhood.[118] There were lying-in feasts, birth feasts, baptismal feasts, churching feasts, feasts when infants were swaddled and another when boys were breeched, birthday feasts and saints' days feasts (not necessarily the same), feasts on beginning school and beginning apprenticeship, betrothal feasts, wedding feasts, feasts on setting up house, feasts for departing on long journeys and feasts for homecoming, wedding anniversary feasts and co-option (to a municipal regency or the board of a charitable institution) feasts, feasts on the inauguration of a lottery and the conclusion of its draw, feasts on the return of a grand cargo or the conclusion of a triumphant peace, on the restoration of a church, the installation of a window or organ or organ loft or pulpit and on the setting of a family gravestone in its floor, feasts on recovering from sickness, feasts at funerals and burials and the reading of a testament, even the *jokmaalen,* feasts of inversion when master and mistress would act the part of servants and wait on their own retainers.[119] And for each there would be particular foods: spiced wine and caudle for lying-in, another kind of caudle of sweet wine and cinnamon for birth parties. Although not every father, wearing his quilted paternity bonnet, would have offered his guests the oysters, celery and caviar that the harried husband of the *Ten Diversions* served up,[120] at the very least a special brew of *kraam-bier* (crib-ale) would be on hand to accompany the new arrival. At weddings it was customary to drink a hippocras, usually made from diluted Rhine wine, spiced with cloves and ginger. And at betrothals, new marzipan would be made from almonds soaked the statutory day and night, then pressed, sugared and blended with rosewater before being cooked over a slow fire.[121]

If the greatest pomp was reserved for the funerals of heads of patrician houses who were taken in slow procession, often with torches, to their burial places in the church, with tolling of bells,[122] the most prolonged forms of celebration occurred on the marriage alliance of regent dynasties. These entertainments could continue for days on end and incur enormous expense. When the young pensionary Johan de Witt married into the illustrious Amsterdam clan of the Bickers, his father, from more modest Dordrecht circumstances, had to take out a loan at punishing rates of interest to keep up his end of the affair.[123] The Synod of Dordrecht in 1618 had urged the enactment of sumptuary laws in restraint of extravagant entertainment, but as in so many other matters, the message of the clergy went unheeded by the magistracy. It was not that they were indifferent to the perils incurred by sumptuary extravagance—rather that it was in the nature of their more humanist inclinations to let the culture regulate itself without legislative intervention. Paradoxically, then, town authorities showed themselves much less ready than their Italian counterparts to impose sumptuary restraints on their citizens. But when they did so, it was, like the Venetian laws, invariably in response to some pressing crisis and so took on the quality of penitential propitiation. In 1655, when Dr. Tulp and Burgermeester Bontemantel succeeded in pushing through Amsterdam's law against extravagant wedding feasts, the measure was enacted against a background of an appalling visitation of the plague and a serious trade depression brought on by defeats and blockades in the naval war against England. Even then, the law was less draconian than might have been the case, limiting celebrations to fifty guests and a duration of two days! The number of musicians permitted was limited to six, and the value of gifts brought to the match was not to exceed five percent of the dowry (a provision that seems to have brought more relief to the groom's family than the bride's). Yet it was the same Dr. Tulp, ever watchful against excess, who was the principal guest at a resplendent banquet on January 28, 1672, at a time when the affairs of the Republic were becoming critical. At his house on the Keizersgracht, close to the Westermarkt (and therefore in sight of the Westerkerk), he was toasted in Burgundy on the occasion of his fiftieth year on the council. Verses by Jan Six were read against a centerpiece of crystallized peacock (in Cats's book the symbol of earthly pride and vanity!) with scented tobacco circulating on dishes of the finest Ming blue ware.[124]

Later the same year, after the traumatic events in The Hague and the apparently unstoppable invasion of Louis XIV's armies, the Amsterdam councillors passed their second sumptuary law. It referred to the financial straits in which the city found itself in this time of crisis (when, in fact, a run on the bank was much in the air), and ordered the abolition of all "unnecessary and sumptuous banquets," both those of the magistracy and regents of charity houses as well as those of the guilds and *schutterij*.[125] And this law was itself proclaimed against a chorus of jeremiads from the Amsterdam clergy who blamed the catastrophe that had befallen the Republic on the wanton style of life that had invaded the great cities of Holland. Ironically, violent censure was directed at the murdered pensionary de Witt who, of all people, had led an exemplary (perhaps too exemplary) life.[126] But in the idiom of the ministry there were "Baal worshippers" throughout the halls of government whose filthy obsession with getting and spending had laid the Fatherland low. The festive mode of relieving the anxieties of abundance could not cope with a Jehovah in so evidently wrathful a temper. And while it was more successful than formal Calvinist dogma at providing an outlet for celebration that could be jubilant without being wanton, customary rather than pagan-hedonist, its very imprecision (unlike dogma) could get the celebrants into difficulties. It was a tricky business, after all—even for Dr. Tulp—to draw the line between morally sanctioned customary conviviality and morally reprehensible gluttony. According to the sermons, of course, the faintest smacking of the lips at the prospect of a capon stuffed with Hormuz apricots had led directly to the prostration of Utrecht before Louis XIV. Like the whale, Louis XIV was the (indirect) courier of God's ire, dispatched to smite an errant people hip and thigh. And even those paintings of Jan Steen's which we most associate with the Dutch festive tradition, awash with beer and cacophonous roistering, on closer inspection turn out to carry symbols of warning: the crutch, the clapper and the chastising rod.

As I have argued elsewhere,[127] neither the saturnalia nor the sermon can be said to have prevailed absolutely within Dutch culture. Its very nature was to keep both in play. It would be an exaggeration to represent good Dutch burghers as constantly hagridden as to whether an extra helping of *hutsepot* could jeopardize the security of the state. Even William III, for all his reputation as a sobersides, was in fact a devotee of The Hague's *kermis*, and was happiest in 1690 when lavishly feasted as Stadholder-King on his return to the Netherlands. What evidently did *not* happen in the Republic was a "triumph of Lent,"[128] in which the militants of the Calvinist Church succeeded in eradicating from popular practice the festive customs they deemed incompatible with God's law. Nor, as has been said of a similar process in eighteenth-century Britain, was capitalist rationality an accomplice in this aim. Indeed as the buoyant economy generated more goods and higher incomes, so the need for morally innocuous ways of digesting them became, if anything, more imperious. Of course the huge weight of excise and indirect taxes was one very convenient way to pay tribute to the common good, but it was less consoling than acts of conspicuous waste committed in the name of the festive tradition. So that, at the end of the seventeenth century, as at the beginning, come the days of *Vastenavond,* when the corpulent jester of the feast, armed with his strings of sausages and trenchers of pies and waffles, sallied forth on his barrel to do battle with *mager* Lent. And who could tell if spit or griddle would prevail?

iii STYGIAN FIRES AND AQUA FORTIS

"Holland," wrote Claude Saumaise, "is a country where the demon gold is seated on a throne of cheese, and crowned with tobacco."[129] Like many other immigrants to the Republic of Letters, "Salmasius" had an ambivalent attitude towards the abundance of his adopted country that sat uncomfortably with his articles of faith. But though this characteristic habit of biting the hand that fed him was all too common, Saumaise's comment did identify an important feature of Dutch culture: its propensity to assume forms that might avert the calamity of uncontrolled luxury. For it was the peculiar condition of the Netherlands to generate a wealth that, given its self-image as the New Israel, had potentially dangerous implications. The fortunes with which it was so lavishly endowed had not come to it as the result of any concerted design to engross the fruits of the earth, but rather as the indirect consequence of prosecuting a war against the Antichrist. The one axiom on which Calvinist clergy and humanist magistracy might agree was that prosperity would remain intact only so long as the divine precepts were obeyed—though naturally they differed on the definition of infractions and the authority for their jursidiction. They also agreed that the same bounty that was indispensable for the security of the Republic could, if set free from its moorings in moral regulation, be the nation's undoing.

This quandary was not the exclusive burden of the Dutch. In varying forms, it was a self-inflicted dilemma encountered in all nascent capitalisms for which, it should by now be apparent, theology—Calvinist or Catholic—offered little relief. In the Dutch Republic, the disproportion between the magnitude of its wealth and the limits of its demographic and territorial resources provoked sharp swings of temper from euphoria to anxiety. Its telling questions—

How to be strong yet pure? How to be rich yet humble?—were by definition insoluble. But it was the job of a conscientious magistracy to provide some sort of moral *modus vivendi* with materialism. And they, as well as other custodians of the national culture, did just that in richly ingenious ways. Commodities that brought fortune, like the carcass of the whale, could be made to intimate an offsetting misfortune. Its bulky substance could even evoke the insubstantiality of worldly prosperity through scriptural and folklore associations as well as the torments of sin and redemptive penance. The food on which humanist morality might choke could be digested into a repertoire of ethical connotations, visual and poetic. It could work for, rather than against, the regulations of a dietary regimen in which moderation was the norm and superfluity and meagerness were both frowned on. Or it could be consumed in festive rejoicing according to the rites and customs that exonerated it from suspicions of wanton self-indulgence. And that was made easier by the fact that some foods—wine and bread, for example—had long been imbued with sacred associations. Other foods were, on the face of it, value free. Even for the most excitable preacher, there was nothing *inherently* sinful about a waffle.

The same could not be said of substances as dangerous and contaminating as alcohol and tobacco. Where the consumption of food could be made to work for moral, rather than amoral, ends, in the case of intoxicants abstinence seemed to be the only alternative to transgression. If, indeed, that was the sole path to salvation, the Dutch were in deep trouble, for their collective addiction to both smoking and drinking—at all levels of society—was notorious. Hardened topers and puffers from abroad buckled at the knees in taverns where the quantities of cheap *kuyte* beer and brandywine being sunk was masked only by the dense fog of pipe fumes that settled on everyone and everything. The smell of the Dutch Republic was the smell of tobacco. In the middle of the eighteenth century the French traveler Grosley counted three hundred smokers in a single modest inn at Rotterdam and complained that the Dutch were so indifferent to the poisoning of confined spaces that the fumes from traveling barges drove foxes from their lairs as they passed.[130] Foreigners were especially repelled by the spectacle of women blowing smoke from between tar-blackened teeth. And as quids of chewing tobacco and snuff joined pipe shag in the early 1700s, the sight of slopping cuspidors indoors and out added a further element of squalor to the nicotine-stained landscape.[131] Diderot wittily combined the Dutch predilection for both fire and spirits by calling them "living alembics, distilling, in effect, themselves."[132] And the standard caricature Dutchman in English prints is barrel-shaped in girth, sozzled with gin and often seen lighting the next pipe with the smoldering embers of the last.

The Dutch reputation for hard drinking went back at least to the early sixteenth century, when Lodovico Giucciardini noted it as "abnormal." Like many later commentators he attributed it to the need to ward off the chilly vapors that rose from the bogs and ditches among which the Dutch dwelled. The English traveler Fynes Moryson also supposed that since "these United parts are seated in the wildest of seas and waters and use excesse of drinking, so they commonly are of flegmatick complections and beget more females than males."[133] Thomas Coryate also linked sluggishness to the alehouse, noting that "whensoever one drinketh to another he shaketh his fellow by the hand and whensoever the men of the country come into an inn to drink they use to take a tin tankard of beer in their hands and sit by it an hour together, yea sometimes two whole hours." It was even possible, visitors noted, to spend time inside a huge, emptied cask, "The Great Tun of Amsterdam, that could seat thirty-two comfortably for a whole day's amiable sozzling."[134] Curiously, most of the seventeenth-century reports of Dutch drinking habits stress their sudden hilarity and raucous uproar rather than torpor or phlegm (though the two tempers are not, of course, alcoholically inconsistent). In 1634 William Brereton was present at the *schutters'* annual feast at Dordrecht and grumbled, "I do not believe scarce a sober man to be found amongst them, nor was it safe for a sober man to trust himself amongst them, they did shout so and sing, roar, skip and leap."[135] Robert Bargrave, in 1655, had an even more alarming experience in the same town, when the room in "the burghers' common tavern" in which he was witnessing a celebration began to revolve. This was less the effect of the brandywine than an extraordinary mechanical device "in which if the wine the goodfellows drink were not enough to turn their brains, there is a moving form which turns a whole Company round the banqueting table as they sit at it."[136] It was a standard refrain in the litany of Hollandophobia that the "Dutch courage" needed to stiffen their spirits in war at sea rendered them riotous, brawling and incontinent on land. At Oxford in 1675 it was reported with barely disguised disdain that the great admiral (Cornelis) Tromp, the scourge of the ocean and terror of the taverns, had succumbed so completely to Oxford porter that he had to be trundled back to his lodgings in a wheelbarrow.[137]

However vividly observed, these are not much more than passing impressions, difficult for the historian either to corroborate or to falsify. Their very unanimity of tone proclaims them as a collective cliché in which the "amphibious" nature of the Dutch—their boggy, soggy moistness and phlegmatic humor—derives from a wet within/wet without complementarity. Hostile caricatures sometimes showed them as frogs washed away in a flood of gin, while one of Cruikshank's nastiest productions in 1794 set buxom Dutch *juffers* in line, stretching out to sea like a human breakwater, downing torrents of gin, which in their turn become flushed away into the tide.

Fragments of data do seem to confirm the visitors' impressions. It is known, for example, that in 1613 there were as many as 518 alehouses in Amsterdam alone, or one for every two hundred inhabitants. And in Haarlem, at the very end of the sixteenth century, the prodigious quantity of 12,508 liters of beer were consumed every day, a third in pubs and two thirds at home.[138] But quantifying consumption is not the point, even were it possible to use dependable sources. The Dutch were not only consumers, they were also traders and producers — it might not be too much to say specialists — in exactly those commodities that their moralists most fervently deplored. For there is no doubt at all that alcoholic drinks and, to a lesser extent, tobacco contributed a great deal to the prospering of the Dutch economy. Any attempt to appease the preachers by restricting the production, transport or use of those commodities other than by taxation was likely to run into stiff resistance. Even efforts to curb Sunday drinking could provoke local wrath. Brereton reported a Mr. Peters, the English minister at Rotterdam, recalling that

> a religious burgomaster two years ago endeavored to reform the profanation of
> the Sabbath and imposed and collected by distress or otherwise from every man
> trading or working on this day. At length the brewers (whereof there are
> abundance in this town) made a head, came into the State House [i.e.,

95. Isaac Cruikshank, *Opening the Sluices or Holland's Last Shift.* British Museum Collection of Political Prints and Satires

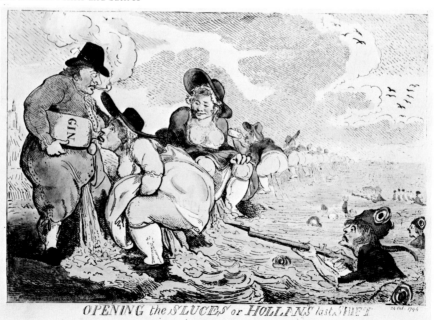

OPENING the SLUICES or HOLLANS last SHIFT

stadhuis—town hall] and in a mutinous manner told the burgomaster that they would not be subject unto his new laws and hereby quashed what was formerly effected, and the hoped for reformation came to nothing.[139]

This was a tale repeated—and not just over drink—throughout the Republic. Where municipal authorities did impose restrictions on drinking hours, they did so for prudential rather than prohibitionist motives. Amsterdam passed thirty such ordinances and bylaws in the first half of the seventeenth century, but they were confined to ensuring that publicans traded only with an official license, the proceeds of which went to the upkeep of the city Spinhuis, the female house of correction. It was typical of the somewhat circular morality by which the magistrates kept their house in order that the proceeds of the drink trade went towards the reform of those who had, as it were, collapsed in its service. Similarly, when Amsterdam passed more draconian measures prohibiting tavernkeeping altogether in certain areas, it was done in the aftermath of some act of public mayhem. In December 1629, for example, houses in the *dolle* Bagijnensteeg and in the *slopjes* and *steegjes* (alleys and lanes) between the Oude Kerk and the St. Jans Kerk, and in Sint Annastraat and the Oude Zijds Kerkhof—none of them very salubrious parts of the city—were forbidden to operate as taverns on pain of a three-guilder fine for every day of a violation. The reason given was that "in the aforesaid pubs [*knijpen en kroegen*] great acts of insolence and wantonness have taken place by those who frequent these places, to the great harm of our commonwealth and our good city."[140]

Respectable brewing was another matter entirely, and a much too powerful interest to alienate in the name of godly rule. In Haarlem during the siege of the 1570s there were already 50 operating breweries, and by 1620 twice that number. In 1590 there were 180 breweries in Amsterdam alone. Delft remained the premium producer of high-quality ale, at least according to its own estimation, though competition was keen to dethrone it. Weesp, Hoorn and Gouda beers all enjoyed their partisans, though under Frederick Henry the allegedly superior quality of Rotterdam water boosted the claims of its local ale to supplant Delftse as the best of Holland.[141] Given the universality of ale as breakfast beverage as well as tavern drink, and the eulogies heaped on it by virtually all medical authorities and popular writers, much was at stake in this local rivalry. It was, in effect, a feature of the characteristic competitions between Dutch towns that also included conscious attempts to display the most elegant patrician houses, most bosky outskirts, most glady canals, most grandiloquent town hall, tallest church spire, most resonant carillon—all dutifully recorded and praised by the local historian. Within this circuit of rivals, the swift rise to fame and fortune of the Brabant ales, centered on Breda, was something of an intrusion, and there were complaints that it owed its edge to unfair advantages: access to relatively cheap semirural labor, the proximity of Flemish hops and freedom in the "Generality Lands" from onerous urban excises. But the relatively modest scale of many of the individual producers deflected this peevishness somewhat. At any rate, nothing was done to check the growth of Brabant ales, other than to impose additional duties when they tried to penetrate Holland markets.

Brewing was a staple of the Dutch economy and enjoyed as such a moral legitimacy denied to distilling. The greater part of the *eaux de vie* and brandies consumed by the Dutch in the seventeenth century were probably imported from France, but there was some distilling of grain and fruit spirits principally for cheap tavern consumption and on shipboard. Gin, concentrated on the port town of Schiedam, did not begin its conquest until late in the seventeenth century, there being just 12 mills there in 1650 but 120 by 1775.[142] Distilleries were looked on by local authorities as dubious operations but, from excise taxes on peat, grain and consumption, were too valuable to suppress. On one occasion in 1637, the peat haulers' guild went so far as to impose a fine of six weeks' wages on any member caught delivering peat to taverns or distilleries where the liquors were made, but there is no indication that even this stringent measure had any effect.

If distilling was a more marginal industry, the wine-carrying trade was central to the fortunes of the Dutch entrepôt economy. Holland and Zeeland were at the hub of an extensive commercial network connecting producers with consumers from Cyprus to Peru. The Dutch shipped Bordeaux to Germany and Sweden, Rhine wines to Russia in the east and Spain in the west, sweet Malaga from Spain and Marsala from southern Italy to England, Burgundies to the Baltic. The several parts of the staple were so intricately interconnected and so ramified into ancillary service industries, that an attack on any part of it (unthinkable though that was), for moral purposes, would have sunk a heavily laden raft of commercial and financial interests ranging from modest artisans to international entrepreneurs. Among those affected would have been coastal and intercity skippers, coopers and stone flask cutters, port cellarers and bottlers, cork importers who brought the bark along with their wine cargoes from the Douro and, not least, the ubiquitous wine merchants who sometimes doubled as apothecaries or tavernkeepers or both.

While not quite so extensively spread through the commercial economy, tobacco was also too important, especially to local economic interests, to permit the enforcement of church-directed suppression.[143] Initially the Dutch drying, cutting and spinning industries centered on Amsterdam, from where tobacco was exported eastward to Russia and the Baltic, using primarily Maryland and Virginia leaf. But by the late 1630s, a striking initiative had taken place that transformed the Dutch role in the international market. A domestic crop began to be raised in the fields around Amersfoort in eastern Utrecht and, shortly after, in the neighboring region of the Veluwe in Gelderland, principally close to the towns of Wageningen, Barneveld, Elburg and Nijkerk. The quality of Dutch leaf was coarser than its Virginia counterpart, but it was ideal for mixing inside an American "wrapper" or for cutting together with the superior material for a much cheaper finished blend. The staple was an immense success, and the 50 or so growers of 1636 at Amersfoort had expanded to not fewer than 120 by 1670.[144] By 1675, around 5–6 million pounds of tobacco were being exported annually, and this figure may even have doubled again by the end of the century. In 1706 two English merchants at Riga, Samuel Shepheard and John Martin, complained that "the tobacco trade is good for nothing and quite ruin'd and that chiefly on account of the vast quantities of Dutch growth imported here and which by the cheapness of it finds consumption."[145] Not surprisingly, then, so far from hampering it with fiscal restrictions, local and provincial authorities relieved it from some excises, ignoring (as public bodies have always tended to do for tobacco growers) any kind of moral implication. In 1636, for example, the States of Utrecht in effect subsidized the growers by abolishing all duties on leaf tobacco destined for export to the spinneries of Holland, and in the next decade the Gelderland *kwartier* authorities did likewise. Indeed one of the most prominent Amersfoort growers, Brant van Slichtenhorst, was both deputy sheriff of the city *and* deacon of the Reformed Church — and a tax officer to boot.[146]

There were other important economic interests engaged in the tobacco industry. The West India Company — associated with the more zealously Calvinist wing of the mercantile community in Holland and Zeeland — on the whole did not see Dutch domestic tobacco as a threat. Rather, it complemented their own imports from Brazil, Venezuela and Virginia/Maryland and expanded their market range. Van Slichtenhorst had important contacts within the Amsterdam chamber of the company and he did business with the Sephardic Jewish families like the Diases and the Fonsecas who dominated the earliest phase of the processing industry from their base on the St. Anthonie Breestraat.[147] By the 1670s, the scale of production in Amsterdam had massively expanded. Information elicited from the Rotterdam firm of van Gowder and Cock for anxious English competitors about the progress of the Amsterdam spinners disclosed that there were between thirty and forty concerns employing a workforce of around four thousand, with the largest retaining as many as two hundred workers — a huge payroll for the seventeenth century. Altogether the Amsterdam tobacco works were thought to have turned over in the region of 12 million pounds by the end of the century, and the most celebrated of the firms, Scholten, was exporting to Scandinavia, Russia, Poland, Prussia and even the Turkish Levant.

To complete the picture there were also the pipe makers in Amsterdam, Haarlem, Gorinchem, Alphen, Groningen and Schoonhoven—but concentrated especially in and around Gouda. Gouda alone employed some fifteen to sixteen thousand workers, or perhaps half of its labor force, in this single industry, and while some of the producing units were small, they were tied together in entrepreneurial syndicates (often family-based) like those of Jan Jacobsz. Verka, and of Burgomaster Jan Govert Cinq, whose long-stemmed clays bore the trademark of a 5 on the base of the bowl.

There were, then, ample economic reasons why public officials in the Republic should have turned a blind eye to the production, carrying and sale of commodities which, as good Calvinists, they were supposed to deplore, if not actually extirpate. When they did interfere with production or consumption, they did so for reasons—fiscal or judicial—that stemmed from the charges of their lay stewardship. This is not to say that they were materialist cynics. But for all its insistence that alcohol and tobacco were the Devil's food, the church had failed to stigmatize their use as moral uncleanness. Indeed, what vexed the predikants was the general evidence that, for the most part, smoking and drinking—with humanist moderation to be sure—were thought of as socially innocuous. In some circumstances (Dr. Tulp's celebratory tobacco, or the silver-inlaid pipes that Govert Cinq made for weddings) their use could actually confer honor and status. At the feast of the Zwannenbroeders in den Bosch, as well as in the wigwams of the Iroquois, there were, literally, pipes of peace. At any rate what foreigners took for besotted addiction passed in the Netherlands as homely custom. Even today the most resplendent cigar shops in the world, redolent of sandalwood and cedar and the fragrant teas that are sold alongside, are to be discovered off the Kneuterdijk in The Hague and on the Rokin in Amsterdam, treated with the due veneration that their august aura commands. When a young Dutchman climbs off his bicycle to roll a cigarette from *half zware shag* he does so with a a studied care that belies the fact of impending incineration. Nothing could be further from vending-machine remoteness than the compulsive scrutiny of aroma and texture. The Dutch may not have been the first users of tobacco in Europe, but they were its first connoisseurs. Not only pipes, but tobacco boxes were made from sumptuous materials like ivory or nutwood and inscribed with favorite mottoes or devices of the owners' choosing.[148] Given this integration of tobacco into the "home life" of the country, it should not be surprising to find them inventing a subgenre of still life painting devoted to "tobacco pieces." And given this evident sensuous pleasure in the stuff, it seems highly unlikely that on *every* occasion a pipe was incorporated into a painting, the beholder was meant to be solemnly reminded of the Psalmist's axiom that "my days are consumed like smoke."[149]

As they did with Ming china and Turkish carpets, the Dutch domesticated the exoticism of tobacco. Perhaps it would be better to suggest that exoticism was at any rate no bar to its absorption into the texture of everyday life. Indeed, tobacco processors were keen to promote variety even further by saturating and mixing the cut and spun leaf with a miscellany of spices and flavorings that were universally known as sauces. These included citron, aniseed, thyme, saffron, lavender, dill, nutmeg, coriander, vinegar, brown beer, mace, fennel, potash, chamomile, prunes and rosemary. The most competitive of the tobacconists would go to almost as great lengths in their inventiveness and secrecy in guarding their patented blend as jealous cross-pollinators of a hybrid bloom. The notion of a "sauce-flavored" tobacco and the efforts expended to make it agreeable to the palate as well as the nostrils suggests that for the earlier part of the seventeenth century it was unclear whether tobacco was a drug, a food or a poison. Chewing tobacco (*pruimtabak*) was not generally available until after the 1660s, and snuff even later. But even as a smoking mixture, the weed could be invested with properties that, if not exactly nutritious, could be hailed as healthful rather than harmful. A succession of humanist doctors and botanists lauded tobacco for its miraculous

96. From Johan van Beverwijck, *Schat der Gesontheyt* (Dordrecht, 1635)

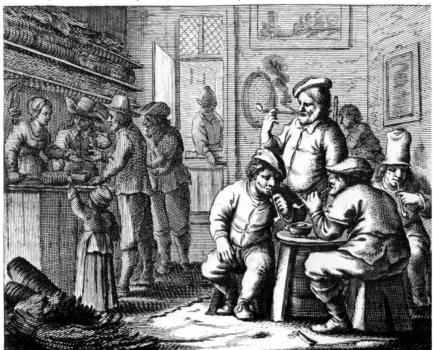

qualities as a panacea, capable of soothing toothaches as well as curing worms. When taken in sap-potion form, along with some sugar, one insisted, it would banish ague and prolong life. In the 1680s Stephanus Blankaart, the Amsterdam physician, and Cornelis Bontekoe both praised its sedative effects and urged its use against, *inter alia,* scurvy, gout, stones and chronic insomnia![150] Van Beintema van Peyma, the Frisian medical writer, went so far as to recommend it for specifically female conditions, not least labor pains. Ysbrand van Diemerbroek, the Nijmegen doctor (his credibility somewhat impaired by being a brother-in-law of Burgomaster Cinq), shared the view that tobacco smoke was an effective prophylactic against the plague and maintained that he had survived the epidemic of 1635–36 by keeping a pipe in his mouth for hours on end, smoking two or three after breakfast, another three after the noon meal and always in the presence of infected cadavers.[151] There was a body of learned humanist tracts, the most notable being that of Petrus Scriverius, translated into Dutch by Samuel Ampzing, that warned against the addictive properties of *Nicotiana tabacum.*[152] But more often the adversaries of the weed, like Constantijn Huygens and Roemer Visscher, simply added it to the list of idle fashions that any devotee of the temperate life should abhor. Visscher's own dig at the habit in *Sinnepoppen* was typical of the relatively gentle tone taken by such attacks and stressed its faddishness rather than anything more sinister as a reason to beware. He even conceded, at the same time, that tobacco "might be good and medicinal for the curing of sicknesses" but added that only a craze for novelty, of the kind that had men eating wooden parrots for bread, could possibly make one suppose it tasted good.[153] Jacob Cats, whom one might expect to have taken a stronger line, also used gentle humor rather than all-out castigation against the vice. His *toebakblaezer* confesses abjectly that "my kitchen is my pipe; my pouch a well-stocked larder/smoking my drink, what need I then of wine?"[154] And he was not the only writer to imply that tobacco could be a desirable alternative to alcohol, though authorities disagreed on whether preference should be given for its stimulant or its relaxant effects. And there must have been the occasional devotee even within the Reformed ministry itself, since the Synod of Schiedam in 1631 felt it necessary to deliver a mild reprimand to its predecessor, sitting at Schoonhoven, for ordering hundreds of guilders' worth of tobacco along with other victuals.[155] And while long-stemmed clay pipes in Holland were certainly not known as churchwardens, the spectacle of a deacon or a sexton puffing away between services was not at all uncommon. Van Slichtenhorst, the first great tobacco magnate at Amersfoort, was himself a church deacon.

It would be misleading, though, to give the impression that smoking became socially acceptable through the route of a commended drug. As Roessingh, the outstanding historian of the domestic crop, argues, by 1620,

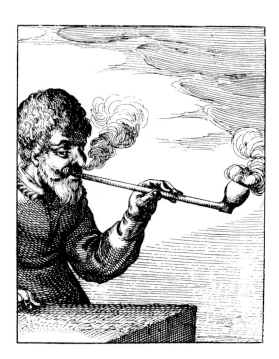

97. Emblem from Roemer
Visscher, *Sinnepoppen* (Amsterdam,
1614)

at the latest, it was already part of social habit for pleasure, rather than as prophylactic or remedy.[156] And even by the time that Cornelis Bontekoe wrote his careful description in 1686, there were some who still believed its use would lead to madness, impotence and stultification. But by and large it had become recognizably ingrained into the pattern of domestic habits in Holland. Indulged in moderation, it was deemed inoffensive by all except the militant clergy and institutional custodians, like the regents of poorhouses in Amsterdam who forbade the practice within their precincts. Heavy fetters penalized violators, but whether inmates were prohibited tobacco as a sin or as a pleasure is open to question. The same patrician regents who frowned on its use by their wards enjoyed their pipes within their own meeting rooms. There were exemplars of the national spirit like the Stadholder Maurice who suppressed the habit in his army or Piet Heyn who did the same in his fleet. But the association between clean living and patriotic energy was offset by the identification of national heroes with homely habits. A tobacco vendor's sign in Amsterdam invoked Admiral Tromp's famous refusal to concede naval superiority with his own claim to have routed the competition.[157] A commonplace observation at home and abroad was that "a Hollander without a pipe is a national impossibility, akin to a town without a house, a stage without actors, a spring without flowers. If a Hollander should be bereft of his pipe of tobacco he could not blissfully enter heaven."[158]

It was precisely this demotion of a sin to a peccadillo that so irked the church, and in the same way it deplored the common tendency to regard alcoholic drink as if it were merely another kind of food. Indeed, that was the way it was treated in cookbooks and household manuals like the *Verstandige Huyshouder,* where detailed recipes for home brewing using fruit and herbs along with hops and barley, in eighteen variations, accompanied advice on how best to preserve melon and walnuts or to concoct a toothsome honey mead.[159] Before coffee was cheap enough for the common people to afford, a morning *boerenkoffie* would consist of a mixture of warmed beer, nutmeg and sugar. And throughout the seventeenth and eighteenth centuries, farmers in Friesland, north Holland and Groningen would be sent off to work on a crack-sharp frosty December morning having breakfasted on a *susenol* of beer and eggs, or, for the strong of gut, a *wip* made from eggs, sugar, warm beer and stiff shots of brandywine. Casual drinking punctuated the daily round of work in such a regular and commonplace way that it was especially hard for the church to intervene. When deals between farmers and buyers were made outside the market (and sometimes in it) they were generally sealed over a tankard of ale in the inn. In parts of north Holland when a traveling merchant came to buy wool, he was made to drink without stopping from a quart flagon into which a coin had been thrown. If he managed to empty the pot and catch the coin in his teeth, the sale was good and he got to keep the coin. If not, he presumably had the coin anyway, though in a place where it could do him no good.[160] Some town councils passed bylaws invalidating commercial contracts made in taverns unless they were subsequently certified by the parties in front of a notary. But at this humble social level, between small town or village custom, which decreed that no sales could be valid without the consecrating pot of beer, and the formal law, which decreed the opposite, there was no telling which would necessarily prevail. Where the farmer was the seller it was custom that had the upper hand. Toasts, it has already been suggested, were important rites of social familiarity and could range in elaborateness from an initial morning greeting in an alehouse to a full-dress hundred-stanza alcoholic epithalamion. The *Huweliksluiter* of 1685, which was, among many other things an anthology of bonhomous cordiality, put it with characteristic breeziness, "the first little glass is for health, the second for taste, the third for a nightcap—and the rest can only be for pleasure." The occasional nip was (and is) known as an *een borrel,* a term of innocent conviviality made even more innocuous by adding the diminutive suffix *je.* The harmless and cheering little dram glass thus held the *vaderlantje* (gin), a sobriquet that thus managed to be both endearing and patriotic. Indeed on some occasions it would have been positively unpatriotic not to have joined in the general carousing. Jan Steen's "Merry Company" in the Rijksmuseum is celebrating the birthday of Prince William III with the toast (inscribed on the paper in the foreground):

Op de gesontheyt van het nassaus basie
in de eene hant het rapier in de andere hant het glaesie

To the health of Nassau's little boss
In the one hand the sword, in the other the glass

And since the public, as well as private, pretexts for *een borreltje* were so common and so frequent, it was very difficult for the church in its arraignments to apply the distinction between mere tipsiness (*beschonkenheid*) and dead drunkenness (*dronkenschap*) with any consistency. "Men drink at the slightest excuse," complained Pastor Wittewrongel, "at the sound of a bell or the turning of a mill . . . the Devil himself has turned brewer."[161]

Under certain circumstances, then, smoking and drinking, so far from being signposts on the way to self-destruction, had actually become familiar characteristics of the national culture—mutually shared manners by which the Dutch recognized their common identity. This was bad news for the custodians of the patriotic scripture, who saw in this blasphemous inversion the work of a diabolical conspiracy. Demons were at large, working through the snares of addiction, and it is not too much to say that the predikants of the church believed themselves to be engaged in a Manichaean contest with the minions

98. Jan Steen, *Prinsjesdag*, 1660. Rijksmuseum, Amsterdam

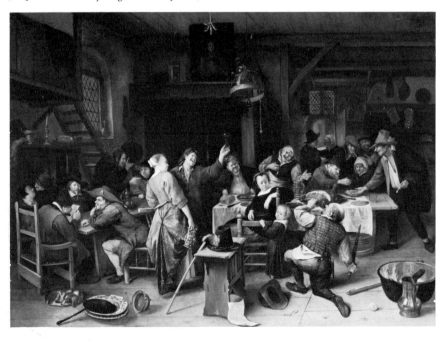

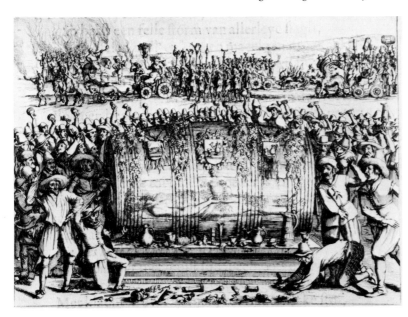

99. *Bacchus Wonder-wercken* (Amsterdam, 1628). Koninklijke Bibliotheek, The Hague

of Satan for the possession of Dutch souls. In one print, the Devil himself lies recumbent within an immense tun that becomes literally an object of besotted idolatry. The unorthodox were particularly suspect of abetting this foul play. It was, after all, the Marrano Jews (experts in subterfuge) on the Breestraat who dominated the spinning and cutting of tobacco and who had beguiled Christian women and children into working for their nefarious trade. Catholics, it was well known, were notorious imbibers, capable of shrugging off their guilt with their hangover in the confessional. As for the odious Remonstrants, their service to the Great Goat was indicated by their compulsive worship of the pipe. Fire, after all, was the Devil's element. Voetius was so exercised by students' enslavement to the vice that in his inaugural lecture at Utrecht in 1634, he spoke of hellish vapors rising like so many Sodoms and Gomorrahs in the sky.[162] And if smoking represented the firing of herbs (*kruyd*), spirits were *a fortiori* even more diabolical, being the burning of two sacred foods: grain and wine. The predikants could see all this with prophetic clarity. What else but a satanic plot could be responsible for the peat cutters consuming the polders with their inexhaustible demand for fuel for the distilleries and breweries? If their excavations went unchecked, a great subaqueous chasm would one day open beneath the reclaimed land and swallow all the unrighteous, who had, literally, undermined the foundations of the commonwealth.

This Manichaean view of the opposition of tavern and church, of the infernal and the celestial, seemed to be borne out by the location of so many alehouses directly opposite houses of worship. Samuel Ampzing, the predikant-chronicler of Haarlem, complained that "Satan had set his cabins in the place where God's work and His holy word were established."[163] And even their choice of names seemed ominous—the Beelzebub at Dordrecht, a notorious haunt of soaks and roughnecks; the Duivel aan de Ketting (the Devil on a Chain) in Amsterdam, where the Undertakers' Riots in 1696 were said to have been "stoked up" by copious libations of Dutch gin and brandywine.[164] Sites cherished by the Calvinist Church, like the old cloister of the Carthusians in Amsterdam, where the first sermon for reform had been preached in 1566, had, a century later, turned into a large inn called De Vink (The Finch), and the street on which it stood De Vinkstraat. Sunday toping was the most abhorrent, and almost too horrid to contemplate was the spectacle of the inebriate defiling the sanctity of the church itself. One Jan Simonszoon was brought before the Amsterdam church council for being so drunk at evensong that "he could not stand and fell upon his face."[165] A certain Jan Barents was so incorrigible in his vice that he was excluded altogether from the Lord's Supper until decently reformed. Worse was the poor example set by public officers giving themselves up to shameless debauchery and drunkenness. Church council records are full of cases of sheriffs, constables and bailiffs (a notorious rout) falling by the wayside. While it was in fact a cherished part of their niggardly stipend, schoolmasters were often reproved for letting tankards of ale stand on their desks in class—and even vergers, undertakers and beadles were reported intoxicated at work. There were, occasionally, bigger, wetter fish caught in the sinners' net. Paulus van Dalem, the captain of one of the Amsterdam militia companies, failed to surrender the keys of the city gate to the burgomaster after the night watch, having fallen into a drunken sleep, and Cornelis Banning, who was one of the three sitting burgomasters, fought a drunken brawl with his patrician rival, Jan Boelens, at a banquet given by the French ambassador.[166] At the very bottom of the sink were predikants who had given themselves over to Bacchus and his *opperheer,* Lucifer. In 1634 Jan Swartenius, the predikant of Erichem, was expelled from his ministry for persistent and abominable acts of drunkenness (as well as brawling in fields, taverns and on the street!).[167] The notoriety of such cases greatly assisted the opponents of Calvinist discipline by disseminating scurrilous rumors that the most zealous of their number were, in fact, secret tipplers, and that the heat of their sermons was in direct proportion to the fire of their favorite peccadillo. There was, for example, much waggish speculation about the color of Jacobus Trigland's nose, a line of folklore similar to the stories that circulated about "drunken William Perkins" in Puritan Cambridge.[168]

None of this means that humanist writers, physicians and magistrates were indiscriminate apologists for Bacchic license. Erasmus, after all, was no soak. They were prepared to defend festive drinking against the prohibitionism of the church when it could be represented as part of the legitimate customs of the Fatherland—commemorative or "immemorial." For all the overkill of its dramatic bravura, Rembrandt's *Claudius Civilis* was painted to a commission to represent the founding oath taken during a ritual feast.[169] But by the same token, smoking and drinking in casual immoderation, so far from binding the community together, could well act as a subversive dissolvent. In voicing these anxieties they were sharing many of the apprehensions of the stricter Calvinists (and there were, of course, devout Calvinists who sat in council chambers and on judicial benches along with more pragmatic colleagues). Where they differed was not only their willingness or reluctance to use the lay arm to punish offenses against sobriety but in their definition of what such offenses were. Calvinists insisted that any and all indulgence in tobacco or alcohol led inevitably down the slippery road to mass ruin; humanists claimed to be able to distinguish through right reason between moderation and excess, feast and debauch. And while Calvinists saw the steady degradation of manners as part of a predestined plan to mortify the sinful and bring the nation to rebirth through atonement, humanists were concerned that the stupefaction of the senses resulted in a dispossession of Christian free will.

Those who had squandered their free will were, by definition, ripe for enslavement, and one way in which moralists linked the corruption of manners to the imperiling of the state was by describing heavy smoking and drinking in terms of betrayal. In the early medical debate on the properties of tobacco, Scriverius and other hostile commentators argued that by inducing deep melancholia the habit rendered men unfit for military service, a view that was presumably shared by that military optimist Prince Maurice. And since it was also alleged that tobacco atrophied the generative function, addicts would be further contributing to weakening the Fatherland by robbing it of future citizens. At a less literal level, the besotted were culpable of frittering away the special opportunity vouchsafed by the Republic's independence of enjoying the blessings of Christian freedom. "Drunkenness is the crime of High Treason against both God and man by the Bereaving of souls of all Good Reason and Sense"—so ran the epigraph to one of the cautionary tales published in the 1690s, and posthumously (though spuriously) attributed to that pillar of republican rectitude, Johan de Witt.[170]

Treason of the senses could take many forms: sexual dalliance, unnatural vice, narcotic stupor, deathlike somnolence or inebriate frenzy. All, however, implied the opposite to the perennial ideal of Renaissance humanism: perpetual vigilance in defense of liberty.

Tobacco had been associated with sexual incontinence virtually since its

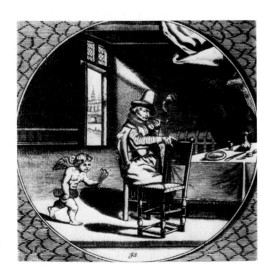

100. Emblem from Jacob Cats, *Alle de
Werken* (Amsterdam, 1659)

discovery in the Americas. The stock visual and textual anthologies of native
barbarism in Brazil and Florida, for example, featured Indians smoking through
rolled leaves, while acts of copulation, cannibalism, public urination and
other sorts of miscellaneous beastliness proceeded routinely in the background.[171]
In less drastic style, tobacco quickly became incorporated into the already
extensive catalogue of aphrodisiac plants. The otherwise conventional Cupid,
in the engraving accompanying Jacob Cats's verse for the listless *toebakblaezer,*
has already exchanged his regulation quiver of darts for a more modish fistful
of pipes. Clay pipes began their long career as phallic symbols (to be displaced
only by the Freudian cigar) early in the seventeenth century. There are even
contemporary instances of symbol and referent joining, as they were to do
many times in the future, in erotically disposed figures carved into stems
made from hardwood or bone.[172] As a source of bawdy innuendo, the pipe
seems to have been inexhaustibly ribald. Jan Steen made the most relentless
use of the device in genre scenes where coarse mirth is prudentially qualified
by faint flushes of embarrassment, perhaps even shame. One of the many
tavern paintings to include a guffawing self-portrait is virtually an anthology of
Dutch smut. No lewd reference to the condition of the girl or to the act
which brought it about has been omitted. Broken egg shells, mussels, an
opened *flapkan* tankard, a gaping bunghole, a scrutinized chamberpot and no
fewer than three pointing handles and stems provide rib-nudging visual
counterparts for the cruel prurience of the cacophonous laughter. There is
eloquent visual communication between the girl and her seducer, a study in
rancid dissipation extraordinary even for Steen, whose second occupation as

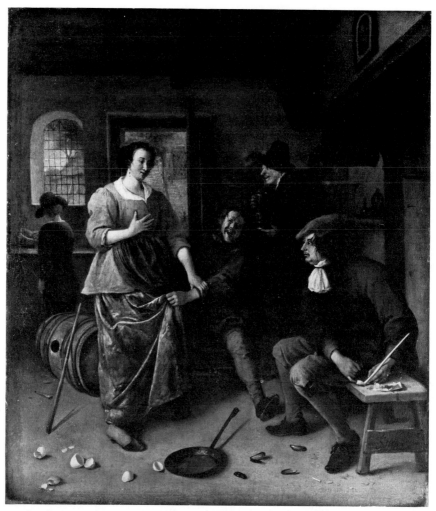

101. Jan Steen, *Tavern Scene.* Courtesy of the Trustees, National Gallery, London

innkeeper enabled him to observe tavern behavior at first hand.[173] Even their body language is telling, reinforcing the distinction between victim and malefactor. While the girl places a hand on the maternal bosom, her wrong-doer pokes a little finger into the bowl of his pipe, reenacting by the obscene gesture the cause of her distress. That same business with finger and pipe bowl recurs elsewhere in a way that suggests general familiarity.[174] In a Hendrik Pot brothel scene of soldiers and whores, the crone procuress uses it to advertise her trade. It was not the only lowlife euphemism for the vagina. The opened *flapkan* was one vulgar colloquialism, and in another bawdy smokers' scene,

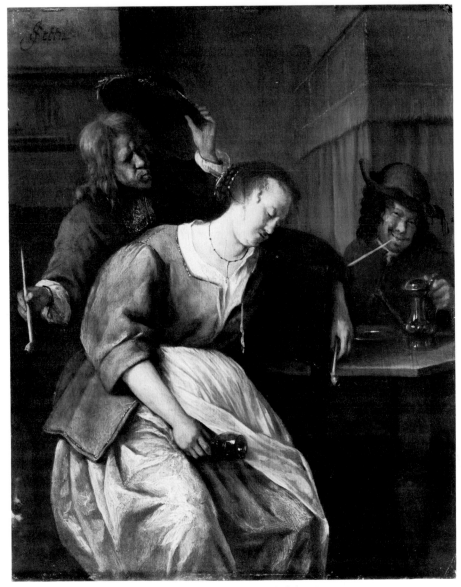

102. Jan Steen, *Man Blowing Smoke at a Woman.* Courtesy of the Trustees, National Gallery, London

where a bed is conspicuously positioned in the background, Steen used a hollow-stemmed *roemer* goblet, strategically positioned, to complement the ubiquitous pipe. From the evidence of other prints, it seems likely that the act of blowing smoke at a woman was already a sexually insulting jest. Even tobacco boxes and pouches could raise a knowing snigger. The wooden boxes in particular were commonly inscribed with an owner's motto, and one inscription included in the perennially popular anthology, *Koddige en Ernstige Opschriften* (Comic and Serious Inscriptions) used two layers of pun but left nothing at all to the imagination. Belonging to a woman, it showed the owner holding a mussel in her hand and declaring

> Deze mossel blijft gedurig gesloten
> Maar de myne die staat altyd open
>
> *These mussels stay always closed*
> *Except for mine which stays always open*[175]

Assuming that the box really belonged to a woman, it seems likely that she herself was a prostitute. At any rate, one of the most celebrated of the Amsterdam brothels of the midcentury went by the name of Marie the Tobacco Vendor.[176] No wonder, then, that smoke could also function as an expression of contempt.

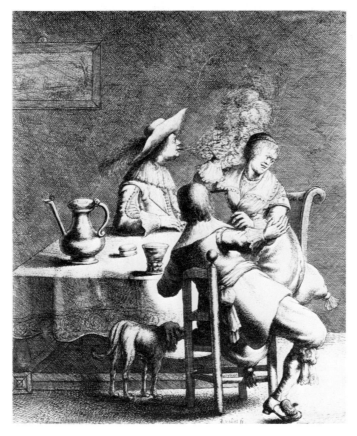

103. Jan van de Vliet, etching, *The Sense of Smell*. Atlas van Stolk, Rotterdam

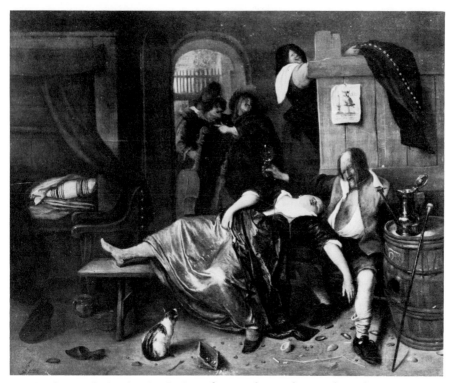

104. Jan Steen, *The Drunken Couple*. City of Amsterdam on loan to the Rijksmuseum

The derision evident on the smirking faces of the smoke blowers in Steen's inn scene suggests their low view of the dormant slattern. In Jan van Vliet's etching, however, it is the smoker rather than the smoked-at who is the object of disgust.

  The drunken sleep became a standard *topos* in Dutch genre painting towards the middle of the seventeenth century. Vermeer's famous *Girl Asleep at a Table* of 1657 was sold in 1696 in Amsterdam bearing the title *A Drunken, Sleeping Maid at a Table* and variations on this theme were painted not only innumerable times by Jan Steen but by Frans van Mieris, Gabriel Metsu, and Nicolas Maes. Art historians have noted that these figures slumped in attitudes of morphic stupor owed something to the classical prototype of sloth or accidie, but Dutch artists set them in the recognizably contemporary milieu of domestic interiors or taverns, and amidst anecdotal detail that reflected peculiarly Dutch preoccupations. The free arm, in many of these pictures, dandles loosely but strategically at the crotch holding the attributes of the sleeper's folly: a pipe or a *roemer*. Where the hand is empty, the debris of their pleasure lies beside them on a table, or haphazardly (and sometimes smashed) on the floor. Far more often the sleeper is observed by the mischievously awake who make him or her the butt of their ridicule and the object of their plunder. In Hendrik Bary's engraving after a van Mieris drawing of 1664 the theme assumes a quasi-emblematic form and bears the title taken from Proverbs 20:1 (*Wijn is een spotter*—Wine is a mocker).[177] Here, the sleeper is doubly observed and doubly ridiculed. The presence of the owl, also presented as an admonishing print in the Steen, recalls two proverbs simultaneously: "drunk as an owl" and "what use are candles and spectacles if the owl will not see?" While the morally myopic owl thus becomes the attribute of the insensate figure, the fool-mocker overturns the pisspot on the reprobate, denoting not merely her blindness to wisdom as the biblical proverb has it, but her degradation.

The London Steen is one of his many studies in dormant negligence and is virtually an *omnium gatherum* of domestic misdemeanor.[178] While the maid (or mother) sleeps beside the overturned flagon of wine and half-eaten bread and fruit, a scene of chaos and dereliction—the unpinning of domestic order—ensues around her. Her own pocket is picked by one child, while three others feed the pie to the kitten, and the eldest girl, perverting the emulation and instruction on which the household regimen should be based, has the parrot

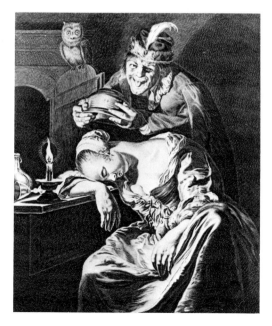

105. Hendrik Bary after Frans van Mieris, *"Wine Is a Mocker."* Fogg Art Museum, Harvard University

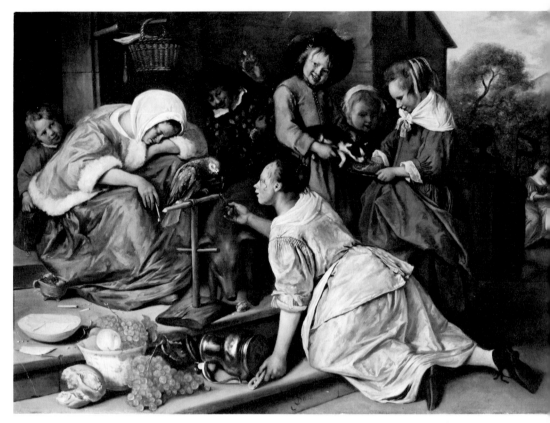

106. Jan Steen, *The Effects of Intemperance*. Courtesy of the Trustees, National Gallery, London

sup from a wineglass, thus imitating vice rather than virtue. While the boy at the rear plucks a rose to signify the vanities of the worldly life and the rupture of innocence, a couple, the woman in *décolletage*, engage in amorous dalliance in the garden bower. Nearby, the instruments of chastisement: the cripple's crutch, the leper's clapper and some birch rods hang in ominous suspension.

These figures are not merely disgraced in their drink-sodden slumber, they are also at risk. The critics of tobacco harped on the dangers of fire, should smokers fall asleep with their pipes still smoldering. Theirs was still, predominantly, a timbered world. But the vulnerability of the sleepers was as much moral as material. The women, in their *décolletage,* are literally exposed, not only to leering lechery, but to the pilfering and sundry other misde-meanors that Steen gleefully chronicles. In their inertia, they become the accomplices of disorder, unfastening the rules of the humanist social code along with their dress. As a helpless observer of these scenes, the beholder is put in the position of a moral spy. Things fall apart; misfortune is in the offing even though skirts are not yet on fire or goblets smashed to smithereens. Impending danger, insensate exploitation is also, of course, richly comic. But in all of these genre scenes, the joke is that of the alarm bell.

At their most urgent, the apostles of vigilance regarded smoking and drinking and the general fecklessness they exemplified as fraught with fatal consequences. Those who began as jolly tipplers, they warned, ended as dead drunks. Grim cautionary tales were used to press the moral home. One of the most sinister of these parables appeared in the collection of moral tales already mentioned as pseudonymously attributed to Johan de Witt and possibly a version of Pieter de la Court's *Zinryken Fabulen* (Meaningful Fables).[179] It was something of a tradition in the Netherlands for the great men of public office (at least from the time of Oldenbarneveld and Grotius) to pass on their wise saws and adages for general consumption. Father Cats, de Witt's predecessor as Grand Pensionary, had been more notable for his moralizing than his statesmanship, but the genre perfectly suited the characteristically Dutch connection between domestic manners and public affairs. The state, the Dutch assumed, was but a dependency of the sovereign town, and that a mere aggregate of households. The "de Witt" fables were probably written by a member of the de la Court dynasty, his allies, but they were at least faithful to the enigmatic personality of the pensionary, being by turns sardonically witty and gravely somber. The tale of the drunkard—that "crime of High Treason against God and man"— was both. He is enslaved to the bottle, and his virtuous wife makes a desperate attempt to reform him. To remind him of the Christian way she has an image of the Savior on the Cross engraved at the bottom of his wineglass. This has the undesired result of doubling his rations, the husband protesting his eagerness at all times to behold the image of the Lord. Logical to a fault, the wife alters the image to that of the Devil. The drinking continues unabated, the husband claiming that he had drained his glass so regularly merely to deny giving the Devil his due. Understandably irked by all this cunning (somewhat at odds with a man in his cups), the reforming wife took drastic action. Lugging the drunk into a shallow, freshly dug grave she placed heavy boards loosely on top. Standing on the planks she then yelled through the cracks that she was a spirit come to haunt the sinner, but should he repent of his wicked ways, she would forgive him and even bring him some nourishment. Unsporting to the end, the husband declined both the deception and the food, "being qualmish," but replied instead that he "would fain drink a glass of wine." That was that. The wife nailed up the boards and left him to rot in his hole in the ground.

This was to take the proverbial characterization of drunkenness as a living grave somewhat too literally. But the lesson of the grim little parable was to point out the *mortal* peril of the sot. Favorite stories from scripture like Jael and Sisera, in which an alert and vigorous woman conquers a dozy and drunken man, reinforced the point, especially when writers like van Beverwijck characterized a hangover as a "nail boring through the temples."

Moralists were concerned with similar states in which right reason and Christian duty were lost on the sinner. And tobacco, it was thought, could induce these dangerously stupefied trances as easily as alcohol. The artists who specialized in rustic or lowlife smoking scenes, like Adriaen Brouwer in the 1620s and 1630s, took great care to record the expressions of deep inhalation or drowsy puffing peculiar to the serious pipe smoker. Some of their figures appear so stunned and insensate with smoke that it has been argued— speculatively—that their tobacco might have been spiked with some sort of opiate or narcotic.[180] The practice of brewers fortifying their products with trance-inducing or hallucinogenic substances like black henbane seed, belladonna or thornapples went back at least to the late Middle Ages and persisted in spite of fierce prohibitions from church and state alike. Tobacco vendors, particularly those catering to a plebeian clientele, merely applied similar formulae to their product though probably with disproportionately narcotic

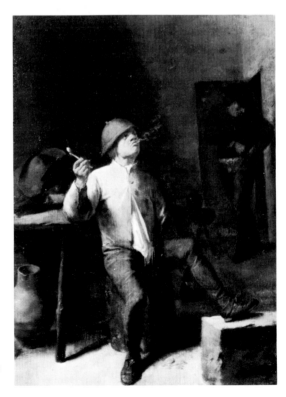

107. Adriaen Brouwer, *The Smoker.*
Rijksmuseum, Amsterdam

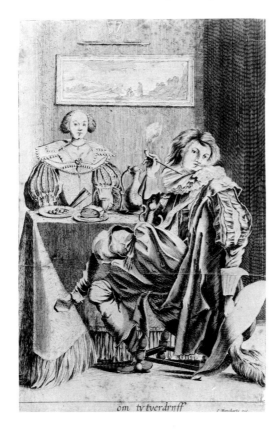

om tytverdriff

108. Cornelis Dansckertsz., *Smoker,*
etching. Bodleian Library, Oxford

effect. Roessingh, the historian of the Dutch tobacco industry, does not rule
out the possibility that some of the merchandise might have been "sauced"
with *Cannabis sativa,* familiar to Dutchmen who had traveled in the Levant and
Indian Orient.[181]

Whatever the mixture, and whether the effect was tranquilizing or stimulating (on which contemporary opinion differed almost as contentiously as
modern), the pictures of dazed pipe puffers were merely a variation on the old
theme of *ijdelheid:* the vain and lethargic passage of the hours. Smoke was
especially suited to these visual tracts on worldly vanity and the ephemerality
of earthly pleasures, since it could evoke the psalmist's reminder that "my
days are consumed like smoke" (Psalms 102:3) or Sartorius's version of the old
Dutch saying *"Des menschen leven gaat als een rook voorbij"* ("Man's life passes
even as smoke").[182] In appropriately delicate emphasis an Abraham Diepraam
drawing has a calendar tacked to the wall behind the smoker. And the legend
at the foot of an engraving by Danckertsz — *om tytverdtrijff* — means "the dissipation (or waste) of time." The futility of other worldly vanities is implied by

the extravagance of the dress and by the presence of food and drink. It may be that the inverted crucifix, hanging from a string of pearls (which in their pristine state connoted chastity) may comment on the scene, and the pastoral landscape (above which rests a Berkmeyer goblet) may represent the fateful moment at which Lot's wife turned for a last glimpse of the scene of her earthly pleasures.

Pipes were an obvious addition to the standard ensemble of didactic objects gathered by *vanitas* still life artists like Harmen Steenwyck. Together with *memento mori* like skulls, emblems of vain folly like shells, and the self-explanatory sand-timers, watches and guttering or spent candles, they signified the ephemerality as well as the futility of the material life.[183] Often they were painted in the somber brown and gray tones favored by the Haarlem monochromatists (though Steenwyck worked most of his life in Calvinist Leiden), and given a murky ground on which the illumination of the spirit could fall. In a kindred sense, pipes contributed to another important genre in the early history of Dutch culture. "Merry company" scenes illustrating the follies of fashion and the sensuous life had been in vogue throughout the High Renaissance, but between 1590 and 1620 the Haarlem mannerists gave them a particularly north Netherlandish expression. Willem Buytewech in particular painted at least five such scenes (out of only nine paintings attributed to him) between 1615 and 1626.[184] Two of these, including the most affecting and enigmatic Rotterdam merry company, included figures with pipes. As a subject of graphic art, "smoking companies" as we might call them, persisted far longer, often as a curious hybrid between the more courtly style of Buytewech and the grosser tavern genres of Dirk Hals. They might even be said to have contributed to the founding of "conversation pieces" and were probably the source for Hogarth's *Midnight Modern Conversation* of 1734.[185] The coarser style of "merry companies" was set in an inn rather than an arbor and was commonly used to illustrate attacks on extravagant costume, gluttony and other worldly vices. In 1628 a typical specimen of the genre, *Bacchus's Wonder-Wercken,* that promised hellfire for those fallen into bad habits, included an engraving by Gillis van Scheyndel illustrating all too graphically the filthy evils of tobacco. Fashionably attired figures fritter away their time in wreaths of smoke against the background of a heraldic device of crossed pipes and a picture of tobacco casks. While victims of the habit make beasts of themselves in the foreground, the whole company is led on in its deluded pleasure by the pipe-smoking ape, the incarnation of folly, lust and sensual gratification.[186] Almost a century later, in 1720, one of the many graphic satires on the swindle of the Mississippi Company developed the theme of "airy" fruitlessness even further. The "bubble" involved the fraudulent sale of land in the southern part of the American colonies, ostensibly for the cultivation of tobacco. So that it was a perfect opportunity for satirists to show pictures of Indians smoking pipes while gullible investors shared those "pipe dreams" while their savings went up in smoke.

The merry companies had a further element built into their iconology. Part genre, they were in a broad sense also history painting, purporting to represent, in a very stylized manner, the last days of antediluvian folly. The notion of the punitive flood, as I have already suggested in Chapter 2, had, for obvious reasons, a special immediacy for the Dutch. And it is worthwhile noting that Buytewech painted his great series during a time of the most bitter domestic contention, which culminated in the execution of Oldenbarneveld and the incarceration of Grotius and the Remonstrant leaders in Loevestein Castle. The debate between the humanist Arminians and the stricter Gomarists was not only about the niceties of predestination and supra- or infra-lapsarianism. It was also much exercised by whether toleration or orthodoxy should have primacy in a godly Republic. And it was a favorite obsession of the zealots that the habits of depraved *ijdelheid* would not merely rot the fiber of Christians, but would bring the whole commonwealth crashing down in disaster, a view in which they enlisted the support of the tobacco-prohibiting Stadholder

109. Gillis van Scheyndel, engraving from *Bacchus Wonder-wercken* (Amsterdam, 1628). Koninklijke Bibliotheek, The Hague

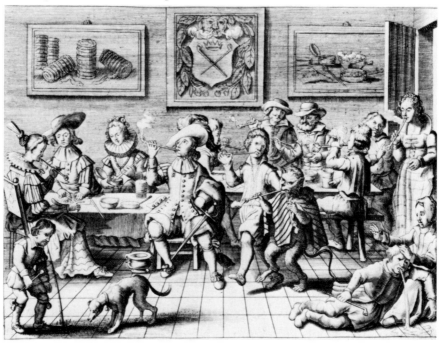

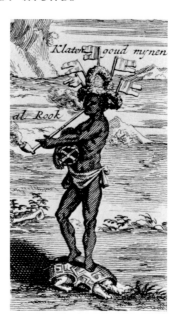

110. Detail from engraving in series, *Groote Tafereel der Dwaasheid.* Author's collection

Maurice. However enigmatic in tone and delicate in symbolism, it seems highly improbable that against this background Buytewech should have wished to advertise the pleasures of casual indulgence. This is far from turning the Rotterdam "merry company" into a visual sermon, but it does not seem too farfetched to assume that some intimation of the cleansing/punishing flood as the wage of *ijdelheid* was implied by its gentle criticism.

The interpretation need not be left to external historical speculation. The composition, after all, is littered with symbolic allusions. The bearded figure in the center wears the attributes of *Hans Wurst* — the presiding figure of comic gluttony on Fat Tuesday. At right the maid brings on a dish of artichokes, celebrated for their power to quicken jaded sensual appetites. To the left of Hans Wurst, a man holds a goblet of wine, while to the far left, another figure in a ruff grasps the mocking pisspot to which the wine will, in due course, revert. Near the debris of *roemers, berkmeyers* and flagons at the bottom right, the most gorgeously arrayed of all the company holds his hat perilously close to the burning coals.

Is this, then, a picture about purity and danger? If it is, then Geestige Willem's (Witty William's) warning bell tinkles rather than tolls, so wryly ingratiating is his collective portrait of human foibles. This, however, does not mean that the painting is dispassionate, much less amoral. The chosen voice of northern humanism was ironic rather than apocalyptic, and if Buytewech was not himself a Remonstrant, his parents almost certainly were.[187] The most explicitly didactic element in the composition, though, may well be the detail which on superficial inspection seems the most purely decorative: the map behind the company. Maps such as that, especially in the fine editions produced by Blaeuw, were already very popular with the well-heeled patrician class who people Buytewech's merry companies. But their inclusion was never merely pictorial or documentary, any more than the choice of a biblical or historical theme for a background painting. This particular map is of the province of Holland and should be read with the extreme tip of the Noorderkwartier at the left, with the line of the North Sea coast running to the right and joining the brim of the pipe smoker's hat. At the center of the map lie the Zuider Zee and the wetlands north of Amsterdam. This was exactly the period when the great reclamation works on the Purmer, Schermer and Beemster were getting under way, transforming inland seas into the lush polders on which the lowing herds that stock Konincks's and Potter's landscapes would graze. Buytewech may or may not have wished to emphasize this changing boundary between the sea and the land, but any map of Holland was

111. Willem Buytewech, *Merry Company,* 1617–20. Boymans-van Beuningen Museum, Rotterdam

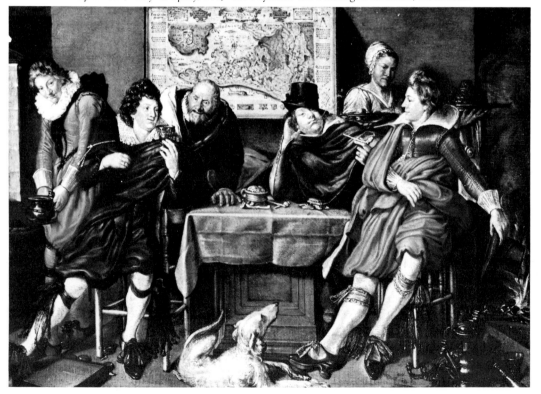

bound to work as a device for turning the picture into an essay *about* Holland and its particular connection between liberty, dryness and virtue. There was no such thing as value-free geography in the Netherlands, and a map such as this could serve humanist ambivalence displaying the work of man as a badge of pride, but simultaneously implying the vulnerability of the achievement. The map and the merry company together transpose the classic connotations of human follies before Noah's Flood into contemporary Dutch circumstances. The text of *Bacchus Wonder-Wercken* reminds its readers that drunkenness as well as idol worship, lust for gold and other unmentionable transgressions had brought about the cleansing wrath of God. And to this list of iniquities was now added the dry drunkenness of tobacco, as the preachers called it. Hollandia and its sentinel lion with upraised sword thus acts as a mute witness of the vain pleasures enacted in front of it.

The ironic reticence of humanist commentary complemented, rather than contradicted, the fulminations of the pulpit. The tide of rhetoric ebbed and flowed with the fortunes of war, or the spectacles of natural calamities like plague and flood. But just as there was no escape from geography, so there was no time during the Golden Century when the forebodings of punishment for success entirely disappeared from Dutch culture. The very signs of prosperity — the swelling girth of the burgher, the finery in which he and his family were portrayed, the pipes inlaid with silver, the festive splendor of a *schutter* banquet, the gilt statuettes supporting the drinking horns of the guilds — all invoked, in the very act of their enjoyment, the transience of worldly euphoria. The whale was both floating bank account and messenger of doom, the precious drinking cup a vessel of patriotic toasts and the accomplice of Belshazzar's downfall.

To be sure, the mass of the Dutch population did not go about in a state of nail-biting, hagridden despondency. Like the Malvern innkeeper of my epigraph, his Amsterdam counterpart was able to discern a providential will that tolerated rather than prohibited the innocent indulgence of appetite. The trick of staying happy in such circumstances was to adhere to the social conventions which distinguished innocent from guilty pleasures, celebrations that were sanctioned by custom or collective ritual rather than casual acts of hedonism. The prints, verses, paintings examined in this chapter all worked to help the Dutch steer their way through a life bursting at the seams with the fruits of affluence without incurring the wrath of Jehovah.

Despite the subtlety and versatility of this humanist response to temptation, there were occasions when the cathartic self-mortification commanded by the predikants seemed more appropriate than gazing on a *vanitas* still life. In 1624 and 1626 there were violent floods in both south and north Holland, so that the author of *Bacchus Wonder-Wercken* could both attribute the calamity to the high tide of sozzling and warn of even greater catastrophes to come were the message to go unheeded

> *Wine and strong spirits*
> *Flood in like seas*
> *Over dam and dike, and great palaces*
> *Over treasure and money*
> *And all our Fatherland's great houses*[188]

In 1651, 1653 and especially in 1658 similar disasters occurred with the massive inundation of the Alblasserwaard destroying the retaining dikes in south Holland on the night of January 30, 1658. In the towns and villages, days of prayer and fast were called; in the squares of Rotterdam and Dordrecht psalms were sung for the safety of the population; stories of the drowned churches of the great St. Elizabeth's Flood of 1472 were revived. And it was for such terrible occasions that the great virtuosi of fire and brimstone reserved their coloratura performances, preaching in church or the open air to huge congregations. Pastor Lydius had his flock chant Psalms 107:17–19, 23–29.

Fools because of their transgression, and because of their iniquities, are afflicted.

Their soul abhorreth all manner of meat, and they draw near unto the gates of death.

Then they cry unto the Lord in their trouble, and he saveth them out of their distresses.

They that go down to the sea in ships, that do business in great waters;
These see the works of the Lord and his wonders in the deep.

For he commandeth, and raiseth the stormy wind, which lifteth up the waves thereof.

They mount up to the heaven, they go down again to the depths: their soul is melted because of trouble.

They reel to and fro, and stagger like a drunken man, and are at their wit's end.

Then they cry unto the Lord in their trouble, and he bringeth them out of their distresses.

He maketh the storm a calm, so that the waves thereof are still.

"Thus Israel found God's grace," *Lydius's Wee-klag* (Lydius's Lament) continued, "after which . . . men bathed themselves in hot tears. So from the pestilential curse, even was Nineveh spared."[189]

And the message from Carpentier, who preached on the Texel storm as "Floods of tears over Jerusalem's present sins and coming wounds," was the same. Only a flood of sorrowful contrition could wash away the flood of divine fury. In 1672 when the catastrophe of which the preachers had relentlessly warned actually seemed to be upon the Republic, and it was forced to *create* a flood by opening the dikes of the *waterlinie* against the advancing armies of Louis XIV and the bishop of Münster, the awful symmetry of the penitential liquefaction seemed complete. The *overvloed* of wealth had corrupted the patriotic spirit; the inundation of drink had brought about the inundation of the polders. To see dry land and freedom once more required the wet eyes of the atoning sinner.

> There is no water strong enough, no *aquae fortis* to quench the fire of God's wrath as strong as the water of penitent tears, that wine of God and Man's rejoicing like unto the drops from the vineyard of the Lord sent to heal all our wounds. . . . For as the Egyptians were smitten for their sins, so the sweet pools of Bethesda shall heal our spiritual lameness. Our outflowing tears of repentance shall wash away the stain on our innermost souls, and shall be even as sweetly perfumed rosewater before the presence of the Lord.[190]

What, though, of the time when the waters had receded just as they had landed the ark safely on the mount of Ararat? For even after the sacred covenant of the rainbow, man had reverted to his habitual state of epicurean iniquity. It was when he was deep in his cups, after all, that Noah turned out to be the first recidivist of the New Age.

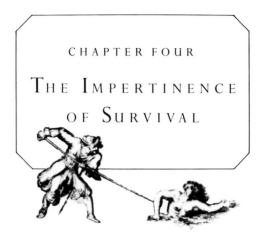

CHAPTER FOUR

THE IMPERTINENCE OF SURVIVAL

The first sight of a large supermarket at a time when Britain was still short produced in me an extraordinary mixture of greed, scorn and fear. There'd be a dreadful reckoning for all this over-abundance sure enough. "You'll pay for this," I thought. "You always do have to pay for your excesses."

RICHARD HOGGART (recalling America in 1955), *Only Connect*

Vigilate, Deo confidentes

Motto of the province of Holland

i BETWEEN MARS AND MERCURY

Republics rarely live up to the innocence of their origins. If born in austerity, they invariably flourish amidst pomp.[1] It may well be their own kind of pomp: aldermanic rather than regal, and consistent with the public abjuring of the rites of monarchy. It may have little in common with court mystique in which the aura of the god-prince is veiled, the better to dazzle his subjects with an occasional radiant glimpse. But, in its own manner, republican pomp

is no less grandiose. It is public rather than secluded, bombastic rather than
magical, didactic rather than illusionist. As a profession of community rather
than an expression of separateness, it offers participation and loyal huzzahs
rather than bowed heads and awed prostration. Yet it too is a device for the
appropriation of power. Deprived of its substance by a ruling patriciate, the
citizenry may be allotted walk-on parts in the performance of its theater. And
regrouped outside the harsh categories of social caste, the actors in republican
ceremonies dutifully re-form as troupes: banner-waving, arquebus-discharging,
parrot-shooting militiamen, guzzling, solemnizing guildsmen, festive con-
fraternities, bestiaries of carnival animals, gesticulating rhetoricians, brawling
"abbeys" of adolescents, euphoric Shriners on Vespas. Their business presupposes an audience and requires appreciative clamor: pageants, processions,
collective benedictions, commemorative feasts, penitential fasts, public executions and, inescapably, long harangues from balconies on dusty city squares.
From the time of Periclean Athens, the captains and the heroes of such
republican pomp remain incorrigibly civic, even when they have been about
martial business. During the second Anglo-Dutch war, de Witt appeared on
the deck of de Ruyter's flagship costumed in gold and silver braid as the
embodiment of the States General, but the incongruousness of the civilian
dressed to kill only provoked guffaws from Admiral Cornelis Tromp.[2] Unlike
the god-kings of baroque Europe, such figures were not candidates for Parnassus,
even though their patriotic service sometimes earned them a reservation in
Elysium. Defunct, they joined the ranks of ancestors and republican paragons:

112. Romeyn de Hooghe, *"Holland."* Houghton Library, Harvard University

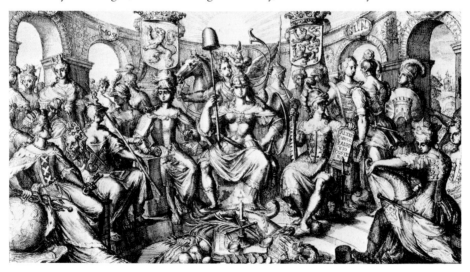

the community's most flattering version of its own personality. Their legendary familiars are not dynastic deities but mythic personifications of the
Republic itself: candy-striped and avuncular in America, potent and lactating
in the French *Marianne*,[3] immemorially miraculous in the Venetian San Marco,
liberated, adamantly enthroned and bountiful in the Hollands Maid. And around
each of these providential personae cluster the fables and chronicles of the
patria that provide it with a virtuous pedigree and comfort it against coming
perils.

At the zenith of its power and brilliance, in the mid-seventeenth century,
the Dutch Republic was no more immune than any other from acts of
elaborate self-congratulation. The Flemish towns from which its culture
descended had married the Burgundian taste for opulence with their own
vernacular tradition of civic pomp to produce Renaissance ceremonies of
unrivaled splendor in the north.[4] And notwithstanding clichés about the
"simplicity" of the Dutch, they developed this ingrained taste for public
solemnities and festivities still further.[5] To this day, public life in the Netherlands
retains a pleasure in ceremony. Conventionally mistaken for royalism dressed
down, it is in fact republicanism dressed up.

In 1667, when the English flagship *The Royal Charles* was hauled back by de
Ruyter to Hellevoersluys, the cup of Dutch glory seemed brimful. In the
circumstances, even for the most hubris-conscious preacher, a lapse into
swagger was understandable, if not altogether wise. From the marble-inlaid
floor of the great Burgerzaal of the new Amsterdam town hall, where Holland
was, literally, placed at the center of the *mappa mundi,* the prospect was
intoxicating. In two or three generations the Republic had risen from a
ramshackle and beleaguered confederacy of towns and provinces into a global
empire of apparently unlimited prosperity and power. "Scarce any subject
occurs more frequent in the discourses of ingenious men," conceded William
Aglionby, who, as a Fellow of the Royal Society counted himself among them,
"than that of the marvellous progress of this little state which, in the space of
about a hundred years . . . hath grown to a height, not only infinitely transcending
all the ancient republics of Greece, but not much inferior in some respects
even to the greatest monarchies of these latter ages."[6] It was, indeed, a
phenomenon. For the Dutch state drew power from federalism when absolutist
centralization was the norm. Its population had trebled from 1550 to 1650,
when most others had stagnated or regressed under the onslaught of plague
and civil and foreign wars.[7] What contemporaries called the "mother trade"—in
Baltic grain—had provisioned their packed towns with dependable regularity
while other urban centers in Europe had suffered from high prices and
intermittent supplies. Dutch fleets covered the surface of the known world,
and their navigators were restlessly extending the boundaries of that knowl-

edge in the antipodes. Charles Davenant, no warm friend of the Dutch, acknowledged that "the trade of the Hollanders is so far extended that it may be said to have no other bounds than those which the Almighty set at Creation."[8] The Republic had accumulated capital and circulated it at rates of three percent when it was a mercantilist axiom that only high rates could preserve a sufficiency of coin. Most important of all, where other states — France, Britain, Spain, Germany — had broken apart in domestic upheavals, the Dutch polity had proved remarkably resilient under stress, effective in administration and ingenious at sustaining the minimal consensus needed to contain discord well within the bounds of civil war.[9] The perennial commentary of foreigners that the intricacies of Dutch federalism were a "chaos" of government spoke to their incomprehension, not to the historical truth.

In all these respects, then, the Dutch Republic was the Great Seventeenth-Century Exception. No wonder its magistrates prided themselves on their good fortune and supposed themselves the darlings of a benign Jehovah. Sometimes they were unable to resist the temptation of addressing commiserating homilies to those unfortunate enough to have to dwell elsewhere. The public tone of the de Witt years of the 1650s and 1660s was, then, more than usually sententious. It was typified by the Grand Pensionary's issuing Solomonic judgments as to which of two squabbling ambassadorial entourages, Spanish or French, ought to take formal precedence in the carriageways of The Hague, should, by some luckless chance, their coaches meet head-on.[10] Throughout the Republic, regents embarked on ambitious programs of redecoration in town and guild halls, expressed in a grandiose classical style commensurate with their swelling sense of self-importance.[11] Many of these had been under way in the 1630s and 1640s, or still earlier, but it was the period immediately following the Peace of Münster with Spain in 1648 that saw the fulfillment of the most extravagant schemes. The grandest of all was, of course, van Campen's monumental new town hall in Amsterdam, where the perennial humanist virtues — stoicism, continence, disinterested justice and patriotic courage — were all displayed in history paintings, sculpture and reliefs in the chambers deemed most apt to their exercise.[12] Lest it be supposed that these visual tracts testified to a becoming humility, they were surmounted on the exterior roof pediments by Quellijn's Parthenon-scale statuary showing, on one side, Amsterdam receiving the tribute of the four continents while the Dutch Atlas bore the globe itself on his muscled back. On the floor frieze of the Burgerzaal, Tasman's most recent discoveries in the Pacific southern seas were very conspicuously designated "New Holland."

Amsterdam's sense of itself as the hub of an empire was not just idle boasting. If it was true that, in the last resort, the city could not survive independently of the Republic, it was equally true that the Republic could not survive without Amsterdam. As by far the heaviest contributor to the finances of the province of Holland, which, in turn, bore between fifty-five and fifty-eight percent of the costs of defending the Republic, the metropolis exercised disproportionate weight within the country as a whole. In 1638 it had welcomed Marie de Médicis, the disaffected *reine-mère* of France, with rhetoric that proclaimed the city itself as her equal, and as though it had its own foreign policy.[13] Since then it had survived William II's armed attempt to cut it down to size, and had reemerged in the mid-1650s as the leading protagonist of those who sought to return the House of Orange's hereditary offices back to the provincial States. It was fitting, then, at this triumphal period, for Amsterdam to have built a seat of government (which was also bank, court and prison) on a palatial scale. In the mid-seventeenth century, only St. Peter's, the Escorial and the Palazzo Ducale in Venice could rival it for scale or magnificence.

As befitted the relative unimportance of national (as against civic) institutions, the central administration of the Republic and indeed of the province of Holland were housed in much less imposing quarters. There was some elegant architecture in The Hague, built in the new Dutch classical manner by Pieter

113. Solomon Savery after Simon de Vlieger, engraving, *Water revels for Marie de Médicis in Amsterdam,* 1638. Bodleian Library, Oxford

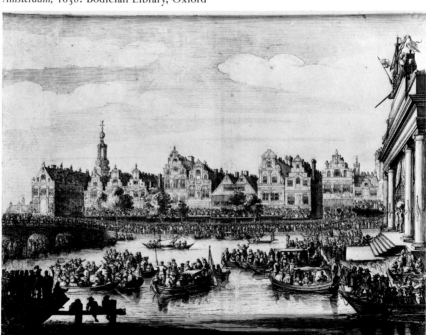

Post and Jacob van Campen, but they were private residences, of Huygens on the Plein, and Johan Maurits (the present Mauritshuis Museum) at the corner of the Vijver. By contrast, the rabbit warren of halls, flanking wings and outbuilding apartments that made up the Binnenhof was, like the Dutch state itself, a peculiar jumble of medieval remains, Renaissance invention and contemporary improvisation. Since the thirteenth century it had been the seat of the counts of Holland and it was they who had built the Gothic Hall of Knights (the Ridderzaal) at its center. Replete with heraldic devices and banners of the seven sovereign provinces, the hall continued to serve as the principal deliberating chamber of the States General. In Dirk van Delen's painting of the "Great Assembly" of 1651, the hall was additionally festooned with captured Spanish flags, hung like congratulatory trophies above the delegates. The cobbled courtyard in which the hall stood was flanked on all four sides by enclosing wings pierced by arched gateways, and on its south side by a small lake, the Vijver. This, in turn, had fed defensive ditches, so that in effect the Binnenhof had evolved as a moated castle in which the service functions had long since outstripped the military. Although some of the

114. Dirck van Delen, *The Great Hall on the Binnenhof During the "Great Assembly" of* 1651. Rijksmuseum, Amsterdam

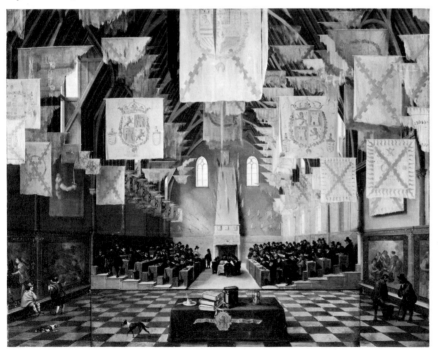

outbuildings continued to serve as barracks for the guard of the States General, the compound was anything but a private or seclusive citadel. In 1660, as now, citizens were free to wander about the courtyard, and many of them set up stalls in its precincts. Inside the Ridderzaal itself, the walls were lined with booksellers and print vendors hawking their wares to customers, oblivious as to whether official proceedings were taking place in the hall itself.

Under Stadholder Frederick Henry there had been a conscious effort to provide the dynasty with courtly residences more becoming to its pretensions, and the entourage evacuated the Binnenhof for purpose-built establishments at the Huis ten Bosch and Honselaarsdijk, both on the outskirts of The Hague. This left the wing-buildings full of the clerks, counting stewards and scribes employed by the province and by the Council of State, the executive organ of the States General. Unlike Huygens, who envisioned dramatic and refined accommodation for the seat of government, de Witt, who worked with a modest staff in one of the bureaus facing the Vijver, had no wish to emulate Olivares or Colbert.[14] But in the ebullient climate of the late 1650s, the States of Holland decided at least to redecorate their own council chamber (now the Eerste Kamer—the upper house—of the Dutch parliament). In so doing it wished to express its own sense of the significance of Holland, not just to the Fatherland as a whole, but to great affairs of state in the world beyond. Predictably, the style chosen for this momentous departure was the high baroque history manner so lavishly used both in the Oranjezaal and in Amsterdam. The deputies were to be seated centrally between two large murals at either end of the chamber, one commissioned from Jan Lievens representing *War Trampling on Religion and Rights*, the other from Adriaan Hanneman and not completed until 1669, representing the Vredesmaagd, the Maid of Peace, draped against Doric columns in an attitude of beatific repose.

The grim, not so say slightly unhinged, countenance of Lievens's Mars made a pointed contrast with the more usual celebration of martial prowess to be discovered in official commissions elsewhere.[15] But, in the manner of its execution as well as choice of theme, neither of the wall murals was especially unconventional. The ceiling fresco, however, was much more disconcerting. For, peering down on the assembly of the States from celestial case lights and balustrades, executed in brilliantly effective trompe l'oeil, were gathered representatives of all the nations with whom the Dutch had commercial as well as political intercourse. Unlike the incarnations of War and Peace, as well as the conventional representations of Commerce, Justice and Wisdom, they were costumed in stylized but recognizable contemporary dress. Their closest prototypes were the representations of the Four Continents that would be used to similar effect by Le Brun on the Ambassador's Staircase and by Laguerre in the Saloon at Blenheim. In both cases, the continents owed much

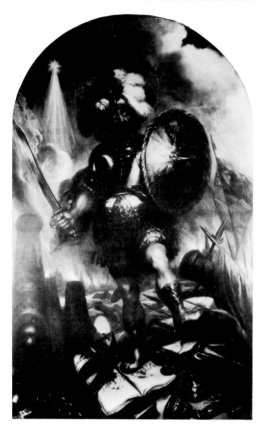

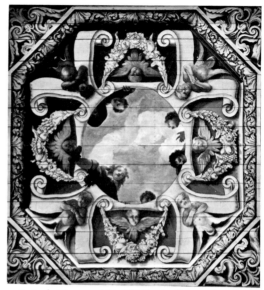

116. A. de Haan and N. Wielingh, *Trompe l'oeuil* ceiling painting for the States of Holland, The Hague

115. Jan Lievens, *War.* Eerste Kamer, Rijksdienst voor de Monumentenzorg

to their personifications in Cesare Ripa's well-known *Iconologia.* But at The Hague the figures were more specified as representatives of the nations: the hirsute Muscovite swathed in sable staring from one corner, the robust Hansa fisherman in worsted and floppy cap in another. Opposite were a Spanish-American don depicted as feudally resplendent, reclining beneath a parasol held by an Indian servant, silk-turbaned Turks and Persians, and an extravagantly fashionable Frenchman, exquisitely peruked, with ribboned mules, smiling deviously into the chamber.

None of this was very flattering. Nor was it meant to be. In the manner of both the Amsterdam roof pediment and the Burgerzaal floor, it was meant to demonstrate the centrality of the Dutch to the commerce of the world, thus complementing the message of the wall murals that proclaimed their arbitration of peace and war. In the most literal style, then, their High Mightinesses sat and deliberated between Mars and Mercury, the god of commerce. The very center of the ceiling fresco, however, was more surprising. It was, in effect, a visual enactment of the province's motto *Vigilate! Deo confidentes* and a warning against unwelcome intrusion. In red worsted hose, one large boot appearing to point into the body of the hall, is the unmistakable figure of the Englishman. Endeavoring to clamber into the Dutch commonwealth, he and his confederates are shown as clumsy, larcenous, greedy and incompetent, a failed burglar reduced to peering enviously down at the proceedings below.

The ceiling of the Statenkamer epitomized the mixture of self-satisfaction qualified by apprehension that colored its proceedings in these years. On the one hand, there was ample cause for rejoicing that Holland seemed to have garnered the fattest prizes of world trade; on the other, a nagging anxiety that they might be robbed of what was "rightfully" theirs by force or by stealth. Along with justice and temperance, the third figure of *waakzaamheid,* or watchfulness, was added to the outsize statuary on the Amsterdam town hall roof. The most likely culprit in any such endeavor was of course Britain. Spain had been transformed from ancestral foe to first line of defense in the south, though not everyone in the Republic was happy about this. But its presence in Flanders and Brabant, once a *casus belli,* was now judged preferable to that of an aggrandizing France. And for this reason the States of Holland, despite de Witt's attempt to persuade them, persistently rejected plans of "cantonment" or partition of the southern Netherlands between the Republic and the French monarchy. Even the Pensionary had little inkling of how deep Louis XIV's displeasure ran at being thwarted in this ambitious plan.

De Witt was a professional calculator, a serious mathematician who published treatises on the elements of the curved line (whatever that is).[16] He was much given to actuarial ruminations on the conjunction of this or that political circumstance and to devising judicious designs to meet such contingencies. Appearing sometimes with abacus and always with notebook in the States, he was, in effect, the first probability theorist to govern a great power. And his probability theory told him that a French adventure against the Republic was out of the question so long as the Stuarts and the Bourbons were kept divided, a task he felt well within his capabilities. British enmity, on the other hand, he knew to be chronic and rooted in the very nature of the Republic's existence, or at least in its prosperity. The problem, he supposed in common with many of his compatriots, was that, in matters of trade, the British were poor losers. Unable to match the Dutch in resourcefulness, industry, or technical ingenuity, they were prepared to bludgeon their way to wealth by the assertion of deliberately bellicose principles and by interfering with the freedom of trade. Peevish envy had turned them into a gang of unscrupulous ruffians who would stop at nothing to burglarize the Dutch warehouse, pretending all the time that some cherished issue of sovereignty had been infringed. That, at any rate, was the message of the Statenkamer ceiling, and it was vindicated by remarks of the blunter anti-Dutch politicians like Monck, who on the eve of the second Dutch war brushed aside all sophistry: "What matters this or that reason? What we want is more of the trade that the Dutch now have."[17]

In the Dutch view, the British were capable of picking quarrels on any pretext so long as it allowed them to suspend the normal conditions of trade, and resort instead to naval bullying. It was not until the reign of Charles I, however, that British naval power was in any strength to make those challenges good, and until the 1650s, their tactics were necessarily confined to a mixture of bluff, diplomatic threats, privateering and isolated raids in the colonies. The Dutch knew full well the weakness of the British position and hence responded with a series of diplomatic overtures which turned into exercises in unlimited procrastination, an activity at which they were the acknowledged champions.

Despite the picayune nature of some of the disputes, there were in fact serious issues of principle dividing the two maritime powers. As early as 1608, James I had challenged the Dutch right to fish freely for herring in what Thomas Mun, the mercantilist pamphleteer, later called "His Majestie's Seas."[18] The all-too-obvious aim was to force the Dutch to share their "chiefest trade and gold mine"[19] (its annual value has been estimated at around one million pounds, or half the total exports of Britain at this time), or else yield up some of that revenue in the form of licenses. The assertion of a maritime sovereignty drew from Grotius the celebrated retort of the *mare liberum*. Rejecting the notion that territorial dominion could be extended to the oceans, he insisted that it was a "due right of mankind according to the laws of nature and of nations" to uphold the undivided freedom of navigation and commerce. "Can the vast boundless sea be the appanage of one country alone, and it not the greatest? Can any one have the right to prevent another from bartering with one another?" The only jurisdiction belonged to the Almighty, who had divided the waters from the dry land.[20]

Against this humanist universalism, British polemicists like John Selden set precedent and prescription. The common lawyers and antiquarians busied themselves among the parchment and eventually claimed to unearth a document of King Edgar's time (A.D. 964) which referred to him as *Rex Marium Britanniae*. However flimsy (or spurious), the document was enough to allow Selden, together with the truculent admiral and mercantilist William Monson, to insist in *Mare Clausum* (1635) that territorial sovereignty in the seas had *always* been recognized in both custom and statute. This the Dutch continued to find preposterous. In the 1660s, de Witt stated flatly that "sooner than acknowledge this imaginary sovereignty of the seas, or even receive from the English as a concession that freedom of navigation and fishing which belongs to us as a right, we would shed our last drop of blood."[21]

While Charles I was on the throne, the Dutch (and the States Party in particular, who were contending with his Orangist allies and kin) attributed obduracy in these matters to the high-handedness of absolute monarchs. They were, however, to be sharply disabused by the Commonwealth parliaments. If anything, their conjunction of aggressive mercantilism and godly patriotism propelled policy towards a more belligerent restatement of the old principles.[22] What was now at stake was no longer royal amour propre but the determination of disadvantaged commercial interest groups to break Dutch domination through the use of state power. The coalition of warrior-merchants was surprisingly broad. It included the secretary of Cromwell's Committee for Trade, Benjamin Worsley, colonial imperialists like Maurice Thompson and William Pennoyer, who had seen how the Dutch had used their own military force to protect their monopoly in the Indies, advocates of domestic industrial protection like Slingsby Bethel, who spoke for the British clothiers resentful at the undercutting of Leiden and of the Dutch passing off Wiltshire and Gloucestershire woolens, finished in Holland, as Dutch goods. The city trading companies were also in favor of some sort of protecting legislation backed up, if need be, with force. The Levant Company was watching its trade to Turkey wither under Dutch competition, and the Eastland Company had always felt itself excluded from a fair share of the domestic market through the overwhelming domination of the Baltic by Dutch freight.

Resisting this rising tide of bellicose protectionism was, paradoxically, Cromwell himself. He had no special sympathy for the Dutch, but after the execution of Charles I in 1649, they were an indispensable element in his design for a league of Protestant powers. At a less grandiose level, they were also important in hunting down royalist privateers and evicting royalist refugees from asylum in the Netherlands. Preliminary negotiations for a proposal of "alliance and union" got as far as an embassy to The Hague in 1650, where, however, it became apparent that the Dutch were initially bewildered and then very suspicious of the ultimate purpose of the scheme. Having set the seal on their own independence just two years before, they were not about to relinquish it to some bizarre diplomatic fantasy of Cromwell's making. Nor were they prepared to compromise on the all-important issue of *mare liberum,* or restrict their own trade in the interests of otherwise British commerce. These reservations led to the collapse of the negotiations and an outburst of indignant polemics complaining, like Benjamin Worsley's *Advocate,* that the Dutch "aimed to lay a foundation for themselves of ingrossing the Universal Trade not only of Christendom but indeed of the greater part of the known world."[23]

The recoil effect from the collapse of Cromwell's Anglo-Dutch design produced the Navigation Act of 1651. This prohibited the import of goods to

England other than in a vessel of either the country of origin or of England. It was, in effect, a statutory salvo aimed directly at the body of the Dutch carrying trade, and it was further primed by the continued insistence that the Dutch offer a deferential salute to British vessels when encountering them in the "British seas."

Both sides appreciated that behind this apparently trivial matter of naval salutes lay weighty issues of sovereignty at sea. Historians have been apt to dismiss the whole fuss as comical posturing, but in the seventeenth century, it should hardly need to be said, the symbolism of state was of the utmost importance. Both the British and Dutch parties understood perfectly well that acknowledging the demand for the salute would be to recognize the validity of the British position on their "proprietorship" of the surrounding seas. And given the Dutch commitment to *mare liberum,* a war over the matter was bound to ensue. This duly happened in 1652, and although on paper the Dutch fleet was more numerous than the British, it became quickly apparent that it was poorly prepared for the kind of broadside-slogging war unleashed by Admiral Blake. Maarten Tromp shone as a naval commander but his battle-readiness had been gravely impaired by the reluctance of the five provincial Admiralties to abandon their thrifty habit of relying on merchantmen that could be expeditiously armed in time of war rather than on a purpose-built war fleet. The needs of convoy also found merchant fleets seriously under-protected. And the result was the drubbing of the Three Days' Battle in February 1653 and a series of further defeats before the States General was persuaded of the urgent need for larger, more heavily armed, custom-built warships.[24]

Given the extent of Dutch losses, the Treaty of Westminster that ended the conflict in 1654 was relatively generous. This was less due to any great magnanimity on the British side than to the heavy losses and expense they had themselves incurred during the war. But the principles of maritime sovereignty were set aside and the occasions for courtesy salutes confined to encounters in the "Narrow Seas" (the Straits of Dover). This meant, in effect, that the Dutch were free to continue their herring and cod fishing around the coasts of Britain, subject only to a periodic licensing. On the other hand, the Navigation Act remained in full force, and between 1652 and 1658 no fewer than three hundred Dutch vessels were seized both in European and colonial waters for infringing its terms. That the British could still be a menace to the essential structure of the carrying trade was underlined when their navy took to apprehending any Dutch vessels they deemed might be carrying goods to or from Spain during the English war with that kingdom. "Free ships, free goods" was almost as sacrosanct a principle as the *mare liberum* itself. Moreover the ugly little conflict that broke out in 1658 when the truculent Swedish king,

Charles X, attacked Denmark in the hope of dividing the lucrative control of the Baltic Sound, threatened the Dutch grain and naval supplies trade — the "mother trade" — at its heart. Predictably the British supported Sweden, somewhat improbably casting Charles X in the unaccustomed guise of a Protestant hero, while the Dutch sent fleets to Copenhagen and to Sweden to ensure that the "keys to the Sound" should not fall into extortionate hands.

All this suggested that the conflicts of rights and riches were far from being satisfactorily resolved. When Charles II sailed from Scheveningen in 1660 in response to General Monck's invitation to ascend the throne, there were some hopes that the new king, who had lived as a fugitive in the Netherlands, would look more considerately on their claims. Great banquets were held in his honor in The Hague prior to his departure, in a transparent effort at ingratiation. Charles accepted the toasts with his instinctive graciousness and preserved his freedom of action. He had, in any case, no obligations of gratitude to discharge towards the States since they had evicted him from their hospitality in deference to Cromwell's peace conditions. And he repaid expediency with expediency by retaining, in his turn, some of the Common-wealth's most vehemently anti-Dutch polemicists, like George Downing. In 1660 a new Navigation Act was passed by the Cavalier Parliament which, while yielding nothing in principle, was more sophisticated in its application. Instead of an unenforceable blanket prohibition on all imported goods in Dutch vessels, the new restrictions applied only to specially designated items such as Baltic naval supplies, colonial goods, Levant cottons and the like.

Just how stringently the act would be implemented was a matter of conten-tion between rival groups maneuvering for control of policy in early Restoration England. Clarendon was not a partisan of confrontation with the Dutch and somewhat astonishingly pulled a treaty out of his hat in 1662 at a time when colonial and commercial relations were rapidly deteriorating. That policy of conciliation disappeared with his fall, however, to be replaced with Downing's taste for confrontation indulged by Arlington and the Duke of York, both impatient for some sort of naval *action d'éclat.* After a series of miniature engagements in Africa, the East Indies and the Caribbean, war resumed in the spring of 1665. At its outset, off Lowestoft, the British fleet inflicted another of the heavy defeats reminiscent of the first war and in which the Dutch admiral Obdam was killed. Rejoicing in Whitehall proved to be premature. For it subsequently transpired that the Dutch had learned the expensive lessons of Cromwell's war only too well. Although the numbers of warships and crew were at approximately similar strengths, the Dutch had reinforced theirs with custom-designed, heavily armed vessels and, more important, had reserves in depth to withstand any British attempt at intervention and blockade. Indeed they turned those blockading tactics on the British in 1666, defeating an attempt to harry an East India fleet returning via Bergen, and landing troops themselves at Sheerness later that year. In June 1666 the Four Days' Battle resulted in the first overwhelming victory for the Dutch fleet under de Ruyter, and although offset by a reverse in July, brought the first indications of willingness to negotiate from a financially stricken British government. It was, however, the traumatic events of 1667, coming as they did on the heels of the plague of 1665 and the Great Fire of 1666, which left them no alternative but to end the war on the best terms they could get. In a swift and almost unopposed action de Ruyter brought a fleet of eighty ships to the Medway naval ports and into the mouth of the Thames itself. The "barrier chain" was broken; the fleet fired, and the flagship *Royal Charles* taken as prize to Hellevoetsluys. John Evelyn traveled to Chatham to watch the triumphant Dutch fleet riding at anchor and thought it "a Dreadful spectacle as any English man saw and a dishonour never to be wiped off." When another squadron appeared at Gravesend in July, it was too much for Sir William Batten, the Surveyor of the Navy. In Pepys's presence he complained, "I think the Devil shits Dutchmen."[25]

The States General did their best not to gloat. De Witt's characteristic reaction on learning the news of the Medway raid was relief: "Now God be praised and thanked for such a great mercy; and may He grant that the arrogance of the enemy be curbed, and the present bloody war be changed

117. H.L. Padtbrugge, *The Raid on Chatham,* from L. van den Bosch, *Leven en Daaden der Doorlugtige Zeehelden* (Amsterdam, 1676)

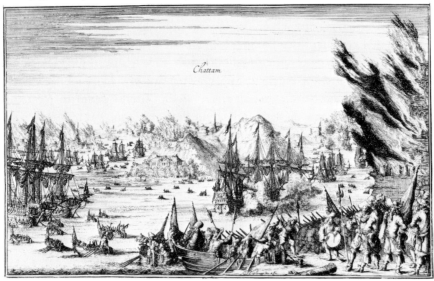

into an honourable and assured peace."[26] The terms accepted by the British plenipotentiaries at Breda in August 1667 were reasonably magnanimous. Both states preserved the colonial acquisitions they had made during the war, which meant, in effect that the Dutch retained Suriname and Pulo Run in the Moluccas, and the British acquired Nieuw Amsterdam (New York) and the middle colonies on the Delaware. While there was no doubt that both the British and the Dutch supposed the latter to have had much the best of this colonial exchange, it had the momentous consequence of shifting British colonial energies towards North America and the central Caribbean in the west and abandoning the Indonesian archipelago in the east in favor of Job Charnock's fort at the mouth of the Hooghly in Bengal. In other respects not very much changed. Further concessions were made in respect of the Navigation Act so that, for example, textiles exported from the German hinterland of the Dutch were to be counted as "Hollands" for its purposes and the whole principle of maritime sovereignty and the fisheries was set aside indefinitely. These terms left many gloomy in Britain. "Nobody," wrote Pepys, "is speaking of the peace with any content or pleasure but are silent in it as a thing they are ashamed of."[27]

It was, in fact, the very reasonableness of the Dutch, their magnanimity in victory, which was so galling to the paladins of the British empire of trade. The more the Dutch preened themselves on their generosity and common sense, the more George Downing burned with inward rage. Their whole deportment during the first two naval wars (the third in 1672 would be very different in that it was a war for the life or death of the Republic), was one of affronted peacefulness. Jacob Westerbaen, the bard of the herring, registered the Dutch sense of wounded dismay at belligerent British conduct in 1652 in his limping verse:

> *We were friends and sworn allies*
> *Neighbors, both of one religion and one belief*
> *Why, then, do you attack us . . . and with hostile fleets*
> *Make war on our commonwealth and plunder*
> *   our fleets?*[28]

Others were less naive. Another anti-British poet saw that whatever the apparent inconstancy of English politics, the aggressive pursuit of the national interest had hardened itself into enduring anti-Dutch feeling:

> *Sea-scouring island, how strange in its changes*
> *Constant only in its will to subjugate the Netherlands . . .*
> *[For we are] the lead in its heart, the thorn in its foot*[29]

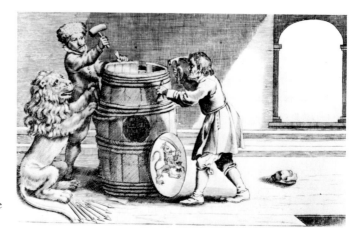

118. Anon. engraving, *Engels-Kuiper,* 1652. Koninklijke Bibliotheek, The Hague

Most vexing of all was the manner of droll condescension adopted in Dutch prints and caricatures (many of them deliberately circulated in Britain to stoke the fires of patriotic resentment) towards the futility of British efforts at changing the "natural" economic relations through acts of violence. In Jan de Mol's *Engels-Kuiper* (English Cooper), published in 1652 satirizing domestic disputes about foreign policy, a perspiring Englishman attempts to barrel in what is not his to appropriate: the God-bestowed riches of the sea. He is frustrated in this by the persistent but evidently well-intentioned and amiable Dutch lion, who also supplies a verse sermon on the futility of the enterprise:

> *Foolish cooper, stay your hammer*
> *In your hand, and become calmer*
> *What men do when they're not wise*
> *May cost their master too high a price*
>
> *Let the peace join together*
> *What revenge will never tether*
> *On every side, man and beast*
> *Are in God's hands, so pray for peace*[30]

It was just this sort of high-minded preaching that, when translated into official utterances, grated on foreign sensibilities. In Whitehall and Fontainebleau, it was often taken to be so much sanctimonious humbug shrouding the bloated reality of Dutch commercial imperialism. In their eyes the *pax Belgica* was nothing more than a disingenuous device for the perpetuation of economic paramountcy, all the more offensive for being defended in the language of the rights of nations and pious altruism. While Dutch herrings slid down the gullet, Grotius stuck in the craw. This sort of rationalization was all the more infuriating because the nostrums of *mare liberum* so freely aired in respect to the European seas and the Atlantic went entirely by the board in the East Indies, where the Dutch guarded their spice monopoly with ferocious jealousy against any interlopers. The "massacre" of the English factory at Amboina in 1623 became, in British anti-Dutch polemics, a byword for the infamy of their empire, a dominion according to its foes based on equal parts of hypocrisy, cruelty and cant.

Some of this criticism was well taken. The Dutch were given to invoking the freedom of navigation as though it were part of a code of natural law to which all states self-evidently subscribed. They then proceeded to apply those principles with what seemed a very elastic partiality. Ostensibly, the king of Denmark was free to impose tolls on the Sound connecting the North Sea with the Baltic as he saw fit. In practice, however, his sovereignty in these matters was limited. Treaties with the Dutch, in particular that of 1649, which offered "protection" against aggression, also laid down special terms for the Republic as a most-favored trader. Dutch vessels were exempt from all tolls on the payment of an annual lump sum as a compounding "redemption" of those dues. In this respect the Companies of the North and of Muscovy, that brought in profits estimated at midcentury to be in the region of three and a half million guilders a year,[31] were almost as much parties to local administration at the Sound as the modern canal companies were to be at Suez and Panama. In a similar manner, commercial interests were reinforced by military engagements. Should the "territorial" power have the temerity to deny passage to Dutch vessels or to seek unacceptable rates, it would be subject to strong doses of naval persuasion. And twice in the 1650s—in 1656 and 1658—the States General sent formidable expeditionary forces to deter the Swedes from forcing Denmark to alter its compliant policy in an anti-Dutch direction.

Issues of territorial sovereignty, then, could be interpreted with a liberal pinch of pragmatism, especially where geography was helpfully indeterminate. Seas and oceans, in the Dutch view, were manifestly "free" and "open," but what of straits, isthmuses, estuaries and archipelagos, many of which were vital strategic points in any commercial network? As long as the Kattegat was controlled by the weak Danish crown, the Dutch were content to accept its jurisdiction, but the ambitious extension of Swedish power under Queen Christina and King Charles X to the left bank of the Sound threatened to make Dutch trade hostage to a much less benign custodian and to undermine their domination in grain and naval supplies. As a result the principles of free passage were more liberally invoked during the Baltic conflicts of the 1650s. When it came to their own straits and estuaries, however, the Dutch were more forthright in asserting the principles of contiguous sovereignty. The forts of States' Flanders were judged non-negotiable possessions in perpetuity because they ensured the indefinite closure of the Scheldt and the crippling of Antwerp's prospects as an entrepôt.

The convenient inconsistencies in the Dutch approach to its vaunted principles of *mare liberum* and "free ship, free goods" were naturally pounced on by its enemies to denounce the Republic for hypocrisy. While always prating of peace and freedom, it was said, they were on the lookout for the spoils of war. Owen Felltham, one of the most truculent of the Cromwellian generation of pamphleteers, went so far as to state that "war is their heaven and peace their hell,"[32] not least because they stood to profit from the embroilment of other states. The prominence of the Dutch in the munitions trade, their near-monopoly of Swedish iron and copper, the great fortunes made by the Trip dynasty in that industry, and the early professionalization under Prince Maurice of musketeers, was all held to be evidence of their pleasure in arms. It was an open secret that the payment of armies during the Thirty Years' War (even armies that fought the Dutch) through bills of exchange discounted on Amsterdam, sustained an enormous business for the city, and that while statesmen and jurists expressed their distaste for piracy, Dutch privateering in the East and West Indies flourished at the expense of rival naval powers, especially the Spanish and Portuguese. What was the immense prize of Piet Heyn's capture of the Spanish silver *flota* in 1629 other than the most spectacular instance of booty legalized by war? Somewhat more implausibly, the well-known Dutch reluctance to be dragged into entangling alliances was interpreted by the uncharitable as a smoke screen for calculated perfidy. This was a bit thick coming as it did from English and French writers defending the premeditated joint attack on the Republic in 1672. Yet one such polemicist argued that it was the Dutch, not themselves, who were the true warmongers and that their low republican ratiocination made it impossible for them to respect the terms of treaties. "The Hollanders are always brooding of wars, and there's no firm league to be had with 'em but [only] impuissance to do hurt."[33]

The Dutch may, I suppose, have been guilty of a double standard in professing an aversion for military force which their own conduct periodically belied. But the fluctuations in policy that were stigmatized as hypocritical were, like so much else in their nation's public life, the product of divided sentiments and contending interests. Those internal debates on the advisability or inadvisability of war, however, were concerned with judging the circumstances in which it might be lawful. That there *was* a distinction between lawful and unlawful war (even when decreed by a prince) was an article of national faith. In this, both polite and popular culture followed Grotius in distinguishing between the immoral war as the plaything of dynastic ambition or the weapon of dogma, and the just war as the defense of legitimately acquired freedom and property. In allegorical prints dealing with matters of war and peace, the Republic, depicted either as the fair Hollands Maid crowned with the hat of liberty, or as a well-stocked and verdant garden (or both), is defended by the Batavian lion rampant, the seven arrows of the Union clutched in his paw, an upraised sword in his right arm. Against him are generally ranged a menagerie of predators: the English, to their displeasure usually personified as a dog, Reynard the French fox (occasionally the Gallic rooster), and Spain represented either as the incorrigible leopard or the devious wolf clad in sheep's clothing. All seek to force an entry into the garden and carry off its fruit, whether by violence or stealth, though sometimes the French fox is obligingly seen at the side of the lion repelling the rest. Between aggressors and defenders there lies only a flimsy stockade or fence, and it was this stockade mentality that pervaded Dutch attitudes to war within their beleaguered Eden. It must have seemed that the long ordeal for their freedom had as a felicitous by-product generated immense riches. But instead of buying them the peace to enjoy that wealth, it had merely stoked up further envy and hatred, and led to yet more wars for its preservation. Even in prints ostensibly

119. Crispijn van de Pas, etching, 1648. *The Courtship of the Hollands Bride.* Atlas van Stolk, Rotterdam

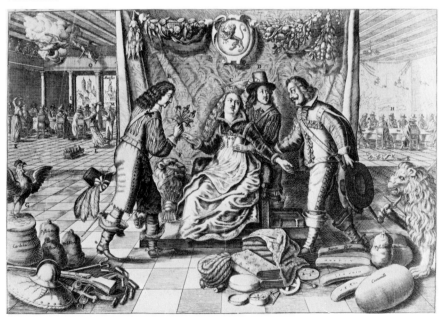

celebrating the peace, this uneasy defensiveness persisted. In the "Hollands Courtshop," a jealous de Witt protects his ward from the mutually dishonorable advances of French and Spanish suitors.

In Jan Vos's euphoric poem of 1662 on "The Increase of Amsterdam" Gisbrecht van Amstel, the legendary founder of the city, hopes that "wealth may find some rest in the shadow of peace," almost certainly meaning the shadow of the great Maiden of Peace that now stood atop the town hall.[34] But in the very same year Pieter de la Court, the Leiden cloth manufacturer and principal author of the pseudonymous *Memoirs of de Witt*, took a much more bleakly pessimistic view of the future. He himself had declared in a chapter on foreign policy that "above all things, war, and chiefly by sea, is most prejudicial, and peace very beneficial, for Holland." But reality was inauspicious. "An *assured* peace, in regard to Holland," he concluded, "is a mere Chimera, a Dream and a Fiction."[35]

Military glory, then, was liable to be regarded with more circumspection than enthusiasm in the Netherlands. "War," said a popular Dutch verse of the 1640s, "is the plague of towns and of the countryside, the monster of the seas. Those who thrive on it burn with hatred and envy."[36] And given the long, grim history of the Eighty Years' War, this could hardly have been otherwise. The midcentury generations, at least outside Brabant and Gelderland, had little direct experience of invasion and the indiscriminate slaughter of civilians that had marked the "forty murder years" after 1570. But there had been protracted sieges and relief marches in Brabant and Gelderland during Frederick Henry's stadholderate in the 1630s, and even those not caught up directly in the theater of war paid through stiff excises the costs of the campaigns. Whole communities, like the south Holland and Zeeland fishermen, were more or less hostage to privateers, and others suffered increasingly through skillfully targeted blockades. Others, like Naarden and Gorinchem, turned into garrison towns with all the mixed feelings that such places sustained towards their guardians.

Even though professional soldiers—including foreign mercenaries in increasing numbers—played a crucial role in the defense of the Republic in the seventeenth century, they went conspicuously without honor in the patriotic culture of the time. The stadholders themselves and their kin in Friesland who played an important role in the army were exempt from the suspicion and scorn, but it was left to their own patronage to indulge in the kind of triumphal military art that so liberally adorned public and court monuments elsewhere in Europe. Until the nineteenth century there was no equestrian statuary in Holland, and though Hendrick de Keyser posed William the Silent as a commander for his tomb in the Nieuwe Kerk at Delft, he is shown seated as for prayer, in the Calvinist manner, paternal and accessible.[37] By

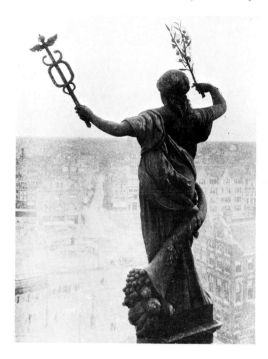

120. Artus Quellijn, *Vredesmaagd*
(Maid of Peace). Royal Palace,
Amsterdam

contrast, there was a profusion of images of peace in both public and private places in the Republic. Hanneman's *Peace* reproachfully confronted Lievens's *War* in the Chamber of the States of Holland. Quellijn's Vredesmaagd atop the Amsterdam town hall was a colossal work of statuary, weighing eight thousand pounds, unprecedented in scale and magnificence in the country. Looming over the Dam, she brought together in her attributes of olive branch, Mercury's staff and cornucopia the paramount themes of Amsterdam's civic ethos: peace, commerce and prosperity. And even while the war with Spain continued it is possible to find imagery eulogizing a desired peace. An allegorical painting of 1640, for example, by Hendrick Maartensz. Sorgh gives greater honor to the heroic group of cabbages and turnips than to the military appurtenances piled up to the right. And while a wolf lies down with the lamb and a lion with the child, it is a cuirassed captain who kneels together with the farmer and his wife before the radiantly illuminated figure of the Maid of Peace.[38]

If war was played down in Dutch history painting, soldiers fared still worse in genre painting. An entire genre of *boerenverdriet*—peasants' sorrow—developed around the theme of soldiers marauding and ransacking the hamlets of innocent and helpless villagers.[39] And it was that kind of treatment that linked the first generation of atrocity prints in the 1600s with their revival by Romeyn de

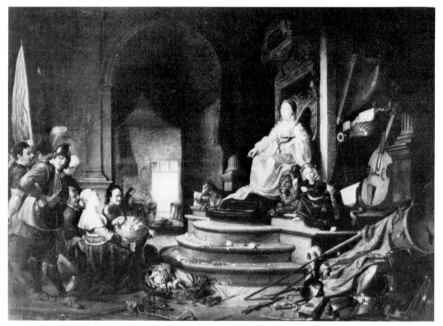

121. Hendrick Maartensz. Sorgh, *Allegory of Peace.* Musée des Beaux Arts, 1640s. Azay-le-Rideau

122. Jacob Duck, *Soldiers Arming Themselves,* mid-1630s. H. Schickman Gallery, New York

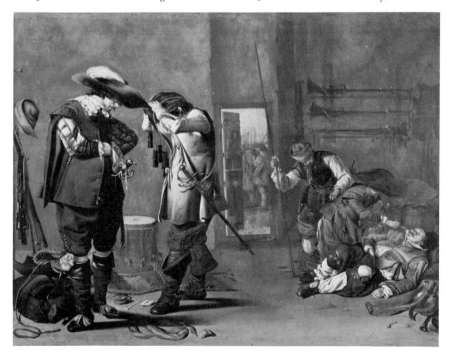

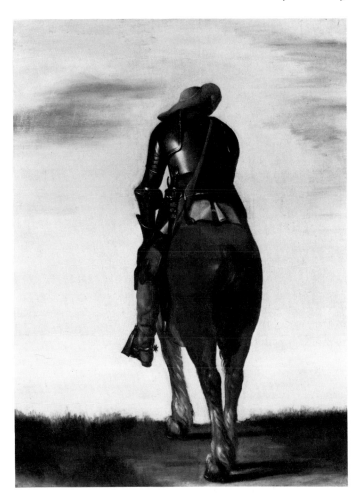

123. Gerard ter Borch, *Man on Horseback*. c. 1634. Boston Museum of Fine Arts

Hooghe in the 1670s. Graphic artists like Goltzius and Jacques de Gheyn in the early years of the war had provided something close to a heroic, or at least a flamboyant, view of the man in arms. But that image had largely disappeared by midcentury, to be replaced by something closer to lowlife burlesque. For they feature prominently as the clientele of brothels in the work of Hendrick Pot. Even the *cortegardje* barrack-room scenes produced by Pieter Codde and Jacob Duck were implacably unheroic. In one remarkably matter-of-fact painting by Duck, soldiers are being roused for the morning muster in a light of such gloomy murkiness that neither the richness of their uniform nor the bleak little tickling joke played at right does anything to relieve it.[40]

This is not to say that soldiers are never shown sympathetically in Dutch art or literature. Gerard ter Borch painted a number of wry pictures of military life, the temper of which is best described as delicate disrespect. The extraordinary *Rider Seen from the Rear* is so unconventional and so ingratiatingly slack in pose that it comes close to a parody of the formal profiles of Renaissance equestrian heroes. (Could it, indeed, have been a source for Daumier's *Quichotte* two centuries later?) In many instances, the warmth and intimacy of ter Borch's regard arises from the artful ways in which he demilitarizes and demobilizes his chosen scenes. None are set in camp. Some, essentially refined variations on the barrack-and-brothel genre, depict rumbustious carousal, or, like the Mauritshuis *Unwelcome Embassy,* the familiar contention between Mars and Venus. And if, anecdotally, the call to arms prevails over the call to love, the heavy reluctance to concede the victory is expressed in the tender sentiment that fills the frame, the déshabillé of the girl contrasting with the unyielding breastplate of the soldier. Armor, in ter Borch's scenes though is to be taken off as much as put on. Helmets sit on writing desks; swords and bucklers go unstrapped; vulnerable bodies are left undefended. Unlike the martial epics that crowded the Hall of Realms at Buen Retiro, these are small paintings colored in soft hues. Unlike the neoclassical heroic style that was to come at the end of the eighteenth century, they are scenes in which the intimate and the domestic and the private dominate the public and the patriotic.

In a similar vein, the most celebrated of all pseudo-military ensembles, the *schutterstukken* militia scenes (whether in the sober and formal manner of the sixteenth-century prototypes, or the flamboyant grandeur of Hals and Rembrandt), are emphatically group portraits of civilians in martial fancy dress. Their ranks are determined by their respective places in the patrician pecking order, and their regimental insignia and emblems and colors are closer to those of the civic corporations and guilds than to battle dress (which had no uniform at all).[41] The gorgeousness of their array was an urban parade, and the *doelen,* even amidst the banner waving and the shouted Sunday drill, stood not as an extension of the military life into the civic, but as its opposite and alternative. The militiaman, the armed civilian, was as intrinsically benign as the professional soldier was malign. He was *of* the community and not a marauding intruder or an unwelcome billet. He could be relied on to bear arms in the Fatherland's hour of need without abusing them to threaten its liberties. That, at least, was the received wisdom, though in 1672 it turned out to be doubly mistaken. In that most frightening of all the seventeenth-century crises, the virtues of the *schutterij* turned out to be exclusively what they were not, rather than what they were. Sunday parades notwithstanding, their effective military value in withstanding the shock of the French invasion was almost nil, and de Witt paid a dreadful price for his overestimate of their mobilization. Somewhat ungraciously, considering his faith in their republican

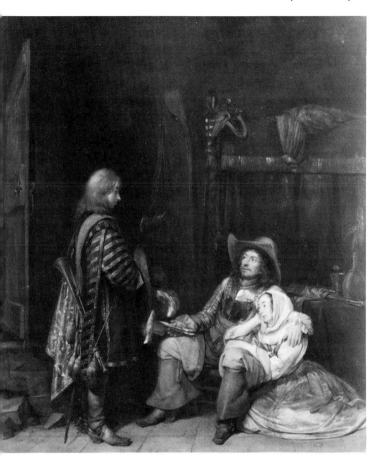

124. Gerard ter Borch, *Unwelcome Embassy*. Mauritshuis, The Hague

ardor, it was the Hague militia (admittedly a notoriously Orangist bunch) who delivered the brothers up to the mob that tore them limb from limb on the flagstones of the Buitenhof.

Ironically, on that macabre day, it was the troops of the regular army rather than the *schutters* that stood between the de Witt brothers and their assassins.[42] And there are occasional glimpses that the civilian ethos sometimes may have affected the conduct of regular troops. Those that were disembarked to occupy the Medway ports in the summer of 1667, for instance, exhibited a thoroughly Dutch regard for the sanctity of property. Pepys reported the local townspeople (who had no reason to whitewash the foe) as surprised by their decorum—"they kill'd none of our people nor plunder'd their houses." This was in marked contrast to the behavior of Lord Douglas's soldiers, who followed the occupation. "The watermen that carried us," Pepys added during his tour of inspection for the navy, "did further tell us that our own soldiers are far more terrible to those people of the countrey-towns than the Dutch themselfs."[43]

This happy vision of a please-and-thank-you army charming the locals into submission with an impeccable display of table manners ought not to be taken too literally. In the Indies especially, the Dutch were quite as capable of brutalizing the natives (if not more so) than the next gang of imperialist ruffians. In the Medway, the troops—or marines, as we should call them— were under the authority of the navy, and some indeed were English seamen who had been prisoners of war and had defected to the Dutch for better wages and conditions.[44] In Amsterdam and other major ports, the popular lore about sailors was that they were a wild and unruly bunch given to dreadful excesses when in dock and best confined to areas of the city that no respectable burgher penetrated. Yet it is also true that *collectively,* and institutionally, the navy was seen as less intimidating and more *vaderlandse* than the army. Much, of course, depended on angle of vision. In the land provinces of the Republic from which many of the troops were recruited and indeed in towns like Utrecht, Amersfoort and Coevorden with long military traditions, the army was not seen as particularly alien. A sizable section of the local population, in garrison towns, of course, made their livelihood from them. The same was true of the navy in the maritime provinces of Holland, Zeeland and Friesland. There, the Dutch fleets were regarded more as necessary extensions of the local economy than as organized institutions of war. The first ships to be used in anger against the Spanish at Brielle, after all, had come from the armed fisherfolk communities of the estuary islands and ports in Zeeland and south Holland (even though their officers were gentry) and had their counterparts in the fishing villages of the Zuider Zee and the *Noorderkwartier.* The first Dutch warships were rough-and-ready conversions of grain ships, flyboats and even coastal barges, and they were crewed by seamen who expected to return to their own occupations once the seas had been made safe. Even when the war turned out to be protracted, those villages continued to supply manpower for the fleets of the Republic, with some "short-term" men serving off and on and going home as the pressures of the family economy demanded. No press gangs were needed in Holland or Zeeland. The navy developed not as a policy of state but out of the spontaneous needs of the maritime communities, and perhaps out of their more emphatic Calvinist sense of patriotic mission. The convoy system, too, was typical in that it was a defensive arm protecting the business of trade rather than promoting belligerent strategy. Even privateering, which to its victims was licensed piracy pure and simple, was an expression of this muddied frontier between war and subsistence.

The image that the Dutch had of their own fleets, then, was defensive and patriotic. It was almost as if it had been a seaborne militia (which in its earliest

days it was). Ships, as has been pointed out in an earlier chapter, were floating
replicas of the ideal Dutch town, complete with pastor, merchant and
skipper-magistrate. Nor was this sense of their being a "home-away-from-
home" much diluted by the increasingly large proportion of foreigners who
made up over 50 per cent of the complement, especially after the expansion
of the fleet following the British success in the first war. Historical lies car
easily become cultural truisms. So that even if in reality it was made up of
Scandinavians and Germans, the navy was perceived as less alien a presence
than the army. Correspondingly its heroics were more popular a subject for
painters, engravers and even decorative artists like silversmiths, tile painters
and glass engravers. It is not too much to say that maritime heroism had an
"audience" in a way strictly inconceivable on land. For during some battles
like the Downs and the Three Days, the population of the North Sea coastal
villages and towns did stream to the shore to see the wreaths of smoke on the
distant horizon and listen, presumably with a mixture of fearfulness and excite-
ment, to the dull thunder of the cannon. For those who could not be there in
person, the sense of vicarious participation was exploited by the early Dutch

125. Romeyn de Hooghe, *Victorious Sea-Battle* . . . 21 *August* 1673. From *Hollandsche Mercurius,* 1674

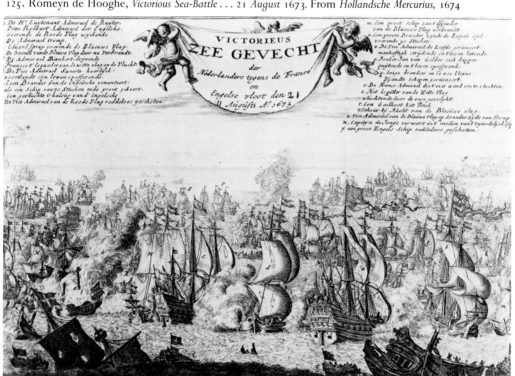

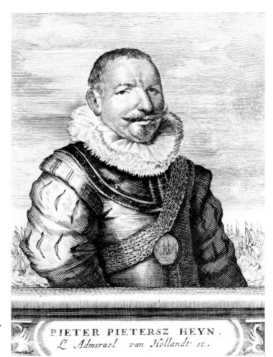

126. Engraving of Piet Heyn, from
L. van den Bosch, *Leven en Daaden* . . .
Houghton Library, Harvard
University

PIETER PIETERSZ HEYN.
Lt Admirael   van Hollandt et.

press, which not only published full narratives of the battles but supplied
superb, pull-out engravings with keys to salient moments and heroes of the
hour.[45]

Naval heroes, moreover, were demotic rather than aristocratic, or at least
were supposed to be. Piet Heyn and Maarten Tromp enjoyed a popularity
wholly different from the Princes of Orange and Captains-General, with the
exception, that is, of William the Silent. Like the first Prince, Tromp was
cultivated as a paternal figure: *"Bestevaer,"* or "dear Father" (a title passed on to
de Ruyter) and he was accorded the extraordinary honor, after his death in
battle in 1653, of being buried near William in the Oude Kerk at Delft. But
Tromp's paternal persona was not meant to be the disembodied incarnation of
a *pater patriae.* Nor did the massive state funeral accorded him and the
grandiloquent tomb designed by Rombout Verhulst mean that Tromp was
simply a figure of elite, official acclaim. For like de Ruyter and Piet Heyn and
van Heemskerk, it was as a flesh-and-blood figure that he enjoyed his immense
popularity with all classes of the population. Books like Lambertus van den
Bosch's *Doorluchtige Zeehelden* (Renowned Sea Heroes) provided the reading
public with stirring biographies of the great men, all stressing their closeness
to the common man even at the height of their fame and fortune.[46] Their

careers, celebrated in jokes, songs, *roemer* engravings, toasts and prints, were meant to demonstrate what the Dutch took to be exemplary home truths about themselves: that with courage, hard work, daring and determination it was possible to rise through the ranks to wealth and renown. In actual fact relatively few naval officers worked their way up in this way. Many, if not most, were the sons of regents, notaries or other officers. But the legends of exemplary social mobility were useful partiotic myths. There were stories, then, of Joachim Swartenhondt, who walked from Bristol to London to escape English rovers, of Jan van Galen, who began as a humble boatswain and became captain at twenty-six, of Piet Heyn, whose father had been imprisoned in the galleys by the Spanish. But above all there was de Ruyter, who went to sea at eleven and who "from a lowly station climbed to the pinnacle of honor and state."[47] De Ruyter was, after Maarten Tromp, the exemplar of exemplars, whose early exploits as a young whaling crewman in the frozen north bore an uncanny resemblance to the apprenticeship of the cult hero of the British eighteenth century, Horatio Nelson. These reputations as salts-of-the-earth were reinforced by emphasis (not always accurate) on their becoming humility, modesty and altruism. In fact the commanders, as often as not, reflected in their political and religious sentiments the divisions afflicting the Republic as a whole. The Tromps, Maarten and his son Cornelis both, as fierce Orangists, disliked de Ruyter, who remained a tenacious States Party republican, and that antagonism came close to destroying the Dutch fleet in 1672. The personal quarrels and bickering that disfigured the naval command were probably aggravated by precisely the sense of amour propre that came with celebrity, but at least in times of dire crisis it could be set aside for the national interest.

The ethos that won public admiration in the maritime provinces, then, was consciously more populist than that of the army, where it never shook off the odium of misconduct among civilians. The navy could even be said to be anti-aristocratic in bias, with the only true patrician, Admiral van Wassenaer van Obdam (appropriately monumentalized in the Nieuwe Kerk in Amsterdam), blown up at the battle of Lowestoft. Indeed it was consistent with the navy's anti-oligarchic tone that both seamen and officers (except for de Ruyter) were much more likely to declare for prince than patricians in any serious domestic political crisis. After the narrow squeak of 1650, Amsterdam and the Holland towns were determined never to sacrifice the strength of the navy for a reinforcement of the army, which they feared might again be used to intimidate them into political capitulation. Paradoxically, de Witt stood the best chance of extracting funds for a large-scale naval reinforcement by arguing that it was an indispensable condition of commercial prosperity. To make the British or the French desist from interfering with the freedom of trade it was imperative to make the costs of such presumption prohibitively high. That was meant to be the lesson of the Medway raid and the peace of Breda. Unhappily, for both himself and his country, Johan de Witt was too blithe in his assumption that naval power could be used prophylactically — to forestall general conflict rather than provoke it. The desired equilibrium by which a certain level of naval force was the guaranteeing condition for restraining the growth of the army remained wishful thinking. There was, of course, more than financial prudence at the back of de Witt's mind in these optimistic calculations. Grotius and Oldenbarneveld had been undone by their opposition to a war policy, and had been dislodged by the army that wanted to fight it. Like those predecessors the Grand Pensionary suspected that great armies and protracted wars existed in a kind of corrupt symbiosis, the latter supplying the former with the rationale for its domestic power. In that classic States Party view, the wars against Spain had not been fought in order that endless dynastic entanglement should perpetuate a state of siege. For de Witt and de la Court a republic worthy of the name fought only wars of survival. The tricky question, of course, was to decide which they were. De Witt's adversary, tutee and successor, William III, after all, drew his legitimacy, both as Stadholder and later as King, as the Captain-General of resistance to the overbearing Apollo of Versailles.

The art of Dutch security, then, was to sustain sufficient force to deter aggression, but not so much as to jeopardize freedom from within. In what this sufficiency consisted, though, was a matter of ancient debate. The policies that the States Party under Oldenbarneveld criticized as rash and excessive were held by their adversaries to be barely adequate for the Republic's survival, much less its dignity. The "war party" in the second decade of the seventeenth century, led by Prince Maurice, fulminated against the truce with Spain as tantamount to treason. Not only was it a bargain with Antichrist, it was also a feckless maneuver that could only serve to strengthen the enemy for a renewed onslaught. Minimal security frontiers, they argued, had to lie in the south, in Flanders and Brabant, if Holland itself was to enjoy any permanent respite. And in this respect strategy was supported by piety. Since the triumph of the orthodox Gomarist Calvinists at the Synod of Dordrecht, their most militant predikants had been calling on the Stadholder to "redeem" the lost provinces of the south. Some of those who lent their purses as well as their voices to the endeavor were themselves Calvinist zealots from Antwerp, Ghent and the Flemish towns and who further contributed to the foundation of the West India Company as a means of harrying the foe in his imperial domains. Indeed it was argued by the likes of Willem Usselincx that the Republic had nothing to lose and much to gain economically from a resumption of hostilities since, *inter alia,* it would also permit Dutch fleets to go on the offensive against the Portuguese in West Africa and the East Indies.[48]

Despite the devastation wreaked by the "Spanish Fury" in the south and the raw memories of the occupations and sieges of the 1570s, it was true, of course, that the war between 1590 and 1612 had indeed coincided with the most spectacular flowering of the Dutch economy. Antwerp's catastrophe, after all, had been Leiden's opportunity, when the capital and skills of the textile industry were transplanted there. Even Pieter Hooft, who was certainly not of the militant "war party," conceded (by way of claiming divine wardship) that "whereas it is generally in the nature of war to ruin land and people, these countries on the contrary have been notably improved thereby."[49]

Yet if there were sanguine expectations of war profits and unlimited booty from the Spanish empire, when the truce was finally and decisively ruptured in 1621, those hopes were dramatically confounded over the next twenty years. Olivares's shrewd policy of waging strategically targeted economic war on the Republic (as well as the more conventional kind) demonstrated only too well just how vulnerable its trading network was to systematically planned sabotage.[50] The very interdependence of the carrying trade which in propitious times was so much a Dutch strength came to seem an extra hazard in that when one link snapped the whole chain could easily fall apart. Through blockade and expulsion the Spanish government deprived the Dutch not only of their Cadiz trade, but of two of the most essential commodities in their long-distance north-south, east-west network: Setubal salt for the preservation of fish, and merino wool to supply the Leiden and Haarlem textiles. Still more serious, the naval supplies which gave Dutch shipbuilders, and thus freight rates, their competitive edge were gravely affected by naval attacks and privateering in the Baltic. The price of shipping Norwegian timber to Holland rose between 1625 and 1645 by 50 percent, and in years of acute difficulty, by a hundred percent, making the unit cost of equipping the carrying trade rise alarmingly. The scourge of privateering, particularly out of Dunkirk, as well as of concerted Spanish naval action also affected the most basic staples of the "mother trade," grain and fish. The Dutch fishing boats were particularly vulnerable to attack. In 1625 the entire herring fleet of the Maas and Goeree was caught by Spanish warships off the Hebrides and 80 boats were destroyed in the one encounter. The States General was obliged to provide expensive convoy protection, but even then it occasionally failed. In 1627 the Dunkirkers destroyed a further 89 boats and took nearly a thousand fishermen prisoner. Between 1631 and 1634, Maassluis alone, one of the two major fishing ports on the Maas and Vlie, lost 162 boats—a disaster which affected two thousand men and cost something like a million guilders' worth of income over seven years.[51]

Nor were the grander elements of Dutch trade spared. In 1642 the whole of the Archangel–Muscovy convoy, with its rich cargo of sable, ambergris, whale train oil and iron, was taken. Nor were the prizes and colonies taken an adequate compensation for the losses. It was only after the Peace of Münster and the conclusion of hostilities that the outward volume of shipping to the East Indies significantly expanded. The Atlantic theater was still more disappointing. Even before the Portuguese uprising in Brazil, which ended with the eviction of the Dutch, the West India Company had proved itself a questionable enterprise. It had been forced to spend well over a million guilders a year in defending the footholds at Recife and Pernambuco, while only four hundred thousand guilders in profits had been made off the receipts from slaving and the sugar and dyewood plantations it supplied.[52] The company had been regarded with some mistrust by the more conservative Amsterdam mercantile community ever since its incorporation. Attracting more investment from the Zeeland towns and from the newer circles of capitalists in the north, many of them Flemish expatriates, it was suspected of being first an agency with which to pursue religious war in the Atlantic and only second as a trading operation. Its perennial need for subsidies during the whole period of its existence did nothing to remove the impression that it was a rash and expensive speculation that could become a millstone round the neck of the Republic. Dutch willingness to accept the expulsion from Brazil but retain the West African possessions taken from the Portuguese, as well as strategic entrepôts in the Antilles and at Curaçao, suggests just how eager the ruling patriciate was to cut losses from its imperial adventures in the west.[53]

Without the additional burden of defending Dutch America there were, after all, ominously accumulating sums to contend with in the European theater. The costs of just treading water in respect of the most vital Dutch concerns was mounting year by year. Apart from the costs of providing convoy protection to the harassed fishing and merchant fleets from the Levant to the White Sea, the elaborate and comprehensive program of fortification on the periphery of the new Dutch state in the 1620s—from 's Hertogenbosch in Brabant through Gorinchem, Coevorden, Naarden and Woerden in central and eastern Holland, up to Zutphen in Overijssel—had eaten up immense sums. Simply maintaining an army and navy adequate for the Republic's minimal needs had become a heavy burden. From 3.2 million guilders as the cost of the campaigns of 1591 against Parma, the year's campaigning in 1622 cost the Republic 13.4 million, and in 1640, with Stadholder Frederick Henry mired down in pointless sieges and minimal marches and countermarches, the bill had risen to 18.8 million.[54] The consequence was a huge fiscal liability imposed on a population of around one and a half million, and taxes that were far more penal than Alva's notorious Tenth Penny, which had done so much to provoke revolt in the previous century. It was a tribute to the strength of Dutch patriotism that it could impose so heavily on its citizens for so long, with very few instances of protest, much less outright revolt. But the governors of Holland were only too keenly aware of their disproportionate role in balancing the Republic's books. Their province bore well over half the Republic's total quota of revenues, and by far the major portion came from indirect taxes: customs and internal excises imposed on a wide variety of consumer commodities from sturgeon to black tobacco, ivory to soap. The frequently expressed hope that trade might be relieved of some of its burdens with the Peace of Münster was certainly typical of the wishful thinking prevalent in the mercantile communities of Holland and Zeeland at midcentury.

For both practical and principled reasons, then, war had come to be regarded in the Dutch Republic with a mixture of aversion and dismay. To say as much of an urban society in the wretched aftermath of the Thirty Years' War when the civilization of the central European towns had all but been destroyed is of course to state the obvious. There was no enthusiasm for the Four Horsemen in 1648. But the marked unwillingness of the Dutch to allow the martial ethos status or dignity in its culture not only separated it from the absolute monarchies, where whims of knightly valor and godlike indestructibility could be entertained at court (and occasionally transformed from masque to policy). It also divorced the burgher Republic from the history of the Renaissance city-states with their appetite for internecine conflict and relish in the *carrozze delle trionfi* (the triumphal cars). Arguably, war had always been seen in Italy as intrinsic to, rather than separable from, the fortunes of trade. Medieval Pisa and Genoa had become formidable powers through supplying the Crusaders with goods and services, and the perversion of the Fourth Crusade into a looting expedition in Constantinople in 1204 had been the making of the Venetian empire in the Levant. Rightly or wrongly, the Dutch understanding of their own commercial power was that it operated independently of, and in spite of, military interruptions. And in this respect, there was some truth to the disdainful assertion of their enemies that policy was made according to the prudential criteria of an enlarged merchant corporation rather than those becoming to a great state. In particular, it was hoped that the causes and the purposes of war could be confined to those two unavoidable matters: the protection of frontiers (as determined by the peace of 1648) and the preservation of conditions by which the Republic's trade could flourish without let or hindrance.

These hopes proved to be idle, not least because what appeared to the Dutch as a modest and unassuming posture seemed to their rivals to mean the indefinite perpetuation of their economic supremacy. A recent historian has gone as far as describing this domination as a global "hegemony,"[55] and while that was not objectively true, it echoes the propaganda of the 1650s.

"Philopatria" Worsley in *The Advocate* not only asserted that the Dutch had tried to engross the commerce of the entire known world for themselves but had done it for the sinister goal *"that they might poise the Affairs of any other state about them"* (emphasis added).[56] If they were innocent of any such dark conspiracy, the Dutch certainly did suffer from a peculiar false consciousness about their use of power. Force in the hands of others was consistently portrayed as an infringement on the laws of nature; force in their own hands was, however, a defense of freedom. Such, alas, is the casuistry of nationalisms that suppose themselves to be divinely appointed. Like other mercantile and industrial empires that followed them in this moral isolationism, they disdained to deal with the rest of the world on its own slightly soiled terms. By adhering instead to the principles that were said to have separated them from the "Old World," they imagined that they might transcend the grubby bartering of *raison d'état*. Unlike nineteenth-century Britain or twentieth-century America, though, geography deprived the Dutch Republic of the insularity, much less continental separation, needed to sustain these high-minded illusions. The *waterlinie* system of inundations offered some kind of defensive shield against future aggression, but one that was rapidly becoming more imaginary than real, as Louis XIV's campaign from the south and east in 1672 was to suggest. The inescapable reality was that the Republic was attached by both geography and economic structure to the rest of Europe, and that it drew its great strength from that attachment, not from separation.

No wonder, then, that when Dutch statesmen pondered on the available alternatives to traditional policies of *raison d'état,* they were immediately confronted by a whole range of ticklish dilemmas. Suppose that there was general agreement with Pieter de la Court's view in *The Interest of Holland* (which there was not) that the only wars to be fought should be wars of economic and political survival. Where did the threshold of survival lie? De la Court thought that it would be politic to "wait until others make war on us," but that defensive confidence presupposed an ability to fortify against all contingencies, naval and military, that the merest glance at the Republic's cumbersome and quarrelsome mobilization belied. It seemed to others reckless folly to wait until armies were massed on the frontiers of the Republic before certifying that such a crisis was indeed a *casus belli*. What of trade wars against the British or the French, who made no effort to conceal their covetousness, both in European and colonial waters? De la Court fondly supposed that since the effectiveness and visibility of Dutch preparations would act as a deterrent, and since any belligerent could expect punitive damage to be dished out to their trade, none would be so foolhardy as to risk the adventure. Instead "they would soon understand that there is more to be gotten by us in time of peace and good trading than by war and the ruin of trade."⁵⁷ This comfortable assumption overlooked the serious harm that had, in fact, been inflicted by the Spanish in the 1630s and 1640s on vital Dutch trade routes and raw material supplies. Other powers, then, might easily draw the conclusion that trade wars *could* in fact yield dividends that peaceful competition (on Dutch terms) could not. The lessons of the first Anglo-Dutch war and the enforcement of the Navigation Act were mostly depressing. On the one hand, the Dutch had felt they could not afford to overlook an infringement of principle that could, ultimately, lead to the destruction of their commercial predominance. On the other hand, the war itself had been a bruising encounter. In the end, it was far from clear what sort of war it might be that the Republic could abstain from on the grounds that it did not touch on their survival. A war between the Turks and the Hungarians, perhaps? (But then there was the Levant trade to consider.)

On the issue of alliances and treaties, the States Party orthodoxy, expressed by de la Court, was that they should be avoided except where (as in the Danish case) they were a convenient device to secure compliance with an economically sound arrangement. This also amounted to a delusion about both the past and the future. The Republic might never have come into existence in the first place had it not had the support, in bleak times, of the French and English monarchies—as they never tired of reminding it. However disdainful they were of being dragged along in the train of obsolete dynastic or religious *idées fixes,* it was naive for the Dutch to suppose they could survive a potential coalition of all those who had reason to wish them humbled. De Witt may have shared Grotius's and de la Court's skepticism about the reliability of treaties made with kings—a contrary version of the monarchical axiom that republics were, by definition, incapacitated from agreements of honor. He was, however, under no illusions that they could be dispensed with altogether. From the first, his primary goal was to exploit as an active participant the alliance system of the European states, so as to preclude any possibility of dangerous isolation. Indeed, from his perspective, the Triple Alliance of 1668 looked just such a foolproof combination. If he ever entertained anxieties about secret collusion, he had only to contemplate the madness of a Franco-British arrangement, which would remove the only major obstacle to *each other's* bid for domination. The trouble was that the Cartesian world in which he lived made no room for exactly the kind of irrationality that could still create policy. There was no Dutch contingency to deal with acts of carefully guarded, unswervingly deceitful conspiracy.

The Grotian plan had also foundered on the impossibility of discerning that set of internationally recognized principles that would secure the Republic's existence as a matter of law. The hope lingered on as a humanist will-o'-the-wisp and as a piety dear to the statesmen who saw themselves as heirs to

Grotius's adjudications. They *hoped* that their Republic would indeed be regarded in time as an emanation of natural law, but de Witt in particular was not especially optimistic. Even de la Court thought such an axiom and the peace it entailed to be "a fiction, used only by those who, like sirens or mermaids, endeavor by their melodious singing to delude the credulous Hollanders till they split upon the rocks."[58] There was, moreover, no court to which to turn, except that of the Almighty on high, in case of disputes. And Calvinists, of course, believed that the working of history was itself a matter of providential design against which only the foolish or the sacrilegious could protest.

Finally, the patriotic assumption that there was a special dispensation evident in the history of the Fatherland and expressed in its power and wealth that might enable it to forgo the vainglorious concerns of mere monarchies rebounded with terrible force on the Dutch. Both the Calvinist Church, which proclaimed the wardship of Jehovah, and the patriciate, which assumed that the house of the Republic was too strong to be blown away by princely huffing and puffing, conspired in the beguiling notion of exceptionality. It sheltered even hard-boiled empiricists like de Witt from a bleak truth: that the singularity on which the Dutch prided themselves was the source for much of the enmity they encountered in the outside world. It is hardly surprising that this issue was fudged, for even had it been squarely faced, what could have been done about it? Were the Dutch supposed to efface their patriotic identity in obedience to purblind hostility? Were they to comport themselves among the nations with humility so as to present a less obvious target? If the rest of the world chose to regard their existence as an impertinence, it was for others to adjust their sights to the unalterable reality of Dutch power and Dutch wealth. The difficulty with this otherwise reasonable stance was that, as any cursory inspection of utterances on Holland reveals, the response of other Europeans was not at all rational. Such was the disquiet caused by the suddenness and magnitude of their irruption into the community of states that the Republic had come to be regarded as a monstrous cuckoo that had been hatched in a modest nest and had then eaten its foster-parents out of house and home. The displeased were now lining up to throw it off its perch. Thomas Mun's tract *Treasure by Foreign Trade*, written in 1624 but published forty years later, also resorted to the ornithological conceit to hint at the vulnerability of the Dutch carrying trade. The United Provinces were, he wrote, "like a fair bird with borrowed plumes, but if every Fowl should take his feather, this bird would rest neer naked."[59] Downing expressed much the same sentiment with his customary brusqueness. "If England were once brought to a Navigation as cheap as this [Dutch] country, good night Amsterdam."[60]

These intimations did not go wholly unnoticed at home. In the midst of their self-celebration, the deputies of the States of Holland might look up at their ceiling and catch the red leg of the Englishman dangling ominously above their heads.

ii "THIS INDIGESTED VOMIT OF THE SEA"

In the last week of September 1665, the plague harvested seven thousand bodies for the charnel houses of London and Samuel Pepys came in for a bit of good fortune. A botched attempt to intercept the Dutch Indies fleet had yielded consolation prizes in the shape of two heavily laden East Indiamen. "Rejoice O England," ran a popular refrain, "Dance and Sing/That's an Ill Wind which none doth profit bring."[61] Delighted with the bounty, the commander of the attack expedition, Lord Sandwich, had followed the old Elizabethan custom of immediately dividing the spoils among his crew. The men evidently helped themselves with a will, since it was reported that following the first onslaught on the plunder the ships floated five feet higher in the water.[62] Even in the high naughtiness of Restoration government this was considered improper, especially when the government itself was desperately hard-pressed for funds. As the new Surveyor-Victualer to the Royal Navy, Pepys was sent to Erith in Kent, where the ships lay, to supervise, in a more orderly manner, the distribution of the prize cargo. But this official commission did not preclude a little business on the side. And together with a Captain Cockes, Pepys took the opportunity to buy up, at bargain prices, job lots of silk and spices, much of it from "dirty wretched seamen" encountered in verminous taverns.[63] As the business, both official and unofficial, proceeded, visions of the loot swam in his greedy brain. But even Pepys was unprepared for what he saw when, on November 16, he toured the holds of one of the Dutch vessels. An oriental cornucopia lay chaotically heaped about the decks, and Pepys duly succumbed to that old occidental fever: the *delirium imperialis*. It was, he wrote, "as noble a sight as ever I saw in my life, the greatest wealth in confusion that a man can see in the world. Pepper scattered through every chink. You trod upon it and in cloves and nutmegs I walked above the knees, whole rooms full. And silk in bales and boxes of copper plate, one of which I opened."[64] Like a child given the key to the candy store, he felt it was too much and yet not enough. Wading thigh-high through the cloves and crunching peppercorns beneath his heel, Pepys was slightly unsettled by this dazzling vision of superabundant swag. There were, however, some sobering considerations. Gossip was already running that men in high places had helped themselves improperly to what belonged to the royal treasury, and even more depressing was the reminder that these two ships were, as far as the Dutch were concerned, merely crumbs on the table, since most of the fleet had made their way safely home. And when the government was so desperately hard-pressed for funds to continue the war, the scale of the resources the enemy could bring to the battles ahead must have seemed daunting.

Pepys's mixture of exhilaration and apprehension on seeing the Dutch prize was typical of contemporaries' reaction to the riches of Holland. Nothing in the common stereotypes of the Dutch really prepared visitors and competitors for the sheer sumptuousness of the culture, nor for their childlike relish in showing it off. Upstart commercial empires were, of course, nothing new. Northerners had long been exposed to the brilliance and swagger of Venetian pretensions, and the lavishness of the great Flemish cloth centers like Bruges in their Burgundian prime had left little to be desired. But the commonplaces about the "sober" Dutch were overturned by the reality. Their merchant princes were supposed to be parsimonious and austere: fustian in apparel and coarse in diet. They were the cheesemongers, the herring picklers, the clod-dish Hogan-Mogans who dwelled in what Owen Felltham called "a universall quagmire" and Charles Molloy "such a spot as if God reserved it as a place only to dig turf out of."[65] To court cultures, devoted to organized prodigality, the unavoidable fact of Dutch wealth was only supportable when it was linked to the consoling stereotype of niggardly avarice. Netherlanders then were toler-ated so long as they cut poor figures—comical in their aspirations to higher things but consumed by their lust for gain. When they presumed to outdo court style with gestures of outrageous ostentation, the reaction of the outdone mixed a deal of anger along with bemused disdain. The christening present of the States General to Princess Elizabeth Palatine, a choker of thirty-six dia-monds and fifty-two pearls (one for each week of the year), was received with polite awe. But another *pillegift* also presented at the court of James I to Henry, Prince of Wales, was more calculated to remind the Stuart court of the power of raw wealth: a massive gold casket brimful of annuity bonds drawn on the Amsterdam market. This mixture of ingratiation and plutocratic vulgarity chafed on the refined sensibilities of a court accustomed to being schooled in the celestial graces by Italianizers like Inigo Jones. When a courtier who was being shown the casket by one of the Dutch emissaries retorted with a laconic *"puf"* he was taken severely to task. *"Non puf est,"* came back the reproof, *"sed aurum purum."*[66]

Some of the rancor which, in the evil temper of a Downing or a Colbert, could reach irrational denaturing proportions, stemmed, I think, from the behavior of the Dutch subverting the consoling cliché of meanness. So long as they were mere Lombards in worsted, bankers to the powers rather than a power in their own right, the scale of their riches could be accepted as a regrettable necessity. But when it was converted into the means by which the Dutch might throw their weight about in the company of monarchs, their wealth ceased to be a joke and became an intolerable threat.

There may have been an additional, murkier source of spleen. The dividing line between unashamedly materialist cultures and ostensibly antimaterialist ones in Baroque Europe was much less rigid than its formal partitions proclaimed. Counter-Reformation popes were no less avid for lucre than Calvinist bankers in Geneva. Those within the European courts who took most offense at Dutch wealth, from Olivares to Colbert, were not those most impervious to money but on the contrary those most eager to amass it. Is it conceivable (and I advance the supposition with all due caution) that the Dutch were made the whipping boys for tender European consciences, disturbed by their own growing fixation with hard cash? Such an exercise in collective guilt displacement — the transfer of odium to an external party which was then made to embody the vice of which one suspected oneself — would hardly have been a unique historical phenomenon. It was, for instance, at the root of much Jew hatred in modernizing societies in the nineteenth century. Some of the stigma attaching to impeccably patriotic German-Jewish burghers in the Wilhelmine period came, paradoxically, from their reluctance to exhibit the cupidity which the capital-hungry Junker class required. In the bizarre circularity of the anti-Semitic mind, the very addiction of Vienna and Berlin Jews to the lofty values of *Bildung* and *Kultur* became a symptom of their innate dishonesty, the gaberdine of Jew Süss always visible through the burgher's frock coat.

There was, in any case, a much more obvious sense in which the Dutch were penalized for being the instruments in a perennial debate about the most expeditious route to prosperity. In such a debate, of course, they were not without advocates and even admirers, however grudging. For John Keymer, Thomas Culpeper and Henry Robinson in the middle of the century and for Josiah Child and William Petty later, they represented a model more worthy of emulation than scorn.[67] In particular their success seemed to make a nonsense of the received wisdoms of mercantilism which these writers were concerned to contest. The Dutch Republic, after all, combined a superabundance of specie with low interest rates, when it was a mercantilist rule of thumb that rates of three or four percent would be bound to "drive out treasure." Even more baffling, they appeared to combine a high population increase with high real wages. Their success at opening up new sources of supply, generating and servicing demand, and connecting new markets with the processing industries of the Amsterdam entrepôt seemed (especially to Josiah Child, who was an advocate for the East India interest) to belie the axiom of an inelastic aggregate volume of world trade — a zero-sum competition.[68] Those like

Roger Coke, who enthused over the Dutch example, also supposed it derived from a refreshingly unclouded approach to the practical world: the ethos in fact of political (and social) arithmetic. Much admiring astonishment was expressed over the aptitude—and the instruction—of Dutch women in business affairs. Coke went so far as to list eighteen characteristics of this new culture, including the education of both sexes in geometry and applied mathematics, the institution of free ports, the liberation from the futile defensiveness of protectionism.[69] All this was grist to the mill of those who saw themselves as the promoters of a commercial ethos, but before the 1690s they remained a small and relatively uninfluential group in the councils of state in both England and France. The unadorned practicality of their recommendations was precisely the reason for their unacceptability in courts still addicted to the more conventional insignia of power and status—in particular, land. Where, as in the celebrated case of Colbert, a minister was a passionate advocate of a mercantile and naval sector, it was not to be inferred from that, that he would take lessons from the Dutch experience. More, not less, protection from competing imports, higher tariffs, the subsidized encouragement of chartered colonial ventures, the encouragement of a domestic shipbuilding industry was the typical response. As for low interest rates, these, it was said by the dogged mercantilists, were the fruit rather than the seed of prosperity, and if the Dutch wanted to waste their capital on exported investment, that was their business. Even at the turn of the century, when a Dutch Stadholder had become King William III; when the Greenwich–Royal Society connection had become institutionalized; and political arithmeticians like Lowndes and Blathwayt were entrenched in the revenue administration, the victory of a "Dutch" party in the political economy was far from assured. For every Defoe prepared to offer a guarded endorsement of the Dutch model, there was a counterpolemic intent on portraying them still as rapacious engrossers of foreign trade. During the long War of Spanish Succession, Tory pamphleteers harped on the Dutch perpetuation of hostilities in their own narrowly selfish interests and accused their defenders of being lackeys of the Bank of Amsterdam happy to fleece the landed gentry to pay for a "Dutch" war. "I cannot trust to the accounts of any Dutchman," complained Harley in 1704, "from whom no sincerity is to be expected in a matter of this nature where, if they speak the truth they must necessarily condemn themselves."[70] Charles Davenant, who had swerved from hostility to admiration back to hostility, also believed that the Dutch had exploited the war for their own enrichment, and more extreme high Tory polemicists like Robert Ferguson continued to refer to their "insatiable thirst for Money" and the part the innocent British had played in the "aggrandisement of that ungrateful nation."[71] In the bestiary of popular xenophobia, the Dutchman was still the gross and comical Nick Frog, the "son of mud who worships Mammon" and who needed a periodic drubbing to be reminded of his lowly station among the mighty of the world.[72]

Harping on the cupidity of the Dutch was especially ironic since uninterrupted fretting about the propriety of capitalism was something of a national trait. The debate conducted in France and England (and even in Spain) as to the relative priority of profit and power was no more than a distorted image of an identical debate perennially joined in the Republic itself. And in those arguments it was never a foregone conclusion, even within Amsterdam, that the champions of the commercial interest would invariably have the upper hand over the Calvinist clergy or the land-war oriented factions of the Orangist nobility. These complications were obscured by the fixed stereotype of the Republic as a pseudo-state devised and managed purely in the interests of Dutch money. Even William III's closest adviser, Willem Bentinck (the first Earl of Portland), who had spent most of his career embattled with the commercial patriciate, was stigmatized by his impeachers as a typically avaricious Dutch peculator. Propaganda is nourished by such denaturing simplifications: the reduction of the feared and detested Other to a few simply recognizable vices. What was striking about the Hollandophobic variety was how far it went beyond the old Catholic style of anathematizing heretics, and even beyond the stock conventions of late baroque name-calling, to something more sinister. At its most bilious, it implied that the Dutch title to freedom and sovereignty was spurious; that their pretensions to statehood were doubtful and had been overindulged through the misguided magnanimity of their allies and protectors. Overgrown and ungrateful, their "reduction" — to what, remained ominously indeterminate — was now an urgent requirement for the dignity and prosperity of all true (read dynastic) states.[73]

Though much of this polemic was seen for the histrionic gesticulation that it was, the Dutch could not afford to treat it as entirely frivolous. It amounted, after all, to the delegitimation of their independence scarcely any time after it had been won. Their characteristic response, however, was not to flee into some more innocuous form of existence, such as the prolonged neutrality that would characterize their diplomacy in the middle of the eighteenth century.[74] As they perceived themselves to be beleaguered, so they asserted with corresponding vigor the very singularity that had given offense. So their "Judaic" sense of providential protection lived in a poisoned reciprocity with the "profane" motives of their neighbors and adversaries. The more the latter bludgeoned and threatened, the more stiff-necked and preachy the ministers of the Dutch Republic became. The consequences were predictable and unfortunate. They would culminate in the disaster of 1672 but had long-term origins. As early as the *mare liberum* issue in 1609, the Grotian style of treating international conflicts as disputes to be adjudicated by reference to some universally discernible and acknowledged corpus of natural law, provoked acts of exquisite Machiavellian lawlessness. Such conflicts remained obstinately the contentions of power, authority, religion, dynastic amour propre and custom — the very issues that Grotius had deemed inadequate pretexts for the prosecution of a just war.[75] Oldenbarneveld, who had held high office by virtue of his legal capacity as Lands-Advocate, was himself the victim of a judicial murder and surrendered the charge of state to the more predictable interests of church and dynasty. At a later date, the more Johan de Witt relied on Cartesian actuarial calculations of diplomatic contingency, the more vulnerable he became to acts of public unreason. He, too, was done to death in the aftermath of a judicial travesty perpetrated on his brother.[76] In striving for the best possible principles by which to arrange their relations with other states, the Dutch succeeded only in bringing out the worst in all concerned. The world they were condemned to live in was the world of their public ethics turned upside down.

It was only to be expected, then, that the favored manner of denigrating Dutch claims to be taken seriously as a sovereign state was the ironic inversion of the very qualities that distinguished those claims. Their amphibious geography, for example, instead of reinforcing national legitimacy, became the butt of ridicule. "Holland, at the creation of the world, was no land for a dwelling place of men," stated the author of *Observations Concerning the Present Affairs of Holland.* Only land, which "yielded bread to eat and wood and stone to build with," was fit for men's habitations, and those that flouted the principle were "usurpers that deprive fish of their dwelling places."[77] Their whole metabolism was adapted to this unnatural dwelling, thought another, for "insomuch that in drawing their breath they must of necessity suck in the water which with long continuance forced all their inward parts coming out of the nose, ears and eyes, so stifling and choking them that it took away their breath."[78] Dutch chroniclers and apologists had argued (retrospectively) that their ancestral freedom from vassalage was owed, in part, to the labor of redeeming "drowned land." Had the separation of dry from wet not been ordained by Providence, it would have been an act of sinful pride if not blasphemy. But as part of a providential allotment and benediction, it conferred a direct sovereignty (as in the Judaic covenant) which acknowledged no human intermediaries. To foreign critics, for whom the historic conquest and possession of land was the essence of nationality, and for whom territory without personal allegiance was strictly inconceivable, such claims were disingenuous humbug. Watery land or land-from-water was in their view as much of an anomaly as the political artifice which had been constructed on its infirm structure. In Andrew Marvell's propaganda poem, *The Character of Holland,* originally turned

out for Cromwell in 1651 but serviceably republished in 1665 for the second
Anglo-Dutch war, the sedimentary nature of the country undermines its
claims to substance:

> *Holland, that scarce deserves the name of land,*
> *As but th'off-scouring of the British sand . . .*
> *This indigested vomit of the sea*
> *Fell to the Dutch by just propriety.*[79]

That sovereignty could not be built on silt was a refrain echoed by all those
who meant to discount Dutch nationality. Napoleon, who abolished it outright in 1810, described the Netherlands as so much "alluvium deposited by
some of the principal rivers of my empire."[80]

Just as muddy waste could not confer the attributes of true *patria,* so it
condemned those who dwelled upon it to a necessarily ignoble existence.
"Degenerate Race!" apostrophized the unfriendly author of *The Dutch Deputies,*
"Sprung out of Mire and Slime/And like a mushroom, ripen'd in small time."[81]
The brevity of Dutch history and the precocity of its fortunes were thus contrasted unfavorably with the immemorial epic of an authentically aristocratic-
dynastic-landed realm and supplied further evidence of its unfitness for their
company. Pierre le Jolle, one of Louvois's hacks, who, in 1672, figuratively
swept his hat to the floor in sarcastic mock greeting to the invaded Republic,
"Vostre Illustrissime Saleté," also reminded anyone so impressionable as to be
overawed by the metropolis that

> Amsterdam, quoi qu'on loue
> Est faite de merde et de boue[82]

The notion that the Dutch were generated from filth similarly stood on its
head their own much-advertised passion for cleanliness. A pamphlet of 1653
titled *The Dutch-mens Pedigree as a Relation, Showing how They Were First Bred and
Descended from a Horse-Turd which Was Enclosed in a Butter-Box* — a typical example
of the genre — had them produced from "dung, out of which . . . within nine
days sprung forth men, women and children, the offspring whereof are alive to
this day and now commonly known by the name of Dutchmen."[83]

The lowness of Their High Mightinesses, the baseness of the *Pays-Bas* was
relentlessly punned on by the court wits of the seventeenth century. The
author of *The Dutch Boare Dissected,* produced for the second Anglo-Dutch war
in 1665, was typical in jesting that "An Hollander is not an High-Lander, but a
low-lander for he loves to be down in the dirt and wallow therein."[84] But the
pig was superseded by the frog as the stock type of Hollandophobic caricature:

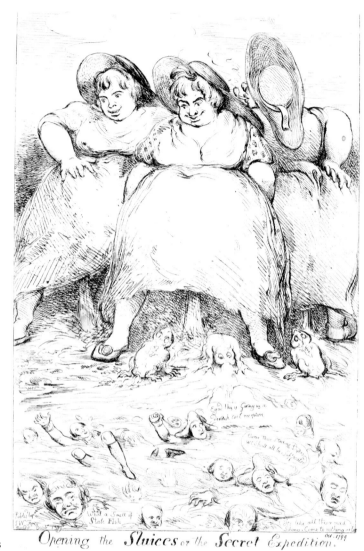

127. James Gillray, *Opening the Sluices or the Secret Expedition* 1799. British Museum Collection of Personal and Political Prints and Satires

ugly, slippery, guttural in utterance and with comical pretensions to higher status in the heraldic bestiary. "Frogs in great number/Their land doth cumber/And such like Croaking People" ran the same broadside. It was only late in the eighteenth century, when France rather than the Republic had established itself as the major naval adversary of the British, that their satires turned to the eaters, rather than the imitators of the frog, for stock abuse.[85]

Another standard theme was the dangerous consequences of the nether-dwelling's proximity to the infernal shades. The apparent paradox of the adjacency of hellfire with the waters was overcome by commentators who noted that the Dutch dredged their waters for the turf (peat) they burned as fuel. It was that same turf, they noted, that fed the distilleries to make the devil's fire-spirits. Lowness, then, could mean a league with unholy powers. The author of the *Observations* concluded in 1622 that the Republic "was the fittest for rebellion in all Christendom," since, through "the great lowness of their dwelling, they are the nearest neighbors to the Devil of any nation living on earth."[86] Owen Felltham, the Commonwealth polemicist, whose *Brief Character of the Low Countries* (1652) supplied the basic arsenal of xenophobic polemics recycled over and again through the seventeenth and early eighteenth centuries, also lingered on the diabolical fishiness of the Dutch. "There is in them," he wrote, "such an equilibrium of mud and water; their riches show them to be Pluto's region, and you all know what part that was the Poets of old did assign him."[87] It was, then, the "universal quagmire," "the buttock of the world, full of veins and blood but no bones in it." Its inability to describe a cut-and-dried border (unlike the reassuringly cliff-girt insularity of Albion) would, in the end, undo it, for there was "such an equilibrium of earth and water that a strong earthquake would shake them into a chaos."[88]

It was this repulsively amphibian habitat which accounted for their ungracious social habits. Coolness of blood bred phlegm and sluggishness, noted a succession of foreign travelers, who fretted and fumed over the time taken to serve dinner or ale. Both Dr. Johnson and Heinrich Heine have been credited with observing that if they knew the end of the world was imminent, they would take themselves off to Holland, for everything there happened ten minutes later. The same coldness of humor was said to breed churlishness of etiquette, a boorish bluntness of manner, a coarse diet of greens and cheese and pickled fish and the celebrated addiction to alcohol, needed to kindle the passions of love and war. "A Dutchman," wrote the author of the *Dutch Boare,* "is a lusty, Fat, Two-Legged Cheese-Worm. A Creature that is so addicted to eating Butter, Drinking Fat Drink and Sliding [i.e., skating] that all the world knows him for a Slippery Fellow."[89] More seriously, this gross insensibility to the refinements of polite society—what Marvell called their "dunghill soul"— made them impervious to the conventions of rank and honor by which the rest of the world went about its affairs. And that made the Dutch untrustworthy and even dangerous. In matters of bond, for example, they could be as slippery as the eels on which they supped. In a conceit on their Israelitish imaginings, the Caroline pamphleteer Henry Stubbes called the Republic "a Canaan, but seated in a Bog and overflowing with milk and water instead of honey." "They might well," he added, "be called the inhabitants of the Promised Land, since they were adept at making promises rather than keeping them."[90]

In matters of rank they were casual if not downright indifferent. Felltham shrewdly took the fixation with armorial bearings (still ingrained to this day) as an indication of the dilution of social hierarchy through common usage. "Escutcheons are as plentiful as Gentry is scarce; every man is his own herald."[91] And both the vestimentary hierarchy of dress and the household hierarchy of masters and servants were violated in the leveling practices of everyday conduct. "They should make good justices, for they respect neither person nor apparel. A boor in his liqor'd slop shall have as much good use as a courtier in his bravery."[92] And "in their families they are all equals and you have no way to know the Master and the Mistress but by taking them in bed together."[93] Marvell reverted to the dikes-and-drains conceit to sneer at the Dutch notion of office:

> *Who best could know to pump an earth so leak,*
> *Him they their Lord and Country's Father speak.*
> *To make a bank was a great plot of state;*
> *Invent a shov'l and be a magistrate.*[94]

This meanness of nature and calling was said to incapacitate them (contrary to a great deal of historical evidence) for the honorable arts of war. In one of the less perceptive observations on the country, the French ambassador in June 1665 remarked that, "It is not, after all, the *métier* of merchants to make war; [for that] it is necessary to have good leaders, good officers and brave soldiers and sterling sailors. The Hollanders lack all those."[95]

If social leveling was proof of the incorrigible ignobility of the Republic, its encouragement of religious heterodoxy was taken to be a more direct menace to the proprieties of the European order. Paradoxically, the militant Calvinism of the Synod of Dordrecht seemed, even to Counter-Reformation Catholics, to be less subversive than the free-for-all asylum of sectaries that masqueraded as principled toleration. With the former, even heretics at least were under the control of established authorities: prince and synod. With the latter, a swarm of dissident sectaries — hostile to any and all established faiths — was allowed to disseminate their heretical nonsense without check or restraint. "Is there a mongrel sect in Christendom," complained another of Cromwell's propagandists, "which does not croak and spawn and flourish in their Sooterkin bogs?" They were, said another, "the greatest patrons of Schism in the world."[96] For some of these writers the root of the evil was the feckless disregard for authority that led to a vicious pluralism, all the worse for being glossed by piety. "They are generally so bred up to the Bible," explained another pamphlet, "that almost every Cobbler is a Dutch doctor of divinity . . . yet fall those inward illuminations so different that sometimes seven religions are found in one family."[97] For other commentators this perverse chaos of beliefs was to be explained by the addiction to low commerce. Amsterdam might masquerade as an asylum, but its commitment to harboring any and every sect was in reality governed by the expediency of commercial congregation

> *Hence Amsterdam, Turk-Christian-Pagan-Jew,*
> *Staple of sects and mint of schism grew;*
> *That bank of conscience, where not one so strange*
> *Opinion but finds credit, and exchange.*[98]

Marvell's depiction of the bargain basement of faiths, an entrepôt of churches, was perhaps the common view of orthodox Protestant and Catholic alike. Even those who themselves benefited from asylum were shocked and dismayed at the heterodox bazaar in which they found themselves. Felltham called it "the Den of several Serpents" in which "you may be what Devil you will so you push not the State with your horns." " 'Tis the Fair of all the sects where all the peddlers of religion have leave to vent their toys, their ribands and their fanatic rattles."[99]

It was that *leave,* that license, which so mortified the absolute monarchies of Europe. If the thesis of baroque absolutism was the subjection of incoherence — in men and matter — to the ordering of hierarchies of court icons, then the willfully jumbled, randomly distributed, matter-of-fact Republic was its antithesis. Worse, it was chaos unconfined, a creeping, pullulating thing, a swarming abomination. So that the outrage it provoked was not just a matter of violating the aesthetic symmetries and Apollonian harmonies of the baroque state. Rather, its loose-jointed toleration was intolerable because it was seen to be intrinsically self-propagating. It was, then, an organic menace, the "pestiduct of Europe" through whose conduits the poison of individualist skepticism might infiltrate the body politic of the European monarchies.[100] Just as with the later, analogous anti-Semitic hysteria, Hollandophobia was possessed by a liquid terror. Commerce was the vector by which it supposed the toxins of unbelief to be carried through an infinity of ducts and waterways, canals and capillaries: unstoppable, formless and lethal. "They are like destructive vermin," wrote another English polemicist, "that will spread o'er the earth like the most poisonous weed."[101] As parasites they battened on sedition and fed off profit. Even in 1712 the parasitic metaphor adhered. The Dutch, said a Tory pamphleteer, were "the crab lice of Europe who would stick until they have drained Britain dry."[102]

To extend sanctuary to the enemies of order was bad enough, but it was the permission and encouragement of license in speech and writing that caused such deep offense that it was listed in the formal causes of war by both French and British monarchs in 1672. It was cited as the most obvious instance of the disingenuousness of the Dutch. While pretending to be the passive receptacle of those ejected from the realms of their neighbors and allies, they were in fact exploiting them to do mischief and "cry down" their dignity. Both Charles II and Louis XIV (like Mazarin and Cromwell before them) were keenly aware of the publication of *"blauwboekje"* squibs and broadsides attacking their administrations and held the Dutch authorities accountable for their dissemination. On the second of February, 1662, for example, Downing, the British ambassador at The Hague, received a note from Whitehall informing him that "We have lately received [advice] of a newsmonger at Utrecht, one van Haecht, which in his weekly books hath of late taken an insolent liberty speaking of His Majesty and his Government." It was the desire of Mr. Secretary that "you would please eye him and if you find occasion, demand redress on it."[103] It did nothing to assuage these grievances that Holland was also the center of publication for satirical prints and engravings, executed not only at the behest of Dutch politicians, but just as readily for the exiled enemies of home governments. But it was the gazettes that constituted the major source of offense. In France, or for that matter in Sweden, Spain or Brandenburg, the control of information on affairs of state *was* the boundary that defined the governing elite and separated them off from the mass of uninformed subjects. Through their fictive third-person reporting of events, and ready publication of rumor, the gazettes (from the 1650s onwards) created the unsettling impression of ironic observation. They transformed state events into public events by making the mere reader privy to the doings of the mighty. For the inventor of Versailles this was lèse-majesté with a vengeance.

It was no mitigation for the Dutch to plead that they were not mischief makers by design, that it was in the nature of their decentralized jurisdictions to be without the machinery for the suppression of opinion. The States General, much less the Grand Pensionary, could not order the magistrates of Haarlem or Amsterdam to prohibit a publication and arrest its author on the grounds that it may have given offense to a foreign power. If this was indeed the institutional state of affairs, retorted the offended diplomats, so much the worse for those institutions. It was high time, in their view, that they were amended, the better to conform to the decencies observed between states. While a sage and dispassionate observer like William Temple fully appreciated that this was tantamount to asking the Republic to become something other than it was, the more common suspicion (firmly rooted in George Downing's mind, of course) was that these bewildering institutional arrangements were themselves a subterfuge for the active prosecution of libelous propaganda. Worse still, the perpetual displacing of accountability for acts that breached international agreements was thought to be a smoke screen behind which the Dutch could do exactly as they pleased. One example of this syndrome should suffice. In 1658 Cromwell's resident at The Hague was informed that the suspicion that Dutch ships were secretly ferrying munitions to the Spanish at Ostend in violation of the Anglo-Dutch treaty of 1654 had been vindicated when Admiral Goodson had caught such a convoy, belonging to Michiel van Diest of Rotterdam, *in flagrante delicto.* The procedure was then as follows. The Resident informed the Pensionary, who informed the States General. But the States General was empowered to do no more than inform the States of Holland (through their deputies) of the affair. The States, in their turn, could ask the Rotterdam magistrates to look into the matter, but on the strict understanding that any restraining or punitive measures would be imposed by their own bench. The case was duly investigated, the offending skipper fined and his goods confiscated. But the proceedings dragged on through the formal niceties which the British took to be a peculiarly excruciating form of procrastination. Their irritation, however, turned to rage when a second sea captain, one Tysen, arrested in Amsterdam, was released with a light fine and a deportation order.[104] When an explanation of this apparently lenient sentence was demanded by the English resident, he was told that on investigation the Amsterdam authorities had discovered Tysen to be a Fleming and as such not bound by any Anglo-Dutch maritime convention. Fining and banishment were then the only appropriate measures in these circumstances. None of this dispelled the impression that Amsterdam was once again colluding in a breach of treaty in the interests of its own commerce. More insufferable still, its magistrates were invoking the holy aura of the law to cover their tracks.

Relations between the Dutch and their neighbors were progressively envenomed after midcentury by countless disputes of this sort, most of them petty, some of them more grave. Were they no more than the mutual bites and scratches exchanged between rival powers living in suspicious coexistence? Or were they, cumulatively, the symptoms of a more sinister incompatibility that would have its traumatic discharge in 1672? There was something more phobic about the vocabulary of abuse against the Dutch than seems warranted by the calculations of commercial competition. Its vitriolic aversion for the upstart and its repeated accusation that Holland had "engrossed" the wealth of the world amounted to a wholesale denaturing of their collective personality. This distorted image of Dutch social identity in turn nourished an animosity that became difficult to assuage, save by some brutal act of obligatory personality alteration. That, indeed, was part of the war aims of 1672. Beforehand, it was assumed that the Dutch did what they did because they were what they were. And what they were was base and dishonorable. French propagandists argued that the Republic had made a separate peace with Spain in 1648 because it was incapable of understanding honorable obligation. "Princes know the difference between right and wrong whereas the Dutch comprehend nothing but what is advantageous and disadvantageous," wrote Stubbes in 1672.[105] And another broadside reiterated the accusation that their deviousness arose from their natural want of majesty. "The Dutchmen have nothing that is royal amongst them; their High Mighties are not Princes, and they have different *iura majestatis* as they have different ends from the generous and sincere part of mankind."[106]

In retrospect it seems peculiarly disingenuous of the spokesmen of *raison d'état* — the hacks of Richelieu, Mazarin, Downing and Albemarle — to have accused the Dutch of inhabiting a world of diplomatic libertinism, or worse, of naked Hobbesian calculation. As with the *Schadenfreude* of commercial cupidity, the Dutch were being made the whipping boys of imperfectly de-Christianized tender consciences. For the truth was that they were being punished for being insufficiently, rather than excessively, Machiavellian. For all their harping on the issue, the separate peace with Spain was not really a *casus belli* for the French, since it was common knowledge that at the time they were contemplating precisely the same course of action. Their pique was at being preempted rather than being confounded. A much more smarting matter was the *noli me tangere* attitude adopted by de Witt when approached by Louis XIV's ministers on the possibility of a joint partition of the Spanish Netherlands. The prudential principle of *Gallicus amicus sed non vicinus,* which evidently preferred a weakened Spain to an aggrandized France on their frontiers, seemed, by definition, to impugn the King's honor and his long-term intentions.

Whatever the turbid mix of crossed ambitions and thwarted designs, it is apparent that by the 1660s, both French and British polemicists were busy canceling the credentials of sovereignty they claimed they had first issued on the Republic's behalf. Versions of the Eighty Years' War were being written in which the native Dutch emphasis on providentially protected self-help was transformed into a freedom that had been absolutely conditional on the disinterested assistance of France and England. In such accounts, the English, in particular, figure as altruistic mentors, rescuing the Dutch from certain extinction, and then graciously waiving any political favors offered as recompense for their military support. There was a grain of truth in this history, since Elizabeth had indeed declined the offer of sovereignty extended by the States General following the death of William the Silent in 1584. Her motives for so doing, however, were as thoroughly expedient as those which had inclined her to send Leicester into the Low Countries in the first place.[107] A century later the Dutch were made to appear ungrateful and impertinent wards. The author of *An Exhortation to the Love of our Country* (subtitled *The Obligations of the Dutch to England and their Continual Ingratitude*) referred to the Republic as "a crazy, sickly province, which we generously raised from the dirt and mire and which we nursed, fostered and brought up, only to be deceived and crossed for our pains and services."[108] "They are so surfeited with England's kindness," said another, "that like a bad spleen, they swell as big as makes Europe lean."[109] According to Jean Racine's account of the Dutch war, their sin had been that "blinded by prosperity, it [the Republic] failed to recognize the hand that so many times strengthened and supported it. Leagued with the enemies of France, it preferred to give the law to Europe and prided itself on limiting the conquests of the King."[110]

It is a measure of later historians' reduction of the Republic to a paradigm of "early capitalism" that they should have assumed the causes of this war to have been primarily economic.[111] Long-standing economic grievances were, of course, an important element in the triangular antagonism and were alluded to in the propaganda of the two allied powers. Colbert was certainly incensed by the attempt to impose a ban on the import of French wines and spirits into the Republic in retaliation for his protective tariff of 1667. But for all his aggressiveness and his long-term ambitions for Antwerp, it seems unlikely that at the outset he thought of war as a means of achieving French economic primacy. Indeed the sorry condition of royal finances and the sobering prospect of domestic competition from a new population of Flemish or Dutch merchants made him pause before contemplating any grandiose scheme of large-scale annexation.[112] Colonial disputes between the English and Dutch in Suriname, Africa and the East Indies had accumulated a backlog of contentious and bitter disputes, but these were as much matters of status and sovereignty as commercial advantage and often turned on issues of extraterritorial jurisdiction and the "persecution" or "torture" of colonial "trespassers." The essential debt that was to be discharged in 1672 was one of honor, and the language in which the *casus belli* was spelled out was heraldic, not mercantilist. "Tired of these insolences the King resolved to punish them," begins Racine's account, and Stubbes was even more forthright in his harangue on royal dignity: "When a Prince is wounded in his reputation, and his Forces are cryed down; when his prosperities are lessen'd and his disgraces increas'd; when endeavours are used to obscure the lustre of his greatness and justice, and his puissance is ruin'd in the eyes of strangers . . . this is the subject of a just war."[113]

In a second, equally violent broadside published a year later in 1673, Stubbes set out in detail the "tongues, outrages and insolences of the Dutch [that] have done England more prejudice than their ships or cannon."[114] They had, he claimed, trailed the English colors "defil'd with excrement" through the streets of their towns and had hung them upside down from the sterns of their ships. Worse still they had rendered the English "cheap and ridiculous by their lying Pictures and libelling pamphlets," that had made "the Ruffian think us a ruin'd nation." In the *Further Justification* he even included somewhat

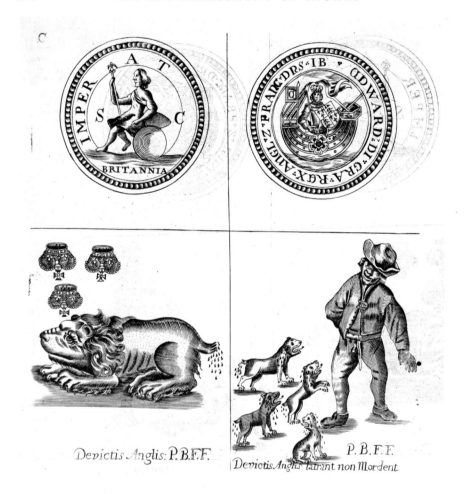

128. The British version of Dutch satires against England, 1673. From Henry Stubbes, *Further Justification.* Kress Library, Harvard University

primitively rendered examples of the "ridiculous pictures and odious medals" that had given offense: a lion with its tail cut to a bleeding stump set on reversed crowns; England personified as an adder whose tail was about to be axed by a Dutch *boer;* the British Phaeton brought low by the United Provinces; and Britannia herself laid at the feet of the Hollands Maid and trampled by the Dutch imperial elephant. All of these "indignities and contumelies" were so shocking and outrageous that the only wonder was, according to Stubbes, that His Majesty had so long endured them before finally making war.

The onslaught of 1672, then, was at least as much one of "wounded

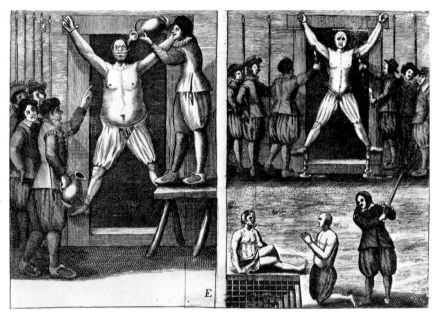

129. *The Massacre at Amboina*. From Stubbes, *Further Justification*. Kress Library, Harvard University

reputations" as of slighted profits. As such it was the war of Grotius's nightmares. Precisely the trifles of dynastic amour propre that he had condemned as insufficient cause for the shedding of Christian blood were now flung in the face of his compatriots. "God preserve the world from such Christian Princes," de la Court had written, "as for a Picture or a medal make no scruple to stir up commotions in Christendom and to cause the effusion of so much innocent blood."[115] And if the British were sensitive to the matter of national honor, it could hardly go by the board at Versailles. The French, too, had heard offensive reports of Dutch insults through iconography. It was said that van Beuningen, the Dutch ambassador in Paris, had had a medal specially minted with himself represented as Joshua arresting the course of the sun at Ai. There was indeed such a medal, showing Britain, the Republic and the Emperor, and bearing the offending motto *Ecquis Cursum Inflectet*, "who will deflect its course?" But it had been minted in Germany in 1668 and, as van Beuningen protested, he had been entirely innocent of its invention.[116]   But the element of princely vindication was paramount. Louis XIV was determined to campaign in person even if it meant seeking the assent of the Parlement of Paris for powers of regency for the queen. He meant to appear before the abject Lowlanders in the full radiance of his majesty, just as Le Brun represented him in the Gobelins tapestry: Apollo in arms, Caesar at the Rhine. Enthroned in his pavilion at Zeist, outside Utrecht, he let it be known to envoys from the States General that among his terms for pacification would be their future obligation to send an embassy each year to Versailles bearing a medallion that would express the depth of their contrition, their subjection to his royal authority and their eternal gratitude for his gracious clemency. Only this abrupt demotion to a tributary status would suffice to expunge the stain of their presumption. Charles II's propagandist, Stubbes, was less baroque in presenting demands, but the temper was the same. The true cause of war, he stated, was "the unavoidable necessity of reducing these insolent, treacherous Dutchmen into a posture as they may not only pay their due submissions with reparations of honour unto our King, but be obliged to continue them by a Treaty. They have no honour to lose, no conscience to stain, no certain principles to recede from."[117]

For all the fulmination, it was never clear either from the secret Treaty of Dover, which had hatched the war of premeditated aggression, or from subsequent discussions between the powers, how far they would have to go to accomplish this salutary punishment. Even the bleak little pun that encapsulated their ambitions: *"Il faut réduire les Provinces-Unies et les faire les provinces désunies,"*[118] was open to maximal or minimal interpretations. But like all exercises in predatory greed, the appetite grew with the eating. Once Utrecht was occupied and the *Te Deums* sung in the reconsecrated cathedral, Louis was invariably inclined toward the most implacable faction in his council, led by the war minister Louvois. However severe the demands, they argued, with virtually half its territory overrun, the King's army within striking distance of Amsterdam and the Republic forced to fight a simultaneous naval and land war, it was bound to capitulate. It was reliably reported that the States of Holland, even behind their redoubt of the *waterlinie,* were leaning towards accepting whatever terms were laid down. Consequently, those terms were draconian—as brutal and uncompromisingly vindictive as any that European powers have inflicted on each other in the course of their history as nation states. The Republic was to cede to the King of France not merely the "Generality Lands" they had already offered (Brabant and States Flanders) but all the territory he had conquered: in effect the three land provinces of Gelderland, Overijssel and Utrecht. Dutch fortified garrisons were to be dismantled and French ones to take their place. Economic aims were to be satisfied with the rescinding of any retaliatory tariffs imposed since 1667 and an indemnity so substantial as to make the Dutch more or less pay for their own chastisement. It was not this, however, that stung most; perhaps not even the dismembering of their territory so much as the crushing annihilation of their sovereignty and national self-respect. French subjects were to be permitted to travel at will through the Republic, in effect subject to no jurisdiction save that of their own King. The Catholic religion was not merely to be tolerated, but priests were to be at the public charge. The truncated Republic was itself to be a proclamation of future dependence, but the cantonment of French troops at Maastricht and Grave, and the adjacency of an enormously aggrandized monarchy, was its iron guarantee.

What was left of the Republic, moreover, was to be a much altered dominion. It was an axiom of the belligerent powers that once Pensionary de Witt and his "cabal" had been disposed of, the subsequent ascendancy of the Prince of Orange would create a state more amenable to their interests. Rendered inoffensive, it was projected as a cross between a serviceable banking state along the lines of Genoa, and a pumpernickel principality like Hanover or Brunswick. The Prince himself was assumed to be a crucial figure in this reconfiguration, and any offense he might take at the incorporation of the ancient domain of Orange in the south of France was to be appeased with some territorial compensation elsewhere. The assumption that William III would be a dependable client of the English and French monarchies was perhaps the most comical delusion among all those that shimmered in the mirage of the Sun King's pyrrhic victory. It was based on the marriage connection between the houses of Stuart and Orange, and William's cordial detestation of his jailor-tutor de Witt, who had attempted to deprive his dynasty of its offices of admiral and captain-general.[119] All of this was fact, but of no significance beside William's unconditional acceptance of the Dutch principle that the stadholderate, even freshly restored, was different in kind from a royal title. It was, in fact, a republican office, and owed its legitimacy to the Prince's ability to incarnate the will of the Fatherland, not the obedience of the nation to the will of the Prince. In the climate of 1672, Orangism meant resistance, not defeatism, especially since the estates of so many of the Orangist nobility were in territories occupied by the troops of the King of France and the Bishop of Münster.[120] Patriotic defiance was not, of course, limited to the traditional partisans of the dynasty. Once the de Witts were a spent force, former opponents of the Prince like Caspar Fagel of Haarlem became convinced that he was the indispensable patriotic symbol around which to rally the irresolute. And in the desperate circumstances of the *rampjaar,* old foes were, at least briefly, reconciled. Cornelis Tromp and Michiel de Ruyter patched up their squabbles long enough to face the unprecedented danger of a combined Anglo-French naval attack. Orangist ministers and those few States Party magistrates who survived the riotous upheavals in the Holland towns united to invoke the totems of the commonwealth. Prayers were offered to the Almighty protector of the *Nederkinderen;* memories of the old covenant rekindled. William himself, for all his taciturn opacity, revealed himself to be a more assiduous pupil of the dead Pensionary than of his dead father, who had indeed shown signs of treating the Republic like a dynastic fief. The new Stadholder's models were older and more reverent. The Prince-Father-Captain and the punishing-healing-redeeming flood had been the old testament in 1572, and they became the new testament a hundred years later.

In all these ways and many more, the convulsions of 1672 reinforced, rather than decomposed, the singularities of Dutch nationhood — at least in the short term. Even the atrocious murder of the de Witts might be seen as a catharsis through which the integrity and cohesion of the community was preserved against extreme strain. The blood guilt, remorselessly invoked by preachers as the price for profane living, was thus displaced onto the heads of scapegoats. The grisly fate of the Pensionary drained off the odium for transgressions that otherwise would have been imputed to the whole nation. And at the same time, the terror of death, both individual and collective, was averted by concentrating a killing on the figure who had presumed to incarnate the stadholderless commonwealth, the fatherless Fatherland. And if de Witt and his brother were slaughtered in the manner of a political oblation, so that the nation could survive, the sacrifice seems to have been heeded. For once they were gone, the dread of collective punishment was replaced with almost callous swiftness by a great surge of patriotic determination focused on the figure of the restored Prince.[121]

The language in which the events of 1672 were enveloped in the public mind was not that of dispassionate Cartesian logic. It was, rather, the shrieking fulmination reserved for moments of national trauma. Even those like Coenraad van Beuningen, de Witt's colleague and ambassador to France, who had personified the calculus of interests, turned inwards to exalted forms of mystical faith, following the shock of the invasion. Sermons and poems ranted of the apocalypse, of the seven-headed beast with ten horns.[122] The book of Ezekiel turned England and France into Gog and Magog (Chapter 38); Daniel 4 transformed Louis XIV into Nebuchadnezzar (Chapter 4).[123] One of the most bizarre purported to be a vision that appeared to van Beuningen, de Witt's long-time friend and diplomatic agent, who in crisis had turned from him to the Prince of Orange (and was himself later to become a mystic, enveloped in chiliastic visions). In the pamphlet Louis XIV arose transfigured as Nebuchadnezzar while the sky caught fire and the earth belched smoke and the King shrieked, "Kill, kill, for the hunt is good."[124] Other *zieners* walked the streets calling for the repentance of the unrighteous, and when the rage and terror of the common people had been appeased by the eviction of the sitting magistrates, crowds in the streets of Holland and Zeeland mortified their flesh with fasts and prayers of contrition.

Once the tide of events had turned somewhat, and the Dutch could bear to face their own history again, their battles at sea and on land were chronicled once more as the deeds of Joshua and Gideon — the latter being in special favor for having prevailed against heavy odds. The famous and spectacular print of the dike-break before Coevorden that swallowed up the Bishop of Münster's army — and in which six hundred peasants and soldiers drowned — was imbued by Romeyn de Hooghe with appropriately pharaonic overtones reminiscent of the earlier treatments of the relief of Leiden.

> *He [the Bishop] broke his solemn vow*
> *So God breaks his dike . . .*
> *Fight no more Bishop,*
> *By Groningen was there fire*
> *And now the water . . .*
> *Fight, fight no more Bishop*
> *Or fight with earth and air*

130. Romeyn de Hooghe, *The Dike-break at Coevorden.* Engraving. Bodleian Library, Oxford

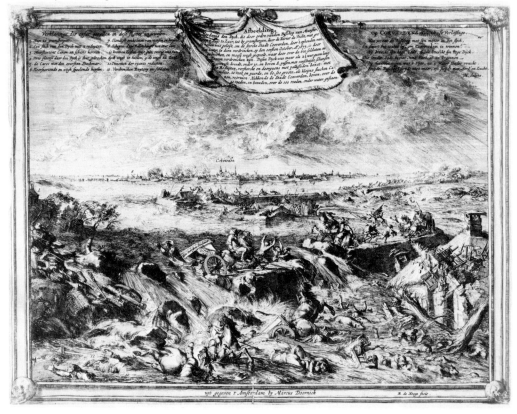

And in a similar vein, the ebb tide that forestalled the junction of the French and British fleets until they could be singly disposed of was attributed to the miraculous intervention of an appeased Jehovah.

Both text and images in the chronicle histories and propaganda sheets of the war rose to new heights of histrionic intensity. Drawing on the old atrocity prints of the Eighty Years' War histories, writers like Abraham Wicquevort (later arrested as a French spy!), Tobias van Domselaer, Lambertus van den Bosch and not least Romeyn de Hooghe himself, all reworked familiar themes to suit the new circumstances.[125] The French now substituted for the Spanish as bloodthirsty and pitiless marauders and Bodegraven and Swammerdam became the theaters of their cruelest excesses as Naarden and Oudewater had been a century earlier. But the narrative manner was strikingly similar. Stories were heavily localized and personalized, and the sacred totems of the family — old age, chastity, parental love — all annihilated. At Bodegraven an eighty-year-old matriarch is stripped naked, assaulted and left to die with a rag thrown over her; at Woerden a blind women is burned alive with her four children

131. Romeyn de Hooghe, *Mirror of the French Tyranny* . . . (Amsterdam, 1673). Houghton Library, Harvard University

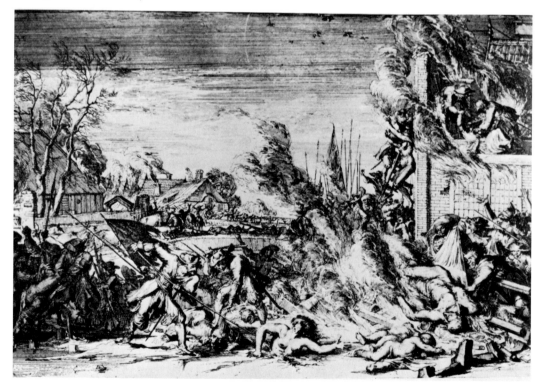

and another woman's genitalia "slit to the navel."[126] If anything the element of sexual horror was even more thoroughly exploited in the French "Black Legend" than in the Spanish. The story of a girl at Bodegraven raped by twenty-eight soldiers appeared over and again, and that of another, whose breasts, nose and ears were cut off after she was raped, and pepper rubbed in the wounds, was confirmed by the confession of a sick French soldier to his Dutch doctor at Nijmegen that he had participated in the torture. And there were consoling heroines in the same vein, like the young woman who burned herself alive "rather than tarnish her chastity."[127]

Where Leiden had been the martyr-town of the 1570s, Utrecht—occupied, desecrated and plundered (together with the garrison town of Woerden)—supplied the bitter history of a pious city subjected to every manner of infamy. There was, however, a subtle difference in the treatment of the two towns. Whereas in Leiden's case it had been the personal heroism of Burgomaster van der Werff that had stiffened the personal resolve of a famished and weakening populace, in Utrecht the regents were often depicted groveling at the feet of a triumphant Sun King while the ordinary citizens were left to pay the price for his entry. And it was on the plight of hostage Utrecht that the fiercest specifically Protestant propaganda was turned. So that in 1673—the turning year of the war—the French decision to hold a "Holy Sacrament" day centering on the Dom cathedral, on April 22, played directly into the hands of the resourceful Dutch propagandists. Virgin Mary banners, of gilt lilies and angels, of triumphal processions with arches bearing the legends *Ludovicus Triumphans* and of good *vaderlandse kinderen* being drafted into abominable Catholic ritual, was in fact no more than the truth and exactly calculated to turn the patriotic stomach and gnash the patriotic teeth. So that from a nation demoralized, divided and traumatized, with the help of a propaganda effort no less important than in twentieth-century national wars, the Dutch rallied around their Prince and their admiral heroes to turn the tide.

The virtuoso of patriotic imagery was Romeyn de Hooghe.[128] While his predecessors of the Spanish "Black Legend" divided into vulgar illustrators of atrocity and mayhem on the one hand, and the mannerist engravers who concerned themselves primarily with allegorical representation on the other, de Hooghe's graphic style combined those two visual vocabularies in an extraordinary explosion of baroque flamboyance. The stock scenes of epic battles, desecrated churches, massacred families and towns put to the torch all reappeared in his work, but were invested with a documentary immediacy and

132. OVERLEAF: Romeyn de Hooghe, engraving, from L. van den Bosch, *Toneel des Oorlogs* (1675). Houghton Library, Harvard University

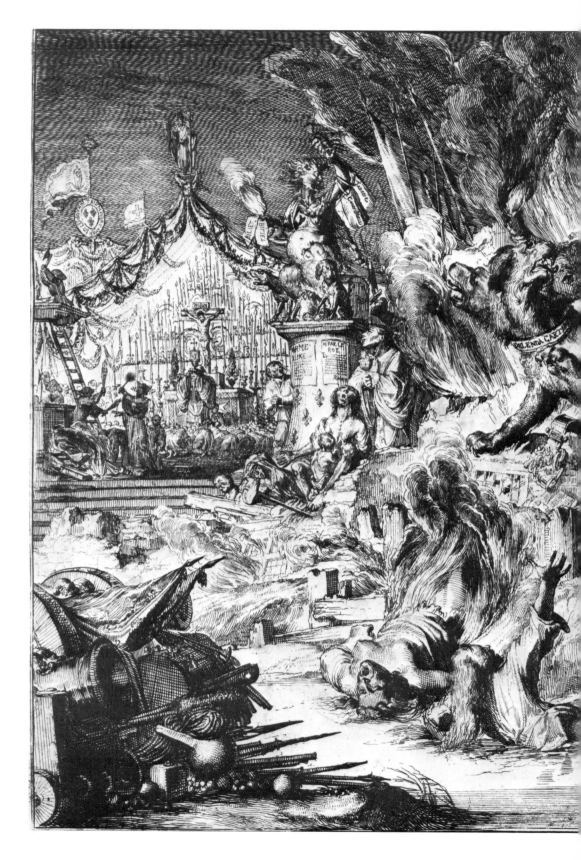

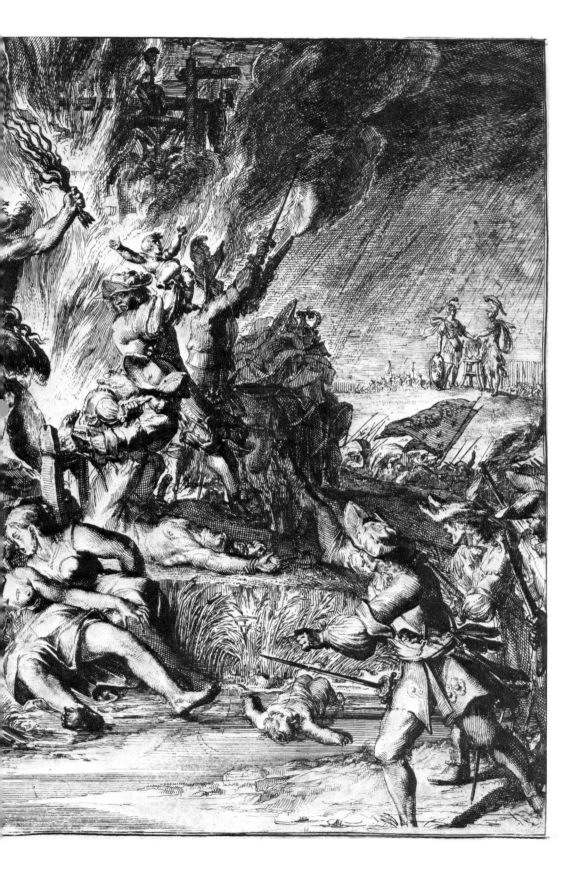

polemical force that the simpler prints in the old Fatherland style could hardly match. When the regents of Utrecht present the keys of their city in an engraving for Tobias van Domselaer's *Het Ontroerde Nederlandt,* their hands gesticulate in fawning subjection before the streaming pennants of Louis's conquest. In the most terrible images of all, originally engraved by de Hooghe for Wicquevort's *Advis fidelle aux véritables hollandais* (1673), a veritable holocaust unfolds in Bodegraven of babies, impaled naked female torsos and peasant heads cudgeled to a gory mess. In the semiallegorical prints, little is spared, and the gesture towards conventions only reinforces the impression of humanity tormented by monstrous power. In one fairly typical print taken from van den Bosch's *Toneel des Oorlogs* (1675), the alliance of hostile states is transmogrified into a three-headed hound wearing a collar with the legend *Delenda est Carthago.* This was the motto adopted by the victors in their early gloating and which sprang to the lips of Shaftesbury (no friend of absolute monarchs) in the House of Lords in 1672.[129] In place of the martial Apollo, a gorgon of repellent aspect is seated on the beast, coiffed with writhing coils of serpents. Around its feet are strewn mutilated corpses, and in the background infants are abducted by soldiers wearing appropriately savage expressions. Farther back still, amid flame and smoke, heads stuck on pikes and corpses hanging from gibbets are seen as troops carrying the banner of the fleur-de-lis advance. In the left background, beneath the pavilion of *Lodovicus Triumphans,* Catholic mass is celebrated before a craven and prostrated congregation as the ax is put to a Calvinist pulpit. On a pedestal nearby stands a figure bloated with "Billets," "Taxation" and "Requisition," while at its feet a cadaverous mother attempts to nurse her child from a dry and withered dug.

Not surprisingly, these images of the French occupation—as much as the reality (which was, itself, no picnic)—cut themselves into the Dutch historical memory. The scar from that wound was kept raw and livid by a fresh generation of chronicler-historians like Basnage and Leclerc, who as *Huguenots réfugiés* had endured their own exodus from their own implacable Pharaoh. And at the level of the popular imagination, not only those villagers who suffered directly from the French troops (or, much worse, the mercenaries of the Bishop of Münster), but also those Hollanders at the *waterlinie* whose herds and lands had been flooded to keep the invaders at bay—all transmitted their bitterness to succeeding generations. After William the Silent and Maurice, William III became the next chapbook hero to figure prominently in the domestic genre. And just as the Spanish ordeal had made it possible for a second (relatively unthreatened) generation to resume a protracted war in the 1620s, so the French ordeal supplied much of the emotional not to say fiscal momentum needed for the thirty-odd years of war against Louis XIV that lay ahead.

For all this, 1672 marks a different sort of caesura in Dutch history.

Historians who have conventionally parenthesized the Golden Century between 1570 and 1670 may not, after all, be far wide of the mark. While it seems likely that by the last decades of the seventeenth century the Republic had already gone beyond its apogee in economic fortunes, colonial energies and demographic growth, I am not here concerned with the economic historian's pastime of spotting the climacteric. It is rather a matter of an alteration in the Republic's sense of its own place in Europe. For if its narrow escape had lent further force to a sense of separation, in the longer term, survival seemed to necessitate reintegration into a system of dependable alliances. The result of this was a dilution of their singularity, and a corresponding relaxation of the jealousies and suspicions that had attended their career at its zenith. The Republic, of course, retained the extreme peculiarity of its decentralized institutions, but in the age of reason this became more the object of commiserating curiosity than bewildered anger. The very existence of the Republic no longer seemed an "engine of sedition" even when it lent its imprimatur to works condemned by more stringent censors elsewhere. Its hauteur somewhat compromised by association with less philosophically lofty polities, the Dutch state seemed an amiable anomaly, already sinking into a reassuringly lethargic obsolescence. Comparisons with Venice began to be apropos.

In what respects did the nation become more acceptably ordinary? The transmogrification of the Stadholder into King William III at Westminster was itself an unplanned answer to the problems that had bedeviled the Cromwellian attempts at union. The two states remained wholly distinct yet bound by both person and interest. While evidently not much loved (except by the Ulster Presbyterians), King Billy was respected for his military tenacity and his surprising aloofness from party favoritism. More important than any of this, he offered himself as an incarnation of constitutional propriety so that, temperamentally stubborn, he was careful never to exceed the limits of a prerogative overexploited by the later Stuarts. Within the anti-Lodovican alliance, the decisive element (and one that survived William III's demise) was not so much the Anglo-Dutch rapprochement, as the intervention of the Habsburg emperor. It was hard to miss the ironic symmetry. That dynasty against which the Republic first defined its founding liberties now became the guarantor of its survival. With the empire, its cadet House of Savoy and sundry other warlords on the make (like the elector of Brandenburg) throwing their weight against Louis XIV, the focus of the alliance shifted gratifyingly away from the Republic itself and towards the more generalized concern of the European balance of power. The Netherlands was seen as merely an early victim of the French King's incorrigible hunger for aggrandizement, and in particular his manipulation of dynastic claims. Even when the fighting itself plowed back and forth in the Flemish fields, the Republic acted more as an

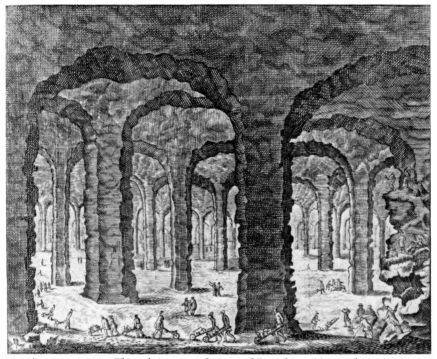

133. Anon. engraving, The subterranean fortress of Petersburg, Maastricht.
Bodleian Library, Oxford

integral partner in a general coalition than as the state for whom the contest was a matter of life and death.

Nor were there any lingering illusions about fighting a peculiarly republican kind of war. De Witt had been reluctant to support a substantial regular army, for fear that it might revert to its traditional role of intervening in politics on behalf of the stadholderian cause. But his understandable political circumspection had left the Republic seriously depleted of troops in a time of emergency. Even in 1671 his pathetic fallacy had been that, in extremis, the Republic could fall back on a variety of quasi-civilian reserves to bolster its regular troops. But the *waardgelder* militias, much less the fantastic pipe dreams of raising Swiss Protestant volunteers or arming fifteen to twenty thousand peasant home guards, were no substitute for effectively mobilized and equipped professional soldiers. From 1688 through to the peace of Utrecht, the Republic fought the War of Spanish Succession (1702–13) much like its allies: with a large army (often of more than one hundred thousand) the majority of whom were mercenaries. The Dutch navy now had to supplement its native crews with even greater numbers of foreigners, principally Scandinavians,

Scots and Germans.[130] It was even possible to use the Republic's still considerable financial resources to subsidize allies to join the fray. All of this meant a further dilution of the myth of republican self-reliance, but Pensionaries of this time like Heinsius surveyed the world and the place of the Dutch in it, with a more prudent and modest vision than had de Witt.

There were other, subtler ways in which the Dutch relaxed their grip on their sense of national singularity. At the same time as they were resisting the military power of France, many among the governing elite of the Republic were capitulating to its cultural tone. Classicism had in fact always played an important part in Dutch literature and especially in architectural design.[131] But the work of van Campen and Post had filtered Italian taste through the Netherlandish tradition, and had come up with something indigenous and inimitable. Towards the end of the seventeenth century, a much more imitative strain set in, especially in literary and artistic style, accentuated, if anything, by the injection of Huguenot graphic artists like Daniel Marot. For the first time, there appeared the signs of an ashamed self-consciousness about the Dutch vernacular—almost three-quarters of a century after Bredero had celebrated its earthy virtues. The academy Nil Volentibus Arduum established itself as a watchdog of refined taste (in the manner of an unofficial Académie royale), committed to scouring the language of vulgar impurities and colloquialisms. A "polite style" of greeting and discourse, heavily adulterated with French gallantries, became fashionable among younger members of the patriciate who made painful attempts to emulate the harmonies of the Alexandrine couplet in the inauspicious medium of urban Dutch. The Amsterdam *schouwburg* even began to turn to the staples of French classical tragedy for its repertory. Gérard de Lairesse performed something of the same function for painting, grafting the formal severities of French classicism onto the more exuberant traditions of Netherlandish history painting.[132] The result was more stilted than monumental. And the desire to affect a *bon ton à la Versailles* spread from habits of gait and posture to dress and an appetite for the ornately sumptuous in interior decoration and hangings.

All these developments widened the distance between the most "cultivated" section of the elite, booted and peruked in the international court style, and the mass of the governed, who adhered to more traditional native manners. And since the period from 1690 to 1740 was also a time in which access to the patrician circles seems to have become more difficult, historians have found it possible to speak of an "aristocratization" of the Republic around this time. Certainly, by 1730, the culture which had once transected social divisions had split into subcultures that corresponded to them. Where once the regent elite had pretended to legitimate its monopoly of power through manners, language and beliefs that were shared with the governed, its rationale was now exactly the opposite. It was through contrast, rather than conformity, with popular habit that it demonstrated its title to rule. This was tantamount to a redefinition of the patrician ethic, and one that was indeed closer to other European aristocracies. But it was, by the same token, a striking and dangerous departure from Dutch tradition. Predictably, it was not long before members of the ruling class itself—as well as those beyond its privileged circles—began to register "patriotic" objections. So that even by the 1740s, writers in the "spectatorial" press were equating cosmopolitanism with excessive remoteness from the *brede middenstand* (the middling sort), and both as a betrayal of the national patrimony.

The year 1672, then, was the second great historical watershed in the life of the independent Dutch nation. And when the trauma had abated, a strange exchange of values ensued. As the Republic ceased to be the great issue of European politics, and as its obtrusiveness as a power diminished, so it began to be perceived as less of a threat and more of a necessary party to the general pacification of Europe. By the end of the wars of Spanish Succession, it had, in effect, become "naturalized" as a member of the community of powers. The three great peace treaties of the wars with Louis XIV—Nijmegen, Rijswijk and Utrecht—were all signed on Dutch soil, but for the last time in European history. And as it came to be considered less peculiar, and so less threatening, the Republic gradually came to feel itself less threatened. Dutch statesmen of the early eighteenth century like Heinsius and van Slingelandt sought means of protecting Dutch integrity that would be less risky than those of de Witt. No more trust in *waardgelders* to reinforce regular troops, no more fantasies of Protestant volunteers, less anxiety about reciprocal troop engagements with foreign powers, less eagerness to make high court judgments on international disputes before the *corps diplomatique*. Instead of the principled vigilance that had been the style of de Witt's conduct of affairs, there were concrete dispositions—barrier fortresses in the southern Netherlands, for example— and treaty guarantees that connected, rather than separated, the interests of the Republic from those of other powers. The aims were now more modest: an economy both of resources and of principles more in keeping with the new sense of the country's limitations.

Historians, too, began to place the history of the Republic into some wider perspective, comparing and contrasting its career with those of other republics, Catholic and Protestant. The similarity between its predicament in 1672 and the onslaught on Venice by the powers of the League of Cambrai in 1505, for example, was already noticed by writers in both states.[133] Even the comments of visiting foreigners were less strained by envy—of either the admiring or the detesting kind. Downing's aggravated spleen was replaced by Addison's accurate reassurance (following Temple) in 1707 that the wars had meant behind the "seeming prosperity of the United Provinces we know they are indebted many Millions more than their whole Republick is worth, and if we consider the variety of taxes and impositions they groan under . . . we shall not think the condition of the people so much to be envied as some amongst us would willingly represent it."[134] And as extolling the virtues of commerce became less controversial, so did praise for its most spectacular incarnation. Similarly, as the thin wedge of enlightened values—religious toleration and scientific curiosity, for instance—forced an entry into the culture of aristocratic Europe, so the Republic became transformed from a cuckoo in the nest, or an "engine of sedition," to an historical *exemplum*. Men of art and letters who came to the Republic as visitors, on publishing business or even as immigrants, affected a polite appreciation that was close cousin to condescension. And the linden-lined canals, the Hortus Botanicus in Leiden, and the great stone bulk of the Amsterdam Stadhuis or the East India Pakhuis, which had once seemed so dazzling and so vexing at the same time, now featured as exhibits on an itinerary to a living museum of the early Enlightenment. Such were the therapeutic charms of the second-rate.

Does all of this mean that there was some involuntary kinship between paranoia and patriotism, between insecurity and national energy? Or, conversely, that release from the anxieties of being exceptional brought with it the sort of culture in which placid mediocrity became the norm? Indeed it does.

Not that this occurred overnight, or even over the interminable period of wars and punctuated truces that began in 1672 and ended only in 1714. At moments of tension during the early eighteenth century, it was a matter of a moment for both parties to revert to the stock antagonisms and mutual suspicions that had been standard form in the classic age of their rivalry. While it is true that the more apopleptic expressions of Hollandophobia— "They hate us because we are for Monarchy and Episcopacy, s'blud Amboyna always runs in my Mind—and Chatham too and the Fishery"—were now *parodies* put in the mouth of an unreconstructed Tory squire by a Whig pamphleteer,[135] nonetheless, the prototype was not so easily disarmed. Towards the end of the war, when the Tories were arguing for an early settlement with France and leaning back to the affiliations of the 1670s, their polemicists, like Swift and the editors of *The Examiner,* continued to chorus the ancient refrains. "We do say that the Dutch are our rivals, and the only formidable rivals of Britain in its trade; we do say that they have never missed any opportunity, either by secret fraud or open violence, to destroy our factories and ruin our commerce: We appeal for the truth of this to former Times. . . . "[136]

Nor was the Dutch tradition of squaring up to the world and proclaiming, unabashedly, its special historic identity, altogether cowed by cautious pragmatism. In 1703, the apocryphal *Fables, Moral and Political,* pseudonymously and posthumously attributed to de Witt, were published for the first time in an English translation. It seems likely that they were intended as an arsenal for those Whig pamphleteers whose cause lay in praising rather than deprecating the Dutch example. Together they formed a lexicon of the national virtues. Fable Three, for example, related the history of "A Frenchman and a Dutchman in the Kingdom of Apes."[137] The monkey monarch invited both to a court ball, and when the preliminaries of "hunting and hawking" were over "they fell to eating, drinking, swearing, cursing, gaming, whoring, talking lewdly and all other excesses." The king then asked his visitors how his realm pleased them. "The insinuating Frenchman, perceiving the vanity of the apes, resolved to suit his answer accordingly and therefore told him that he was astonish'd at the great prudence, courage and eloquence he had observed in all his subjects, and that their way of dressing and eating surpassed all that he had seen elsewhere. That the horses, hawks and hounds of his country were not to be matched, but above all that the ladies were passing fair and that in short he fancied himself to be in an earthly paradise and that his whole ambition was to be admitted into the number of His Majesty's most humble slaves." The consequence of these remarks was that the Frenchman was immediately made a member of the king's privy council.

The Dutchman was, however, made of different stuff, thinking "that he should gain more honour by telling the plain truth of the matter. . . . He therefore roundly told the Ape that he had not seen the least pattern of good government, and that all his country had presented him with nothing but a scene of lewdness and debauchery, and he plainly saw that apes were nothing but apes and all their actions apish and there was no comparison between their ways of living and those of Rational creatures." The consequence of those remarks was that the candor of the Dutchman was repaid by his being immediately put to death.

And in case the moral remained at all veiled, the "explanation" contrasted unfavorably the craven flattery of the slave-Frenchman with the upright, liberty-addicted Netherlander: "By Dutchmen we mean men who are born and bred under a free government, and who will not easily be brought off from their old ways of living and talking, though it should be their misfortune to be removed into the dominions of Kings and sovereign princes."[138]

This was fighting talk, Tromp's broom tacked once more to the bowsprit. But at the same time that it warmed the cockles of the old *Vaderlands-gevoel,* it hinted, prudentially, of calamities in the offing. The Dutchman of the tale, it is true, died an honorable man. But he died.

CHAPTER FIVE

THE EMBARRASSMENT OF RICHES

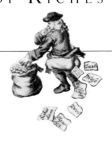

For it too often happens that riches bring self-indulgence, and superfluity of pleasures produces flabbiness as we can see in wealthy regions and cities (where there are merchants). Now those who sail to distant places are no longer content with home comforts but bring back with them unknown luxuries. Therefore because wealth is generally the mother of extravagance, the prophet mentions here expensive household furnishings, by which he means the Jews brought God's judgment upon themselves by the lavish way they decorated their houses. For with pictures he includes expensive tapestries like Phrygian embroidery and vases molded with exquisite art

JOHN CALVIN
Commentary on Isaiah 2:12, 16

Let a merchant hold fast to this precious maxim: honor before gold   GODFRIED UDEMANS
Spiritual Rudder of Commerce

Here lies Isaac le Maire, merchant, who during his affairs throughout the world, by the grace of God, has known much abundance and has lost in thirty years (excepting his honor) over 150,000 guilders. Died as a Christian 30 September 1624

Epitaph

i CORNUCOPIA

Amidst lengthening afternoon shadows, an unhurried *au revoir* is in progress. A handsomely gilded and studded coach awaits its passengers before the gate of a Dutch country house. An elegant skirt is gathered as its wearer prepares to mount the carriage steps, leaving her companion with an expression of disconsolate reluctance. Men loiter over their farewells, an affectionate arm slung over a departing shoulder. Business may impend, but like the serving boy waiting uncertainly with a jug of last refreshment, it forbears to intrude.

Whatever else it may be, Ludolf de Jonghe's conversation piece is hardly a specimen of a Calvinist culture. The work ethic could not be more agreeably remote. If anything, it is a poem to the Dutch leisure ethic: an arrangement of Corinthian pilasters, rustling satin, sleek hounds and afternoon breezes. A delicious satisfaction with the material world saturates the canvas. Though it may have stirred the Calvinist ministry to denunciations of epicureanism, such innocent bucolic pleasures evidently became fashionable among the well-to-do by the 1660s.[1]

The English traveler William Aglionby discovered this world of small delights when he discovered Leiderdorp. The village lay, as its name implied, on the outskirts of Leiden, then at the peak of its fame and prosperity.[2] Together with a constellation of busy hamlets—Oegstgeest, Souterwoude and Achterhoven—it had long been a supplier of dairy and horticultural produce for the city (now swollen to eighty thousand souls), and a way station for the busy barge traffic east to Gouda and Amsterdam. But when Aglionby visited Leiderdorp in the summer of 1660, it was already outgrowing its humble standing as a cabbages-and-ale parish. Less of a market garden and more of a garden suburb, it was becoming the kind of bosky retreat recommended by humanist doctors like Johan van Beverwijck for the reinvigoration of jaded

134. Ludolf de Jonghe, *Farewells Before a Country House.* Formerly Gallery P. de Boer, Amsterdam

135. Anon. engraving. *Ockenburgh* from Jacob Westerbaen, *Alle de gedichten* ('s Gravenhage, 1672). Houghton Library, Harvard University

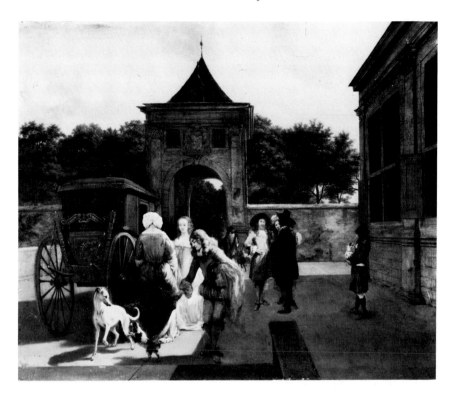

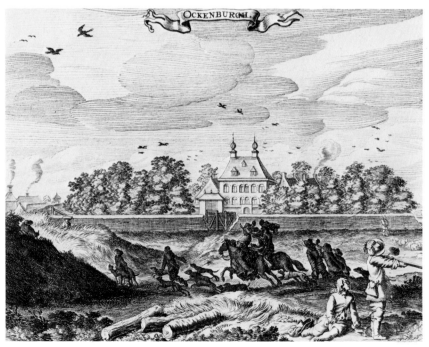

urban bodies and souls. Between water meadows and copses of elm and beech stood handsome villas, very much like that depicted in de Jonghe's painting, built for the patricians and cloth manufacturers of Leiden. Both their form and function owed a good deal to the Palladian prototypes of the Veneto, modified by the fashionable Dutch classicism of Pieter Post and Jacob van Campen, and correspondingly more generous with rose brick and Bentheim limestone than with marble. Like the Italian villas, they were designed to give the agreeable illusion of the pastoral without any of its rustic inconveniences, being light, spacious and harmoniously proportioned. Leafy parks offered the prospect of salubrious promenades with dogs bred for genteel companionship and occasional hunting. Kempt tenant farms gave the man of business the chance to play the squire, in keeping with the title of Heer he bought along with the property, and the coat of arms he had emblazoned above the gateway. Above all, the *buitenplaats* was a cleansing repose from the soiling commerce of the town.

Leiderdorp was neither the earliest nor the grandest of these clusters of elegant country mansions. The richest and most self-consciously cultivated among the patriciate had spilled out from their crowded cities in search of bucolic arcadia as early as the 1630s, though the momentum of building accelerated considerably after 1650.[3] The Haarlem elite chose to remove themselves to the bracing ozone of the dunes, where a wealthy confectioner bankrupted himself in creating the grandiloquent Elswout in 1634–35, but it took another twenty years before the house was completed for its new owner, Gabriel Marcelis, an arms merchant and consul for the king of Denmark. The

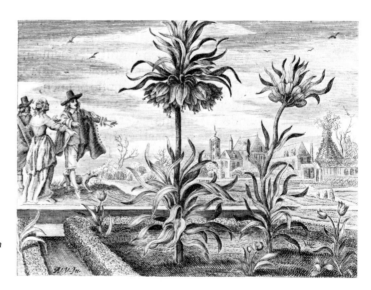

136. Adriaen van de Venne, engraving from Jacob Cats, *Ouderdom en Buitenleven* (in 1655 edition of complete works)

Coymans family, with their roots in Haarlem but with branches flourishing in Amsterdam, built De Kruidberg, also amid the dunes, in the 1640s. But the major impetus for the country retreat came from court-hating courtiers around the Stadholder and the States General at The Hague. Italianate inspiration, horticultural enthusiasms and the affected convention of opposing the corrupt decadence of court life with the moral rejuvenation of the country all combined to encourage urban flight. Constantijn Huygens, Stadholder Frederick Henry's secretary, and Jacob Cats both expended a great deal of money and even more lines of poetry on, respectively, Hofwijk (Away from Court) and Zorghvliet (Fly from Care). Cats, who was a great advocate of rural therapy for urban ills, also kept a house, De Munnikenhof, in his native Zeeland, near the village of Grijpskerk. Zorghvliet was rather grander, and there are occasional signs that his Calvinist conscience was at least a little defensive on the subject. He liked to put it about that it was seated amid a mere sandy waste (where in fact it was watered by a prolific little brook) and that any pleasures he might derive from the property were the fruits of decently Georgic toil.[4]

There was nothing apologetic, however, about the villas on the River Vecht between Amsterdam and Utrecht, where stunning houses sprang up in dense and elegant competition. Joan Huydecoper, one of the most powerful and enduring of the Amsterdam regents, had Philips Vingboons build, probably in 1639, what became the cynosure of admiration along the "Zegepralende Vecht": Goudestein.[5] In 1640, Huydecoper acquired the title of Heer of its adjacent village, Maarsseveen, and added a cupola to the house in proclamation of his promotion. In 1674, Jan van der Heyden painted the house, set by the river, complete with its urn-surmounted gateway and a facade with a relief-bust of the lord of the manor set into the pediment.

Alongside the splendor of the Vecht, Leiderdorp could boast only more modest residences, but what nevertheless struck Aglionby was not merely their elegance, but the unconcealed relish with which their owners showed them off. The village, he wrote, has "more palaces than country people's houses. Tis here where we must admire the magnificence of the citizens, for one would think that there were an emulation between them who would show most marks of riches by their expenses."[6] When going on to describe other towns in Holland he reverted to the same vein, for it was evidently the visible opulence of people and places that made a deep impression on him. Leiden he thought extraordinary in being so bountifully endowed with riches of both scholarship and the purse. The Hague was a "place which by the breadth of its streets, the nobleness of its buildings, the pleasant shade of its trees and the civility of its inhabitants, may justly claim the title of the most pleasant place in the world and may make all men envy the happiness of those who live in it." As for Amsterdam, "Tis commonly said that this city is very like Venice.

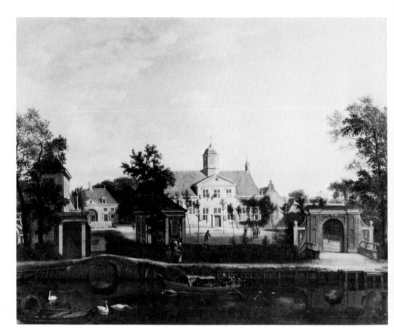

137. Jan van der Heyden,
Goudestein. Wellington Museum,
Apsley House, London

For my part I believe Amsterdam to be much superior in riches. . . . " Nor was
this merely a matter of comparing aristocracies, for Aglionby noted that signs
of prosperity and ease extended right through the population. And he was
shrewd in observing that the glitter of ornament was set off to good advantage
when surrounded by a modest ground. The country people he encountered in
the heart of Holland wore black fustian, but their wives sported gold rings and
bonnet pins. It was "not rare," he supposed (with pardonable exaggeration),
to "meet peasants worth ten thousand pounds."[7]

From all this it may be assumed that William Aglionby was virtually an
uncritical admirer of the Republic, though like many of his contemporaries
somewhat bewildered by its governing institutions. Doubtless his head was
turned by what he saw and enjoyed, but his account is nonetheless remarkable
for its emphasis, not only on the riches of the country, but on the delight the
Dutch had in exhibiting their good fortune. By the time that Joseph Marshall
traveled much the same route a century later, in the 1760s, the pleasure of
spending seemed to have become established as an addiction of the well-
to-do. He commented:

> I know hardly any country where they spend their money more freely to pass
> their time agreeably and enjoy whatever their rank and fortune entitle them to.
> You see everywhere good houses, well-furnished, plentiful and elegant tables

kept, numerous servants, equipages as common as elsewhere, rich dresses . . . and in the education of their children no expense spared. In a word you view not only the conveniences of life, but those improvements, those refinements which rich and luxurious ages only know.[8]

This vision of the Dutch elite as free-spending prodigals seems strangely at odds with the more conventional picture of them as Europe's most tightfisted burghers. Josiah Child was more typical of the general run of foreign commentators when he wrote of "their parsimonious and thrifty living which is so extraordinary that a merchant of one hundred thousand pounds estate will scarce spend so much per annum as one of fifteen hundred pounds estate in London."[9] This commonplace, echoed innumerable times in the seventeenth century, further held that the Dutch owed much of their economic success to an ingrained aversion to conspicuous consumption. "They are frugal to the saving of an egg-shell," wrote Owen Felltham with his usual mixture of envy and jeering.[10] But if the evidence of travelers' eyes, especially in the second half of the century, seemed to belie the stock image of an austere and ascetic way of life, the discrepancy could be explained, in the manner of Sir William Temple, by an unfortunate falling off from older, stricter ways.[11] By the 1660s, it was commonly said, the frugal and modest habits, which had originally created the foundations of Dutch prosperity, were now being squandered in a show of worldly vanity and luxury. This was no more than the latest version of the Roman stoic lament for the sybaritic corruption of republican virtue. That it was much rehearsed by Dutch moralists throughout the seventeenth and eighteenth centuries is not in doubt, but whether the flocks ever heeded their Jeremiahs (except in times of national crisis) is more doubtful. The same collective personality that heard diatribes against Queen Money and Dame World from the pulpit rejoiced in flaunting its power on their streets and in its homes. And that peculiar ambivalence was as true for the sixteenth century as for the eighteenth. Both Lodovico Giucciardini early on and Thomas Coryate towards the end of the sixteenth century were so much lost in admiration at the spectacle of Netherlands towns that it seems unlikely that there ever was a golden age of gold-hatred. At Gorinchem, Coryate went into raptures over "the sweetness of the situation, the elegancy of the buildings, the beauty of the streets, all things whatsoever did so wonderfully delight me that as soon as I entered into one of the longer streets, I methought I was suddenly arrived in the Thessalian tempe or the Antiochan tempe."[12] And while the majority of economic writers in the seventeenth century may have argued a connection between frugality and prosperity, there were some at least (like Nicholas Barbon, John Houghton and Dudley North)[13] who thought display — or the gratification of wants — wholly compatible with the national fortune.

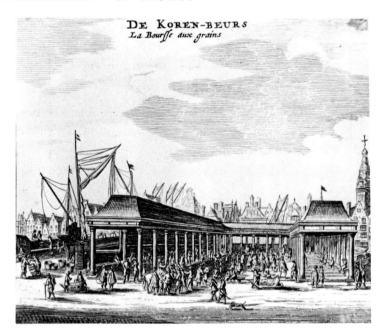

138. I. Veenhuijzen, *The Corn Exchange.* Author's collection

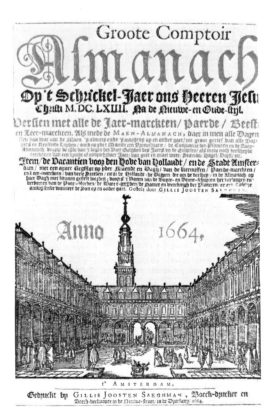

139. Woodcut, title page from *Groote Comptoir Almanach* 1664. Atlas van Stolk, Rotterdam

There was, then, a minority school in England which remained hostile to the manipulation of demand as a contribution to economic productivity. But it would have been eccentric for them to have cited the Dutch in vindication. No inhibitions of this sort, however, deterred the mischievous genius of Bernard de Mandeville. Born in Rotterdam, Mandeville knew his former compatriots better than their self-proclaimed admirers, and in *The Fable of the Bees* invoked the cliché of their supposed austerity as a prime case of humbug. "The Dutch may ascribe their present grandeur," he wrote, "to the virtue and frugality of their ancestors as they please, but what made that contemptible spot of earth so considerable among the powers of Europe has been their political wisdom in postponing everything to merchandise and navigation [and] the unlimited liberty of conscience that is enjoyed among them. . . ."[14] History, rather than piety, rationality rather than zeal, humanism rather than Calvinism, he thought, supplied the answers. Frugality, if it was ever put on, he continued, was less a conscious choice than the consequence of the "hardships and calamities of war." Once these involuntary impositions were removed in peace, their manners naturally gravitated towards the sensuous and the epicurean:

> in pictures and marble they are profuse; in their buildings and gardens they are extravagant to folly. In other countries you may meet with stately courts and palaces which nobody can expect in a commonwealth where so much equality is observed as there is in Holland but in all Europe you shall find no private buildings so sumptuously magnificent as a great many of the merchants' and other gentlemen's houses are in Amsterdam, and in some of the great cities of that small province, and in the generality of those that build there, lay out a greater proportion of their estates on the houses they dwell in than any people upon the earth.[15]

The case for the Dutch as commodity fetishists ought not to be overstated. Mandeville — who delighted in turning received wisdoms on their head — was not suggesting that, compared to the Amsterdam town hall, Versailles was a dingy hovel, and neither am I. As he pointed out, to measure Dutch conspicuous consumption by the prodigal standards of a royal court is to compare like with unlike and end up confirming the self-evident. But to discover whether religion had the particular effect that Max Weber claimed is to undertake a different and more challenging comparison. It is to establish whether, compared with other commercial cultures, and, in particular, non-Calvinist ones like Venice or Antwerp or eighteenth-century London, the Dutch behaved differently in their pattern of personal consumption. On the notional index of European parsimony which informs most casual accounts, the Dutch seem to figure below the Genevans but above the Venetians. This may be to mistake rhetoric for reality, sermons for social action. For all the pungency of the polemics against worldliness and luxury, there seems no reason to assume that the "core" groups of Dutch society, from the patriciate at the top to skilled artisans and tradesmen at the bottom, showed any special propensity to avoid consumption in favor of savings and investment. So whatever Calvinist attacks on Dame World did do (and we shall come to that further on), they do not appear to have diverted capital from expenditure to productive enterprise. This is not to say that in the glut of capital that washed around midcentury, there were not high rates of capital accumulation, merely that it is difficult to attribute that, directly or indirectly, to the teaching of the ministry.[16]

At any rate, there were some Dutch writers who were not in the least shy of celebrating the Republic as a consumer's paradise: the great *emporium mundi.* Advertising the attractions of a Dutch town—not merely its public monuments and churches, but also commercial buildings and private residences—became an obligatory feature of urban panegyrics. These were commissioned and published from the first decade of the seventeenth century for the express purpose of civic bragging, somewhat in the manner of modern chamber of commerce publicity literature. City notables expected to see themselves the objects of fulsome dedications just as they expected to have their group portraits painted as officers of the *schutterij* or regents of the city orphanage. And there was no shortage of impecunious hacks ready to oblige. Their models were city descriptions and eulogies produced in Italy, Flanders and Brabant during the Renaissance. They more than matched them for florid verse hyperbole, but the Dutch versions tended to be less antiquarian and more brazen in their vulgar euphoria. They were almost all written in the vernacular and in a plodding rhyme that could deal equally well with local mythology and history (especially heroic martyrologies from the Eighty Years' War), biographies of urban worthies and careful topographical description. Most often, even in the cheaper quarto and octavo formats, these *lof en beschryving* (praise and description) books, included copper engravings of varying sophistication depicting bird's-eye views and individual city sights. The more ambitious and detailed of these prints, like those by Simon de Vlieger, Jan van de Velde II and Claes Jansz. Visscher, were produced both for book illustrations and to be sold in loose batches. Engravings and woodcuts of a more humdrum variety, like those turned out by Veenhuijzen in the 1650s for Tobias van Domselaer's *Beschryving van Amsterdam*, were simply stock-in-trade for publishers who reused them over and again in different small-format books and editions. Not infrequently these gazetteers included practical information for the traveler such as opening times of the Bourse, estimated sailing and arrival times of long-distance merchant fleets, the locations of churches of different denominations (other than the formally forbidden Catholic conventicles), and in some cases even the timetable of the *trekschuit* barges that conveyed passengers to and from the town.[17]

The best known of the early panegyrics were Johannes Pontanus's *Rerum et Urbis Amstelodamensium* (1611), translated into Dutch in 1614, and the predikant Samuel Ampzing's *Lof en Beschryving van Haarlem* (1628). But others for Leiden, Delft, Dordrecht and Rotterdam followed.[18] By the middle of the seventeenth century, it was Amsterdam's eulogists, predictably, that waxed most lyrical about their hometown. When other cities of antiquity were invoked by the versifiers they were made to fade into the shadows cast by Amsterdam's contemporary brilliance. A famous boast about the Bourse was repeated on prints, plaques, medallions:

Roemt Ephesus op haer kerk
Tyrhus op haer markt en haven
Babel op haer metzel werk
Memphis op haer spitze gaven,
Romen op haer heerschappy
Al de werelt roemt op my

Ephesus' fame was her temple
Tyre her market and her port
Babylon her masonry Walls
Memphis her pyramids
Rome, her empire
All the world praises me[19]

And if there was no longer any need to make respectful obeisances to antiquity, neither did poets or orators crook the knee to royal pedigree. When Marie de Médicis, the French *reine mère,* made her famous entry into Amsterdam in 1638, the humanist scholar and orator Caspar Barlaeus in his address pointedly equated "the quality of her blood and that of her ancestors" with "the greatness of this city in trade, and the good fortune and happiness of its citizens."[20] The lavish entertainment organized for her benefit, including water tournaments, banquets, fireworks and spectacular allegorical masques staged on floating islands moored in the IJ (see fig. 113), were all meant to rub home the lesson of that new parity. Even in matters of grandiose conspicuous waste, Amsterdam needed no tuition from aristocracies.

Barlaeus, Vos and Joost van Vondel, who composed long lyric eulogies commemorating the building of the new town hall and the *Increase of Amsterdam* all represented the enthusiasm of polite culture. At the other end of the spectrum, and in some ways more typical of popular taste, was Melchior Fokkens's *Beschryving der Wijdt-Vermaerde Koop-stadt Amstelredam* (Description of the widely renowned merchant city of Amsterdam). A successful history-and-gazetteer which went through three editions shortly after first appearing in 1662, Fokkens's book was the literary equivalent of Quellijn's triumphant statuary in the town hall pediment: a trumpet blast of self-congratulation.

> So, Amsterdam has risen through the hand of God to the peak of prosperity and greatness. . . . The whole world stands amazed at its riches and from east and west, north and south they come to behold it.
>
> The Great and Almighty Lord has raised this city above all others . . . yea he has even taken from them the shipping of the east and the west (for in former times Antwerp and Lisbon also flourished) and has spilled their treasure into our bosom.

While other cities exhausted themselves in foreign and domestic wars "through the din and thunder of shot," Amsterdam had flourished. This was no more than her due, since she had from the first opened her gates wide to shelter the

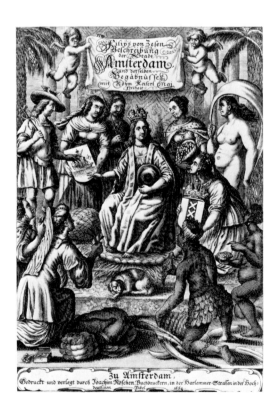

140. Title page of P. von Zesen, *Beschreibung der Stadt Amsterdam,* 1664. Houghton Library, Harvard University

persecuted and oppressed of neighboring states. In time she had become simply "the greatest and most powerful merchant city in all Europe. . . . Truly it is a wondrous thing that it may be said that from a child and scarce e'er grown in its youth, Amsterdam has become a man so that our neighbors and foreigners are struck with wonder that in so few years Amsterdam has grown to such glorious riches."[21] There is a great deal in this vein of adolescent crowing, much of it emphasizing the magical aspects of the transformation from "morass and slime" to "pearls and gold." Amsterdammers evidently enjoyed (and still do) the paradoxical nature of their habitat, captured in Huygens's famous verse oxymoron of "upside down masts of wood [the piles on which the city was built] . . . swamps full of stone, sacks full of gold." They were also much given to dwelling on the prolific bounty of their trade:

> *What is there that's not found here*
> *Of corn; French or Spanish wine*
> *Any Indies goods that are sought*
> *In Amsterdam may all be bought*
> *Here's no famine . . . the land is fat.*[22]

It was, of course, a promised land, "as it was said in olden times, a land flowing with milk and honey, truly that is Holland and here in Amsterdam where there is a land and a city that overflows with milk and with cheese."[23]

This much is conventional bombast, but the real interest of Fokkens's account is the richly detailed description given of the worldly pleasures to be sampled in Amsterdam. Along with the usual survey of public buildings and monuments, he lists streets and districts specializing in particular wares as though he were addressing himself to the prospective shopper. (And indeed a novelty of Marie de Médicis' visit in 1638 had been her descent on the Amsterdam shops, where, it was reported, she haggled like an expert with the shopkeepers.) On the Nieuwe Brug, Fokkens tells us, are to be found bookshops, stationers and nautical goods purveyors dealing in charts, maps, pilots, sextants and the like. In the same area may be found hardware and ironmonger shops, dye-shops and apothecaries with precious and arcane physics from Palestine, Greece and Egypt. On Bicker's Island in the IJ are ships' chandlers and salt-refining houses, on the Singel Canal the market where farmers bring their horticultural produce by barge and where the coastal packets from Flanders and Zeeland dock. In the Nes are the famed pastry shops and bakers; in the Kalverstraat print shops and haberdashers; in the Halsteeg cobblers and bootmakers. The Warmoesstraat, the ancient medieval heart of the city that connected the old dock and wharf area on the IJ with the Dam and the Rokin, was the center of fabrics and fine furnishings crammed with stores of all sizes.

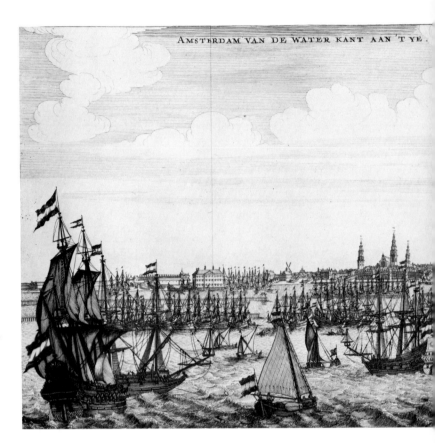

AMSTERDAM VAN DE WATER KANT AAN 'T YE.

141. The port of
Amsterdam seen from
the IJ. From Caspar
Commelin et al.,
*Beschryving der Stad
Amsterdam,* 1665.
Houghton Library,
Harvard University

On two hundred houses, Fokkens notes, there are two hundred and thirty shop signs (the *uythangboord* had become so much a popular decorative art in Holland that whole books were devoted to anthologizing them).[24] In the cornucopia of the Warmoesstraat, the dedicated shopper could purchase Nuremberg porcelain, Italian majolica or Delft faience; Lyons silk, Spanish taffeta, or Haarlem linen bleached to the most dazzling whiteness.

The more handsome and opulent the wares, the more lyrical Fokkens's account becomes. He singles out one craftsman, Dirk Rijswijk, for his prodigious work in creating tables of dark "touchstone" inlaid with designs of mother-of-pearl. Rijswijk's pearl tulips and roses were so fine, he boasts, that not even the most skillful painter could match their detail and luster.[25]

The cheerful vulgarity of Fokkens's shoppers' tour is reinforced by his habit of noting, now and again, prices and values. It was evidently hard cash value, as much as aesthetic gorgeousness that excited him, and that he cited to impress his provincial readers and perhaps to advertise the going rates for the most desirable Amsterdam residences. The house of Wouter Geurtsen on the Rokin was so fine that it then rented for sixteen hundred guilders. Beyond, on the

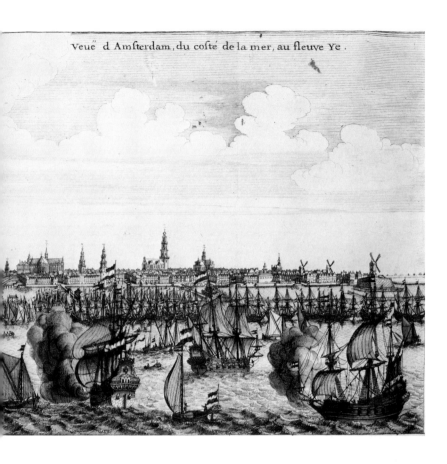

Veuë d Amſterdam, du coſté de la mer, au fleuve Ye .

Prinsengracht, houses might commonly be let for twelve to fifteen hundred. But it was for the most fashionable of all addresses, the Herengracht, that Fokkens reserved his most breathless acclaim:

> Here you will see no houses with open shops; all the buildings stand tall . . . some of them two, others three and four stories high; sometimes their great cellars filled with merchandise. Within, the houses are full of priceless orna- ments so that they seem more like royal palaces than the houses of merchants, many of them with splendid marble and alabaster columns, floors inlaid with gold, and the rooms hung with valuable tapestries or gold- or silver-stamped leather worth many thousands of guilders. . . . You will also find in these houses valuable household furnishings like paintings and oriental ornaments and decora- tions so that the value of all these things is truly inestimable — but perhaps fifty or even a hundred thousand.[26]

One room alone, he guessed, might have three or four thousand guilders' worth of objects in it.

These estimates should be taken with a generous pinch of salt, for they were more the product of Fokkens's naive enthusiasm than any careful inventory. But his catalogue of domestic treasure is less important as a reliable description than for what it reveals about Dutch attitudes toward the worldly goods and pleasures denounced by their clergy. This can only be characterized as a lust for consumption, and one which the craft industries, not only in Amsterdam but in Delft and Haarlem, did their best to gratify.[27] The appetite for ornament and decoration did vary, it is true, in different regions of the country. In the market towns of Friesland or Zeeland, it would have been regarded as suspiciously impious to parade one's wealth in ways that went unremarked in Amsterdam. But despite these variations it is obvious that this was not the austere pleasure-denying culture of the historical cliché. In fact it seems likely that the market for decorative and applied arts was more highly developed in Holland than anywhere else in mid-seventeenth-century Europe. While it is true that Venetian mirrors, Turkish carpets, Persian silks and Japanese lacquerware were all re-exported, it is also true that the domestic market was buoyant, especially in the last half of the century. Indeed, the demand had penetrated below the wealthiest elite, so that indigenous workshops in Amsterdam were turning out imitations, particularly of mirrors and lacquer boxes, at cheaper prices. In the de Hooch *Family Making Music* of 1663, it is impossible to tell the fine ware from the Amsterdam product, though in other respects, the parlor is a visual transcription of one of Fokkens's descriptions. On top of the oak armoire stand Kang-hsi porcelain pots; and the rug on the table is apparently a Transylvanian church weave.[28] The wall at the rear is hung with tapestry, and to the left is a marbled interior porch with Corinthian columns *and* Ionic scroll work. The child seen through the open door wears a version of her mother's expensive and brilliant costume. And, since this was certainly a commissioned family group, it hardly shows much reticence in the display of wealth.

Even in less grandiose households, there was nothing plain or simple about taste in domestic possessions. If anything, Dutch sensibilities, from the *early* part of the seventeenth century, veered toward profuseness, elaboration and intricate detail. Before advocates of Italian classicism like Salomon de Bray and Pieter Post imposed their more severe harmonies on local style, their Mannerist predecessors like Lieven de Key and Hendrick de Keyser were capable of taking the old "Flemish" taste to eccentric extremes. The link between southern and northern mannerism was the gifted family of Vredeman de Vries. Hans Vredeman de Vries published his *Variae Architectura Formae* in Antwerp in 1560, and it rapidly became the handbook for the extravagant architectural detailing and molding that swept from the Netherlands through northern France to England. His book purported to convey the elements of

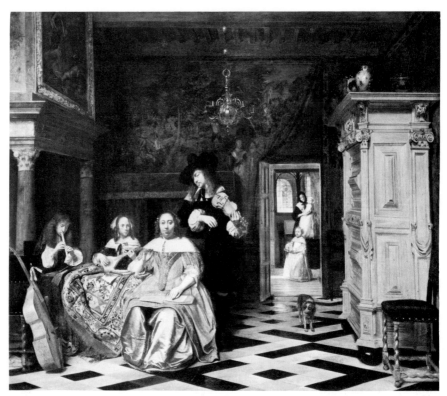

142. Pieter de Hooch, *Family Making Music,* 1663. Cleveland Museum of Art

Italian architecture but in fact introduced fanciful variations wherever possible, breaking pediments, substituting bizarre exotic statuary for regular-order columns and making abundant use of the grotesque. Karel van Mander, writing in 1608, regretted that "this rein is so free and this licence so misused by our Netherlanders that in the course of time in building a great heresy has arisen among them, with a heap of craziness of decorations and breaking of pilasters in the middle, and adding on pedestals, their usual coarse points of diamonds and such lameness, very disgusting to see."[29]

Many of Hans Vredeman de Vries's designs remained in the realm of fantasy, or were confined to draftsmen's exercises or theatrical ephemera. But his son Paul's publication of the *Verscheyden Schrynwerck* (Diverse Cabinetmaking) in Amsterdam in 1630 ensured that watered-down versions of the Vredeman de Vries designs for buffets, beds, cabinets and interior porches did take shape in the joiners' shops well into the second quarter of the century. In the 1663 de Hooch family group, there is a good example of the heavily embossed, incised and fruited oak cupboard that typified large free-standing Dutch

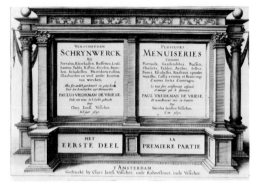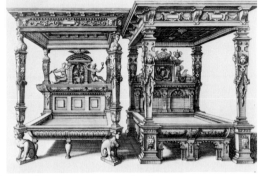

143. and 144. Claes Jansz. Visscher after Hans Vredeman de Vries. From *Verscheyden Schrynwerck* (Amsterdam, 1630). Bodleian Library, Oxford

wardrobes. And in gardens, where there was more freedom to indulge whimsy, architectural gateways, arches and tempiette continued to boast heavy strapwork conceits, scrollwork and scalloping. The goldsmiths of Amsterdam and Utrecht also turned out ewers and standing salts of startling extravagance, creating the wavelike forms of the "lobate" and "auricular" styles peculiar to Dutch craft of this period. Even when mannerist decorative style in the applied arts finally went out of favor in the 1670s, elaborate ornament was by no means banished from well-to-do Dutch salons and parlors. The engraved illustration of prizes for a lottery organized by Henricus van Soest and meant to stimulate demand from potential ticket-holders, shows a throng of well-dressed burghers viewing a glittering array of luxury goods. In the advertising text of the print these included a room of "tapestries showing the twelve months of the year, finely worked with gold and outstandingly beautiful; bedsteads with velvet draperies, all preciously embroidered, along with many other beds and couches . . . rare bureaux and cabinets; diverse fine clothing; and other pearwood seating, inlaid with silver and gold and other rarities."[30] And all these treasures, the text implies, were only one part of the offered prizes.

Lottery prizes give some indication of those luxury wares most coveted by the Dutch *burgerij*. The lottery itself offered a rare opportunity to acquire those treasures, without incurring any of the odium that normally went with hankering after gold and silverplate. They were civic occasions, usually organized by the local magistracy to raise funds for some charitable or public municipal purpose. In Amsterdam, for example, in 1601, a lottery was held to build a new madhouse; in 1606, the Pellikanisten (Pelicans) Chamber of Rhetoric at Haarlem organized a lottery with the help of brother rhetoricians to build a new old-age home for men. The entire business was officially sanctioned by a license granted by the States of Holland or Zeeland and blessed by the church as a form of charitable donation.[31] It was also carefully and publicly regulated, great care being taken to avoid any fraud through special commissions established to ensure that prizes had actually been ordered from the goldsmiths. In a similar fashion the draw itself, which sometimes went on for weeks, day and night, was held in a prominent public place where the proceedings could be scrutinized by the citizenry. It was a brilliantly ingenious Netherlandish occasion (which had begun long before in fifteenth-century Flanders) in that it harnessed the most unblushing worldly appetite for godly ends. Even the principle of the draw itself met both humanist and Calvinist criteria for providential dispensation, exemplifying either the vagaries of Fortuna or the predestined allotment of a portion, depending on one's religious inclination. A print by Claes Jansz. Visscher exemplifies this delicate moral balance between godliness and greed. The engraving was probably executed to attract subscribers in Haarlem and Amsterdam to the lottery organized in 1615 for the building of a new almshouse at Egmond-op-Zee. The fishing village had suffered, as the *lotterij-kaart* brochure made clear, from the double ravages of war and storm floods, and had left a number of poor and needy widows and orphans without proper means of support. Accordingly, Visscher's print shows two such hard-up fisherfolk in attitudes of becoming modesty and humility. Incongruously to the modern eye, but evidently not to

145. Lottery card, 1660s. Bodleian Library, Oxford

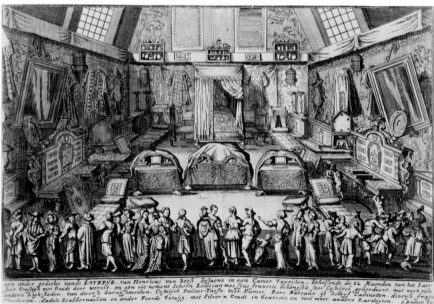

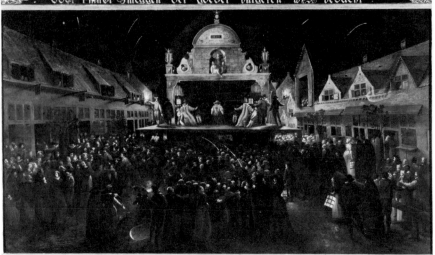

146. Gillis Coignet, *Drawing of Lottery on "The Russland,"* 1592. Amsterdam Historical Museum

147. Claes Jansz. Visscher, lottery card for Egmond-aan-Zee, 1615

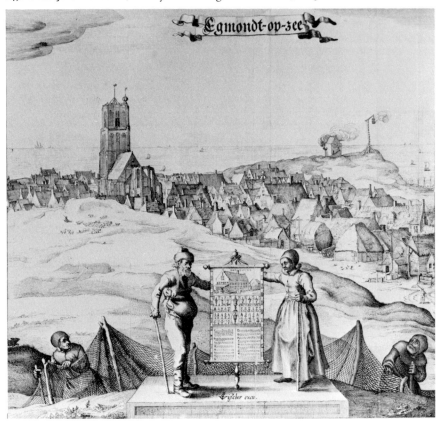

the seventeenth-century Dutchman, the intended recipients of the charity display the print within the print—the *lotterij-kaart* itself, with a picture of the Gasthuis above a great hoard of prizes: engraved goblets, standing salts, beakers and tankards. And while it was not uncommon to include annuities or even stock in chartered companies along with the more tangible prizes, these items of precious ware generally made up the bulk. In the lottery held in 1662 for the poor of the Zeeland town of Veere, for example, there were 6 major and 828 minor prizes, as well as special bonuses for "the best and shortest rhymed motto" (indecent entries strictly forbidden).[32] The six major prizes were as follows:

First:	a silver table service of dishes, plates, ewers, tankards, candlesticks, and [surprisingly] forks as well as other pieces to the value of fl. 4,000
Second:	a golden chain to the value of 1,000 fl. plus 2,000 in cash
Third:	a silver ewer and beaker, to the value of fl. 600 and 1,400 in cash
Fourth:	a silver breadbasket (fl. 300) plus fl. 1,000 cash
Fifth:	three silver candlesticks, each fl. 100 plus fl. 500
Sixth:	two mirrors, each fl. 100 plus fl. 200 cash

The minor prizes consisted of twelve silver sword handles and dagger hilts, assorted wine goblets and beakers, oil jars in silver, standing salts and cellars, ice buckets and (at fl. 24 each) sets of women's petticoats.

This represents a fairly typical sample of prizes offered in the more modest lotteries. The grander events in Amsterdam and Middelburg—and the grandest of all, which had taken place in Antwerp the previous century—ran to hundreds of thousands of tickets and an extraordinary catalogue of loot. While the Dutch lotteries proper seem to have petered out toward the end of the seventeenth century and eventually became institutionalized as a conventional form of supplementary revenue-raising, the earlier prize lists testify eloquently to the widespread popular enthusiasm for providentially distributed opulence. Ostensibly, of course, the lottery appeared to be an occasion for the random equalization of precious goods. In fact, since there was no upper limit to the number of tickets that could be bought, the haves stood a much better chance of adding to their fortunes than the have-nots. But the subscribers' books that survive for some of the lotteries make it clear that all kinds of conditions and ranks made strenuous efforts to procure as many tickets as they could, turning in not merely cash, but all sorts of possessions for a lump purchase. The painter Maarten van Heemskerck—who was very much preoccupied with the subject of wealth—supplied one of his paintings, an *Adultery of Mars with Venus*, to buy a hundred tickets for the grand Middelburg lottery of 1553.[33] Other people brought other things appropriate to their occupations. Farmers turned in livestock, cheeses, horses and cartloads of peat. Merchants used woolen and linen textiles, casks of ale or wine or, in one case, a sack full of hair to buy swatches of tickets. Weapons, boots and other articles of clothing were all acceptable. And some of the objects used for purchasing tickets—such as jewelry or tapestries—suggest that for the better-off buyer, the lottery was a calculated gamble in which they hoped to exchange luxury goods of smaller value for those of greater.

All of this suggests that the Dutch were no more immune to the temptations of opulence than other Renaissance and baroque cultures. Calvinist sermons do not seem to have prevented them from spending freely on decorating their bodies with fine clothes and jewels and their houses with fine art and furnishings—though the latter came more cheaply than the former. In 1612, for instance, Pieter Stael, a painter in Delft who belonged to the more militant Gomarist Calvinists in the town, agreed to paint a *Sodom and Gomorrah* in return for a pair of coral-red striped breeches, decorated with passementerie-work.[34] A century later the house inventory of Remmert Clundert, an Amsterdam tradesman, prepared for the bankruptcy commissioners, included as its most expensive item a blue damask house robe valued at ninety-five guilders.[35] And even when costume was black and white in deference to the strictures of the predikants, the black was very often satin or velvet, sometimes discreetly trimmed with fur. The white would have been lace or linen bleached to the most dazzling purity in Haarlem. If their floors were set with black and white lozenges, the material was most often contrasting marble. This was, to be sure, the manner of the rich, but there is no reason to suppose that, given the means, those lower down on the social scale would have behaved any differently. When shopkeeper turned merchant, or merchant turned landowner and rentier, each eagerly adopted the manners of the grander group and extended his acquisitiveness accordingly.

If the consumption of the Dutch has generally been represented as inconspicuous, that may be because conspicuousness in the Renaissance and baroque has been equated either with court culture or else with the Italian style of civic display. In fact, there had always been a rich tradition of ceremonial waste in the Netherlands, and one that was made more elaborate by the influence of Burgundian culture in the fourteenth and fifteenth centuries. Sixteenth-century Antwerp, where this Netherlandish idiom of ceremonious show reached full flower in the *ommegangen* processions on saint's days and the *landjuweel* competitions of the chambers of rhetoric, yielded nothing by way of ostentation to its southern counterparts.[36] Amsterdam, in turn, inherited this passion for public pomp and circumstance, and in the weekly parades of the *schutter* militia companies, or the banquets, fireworks displays and open-air theatricals that marked historic occasions, indulged it to the full.

The most important, and effective, stage on which the Dutch patrician displayed his wealth, however, was his own home. It is to the interior of the canal houses that the historian must look to judge whether the hyperbole of Fokkens and Mandeville was real or misplaced. Even their overall proportions and exterior appearance, though, bear some comparison with Italian and French counterparts. But where the Venetian palazzi typically presented their longest dimension as a facade, parallel to the canal, that of Dutch houses lay at right angles to it. Constraints of space in rapidly crowded cities like Leiden and Amsterdam were partly responsible for the convention that depth should be greater than breadth. But Dutch taste and the legacy of much less pretentious late-medieval establishments conditioned a preference for interior, rather than exterior, display. Even when Amsterdam embarked on the construction of the radial canals, designed to create expensive residential units, the "royal measure" laid down by the *stadsfabriekmeester* and the city fathers only offered a frontage of thirty-odd feet as against a depth of a hundred and ninety.[37] There were, of course, many ways for determined architects and their clients to evade or at least circumvent these constraints. Philips Vingboons specialized in creating a peculiar trapezoidal shape of house, like that of 1638, at Herengracht 138, where the left side of the central and rear rooms was broader than the front. By the time that the lot reached the garden it was almost a third as broad again as the facade. Families who were determined to impress with a facade of imposing proportions could collaborate on an early form of condominium, with two interior houses united by a single continuous facade, usually borrowed from Palladian stylebooks. Jacob van Campen built such a house for the brothers Balthasar and Johan Coymans in 1642, and Justus Vingboons an even grander house for the brothers Trip on the Kloveniersburgwal in 1662. The Trippenhuis (or *huizen*) had two separate front doors but one running facade unified with colossal Corinthian pilasters, heavily and uniformly embellished windowsills, and a single, pedimented gable.

Even when facades remained modest, it was possible to ornament the exterior between the window spaces, and especially on the gable, where a riot of sculptured or molded detail was allowed free rein. Gable decoration was the heraldic blazon of the mercantile burgher, and house owners commissioned all kinds of self-promoting devices to sprout from their roofs. Coats of arms, allusions to trade or even emblems from astrological bestiaries might appear, especially as the earlier *trapgevel* (step gable) became transformed into the more elaborate and profuse *halsgevel* ("neck" gable) of the midcentury. For the Trip brothers, Justus Vingboons had sculpted into the pediment gable crossed

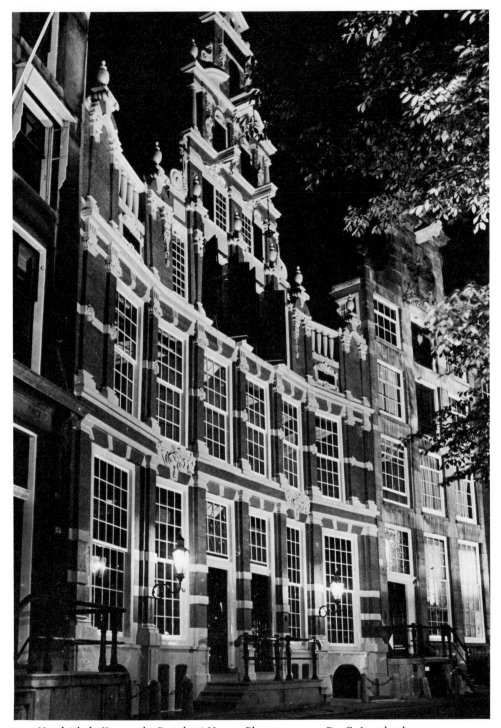

148. Hendrick de Keyser, the Bartolotti House. Photo: courtesy Dr. G. Leonhardt

mortars proclaiming the armaments trade by which the dynasty had made its prodigious fortune. Sometimes architects who were also masons and sculptors would be commissioned to create custom-ordered sculpture for exterior ornament, like the busts that de Keyser produced for Nicolas Soyhier's house on the Keizersgracht, or the cascade of decoration with which he adorned the Bartolotti house on the Herengracht.

The Bartolotti house is the most splendid example of the grand style of patrician building that survives from the early seventeenth century (1617–18). Its Italian family name does not, in fact, announce an alien Mediterranean presence on a northern canal, for its decorative richness was a purely Dutch affair. De Keyser seems to have begun it for a speculator called Keteltas (Kettlebag!) but the property was finally designed and completed for a West India company director and Levant trader, van den Heuvel, who had deferred to his mother-in-law's wish and had taken the name of her late Bolognese Calvinist husband in return for a substantial legacy.[38] In its day, it was the last word in triple-storied stateliness.

It is, moreover, possible to reconstruct both the shape and the contents of the house, from an inventory made for tax purposes on the death of van den Heuvel/Bartolotti's daughter-in-law, Jacoba van Erp, in 1665.[39] And from the astonishing document it is apparent that, if anything, the most grandiose high-life interiors of Metsu and de Hooch understated the quality and the quantity of fixtures and furnishings that crammed the Dutch patrician's house.

Unlike the Venetian *piano nobile*—and in fact unlike most patrician canal houses of the van Campen/Vingboons era—it was on the ground floor that the most imposing rooms were located. De Keyser's Tuscan doorway, with broken rusticated arch, led into a nearly square, spacious *voorhuis* receiving lobby, where two maps of the West India possessions were hung, advertising Bartolotti's connection with the company. In that same room were a large landscape and twelve other paintings, a density of visual decoration that was typical of the whole house. The widow van Erp's modest bedroom, for example, contained twelve paintings, and even one of the maids' rooms had seven—the latter adding up to a mere one guilder's worth, in the estimate of the assessor.[40]

The furniture for the *voorhuis* was quite sparse as befitted a waiting area: a mirror, wooden bench, an oak buffet and eight red leather chairs. A room off to the left, a *zijkamer,* or side chamber, was more comfortable. It was hung with gold-stamped leather and contained an East Indian cabinet, a round nutwood table covered in typically Dutch style with a Turkish rug, a further nutwood buffet, twelve chairs and yet another smaller cupboard. There was also a harpsichord, suggesting that this might be the family room, used for musical parties. As well as the leather wall-hanging, there were fifteen paintings and a large ebony-framed mirror. In the corresponding right *zijkamer* hung tapestries assessed at 900 guilders *tax* (about the cost of purchasing an entire house for a small tradesman). In the same room were twelve chairs including four armchairs upholstered with the same tapestry, a round ebony table, another large mirror and an ebony buffet containing "all the finest and best tableware," suggesting this might have been the *eetsaal* (dining room), a function that was already separate from other social activity in the Dutch house. To the rear and right of the *voorhuis* lay the "great hall" of the house, used for more formal and festive entertainment, with a long oak table, twelve red velvet-upholstered chairs, yet another ebony-framed mirror and with red serge curtains against the windows. Above the mantelpiece was a painting of the Nativity with wooden angels on each side, and below, a great iron hearthplate. Paintings of the family's children as well as several portraits of the princes of Orange hung on the walls. The widow's room, also thoughtfully situated on the ground floor, was more old-fashioned in style but amply *gezellig* nonetheless. It had three full-length curtains, a long oak table, another rectangular table covered with striped cloth, four armchairs, another four wooden chairs, a reading lectern to hold a Bible, a cabinet, an eight-sided mirror in a tortoiseshell and ebony frame, a large couch with iron scroll feet, a bedstead and a small harpsichord.

This is an extremely abbreviated account of a very long inventory of possessions. Even on this floor, the list overlooks the long gallery, crossing the breadth of the house, lined with oak chests and nutwood chairs, bird cages, maps, and prints and drawings of Amsterdam. The upper stories all boasted receiving and retiring rooms of similar opulence, filled with solid furniture, expensive fabrics, highly wrought bedsteads and cartloads of works of art. Obviously, the Bartolotti house was typical only of the wealthier elite, though the residences of most of the great regent families would have hardly been any more modestly appointed. The Huydecopers on the Singel, the monumental mansion that Vingboons put up for Ioan Poppen on the Kloveniersburgwal with its forty-foot "state room," the van Nijs' house on the Keizersgracht and those of the Bickers, Corvers, Backers and Valckeniers all competed with each other in dynastic splendor. Neither the degree nor, for that matter, the kind of religious commitment seemed to affect this patrician life-style. Poppen turned Catholic and converted his state room to a chapel; Bartolotti/van den Heuvel, wallowing in his burgher palace, belonged to the more militantly Calvinist group within the city and had a plaque inscribed *Religione et Probitate* set into his outside wall. Hostile factions met at the draper or the goldsmith.

It is much more difficult to generalize with any degree of confidence about the spending patterns of the "middling sort"—tradesmen, petty officials, notaries—who enjoyed a comfortable but not luxurious existence. Probate records and marriage contracts, itemizing inventories, lie in the notarial archives of most Dutch towns, but are notoriously difficult to use, except at random, without prior indication of the clients' identity.[41] Lists of goods (sometimes with prices) sold at auction from bankrupt estates are another valuable source but by definition may describe life-styles that were atypically prodigal. While research in all these archival sources is still in its early days, it is possible to hazard a preliminary impression of the "middling" household from documents that are already known. One should beware of confusing this group with all professionals, for within a single skilled occupation the very rich and the very humble coexisted. Frans de Vicq, for example, was an Amsterdam physician rich enough to have a spectacular Italianate house built for him on the Herengracht in the late 1660s, while a small town doctor-surgeon lived in much the same style and house as a draper or master brewer. Households with incomes between fifteen hundred and three thousand guilders a year could be called comfortable—a master carpenter in Amsterdam earned by contrast around five hundred in midcentury.[42] A prospering tradesman would have bought a house, if he had not inherited it, for perhaps a thousand and filled it with another thousand's worth of movables. These would have included at least two beds, two or three tables, two or three

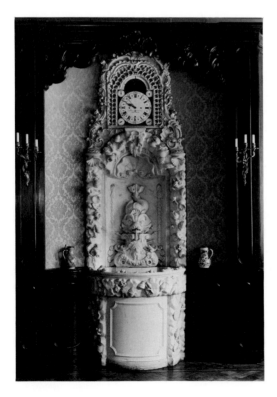

149. Late 17th-century water fountain, the Bartolotti House. Photo: courtesy Dr. G. Leonhardt

wardrobes or cabinets, heavy drapes and curtains, some lace curtains, the obligatory Delft earthenware and tiles, a dozen or so candlesticks, brass or silver, pewter dishes and tankards, many paintings, a few books — at least the States Bible and the works of Cats — and a prodigious amount of linen, both for bed and table.

A tailor on the Prinsengracht, one ter Hoeven, whose household was sold in the spring of 1717, was, I think, reasonably typical of his social group. Although his address was in the heart of a well-to-do district of the city, he practiced his trade in his house, and probably did not occupy all of it. The list of his goods is a documentary equivalent of an interior by Jacob Duck or Quirijn Brekelenkam. They included: five paintings (worth five guilders in total), three tables, a cradle and a child's chair, assorted books, Delft earthenware and tiles, pewter tankards and plates, a spinning wheel, seven lace curtains, two beds and a sleep bench with mattress, an oak wood chest, linen cabinet, several cushions, two mirrors (one broken), twenty-odd chairs (some of them for work), six sets of bed linen, forty-one napkins and a birdcage.[43] A similar household, belonging to Jan van Zoelen and Neeltje Zuykenaar, whose joint goods made less than a thousand guilders, was even better equipped. It included four tables, eighteen chairs for the family and another set for work, eighteen sets of bed linen, twelve table covers and thirty-five napkins, the inevitable Delftware and a large battery of spoons, forks, copper pans and kettles. It seemed to have only one book, but with a binding inlaid with silver and worth nine guilders.[44]

These relatively modest households could be well stocked with furnishings because, by the standards of other European urban societies, they were fairly cheap. As an item of family expenditure, clothing was a good deal more expensive.[45] A straight-back chair could sell for as little as twenty stuivers, a simple table for just over a guilder. By far the most expensive single item in the house would be a bed. The simpler wall-beds sold for between fifteen and twenty-five guilders, while a more ornate, free-standing bed, together with its canopy hangings, might cost a hundred guilders or more.[46] Humbler households made do with a single cupboard or wall-bed and *rustbank* couches with mattresses or boards for the children and/or a maidservant. Those would only set the household back three to five guilders. The other major items of expense in the heavy furniture category were cabinets and cupboards. Oak chests could be had for as little as ten guilders (two weeks' wages for a craftsman) but virtually all burgher households aspired to (or, more usually, inherited) the great wooden carved cabinets and wardrobes that were the hallmark of solid prosperity. A decent linen cabinet (for there was much linen to store) might cost twenty guilders new or fifteen at auction, a fancier carved nutwood model, as much as fifty or sixty. One such piece together with a chest would suffice to announce middle-class credentials, though it is common in quite modest inventories to discover three or four.[47] The most common "luxury" items in middling households were the mirrors that the clergy denounced as the tempters of devilish vanity. They were cheap and they were ubiquitous, especially once domestic glaziers and carpenters were producing copies of Venetian prototypes. A small glass might cost as little as three guilders; anything framed in ebony or tortoiseshell, or cut to unusual design (octagonal frames were popular in the mid-century) might cost ten to fifteen guilders.

It was perhaps in their kitchens and parlors that the Dutch middling sort were most lavishly equipped. Pots and pans were, in fact, quite dear and were very often an important part in a bride's dowry. A large iron stew pan, for the family *hutsepot,* might cost a guilder and a half or two, and a kettle or tart pan more like three guilders. The biggest pans fetched five guilders even at auction. In middling households, copper was kept for somewhat grander uses — a bed-warming pan, for example, which might cost seven guilders, or a tea kettle (after the 1680s), which might cost five. Copper was also used when vessels had to be light enough to carry, so that *doofpot* (fire extinguishers) were made from it and were correspondingly expensive. Another obligatory item was a flatiron, which cost around three guilders. The standard eating and drinking vessels were pewter and were cheap. A set of four bowls and spoons could be had for four guilders, while eight pewter half-pint tankards cost only one guilder thirty-five at auction (perhaps battered). Silver spoons were, of course, very much more expensive, and the possession of any silverware would indicate an important step up the hierarchy of domestic display. Each spoon might cost around seven guilders in the midcentury, and a set of six could be had for forty guilders. Glassware varied a good deal in price. Standard *roemers:* the hollow-stemmed green, gold or blue raspberry prunted goblets so dear to still life artists were surprisingly cheap. They made up basic tavernware and could be had for not much more than a guilder the dozen. But the sturdiness of pewter and its durability may account for solid tankards showing up much more frequently in middling-sort inventories. Special glass goblets, engraved for betrothals, birthdays or historic anniversaries, were more prized. They could cost as much as five guilders and as wine or water jugs could be further embellished in the German manner, adding silver handles and bases. Brass was most commonly used for candlesticks, though iron was available for the poorer houses and copper for the richer. Delft earthenware shows up with increasing frequency after midcentury, though the fact that inventories often included pewter plates and dishes along with china suggests that the latter was more usually kept for display or festive, rather than daily, use. Delft tiles were, of course, a cheap form of domestic decoration. Early in the century, the polychrome tiles that tried to imitate the hues of Italian majolica remained relatively expensive—one and a half to four stuivers each, or a thousand for seventy-five to a hundred guilders. But once the famous blue and white turned to a cheap imitation of Ming instead as a standard product, it rapidly established itself as a favorite for all but the poorest parlors and kitchens. By the 1660s they could be had for twenty-five guilders per thousand, so that a skilled craftsman could decorate a large kitchen parlor, starting at the base of the walls to keep damp at bay—for something like three weeks' wages.[48]

Finally, there were the pictures that hung in such profusion in middle-class households and that provoked so much surprised comment from foreign visitors. John Evelyn's remark of 1641 has been quoted so many times that it has given rise to suspicions of atypicality. But in fact many other travelers—Peter Mundy, Jean de Parival, William Aglionby—commented in much the same vein that "pictures are very common here, there being scarce an ordinary tradesman whose house is not decorated with them."[49] At the cheapest end of what was, in effect, the first mass consumers' art market in European history, engravings sold for a few stuivers each, or more commonly in sets. Emblem books and illustrated histories were also relatively inexpensive in all but the very grandest folio editions. (See Appendix 2.) The most splendid of all, the Cats *Alle de Werken,* in the 1659 Schipper edition, sold at auction in Zeeland for seven guilders and fifteen stuivers in 1687. Perhaps more typical was an earlier auction at Middelburg in 1658, when a copy of de Brune's *Emblemata* with plates fetched just two guilders and a separate copy of Cats's *Self-Strijt* only fifteen stuivers.[50]

Etchings varied a good deal in price, though Rembrandt's "Hundred Guilder print" was altogether exceptional. Oil paintings on wood or canvas also had a wide price range, and tax assessors and auctioneers took size and the quality of the frame into account when they made assessments. A "sea battle" and a "man, with child and small bird" sold at an Amsterdam auction in 1681 made, respectively, twenty and twenty-five guilders, almost certainly because they were specified as being in gilt frames.[51] This was not the case for most paintings, and their presence in many if not most inventories, where the total value of movables was a thousand guilders or even less, tends to confirm the popular generalization that in the Dutch Republic it was common for burgher families to own works of art. It seems likely that they were thought of more as works of craft, just as most painters were thought of as craftsmen and rewarded accordingly.[52] The walls of households were covered with pictures of children at play, winterscapes, ships and Bible scenes, just as tiles covered the parlor with the same kind of anecdotal or gently moralizing matter. As most art historians have correctly surmised, low-life scenes, barrack room and brothel scenes, interior genre and "maidservant" pictures seem to have been the cheapest. In an auction of 1682, a *slagtyd* country scene fetched two guilders ten stuivers, while a brothel scene (specifically described as such) went for just one guilder ten.[53] (In the same inventory a mirror with an ebony frame fetched ten guilders!) Small landscapes could also be cheap. A view of watermills — perhaps in the Ruisdael/Allaert van Everdingen manner — fetched only one guilder, and a townscape two. An average price for a small landscape seems to have run between three and four guilders, and the same was true for a seascape (other than the grandiose battle pictures). Landscapes in the 1670s and 1680s in a grander manner and in larger format, either the "Italianizing" style of Cuyp or the fashionable Wouwerman hunting and hawking pastorals, were in demand at the upper end of the market and could be much more expensive. In another sale in 1681, for example, a "Bruegelachtig" landscape — by which might have been meant Jan, rather than Pieter the Elder — fetched thirty guilders. Still lifes also varied considerably with their size and subject. Elaborate, high-finish *fijnschilder* studies of the kind popularized by Kalf and van Beyeren might fetch six or seven guilders, while smaller pictures of fish or flowers could go for three or four. Portraits and history paintings (which appear less frequently after midcentury) were, as might be expected, the most expensive, and commissioned *portraits historiés* the most expensive of all. But even in the 1680s it was still possible to buy modest histories for less than the price of an elegant mirror and much less than an oak buffet. A "Roman history" at the 1682 sale fetched only five guilders, while a "landscape with Jacob [Isaac?] and Rebecca" from the large collection of François van der Noordt made only nine.

Compared with kitchen utensils and small furnishings and decorations, personal clothing was rather more expensive in its unit cost. A pewter bowl would cost a few stuivers while a woman's chemise would cost about a guilder. The pattern of acquisition for middling households, to judge from inventories, seems to have been to have a narrow range of items, but each present in large numbers. It was not uncommon, for example, for a *huisvrouw* to own thirty or more bonnets. Starched linen was the staple fabric of the Dutch household. Twelve or fourteen sets of bed linen for two or three beds, and thirty or forty napkins, even a dozen handkerchiefs (called, more explicitly, "nose cloths") was not at all unusual. The wardrobe of the wife of Remmert Clundert of Amsterdam in the early eighteenth century included thirteen chemises, five skirts and three petticoats, with two fine damask dresses, one black and one blue, for special occasions. While each of the ordinary skirts cost around two guilders, the dress costumes represented a considerable outlay, priced at twenty and ninety-five guilders respectively. Men's dress followed the same cost pattern. Shirts were around a guilder a piece; a house-gown about ten guilders and an elaborate coat and vest at the end of the century could run to forty or fifty guilders (without brocade).[54] In this bracket of household goods of between a thousand and two thousand guilders, the evidence of the Amsterdam inventories suggests that around two-thirds of movable assets were in domestic goods and furnishings and a third in clothes. For the many among the Dutch middling sort, the display of status and fortune was expressed primarily in home comforts.

As we have seen from the Bartolotti inventory, the rich did not stint in the decoration of their homes. And the more elaborate furnishings favored in the later seventeenth century provided new opportunities for conspicuous consumption within the house. Stamped leather wall-hangings were beginning to be replaced by painted silk or paper on which the pastoral arcadia of the Wouwerman type might appear. Fabrics like moiré and satin were substituted for the older velvets and says. But however grand the house or magnificent its furnishings, once a certain threshold of wealth had been reached, the urge to proclaim status required a different kind and quality of expenditure. In the early years of his tenure as Receiver General of the Republic, 1685–89, Cornelis de Jonge van Ellemeet had an income of around twenty thousand guilders a year, half of which he spent on various kinds of personal consumption.[55] Ten years later he was earning over *sixty* thousand (an extraordinary increase, even by Dutch standards), of which some seventeen thousand went on consumption. His average annual expenditure on furniture alone doubled from around a thousand to two thousand. In 1699 he spent twice as much on a single carpet as he was paying for a whole year's worth of labor from the handyman who was looking after his rural property.[56] Despite this prodigality his income always rose faster than his expenditure, and the proportion saved from just about half in 1685 to two-thirds in 1704. In that latter year, he was earning fl. 93,342, spending fl. 19,886 and paying fl. 10,688 in direct taxes. This success in saving, though, owed little to any Calvinist abhorrence of conspicuous consumption and a great deal to unlimited opportunities for profiteering in a time of high wartime demand and inflation—he was, one should keep in mind, Receiver General of the United Provinces. From the 1680s onwards, when he and his equally well-endowed wife Maria Oyens settled into their fifteen-thousand-guilder house on the Lange Vijverberg in the very center of The Hague, they spent freely on virtually everything that could be acquired to accommodate a patrician life-style. Their only economy seems to have been household servants, which numbered a paltry four, although new livery was periodically bought for them.

De Jonge van Ellemeet's expenditures were of a different order from the Amsterdam burghers'. Even his pictures were much more costly. Constantijn Netscher was hired to paint his three children for sixty-three guilders, and his taste in history painting ran to the sixteenth-century northern masters. A Frans Floris crucifixion cost him twenty-nine guilders. A single purchase of drapes for the "upper dining room" in 1690 cost three hundred guilders, and four armchairs in 1713, two hundred. When, in 1702, he finally decided that his high status required a coach and four to show it off, it set him back fl. 2,593 — by the standards of the time a princely sum. Plate and jewels were acquired with similar avidity, a set of a dozen silver plates costing more than eight hundred guilders. Diamonds, though, were de Jonge van Ellemeet's special weakness. The thriving cutting and polishing industry in Amsterdam, as well as Dutch control over the supplies of precious stones — not just diamonds, but Brazilian emeralds and East Indian sapphires — had made the Republic the center of the international market in costly gems, and patricians like de Jonge van Ellemeet had no trouble, either moral or material, in acquiring a growing hoard. In 1687 he bought his wife (who had brought a number of jewels to the match as part of her dowry) a diamond for fl. 487. In 1691 he spent nearly two *thousand* guilders on a string of twenty-one stones, in 1696 a heart and eleven small stones for a mere five hundred, and three years later, a single colossal *bloksteen* for fl. 1,115. Gold objects were acquired on an almost casual basis. When his gold purse was stolen from him at the Haagse *kermis* he replaced it with another for about two hundred guilders without, it seems, turning a hair.

The swagger and glitter of de Jonge van Ellemeet's life-style was, of course, exactly the kind of profligate behavior most deplored by ministers and moralists. Spending sprees, and the addiction to opulence, they warned, could have only one end: a material and moral enfeeblement that would inevitably culminate in collapse. The wages of fecklessness would be the old, familiar horrors: war, invasion, servitude and a new, punishing deluge.[57] As a prophetic corrective to the consuming passions of the Dutch, these warnings played an important part in their culture. But the assumption that high spending was squandering the national patrimony belongs more in the realm of sermons than of economic forecasting. It took for granted the old mercantilist axiom that there was a fixed stock of capital that could be allotted either to productive or unproductive ends. High rates of consumption would eat into the resources that otherwise could be made fruitful through investment. But, as Mandeville shrewdly understood, this was not necessarily the way in which early modern economies prospered. High rates of consumption might actually encourage turnover of both labor and capital and coincide with, rather than exclude, capital formation. Much, of course, depended on the overall growth of the economy, and without gross national product estimates, the rhythm of that growth is hard to assess. But the "pessimistic" view of capital increasingly sucked into nonproductive enterprises has conventionally held that the Dutch economy began to stagnate in commerce and industry, as early as the 1680s.[58] This now seems an absurdly premature judgment. What began to go, towards the end of the century, was the Dutch edge over other nations' cost factors in shipbuilding and freight, but commerce in the Atlantic, the Levant and the East Indies remained buoyant throughout the eighteenth century. And when the Dutch economy did begin to suffer from competition, it was less the consequence of a decadent life-style than the force of external circumstances: war and the steep costs of imperial protection.[59]

Despite prevailing stereotypes, then, the Dutch economy in its prime did not turn on the habit of thrift. There is as much reason to describe it as a spend-and-prosper economy as a save-and-prosper economy, for savings and spending were not in the least mutually exclusive. What were, by European standards, high real incomes — in social groups from skilled artisans to rentier patricians — permitted correspondingly higher levels of disposable income to be available for consumption. But, paradoxically, the more that was spent absolutely on consumption, the *smaller* its proportion of overall assets. The carpenter who made six hundred guilders a year probably (according to Posthumus) spent half of it on food, while Cornelis de Jonge van Ellemeet, making nearly one hundred thousand guilders, spent one-third of that on food for his household![60] In between, the proportions varied a good deal, not merely with station but with inclination. One of the Delft artists studied by Michael Montias retained only ten percent of his assets in movables like jewelry and furniture, while Boudewijn de Man (also a Receiver General) and a collector had nearly a third in "consumer durables."[61] In the marriage contracts and inventories of the great Amsterdam dynasties of the midcentury, jewelry, hard cash and belongings account for between twelve and twenty-five percent of capital assets. When Cornelis Backer married his second wife, Catherina Raye, in 1660, for example, he had as much money tied up in jewels as in merchant venture shares (respectively, fl. 6,000 and fl. 7,000) and only fl. 3,000 in other kinds of stock.[62] In fact a great deal of wealth was held in forms that could, depending on moral viewpoint, be characterized as either productive or unproductive: urban and landed property (even swamp, held speculatively for reclamation or peat-digging), annuities, provincial and municipal bonds and debentures, bills of exchange and, especially, short- and medium-term loans contracted for unspecified purposes. A typical portfolio of an Amsterdam capitalist would have included all these investments, with proportions shifting from year to year and sector to sector as personal needs and judgment commanded. Louis Trip, for example, transferred capital from trading concerns in the 1650s and 1660s, first to commercial stock, but then, in increasing allotments and quantities, to the relatively risk-free areas of public loans and property.[63]

One part, then, of Max Weber's famous proposition, that the Protestant ethic restrained consumption to the advantage of capital accumulation, does not seem to hold true for the Netherlands, the most formidable capitalism the world had yet seen. Louis and Hendrick Trip—as near to the ideal type of commercial and industrial baron as one could imagine for the seventeenth century—spent a quarter of a *million* guilders on their regal Vingboons house. But this is not to say that Calvinism meekly concurred with a riot of epicureanism. Quite the opposite was the case. Its voice, denouncing the iniquities of Dame World and the profanities of Queen Money, could be heard thundering from pulpits through the length and breadth of the Republic. But to what end, and to what effect? It warned, but it seemed helpless to restrain. And if it could not restrain, did it then, as Weber also argued, sanction the increase of riches as the outward sign of salvation?

ii IN THE REALM OF QUEEN MONEY

How much prosperity was good for the Dutch? On the face of it, in the most miserable conditions that Europe had experienced since the fourteenth century, the question was absurd. The Republic was an island of plenty in an ocean of want. Its artisans, even its unskilled workers and its farmers (for it seems a misnomer to call them peasants) enjoyed higher real incomes, better diets and safer livelihoods than anywhere else on the continent. Their only shared misfortune with social equals elsewhere was the plague, yet even its visitations seemed somewhat lighter in Amsterdam than they did in London. In the worst week of the pandemic in 1664 in Amsterdam there were 1,041 burials compared with 7,000 in the late summer of 1665 in London, a city twice its size.[64] Replacement from immigration, moreover, ensured that Amsterdam suffered nothing like the depressed conditions of Venice, which lost a third of its population to the terrible plagues of the 1630s. The country's riches seemed invulnerable to the scourges that fell upon the rest of the world with merciless intensity. Capital begot capital with astonishing ease, and so far from denying themselves its fruits, capitalists reveled in the material comforts it bought. At midcentury there seemed no limit, certainly no geographical limit, to the range of its fleets and the resourcefulness of its entrepreneurs. No sooner was one consumer demand glutted or exhausted than another promising raw material was discovered, the supply monopolized, demand stimulated, markets exploited at home and abroad. Would the tide of prosperity ever ebb?

150. OVERLEAF: Engraving. *New Church on the Botermarkt.* Bodleian Library, Oxford

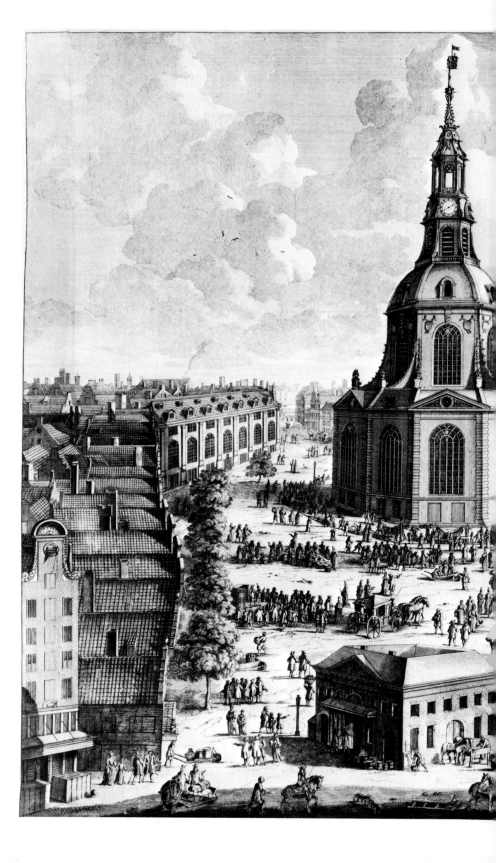

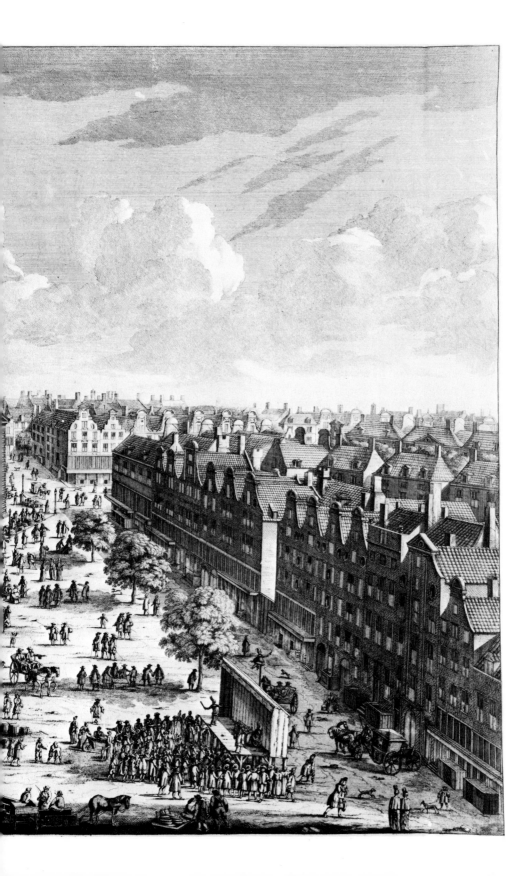

And that was just the problem. If the Dutch ever imagined their ruin it was not at the hands of some neighboring predator power but at their own. They could be the authors of their own undoing simply by overdoing things. Their ministers tirelessly reminded them of this, of the example of Israel where the corruption of Baal had been the herald of disaster. Calvin's commentary on Isaiah's denunciation of Tarshish warned that if the Jews are to learn to submit themselves to God they must be stripped of their wealth."[65] And the notion that, if their cup ever ran over it would spill into a punishing flood was deeply embedded in national folklore. When William Aglionby, that connoisseur of Dutch affluence, visited the thriving rural hamlets of the Betuwe in south Holland, he noticed that the farmers spoke of the great inundations of the fifteenth century as though they were but yesterday. Throughout their talk there ran a vein of fearfulness, a rustic version of humanist pessimism. Aglionby listened carefully, even though his Royal Society Baconian intellect was amused by its droll irrationality: "As it happens, often, that when we are ignorant of the cause of a thing, we are apt to attribute it to some invisible, super-natural power, as to our sins that provoke God's anger, so some have said that these villages were drowned because they did make ill use of their great riches, that they would not wear any other than golden spurs and lived in great mag-nificence."[66]

So riches seemed to provoke their own discomfort, and affluence cohabited with anxiety. This syndrome, at once strange and familiar to modern sensibility, did not originate with the Reformation, nor was it peculiar to the Netherlands. Both the Roman stoics' criticism of luxury and avarice (encoded in Italian sumptuary laws from the thirteenth century onwards), and the repeated attacks of Franciscans on church and lay wealth were absorbed into northern humanism. But when Erasmus came to assail the vanity of worldly riches and power, he had turned from the quietist tradition of retreat that he had experienced firsthand in the monastery of the Brothers of the Common Life at Steyn. Nor was he at all attracted by the Franciscan tradition of mendicant purity. The Erasmian confrontation of wealth denied shelter and refuge from the trials of the material world; instead, it commanded an encounter with them. The new *miles Christianum*, the Christian knight, had to meet his enemies — cupidity, lust, pride and vanity — head-on in the lists of day-to-day business. Going into the world, the better to master its vanities, was the quotidian ordeal to which Erasmian humanists subjected themselves. The awful risk that in so doing the things of the world might master them was ever present, especially for men like More, who accepted high office, but it was a risk from which they were not permitted to abstain.[67]

The sensibilities of Flemish capitalists in the sixteenth century — and their outlying satellites in the north, in Haarlem and Leiden — were, then, ambivalent.

A great deal of money was spent in formal, ceremonial attacks on money. In 1561, the annual procession through the city, the *ommegang* of the Feast of the Circumcision staged by one of its chambers of rhetoric, was devoted to the *circulus vicissitudinis rerum humanorum* — the fatal cycle of worldly fortune.[68] The artist (and lottery speculator) Maarten van Heemskerck left designs for the eight allegorical triumphal cars and retinues. They were engraved in 1564 and, together with surviving "ordinances" for the festival, provide a detailed description of the event. Beginning with the triumph of the world, and moving successively through riches, pride, envy, war (a crucial break), then want, humility, and peace, the cycle is ominously resumed as peace mothers riches in the final "triumph."[69] Only God's Last Judgment could interrupt the fatal cycle — and, interestingly, van Heemskerck did not provide a design for its representation. The theme was an ancient humanist favorite, but its immediate relevance to their own interests and preoccupations could not possibly have been lost on the burghers of Antwerp. A century later, ministers and moralists continued to utter warnings and prophecies couched in identical terms.

Within this Christian humanist chronology, wealth obviously played an all-important part. The second triumphal car featured Opulentia riding Fame, accompanied by all the usual undesirable traits associated with her victory. Her charioteer was Guile, her steeds Fraud and Rapine, her attendants Usury, Betrayal and Lust. At the rear, in front of Idle Pleasure (Vana Volupta) walks the figure of False Joy blowing the bubbles of her ephemerality. She would, in fact, walk right through the iconography of capitalist speculation — that fairground of the popping bubble.

Ilja Veldman has argued persuasively for a close association between these themes and the moralizing literature of Dirck Volkertszoon Coornhert.[70] Coornhert was indeed one of the crucial connections between the moralizing humanism of Flanders, the social ministry of the Netherlands magistracy and its transplantation north to Haarlem and to Amsterdam. His *Comedie van de Rijcke Man* (The Comedy of the Rich Man), published in 1550, and the insistent strictures of his *Zedekunst dat is Wellevenskunst* (The Art of Morals, the Art of Right Living) — next to Erasmus's works, the Bible of the Dutch humanists — were wholly in keeping with the ceremonial polemics against wealth. Many of the diatribes against riches in fact went beyond criticisms of sumptuary excesses or usurious avarice to an attack on the pecuniary ethos itself. In Coornhert's *Roerspel der kettersche werelt* (1550) Everyman is dressed as a rich merchant, and is converted by Money to the belief that physical and spiritual salvation can be acquired by riches. Falsehood then instructs him that the ways to win it are (naturally) through deceit, usury and theft.[71] This attack on the odious nature of wealth itself appears even more unequivocally in another series of Heemskerck prints inspired by Coornhert's teaching, the *Divitum*

Misera Sors (The Unhappy Lot of the Rich), engraved by Philips Galle in 1563. This, too, appears as a procession, and may have been staged as such by a chamber of rhetoric for public edification. It begins with a rich man attempting vainly to enter the gate of heaven while a camel is lined up for needle-threading. In the third print, figures embodying the evils of wealth—Lucullus, Crassus, Croesus and Midas—are shown with the respective attributes of their folly. And in the fourth, Queen Money, Regina Pecunia, has her chariot drawn by Fear and Danger while guarding Robbery beneath her mantle. Behind her, the fool stares directly at Pandemia—the figure of "all the people," who balances the world on her head with its inverted cross and cornucopia, while Theft relieves her of her money bag.

Many of these symbolic themes: the ephemerality of the bubble, the robbery of the vain and foolish, the folly of Dame World and the despotism of Queen Money were to enjoy an extraordinarily long life in the culture, both verbal and visual, of the Netherlands. Nor, despite their allegorical richness, were these emblems mere conceits intended only for a lettered and leisured elite that could afford to frown on cupidity. Coornhert, like Erasmus before him, was concerned to drum his moral lessons into the minds of children of

151. Philips Galle after Maarten van Heemskerck, 1563, *Divitum Misera Sors.* Kress Library, Harvard University

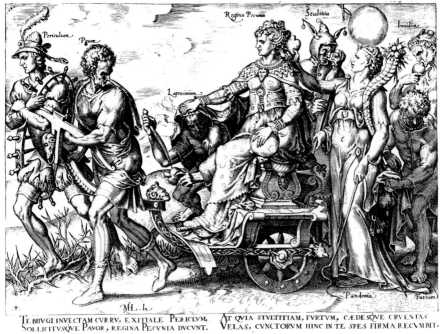

all classes, and specified that the *Zedekunst* was not for learned scholars, but for "untutored persons, desirous of learning."[72] Other prints dealing with related themes, like Pieter Bruegel the Elder's image of capitalism as all-out war, *The Battle of the Strong Boxes and the Money Bags*, or the northern artist Cornelis Anthoniszoon's woodcuts *The Misuse of Prosperity*, were evidently intended for a popular audience.

None of this, of course, is inconsistent with the view that while humanist Catholicism continued to make life difficult for the assertion of capitalist values, the Protestant ethic made room for them. But even if the Calvinist clergy, as Weber has it, allowed this to happen *unintentionally,* it is certainly not apparent from the tenor of their remarks about the place of money in the Christian life. Indeed, there seems to be no real break at all in the uninterrupted flow of polemics against wealth from Flanders to Holland, from Antwerp to Amsterdam. Although there was, in the end, no place for Coornhert in the reformed Republic, his teaching was imprinted on the manners of the people, even as they were busy making their fortunes. Nor can the Calvinist clergy be supposed to be neutral in the matter, allowing the consecration of the "calling" and the uncertainty of membership of the Elect do capitalism's

152. Jan Galle after Pieter Bruegel the Elder, *The Battle of the Strong Boxes and the Money Bags*. Kress Library, Harvard University

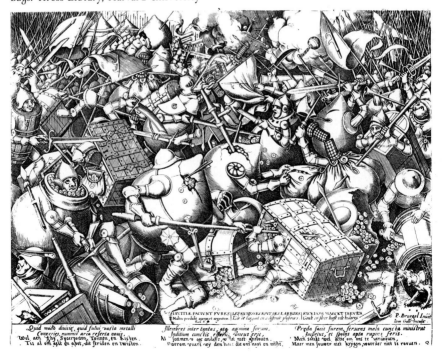

work for it. The predikants would not stand idly by while the Golden Calf was erected amidst Israel's tents. Far from tacitly endorsing finance capitalism, the Dutch general synods did their level best to proclaim their disapproval. Bankers were excluded from communion by an ordinance of 1581, joining a list of other shady occupations—pawnbrokers, actors, jugglers, acrobats, quacks and brothel keepers—that were disqualified from receiving God's grace. Their wives were permitted to join the Lord's Supper, but only on condition that they publicly declared their repugnance for their husband's profession! Their families shared the taint and were only permitted to join communion after a public profession of distaste for dealing in money. It was not until 1658 that the States of Holland persuaded the church to withdraw this humiliating prohibition on "lombards."

While bankers remained under the presumption of usurious practice, Dutch Calvinism did consider the possibility that a Christian merchant might not be a contradiction in terms. The most important of those tracts specifically devoted to reconciling commerce and godliness was the Zeeland predikant Godfried Udemans's *Geestelijke Roer van 't Coopmans Schip.* Since this large work discussed the godly mission in the Indies, the conduct of sailors and officers in both merchant and war fleets and Christian behavior in dealing with unbelievers like the Turks, its punning title meant both "The Spiritual Rudder of Commerce (Koopmanschap)" and "The Spiritual Rudder of the Merchant's Ship." Superficially the book seems written to vindicate the Weber thesis, with its frontispiece of a benign tetragrammaton shining down on the Amsterdam bourse and its avowed aim of pacifying the uneasy conscience of the merchant by showing him the Right Way.[73] But its definition of "righteous" commercial practice was so hedged about with prohibitions and traditional scruples that it was, in the end, no more economically permissive than the classic humanist texts—Cicero, Seneca and the Stoics—that it cited as freely as scripture. There was no room, for example, for vertical mobility, the small merchant being forbidden from emulating the "great merchant" lest he become guilty of the sin of envy. And envy, it hardly needs saying, was the fire of competition. Excessive risk was frowned on as the irresponsible squandering of capital; futures trading was regarded as immoral gambling, and there were circumstances in which it remained unlawful for a good Christian to make a profit at all: on the resale of a house, for example.[74] And it was precisely the most aggressive and successful practices of Dutch capitalism: monopolies, price regulation, real estate speculation, international munitions trading, etc. that were specifically stigmatized as un-Christian and belonging to the realm of cupidity rather than true commerce. Aversion to monopoly did not, however, mean that Udemans meant to encourage individualism. On the contrary, his golden maxims for the merchant were entirely those of traditional Christian and humanist teaching: do unto others as you would be done by; "honor before gold"; be true to thy bond; always work for the interests of the *patria* — the *Vaderland* — "for men must also know that they are born for each other, since we are taught that the commonwealth must be advanced by the exchange of our gifts [i.e., goods] . . . and by our knowledge, skill and industry."[75]

Godly righteousness and the community, then, not the individual, much less his anxiety about membership of the Elect (on which subject nothing was said in Udemans's six hundred pages) were the arbiters of right commercial conduct. And even in respect of matters like poverty, this wholly typical Calvinist work followed a wholly traditional humanist line. "Let a merchant take for his maxim: honor above gold, for it is better to be a poor man than a liar . . . For an honorable man is and will always remain a burgher even if he be poor, but if he outlives his honor, that is a living death."[76] For many of the Calvinist clergy a truly Christian capitalism seemed to be a will-o'-the-wisp. And they spent far more time denouncing gain than in praising it. Sermons that explicitly contrasted the profane greed of finance with the humility of the Elect rained down on well-heeled congregations. Their effect, however, was always in doubt. In 1655 the Hague predikant Simonides castigated hypocritical businessmen whose piety ended at the church door. "When he goes home from Church, does he take God's Holy Book with him to ponder the sermon? No. Instead he picks up the day's gazette and busies himself with calculations of interest and the liquidations of debts. It would be better that on the Lord's Day he gave some accounting of himself and instead of reckoning his money reckoned up his sins."[77] Jacobus Lydius likewise inveighed against "money hounds" and against the "acts of cunning, dodges, deceits and devilry" common among merchants who "sin against the old name of honor."[78] Others were provoked by the tide of gold washing into the precincts of the church itself in the form of overelaborate Bible bindings or fancy pew decorations. Even organ lofts were scrutinized for undesirable embellishment.[79] Trigland in Amsterdam was particularly incensed by any wanton display of ornament in his congregations, earrings arousing his mighty wrath. "How can it be that God's people could be so ornamented with silver and gold?" he asked rhetorically, and how could decent Amsterdammers come to divine service got up in satin, brocade and damasks, "worked with gold, silver and I know not what fancy decorations and geegaws." Amsterdam, he warned, should think on the fate of Antwerp and be chastened. His favorite text was Zephaniah 1:11, "Howl, ye inhabitants of Maktesh, for all the merchant people are cut down; all they that bear silver are cut off."[80]

Humanist criticism of worldly wealth and high living persisted alongside church doctrine, both as learned history and popular lore. A typical piece of ephemera, the *Gedachten op Gelt* (Thoughts on Money) anthologized proverbs and sayings about money on a couple of sheets. Most of them, predictably, were unfavorable:

> *Money is set so high in price*
> *Makes villains pious and idiots wise*
>
> *Because men honor rich young sires*
> *Money is by fools desired.*[81]

Jan Krul's *Wereld-hatende nootzaakelyke* (On the Necessity of Unworldliness) sounded the same refrain, reviling *"snoode geld"* (base money): the betrayer of loyalty, the corrupter of justice, the perverter of affection between the sexes. In the spirit of Quintijn Metsys's couple rather than Van Eyck's *Arnolfinis*, prints and paintings reverted time and again to the theme of the degradation of love by money.[82] A marriage contract between a rich widow and her suitor is sealed by a female incarnation of the Devil spewing coin, and with the dugs of *gierigheid*, avarice. Krul's text has money closely related to pride and worldly folly:

> *What is, alas, the world's bait*
> *But golden crowns, pearl-encrusted?*
> *What is the world's only pride*
> *But base sorcery, ne'er to be trusted.*[83]

And Queen Money reappeared over and again to the seventeenth-century Dutch, as she had to the sixteenth-century Flemish and Brabanters, as the epitome of vanity and ephemeral pleasure. In Abraham Bloemaert's *Opulentia* of 1611, she resumes the familiar symbolic motifs: the bubbles, evanescent smoke and the heaps of treasure—coin, chased cups and tankards—that signify her realm. In an alarming painting by Hendrick Pot, she appears again as Avarice, clutching a standing salt cellar with white knuckles in a blasphemous parody of prayer. Her pinched cheeks are juxtaposed with swollen money bags. Within there is coin, plate and death; without, light, trees and resurrection. In a more popular source of 1630, one of Cats's emblems, Adriaen van de Venne has Mevrouw Geld, Dame Money, laying down the law to all mankind. She is seen seated on a canopied throne wearing the crown and pearls that Krul abominated, and surrounded by the usual regalia of sacks and chests brimming with coin. In her right hand she holds a balance in which, it is implied, are weighed not only the pieces of gold but the souls of all those in her thrall. Around her gathers a craven throng in varying attitudes of ingratiation or brute greed. They comprise the trading nations of the world; the exquisite Italian,

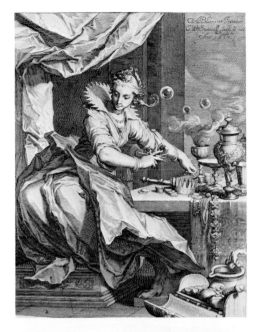

153. W. Swanenburgh after Abraham
Bloemaert, *Opulentia.* Kress Library,
Harvard University

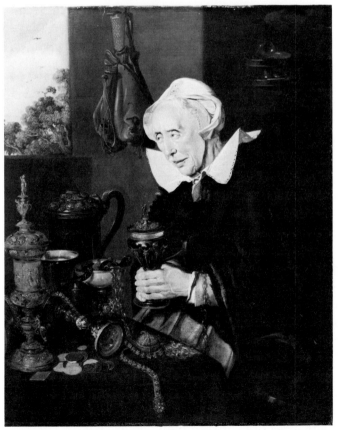

154. Hendrik Pot, *The Miser.*
Rheinisches Landesmuseum, Bonn

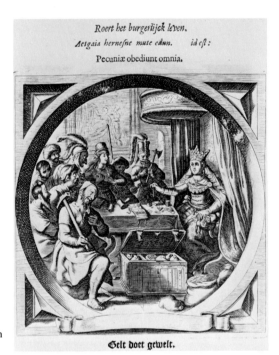

155. Adriaen van de Venne,
emblem from Jacob Cats,
Spiegel van de Oude en de Nieuwe Tyt
(in *Complete Works,* 1655). Houghton
Library, Harvard University

the turbaned Turk and the fustian Hansa all being easily identifiable. In the
background, within the usual secondary-comment frame, Danae receives her
lover, Jupiter, as a rain of gold.

The official creeds of both Calvinism and humanism, then, were agreed
that lucre was indeed filthy, and that devotion to its cult constituted a kind of
polluting idolatry. In its extreme forms of avarice and cupidity it could
unhinge the conscience and reason and turn free souls into fawning slaves.
This strong sense of the reprehensible nature of money-making persisted, even
while the Dutch amassed their individual and collective fortunes. The odd
consequence of this disparity between principles and practice was to foster
expenditure rather than capital accumulation, as a way to exonerate oneself
from the suspicion of avarice. Admittedly, the forms of such expenditure had
to be collectively sanctioned and regarded as morally unblemished by clergy
and laity alike. But that might extend from obviously virtuous expenditures
like philanthropy, to less sacrificial gestures, like lending to public institutions
at low rates and on long terms, or even to the need to provide a comfortable
domestic milieu in which a patriotic Christian family might be raised. Louis
de Geer, who was certainly both an ardent Calvinist and energetic entrepreneur,
managed to accommodate a dignified life-style with pious expenditure, in just
these ways. He bought the House with the Heads from the Soyhier family on
the Keizersgracht and stocked it with expensive nutwood furniture, much of

it imported from France and Italy. But in compensation, his self-tithing for the poor was widely known, as was his sincere help for Calvinist refugees from the central European theaters of the Thirty Years' War. When, in 1646, he drew up a "testament" for his children and heirs, he admonished them to "fear God and keep his commandments and think on the poor and oppressed; then you shall enjoy God's blessings." And he reminded them that when he had come to the Republic, in hard-pressed times, he had made an oath before God to give two hundred guilders a year to the poor for every child of his own. God had heard his prayer and had prospered him, and he, in his turn, had kept his oath. He commended his children to do so in their turn.[84]

In some respects, it is true, de Geer approximates Weber's "ideal type" of pious entrepreneur. But it is important to understand that so far from his religion accommodating his business, it generated a great deal of moral discomfort. That discomfort was only made more tolerable by acts of conspicuous expenditure on both pious and personal objects. So instead of religious anxiety inhibiting consumption (as it certainly meant to do) it might just as well have inhibited profit and capital accumulation, and indirectly encouraged expenditure. This was, I suppose, highly paradoxical, but no more so than Weber's own ingenious formulation.

Does all this mean that, for all its rant and cant, the strictures of the Calvinist church against the corruption of money went *un*heeded, except for the occasional propitiatory gesture of philanthropy? Or was all the hellfire but a smokescreen behind which the church actually colluded in the realities of business as usual? Not quite. The official doctrine that money brought more evil than good into the world, and that riches, like works, were of no avail for salvation, manifestly remained orthodox teaching. But the church was severely handicapped when it tried to enforce its dogma on social and economic matters. The records of the local and provincial synods are full of angry denunciations of Sunday trading, violating the Lord's Sabbath under the noses of the magistracy. In his alphabetically organized *Black Register of a Thousand Sins* the Hoorn predikant Jacobus Hondius had "All those who practice Sunday work" under *A* and from *B* through *D* listed (*inter alia*): bakers, linen-bleachers, surgeons, mint assayers, diamond polishers, etc., etc.[85] But it was very rare for local magistrates to prosecute malefactors with any serious zeal or consistency. So when the church identified sinners, it had only its own ecclesiastical discipline with which to admonish them. The force of that censure should never be underestimated, but of course it depended on the malefactor's membership of a known Reformed congregation, and neither that membership nor residential continuity was at all guaranteed. Where the offender was known to belong to a specific congregation, there was a series of disciplinary measures, escalating in gravity, to which he or she could be subjected. At the first report of the offense, the suspect sinner would be visited in private by two members of the church council in a "brotherly conversation." If the report was confirmed, a warning and rebuke were issued. If the transgressor proved impenitent, he would receive a second visit from the verger or the predikant himself; then after a case hearing at a full meeting of the council, would be denied communion on either a temporary or indefinite basis. The final punishment for hardened offenders was the full gravamen of the "censure": a public eviction from the body of the church, and a formal publication of the ban. Where there was any hope of repentance, an intimidating ritual was arranged with the sinner surrounded by a circle of the righteous (usually the council) and asked, for a final time, whether he would repent and so be reprieved from the excommunication.[86] While this all sounds forbidding, the number of eminent and wealthy (not to mention obscure and poor) figures subjected to the ban suggests that it did not strike terror into the hearts of all believers. The Amsterdam church councils, for example censured the entrepreneur and speculator Isaac le Maire, the secretary of the Admiralty of Amsterdam, Jacob Laureszoon Reael, and at least two founder members of the East India Company.[87]

There were a few occasions when a "pious" faction within a ruling elite could push through civic ordinances and bylaws that were in conformity with church teaching on social matters. But the intrusion of this "Genevan" style of Calvinism into the more pragmatic atmosphere of government in the big commercial centers like Amsterdam and Haarlem depended crucially on abnormal circumstances disrupting the consensus. As we have seen, it was only against the background of a fierce visitation of the plague, defeats in the war with the English and a commercial depression that Tulp and Bontemantel could have hoped to pass their sumptuary legislation in 1655.

More typically, the church had only its own congregational discipline with which to enforce its teaching on social and economic matters. In the absence of anything stronger it was restricted to the auxiliary role of censuring offenses that the judiciary had an independent interest in prosecuting. These were the sort of economic malpractices that, long before Calvin, or indeed the Reformation, humanist magistrates in the Netherlands had considered as abuses and had sought to punish with the full severity of the law. False coining and clipping, for example, or the debasement of coin with tin or lead instead of silver (a widespread practice in a country where specie overflowed and mints were, literally, two a penny) was punishable by death. The church helped the magistracy in Amsterdam by attempting to discipline those offenders who, it was thought, were minting false coin on the borders of the Republic at Roermond in Limburg or Emmerik in Cleves, and shipping them to Dutch commercial centers. Other similar offenses against the canon of both church and state (and which Udemans listed as his cardinal commercial sins)[88] were: embezzlement, fraudulent sales, the conversion of stock or merchandise, falsification of contracts or notarized documents (all involving false oaths), *lorrendraijerij* (trading with the enemy), absconding without paying rent, failure to honor the terms of a loan, or excessive interest asked of it, the practice of monopolies, *arch-listig* (super-wily) contracts, smuggling, tax evasion, and the deliberate incurring of ruinous debt and fugitive bankruptcy (the last distinguished from unfortunate insolvency). Given the division of the Dutch Republic into myriad local jurisdictions, each with its own excise tariffs, and with striking variations in weights and measures, smuggling amounted to a minor industry in a wide variety of commodities but especially in consumer products and foodstuffs. The church attempted to come down hard on butter and sugar smugglers, and to seek out establishments where untaxed ale was being consumed. In at least one case they censured a Dirk Martens who had soap relatively cheaply made in Haarlem and then smuggled it into Amsterdam in locally made and stamped vats.[89]

In all these cases, the Reformed Church was acting as a spiritual constable for the lay authorities. But that is not the same thing as claiming it to be an instrument in the hands of market capitalism. For both ministry and magistracy subscribed to a system of careful regulation, designed to cleanse the world of money of its most blatant impurities. Normally, this meant acting in favor of insulating Christian society against the threat of a free market in either capital or labor. Both church and municipal authorities, for example, vigorously defended the guild system against any attempt to disrupt it by using immigrant labor. In the case of the cloth shearers of the Holland towns, there was a special coincidence of interests, for they were notorious for Sunday labor. Many of them came from the southern provinces and during the late 1620s made some effort to organize themselves into "synods," which could negotiate freely with textile manufacturers wherever satisfactory work and wages could be found. In 1638 such combinations were formally denounced as *complotterye* by both the lay and clerical authorities.[90] In a similar way, the church set its face against high interest rates. In this matter it had a perfectly respectable authority in Calvin himself, who was deeply suspicious of the lawfulness of rates over five percent.[91] There was a good deal of debate within the church itself over what constituted righteous conduct in interest, some ministers insisting that *all* interest was to be considered an immoral generation of profit from unfortunate circumstances. The Leiden divine and writer on economic matters, Johannes Cloppenburgh, liked to refer repeatedly to Leviticus 25:37, "Thou shalt not give him thy money upon usury, nor lend him thy victuals for increase," or Ezekiel 18:8, "He that hath not given forth upon usury, neither hath taken any increase . . . hath executed true judgment between man and man." But in *De Foenore et Usuri* he also tried to establish a tariff according to the circumstance of the loan and the social standing of the borrower.[92] This ran opposite to market principles (though exactly true to Calvin's own teaching), in that the humbler the borrower and the more negligible his collateral, the lower the rate was decreed to be. Thus while merchants might be legitimately charged eight percent for relatively risky projects, farmers ought never to be charged more than four percent and the truly needy nothing at all.[93] This was indeed the thinking of the magistrates and regents who founded the Bank van Lening in 1614 specifically for small loans and as a way to avoid the clutches of the pawnbrokers. The relief sculpture on its facade shows a poor woman receiving help and the inscription advises the well-off to go elsewhere.

To the most hard-boiled capitalists (as well as to the most skeptical historians), this might still seem an obliging apologia for the world of money that the church professed to despise. But it was not, I think, a rationalization for tooth-and-claw capitalism so much as a defense against it. It was also a way for lay and clerical governors to live with what otherwise would have been an intolerably contradictory value system, a perennial combat between acquisitiveness and asceticism. In this working compromise, the regents acknowledged the need for some sort of antipecuniary ethic to restrain capitalism from anarchy and abuse, and the church recognized that, however perilous for a godly Republic, Dutch wealth was a fact of life and could be made to work for righteous ends. By default, then, Calvinist social teaching collapsed back onto its humanist origins. While it continued to reject, as adamantly as it could, the notion that good works might assure a state of grace, they were nonetheless endorsed as an obligatory feature of right living. While the Erasmian *via media* may have lost the battle of doctrine, it succeeded in becoming the norm by which the dangerous realm of Queen Money was patrolled.

This working collaboration with the patrician regulators of the economy was not without periodic strain. On occasions, the church found itself in the position of having to discipline some of its own enthusiasts for offenses against the ruling code of economic propriety. Isaac le Maire, one of the most conspicuous of the southern capitalists who had emigrated north, was especially notorious for infringing those rules. In 1604 and again in 1605, he was the subject of an inquiry by the Amsterdam consistory, both over domestic matters and sharp practice in accounts, during which time he was forbidden communion and subject to a fine. An initial stockholder in the East India Company, to the tune of sixty thousand guilders, he was forced to withdraw and sign an engagement not to undertake any independent expeditions either to the Cape of Good Hope or to the Magellan Straits. Kept at arm's length from the charmed circle of colonial and commercial enterprise, le Maire then organized a ring to conduct bear operations against the East India Company, some of whose members were other old Antwerpers like Reinier Lems or had married into le Maire's family. In an even more unorthodox move he took to trading *in blanco* on the bourse in paper relating to commodities he did not yet possess: a beginning, in effect, of futures trading. If none of this conduct was calculated to win le Maire popularity or respectability, it also failed as a strategy of economic revenge. The bears bankrupted themselves; were in some cases convicted of fraud; le Maire was exiled to Egmond and the ships commissioned for his "Australian Company" were confiscated by Coen at Batavia on the orders of the East India Company. Le Maire probably lost in the region of a million and a half guilders in his efforts to break the orthodox colonial system. But in the reckoning with the Celestial Accountant, the destruction of great fortune was preferable to its accumulation, provided that insolvency had been incurred, as it were, in good faith. So that le Maire could boast in his curious epitaph in 1624

> *Here lies Isaac le Maire, merchant, who in his*
> *affairs throughout the world, knew much abundance*
> *and lost, in thirty years . . . over fl. 150,000*   [a zero was omitted]
> *Died as a Christian, 20 September 1624*[94]

The renegade individualist, the arch-capitalist, then, was very much an offender against both the commercial and ecclesiastical codes of decorum. Nor did the elders of Amsterdam capitalism believe that religious zeal was an entitling qualification to break their highly regulated practices. In fact, the intrusion of the *roervinken,* or firebrands, as Burgomaster Hooft disparagingly called them, was unwelcome for several reasons. It threatened to disturb Amsterdam's delicate balance of congregations on which, it was traditionally supposed, its prosperity depended. And the more ardent among the southerners, like Usselincx, were not only adamantly opposed to the 1609 truce with Spain, but cherished notions of converting the business of empire building into a great missionary cause of faith and settlement. Even in the 1640s, those who continued to hold that view attempted to buy up enough East India stock to carry the day, and they were supported by the urgent counsel of a succession of governors general at Batavia, from Coen and van Goens to Speelman and van Diemen. Paradoxically, it was the *less* Calvinist group of patricians who upheld the more purely commercial principles of maximum profit with minimum risk and who disliked intensely the instruments of trade being appropriated for some obscure fanatical purpose. In this peculiar situation the church had to exercise some prudence. Not surprisingly, its embattled ministers in Amsterdam were among the most aggressive in urging a godly policy, and they found allies in the militant faction within the regents led by the Pauw family. But when synods came to consider matters, they trod more carefully, not least because some divines were themselves subscribers and stockholders of the East India Company. Plancius, who was a great cartographer as well as doctor of the church, invested as much as six thousand guilders, making him a *hoofdparticipant.* He also acted as a subscription agency for other predikants who were interested investors, but in deference to church concern, declined an active role in directing one of the chambers.[95] Schemes were set afoot by agents of the French crown to detach Plancius, and together with the immense capital of Moucheron, le Maire and Usselincx, create a rival company operating under the protection of the king of France. There was no question of this flirtation ever being reciprocated from the Dutch end, particularly when the militant Calvinists were so closely tied up with the cause of the Stadholder. And there was even less question of the church lending itself to anything that could be construed as subverting a company that had been chartered by the States General. But the mere fact that such a scheme could have been plausible in the first place suggests just how alienated the southern faction must have appeared to be.

Held at arm's length by the more established conservative pillars of the Amsterdam trading community, with their tight hold on the gold mine of Baltic staples, the southerners turned, either by inclination or default, to the more high risk, speculative fringes of the Dutch economy. Moucheron, for example, was prominent in real estate speculation (necessarily involving bribery) in Utrecht and in underhand negotiations for military contracts. When an opportunity arose for him and his friends to participate in a more legitimate venture — the West India Company — they plunged into it with a recklessness and a fervor that their enemies thought irrationally uncommercial.[96] Moucheron, in particular, was stubborn in subsidizing the doomed venture in Brazil, where the costs of maintaining a force of military occupation against the Portuguese were out of all proportion to the expected returns. In the end it resulted in his ruin, a major financial crash and an outbreak of self-congratulatory nodding among the wiseacres of the *grachten.* For the Bickers and the Hoofts, these godly plutocrats, with all showy zeal and plutocratic heavy-handedness, were doubtful types: less shady than the Marrano Jews perhaps, less secretive than the Mennonites, but as businessmen, fundamentally unsound.

In essence, then, the more passionate his Calvinism, the less likely was an entrepreneur to fit into the older *modus operandi* of Amsterdam capitalism. One ought not to generalize in this anti-Weberian vein too glibly. In other areas of the Dutch economy — the textile manufactures of Leiden, for example — industrialists of southern origin had much less difficulty in squaring their devotions with commitment to profit. Indeed, in their exploitation of the labor of women and children and in their "integrated" approach to labor, from supplying it with inferior housing to subsidizing the infirm, the Leiden entrepreneurs came very close to Weber's ideal type and, for that matter, the archetypal hard-driven capitalist of the industrial revolution. Farther south, in Rotterdam and Zeeland, a somewhat more ardent approach to religion dovetailed with a shared dislike of Amsterdam monopolists—and a natural eye to the Atlantic—to recruit allies for the West India Company zealots. Udemans, for example, was a formidable propagandist for the cause in Brazil, just about to collapse. But with all these caveats, it remains true that the concentration of economic activity around Amsterdam and north Holland was governed by very pragmatic working arrangements. Many of these were not at all to the church's liking, but it could do little but passively concur.

Chief among such practices were monopolies and rings. The church made no secret of its hostility to these combinations, Petrus Wittewrongel stigmatizing them as "scandalous in the sight of God and man."[97] Not that the church, any more than the southern enemies of monopolies, were, by that token, early champions of laissez-faire. The former simply held that syndicates, or contracts, arranged to lock up the supply of a given commodity or artificially support a price, were, in effect, conspiracies against the consumer and thus forms of unrighteous dealing. The southerners (especially Usselincx) became indignant about such abuses, but in all likelihood would have emulated them, had they ever been given the opportunity.

Whether it was desirable or not in principle, in practice Dutch capitalism depended crucially on an elaborate and extensive system of protection. Violet Barbour was quite right in judging this dependence to be closer in ethos to medieval or Renaissance trade than any anticipation of modern economic behavior (though whether any modern economic system has flourished through devotion to perfect competition is a moot point). But buffer stocks, acquired to regulate prices, and with the deliberate object of preempting competition, were part and parcel of the staple market. P. W. Klein, whose study of the Trip family is the most outstanding account of the Dutch entrepreneurial ethos, is justified in arguing that "the generally accepted idea of entrepreneurs as individuals who are always ready to take risks appears open to question. In reality they always made every effort to avoid risks."[98] Risks, after all, were built into the very circumstances of their national existence, and the perpetual effort to protect themselves from further hazards was deeply ingrained in Dutch mentality. For all the bravura and exploratory ingenuity of the great mariners, navigators and colonizers, their work was firmly bound within the Dutch imperative of opportune force for minimum risk. This held true whether the issue was the uprooting of clove trees in the East Indies to protect a price in Amsterdam or the down payment in hard specie for exclusive rights to an entire Norwegian forest. The object was always to

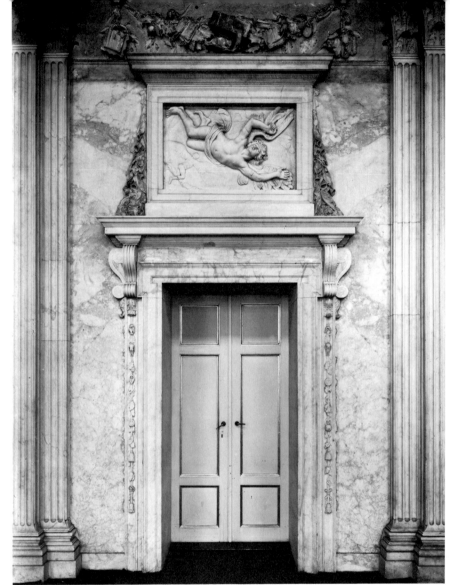

156. Artus Quellijn, doorway of the Bankruptcy Chamber. Royal Palace (formerly Town Hall), Amsterdam

preempt competition, monopolize supply, control all the conditions of a trade, from production of raw material to the terms of domestic or international sale. The Trips were masters of these kinds of arrangements. They managed to obtain exclusive rights to import Swedish tar by negotiating with a firm which itself had the export monopoly. But that firm was financed by the Trips, their major customer, who also organized the freight. The whole business, then, was more akin to an international corporation trading between its own subsidiaries, than business done between genuinely different parties.[99]

Where possible, family loyalties were called on to protect business from outside competition even more effectively. The brothers Trip were famous for their division of the world between their respective concerns (primarily iron and the Baltic staples for munitions) but with branches in the Levant and Muscovy trades. And their marriage alliance with the de Geers was meant to lock up the northern arms market even more tightly. Only Louis de Geer's determination to compete on his own terms fitfully threatened that control.

Dutch commerce, then, ran smoothly, not from the spontaneous harmonization of individual enterprises, but from a carefully and closely controlled system of regulated practices. However much it disliked monopolies, the church never meant to sabotage them in the name of some freer or more just economic principle. On the contrary, its own insistence on the dangers and lures of money was best served by becoming an accomplice, rather than an antagonist, of the regulators. They had, after all, a common foe: money itself. Once set free from her watchmen, Queen Money could wreak terrible havoc on a Godly Republic. She had the power to set brothers at each other's throats, unhinge the reason of the wise and seduce the virtuous. To accomplish all this she had, in her armory, the base instincts of avarice, envy and greed—the curse of *pandemia.* The force of raw money unconfined, magistrates and ministers agreed, was that of diabolical possession.

iii MONEY UNCONFINED: "I INVEST, HE SPECULATES, THEY GAMBLE"

Of all the sculptured reliefs that festoon the interior of the Amsterdam town hall, none is more startling than the decoration over the door of the Bankruptcy Chamber—the *Desolate Boedels Kamer.* Like the motifs allotted to other chambers—the figure of discreet Silentia for the town secretary's office, the Judgment of Solomon for the *vierschaar* tribunal—it alludes, allegorically, to the business of the chamber. The plaque has a familiar humanist theme: the Fall of Icarus, symbolizing the reward for high-flying ambition and folly. But it is the decoration above the plaque that is more unconventional. It is the place where reality bites into platitude, for hanging in garlands are the actual, rather than emblematic, attributes of financial disaster. Empty chests, unpaid bills, worthless stock lie strewn around while among the detritus of a fortune scuttle a family of hungry rats.[100]

Like so much else in the town hall, this strikingly literal admonition is a humanist rather than a Calvinist document. The fall of the bankruptcy was itself akin to a turn of the wheel of Fortuna, a restoration through calamity of decent equilibrium. The array of collapsed assets presupposed a free will capable, through following the golden mean, of avoiding that fate. Similarly, the lengthy and complicated process of the bankruptcy itself was a road through the display of willful misfortune towards redress and restoration. Its object was less the punishment of the delinquent than his or her rehabilitation and the repair of the damage done to the economic balance of the city. It was a balance between prodigality and avarice, between risk and security that had to be upheld, and the eventual aim of the bankruptcy proceeding was, in its legal terminology, a reconciliation between the defaulter and his creditors. This was settled through an agreed percentage of outstanding debts being paid off after the proceeds from an auction of sequestered effects had been applied to the sum. In specifying terms, the "curators" of the settlement would take into account the nature of the debts, how they had been incurred and the overall means of the debtor, including future earnings capacity. Family fortunes — such as dowries — were considered as adhering to individuals and were protected from the consequences of a husband's bankruptcy unless specifically indicated otherwise in a prior marriage settlement. Terms of agreement varied widely from quite severe outstanding charges (for the profligate) or nominal percentages for those at the humbler end of the social spectrum. Though the creditors may have resented what they considered penal terms being imposed on them, there was no other legal course open to them, so that, after pleading haggling it was the curators who had the last word. In the end, a formal ceremony was convened in which both bankrupt and creditors signed their "reconciliation" before a notary behind the door with the rats and the empty strongboxes.[101]

The officials who exercised this arbitration were both judges and stewards; as much as the city sheriff or the deacons of the orphanage they were entrusted with a wardship. Their responsibility was not only to equity but to the civic peace, and that meant keeping the humanists' golden rule of balance forever in mind. And for the oligarchs in the *vroedschap* that appointed them, there were analogies between political and financial discretion. In the realm of power, equilibrium required that no single faction monopolize offices, and that no group (however disagreeable their views to the majority) be absolutely alienated from the ruling elite. Equally, in the realm of money, the wardens of civic peace had to chart a careful course between the "safe" and "unsafe" zones of the economy. Without security, there could be no sustained prosperity, but without risk, there could be no growth.

What were "safe" and "unsafe" zones? The former were areas of activity that were regulated by public authority or protected by it from the consequences of undue risk. The latter were enterprises of high risk and high profit — the East and West India trades or the options trade at the bourse. The city chamber of marine insurance—a few doors down from the *Desolate Boedels Kamer* in the south gallery of the town hall—was a good example of a heavily patrolled safe zone. But the safest place of all in Amsterdam was its Wisselbank, founded in 1609 (significantly, the first year of the truce with Spain). It was created as an instrument to facilitate payments in Amsterdam's rapidly growing foreign trade.[102] But its success in persuading merchants both at home and abroad to make payment in bills drawn on the bank depended crucially on its identification as a public rather than a private institution. In this respect, its impersonality and its corporate status were in sharp contrast to the private banks of the Venetian Rialto or the dynastic court banks of Genoa and Augsburg. It was, in fact, a citadel of right-dealing humanism: adjudicating and conserving, its viability tied up with the integrity of the magistracy itself. Appropriately, its commissioners had their office in the town hall, and its deposits and specie reserves were kept in the vaults. The bank, then, was literally, as well as figuratively, at the foundations of the city's power. Above all, it functioned as a stringently conservative institution, avoiding any kind of issuing role or any venture lending. Its primary concern was to keep the *agio*—the difference between bank money quotations and that for current specie—as high as possible, if necessary by calling on obliging and publicly concerned syndicates to make deposits at times when withdrawals were anticipated. For all the global ramifications of the bank's payments, even by the end of the seventeenth century it had only two thousand depositors. And since business was exclusively a matter of transfer between accounts, there could never be any question of the bank being caught short by withdrawals unmatched by proper reserves. It was this sacred dependability which made Amsterdam bank money so desirable a form of settlement for business, even though it actually *cost* depositors to have accounts, rather than paying them interest. (Fees for opening accounts and for transfers were meant to defray the costs of administration and service.) "Without doubt," wrote the English commentator Onslow Burrish, "the only reason why persons are contented to deposit their money upon such terms is a firm belief that it remains sacred, untouched and unapplied to any use whatsoever. The magistrates of Amsterdam, all those concerned in the government of the Bank and in general the whole body of the Seven Provinces, take pains to propagate this opinion and appear, at least, to be of the same mind themselves."[103] And this solid surety was able to withstand even the most alarming crises of public affairs. In 1672, when, for good reason, a general fear circulated that a run had already started, the indignant commissioners took decisive steps to pre-empt a panic. In an ostentatious display of affronted honor, customers were invited to inspect the vaults if they so wished, and check if accounts could not be tallied with hard money down to the last stuiver. This public gesture had the desired effect, but the magistrates took the offensive against nervous skeptics by declaring "that those who continued to distrust them, and to break the public credit by making their demands at a time when the State was in so great an exigency, should be stigmatized as bad subjects, and should not be permitted to replace their money in the Bank when the storm was blown over."[104]

The bank was the watchdog of capitalism in Amsterdam. Its overriding concern was not to generate funds for enterprise, but, on the contrary, to control the conditions under which they could be exchanged—hence its title. Its very existence testified to a determination to neutralize the worst evils associated with the unconfined world of money: usury, default, counterfeit and other kinds of fraud. Its working motto was probity, not profit. Yet however admirable, the guardians of the economy could not afford to impose a regulation so stifling that it choked off all incentives for enterprise. And if anxiety about the amorality of money loomed large in the mentality of the magistracy, they were not immune to a contradictory strain in the culture: admiration for heroic materialism. This was especially marked (and rendered innocent) when some spectacular act of geographical discovery was involved, with the result that colonial ventures posed peculiar problems for the conscientious city fathers. On the one hand, they indisputably brought immense treasures and profits to the city and the Fatherland, and prizes, moreover, taken from the Iberian enemy. But on the other hand, the uncertainties surrounding their delivery, and the high costs of sustaining a colonial presence in the Indies or Brazil, all made that kind of trade, if not actually unsafe, then very often unsound. This was particularly obvious when compared with the dependable Baltic staples secured over relatively short distances at low unit cost.

For Calvinist ministers and moralists, the dangers were justified less by the prospect of high returns, than by the opportunity to rout the hosts of Antichrist in distant waters and to bring the natives to the true Gospel.[105] But even they shared the misgivings of the magistrates at the low condition and motives of those attracted to service in the Indies. Paradoxically, it was the very brilliance of the more celebrated voyages to the East that had given colonial exploits a fabulous aura and had drawn the credulous towards visions of unimaginable treasure. In fact, that treasure was regularly displayed at the wharves and warehouse of the company and listed in the Amsterdam courants in detail almost calculated to make the palm itch and the mouth water. On June 27, 1634, for example, the spring sailing (God be praised) arrived in the Fatherland and according to the courant unloaded:

> 326,733½ Amsterdam pounds of Malacca pepper; 297,446 lb. of cloves; 292,623 lb. of saltpetre; 141,278 lb. of indigo; 483,082 lb. of sappan wood; 219,027 pieces of blue Ming ware; 52 further chests of Korean and Japanese porcelain; 75 large

vases and pots containing preserved confections, much of it spiced ginger; 660 lb. of Japanese copper; 241 pieces of fine Japanese lacquer work; 3,989 rough diamonds of large carat; 93 boxes of pearls and rubies (misc. carats); 603 bales of dressed Persian silks and grosgreins; 1,155 lb. of raw Chinese silk; 199,800 lb. of unrefined Kandy [i.e., Ceylon] sugar.[106]

Though the sight or the report of this immense bounty may have whetted the appetite of the ambitious, it was not the simple fact of the cargo that, for the more conservative, constituted the "danger" of the business. Rather, it was the vision of untold riches acquired without labor, wealth that existed merely to service vanity or fashion. It seemed to offer a magical rather than methodical route to fortune and so acted as a bad example to citizens easily led astray by the follies of the world. More specifically, it excited a trade in East Indies stock on the bourse that was notorious for its speculative fickleness.

The Amsterdam Bourse was the moral antithesis to the bank. It was as hazardous as the bank was secure. The only places less safe for money were the *musicos* and gambling dens in the slops and stews to which it was constantly being compared. If the bank was the bastion of prudent conservatism, the bourse was a playground for unrestrained passion and reckless enthusiasms. The bank was the church of Dutch capitalism; the bourse was its circus. Like so much else in Amsterdam, both its architecture and its commercial practices were transplanted from Antwerp. The Flemish city in its day had been famous for its addiction to gambling, and in this too, its Dutch stepdaughter followed suit. Wagers were made on every conceivable opportunity, from the outcome of a siege to the sex of an impending baby. They were made on the street, in taverns, at home, in barges. The stakes could be a house full of furniture or a tankard of ale. It was, perhaps, Fortuna's domain, held against all the doctrines of predestination that the church could muster. The line between casual betting and organized trading in stock was often blurred. While the many who had subscribed to a particular merchant venture (often in small shares — as little as one sixty-fourth) had a real interest in the return of a cargo, those who traded in paper were gambling less on the actual outcome of a voyage and making a profit on its commodities than on short-term price fluctuations on the exchange. News was of the utmost importance in these floating transactions, and the regular publication of the courants supplied political and military intelligence to help investors make informed decisions. Strategically placed relatives or correspondents in ports across the globe helped pass on relevant information, but professional punters on the bourse regularly used couriers, eavesdroppers and spies in the coffeehouses of the Kalverstraat to glean tidbits about an enterprise's prospects, or indeed to propagate optimism or pessimism as their stance required.

All this was regarded with spurious piety by the city fathers. They considered the Bourse a sink of iniquity but understood well enough that it was
indispensable to the operations of the city's trade. Even by the first years
following the creation of the East India Company in 1602 (although of course
the bourse traded in all manner of stock), it had become plain that the old
informal dealing in open-air markets on the Warmoesstraat and near the Oude
Kerk would no longer suffice. The new Bourse was built on the Rokin in
1608, not a stone's throw from the town hall and the weigh house (Waag)
— the symbols of paternal jurisdiction over the economy. Confined within its
handsome Flemish-mannerist colonnaded court, the Bourse was more or less
left to its own regulation. Rules were not so much devised by the city for the
exchange, as barriers set between it and the rest of the town's commerce.
They were barriers both in time and place. The Bourse was the only licensed
place for such dealings, and its business was carried on only between the hours
of noon and two o'clock. Opening and closing times were strictly regulated
by the great clock tower that dominated the courtyard, and members could be
fined for arriving after the appointed hour. Although paintings like those by Job
Berckheyde and Emmanuel de Witte showed sedate enough gatherings, written
accounts give a more outlandish impression of behavior at the Bourse. They
also seem to anticipate the frenzied histrionics that characterize stock exchanges
over the centuries and wherever they have taken root. The most vivid such
account is the *Confusion de Confusiones,* written by a Marrano Jew, Joseph de la
Vega, who evidently knew the Bourse very well.[107] He emphasizes the bizarre
nature of its proceedings, the compulsive behavior of the members, their
irrationality under pressure and the theatrical self-consciousness that they
adopted for their business. Such was its reputation as an undignified bazaar,

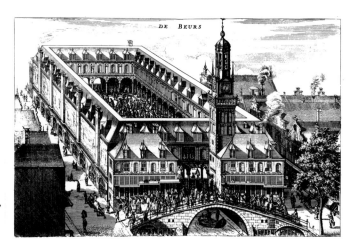

157. *The Bourse,* from Commelin
et al., *Beschryving der Stad Amsterdam,*
1665. Houghton Library, Harvard
University

that the great lords of capital who themselves enjoyed substantial dividend income from share trading disdained to set foot in the place, delegating the daily business of buying and selling to professional brokers. With interest rates in public stock so low — rarely fluctuating much beyond three and five percent — and capital so fecund, there was an evident need for short-term investments with higher yields. And the brokers provided for many clients at a time, the expertise and the continuous presence at the exchange to service that demand on commission. In short, they did then very much what stock-brokers do now, living off their knowledge, not just of the commodities represented by stock, but of the peculiar ways of its trade at the Bourse itself. Indeed they had an interest in perpetuating the faintly unsavory mystique of the Bourse that they then claimed to penetrate.

It was the business of the brokers, buying or selling large batches of *actien* for substantial clients, that set the ebb and flow of prices for the day. But in their wake swam an altogether different kind of investor: the petty speculator, trading strictly for himself and hoping to make quick killings from antici-pating price movements. It was his flamboyant behavior that generated the atmosphere of high-pressure dealing, which the *Confusion* found so eccentric. The brief period set for business intensified this even further, especially during the last half hour — for at half-past one the cashier began to tally the prices of large shares for the day. The relatively ceremonious ritual by which a seller opened his hand and a buyer shook it, a second exaggerated handshake confirming the price, degenerated into a manic display of wild and speedy hand slapping. "Hands redden from the blows . . . handshakes are followed by shouting, insults, impudence, pushing and shoving."[108] The Bourse was no place for the timid, nor for those reluctant to put on the kind of show that their current status as bears (*contremines*) or bulls (*liefhebbers*) demanded. The more skilled performers would deliberately draw attention to themselves as if they were secret guardians of an unbearable mystery. A typical speculator "chews his nails, pulls his fingers, closes his eyes, takes four paces, and four times talks to himself, raises his hand to his cheek as if he has a toothache and all this accompanied by a mysterious coughing."[109] Such nerve-racked punters were specialists at moving small batches of shares, or packets of split shares at low prices (the *ducatoons*). And they lived off their wits rather than their means, since it became common practice to offer shares which either were not yet in their possession or for which they had not yet paid, on the assump-tion that they could be off-loaded for a profit by the time their initial obligation fell due. This was sailing very close to the wind — indeed it became known as trading in the wind or *in blanco,* and it aroused the indignation of the magistracy as well as the church, which condemned it as a form of fraud. But it was only when le Maire took to practicing it on a large scale that the States of Holland were moved to a formal prohibition. In fact the practice seems to have revived (albeit covertly) as soon as the heat from a notorious scandal died down.

Trading in the wind was represented by its critics as a sinister deviation from the proper conventions governing the buying and selling of stock. It was, they said, an invitation to prodigality and deceit. But this moralizing aside, it was in fact only a more extreme form of the practices which arose naturally in an economy where delivery times were bound to be uncertain and prolonged. It was certainly no more improper than governments spending money (usually on building or campaigns) by "anticipating" (that is, realizing, through whatever source delivered the cash) revenues for coming years. In an international entrepôt like Amsterdam, where a glut of capital washed around looking for places to settle, and where rumor and gossip made and ruined fortunes, it was virtually impossible to stifle impromptu speculation. If it was driven from the Bourse, the chances were that it would develop spontaneously elsewhere. For those long time lapses between the "sighting" of a commodity and its actual appearance were unbearably inviting to those in a position to manipulate rising or falling expectations. And from their ingenuity, and from the impatience of the small punter to see his fortune magically transformed, there arose the great speculative manias of the seventeenth and early eighteenth centuries. More than any other phenomena, they revealed to an unnerved elite just how fragile their system of controlled supplies and buffered prices could be when faced with pressure from spontaneous market demand. Speculation was Queen Money's revenge on her guardians. Confined by regulation, she could be set at large by the headlong rush of thousands of devotees, eager to squander what disposable income they had in the irrational hope of instantaneous wealth. Often these were quite modest folk—smallholders or artisans— and their delusions seemed to the patriciate all the more dangerous for that. Their follies were represented, in tracts and prints, not just as wishful thinking, but as a kind of economic anarchy that threatened to destroy the entire, carefully maintained edifice of regulation.

The most spectacular, and certainly the most alarming of these speculative breakouts, was the great tulip mania of 1636–37. It has been the subject of much astonished and bemused writing, perhaps because of the apparent incongruousness between the banality of the flower and the extravagance of its treatment.[110] Only a deeply bourgeois culture, it is implied, could possibly have selected the humble tulip—rather than, say, emeralds or Arabian stallions—as a speculative trophy. But there was nothing suburban about tulips in the seventeenth century. They were, at least to begin with, exotic, alluring and even dangerous. It was precisely at the point that their rarity seemed capable of domestication for a mass market that the potential for runaway demand could be realized. It was this transformation from a connoisseur's specimen to a generally accessible commodity that made the mania possible. And there were other properties, inherent to the bulb, that distorted the process by which an exotic object entered the commonplace life of the culture. The key was reproducibility. Ming porcelain and Turkish rugs were also part of this enrichment of consumer supply, by which expensive rarities were adapted, through domestic manufacture, for a general market. But the blue and white Delftware, and the Flemish carpets which typified this kind of enterprise were at best an approximation rather than a reproduction of the originals. Perception of this difference meant that two tiers of goods established themselves to cater to different clienteles: originals for the monied elite and adaptations for everyone else. The democratization of taste in the applied arts also meant a certain vulgarization, which was cheerfully accepted by the Dutch.

The tulip, though, was a different matter. It, too, was an imported luxury, originating in Turkey, but it could be literally transplanted with ease, and reproduced horticulturally ad infinitum through the splitting of outgrowths. Highly prized varieties—the flamed and striped blooms like Semper Augustus—were jealously guarded from casual imitation. But what would otherwise have been a practice not unlike the careful preservation of buffer stocks to preserve price differentials was continually subverted by trade in outgrowths and the efforts of growers themselves to produce new and more handsome varieties. In these conditions it was virtually impossible for any hypothetical guild of growers to have maintained control over production in the manner of other manufacturers or merchants. Indeed, their own professional interest in experimenting with unlimited combinations of hues, petal shapes and sizes, created a huge range of varieties, destined to attract not just the wealthy connoisseur but thousands of small buyers. The units of sale encouraged this expansion of the market. Initially, while the trade was in the hands of gentlemen horticulturalists and their estate gardeners (between the first decade of the century and the 1620s) sales were confined to large and expensive units: whole beds, or else by weight per thousand "aces" (1/20 gram). As the market quickly expanded in the late 1620s and early 1630s, it became possible to buy by the Amsterdam pound, by the basket or by a small number of aces. This in turn opened up a business in the *vodderij*—the hitherto despised "rags" of the more common types. Unlike other "decorative" goods, then, there was a continuous chain connecting the most prized blooms at the top of the market, with the most modest reds and yellows, like Gouda, that became the stock of the mass trade. The tulip simultaneously retained its associations of precious treasure yet was a prize in some form within the reach of the common man. For a modest outlay he could be drawn into the nexus of buying and speculating which, like all gambles, became quickly addictive.

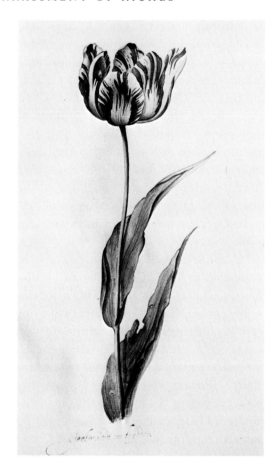

158. Judith Leyster, "Yellow-Red
of Leiden" from Tulip Book. Frans
Hals Museum, Haarlem

There was one further aspect to the production of the bulbs that made them
ideal objects of speculation. This was their dependence on the passing seasons.
For genuine amateurs, the buying season was confined to the period between
lifting in June and the next planting in October. It would have made no sense
at all to have bought for delivery some months away. However, once growers
were tempted into satisfying increasing demand by selling outgrowths, these
could *only* be separated and thus supplied after a wait of a few months at least.
So buying in the winter for future delivery became acceptable, and very quickly
— it seems, around 1634 — extended to the "future" sale of whole bulbs. With
a long period prior to delivery, it was inevitable that buyers should be tempted
into an interim deal, either selling again to a new buyer and realizing a profit
or else upgrading their own stock. They did so, of course, without ever laying
their eyes on the blooms or the bulbs, and before long buyers approached
potential sellers whom they *knew* had not had possession of the stock. They in

their turn offered a "paper" price contingent on delivery, meaning to pass their "paper" sale on to yet another third party. As prices based on expectations rose with the impending spring, so the turnover of what was in effect a trade in tulip futures quickened. By early 1637, the height of the speculation, the point of the purchase had long since ceased to be a tulip bulb and instead had become a negotiable piece of paper with a notional delivery date upon it, like some very doubtful bill of exchange. The closer to delivery that the deal was made, the higher the risk of the buyer having to settle with a grower, but the more dazzling the possibility of realizing a profit from prices that rose by the day and the hour. At this point, the craze had gone into orbit on its own thrust, and it took an act of intervention from a public authority to bring it sharply back down to earth—with a tremendous crash.

There are, then, four phases to this extraordinary story: the phase of the connoisseurs and scholars, the phase of the professionalization of the growers, the mass invasion of speculators and, finally, the intervention of regulators anxious to return Queen Money (dressed as Flora) to obedient confinement. There is nothing mysterious about the tulip's arrival in western Europe. It came to the Netherlands in the sixteenth century at a time when commercial and cultural contacts between the Ottoman Levant and the Habsburg empire flourished notwithstanding their official bellicosity. Ambassador Busbeq saw it growing in Adrianople and agents and diplomats as well as merchants brought the bulbs to the gardens of courtiers, scholars and bankers in Antwerp, Brussels and Augsburg in the 1560s.[111] Joris Rye, who was a botanist as well as a merchant, cultivated varieties at Malines, and by the 1590s it had appeared in gardens in the north, perhaps even the *Hortus Botanicus* at Leiden University, where Clusius and Johan van Hooghelande both experimented with different hues and sizes. In this early period, its cultivation was essentially an aristocratic taste—a novelty that caught on from Paris to Prague, where that passionate innovator the Emperor Rudolf II indulged his curiosity. Both Boisot, the admiral of the Beggar Fleet, and Philip van Marnix, among the entourage of William the Silent, were fanciers, but it was not until the publication of the first substantial catalogues that admiration of the flower moved out from court and humanist circles to a wider group of aficionados. Emmanuel Sweerts's *Florilegium,* published in Frankfurt in 1612, included around a hundred plates reflecting the varieties that he was already selling in Amsterdam. But it was Chrispijn van de Pas's *Hortus Floridus,* published in both Dutch and Latin editions in 1614, that promoted the reputation of the flower throughout Dutch and German towns on the lower Rhine.

By the early 1620s, tulips were established as the unrivaled flower of fashion throughout northern France, the Netherlands and western parts of Germany. In an age extremely conscious of hierarchy, it was not long before an informal system of classification arranged varieties according to rank, from the most noble to the most common. Superior ranking did not necessarily (though often did) indicate rarity, but rather flamboyance and subtlety of color combinations. It was the flamed and irregularly striped varieties that were most admired and were grouped into three aristocratic estates according to dominant hue: the roses (red and pink on white ground), the violets (lilac and purples on white ground) and *bizarden* (red or violet on yellow ground). At the very head of this nobility were the imperial rarities, the Semper Augustus (red flames on white) and the attempted clone, the Parem Augustus. There were also Viceroys, but in the Netherlands, where royalty had gone out of favor, inventive growers appropriated heroic titles for their flowers that cast a reflected patriotic luster on themselves. Thus admirals and generals (for the tulip was always anthropomorphized as male) sprang up everywhere. General Bol and Admiral Pottebacker were not, then, named for military heroes but rather admiral and general tulips named for the growers Pieter Bol of Haarlem and Henrik Pottebacker of Gouda. Tulips could inspire even fancier conceits from poets, one comparing *Tulipa clusiana*, with its carmine-tinted white petals, to the "faint blush on the cheek of chaste Susannah."[112]

In this stage of the flower's debut in northern Europe, tulips were either admired or scorned as an elegant extravagance. Those critics (especially Calvinist preachers) who attacked the follies of outrageous ruffs and beribboned hose or overwrought bedsteads, saw the tulip as yet another dangerous addition to the lengthy catalogue of vanities that were subverting the godly Republic. There are, it is true, occasional exceptions to their hostility in the iconography of moralizing texts. One emblem seems to have imported the oriental Sufi association of tulips with eternity. It shows an image of virtue rather than vice: an elderly widow awaiting her end with her attribute of honorable industry, the distaff, and that of fidelity, her (equally aged) dog. The imminence of her end is symbolized in the scaly hand of death grasping the stem of the tulip. A connotation of virtuous resignation, however, is rare. Much more typical was the association of the tulip with worldly folly. Roemer Visscher's *Sinnepoppen* used it for the motto "A fool and his money are soon parted" almost twenty years *before* the speculative mania got under way.[113] At a time when a single bulb of Semper Augustus might easily fetch a thousand guilders, the sentiment was easily understandable.

Even by the late 1620s, the tulip remained for the most part a costly flower, produced either by gentlemen botanists for themselves or a small number of professional growers for their patrician clientele. Adriaan Pauw, the Pensionary of Amsterdam immediately after Oldenbarneveld's demise, was typical in planting out beds at his rural retreat at Heemstede soon after its purchase in 1623, and became an enthusiast in his own right, producing new red-and-white-

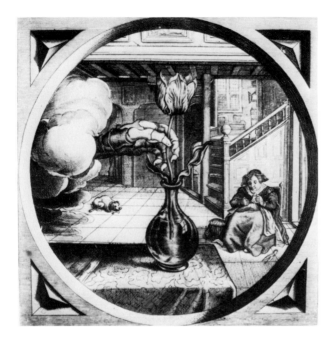

159. "Widow," from Jacob Cats, *Houwelijck,* 1658. Houghton Library, Harvard University

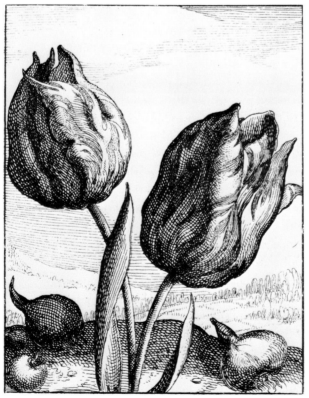

160. Claes Jansz. Visscher, emblem from Roemer Visscher, *Sinnepoppen* (Amsterdam, 1614). Houghton Library, Harvard University

striped hybrids. The most inventive and prolific among the professional growers, like Abraham Catoleyn in Amsterdam and Pieter Bol and Jan Quackel in Haarlem, established specialist reputations, both from the bulbs named for them in the catalogues and through their well-connected clientele. But around the beginning of the 1630s, a second generation of horticulturalists began to break out from this relatively genteel and circumscribed trade and to change the conditions of distribution and sale. Some of these men had served their apprenticeship as gardeners to the older professionals and now struck out on their own with rented lots and aggressively entrepreneurial ambitions. Barent Cardoes, for example, had been Pieter Bol's head gardener and left in his thirties to become an independent grower near Haarlem.[114] The countryside around that town with its rich alluvial soil, was becoming the heartland of bulb production and within Haarlem, on the Houtweg, many of the newer men like Jan van Damme set up shop for direct trading. At the same time they rented more land (in van Damme's case, from a local almshouse) to ensure that they could supply the anticipated new demand. There was no guild control over their trade, their product or their prices. Marginal entrepreneurs who would have found it difficult to enter older crafts and trades, could, with their specialized knowledge, quickly make their way among the bulb men. The Portuguese Jew Francisco Gomez da Costa, for example, was a major grower at Vianen specializing in brilliant, highly variegated *bizarden*.

The new dealers geared themselves to supplying a much broader range of stock, from the high-price hybrids to the gaudier, single-color varieties like the Switsers and the Yellow Crowns that sold for a few stuivers the ace. Differences in both weight and price were enormous, so that potential customers could pick and choose according to their means. The Leiden Yellow and Red (see fig. 158) was inexpensive per ace, but might weigh as much as five hundred aces (100 grams). The Generalissimo, one of da Costa's specialties, which became rapidly popular, was a small bulb, averaging around ten aces, but cost nine guilders the ace. Adjusting the units of sale so that bulbs could be bought by the basket, the pound or even individually expanded the market still further. And, not content with trading directly from nurseries or from shops, growers had itinerant salesmen work village fairs and markets remote from the major bulb centers in Holland and Utrecht. By the winter of 1635 buyers of tulips included all sorts and social groups, from merchants and shopkeepers to skilled workers and artisans. It has been suggested that a labor shortage following a severe visitation of the plague between 1633 and 1635 had suddenly improved real wages to the point that some additional disposable income was available for "luxury" purchases. Be that as it may, it seems that by this time weavers and carpenters, millers and smiths and barge skippers had all been caught up in the horticultural craze.

The result of deliberate market innovations and the extension of production to cover cheaper varieties had produced something like an explosion of demand during the course of 1634 and 1635. The popularization of the tulip had touched a deep well of consumer hunger in the Dutch that could only be assuaged by colorful novelty and conspicuous expenditure at home. The growers had succeeded beyond their wildest expectations. They had invented a national cliché. The effect on prices was extraordinary. Initially, during 1634, the introduction of many new varieties had the effect of depressing prices to the point at which they became accessible to the popular market. The sudden surge of demand then swung them abruptly in the opposite

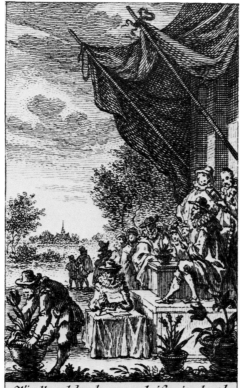

Windhandel, dwaaze drift uit dartle
weeld geboren,
Kan dan een purpre bloem zo 't oog
en hart bekoren ,
Dat men beroep verlaat, zyn goed,
en huis en land
Om een verwelkbre bloem, een tulp,
verkoopt, verpandt ?

161. S. Fokke, etching. Atlas van Stolk, Rotterdam

direction. Seasonal unavailability, as well as the strain on production to keep pace with demand, further accelerated the price rise. By lifting time in 1636, many varieties—even common ones—had trebled in price. A Gouda that had cost thirty stuivers in December 1634 fetched more than fl. 3 two years later. An Admiral de Maan that had sold for fl. 15 cost fl.175 after the same period. A fl. 40 Centen went for fl. 350 just a few months later; a Scipio bought for fl. 800 sold weeks later for fl. 2,200. Such cases could be multiplied indefinitely.[115]

Before long, payment was made in kind, partly as a reflection of down-market customers who could offer more in the way of stock than ready cash to snap up desirable buys. Quite frequently they were obliged to part with their goods on making the purchase and then promised to pay a balance in cash on delivery of the bulb. A quarter of a pound of White Crowns, for example, were bought for fl. 525 to be paid on delivery together with four cows paid at once. A one-pound Centen was paid for by fl. 1,800 and immediate transfer of a "best shot coat, one old rose noble and one coin with a silver chain to hang round a child's neck."[116] A Viceroy that had been bought for fl. 900 was resold while still planted out for fl. 1,000 on delivery and the immediate exchange of a suit and coat. The different kinds of goods offered give some indication of the wide range of occupations and social status of buyers. In all likelihood it was a farmer who paid fl. 2,500 for a single Viceroy in the form of two *last* of wheat and four of rye, four fat oxen, eight pigs, a dozen sheep, two oxheads of wine, four tons of butter, a thousand pounds of cheese, a bed, some clothing and a silver beaker.[117] Tools and stock in trade were commonly offered. Just as van Heemskerck had bought his lottery ticket with a painting, so Jan van Goyen—on the very eve of the crash—paid a Hague burgomaster fl. 1,900 for ten bulbs, and promised, in addition, a picture by Salomon van Ruysdael and a history painting of Judas by himself. By 1641, four years later, he had still not delivered the picture nor had discharged his debts and died insolvent.[118] At the top end of the speculators' market extraordinary deals were made, all carefully notarized. A Semper Augustus of 193 aces was bought for fl. 4,600 and a coach and dapple gray pair (around fl. 2,000 value on their own).[119] The few bulbs of that most prized variety were thought to fetch fl. 6,000 each at the height of the mania. Tracts of land, houses, silver and gold vessels and fine furniture were all commonly traded as part of the increasingly feverish tempo of transactions.

The hysteria about the bulbs was real enough. Small growers went to elab-orate lengths to protect their investment day and night. One horticulturalist at Hoorn in north Holland rigged up a trip wire in his garden to which he attached an alarm bell to alert him to intruders.[120] But the point at which the speculation caused serious concern among both professional growers and city magistrates was late in 1636, when it was transformed into a pure *windhandel*, a paper gamble. Since the inflation period of any given bulb was constantly contracting (prices doubling or trebling by the week or day), the object of the exercise became snapping up paper delivery obligations and then off-loading them again for a choice markup. Speed of turnover depended on the punter's hunch as to whether his contract would continue to appreciate or whether he would be better off realizing his profit quickly. The latter was not always straightforward, since many buyers made offers conditional on delayed payment terms, so that in effect sellers were dealing with stock they did not yet possess for prices they could not realize. Not only their stock, but their profit was paper "in the wind."

As the satirical poems, dialogues and prints issued copiously after the crash make clear, the elite viewed this degeneration of business into gambling with deep misgivings — and the church, of course, with unconcealed horror. It was the contagion of *pandemia:* the gullible masses driven to folly and ruin by their thirst for unearned gain. It was, in their view, money run amok, a kind of anarchy in which all the conventions and rules for virtuous and sober commercial conduct had been thrown to the wind. But what is actually striking about the popular-speculative phase of the tulip mania is how quickly it improvised highly ritualized and formal conventions in which to conduct its trade. Deals were not struck in fly-by-night casual circumstances at street markets or horse fairs at all, but in formally organized groups known as Colleges that convened at specific taverns at specific times. The *Dialogues between Waermondt and Gaergoedt* make it clear that these were created by people for whom formal notarial contracts would have been needlessly expensive and who wished to be free of official regulation. But the rules that they devised at their own College gatherings were hardly less elaborate. Their resemblance to guild ritual and artisans' initiation lore reinforces the impression that these were authentically popular institutions in which the common people could play at a pastiche form of stockbroking.

Newcomers — prospective buyers or sellers — had to be introduced to a company where, the dialogue said, "some will say 'a new whore in the brothel' but take no notice."[121] There were three methods of buying, the simplest through Dutch auction, at which the seller began with a high price and reduced it until a bid was offered. The more common method of dealing, though, was either "through the plates" or "through the nought." In the former, wooden discs with value units inscribed on them were circulated, those receiving them having to make a bid. Sellers were forbidden to offer their own goods directly but to intimate in some strangely roundabout way they they would sell for a price that had been offered. When some sort of convergence was noted, the two parties and proxies haggled together privately, marking their agreed price with chalk marks on the discs. If the deal went through, the marks remained; if not, they were wiped off by one party or the other. Whoever withdrew paid a small fee to the other as compensation. "In the nought" had the seller draw a design on a slate and place a sum of money in it to act as a premium incentive to whoever bidded highest at auction.

Whichever procedure was used, a good deal of obligatory conviviality accompanied the deals. Wine money was fixed at half a stuiver per guilder of the transaction—with a maximum of three guilders. In the event of a successful sale, it was, surprisingly, the buyer who then stood the rest of the company to drinks. If deals flowed thick and fast (as they must have done), these petty cash sums could mount up so that Gaergoedt reported that "I have been on several journeys where I brought home more money than I brought to the Inn. And then I had eaten and drunk wine, beer and tobacco, cooked or roast fish, meat, fowls and rabbits, and sweets to finish, and that from the morning to about three or four at night."[122] Even in the underground economy of the speculators' Colleges, then, the Dutch instinct for offsetting the fickleness of gain and loss by shared festivity and shared obligations rose to the surface. The "wine money" not only paid for edibles, but for heat, light and "the girls" (presumably serving). In an uncharacteristically pious aside, Gaergoedt also wrote that it was used "to remember the poor." Even a weaver, out of a night's flirtation with those dangerous ladies Pecunia and Fortuna, felt the need to protect himself with a gesture of redemptive charity.

None of this made the phenomenon any less alarming to the governing class. Genuine tulip fanciers steered clear of the *windhandel* in the Colleges, and as the pace of dealing became more manic, growers began to be concerned lest a crash leave them saddled with worthless stock in their beds. It must have been difficult for them to judge whether any kind of intervention would make such a disaster more or less likely. And when it duly took place it remains unclear whether it was in response to rumors of official action, or vice versa. At any rate, the first warning noises were sounded in Haarlem, probably on February second or third, at which time people were being advised to stop buying. By the fourth of February, amid conditions of general panic in Haarlem, bulb prices were dropping by the hour, and at the end of the week there was talk of stock becoming unsalable. As for tulip futures, these had become worthless the moment that the price decline set in. It is not surprising, then, that the initial action came from the growers themselves faced with the prospect of their reputations tarnished as quasi-speculators and their stock-in-trade collapsed in value. Once aroused, they worked at what by Dutch standards was lightning speed. An early meeting was convened at Utrecht on the seventh, which in turn appointed delegates from all the major growing centers to a conference in Amsterdam on the twenty-fourth. They included Gomez da Costa from Vianen, Barent Cardoes from Haarlem, Jacques Baalde from Leiden and François Sweerts from Utrecht. That meeting resolved (with Amsterdam's dissent) that all sales prior to November 1636 should be deemed bona fide. Subsequent to that date, buyers who had paid ten percent of the asking price might have the option of withdrawing from the contract. In effect, this was a preemptive move, designed to secure for the growers a reasonable degree of protection for goods they had already sold on paper but were waiting to deliver. But unless public officials concurred, the agreement could not be enforced. The High Court of Holland, to which the States referred the matter, was much less inclined to be charitable to the men whom public opinion saddled with the responsibility for initiating the craze and were now trying to escape the worst damage. At the end of April 1637 the court effectively ignored the Amsterdam resolution by setting aside all deals made since the planting of 1636, while sending any disputed contracts to the jurisdiction of individual town magistrates. The ten-percent condition was overruled, but growers were permitted to attempt to sell languishing stock to third parties at the risk of clients who had notionally bought the bulbs. In the circumstances of what amounted to a moratorium on payments, those efforts, where made, were unlikely to meet with eager buyers. Thus the growers were stuck with much of the financial damage for the crash, since they could neither find new sales nor do much to recover sums from the customers of autumn 1636. By January 1638, it was apparent that if ever horticulture was to be restored to more normal conditions, some further regulation was needed. That adopted by Haarlem in the spring of that year was fairly typical of other towns and was upheld by the States of Holland. A commission of five was empowered to summon parties to disputes over contracts and to hand down arbitrations. Initially the aim was to reconcile the parties, but very quickly it became necessary to make judgments binding, however dissatisfied either or both of the parties might have been. Any outstanding contracts could be liquidated by the flat payment of three and a half percent of the original purchase price. This may have fallen far short of the growers' claims—they argued that they were being penalized for the fecklessness of the masses—but it was, after all, some form of compensation. And the growers retained possession of the bulbs themselves, which, once the mania had abated, reverted to the old price hierarchy as real, rather than artificial, market conditions dictated.

In any event, the magistrates of the Dutch towns saw niceties of equity as less pressing than the need to de-intoxicate the tulip craze. Their intervention was hastened by the urgency of returning the genie speculation to the bottle from which it had escaped, and corking it tightly to ensure against any recurrence. To some extent, they could feel satisfied that the ineluctable operations of Fortuna had already punished the foolhardy by taking them from rags to riches and back again in short order. But they still felt impelled to launch a didactic campaign in tracts, sermons and prints against the folly, since its special wickedness had been in leading the common people astray. To the humanist oligarchs, the tulip mania had violated all their most sacred tenets: moderation, prudence, discretion, right reason and the reciprocity between effort and reward. It had offered the dreadful spectacle of the multitudes following their herd instincts untempered by the sage hand of regulation or instruction. So they represented it as a kind of economic alchemy whereby fools imagined they might turn mere onions (the bulbs) into gold. At the close of the *Third Dialogue* between Gaergoedt and Waermondt, the boastful Gaergoedt says that the flowers surpass "gold and silver, pearls and all the costly stones." The more down-to-earth Waermondt then cautions that "It is true if you consider their beauty when in existence and take into account by whom the trade is run. But not when you look at their perishability and consider by whom silver and gold, pearls and gems and artistic works are esteemed, because the latter are esteemed by great people, the former by common folk."[123] To the "great people" there was even something sinister about a phenomenon that had so dispossessed men of their senses. Some tracts represented it as a kind of heretical social church, complete with its own special incantations, primitive beliefs and ritual practices. It was, in effect, the economic world turned upside down, a Bourse of Fools.

In keeping with a traditional Netherlandish idiom, then, much of the didactic material satirized the ambition and deluded vanity of those simple-tons who hoped tulips might work a magical transformation of their fortunes. Following Erasmus, the author of the *Dialogues* put in the mouth of Gaergoedt all the follies that the humanist found most reprehensible. He boasts of mortgaging his house to acquire the capital to launch the speculation, of leaving his life as a weaver behind, of looking forward to ease and luxury. Waermondt (True Mouth) is appropriately more cautious, scoffing at those "who thought they would be rich this summer" and who already indulged in great extravagance, like the ordering of coaches and horses. But skeptic though he is, he is lured irresistibly by the prospect of quick gain

> Vainly have I done such hard labor and have many parents slaved and toiled. What need is there for merchants to have any or to risk their goods overseas; for children to learn a trade or for the peasants to sow and to work so hard on the soil; for the skipper to sail on the terrible and dangerous seas; for the soldier to risk his life for so little gain if one can make profits of this sort.[124]

In other words, everything decent in Dutch life: the proper relation between labor and reward, the sacrifice of parents for children, the ventures of merchants—the *trials* that were at the core of the humanists' view of the world—all would be fatally undermined by the wickedness of speculation.

And the poor who were most in need of such moral guidance were the most in danger of being ensnared by folly. Hence the graphic illustration of the peril in Nolpe's *Floraes Geks-kap* (Flora's Cap of Fools), one of many prints in 1637, which grafted the new style of documentary narrative onto the older tradition of illustrated follies and vices. While Flora is driven off seated on an ass "for her whorish immorality," as the text below explains, her acolytes in the company of tulip fanciers do their business within an outsize fool's hat reminiscent of the hats that make up the bizarre habitat of Pieter Bruegel's print on *Pride*. For its inn sign, the hat pavilion flies a *kermis* flag proclaiming it to be "*In de 2 Sottebollen*," a pun signifying both fatheads or crazies and foolish bulbs, and showing two jesters wrestling. Ragged peasants haul off bulbs by the cartload or basket while a fop pours bulbs pell-mell onto the unpromising ground below. To his left a demon is seated—the evil spirit of the craze— holding an emptied hourglass while over the fop's head he suspends a pole with another fool's cap and attached contracts and delivery notes. Both are seen against the background of a ruined and derelict building. And in case any of this was lost on the reader, the title legend of the print is: "Illustration of the amazing year of 1637 in which one fool and another hatched a plan to become rich without property and wise without understanding."

The moralizing device of the fool's hat appeared in many other prints scorning the tulip mania. In the most famous of all, attributed to Crispijn van de Pas, Jr., *Floraes Mallewagen* (Flora's Car of Fools), three of her attendants: Lekkebaard (Sweet Beard), Graagryk (Eager for Wealth) and Leegwagen (Traveling Light), wear jester's costume festooned with the flowers, while the cap appears yet again on the flag at the back of the car: Simon Stevin's *zeil-wagen*, or wind chariot, that had itself been the subject of satirical and ominous prints around 1602.[125] Nothing could have been more suitable for a satire on the *windhandel* —the airy trade or flutter—than the wind car. But the print also belongs to the tradition of the Antwerp *ommegang* triumphal procession of the vices and virtues, but instead of using allegory to reinforce some generalized humanist moral on the dangers of wealth and greed, it has been harnessed to specific and topical narrative history (somewhat in the manner of the stranded whale prints). *Flora's Mallewagen* is, in fact, typical of the symbol-laden graphic journalism of which the Dutch were particularly fond, and which laid the basis for the political prints and satires of the next generation.[126] The history of the tulip mania is related in four cartoons at each corner of the print, representing, top left, the grower Pottebacker's nursery at Haarlem and, bottom left, a company of tulip fanciers meeting in a tavern in the same town while two women drink and stoke an already roaring fire in the background. None of these obvious allusions would have been lost on the emblem-hungry Dutch, who "read" these prints very much like a news gazette rather than as

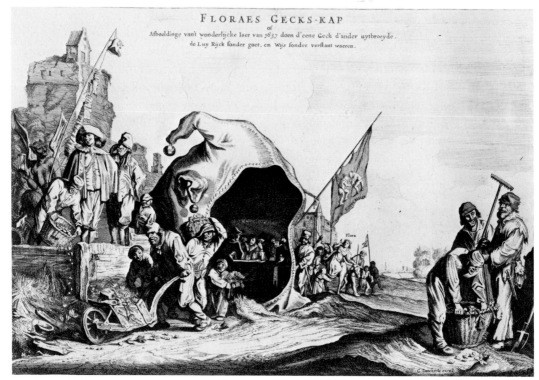

162. Pieter Nolpe, *Floraes Geks-kap,* 1637. Atlas van Stolk, Rotterdam

fine art. At the right, the business rapidly degenerates; at top is a Hoorn company where carousing accompanies the trading in bulbs, and at bottom right, the reckoning catches up with the speculators, one of whom scratches his head as he forlornly comes to his senses. The central part of the print is packed with references to folly, calamity and idle fashion as well as particular allusions to the tulip craze. Over the whole scene, tacked to the top of the mast of Flora's Chariot—for this is a Dutch wind-sail car that was driven along the dunes—is the flag of *kermis,* the *verkeerde wereld,* world turned upside down, with the inverted cross attached to a globe. The climbing ape refers to a proverb attacking foolish ambition—he who would climb must expect to show his naked buttocks—while the *kak* on those below needs no oversubtle elucidation. Flora herself is dressed like her common counterpart, Crijn in the *geks-kap,* as a courtesan, and carries as her attributes the most sought-after of the bulbs—General Bol, Semper Augustus and Admiral van Hoorn. Many other of the varieties that were most inflated in price, like Viceroy, Spinnecoop Verbeterde and Admiral de Maan, lie strewn on the ground beneath the chariot. The town in the background, recognizable from St. Bavo's tower, is

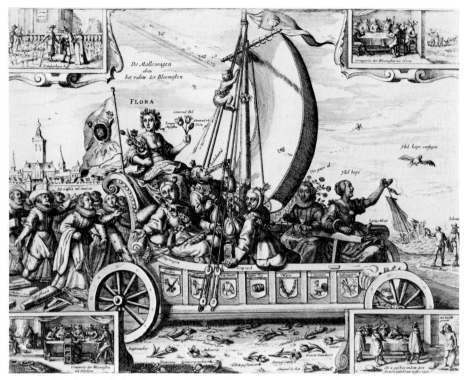

163. Crispijn van de Pas Younger, *Floraes Mallewagen*, 1637. Kress Library, Harvard University

Haarlem, and inn signs like the White Doublet and the Little Hen attached to the chariot refer to the best known dens of the tulip fanciers in the town. Accompanying Flora, Graagryk flourishes his moneybags while Lekkebaard drinks to the gullible. The two women are Ver Gaet al (Forget all), who weighs bulbs as Idle Hope releases the bird Idle Hope Flown Away, a symbol that also commonly denoted the loss of innocence. At the rear of the car, fashionably dressed burghers, distraught at the *valete* of the *bloemisten*, plead to be let on board, while out in the shallows the wreck of the enterprise is depicted with a crew abandoning their foundering car as a Zaantvoort peasant watches and the sheriff approaches.

For all the crowding of the imagery, none of this would have been the least bit obscure to a Dutch audience familiar with both the contemporary news and the perennial symbolism. Like much graphic satire it was meant both to instruct and amuse, but especially to warn against repetitions of the folly. When, in the 1730s, the sudden popularity of fine hyacinths seemed, for a while, to threaten a recurrence of the craze, the old tulip satires were reprinted for a new generation of speculators.[127] Indeed, the imagery of

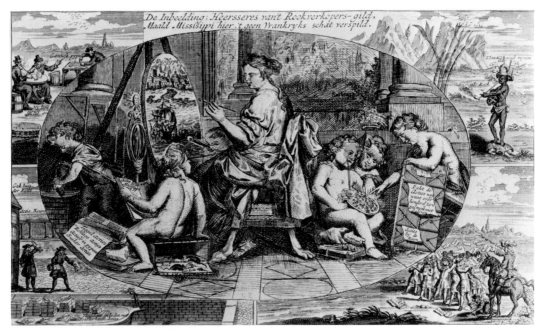

164. and 165. Engravings from series *Het Groote Tafereel der Dwaasheid* (The Great Mirror of Folly), 1720. Author's collection

speculators' folly that had begun with the original seeding of Netherlandish capitalism never really left it. Nor was it confined to flowers. In 1720, when thousands of small investors saw their capital blown away in the Mississippi Company swindle — the Dutch version of the South Sea Bubble — there was once more a great outpouring of moralizing prints, anthologized as *Het Groote Tafereel der Dwaasheid* (The Great Mirror of Folly). [128]   Like the tulip prints, these combined allegory with topical satire to ridicule the credulous, vilify the fraudulent and, by contrast, uphold what were according to the lights of humanism proper standards of economic conduct. A pair of prints, featuring the muses of painting and Fame/History, incorporated many of these now familiar *topoi*. While an image (read, deceit) is painted of a laden cargo vessel arriving at a rich port called Mississippi, putti blow bubbles (ephemera) as they take charge of stock. Beneath the stool of the bookkeeper, the rats of bankruptcy nibble away, and the claw feet of the painter's throne recall the cloven hoof of the demon speculation. Outside the tondo frame, reality proceeds as the "gold mine" literally goes up in smoke in the pipe of a Mississippi Indian — the fraud involved land that was alleged to bring with it a tobacco bonanza. In the cartoon below, a broker distributes worthless stock while his horse shits coin. The process is reversed in the pair where (top left) a

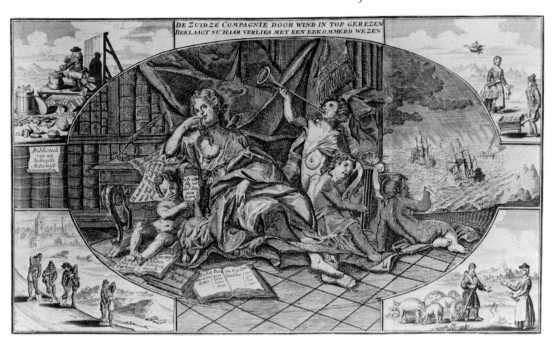

broker consumes money but shits stock bearing the names of the town chambers where it was sold, so that "buyers can enrich themselves with cabbage, roots, herring." Surrounded by books bearing debts, the ships of the company founder in heavy seas as investors are reduced (bottom left) to penury. Idle Hope Flown Away reappears top right, as below a fishwife offers to exchange a single fish for a swine from someone recognizable from stock Dutch anti-Semitic abuse as a *smous* (Sheeny) director.

The *carrozze delle trionfi* — the triumphal cars of van Heemskerck's procession — remained the durable symbols of capitalism destroying its captive believers. In a much simpler print it is John Law who drives the chair, and a pair of Gallic roosters have replaced van Heemskerck's Fraud and Rapine in its shafts. While an investor in this print stands in a "castle in the air" he loses his wig along with his fortune in the wind in which he had traded (fig. 166). The chariot bears the names of the destinations of investors — the poorhouse and the hospital — a theme that is echoed in the most elaborate of all the *windhandel* prints, that by Bernard Picart. At the rear, crowds are shown ushered into the sickhouse, the madhouse and the poorhouse, bearing the arms of Amsterdam — the center of the speculation. The crowd in the left foreground represents the rich and foolish among their seducers — including one holding a magic lantern

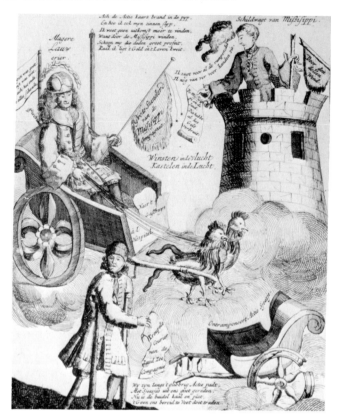

166. Engraving from
series, *The Great Mirror
of Folly*, 1720–21

—while on the right they pour out of the coffeehouse of the rue Quinquempoix
in Paris, where the speculation began to wheel out Fortuna's chariot. This has
turned into a kind of juggernaut, pulled by the symbolic figures of the
imbroglio—the Indies, West and East, the bank and the Mississippi Indian
among them—and trampling both the account book of the company and its
holder beneath wheels, the spokes of which are its chambers. The heraldic
bestiary of the Dutch lion, the French cockerel and the British lion are
reduced to ludicrous proportions on Fortuna's chariot, which is driven by Folly,
in the guise of (unchaste) Diana complete with whalebone hoop skirt—
"another of the foolish fashions of our time," explains the text. In the clouds
surveying the scene fame blows its derisory trumpet, while the devil blows
bubbles and naked Fortuna herself bestows her favors—the stock—on the
crowds below.

Despite, or possibly because of, its withering satire, Picart's print was a
tremendous success. It was done in an English version set in Change Alley,

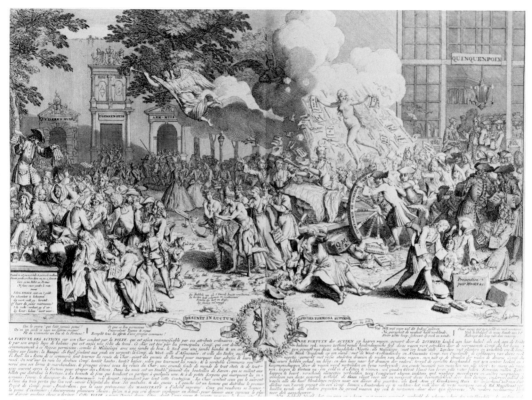

167. Bernard Picart, *Monument Consecrated to Posterity*, 1721. Author's collection

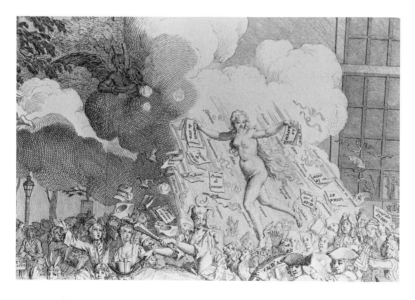

168. Detail from Picart, *Monument . . .*

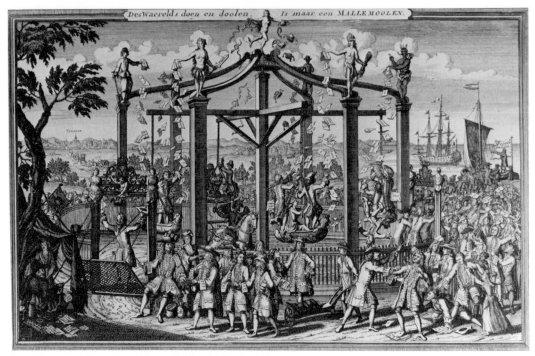

169. Engraving from *Great Mirror of Folly*. Author's collection

Jonathan's coffeehouse substituting for the rue Quinquempoix, and Bedlam for the Amsterdam madhouse. Other prints in the *Tafereel* were evidently prototypes for English satires and lampoons on the South Sea Bubble. Hogarth's *"Who'll Ride?"* may have owed something to the torture wheel in Callot's *Grandes Misères de la Guerre*, but there was a much closer source to hand in Picart's *Mallemoolen*, the Carousel of Fools, with the devil riding on the roundabout horse, as a ship departs for the never-never land of Pepperlandia.

"Des Waereld's Doen en Doolen/Is Maar een Mallemoolen" — The Ways of the World Are But a Fool's Merry-go-round — runs the inscription, a sentiment, by 1720, hoary with ancient authority. It was in reality nothing much more than Erasmus dragged to the stock exchange and made to survey the awful spectacle of men's greed and stupidity. Nothing would have surprised him less. But the unbroken tradition of moral comment on the madness of money — from Bruegel's war of strongboxes and moneybags to Picart's elaborate baroque spectacles of mass delusion — can offer two lessons, somewhat in opposition to each other. On the one hand, the frequency with which the adages were invoked in this capitalist iconography suggests how tenuous was the hold of humanist regulation on commercial and financial ebullience. But on the other hand, it also suggests an impressive degree of determination to contain economic behavior within the bounds of "safety" and propriety. As in so many other departments of Dutch culture, opposite impulses were harmoniously reconciled in practice. The incorrigible habits of material self-indulgence, and the spur of risky venture that were ingrained into the Dutch commercial economy themselves prompted all those warning clucks and solemn judgments from the appointed guardians of the old orthodoxy. It was their task to protect the Dutch from the consequences of their own economic success, just as it was the job of the people to make sure there was enough of a success in the first place to be protected from. This moral pulling and pushing may have made for inconsistency, but it did not much confuse the artisan, the merchant or the banker in their daily affairs. The peculiar coexistence of apparently opposite value systems was what they expected of their culture. It gave them room to maneuver between the sacred and profane as wants or conscience commanded, without risking a brutal choice between poverty or perdition. And they certainly did not need Calvinism to tell them that riches had better embarrass, but need not lose them salvation. That lesson had been drunk with Dutch capitalism's mother's milk, in the earliest accounting between northern trade and the Christian gospel. Nor did it take any lofty wisdom to see that the world was not torn asunder between abstinence and indulgence. Any fool could see that the *same people* embodied, at different times, in different places, the values appropriate to their impermanent role — be they commercially minded ministers like Sylvius, or pious captains of industry like de Geer (making his will); that the pilloried speculators were close kin to the tolerated stockbrokers; that the banker and the bankrupt were separated only by Fortuna's whim. This was the opposite of predestination. And it may have given comfort to those who, as they were about to cross the threshold of that cold chamber of Desolate Boedels, looked up and saw marble rats nibbling marble bills. In Holland, after all, solemnity was never very far away from farce, and perhaps to the irreverent those rats seemed reassuringly comic.

PART

THREE

LIVING AND
GROWING

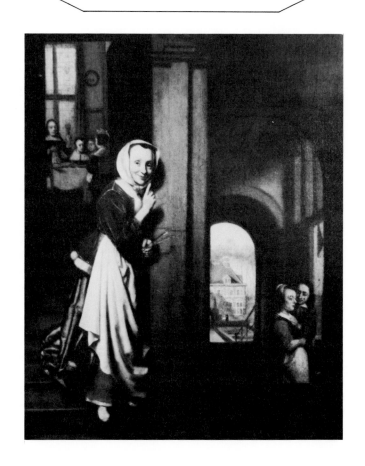

CHAPTER SIX

Housewives and Hussies:
Homeliness and Worldliness

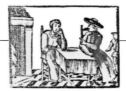

i CLEANLINESS AND GODLINESS

If lucre was filthy, insolvency had the saving grace of being clean. In Dutch, going broke was rendered as *schoon-op,* to be cleaned out. And what was clean, at least etymologically, was also beautiful. So that *zuiver schoon* would do as well for a scoured pot or a starlit night. *Natuurschoon* was and is a favorite term for a pleasing landscape.[1] No visitor to Holland, from Fynes Moryson to Henry James, failed to notice the pains that the Dutch took to keep their streets, their houses and themselves (though there was less unanimity about this) brilliantly clean. The spick-and-span towns shone from hours of tireless sweeping, scrubbing, scraping, burnishing, mopping, rubbing and washing. They made an embarrassing contrast to the porridge of filth and ordure that slopped over the cobbles of most other European cities in the seventeenth century. "The beauty and cleanliness of the streets are so extraordinary," ran an English account, "that Persons of all ranks do not scruple, but even seem to take pleasure in walking them." Women could walk, if they wished, in mules without fear of besmirching them "for the streets are paved with brick and are clean as any chamber floor."[2] Even the most grudging admirers were forced to concede that the Dutch set great store by the spotlessness of their habitat. Their cabin beds were so fearfully high, observed the author of *The Dutch Drawn to Life,* that one risked breaking one's neck getting out of bed at night to answer a call of nature. But should such a misfortune occur, "this comfort at least you will leave your friends, of having died in clean linen."[3] Owen Felltham, Cromwell's propagandist, and so no friend of the Dutch, thought their house fronts so polished that "every door seems studded with diamonds.

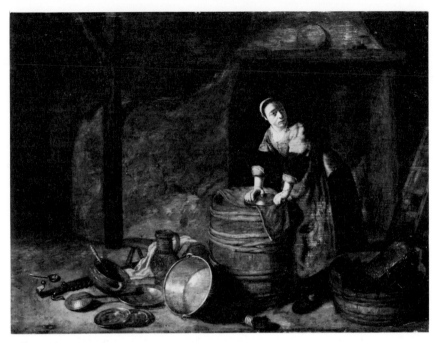

170. P. van den Bosch, *Serving Maid with Pots and Pans.* Courtesy of the Trustees, National Gallery, London

The nails and hinges keep a constant brightness as if there were not a quality incident to iron."[4]

Within the house, too, a cleaning regimen was followed with almost military precision. And its timetable was extraordinarily elaborate and exacting—a whole department of human activity specified in relentless detail. The popular household manual, *The Experienced and Knowledgeable Hollands Householder* (De Ervarene en Verstandige Hollandsche Huyshoudster), devoted an entire chapter to the holy rite with strict instructions on the several tasks to be tackled each week.[5] The steps in front of the house, the path leading to the house, if any, and the front hall were all to be washed every weekday early in the morning. On Wednesdays, the entire house was to be gone over. Monday and Tuesday afternoons were devoted to dusting and polishing reception rooms and bedrooms. Thursdays were scrubbing and scouring days, and Fridays were assigned to the uneviable job of cleaning the kitchen and cellar. Besides these standard chores, dishes had to be scrupulously washed after each meal, and the household laundry done each day. Such were the demands of this regimen that it was laid down that when sheets were folded it was imperative that the end used for the feet never be accidentally turned so that it could be used for the head. Pillows had to be plumped up each day and let stand for the specified hour to permit the feathers to breathe, to avoid lumpiness. Chairs and tables ought to be carefully cleaned, cobwebs removed in summer, the floor inspected inch by inch for telltale signs of insect eggs or droppings, and appropriate antibeetle or louse measures taken, with lye on the floors or a mixture of chalk and turpentine on the walls. Moths could be repelled with camphor, and flies and wasps lured away by a strategically placed honeypot. There was even an entire routine devoted to cleaning domestic animals. Cats were said to be too disgusting to be compatible with a decent household, and though dogs had their unsavory habits as well, these were offset by their importance in helping the security of the house.

This is all very banal in the twentieth century. But in the seventeenth it all seemed a bit much: the product of an obsession rather than a reasonable concern for salubrity. And it seemed especially bizarre when the compulsion overrode the normal conventions of social decorum. It was one thing (though tiresome) to be absolutely prohibited from spitting, either before or within the house, "as though it were an inexpiable crime."[6] But it was positively presumptuous to be obliged to doff one's shoes on entering and replace them with fastidiously provided slippers before being received.[7] Sir William Temple was amused by the story told of a magistrate visiting a house where the "strapping North Holland lass . . . marking his shoes were not very clean, took him by both arms, threw him upon her back, set him down at the bottom of the stairs, pulled off his shoes, put him on a pair of slippers that stood there, all this without saying a word; but when she had done, told him he might go up to see the mistress who was in her chamber."[8] This was related by a Dutchman in gentle self-deprecation, but it became part of a travelers' mythology in which the Dutch were all too ready to ignore the polite conventions of rank in the interests of a clean floor. And while travelers were astonished to behold the daily ritual of washing not merely the *stoep* but the pavement in front of the house, it also made them feel a little uneasy. Such devotion to wholesomeness did not seem quite normal. De Blainville thought the North Holland custom of washing cow stalls "several times a day" and tying their tails to a post "that they may not dirty them by their urine and dung" just one of the "extravagancies" of "excessive neatness" that he found bizarre and disturbing.[9]

If contemporaries ever stopped to ask themselves why the Dutch, in Thomas Nugent's words in *Grand Tour*, were such "perfect slaves to cleanliness," they sometimes arrived at the same functional conclusions as the modern historian. It was, said another writer, "the extreme moisture of the air . . . for without the help of those Customes, their country would not be habitable by such crowds of people but the air would corrupt upon every hot season and expose the inhabitants to . . . infectious diseases." And that same moisture "makes all metals apt to rust and wood to mould which forces them [the Dutch] by continual pains of rubbing and scouring to seek a prevention and cure."[10] There is something to be said for this simple common-sense explanation. The Dutch were certainly concerned to ward off both contagion and decay. But what is conspicuously missing from their own accounts is much sense that the dampness of their geography dictated their exercises in relentless ablution. In fact their climate was actually no more sodden than in many neighboring lands in Germany, Flanders, or even northern France and England, where the people seemed notoriously indifferent to the cleanliness cult.

Something more than material considerations, then, was at work in this mass devotion to purity. And the shrewder commentators on Dutch manners stumbled on it when, like Parival, they alluded to the *"idolâtre excessif"* of housewives to the rites of cleanliness.[11] For the laws that commanded the Dutch to conspicuous observation of their washing rituals were moral rather than material. And they were deeply associated in the collective mentality with the polarities of pride and shame, solidarity and alienness. In 1702 Samuel Paterson noticed that "the smallest filth in the streets would be decreed a reproach . . . to anyone that would suffer it to lie at his door."[12] The threshold of shame about tainting the neighborhood was very low indeed in Holland. In some towns it was the neighborhood authority, the *buurt,* that was formally responsible for keeping streets, and sometimes canals, clean. Because their jurisdiction was so small and their watch so omniscient, it was relatively easy to identify offenders against the communal canon. And there were legal sanctions to back up neighborhood odium. Any person injured or soiled by refuse and filth thrown from a window to the common street might claim double reparations before the magistrate. (On a side street, the warning cry of *"garde à l'eau"* was thought sufficient to protect householders from those claims.[13]) But in the eighteenth century, moralists accused those who polluted canals and avenues of, in effect, a kind of social treason: of being in league with the civic enemy, contagion that stood at the gates. To be filthy was to expose the population to the illicit entry of disease and the vagrant vermin that were said to be its carriers. To throw a dead cat in the canal, to harbor an illegal immigrant, or to neglect one's duty of washing the pavement were all tantamount to delinquency—as if one had opened the gates to an army of infected marauders.

Conversely, to be clean was to be patriotic, vigilant in the defense of one's homeland, hometown and home against invading polluters and polluted invaders. The Dutch could not help brandishing their brushes in the faces of grimier, heathen folk. In 1667 Samuel Pepys reported that the Dutch master of a captured prize that had been laid up in an English dockyard "come on board

Afkomſt ſeyt niet.

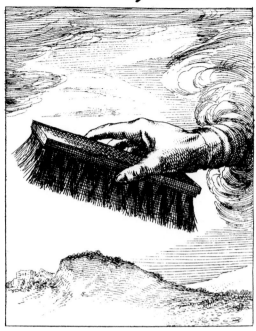

171. Claes Jansz. Visscher, from Roemer Visscher, *Sinnepoppen*. Houghton Library, Harvard University

and look about in every corner and find that she was not so clean as she used to be, though methought she was very clean."[14] Nor was it accidental that Admiral Maarten Tromp tacked a broom to the bowsprit of his flagship. Tromp was a fervent Calvinist, devoted to "sweeping the seas" of tyrants, papists, privateers and (in the English war) bullies. The adoption of cleansing utensils as the badges of patriotic bravura was a deliberate Calvinist conceit with which to taunt their enemies, and emphasize the purity of their new calling. The scrubbing brush in Roemer Visscher's *Sinnepoppen* bears the legend *afkomst seyt niet*—pedigree counts for nothing—and wipes history's slate clean of inherited allegiance. The brush stood as a heraldic device for the new commonwealth, cleansed of the impurities of the past. To have been slaves was to have been dirty. To be free is to be clean. The Dordrecht poet and schoolmaster Pieter van Godewijck put into the mouth of a magistrate's daughter a verse that creates a whole armory of household utensils mobilized in the defense of purity

My brush is my sword; my broom my weapon
Sleep I know not, nor any repose. . . .
No labor is too heavy; no care too great

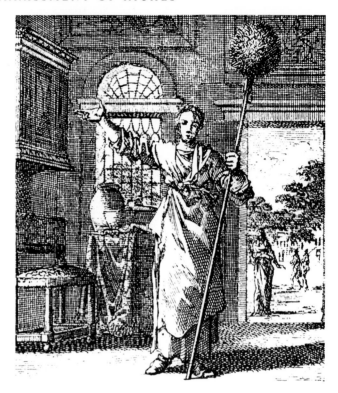

172. Jan Luiken, from *Het Leerzaam Huisraad* (Amsterdam, 1711). Harvard College Library

> *To make everything shine and spotlessly neat*
> *I scrape and scour; I polish and I scrub . . .*
> *And suffer no one to take away my tub*[15]

When Jan Luiken depicted the rag mop (*Het raagbol*) in his emblem book of the godly household, *Het Leerzaam Huisraad,* he borrowed the convention of the Hollands Maid from countless history prints and medallions, substituting the mop for her usual attributes of the pike surmounted with the hat of liberty.[16] In the background, surely not by chance, two soldiers or militiamen stride by the open door.

To be clean, militantly, was an affirmation of separateness. What was cleansed was the dirt of the world that had obscured the special meaning of Dutch history and the providential selection of its people. Dirt made things general and undifferentiated; cleansing exposed distinctness. Abraham Bloemaert's peculiar choice of the ritual purification theme for his drawing of 1616, in the context of the special meaning of the Netherlandish exodus, could only have alluded to their collective reconsecration as a new Chosen People.

To clean was to differentiate and to exclude. In her essays on *Purity and*

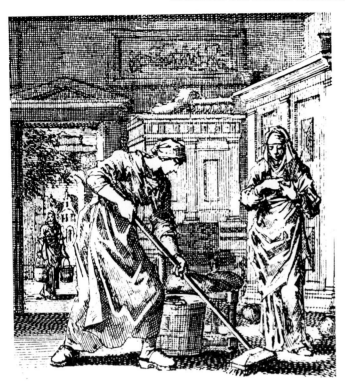

173. Jan Luiken, from *Het Leerzaam Huisraad*. Harvard College Library

Danger[17] the anthropologist Mary Douglas treats the Jewish dietary laws as a classifying system that reinforced the separateness of the Hebrews by establishing rigorous distinctions between clean and unclean orders of beasts. One criterion for impurity was anomaly. Creatures whose attributes were other than those designated for locomotion in their proper element (air, water, earth) at the Creation were deemed anomalous and therefore impure. So sea creatures, like shellfish, that had no fins or scales or that crawled instead of swam, became taboo.[18] In another essay in the same work, dirt is defined anthropologically as "matter out of place."[19] While the Dutch did not take their metaphorical identification with the Children of Israel so far as to introduce an enforceable code of prohibitions in food and dress, the more demanding Calvinists in particular did attempt to establish godly norms of social behavior that were laid down as fitting for the new Chosen People. Conformity to those norms guaranteed the perpetuation of the covenant; deviation from them, the downfall of the commonwealth. So that their flock was repeatedly commanded to guard against the pollution of their consecrated manners and customs, and to weed out impurities wherever they might be discovered. In his *Emblemata,* Johan de Brune warned against unchastity (of thought as well as deed) by recalling that the Children of Israel had been admonished always to uphold "cleanliness and godliness in their lives."[20] Along with Luiken's emblem of the *luiwagen,* the long-handled scrubbing brush, came the text from James 1:21 "Wherefore lay apart all filthiness and superfluity of naughtiness."[21]

What were the forces of soiling that the Dutch were required to subdue and expunge? While the Calvinists pretended to a monopoly of militant virtue, in fact those forces turned out to be the old adversaries of the Erasmian Christian warrior: the appetites of the flesh, the lure of wealth and the follies of worldly vanity. In one of the many misogynist satires of the later seventeenth century, *De Beurs der Vrouwen* (The Stock Exchange of Women), various vices and follies exemplified in female behavior are assembled in their respective niches in the colonnade of the Amsterdam bourse. Significantly, the only women that are presented as unambiguously virtuous are the cleaning ladies, wielding their brushes and pails beneath the legend *Opwacht,* or Lying-in-Wait. "These womenfolk, neat and clean from without, mop and scrub, wash and scour and polish and wipe all the walls, the beams, and the pillars that hold the building up. While their hearts and souls shine from their ardor for this work . . . for *the impure heart can never be freed from dirt.* "[22]

In the moralists' canon, the polluters came in two guises: internal and external. The external threat came from alien cultures, especially pagan, that might seduce the unwary into iniquity, or like the papist tyrants, might attempt to force their heathen idolatry down the throats of the pious. (In colloquial Dutch, the rag mop was also known as either the Pope's or the Turk's head.) But in some ways, it was the threats from within that were more insidious, precisely for seeming so innocuous. "Look also, to subtle things," ran Luiken's legend for the rag mop, "that seem but slight to lazy eyes, and mop them up with your own hand. The cobweb of the vile spider that hangs and sits in all the senses, where dirt and base matter gather."[23]

It would be foolish to suppose that each time a Dutch housewife picked up a mop or broom she was made to ponder on the eternal verities or the state of the nation's soul. But on the other hand it would be unhistorical to assume that domestic chores were a trivial business, unburdened with any moral overtones. I don't mean to argue on that emblems and aphorisms managed to yoke together two otherwise remote and disconnected realms of the sacred and the mundane. On the contrary, their moralization of the domestic reflected a culture in which those worlds were already felicitously confused. The intrusion of the moralist into the kitchen and the parlor was an old Netherlandish tradition, recorded in early sixteenth-century graphic art and still more venerable proverbial lore.[24] But it was the work of the more aggressively Calvinist moralists of the first century of Dutch nationhood to make the fortunes of their commonwealth contingent on their observance. They were

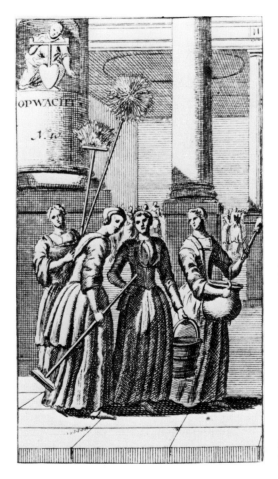

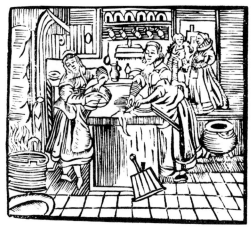

175. Woodcut from Jacob Cats, *Proteus ofte Minnebeelden* (Amsterdam, 1628). Houghton Library, Harvard University

174. From "Felicius Publius," *De Beurs der Vrouwen* (Amsterdam, 1690). Koninklijke Bibliotheek, The Hague

also more systematic in replacing a symbolic vocabulary that had been devised by and for a cultured elite, by one which in its use of commonplace references would be accessible to those with only the bare rudiments of literacy. Jacob Cats, the Pensionary of Holland and uncrowned king of pious doggerel, was the most successful of those who projected their homilies at the humble as well as the mighty. In the preface to *Proteus* he advertised the particular qualities of Dutch domestic emblem literature. "If someone should ask me what are Emblemata, then I should answer in the following way: they are mute pictures which speak, little mundane matters that are yet of great weight; humorous things that are not without wisdom; *things that men can point to with their fingers and grasp with their hands* [my emphasis].[25]

Accordingly, this tangible symbolism discarded a great deal of the classical and allegorical forms that had been inherited from Alciati and the Italian emblematists in favor of a more homely repertoire of images. To praise moderation and poke gentle fun at the spurious enthusiasm of unlikely

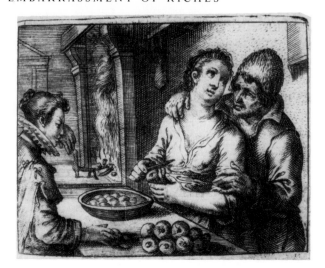

176. Emblem from Cats,
Proteus ofte Minnebeelden,
1628. Bodleian Library,
Oxford

converts, Cats used the emblem of sluttish maidservants won over to new ways, scouring the underneath of the cooking pans.[26] And where the symbolic botany of "high culture" emblems was made up of poetic items such as vines and roses, Cats's warning against the perils of décolletage (*Nuda Movet Lacrimas*) turned instead to the onion, the peeling of which produces tears.[27] In both versions of the print the admonishing knife pointed up the moral. It was this unrefined literalness, the domestication of the senses, which lent Dutch emblem imagery its popular appeal. Where the physical labor of the home could be used to suggest moral strenuousness it was graphically exploited. Roemer Visscher used the image of the butter churn to commend hard work as the only route to success: *"In de rommelingh is de vet"* (only from commotion comes the fat). Adriaen van de Venne's use of the same image for the frontispiece of Cats's *Christelijke Self-Strijt* (Christian Self-struggle) was even more ingenious in that it vividly communicated the tireless perseverance and strength needed to master fleshly self-indulgence. Scripture and kitchen were brought abruptly together since the *exemplum* of such determination was Joseph's rejection of the sexual overtures of Potiphar's wife. Typically, Cats milked the dairy conceit for all it was worth. The cream, he explained, was the spirit, while the whey stood for fleshly pleasure. The two necessarily lay side by side: "The spirit is not alone; the flesh is not unto itself." Both lay side by side within the soul.[28]

These images were self-consciously homely (the Cats emblem is specifically set in a modest kitchen parlor), because the home was of supreme importance in determining the moral fate, both of individuals and of Dutch society as a whole. While the ethos of other seventeenth-century states was

In de rommelingh ist vet.

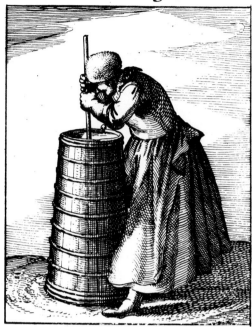

Sinne-Beeldt Openende de heymenisse
ende rechten aert des

CHRISTELICKEN SELF-STRYTS.

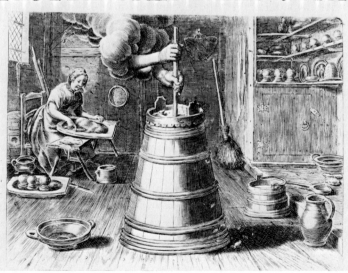

built around the aura of a dynasty, or the historic privileges of a city commune, in the Netherlands it was the family household that was "the fountain and source" of authority, as Dr. Johan van Beverwijck put it.[29] In other words, the home was the irreducible primary cell on which, ultimately, the whole fabric of the commonwealth was grounded. "The first community," wrote van Beverwijck, citing Cicero, "is that of marriage itself; thereafter in a family household with children, in which all things are common. That is the first principle of a town and thus the seed of a common state."[30] And there was an economic as well as a political analogy, for the art of household management was commonly reckoned a basic training for broader economic skills. "This art," wrote the author of the popular manual *The Experienced and Knowledgeable Hollands Householder*, "was the very foundation of our prosperity and is still today the basis on which every household must be built."[31] Domicile conferred the attributes of citizenship: membership in a religious congregation, in a guild, eligibility for the *schutter* civic militia and for the giving and receipt of charity. To possess *poorterschap*, the certification of residence, was, far more than a vote, the indispensable insignia of an active role in the life of a Dutch urban community.

Home, then, was both a microcosm, and a permitting condition, of the properly governed commonwealth. Dutch art was unique in the seventeenth century in presenting interior views of public buildings, both ecclesiastical and secular, which abolished the distance between governors and governed, shepherds and flock. In Pieter de Hooch's interiors of the Amsterdam town hall, families promenade in the council chambers as though they owned them, which in a sense they did. In at least an informal sense, authority in the Republic can be thought of as infinitely descending or devolved. Holland and Zeeland were made up (with the exception of the noble delegation) of sovereign towns, which in their turn were aggregates of neighborhoods. The *buurten* or *wijken*, with their elected officers, tax feasts and ceremonies, were themselves composed of linked streets of homes.[32] And in a more formal sense, the authority of the town rested on its obligation to protect its households and to provide those conditions in which they might best increase and prosper.

Demographically, too, the family household was exceptionally well defined in the Netherlands. As far as figures permit reconstruction, it seems that Dutch homes were, on average, smaller, more tightly organized and more independent of extended family intervention than elsewhere in seventeenth-century Europe.[33] While the rule of Mean Household Size for the period, according to the Cambridge Group for the History of Population, was 4.75; in Gouda, for example in 1622 it was 4.3 and in 1674, 3.6.[34] The average number of children in any such household would have been two, and the percentage of homes with living-in relatives was only around five to six percent. The figures were compressed further by the large number of seventeenth-century households where the head was either a widow, widower, or an unmarried man or woman—something like forty percent in the Noorderkwartier.

179. Pieter de Hooch, *Interior of the Burgomasters' Chamber, Amsterdam Town Hall*, 1664–46. Thyssen-Bornemisza Collection, Lugano, Switzerland

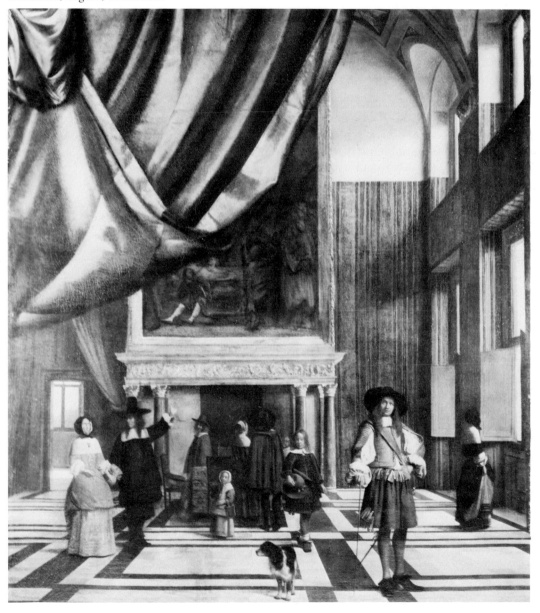

The home, then, was social and political bedrock, and was repeatedly compared in moralizing literature to a little realm in which the father as lord might expect obedience *conditional* on his lawful governance and right conduct. Its hierarchy and division of labor was established on a reciprocity of duties and obligations that had as their end a prospering Christian peace and the procreation of more virtuous households. In this sense it seems mistaken to speak of the bourgeois household as the cradle of individualism. For it was never instituted as an extension of the patriarchal will or interest, but as a *gemeenschap,* a little society or community, with its own collective personality — or as Cats would have said, soul. If it provided the basic molecular structure from which the body politic was built, there were nonetheless indispensably interrelated atoms within each and every molecule.

When properly established and run, the family household was the saving grace of Dutch culture that otherwise would have been indelibly soiled by materialism. It was the crucible through which rude matter and beastly appetite could be transubstantiated into redeeming wholesomeness. When food, lust, sloth, indolence and vain luxury were subdued by the domestic virtues — sobriety, frugality, piety, humility, aptitude and loyalty — they were deprived of their dirt, which is to say, their capacity for inflicting harm or jeopardizing the soul. Home was that morally purified and carefully patrolled terrain where license was governed by prudence, and the wayward habits of animals, children and footloose unmarried women were subdued into a state of harmony and grace. "Blot out all mine iniquities. Create in me a clean

180. Emblem from Jan Luiken, *Het Leerzaam Huisraad.* Houghton Library, Harvard University

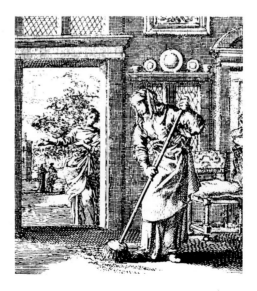

heart," runs the text from Psalm 51 that accompanies Luiken's washtub. But to ensure the pristine sanctity of the home meant perpetual vigilance. "Home" existed in the Dutch mentality in a kind of dialectical polarity with "world," and in particular the street, which brought the mire of the world, literally, to its doorstep. The obligation to wash the pavement in front of the house, then, was not just a legal civic duty, that is to say, a public obligation, it was also a way to protect the threshold of the inner sanctum. The poem supplied for Luiken's scrubbing brush speaks of "the tread of dirty feet that the scrubber must purify." But into the open house of the heart, it goes on, may be brought all

> *The mud, filth and stains*
> *From untrodden ruts and paths*
> *From East and West; here and there*
> *The whole day long, to and fro*
> *From market, streets and alleys*
> *Not just from the world's domain*
> *But also from the hellish realm.*[35]

The struggle between worldliness and homeliness was but another variation on the classic Dutch counterpoint between materialism and morality. To earn their living the Dutch were obliged to travel, whether from village to market town or from Amsterdam to Malacca. Indeed, during the seventeenth century they were the world's greatest travelers, extending the known surface of the globe from the Arctic Sea to the antipodean isles of Tasmania and Nieuw Zeeland. Yet their efforts at empire building were hampered by their notorious reluctance to become settlers. While colonists from other nations showed some eagerness to escape from poverty or persecution or both for virtuous utopias or imagined eldorados overseas, the Dutch were in the opposite position. Their colonial outposts in the East Indies filled up with what the governors of the company lamented were the refuse of society.[36] Only for the most disadvantaged groups in Dutch society (and there were perhaps more of these than is sometimes acknowledged) was there any incentive to leave home. Home was where peace, virtue and prosperity were ideally to be found. It is not surprising, then, to find that the figure of Dame World standing on the globe is transformed in van Beverwijck's *Wtnementheit des Vrouwelijke Geslachts* (On the Excellence of the Female Sex)—into an emblem of domestic bliss. By his lights, the ideal wife could be compared to the tortoise in that she conquered the home/world tension through the solution of the mobile home. In the background of the print, Adam delves outside while Eve spins within. Cats also adopted the tortoise as an emblem of *zedigheid*, morality, for his *Coat of Arms for the Maiden,* arguing that if the

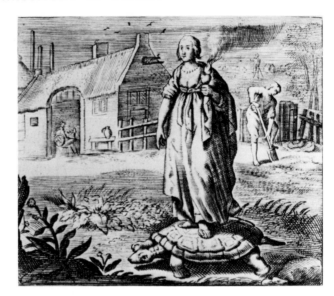

181. Anon., from Johan van Beverwijck, *Van de Wtnementheyt van de Vrouwelycken Geslachts* (Dordrecht, 1643). Houghton Library, Harvard University

T'huys beſt.

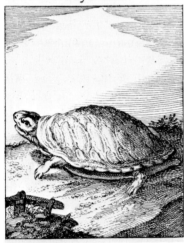

182. Emblem from Roemer Visscher, *Sinnepoppen*. Houghton Library, Harvard University

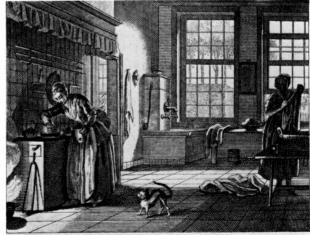

Z 3   Z z.
Zout geeft ſmaak aan alle ſpys: *Zeep* waſcht alles **rein**.
Kind, denk dat Verſtand en Deugd ook zo noodig **zyn**.

183. From J.H. Swildens, *Vaderlandsch AB Boek* (Amsterdam, 1781). Houghton Library, Harvard University

virtuous wife were obliged to leave home, she should at least conduct herself as if it were always with her. In Roemer Visscher's emblem, the axiom has been still further compressed to [East, West] *T'Huys Best*.[37]

The well-kept home was the place where the soiling world subjected to tireless exercises in moral as well as physical ablution. Once across its threshold the most hard-boiled, street-wise trader could expect to discover the moral equivalent of slippers: the comfort of untainted virtue. That threshold, moreover, need not be literal. Very many, if not most, businesses and trades were still carried on within the physical precincts of the house, but the division between living and working space in middle-class households was nonetheless clearly demarcated and jealously guarded.[38] The transformation from work-at-home to the virtual cult of housework that was commended and detailed in many manuals was pleasing not just to Calvinists, obsessed as they were with bleaching out the merest specks ingrained in human nature. It would also have satisfied the older, Erasmian humanist tradition in which the material world must needs be accepted, the better to test the resolution of Christian principle. In an eighteenth-century ABC, salt and soap coexist, not just as both belonging to the letter *Z* (*zout en zeep*), but as twin aspects of the human condition. Salt is made to stand for worldly understanding, without which experience would be bland and unedifying, soap for virtue that washes all clean (when understanding has led the soul down dangerous paths?).[39]

Dutch art was the first to celebrate this ideal ordering of the family home, as well as to satirize its disruption. Because he was a Catholic (as well as a tavern keeper) it may have been easier for Jan Steen than for other artists to perform both functions simultaneously. While the real nature of his intentions remains notoriously elusive (and has produced the kind of solemn scholarship — including my own — that he would have found irresistibly comic), Steen produced genre scene after genre scene of domestic uproar.[40] One of the best known is *The Disorderly Household*. The picture is, in effect, a catalogue of domestic vices, the virtuous household turned upside down, with every conceivable transgression set down with uninhibited gusto. At its center, those who should have the home in safekeeping have abandoned it to sensual self-indulgence. The presumptive mother sleeps before a plate of oysters, the drug of Eros, while the father sets his red-hosed calf on the lap of a *lichtmis*, whose light virtue is announced by the feather in her hair, her beauty patches and inviting décolletage. As in so many other genre paintings of this kind, the action (or inaction) functions as an exemplary charade, acting out the anthology of proverbs and epigrams to which the Dutch were so devoted. Johan de Brune's *Emblemata* had warned that *"een hoeren schoot is duyvel's boot"* (the lap of a whore is the devil's barque),[41] and the diabolical smirk, as much as his five out-turned fingers — denoting the five senses — announce the triumph of worldly pleasure over domestic purity. Accordingly, those who should be protected from the world have become its creatures. One child gleefully holds up a coin; another steals a purse. An ape acts (in the manner of the proverb) as "the thief of time" while the hat "thrown before the door" embodies the epigram of fecklessness. Hanging over this scene of delinquent chaos, though, are the symbols of punishment—the leper's rattle, the cripple's crutch and the scourging birch. In carefully careless adjacency in the foreground are arranged the cards (including the ace of hearts), symbols of dissipation and pagan Fortuna, and the slate on which is chalked the score, or *rekening*.

As in so many of these scenes, Steen included a likeness of himself, and given his combination of occupations, it is just conceivable that his own home might have been the scene of the sort of unbuttoned havoc painted in the festive pieces like the *Egg Dance; The King Drinks* (Twelfth Night) or the St. Nicholas Feast paintings in Amsterdam. Whatever Steen was up to, however, it was surely not picaresque autobiography. (He was also, it should be recalled, the painter of histories from the Bible, including both a *Moses Striking the Rock* and a *Belshazzar's Feast*.) For the cultural historian, though, it makes no

184. Jan Steen, *The Disorderly Household.* Apsley House, London

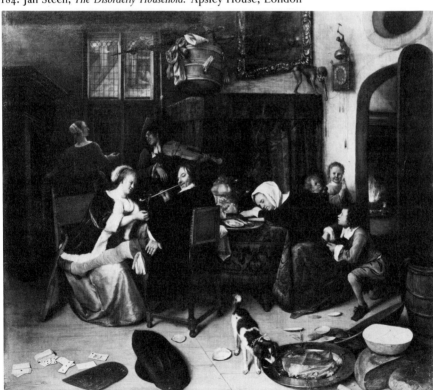

difference whether he was moralist or merrymaker, or whether the second quality was an intrinsic element of the first. The comic shock of his disorderly households lay in their erasing the frontier between houses of license and homes of virtue. The dirt of the world has invaded the sanctity of the home as its guardians carouse or give themselves over to drunken sleep. With vigilance suspended, vice is able to put "matter out of place" (as Lord Palmerston put it) and substitute license for discipline, dirt for cleanliness. One would be tempted to call the spectacle an Erasmian nightmare, were it not that Erasmus himself was the virtuoso of preaching morality through presenting the *self-evident* triumph of folly.

Just as Steen was capable of turning out unambiguously pious history paintings, so Pieter de Hooch was both the painter of merry companies featuring greater or lesser transgressions, and of the idealized apple-pie domestic interior. Some, like the well-to-do group in *Family Making Music* in the Cleveland Museum, used the convention of a musical gathering to symbolize the harmony of the household. The opulence of their dress and the splendor of the furnishings are carefully offset by the image of modest virtue in the background, with the child bringing a basket of fruit and a modestly attired nurse holding the baby. Less formally posed genre scenes conformed more easily to the conventions of domestic peace and cleanliness. The Rijksmuseum's *Interior with Two Women at a Linen Chest* anticipated one of Luiken's panegyrics to clean linen and right living and perfectly conveyed the neutralizing power that kempt housekeeping exerted over dangerous affluence. At the precise frontier between home and the world, Mercury, the guardian deity of commerce, stands holding a money bag on the frame of the doorway. In a slightly more humble setting, the Luton Hoo interior combines all the virtues, just as Steen's scenes collects the vices. Sunlight streams into an impeccable but modest room, its hearth decorated with Delft tiles and a Bible scene hanging above an idealized image of a mother nursing her child. In the foreground a maid is busy sweeping a floor which already appears to be spanking clean. The overwhelming feeling is that of domestic consecration: godliness in a sun-bathed face and a pure, bare, plank floor. Above the head of the nursing mother, the window frame casts the shadow of the cross. And directly above that, hangs the ultimate emblem of a world purified: the Christ crucified.

More often than fathers, it is mothers who figure in Dutch paintings and prints as the protectors of the pure household. Indeed, Cats and the manual writers insisted that this was a mother's vocation. It was they who patrolled that dangerous frontier between the dirt of the street and the cleanliness of the home, who set maids scrubbing or who plunged themselves into the daily ritual of banishing compromising grime from the premises. But their grooming extended to the members of the family who were most likely (in either their

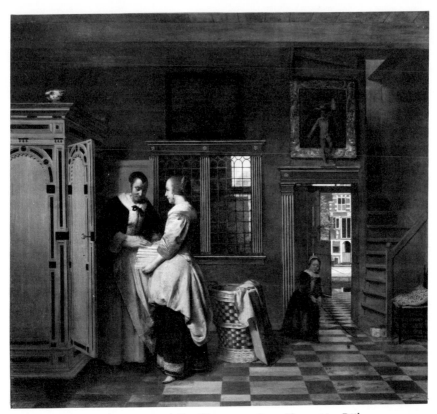

185. Pieter de Hooch, *Interior with Two Women at a Linen Chest*, 1663. Rijksmuseum, Amsterdam

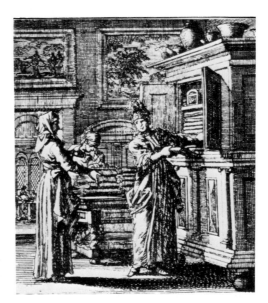

186. Jan Luiken, emblem from *Het Leerzaam Huisraad*. Houghton Library, Harvard University

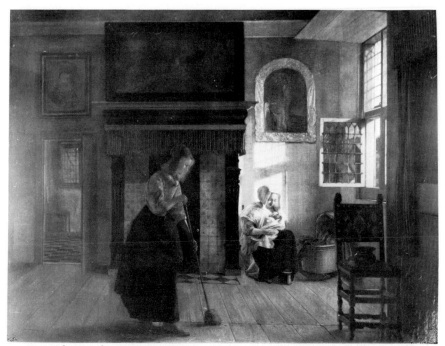

187. Pieter de Hooch, *Mother and Child by a Window with a Woman Sweeping*. The Wernher Collection, Luton Hoo, Bedfordshire

innocence or their incorrigible fecklessness, depending on which kind of Dutch moralist you were), to bring dirt along with them: the children.

Some of the most affecting family scenes in Dutch genre painting are of children submitting to their mother's inspection of their heads for nits and lice. Gerard ter Borch painted two: one as much an image of domestic virtue as a lace worker or a distaff spinner, the second in the much more unusual setting of an impoverished knife grinder's yard. This is all the more extraordinary for being anything but the idealized image of the kempt bourgeois household. It is, in fact, one of the few authentic pictures of the kinds of hovels in which many of the poorest artisans and semiskilled laborers lived in Dutch towns. Yet, for all the dereliction and squalor, it is also unmistakably an image of domestic virtue. It is virtue offered within the same canvas, at work and at home, the knife grinding itself invoking the universal image of hard unremitting toil, and in the foreground the mother at the threshold of the dwelling, occupied with the *moedertaak,* her labor of love. *Purgo et Ornat* ("It Cleans and It Beautifies"), runs the legend with Visscher's comb, the latter being conditional on the former.[42] In de Hooch's scene in the Rijksmuseum, none of the misery so truthfully set out in ter Borch's picture threatens the

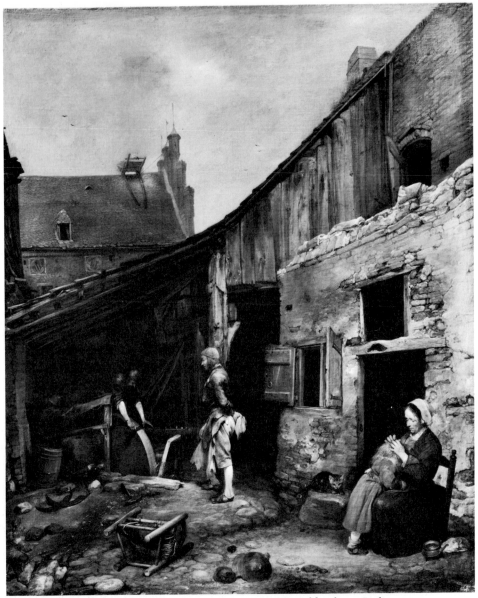

188. Gerard ter Borch, *The Stone Grinder's Family*, 1653–55. Gemäldegalerie, Berlin

scene of unblemished domestic tranquillity. Under the kind of safe housekeeping depicted here, the home was indeed Christian arcadia: the bed spotless, unrumpled and without stain or suspicion, the copper bed-warming pan polished to a state of brilliance, the Delft tiles modest and pure. And, for once, the scene included an exemplary puss who would no more soil the pristine purity of the floor than it would turn into a devil's companion.

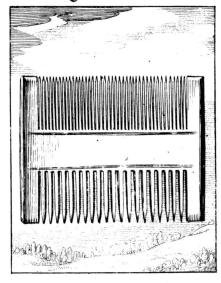

Purgat et ornat.

189. Emblem from Roemer Visscher,
Sinnepoppen. Houghton Library,
Harvard University

190. Pieter de Hooch, *The Mother's
Task,* 1658–60. Rijksmuseum,
Amsterdam

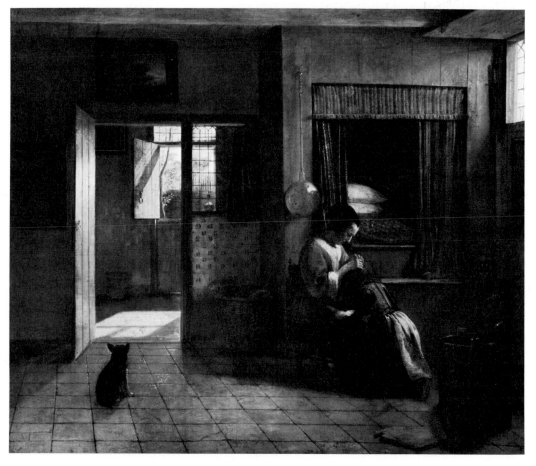

ii   THE HEROIC HOUSEWIFE

For wife, I'd wish a middling mate
Not too high born nor low estate
A wife not proud of her high birth
Yet from a line of solid worth
A wife not rich or mighty grand
But like to me in goods and land
A wife not proud nor haughty high
But modest yet in her own eye
A wife that by all virtue goes
Yet of her gifts but little knows . . .
No slut at home no doll outdoors
A wife that puts her best step forth
In virtue fair. . . .
A wife that honors neighbors close
But seldom out of doors doth go
A wife, a still and peaceful wife
A foe to all that's woe and strife
A wife that never breaks the peace
And ne'er too loud or shrill of speech,
A wife who'd rather suffer pain
Than cry or utter a vile name
A wife that never grunts with food
Or goes into a pouting mood.[43]

Such was Jacob Cats's recipe for domestic bliss, set out in *Houwelick*, his long verse panegyric to the married state. Discovering such a paragon was, he conceded, a tall order, but well worth the trouble of the search. He himself had once been smitten with ardor on seeing such a pearl of virtue in church. His ardor cooled dramatically, however, on discovering that her line was of less than "solid worth," her father, in fact having been a bankrupt. A bona fide bride that stood up to close examination, though, was indeed a treasure beyond price. For the *Christelyke Huyswijf* would be, *inter alia*:

> *a sweet plant; an upright fig tree;*
> *a bright lamp; a golden chandelier (that all the house*
> *doth shine)*

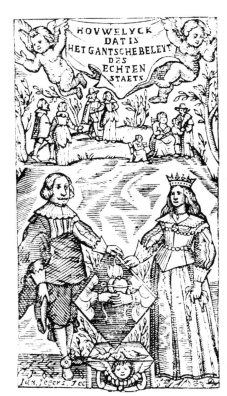

191. Anon. woodcut. Title page of Jacob
Cats, *Houwelijck* (Amsterdam, 1655).
Houghton Library, Harvard University

> *but most upon th'attached pair*
> *a vineyard (for cooling lovers' heat)*
> *the vine itself (full of fruit and gladness)*
> *a beauteous jewel that glistens in the night*
> *a rich stone yet wondrous soft;*
> *a richly laden ship; a golden crown; David's harp; a*
> *fragrant garden . . .* [44]

And a good deal besides.

The list of superlative metaphors runs on until it exhausts the repertoire of
Renaissance clichés. No doubt "Father Cats's" advice to aspiring brides was
meant kindly as an ideal on which they might model their conduct. But how
painful might it have been to suppose one fell short of the specified desiderata
of "the spirit of Sarah, the virtue of Ruth and the humility of Abigail."[45] Such
was the heavy burden of expectations thrust upon Dutch women by male
stereotypes of the virtuous wife. Those assumptions were not of course
peculiar to the Netherlands, but the importance of the family home was so

paramount there that they worked within Dutch culture with particular force and intensity. Customary male markers of patriarchal dynasticism, the residue of a feudal warrior ethos or the accumulation of a territorial estate all being less important in the Republic, the aura and status of a family household assumed correspondingly more significance. And within that household, it was the wife that was held responsible for the contentment or disarray of the domestic regime. Just as the home itself was supposed to cleanse the external world of its impurities before being admitted across its threshold, so the wife within was its chief cleansing agent and moral, as well as mundane, laundress. Indeed, male anxieties or ambiguities about the propriety of their worldly affairs intensified their assumption that it was their work to make the home a safe place for Christian virtue. They demanded that their wives be therapists for the pain of commerce yet not be ignorant of its practicalities. They demanded, in fact, the impossible.

When women of the flesh-and-blood kind (rather than Cats's poetically imagined paragons) failed to meet these exacting standards, the disappointment was often put down to the difficult nature of the raw material. For marriage and housewifery were recommended by the moralists with such urgency as the only fit end for women because, left to herself, the female was a dangerously unsound vessel. Unconfined by marriage and conjugal duties, woman was thought to be a bundle of animal instincts: inconsistent, deceitful, easily seduced into vanity, prone to sensual self-indulgence and quick to unreasonable rage: in short a bad lot, and altogether unsuitable for the guardianship of the family.

Trouble could be expected whenever the boundaries between world and home, street and hearth, were not strictly observed. Women, thought Dr. van Beverwijck, were anatomically designed for "inner" or domestic things, their flesh being softer and muscles weaker than that of men. Males, on the other hand, were made of tougher sinew and bone, the better to withstand extremes of heat and cold, and the knocks and shocks of trade and travel.[46] In *Vrouwe*, Cats prescribed this separation of realms without mincing words:

> *The husband must be on the street to practise his trade*
> *The wife must stay at home to be in the kitchen*
> *The diligent practice of street wisdom may in the man be praised*
> *But with the delicate wife, there should be quiet and steady ways*
> *So you, industrious husband, go to earn your living*
> *While you, O young wife, attend to your household.*[47]

Those that scorned this division of spheres were stigmatized as *uithuizige vrouwen*, women of the world—if not of the street. And they were likely to exhibit all the hallmarks of the unmediated female. a lust for shopping, a relish for malicious gossip, an uncontrollable temper, unseemly cravings for rich, sweet food and strong drink (or even tobacco) and perhaps even more unmentionable weaknesses of the flesh. So that alongside the stereotype of the demure housewife, prudent and chaste, there existed its polar opposite, the equally unreal spectacle of the vicious virago—woman omnivorous and unconfined. If genre paintings of women at the distaff—the perennial emblem of domestic virtue—exemplified the serenity of the one type, the visceral tradition of Bruegel's *Dulle Griet,* where an army of harpies wielding the weapons of the kitchen "plunders at the mouth of hell"[48] continued, a century later, to disturb the family peace. Jan Miense Molenaer (married to the painter Judith Leyster) produced a series of studies of the five senses drawn from domestic life which, though comically raucous, were also a little too rough to be simply jolly. In *The Sense of Touch,* for example, a husband surrendering the breeches of his authority is being thrashed by a wife wielding a clog with deadly force.

These opposite stereotypes, joined at the hip, showed remarkable staying power in Dutch culture, even though social reality—a much subtler phenome-

192. Jan Miense Molenaer, *The Sense of Touch,* 1637. Mauritshuis, The Hague

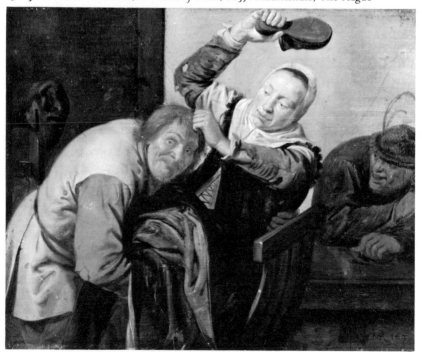

non—kept breaking through. Foreign visitors were themselves affected by it, since they often commented on the peculiar adjacency of virtue and vice in the world of Dutch womenfolk. John Ray paid lip service to their reputation for housewifely sobriety but noticed as well that "the common sort of women [not to say all] seem more fond of and delighted with lasciviousness and obscene talk than either the English or the French." He supposed, however (like Cats), that the rude were translated into the righteous with their marriage vows, for "the women are said not much to regard chastity while unmarried, but once married none more chaste and true to their husbands."[49] Contrary to what one might have expected from reading the moralists, the frontier between the proper and the improper could be very elusive. It was not clear to Thomas Nugent which were the more immoral: the whores who had been placed in the Amsterdam Spinhuis for redemption, or their custodians, who for "a trifle of money" permitted access—through a barred partition—"on which occasion it is customary for them to entertain their visitors with such abominable discourses and indecent actions as are shocking to any men of sense or morality."[50] Their exposure was intended by the humanist fathers, of course, to be an exercise in salutary shame. What was obvious by the time of Nugent's visit in 1737 was that it had become instead a matter of prurient pleasure in which their ostensible guardians shamefully colluded.

More disconcerting was the apparent freedom that apparently respectable Dutch women enjoyed in comparison with their contemporaries elsewhere. Public kissing, candid speech, unaccompanied promenades, all struck foreigners, and especially the French, as shockingly improper, even though they were repeatedly assured of the impregnable chastity of the married woman. John Ray was disconcerted to find that "the women even of the better sort do upon little acquaintance easily submit saluting with a kiss: and it is familiarly used among themselves either in frolics or upon departures and returns though never so short."[51] Coste d'Arnobat believed that such things were only possible because the Dutch woman was wholly dead to the passions, refraining from adding (as did many others) that the dampness of the climate and the coldness of their blood was to blame.[52] Aglionby observed a very free form of night courting in the Noorderkwartier known as *kweesten*,[53] where "a young man shall sit a whole night by his mistress and never hold a discourse in any ways offensive to her honor."[54] This custom was not the new freedom but an old tradition of communal social scrutiny and trial that persisted in the remoter parts of north Holland, Friesland and especially on the islands of the Texel, Vlieland and Ameland. And though "bundling," its equivalent in Wales and parts of England, was equally known to a seventeenth-century observer of manners, it still seemed a gratuitously dangerous test of virtue. Outside the house, women assumed an informality that seemed much too audacious for their own good. At the end of the sixteenth century, Fynes Moryson had been aghast at Frisian women embracing and defecating in public, assuming regular control over the family budget, skating at night until the city gates were locked, and most astonishing of all, feasting through the night in taverns ten or twenty miles from home.

> This they do without any suspicion of unchastity, the hostesses being careful to lodge and oversee the women. In like sort, mothers of good fame permit their daughters at home after they themselves go to bed, to sit up with young men all or most part of the night, banqueting and talking, yea with leave and without leave to walk abroad with young men in the streets by night. And this they do out of a customed liberty without prejudice to their fame whereas the Italian women, strictly kept, think it folly to omit every opportunity they can get to do ill.[55]

It was all very baffling to jealous Catholics and repressive Puritans alike. Dutch moralists (exclusively male) seemed insistent that their common-wealth stood or fell by the untarnished virtue of their women. And yet the way they thought to achieve it seemed by allowing them greater, rather than fewer, liberties than elsewhere. Only the earliest apostles of the eighteenth-century cult of unaffected sensibility found such conduct both intelligible and exemplary. For they saw the freedom and informality of Dutch women as innocent candor rather than reckless license. Their very artlessness suggested a fortuitously blessed escape from the heavy artifice and affectation that women were still bred to in polite society. Joseph Shaw, traveling in the country in 1709, was enchanted with what he saw. "I have never observed," he wrote, "so much public modesty . . . conducted with so great wisdom as among their women who have the penetration of angels." They seemed endowed with "a wondrous stock of good sense without affectation of wit; with much good nature and yet an extraordinary Chastity to be overcome by nothing but the most vigorous, violent impetuous and irresistible sallies of nature."[56] This was bound to impress a man coming from a culture where wit was dangerously synonymous with libertinism, Nor, unlike the French commentators, did Shaw suppose that this cheerful embrace of virtue was the logical consequence of a lack of charm. (Diderot was later to remark that the rest of a Dutch woman removed the incentive to discover whether the reputation of their prodigious bosoms was true or false.[57]) Shaw, on the other hand, claimed that "nowhere [were there] to be seen such beautiful faces yet they are entirely free from vanity." They might be plain in habit and boast neither "patch nor paint" but they aimed straight for the heart "and know no other way to recommend them-selves to inspire and kindle passion or charm their lovers but by the admirable qualities of piety, good nature, innocence, truth and integrity." This was in strong contrast to his glimpse of the other, more heavily applied face of Dutch womanhood in the Spinhuis. There he saw more than a hundred fallen souls "clothed in the gay habiliaments of love, adorned with plumes of feathers on their heads, patched and painted and just as they used to charm and coax the fond, admiring and deluded gulls who know not the fatal Arts of women."[58]

Joseph Shaw was so struck by "the plain downright honesty and truth" of Dutch women that he supposed it to be one of the chief reasons for the "great power and happiness" of the Republic. They were handsome without being vain, educated without being pedantic, even practiced in matters of money without being avaricious or prodigal. When he approached a venerable matron of 104 in the Oudevrouwenhuis and offered her a guilder piece, she declined it, saying "I knew how to spend it better than she did, for her part she knew not what to do with it."[59] All this was too good to be true. (And indeed it was, of course.) But when Shaw wondered why Dutch women seemed both more moral and happier than those in England, he attributed that to their "being better provided for by the laws of their country than in other nations [so that they] are not forced to trust to their wits, nor put on those poor pitiful shifts to jilt mankind and bubble their husbands for money."[60]

And if it is true that Dutch women were in the vanguard of a new world of "affect" that heralded the rise of the "companionate family,"[61] that institutional liberality certainly seems to have helped them along the way. There was no reforming self-consciousness about this at all. Some of the legal provisions which, for example, enabled women to inherit and bequeath property in their own right had survived from the Middle Ages.[62] But the humanist and Protestant ethos, often taken to have imposed grimly unyielding patriarchalism, turns out, in the Netherlands, as well as in Germany and Switzerland, to have been responsible for their more generous treatment.[63] There *was* a good deal of formal subjugation—women were excluded from all political offices—but within these limits they managed nonetheless to assert themselves, both individually and collectively, in public life. In particular they played an important role in charitable institutions as regents of orphanages, hospitals, old age homes and houses of correction. In these capacities they formed networks of family alliances and offices analogous to, but not necessarily identical with, the regent coalitions of their husbands.

If they were formally subject to their husband's legal authority, with their marriage portion merged into the common property, they generally retained the right to its reversion in particular circumstances. On a husband's death, for example, it was common for the widow to recover her full portion together with personal possessions (such as clothes) acquired in the marriage and the gifts that had come from the husband's side at the match. In 1655, when Christina Gillon married the Amsterdam regent Cornelis Backer, their marriage settlement carefully specified the 35,286 guilders she had brought to the match (out of a total estimated 77,030 guilders joint estate), a fortune that included jewels, cash, bills and annuities. The assumption was that were she to be predeceased by her husband, that amount would immediately revert.[64] Usually, property that was acquired during the course of the marriage, such as real estate, furniture and the like, was deemed joint. The law ensured that where a marriage was without child heirs, the widow had right to all her own property plus half of the common estate. Some couples, at the insistence of the bride — and her family — went further in reinforcing her claims. When Sara Hinlopen, the widow of Albert Geelvinck, married Jacob Bicker in 1695, she came to the match already laden with property and obligations, to her children by her first marriage as well as herself. Their agreement stipulated that no property was to be held in common, but that in event of a separation or death without heirs, property would revert to the respective blood line. Profits and losses on their respective properties were to be divided half and half, but their titles remained separate. Jacob Bicker must have wanted the match very badly, for he agreed to even more farsighted contingencies for the bride. Should he predecease her without joint heirs, a specific amount of property plus twelve thousand guilders (no mean sum) was to be set aside for Sara's *new* dowry. Bicker was not entirely defenseless himself, though, for he in his turn specified that should his wife die first, the six thousand guilders' worth of jewels he had given her as a bridal gift went straight back to his side of the family.[65]

There were circumstances other than death in which a wife could reclaim her own share of the married estate. If she believed her husband to be squandering her portion irresponsibly or in some other way abusing his right of legal guardianship, she could appeal in law to have their property formally divided with full reversion of the dowry.[66] Women could and did have recourse to legal process — though if unmarried and below their majority of twenty-five, they needed a guardian of standing through whom to proceed. But the Dutch legal system was not unsympathetic to women filing claims against male abuse. Unmarried pregnant women or mothers could sue the putative father, for example, in *vaderschapsacties* — paternity suits.[67] Their aim was either to oblige the malefactor to marry the wronged party or, if he was married already, to provide a dowry, costs for the delivery of the child and in some cases an arrangement for its regular maintenance. So long as a woman was bringing such an action against a man of roughly her own social standing she stood a much better than even chance of success. In Leiden, for example, between 1671 and 1795, fifty-seven women won their cases, as against twenty-one who lost.[68] There were, of course, very many — principally housemaids — who were made pregnant by their masters or other members of the household, and their chances of legal redress were weaker. Even if the accused was unmarried, it became more realistic to ask for dowry, birth costs (perhaps two to five guilders) and some maintenance of twenty or thirty stuivers a week. The dowry awards might vary according to the means of the defendant and the social expectations of the plaintiff. Young housemaids might receive a few hundred guilders, while *burgerdochters* who could persuade the magistrates that their betrothal vows had been cruelly abused might be treated more handsomely—perhaps between five hundred and a thousand. For the poorer girls, of course, any dowry at all was a boon, and, predictably, housemaids were accused of deliberately ensnaring employers' sons to set themselves up with a dowry.[69] Often, the mere threat of exposing a respectable family to public ignominy in court was enough to ensure an adequate settlement. And there were other stratagems available to a woman determined on justice. She could threaten to have the child baptized in its father's name, or if a girl, to give it a feminized version. In cases of extreme courage or desperation she could even threaten to bring it to the father's house.[70] Where the odds were really stacked against a female plaintiff was when the accused malefactor was himself a high officer in the town. And even in this case, the factional divisions that were commonplace within the Dutch regencies meant that, on occasions, jealous rivals might seize the opportunity of a scandalous case to blacken their enemy's reputation. Johan van Nispen, for example, who had been a member of the regency in Flushing in Zeeland for sixty years, was prosecuted by the town sheriff for misconduct with his maid and duly convicted by the bench of magistrates. Van Nispen, however, himself appealed to the provincial high court on the grounds that the case was animated by political malice, and was duly vindicated.[71] But overall, the predicament of a sexually wronged woman was not completely hopeless. In Leiden in that same period (1671–1795), of all cases brought, twice as many women succeeded as failed.

Women who were wronged during their marriage also had some recourse to legal assistance. In cases of adultery or "willful desertion" they could seek a "separation of table and bed," leave to live apart, effectively annulling the marriage. When church councils took up the complaint, adultery was usually considered sufficiently grievous a sin to permit divorce and remarriage. "Willful desertion" could, of course, include bigamy, and there were other categories—the husband's contraction of venereal disease, or gross physical cruelty to the spouse, which gave grounds for separation. It remains difficult to know how many such cases were brought during the seventeenth century. The following century witnessed an explosion of separation suits brought for adultery,[72] but earlier on there were surprisingly few: nine cases in all in Leiden between 1671 and 1680, nineteen the following decade. Whether this suggests a slighter incidence of marital disharmony or a greater reluctance of wronged spouses to initiate proceedings is impossible to judge.

Women could also make commercial contracts and notarized documents
and so had all the formal qualifications needed for active commercial or
business dealing, an opportunity of which many availed themselves. Shaw
noted that they "were generally bred to accounts, and affairs and labor as much
as their husbands."[73] Widows, in particular, especially in the great trading
families like the Trips and the Bickers, were renowned for their astute
handling of family property. But further down the social scale — at the level of
shopkeepers, for example — it was not at all uncommon for wives to handle
business and money affairs during their marriage. In Jan Mol's misogynist
satire *Beigt der Getrouwde* (The Marriage Confession)[74] it is the wife who becomes mistress, first of the family budget, then of the drapery shop, as the forlorn husband sinks further into impotent dissipation. Indeed, she argues that
since it was her fortune on which the marriage was based, it should hence-
forth be hers to direct. In 1742 when a general tax assessment was made, fifteen percent of all taxable enterprises in Amsterdam and twenty-four percent
in Leiden were those of women. But it also seems that the great majority of
these incomes were those of widows rather than married women trading on
their own. Indeed, it is still the case that while the Netherlands has one of the
oldest and richest traditions of feminism in Europe, it has one of the lowest
percentages of mothers in the workforce — a good deal lower, for example,
than that of either Italy or France.

Protection against abuse (including wife beating) and a measure of redress
against despoliation of dowries did not make Dutch wives in any sense the
peers of their husbands. Nor was there much danger of a widows' cartel to beat
their way into male-dominated commercial houses. In fact, wives and widows
were at their toughest when backing the claims of their dynasty — in marriage
settlements, wills and the like — against the claims of rivals. Any degree of
extra security and independence they may have enjoyed (and that struck
foreign observers as superior to the position of their contemporaries in
England and France) was conditional on their confinement within the household realm. Yet within those formal limits, Dutch women managed to register
their presence with such vigor that in subtle ways they did alter somewhat the
scale of sexual inequality. Any choice of occupation other than that of
housewife was dictated either by their husbands or exigency or both. But it
could lead, nonetheless, to status and reputation (as well as income) in their
own right. When her surgeon husband died in 1692, Catharina Schrader was
thirty-eight and a mother of six young children. She had no choice but to put
the rudimentary obstetric skills with which she was only too familiar and which
her husband had helped her refine, to work. But those bleak circumstances
propelled her into a career as midwife in the Frisian market town of Dokkum,
where she became a renowned figure, attending to the families of nobles and
poor farmers alike. And although she was formally subordinate to the "master"

physicians with whom she worked, it was Vrouw Schrader rather than they who was the indispensable presence at the childbed.[75]

And there were opportunities to make other reputations, however circumscribed. In 1655 the first actress appeared in the Amsterdam theater, strengthening the clergy's view that it was the sink of the vilest iniquity. But Adriana Nozeman went on to make an illustrious career there nonetheless.[76] And at the summit of cultivated society, it was possible for a whole family of gifted women to make a powerful mark as learned savants and poetic muses. Roemer Visscher, the merchant author of the *Sinnepoppen*, turned his house on the Engelsekaai in Amsterdam into a kind of literary and philosophical salon in the second two decades of the century, with his daughters Anna and Maria "Tesselschade" as presiding doyennes. This, too, was in the old humanist tradition to which Visscher, an old friend of Erasmians, like Coornhert and Laurens Spieghel (and like them, a Catholic who detested both the Counter-Reformation and the Calvinist catechism), belonged. The saturation of the Visscher girls in a classical education recalled Thomas More's Platonic exercises with his own daughters. Like them, too, Anna and Tesselschade (there was a third, Geertruid, whose lesser aptitude presumably exempted her from these bookish games) were polished to dazzle visiting luminaries who invariably ended up becoming suitors and deluging the girls with lyric bouquets. Maria managed to overcome the laboriously witty sobriquet of Tesselschade with which her father saddled her, naming her for the Texel "wreck" he survived on the day of her birth. For by all accounts, she was exceptionally comely, as well as gifted in viol, lute and harpsichord and song. Like her sister, she was a skilled translator and commentator from Latin, Greek and Italian (Tasso into Dutch being no mean feat) and a fair poetess in her own right. When some of the older chambers of rhetoric in Amsterdam decided to merge in 1630, it was Tesselschade who won the poetry competition to celebrate their union in the new Coster's Academy. Not surprisingly, then, her list of admirers reads like a directory of Dutch letters in the first half of the century: Bredero, Heinsius, Barlaeus, Vondel Constantijn Hughens and Hooft being merely the most eminent. After their father's death, both sisters were co-opted by (indeed they became indispensable members of) Hooft's celebrated literary circle at the castle of Muiden. In her widowed years in the 1640s, Tesselschade returned to Amsterdam, where she reestablished her presence as a reigning dowager of the arts, one-eyed (she had been hit by a spark from a blacksmith's anvil), prodigious and imposing. When she died in 1649, Huygens wrote of her "immeasurable qualities" and compared her to the sun.

If Tesselschade was supposed to embody beauty and brilliance, Anna, as she was only too aware, was called on to play the role of virtue and wisdom. But in Zeeland, where she was saddled with the slavish admiration of the besotted

Cats, she carved out her own reputation. Cats dedicated his *Maagdeplicht* (The Duties of a Maiden) to her in what even by the standards of the time was an embarrassingly fulsome eulogy, its delicate sentiment imprisoned in the leaden boots of his plodding meter. A frontispiece engraving bore the "Maagdewapen," the arms of the maid in which the lamb (for simplicity) and the puppy (for aptitude) were the heraldic supporters of a shield in which industrious bees were set. For Cats, Anna Roemers Visscher was the incarnation of all such gifts, even though she took his advice on maidenly prudence excessively literally by keeping his overtures at a very long arm's distance. And in the more provincial (and much more Calvinist) circles in Middelburg, Anna swept all before her. In 1622 she was welcomed by a grandiose civic reception arranged by the town secretary, Simon de Beaumont, who produced (as seems to have been obligatory) a poem on the occasion. For flattery he turned to the old humanist conceit of a man and a woman, measured in a beam balance.

> *What! shall a maid that shorter is than I*
> *Small of waist and fine of limb*
> *Whose hands are wondrous fine*

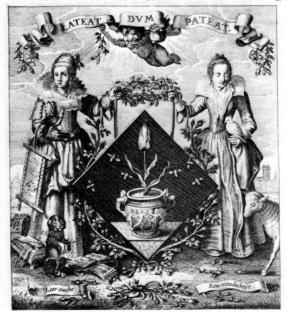

193. Experiens Silleman, engraving, "Maeghde-Wapen" from Jacob Cats, *Alle de Werken* (*Complete Works,* 1655 folio ed.). Houghton Library, Harvard University

And aspect so trim . . .
Weigh more in the scale
Than a man there set

As a graduate of Hooft's *Muiderkring,* Anna was an old hand at parrying these labored though well-meaning tributes, and, quick as a whip, she produced a response that graciously accepted the compliment while deferring to the male's sense of worldly self-importance.

I sleep in peace the whole night long
I relish all my food and drink
Then how should I not weigh more
Than men made lean with worldly care[77]

It is hard not to see this as ingratiating. And while they strayed far from the conventional realms of Dutch housewifery, the talented Visscher women did not really pose a serious threat to male sovereignty over female options. In some ways they even reinforced them, for though they were the apples of their father's eye, Roemer Visscher himself made sure they remembered that he was the trunk from which they stemmed. While less remorseless in its insistence on the male "lordship" of the household than Cats's *Houwelijk,* there is nothing in *Sinnepoppen* to encourage the emancipation of a truly independent female spirit. Both Tesselschade and Anna settled down to respectable marriages — the sought-after beauty defying her name by marrying a sea captain at Alkmaar. Anna, who had enjoyed the courtly airs at Muiden as much as anyone, accelerated the family's upward mobility by marrying Dominicus Boot, a literary nobody, but sheriff and dikegrave of the Wieringerwaard on the northern tip of the Noorderkwartier. In most respects, then, their unofficial careers as learned women remained ornamentally designed to please men. In this respect they were perhaps closer to the salon wits of the eighteenth century than the truly independent women writers of the nineteenth. And it is not fortuitous that the first collective portrait of the Muiden circle to include the Visscher sisters along with the male luminaries (indeed, with Tesselschade as the most prominent of all) was J. C. Kruseman's anecdotal painting of 1852 in the Rijksmuseum.[78]

There was at least one independent female spirit whose exceptional gifts took her well beyond the conventions of literary mutual admiration societies. This was Anna Maria van Schurman, "the learned and most noble virgin" of Utrecht. In some ways, the comparison with the Visscher sisters is unfair, for Anna Maria was of a later generation that doubtless profited by their acceptance. Though she became well known in intellectual circles — to Descartes, among

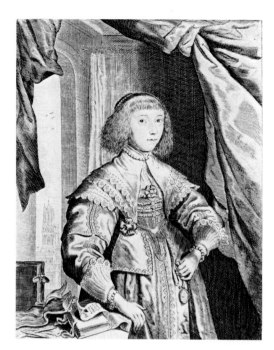

194. Portrait of Anna Maria van Schurman from Cats, *Complete Works,* 1655. Houghton Library, Harvard University

others—and had her portrait painted by the fashionable Michiel van Mierevelt, throughout her life she remained concerned more with inner truth than outward repute. Born in Cologne, her family settled in Utrecht as religious refugees and the presence of the university and the communities of scholars that lived on its fringe provided Anna Maria with opportunities to imbibe all the learning that her prodigious talents could soak up. She did the acceptable things like glass engraving, poetizing in Latin and Italian, and less acceptable things such as portrait painting and copper engraving. She was talented enough at these skills to be admitted to the Guild of St. Luke, in Utrecht, in 1641. Fluent in Hebrew, Greek, Arabic, and Syriac, she wrote in an incisive, spare Latin style, of which it is certain Erasmus would have approved. Her published disquisitions and editions concerned issues in moral and metaphysical reasoning, much of it argued in impeccably careful syllogistic logic. But later in life she turned from formal proofs to inward pietist doctrine and, introduced to Jean de Labadie, married him secretly in 1661, at the age of fifty-four, ten years before her death.

Inevitably, her fame and gifts fanned the ardor of Cats, who was irresistibly drawn to brilliant blue-stockings. Just as inevitably she spurned his offers, Cats consoling himself by assuming that her impregnable maidenhood was the stumbling-block. Intellectually, Anna Maria would in fact have devoured him alive, being not at all warm to men who graciously gave women the *permission* to acquire learning. A short, sharp Latin tract, translated into English in 1659 as *The Learned Maid, or Whether a Maid May Also Be a Scholar,* was exceptionally courageous in its time for arguing, through logic, the evident right of women to exercise their intellect. It was also marked by an affecting degree of social realism, acknowledging that there were certain "necessaries" required: "an indifferent good wit" and the spare time and means to be able to use it. "For some maids are ingenious; others not so; some are rich; some poor; some engaged in Domestic cares, some at liberty."[79] She was also prepared to concede that some subjects were more suitable than others, especially those that were conducive to the moral virtues, though this allowed a broad curriculum — grammar, logic, rhetoric, physics, metaphysics, history, Hebrew and Greek. Mathematics, music, and painting were also deemed proper and at all events preferable to the "pretty ornaments and ingenious recreations" that now passed for suitable pastimes for young women. Military matters and those of the law Schurman thought rated a low priority, but reluctant to give any hostages to male adversaries, insisted that "we in no wise yield that our maid should be excluded from the scholastic knowledge or theory of those, especially not from the most noble doctrine of politics and civil government."[80] Nor did she have any patience at all with those who supposed that women's minds were somehow not ordained for bookish learning, or that they were in any sense the inferior to Adam by being made of his rib. "God hath created woman also," she affirmed as if refusing to cast her eyes down in deferential demureness, "with a sublime and erected countenance," and "whatsoever perfects and adorns the intellect of Man, that is fit and decent for a Christian woman."[81]

Schurman's little tract, then, represented the first stirrings of an authentically independent female spirit in Dutch culture, and perhaps it is not too much to say that only in the Republic could a work of such boldness have appeared in the 1650s. It was not so much that the Dutch positively invited their women to stand forth in their own right. As we have seen and are about to see, the whole prospect of the independent woman made even the more broad-minded types distinctly nervous. But there was more room in the republic of letters for such unorthodoxies to emerge unprosecuted if not exactly unchallenged (Schurman's foes were many). And there are indications elsewhere in Dutch culture, especially perhaps in its art, that women could be seen for what they were, rather than for how they ought to be.

Calvinist iconoclasm had done some of the work in eradicating from northern Netherlandish art at least one prototype of the idealized female: the Blessed Virgin. Others remained, though, for biblical heroines and allegorical incarnations were still an essential ingredient in the history painting that flourished in the Republic alongside more vernacular genres. The publication in 1644 of a Dutch edition of Cesare Ripa's *Iconologia,* with its extensive repertoire of allegorical personifications of the human qualities, may even have supplied female typology with a new baggage of symbolic association. And there were local patriotic versions of those types borrowed for sculptural ornament or history prints, ranging from the traditional Hollands Maid and her six sisters to the Maid of Peace that became popular around 1648 and which Quellijn placed so prominently on the roof of the Amsterdam town hall. Much of the iconographic interpretation of Dutch genre painting has taken Ripa's symbolic prototypes, along with Cats and other emblematists, as the source of meaning attributed to apparently anecdotal or descriptive compositions. And while this methodology has provoked great argument among art historians, it is wholly consistent with the distinctive concerns of northern humanism to infiltrate classical and Christian wisdoms into the business of daily life. So, paradoxically, the very success of moralizing in paintings depended on the skill with which the artist could record quotidian reality. It is this delicate tension between necessary means and required ends that makes the judgment of motivation in genre painting so difficult. It also makes the dichotomy between a descriptive and a prescriptive interpretation unnecessary.[82] What is certainly apparent in Dutch pictures of women at their domestic chores, reading letters, or being courted, is that artists went to unusual pains to trace expression of feature, bodily attitude and gesture in the female with a relaxed clarity that is missing from the conventions of classical and baroque depiction elsewhere. It may be (though I think not) that Brekelenkam's wonderful *Confidential Conversation* in the Rijksmuseum comes heavy with allusions to the *levenstrap,* the ages of woman that also appear in the frontispiece of *Houwelijck.* But what gives the picture its vivacity and intimacy is much more simply the candor and scrupulousness with which feminine gesture has been recorded in three variations: placid attentiveness (in profile), the maid's less polite hand on hip, and the emphasizing gesture of the matron—all three bound together by a triangle of gossip.

There were some signs, then, of a view of Dutch women that was relatively unclouded by cultural stereotype. The nagging preoccupations with virtue and vice still provided the frame of reference within which genre painters selected their subject matter, but the degree to which they allowed it to dominate their more purely pictorial concerns was a matter of their own judgment. And it should be borne in mind that because of the Reformed Church's distaste for images, few painters were likely to imbue their work with self-consciously Calvinist sentiment. It is altogether easier to spot the Catholics, Remonstrants, Collegiants and the like among the fraternity of Dutch artists than the militantly orthodox.[83]

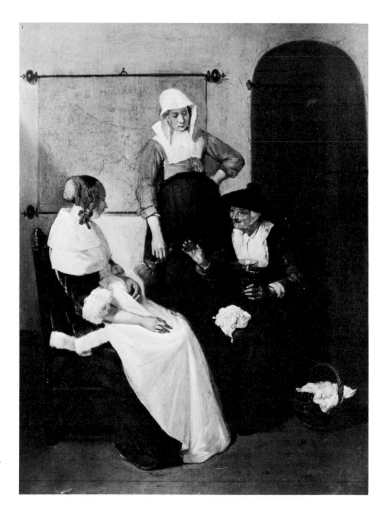

195. Quirijn Brekelenkam,
Confidential Conversation.
Rijksmuseum, Amsterdam

Whether enclosed within these preoccupations or freed from them, depictions of Dutch women were of course overwhelmingly male depictions. Was
there any equivalent of Anna Maria Schurman in the visual arts, an authentically female vision of their own sex? There were certainly women painters in
the Republic, but just as opportunities for women writers and poets were available so long as they obeyed male assumptions about ornamental propriety, so a
significant number of successful women artists turned to the genres that were
closest to purely decorative skills. It was but a short step from glass engraving
and needlework to the kind of brilliant flower and fruit still lifes that made
the reputation of Maria van Oosterwyk and Rachel Ruysch. But there were
nonetheless at least two striking exceptions to this rule of innocuousness, one

belatedly celebrated and the other still virtually and undeservedly unknown. For a long time, Judith Leyster's career—about which we are still poorly informed—remained almost completely hidden. What is known, though, comes as a distinct surprise. A daughter of a brewer, and so without the kind of entrée that the Visscher girls enjoyed, Leyster seems to have made her way much like any male painter, and, more impressively, she did so in the second or third decade of the seventeenth century. She was admitted to the Haarlem Guild of St. Luke in 1633 at about the customary age (her early twenties) and had pupils in her studio including Willem Wouters. Three years later she married the painter Jan Miense Molenaer, and some of her work, like his, is marked by a kind of affectionately ironic view of the dangers and pleasures of family life. Before her independent identity was made clear, some of her jocund studies of topers and music-making were given to Hals. The manner is very close, but perhaps even more than Hals, she adapted the Caravaggist style of large and looming figures brought close to the picture edge in dramatic lighting and heroic posture to the unheroic and anecdotal affairs of everyday life. But did her sex make any particular difference to what and how she painted? There are, at best, tantalizing and speculative answers. Frima Fox Hofrichter has argued plausibly that her *Proposition* of 1631 diverges from the tradition of such paintings (which in the Utrecht Caravaggist idiom were unambiguously venal) by making the woman an "embarrassed victim" rather than a colluding participant.[84] Certainly there can be no question that Leyster

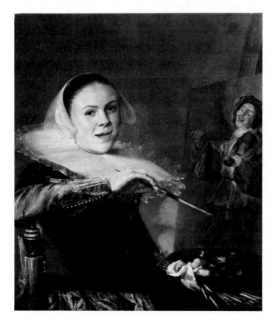

196. Judith Leyster, *Self-Portrait,* 1635. National Gallery of Art, Washington, D.C.

painted her woman as the embodiment of the domestic virtues approached by worldly vice, nor that the brilliance of the light cast from the rush holder onto her face was meant as more than an exercise in Caravaggist chiaroscuro. But the most explicitly assertive work, in which the woman painter invites us to confront the excellence of that small miracle, is her own self-portrait. There is in this unaffectedly cheerful countenance not the least trace of demure self-effacement. Indeed Leyster's use of the "lodestar" pun in her autograph signatures called even more attention to her own particular identity. And in the study of the "merry fiddler" in progress on her canvas, and the startling combination of graceful dress with professional craft, there is a kind of innocent and contagious self-congratulation that the high spirit of the piece defies the beholder not to applaud.

In contrast to Judith Leyster's unabashed declaration of "I am what I am," Geertruid Roghman has registered only the faintest presence in the history of Dutch art. Scholars even remain unsure whether she was the sister, daughter or niece of the more famous landscapist Roelant Roghman. But she produced around the middle of the century a series of engravings of domestic work that have no precedent or parallel in Dutch or for that matter any other sort of art until the nineteenth century. To be sure, they follow moralizing conventions by incorporating in at least some of the prints the stock metaphors of virtue: the distaff for diligence and the reminders of *vita brevis*—skull, book, candle snuffer and clock. Unlike the standard genre treatment, however, it is the rugged and painstaking quality of the work itself that overwhelms everything else in the compositions. There is a solemn inevitability about the regard paid by the younger to the older women at their work that is not altogether lighthearted. And while a moralist like Cats might have found the print of a woman bent over her pots quite as edifying as the butter churn of *Self-Strijt,* the very anonymity of that broad body seen from the rear imparts something altogether more serious and rugged than tasks done to oblige male desiderata of the virtuous wife. Nor do they in the least resemble the range of cheerful tasks and spiritual lessons catalogued in Luiken's *Leerzaam Huisraad.* Domestic work was supposed to make husbands feel that the comfort, the *gezelligheid,* of their home was being attended to, but these are pictures that make men feel distinctly uncomfortable. For once it seems not too much to say that only a working woman could possibly have produced them. For they are images that strip domestic life of its moral ingratiation, its obliging therapy for male materialism and guilt, and instead proclaim it to be an involuntary division of hard physical labor.

Buried not far below the apparently placid surface of domesticity, there may be discerned something like an heroic strain in the lives of Dutch women. And not all Dutch men were indifferent to it, either. Assimilated into

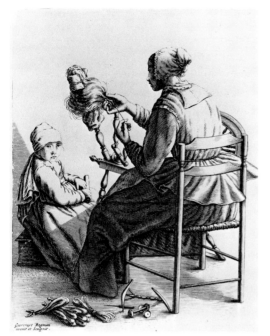

197. Geertruid Roghman, engraving, *Woman Spinning*, 1650s. Atlas van Stolk, Rotterdam

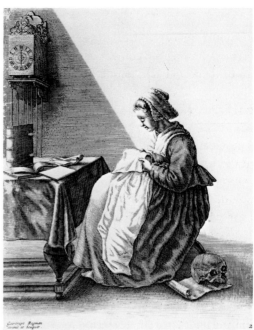

198. Geertruid Roghman, engraving, *Woman with Vanitas Objects*, 1650s. Atlas van Stolk, Rotterdam

199. Geertruid Roghman, engraving, *Woman in Kitchen Interior*. Atlas van Stolk, Rotterdam

200. Geertruid Roghman, engraving, *Women Sewing*. Atlas van Stolk, Rotterdam

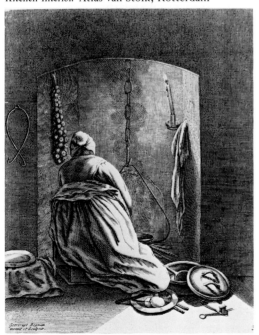

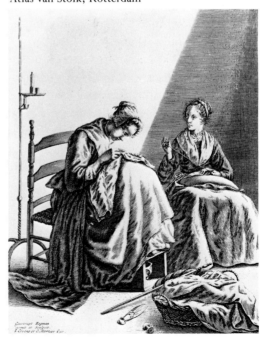

the popular history and patriotic folklore of the country were a number of stories celebrating the courage, strength and resolution of women. To be sure, many of them, like the famous episode of Grotius's wife smuggling him out of his prison at Loevestein in the sublimely appropriate conveyance of a book chest, were grist for the mill of those who preached wifely loyalty and devotion above all other qualities. But other stories stressed the sheer audacity and physical bravery of women, converting the demonology of the virago into the boldness of the patriotic heroine. The print of Kenau Hasselaer Simons, for example, leading an army of housewives to confront the Spanish besieging Haarlem, uses the same formidable *batterie de cuisine* as grim-visaged *Dulle Griet,* but for a wholly laudable purpose (see fig. 39).

Dr. van Beverwijck at any rate had no doubts at all about the fortitude of women. His *Van de Wtnementheyt des Vrouwelycken Geslachts* (On the Excellence of the Female Sex) recorded many instances of their martial heroism—not merely at Haarlem: the women of 's Hertogenbosch, led by "Trijn van Leemput" (Catharijna Bergen), the wife of one of the city's magistrates, who mobilized another women's legion against Alva in 1576, and those at Dordrecht in the fifteenth century who fired cannon from the city walls. But the book is far more than a scroll of female valor; it is an extraordinary eulogy of all the qualities of the sex. It was so fulsome, indeed, that Anna Maria Schurman, to whom it was of course dedicated, felt the need to try to dissuade the doctor from the compliment. Apparently she felt some responsibility for the embarrassment, having egged him on make the invidious comparisons. With characteristic grace she tried not to seem churlish, for "truly I admired your overflowing kindness whereby you have been pleased not only by your elegant style to assert that which alone I lately requested of you, the glory of learning and wisdom to our sex, but to so favor our cause as to equal us everywhere to Men, that I may not say to prefer us."[85] But she was reluctant, she said, to embarrass the doctor's cause by being held up as the embodiment of the best of her sex.

Van Beverwijck of course ignored Schurman's modest complaint and editions of the book duly appeared with her portrait at the frontispiece. For all his free borrowings and anthologizings from scripture, the classics, popular travel lore and the like, van Beverwijck's work was not just meant for the literati. It was published in octavo with simple woodcuts as well as quarto with finer engravings. And van Beverwijck himself was a powerful and influential figure, in many respects rivaling Cats as a source of popular wisdom. Like many physicians, he enjoyed not only professional authority by virtue of his vocation but some degree of political power. He was a regent of Dordrecht, a member of the governing circle of "The Forty," and one of Holland's delegation to the States General. His *Schat der Gesontheyt en Ongesontheyt* (The

Treasury of Health and Sickness) was the standard work of home and clinical medicine, ranging from moral accounts of the humors and the relation between "sound" diet and way of life and longevity, to detailed anatomical instructions for the dressing of wounds or the tending of particular sicknesses and diseases.

What he had to say about women, then, would be heeded, and what he had to say was, to put it mildly, unorthodox in its unqualified enthusiasm. He began by repudiating the first principle on which advocates of female inferiority had always based their case: the creation of woman from Adam's rib. Houses, he replied, are built from wood and stone, but as houses they become incomparably greater than their individual parts or even their sum. So, woman was not made from mere fleshly matter but was endowed with a soul which in every respect made her the equal of man.[86] Historical and contemporary instances were then adduced to show that they could be as learned as men (Sappho and the "Dutch Sappho," Anna Visscher) and for that matter were a great deal more loyal and constant than men. While he deferred to no one in his praise for the housewife, van Beverwijck also contradicted the notion that that was the only fit calling for women. "To those who say that women are fit for the household and no more, then I would answer that with us, many women, without forgetting their house, practice trade and commerce and even the arts and learning. Only let women come to the exercise of them and they shall show themselves capable of all things."[87] And to those who argued from nature that women were physically unsuited to the affairs of the world, he borrowed from Montaigne's style of skeptical relativism, citing Herodotus to the effect that in periods of Egyptian history, it was the women who had been responsible for commercial affairs while men sat at home spinning. "Men carried their packs on their heads while women carried them on their shoulders," and as a clinching argument, "the men made their water sitting down, the women standing . . . whereby it appears that it is not out of nature but from custom that women forbear [from worldly things] but are certainly capable of them."

There was surely no question, van Beverwijck wrote, that women were the more pious and dignified of the sexes, the more susceptible to shame and the more vigilant in protecting their honor. But he added that from his experience as a physician he knew that women were also more capable of standing pain, of which the greatest imaginable was that of every childbirth. And despite that suffering, the spontaneous love and devotion of a mother to a child was itself well-nigh miraculous, apparently blotting out all memory of the miseries endured during birth. And the natural affection between mother and child was physiologically proven, he thought, by the fact that while in other animals infants hung beneath their mother's belly, in women the child was suckled above at the breast—in order that she might fondle and kiss the babe.[88]

However influential and respected he may have been, it would be idle to pretend that van Beverwijck's feminism was at all typical even of the enlightened opinion of his time. What was startling about his book was its willingness to flirt with role exchanges in ways that ran right against the grain of both humanist and Calvinist orthodoxy. Yet there were particular features of his argument which, put in a more conjugal context, were wholly acceptable to conventional wisdom. The rather sanctimonious little manual the *Deughdelijcke Vrou* (The Virtuous Woman), for example, agreed that women should be encouraged to be literate and to read widely, but very much to the end of making them the complete wives and mothers.[89] Not all books, "but alone good books" (those that would kindle godfearing virtue), were to be permitted and all "curiosities" carefully avoided. The point of reading was to enhance a woman's moral self-consciousness, since it was among the most ignorant that shame seemed to be least developed.

A kind of *burgerlijk* consensus about marriage and the relation between the sexes crystallized somewhere between the poles of van Beverwijck's feminist enthusiasms on the one hand, and the doctrinal severities of Calvinist dogma on the other. Throughout this book I have tried to show how cultural norms that the Dutch community took as their collective rule book were generated from the encounter between apparently irreconcilable imperatives. Both sets of principles: the humanist and the Calvinist, the ecclesiastical and the secular, remained conceptually separate and intact. But the unavoidable concessions that moral commands had to make to social obligations resulted in a much more flexible daily code. To be a Dutch burgher meant avoiding being either godless or helpless. The command to be sober, for example, was modified by the fortunes to be made in the wine-carrying trade. But the dilemma was resolved by appeals to festivities that were licensed as patriotic or communally appropriate (see Chapter 3). Money-making, which the Calvinist Church so detested, was tolerated by distinguishing between proper and improper ways of making fortunes, and the concept of wealth as stewardship. To be rich was to show that one was truly eager to give one's wealth away (see Chapter 5). Similarly, the notion of the male's lordship over his wife and house and the strict division of realms of home and world were qualified by the understanding that a strong household required a strong mistress and that it was not best served by a regime of partriarchal enforcement. Wife beating, to the surprise of some foreign visitors, was severely frowned on, and a stream of commentators had written against it. On his trip, Aglionby discovered that the *buurt* could supply its own intervening controls by imposing fines (in kind, a ham) on known wife beaters (and double on wives who roughed up their husbands!).[90] Its definition as a crime of affray was just one instance of how the church, now that it no longer considered marriage as a sacrament, had devolved authority for its regulation to the lay power (while still reserving for the church councils a good deal of scrutinizing and admonishing force).

The church itself, in fact, was less militant on the subject of wifely submission than some of its Puritan counterparts in England.[91] Together with the procreation of children and the avoidance of fornication, it asserted, there was a third reason for the institution of marriage, namely, companionship (*gemeenschap*). The Amsterdam predikant Petrus Wittewrongel, whose *Oeconomia Christiana* is a standard example of Calvinist teaching on marriage, was quite specific on the topic. Citing Genesis 2:18, the preacher concluded that God had specifically made woman to be a helpmate for man and that "just as a head cannot survive without a body, so a groom cannot survive without a bride." Like Ruth and Boaz they should cleave to each other and never be separated. Wittewrongel laid great stress on the departure from the parental household and the establishment of a new conjugal home as an essential feature of a newly shared life.[92] With his endearing compulsion for translating any abstraction (however plain) into a homely, tangible image, Cats made the same point by comparing a husband and wife to two millstones who had, perforce, to grind together to fulfill their purpose in life.[93] Marriage was companionship

> in care and in joy
> in bustle and in rest
> in loss and in gain
> in recreation and in work
> in risk and in fortune.[94]

At the core of the marriage bond was affection, tenderhearted sentiment, love. Humanists had long held this to be so. Grotius insisted that *"non enim coitus matrimonium fecit sed maritalis affectio"* (matrimony is made not merely by coitus but by the affection of marriage).[95] Calvinist teaching, at least in Holland, did not at all subordinate love to obedience but rather exalted it as the indispensable quality for a godly union. Wittewrongel stated that the obligation of man and wife "must be to be tied to one another through a very dear and affectionate marriage-love." Through the "kindling of love in all friendship and dearness, they should warm each other's hearts with conjugal feeling and love."[96] Hearts as well as bodies should be united in this tie, for fidelity in affection ensured true purity in the married home. So that a typical marriage advice manual for newlyweds had, as its engraved frontispiece, the bride and groom exchanging burning hearts.[97] The true test of their love was that they should take pleasure in no one's company more than that of their spouse. And foreign visitors were often surprised and embarrassed to witness the outward signs of married friendship. De la Barre de Beaumarchais dined with a burgomaster of Alkmaar who went so far as to compliment his wife on the meal, to which she responded with a kiss. Marriage for these people, the Frenchman concluded, "is as charming as it is holy."[98]

To be authentic and enduring, these feelings had to be mutual. If the husband was often compared to a king in a little realm, his wife shared at least some of that domestic sovereignty. A wedding song in one of the popular song anthologies, *The Little Holland Goldfinch*, warbled "a house-guardian [*huis-voogd*] and his house friend/May be likened/Unto a King and Queen/For their home is like a kingdom/And the children their happy subjects."[99] Another compared the wife to a viceroy placed in charge of domestic affairs so that the husband could be free for his business. The division of labor was set out as complementary, "men must earn and see that no one is in want; women must spend and provide."[100] The husband's authority was symbolized in constabulary tasks: locking up last thing at night, making sure the home had arms to protect it against intruders, keeping a lantern handy in case of nocturnal disturbance, and checking the doors and windows when a storm was expected. The wife, on the other hand, was the administrative steward supervising the domestic servants, drawing up and executing the weekly timetable of cooking, cleaning and shopping, seeing to the inventory of furniture and utensils and making replacements when necessary, making sure that the children were properly and cleanly dressed, ensuring that there was a decent supply of medicines, herbs and simples in the house to cover all medical troubles, especially those of the children, preparing the festive calendar through the year along with the appropriate foods and ales, and even organizing and tending the shrubs and bulbs should the house have a kitchen or flower garden.[101]

As if this were not enough, a wife was also supposed to be a privy counselor: the person to whom a husband ought immediately to turn for advice and help on anything of importance, *either* domestic or worldly. And the obligations of reciprocity were symbolized in the old betrothal custom of exchanging medallions, coins, or spoons, on which the bonds of mutual love were often engraved. And while obedience was required from a wife, it was not unconditional. "If the man is the Head, then the woman is the neck on which it rests," said one work, somewhat bleakly.[102] That neck, though, was not to be stretched in meek submission. Violent, drunken or otherwise unwholesome conduct in the husband had to be lovingly corrected by the loyal wife through pious example and respectful admonition. Wives who had the misfortune to discover the stain of vice in their spouse only after they had wed were consoled by the commonplace that many a reprobate who had dissipated his life in "*wijnte en trijntje*" (i.e., in wine and women) had been reformed after his marriage through the firmness and love of a good woman.[103] So that her doing his will should not be thought of as subjection but rather an honorable duty, the object of which was to make the home a more pleasurable place than the tavern or the stews. If the wife took care to keep the table well supplied, even when unannounced guests were brought home, and the household clean and safe, then the most hardened sinner could not but be tenderized by this brimful cup of conjugal joy. If, in spite of all these efforts, the delinquent was deaf to his wife's entreaties and truly incorrigible, his faults could be brought to the attention of either the church council or the magistrates or both. And it was not uncommon for despairing wives to bring their own husband's case before the *kerkraad* in the hope of chastening his way of life before ruin descended on their house. In more normal circumstances a wife was bidden to show respect and courtesy and try at all times to speak to her husband in a "soft and friendly manner" and desist from anger and bitterness. But at no time was a wife expected to be tyrannized by her spouse. "In our Netherlands, God be praised," exclaimed Cats, "there are no yokes for the wife, nor slaves' shackles or fetters on her legs."[104]

That marital affection included physical tenderness no one doubted. But writers were less unanimous on the perils and pleasures of the flesh, even within the marriage bed. The more stringent Calvinists thought it was possible to taint the bed with fleshly excess and made pointed references to unions they deemed unnatural. They even supposed it was possible to commit adultery with unclean thoughts or unorthodox postures. Copulation from the

201. "The Marriage Bed Should Be Unstained," from Johan de Brune, *Emblemata of zinnewerck* (Amsterdam, 1624). Houghton Library, Harvard University

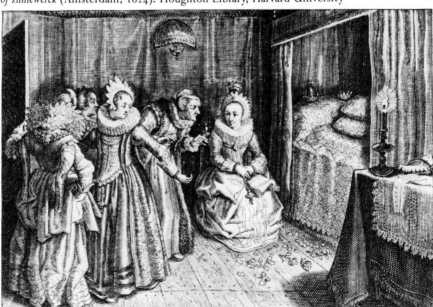

rear, for example, was abhorrent, since it simulated the mating of beasts. One book, while upholding that view, managed to include the enticing item of information that the Cyrene Whore had listed twelve positions in which pleasure might be prolonged.[105] By the same token, though, orthodox marital sexuality was regarded as "chaste," a kind of prolonged virginity. "The marriage bed is no gutter for vile lusts," warned Johan de Brune, "but those who use it well, may stay a maid."[106] It was certainly allowed that sex, or "fleshly conversation," as it was happily euphemized, was for the physical expression of married love (and the avoidance of fornication) as well as for the procreation of children. Indeed, failure to consummate on the part of either partner came to be considered reasonable grounds for a "separation of table and bed." Van Beverwijck, of course, was unblushingly enthusiastic about it and quoted the case of a "certain doctor" who had been asked by his own wife whether it was better to make love in the morning or evening. (Van Beverwijck had worried in print over the effects on digestion of strenuous activity.) He responded that while it was indeed healthier in the a.m., it was probably more fun in the p.m., so why not do it in the morning for health and in the evening for pleasure?[107] This could be overdone. The extraordinarily frank sex manual, *Venus Minsieke Gasthuis,* a Dutch version of the physician Nicolas Venette's *Tableau de l'Amour Considéré dans l'Estat de Mariage*, published in 1687, and which went into seven editions by 1715, warned that four or five ejaculations per night was the maximum for health and for the production of fertile semen.[108] The very existence of this work in a relatively cheap illustrated quarto edition, with its guide to sexual health, pleasure and the avoidance of disease, is striking evidence that knowledge of the biology of reproduction—within of course traditional seventeenth-century limits—was available to the reading public. As usual, in the Galenic-Aristotelian tradition, both men and women were said to have *ballekens:* the male testicles being nicely compared to pomegranates, full of seed, and the ovaries being their counterpart in the female. But at least the external anatomy was objectively described with the clitoris clearly understood as an organ of pleasure. Sensationally, the author insisted that he had known of an eight-year-old girl whose clitoris was as large as "half a little finger."[109]

Most modern historians of the family have assumed an evolution from "patriarchal" to "companionate" styles of marriage, and have busied themselves with tracking experience along a line drawn between that point of departure and its destination.[110] By these lights, the seventeenth-century Dutch seem to have been indeed pioneers on the frontier of friendly, loving marriages. But it may also be that the categories are themselves too exclusive to allow for the complicated mingling of both "patriarchal" and "companionate" sentiment. Dutch writers—and for that matter humanist reformers and Protestant moralists before them in sixteenth-century northern Europe—had all taken pains to insist that deference to the husband as lord of the household was conditional on his reciprocal obligation to confide the governance of the home into his wife's charge and to abstain from all conduct that would bring house and family into disgrace or ruin. Marriage, in short, had already become a true partnership.

If the Dutch *burgerij* were not all that unusual in viewing their marriages in this way, they were certainly the first to give it pictorial expression. As in so many other spheres of social activity, it is in visual rather than textual evidence that the most eloquent confirmation of a new informal tenderness and a reciprocal friendship may be found. There had, of course, been marriage-pair portraits before the seventeenth century, though it was in northern France and Flanders that the genre replaced pendant donor portraits within a single frame. From the very famous van Eyck *Arnolfini* portrait through the sixteenth century, such portraiture had retained a wealth of symbolic allusion to the specifically Christian obligations of the marriage, reflecting the Catholic teaching that marriage was a holy sacrament. Even when the Reformation had disposed of that, pair portraits retained much of the symbolism shorn of its specifically sacramental associations. Gloves, rings and bunches of grapes grasped by the stem became symbols for marital fidelity and steadfastness[111] and traveled from emblematic frontispieces like van de Venne's grapes in *Houwelijck,* to the prop wardrobe of pair portraiture. Into the early seventeenth century, sitters still wore the demeanor of solemnity. For as David Smith has observed, without an obvious model for secular marriage poses, the formal gestures and demeanor of Italian court portraiture were adapted for domestic commissions.[112] As a consequence, many of the late sixteenth-century and early seventeenth-century studies wear that grave and statuesque formality. Such self-images present the ceremonious aspect of marriage rather than its intimacy: dynastic icons rather than domestic memorabilia.

All this had dramatically changed by the middle of the seventeenth century. Even by the 1630s both Rembrandt and Hals were experimenting with more dynamic and companionable poses. Anecdotal elements crept into the pair portrait, anticipating the true conversation pieces that would be the hallmark of the "companionate" marriage portrait in the later seventeenth and eighteenth centuries. Husbands were shown interrupted at their work, sometimes reluctantly, sometimes, as in Jan de Bray's smiling Margarieta van Bancken tempting the publisher Abraham Casteleyn, more playfully.[113] The alteration of mood was not abrupt. Many pair portraits, especially of the highest members of the elite, retained the stiff decorousness of the earlier style. And the emblems of conjugal devotion were preserved in more informal settings. Sometimes the one elided subtly into the other. Frans Hals's famous pair of

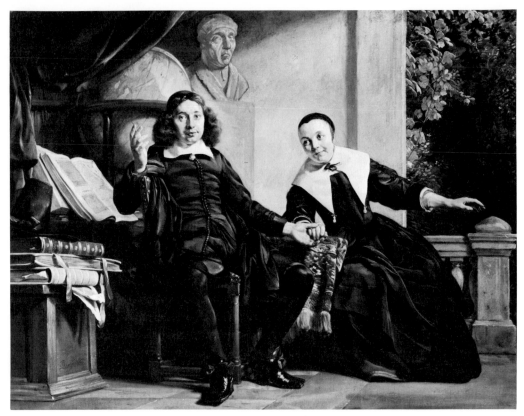

202. Jan de Bray, *Abraham Casteleyn and Margarieta van Bancken*, 1663. Rijksmuseum, Amsterdam

Isaac Massa and Beatrix van der Laen shows the couple informally posed against the setting of a park which on careful inspection turns out to be the standard Renaissance bower and garden of love complete with fountain.[114] Other emblematic motifs—the ivy and the thistle—allude to proper marriage roles. What seems to be the casually affectionate gesture of the wife's arm draped across her husband's shoulder is in fact a studied echo of symbolic vine twined about the sturdy tree. Despite the crowding of this formal, symbolic visual vocabulary, it is the affectionate pleasure of married companionship that remains the most arresting feature of the painting's tone. The warmth and spontaneity of the couple seem actually strengthened, not weakened, by the painting's aim to give physical expression to the married idyll. Similarly, as the manner of joining right hands became more freely rendered—in caresses, entwined fingers or one placed protectively over the other—symbolism receded before the delicate allusions of body language. (Foreigners were quick

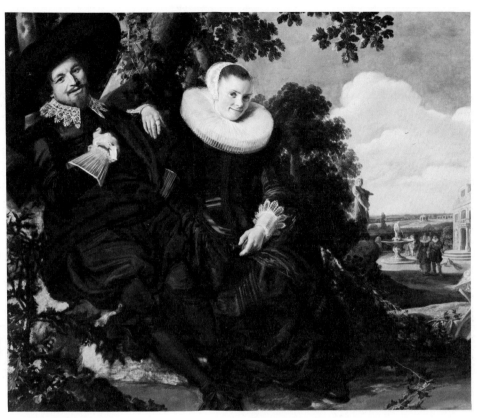

203. Frans Hals, *Couple in a Landscape* (Isaac Massa and Beatrix van der Laen), 1622. Rijksmuseum, Amsterdam

to note the horrid spectacle of couples freely caressing each other or prome-nading hand in hand even though they appeared to be of respectable society.) Before long, the ways of expressing loving companionship became rich and elaborate. Couples posed in *portraits historiés* as biblical pairs, Isaac and Rebecca being favorites, or as figures from antiquity. But what is striking about that transformation is how informality necessarily equalized the roles of the two partners. And gradually, the gentler, more companionable manner came to invade even the conventions of the older pendants. By the time that Hals came to paint Stephanus Geraerdt and Isabella Coymans, for example, neither he nor, presumably, they had any inhibitions about turning the figures in half profile to meet each other's gaze. And instead of an expression of sacramental gravity, they feast their eyes on each other with pleasuring smiles. It is, surely, a fresh moment in the history of European marriage, this urge to celebrate and cherish the warmth of wedded friendship.

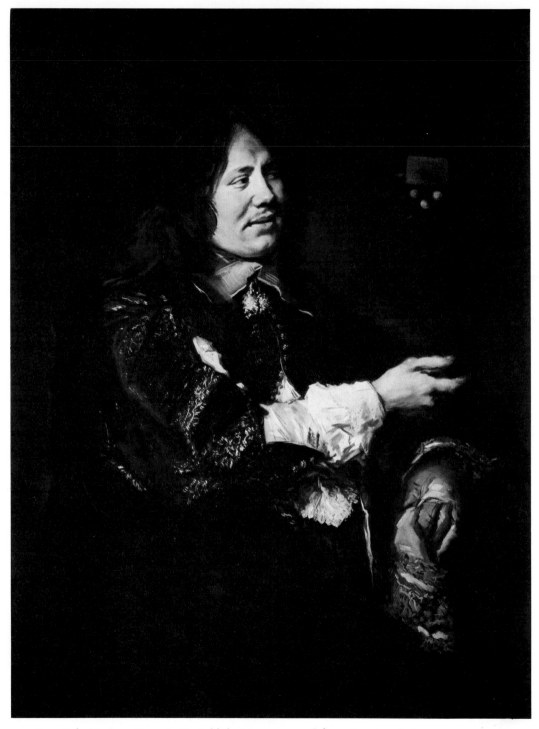

204. Frans Hals, *Stephanus Geraerdt*. Koninklijke Museum voor Schone Kunsten, Antwerp

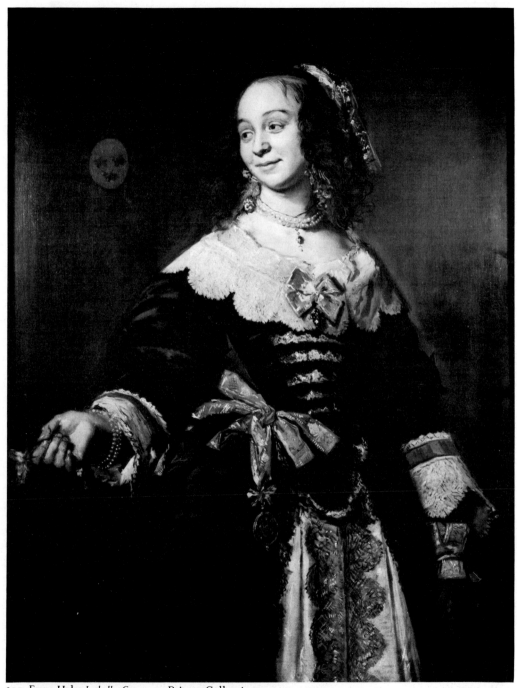

205. Frans Hals, *Isabella Coymans*. Private Collection

iii TEMPTATIONS AND TERRORS

To judge from their art there were no wrinkles quite like Dutch wrinkles. Never before had painters lingered with such meticulous fascination on the crumpled, eroded faces of old women. Nor had etchers ever scratched their burin needles on engraving plates to mark female features with ruts and folds, hollows and crannies. Crowsfeet track mercilessly over cheekbones, frown lines crevice the brow, skin is puckered and pulled over shrinking gums. Their art explored an entire geography of the ancient face, but as always in Dutch culture, it was a moral topography. For in genre painting in particular, there were wrinkles of vice and wrinkles of virtue. Old women are no longer just *exempla* of the transience of vain beauty, as they had been in Giorgione's *Col*

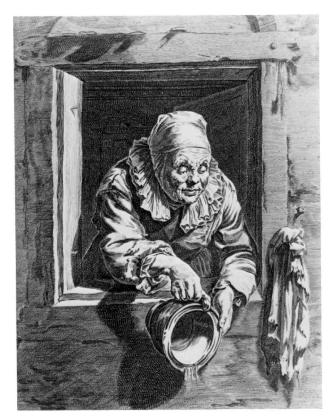

206. Hendrick Bary after Frans van Mieris the Elder, *"Goore Besje."* Atlas van Stolk, Rotterdam

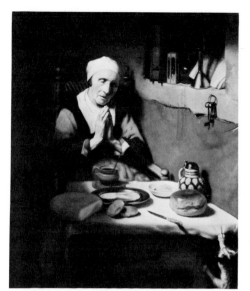

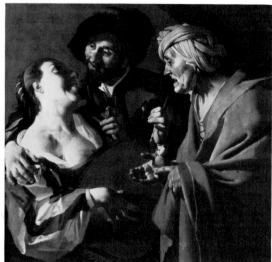

207. Nicolas Maes, *Prayer Without End.* Rijksmuseum, Amsterdam

208. Dirck van Baburen, *The Procuress,* 1622. Courtesy of Museum of Fine Arts, Boston

Tempo, or exercises in the brutal adjacency of fashion and ugliness, as in Leonardo's and Quinten Massys's grotesques. Instead they were incorporated into the great Dutch obsession with appetite and dirt. Frans van Mieris's "Sleazy Bess" is despicable because, her honor lost, she throws her own filth on "respectable heads." But her vileness is so visibly written in her "wrinkled hide" that the legend below the print orders her "away from our sight."

Two kinds of old women feature most commonly in genre painting: the solitary matron saying grace over a humble meal and the leering procuress presiding over a sexual transaction. They stand, of course, for lives led in piety and sin, but they also embody opposite norms of fleshly indulgence. Maes's old woman, like all of the same type, awaits death in virtue, stripped of the deluding folly of things. Her meal is lenten, the sparse and sacred food of herring and bread. And these dowagers are poor. Money, like food or the burden of their own sensual life, has happily fallen away from them. They are ready for the life of the spirit.

The procuress may sometimes be depicted as withered and shriveled, but in the evil corruption (rather than the virtuous depletion) of appetite. And where old women of virtue subtract matter from their lives, the harridan (who is closely related, as a type, to the miser) aggregates it. Following the old Netherlandish idiom, vicious women are both insatiable and avaricious. Once their own sensual appetite is jaded, they transfer its urge from lust to commerce, from sex to money. Pieter Huys's Flemish painting is just one of the

209. Pieter Huys, *Woman Enraged.* On
loan to the Worcester, Mass., Art Museum,
Courtesy of Alexis Audette, formerly Julius
S. Held Collection

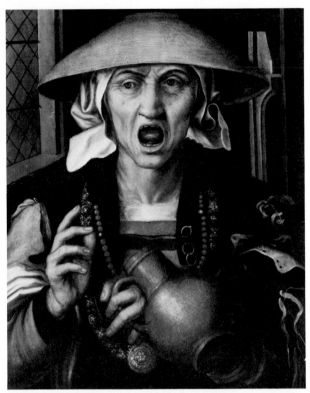

210. Hendrick Pot, *Brothel Scene.*
Courtesy of the Trustees, National Gallery,
London

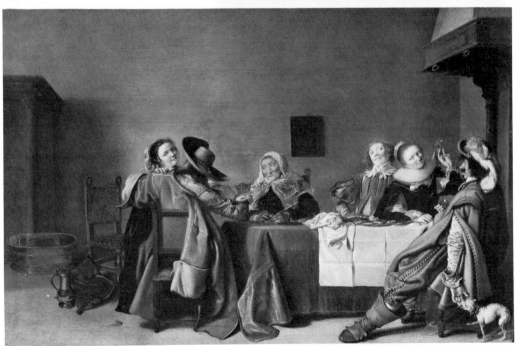

late sixteenth-century prototypes that showed Ira (rage) with both the emblems of avarice and sexual appetite (the open jug) converging on the gaping succubic mouth. Hendrick Pot's brothel keeper, watching her whores flirt with their soldiers, packs her pipe in the standard obscene mimicry of copulation, while her dog licks the unsavory fingers of a collapsed client. In other brothel scenes, whores or their keepers rob and steal (like *Dulle Griet*): takers disguised as givers.

These polarities have been made hard and fast in the opposite types of old women shown in Dutch art. But young women are not so obviously classified. There are certainly those whose work—at distaff and spindle or with bobbin and lace—proclaims their domestic virtue. And there are those whose décolletage, gesture with a wine glass held at the base of the stem, feathered headdresss or exposed red stocking advertises the opposite. But then again there are very many young women in genre paintings—especially those whose dress suggests their higher social station—who belong to an altogether more elusive and ambiguous domain: that of temptation. Metsu, ter Borch, de Hooch, Maes, Netscher and Dou all probed the shadowy zone dividing innocence from worldly knowledge. It is a realm cut loose from the certainties of purity and pollution, one where the first indelicacy is risked, the first forbearance tested. In the parlors of temptation, mirrors are gazed into, letters dreamily perused, fruit tantalizingly beckons, music seduces and *roemers* beg to be filled to the brim. Flirtation, innuendo, suggestion and ambiguity abound, and the hard light of moral guidance is refracted through intervening opportunities.

The difference between emphatic and ambiguous eroticism could be exemplified in the tone and treatment of subject matter of Steen's so-called *Disreputable Woman* ("*La Ribaude*") at St. Omer and ter Borch's *Soldier Offering a Young Woman Coins* in the Louvre.[115] Both prominently feature coins held in the palm of the hand, though in the Steen they are a female demand and in the ter Borch a male offer. Steen leaves absolutely nothing to the imagination in the presence of the smirking procuress; the bursting undress of the girl and the spread of her unhosed legs as she sits on the bed. Though the stock erotic cues are present in the ter Borch—the dish of oysters, the ripe fruit and the goblet waiting to be filled—the outcome of the action is much less determined. The soldier's knee brushes against the girl's satin dress as against the more wanton contact in the Steen brothel scene. Her own eyes are on the coins, registering neither outrage nor greed; Steen's girl confronts the beholder with a knowing expression. In the one, the issues are done with; they merely await settlement. In the other, they are clouded. There the canopy bed separates rather than couples the two figures. In Steen's world there is choice but no dilemma. In ter Borch's, the sensuousness of the outer world—of fabric, fruit and flesh—is in unresolved contention with the inward world of reflection.

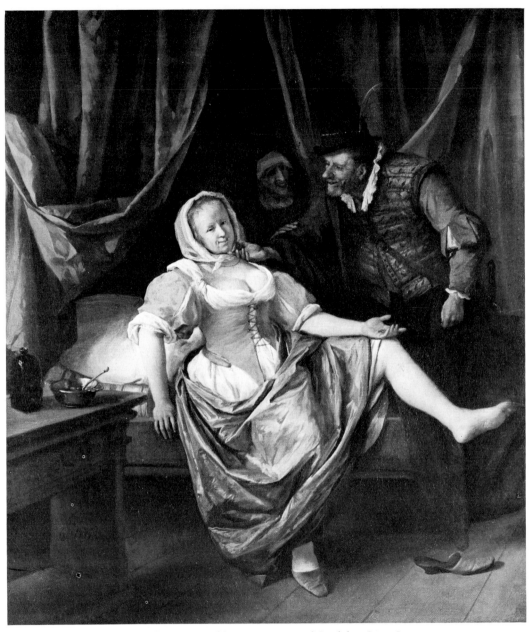

211. Jan Steen, *"La Ribaude"* (The Disreputable Woman). Hôtel Sandelin, Saint-Omer

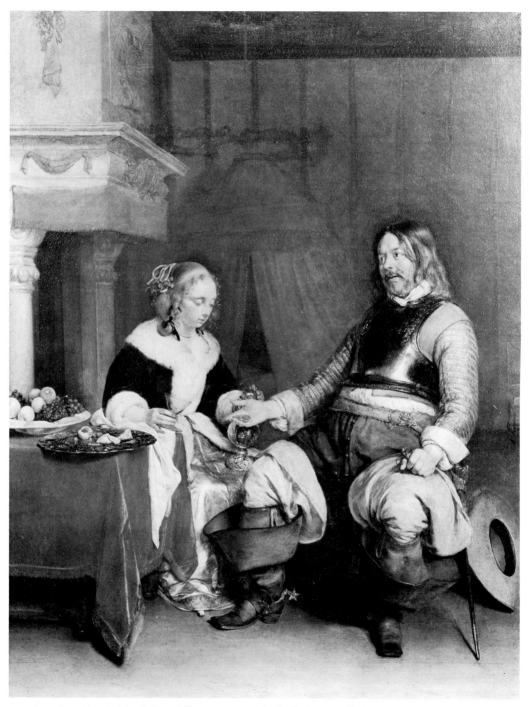

212. Gerard ter Borch, *The Gallant Officer*, 1662–63. Musée du Louvre, Paris

For the Dutch moralists, young women were the choice prey of the Tempter. Their allure, their weakness and their vigorous instincts all exposed them to daily trials. In due course, marriage would offer a secure haven, but the mean age of first marriage for women in seventeenth-century Amsterdam was twenty-four to twenty-eight (though in the early seventeenth century half of all brides were twenty to twenty-four) and eighteen was probably considered the age of sexual maturity.[116] There was, then, a period of prolonged and intense peril before the maiden was safely installed in conjugal bliss. The moralist writers all recognized how tricky bringing off a good match was, but their profusely offered but inconsistent advice was not calculated to soothe a fretful parent's anxieties. On the one hand, Cats opined, it was crucial not to marry the first suitor who presented himself ("marry in haste, repent at leisure") or to imagine that puppy love (calf love, in Dutch) was the real thing. On the other hand, as he graphically put it, a nubile maiden was like a chestnut on the fire — ready to explode if not cooled down, for marriage was constantly described as cooling water poured on the burning heat of lust. One of Cats's more unfortunate images compared the urge of the flesh to "the great lamprey that burns in the ocean."[117] Perhaps to avoid the scalding connotations of striking while the iron was hot, his image for acting expeditiously when the right man came along was another briny simile: that of a gull skimming the waves to spy the perfect fish.[118]

For the maid herself, there was no shortage of instruction, much of it

213. Emblem from Jacob Cats, *Spiegel van de Oude en de Nieuwe Tyt* (Rotterdam, 1627). Houghton Library, Harvard University

214. Emblem from Cats, *Spiegel van de Oude en de Nieuwe Tyt* (Rotterdam, 1627). Bodleian Library, Oxford

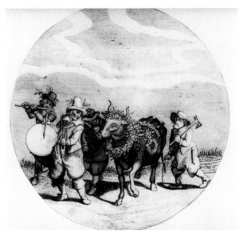

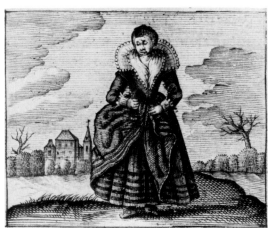

striking a rather mournful note. Beware the idle pleasures of youth, declared one emblem, for they are like nosegays on the festive ox — behind the garlands and the drums lies the grim reckoning of the butcher's ax. Be not vain in thy beauty, for it is a summer fleeting thing, like the petals of the rose:

> *Blond turns to gray*
> *Light-hearted becomes grave*
> *Red lips will turn blue*
> *Beauteous cheeks will be dull*
> *Agile legs become stiff*
> *And nimble feet halt*
> *Plump bodies lean*
> *Fine skin wrinkled*[119]

With these depressing certainties in mind, the young maid should look for enduring virtues in her intended, rather than those of fly-by-night passion. Love could be like the spider's web, so don't fly in hastily if you want to get out. And above all, shun anything daring like low necklines, high fashions or bold caresses. Elegant addresses or flattering sonnets were also to be treated with the greatest circumspection. ("With sweet words are hearts broken.") *Maagdeplicht* told the cautionary tale of the smith's daughter who was so swept off her feet by the eloquence and ardor of a young student that "when he came at night and stood before the door/He joked and played all too free/ And stayed the whole night o'er."[120] Even if it seems that the young man's heart would break, so passionate and tragical he may appear, it was crucial to keep him at arm's length if the maid was to preserve her most priceless treasure.

Best of all, a maid destined for a good match ought not to go freely around town by herself, lest some of the world's dirt muddy her good name. One of the most rueful of all Cats's exemplary sluts was the "French maiden" (*Franse vryster*) who laments her soiled frock and tarnished honor. The nineteenth-century doggerel moralist Robert Fairlie (who not surprisingly took up Cats in a big way) rendered her speech in a faithfully canting style:

> *How I've splashed and soiled my gown*
> *With this gadding through the town*
> *How bedraggled is my skirt*
> *Traipsing through the by-streets' dirt . . .*
> *Come girls here, come all I know . . .*
> *Playmates mine, advise me, show*
> *How shall I remove the stain*
> *And restore my gown again?*

For wherever I may go
People will look at me so
And think, perhaps, such dirt to see
I'm not what I ought to be [author's emphasis].[121]

How obedient to these gloomy strictures were young Dutch men and women? From the sparse data available, it appears that illegitimacy rates in seventeenth-century Holland were very low. In Rotterdam and Maassluis around 1700, fewer than 1 percent of baptized children were illegitimate. And even when that percentage rose, in keeping with general bastardy trends across Europe, they barely reached 3 percent in the 1770s, and in the economically stricken 1790s, 6 percent.[122] These figures do not, of course, give much idea of *overall* illegitimacy rates, expressed as they are, as a percentage of the *baptized*. And if the definition is altered to prenuptial conceptions — infants born seven months or fewer after marriage — a very different picture emerges. In the Gelderland region of Duiven, for example, "early" births are mentioned in 14.3 percent of all marriages between 1666 and 1730; in Maasland (south Holland) the figure rises to 19.8 percent for the later period of 1730–95. So there may have been more "*vuile bruiden*" (dirty brides), even among the "respectable" classes than the propaganda of virtue suggests. In at least one fascinating case, a wedding portrait that presented a wife as the usual paragon of Christian restraint was belied by the facts. For when Reynu Meynertsdr. Seymens of Enkhuizen sat for her wedding portrait in 1595, she was already four months pregnant by her intended second husband, the explorer-mariner Jan Huygen van Linschoten.[123]

While it seems rash to speculate on the basis of such slight evidence, these findings seem consistent with the impressions of foreign visitors: a strikingly free and unpatrolled playfulness between the sexes, *together with* a strict attention to marital loyalty. At the time of her courtship Reynu Seymens was thirty-one and a mother of three. Her lover's voyaging career may well have hastened their consummation. For the most part, though, young Dutch burghers seem, then, to have been flirtatious rather than promiscuous. It was only in the eighteenth century (as elsewhere in Europe) that the line was crossed between playfulness and sexual experiment by the betrothed. In the earlier period, what may seem like daring liberty — as in the night courting in Brabant, Holland and Friesland — was usually a communally authorized encounter with understood limits as to what might be ventured and what prohibited. And the country towns of the Noorderkwartier seem to have preserved a whole variety of occasions for publicly regulated courtship. At Schermerhorn, according to the (slightly questionable) East Indies veteran and ethnographer Piet Neyn, a custom not unlike the French *veillée* persisted where, on an appointed day, eligible bachelors and girls would line up on either side of a room — perhaps a barn or weigh house — and a broker would move between the lines cataloguing the virtues of available partners and attempting to negotiate matches. When a match was successfully made, the future groom would pay for the cost of the evening's entertainment, which usually included sugar and spiced ales and caudles and a saffron and spice *rijstebrij*. Neyn even suggested that this represented a form of licit betrothal with cohabitation following shortly thereafter and before the match would be officially licensed.[124] Similar "markets" for bachelors and spinsters were said to have been a practice at other small country towns in the region like Schagen, where on *kermis* day prospective partners would line up in the church square with a regulating "official" weeding out all those deemed too old, too young or not native.[125]

It was the individualization of courtship rituals that most worried the guardians of morality. For the undisciplined exuberance of urban life in commercial Holland offered innumerable opportunities for mingling between the sexes away from the baleful eye of the church elders. Some of the potential damage could be limited when the town green happened to be located at the *kerkhof,* the square directly in front of the church. Though ministers were incensed to note that all kinds of scandalous frolics could take place apparently undeterred by the looming presence of the spire behind. And there were many other, bolder excursions, many of them customarily taken on Sundays: skating parties, wooden parrot shooting or country picnics. At the North Sea shore there were beach parties in which young men hoisted girls aloft and carried them into the waves. Le Francq van Berkhey particularly mentioned the free courtship habits of the coastal villages, which he said led "to many a bride becoming pregnant before the marriage day but which was not reckoned shameful when it was certain that the lovers were true and steadfast and would make a good marriage."[126] Apparently innocent games could in fact be physically rousing, like Head in the Lap where a young man laid his head in a girl's lap while he tried to guess the identity of those who, in playful turns, smacked his rump. But the church reserved special anathema for dancing schools that actually instructed the young in unseemly conduct. Scripture, they reminded the flock, was full of awful warnings on the conse-quences of dance: the daughter of Jephtha, Salome and Diana. The Synod of Gorinchem in 1652 objected strongly to "ill-considered outings by young people" and drew special attention to the moral dangers of goose-pulling tournaments[127] (a pastime in which horsemen attempted to seize an inverted greased goose suspended from a crosswire). At more refined levels of the patriciate, music parties and poetry readings were cultivated alternatives, and we know of at least one circle of gallants in which the young women played as dominant a role as the men: the "Ordre de le l'Union de la Joye," into which the young Johan de Witt was inducted in 1653.[128] All of these activities made it possible for the young to socialize in groups, often unaccompanied by parents, though rarely in isolated couples. Of course this freedom could be abused — especially as the century progressed and restrictions on conduct were relaxed — as a courtship tactic aimed as much at parents as at the opposite partner. The Synod of Schiedam in 1651 complained that "many young people go out walking with each other to force their parents or guardians to consent to marriage."[129] Some, it added, would even sleep together to oblige their parents to cover the indecency with the marital bond. Seven years earlier the Synod of The Hague had lamented that this scandalous liberty had become so widespread in some places that "of forty or so [young] persons scarcely four come to an honorable estate [i.e., marriage] with decent conduct."[130]

This was indeed a breach in the church's defenses against horrid lust, for while all unchastity was considered the most loathsome sin, a tainted marriage was still preferred over the worse transgression of continuing to live in unlawful cohabitation. Even as early as 1581 the Synod of Middelburg decided to issue the most severe reprimand to such sinners, but to allow a marriage to go forward even where sexual misconduct was known.[131] This was in the event that both parties were in their majority (twenty for a woman, twenty-five for a man) and both refused to break off the liaison. The best cure for such impropriety, though, church and lay moralists agreed, was prevention. And that was in turn better managed in a gentle rather than a heavy-handed fashion. The Politieke Ordonnantie of 1580, on which the marriage laws of the next two centuries were based, made the marriage of minors conditional on parental assent, and since most men and women married either on the threshold of or just after their majority, it is evident that parents' counsel played an all-important role in their decision. Indeed, while pre-Reformation law deemed elopement as *raptus,* or abduction, and subject to criminal proceedings, it did not render such marriages invalid. The 1580 legislation was stricter on this offense, but cases of abduction were treated differently depending on the age of the parties and the degree of force used. Friedrick Conincx, an ex-cornet who had eloped with an underage girl in 1646, got off lightly, whereas Willem Rosenberg, who had contracted a clandestine marriage with a maid in 1653, was sentenced to a ban "on pain of death." And in May 1664, Roelof Colstenstede was actually condemned to be hanged for a violent abduction.[132] For the thwarted lovers there was the desperate remedy of a flight to the enclaves of semifeudal or communal jurisdiction that were free of the sovereignty of the provinces in which they were geographically situated. In Ravenstein, Culemborg and Vianen, for example, a cottage industry of instant marriage prospered on the unresolved friction between parents and rebellious children. In one such case documented by Haks, an impenitent daughter, Cornelia van Velthuysen, who had eloped with Aernout van Craeyvanger, rebuffed her father's efforts to have her return home from Culemborg unless he supplied a written assent to the match.[133] And there were at least some cases where *parental* "abduction" could be punished by the law: where stepfathers had attempted to marry off stepdaughters against their will for the sake of a profitable match. In 1626, for example, Anna van Swanenvelt and her second husband, Roeland van Leemputten, attempted to marry off his stepdaughter without the knowledge of the guardians assigned by her late father's will and expressly against its conditions. The marriage was annulled and the stepfather whipped in the pillory after begging forgiveness on his knees from the offended guardians.[134]

It is not clear from the court record whether the girl or the guardians were deemed the injured parties in this case, but at betrothal the couple was supposed to come to the match "without force or deceit," in the words of the bann. And there is evidence to suggest that while parents did indeed have the veto on their children's choice, they were not supposed to stand in the way of matches which were by most lights at all suitable. What was deemed manifestly unsuitable? A match between partners where the social discrepancy was considered too compromising—for example with a servant or a predikant. One of the most famous of all such attempted *mésalliances* occurred in 1653 when the sixteen-year-old daughter of a Delft regent, Agatha Welhoeck, became enamored of a widower predikant, Arnoldus Bornius, twenty-four years her senior.[135] Her father not only refused the match out of hand but forbade her even to mention the subject, and since Bornius himself was all too conscious of his vulnerable social position in the town and of the weight of the law on the father's side, that might have been that. As young as she was, however, Agatha was made of sterner mettle and proceeded to wage a determined campaign against her father's obduracy. When he took an oath beseeching God never to have mercy on his soul should he ever assent to the match, Agatha persuaded Arnoldus to preach a sermon on the validity of oaths. Geraldo, the father, retaliated by attempting to leave the church for the Walloon Reformed Confession and subjecting his daughter to a humiliating round-the-clock scrutiny. When he attempted to confine her to the house to prevent visitations (that were exemplary in their virtue), Agatha resorted to legal tactics to try to set aside her father's obstruction—since she was now over twenty—and fled to The Hague the better to have her case heard directly by the high court of the province. On May 1, 1662, Agatha wrote a touching letter to the justices of the court testifying that she had "fulfilled all the proper duties of a child" towards her father and had besought him "with prayers and supplications to give his fatherly consent." But despite her pleas and those of friends, burgomasters in Delft and even predikants, he "would not move from his vow." She then petitioned the court "according to the laws of the land" to assent to her marriage to the "learned and godly man with whom I find the greatest contentment with which anyone could be blessed, and who as well accords with my humor as I believe two true souls have ever lived."[136]

The high court was obviously unmoved by these heartfelt pleas, for it found for her father and treated her as a fugitive in accordance with the Delft magistracy, effectively ending her active campaign of resistance and returning her to the custody of the parental home. Agatha's passive campaign continued until Welhoeck's death in 1665, though he pursued her from the grave by committing his widow to the same obdurate denial. And in that same year a pamphlet appeared publicizing the senior Welhoeck's version to try to preempt any new evasive action.[137] Her parents were not able to restrain Agatha from leaving Delft and moving to Alkmaar, beyond the bans of the Delft church and magistracy. But it was not until 1670, seventeen years after she had fallen in love with her predikant, that they finally married at Schermerhorn—when he was fifty-seven and she thirty-three, and they were able to enjoy at least nine years of the marriage for which Agatha's fierce resolution had worked so hard and so long.

The Welhoeck case demonstrated that while popular sympathies in such family disputes often sided with thwarted young love (for Welhoeck senior was insulted on the streets of Delft), institutions were not often prepared to set aside the rules of parental assent for individual grievances, however well founded or persistently prosecuted. There were exceptions to this rule. A firm of advocates in Amsterdam, De Wilde, Molijn and Coningh, specialized in defending the rights of young couples of legal age whose wishes were unreasonably thwarted by their parents. Their most famous success concerned Coningh's own sister, Alida, who defied no less a magnate than Andries Bicker. She married his son Gerard in 1656 despite the Bickers' distaste for their in-laws, whose family had included an innkeeper and a dancing master![138] If the issue of social imbalance could sometimes be a matter for personal rather than formal judgment, there were other criteria for improper matches that were less arbitrary. Marriage out of the faith, for example, was frowned on by law and convention alike, so that marriages with Jews or Muslims remained illegal until the Batavian Revolution. Marrying out, warned minister Hondius, invariably led to "unquiet households," and Dusseldorp, citing Leviticus 20:15, went so far as to equate it with sodomy![139] Other reasons for which a parent might exercise restraining pressure—and for which a notarized betrothal might reasonably be broken off—were the discovery of sexual misconduct with a third party, the disclosure of a bodily infirmity or infectious disease (guess which), or more contentiously, a concealed bankruptcy or reports of undischarged debts. All the evidence that Donald Haks has gathered, however, for towns in Holland, suggests a good deal of social as well as religious endogamy.[140] Where one partner had greater means than the other, it was more likely to be the man, and in thirty-nine percent of such matches, fortunes were deemed equal. A considerable amount of moral and imaginative literature was still devoted to the humanist axiom that marrying for money rather than love was an offense against both God and nature, and that when either young men or women tied themselves to ancient misers they were dooming themselves to a "living grave." One of four drawings of the human follies made by Karel van Mander attacked a "marriage commerce" in which parents literally weighed their prospective son-in-law in the balance and found him wanting. And from the care that we know went into dowry strategies and the making of notarized marriage settlements, it is obvious that compatibility of fortunes was an essential part of satisfactory matchmaking, especially since the newly-weds were much more committed to the immediate establishment of an independent household than couples in most other European societies. It was not absolutely unknown, but certainly uncommon, for a lover to "declass" him- or herself by marrying below station. While marriages were meant to be based on affection, indeed, on love, it was an ardor that could be quenched by economic embarrassment.

Jacob Cats's own youth in Zeeland provides one of the best examples of passion mastered by prudence. In his autobiographical verse memoir, *Eighty-two Years of Life,* he recalled that as a young lawyer, at Middelburg, while listening to a sermon in the Walloon Reformed Church, he saw a young maiden

> *And straight in my heart a lover's fire ignited*
> *She seemed to me so sweet and passing wondrous fair*
> *That in my inmost blood I felt a raging fire.*[141]

Although romantic feeling is said by social historians to have been an invention of the eighteenth-century sentimental novel, there is virtually no cliché of its repertoire omitted by Cats's description of his infatuation. As well as causing the spontaneous combustion of his senses she "opened Heaven before my soul." And he responded in turn by "bringing none but velvet words/Embroidered on all sides with gold and silken thread." The girl did nothing to resist Cats's feverish courtship and agreed to see him. But when he discovered that her father was a bankrupt, his ardor disappeared as abruptly as it had arrived, leaving him to ruminate on the sadness of life—and the suddenly deserted object of his attentions—with rather more bitter conclusions! He eventually married Elizabeth van Valkenburgh, the daughter of a wealthy

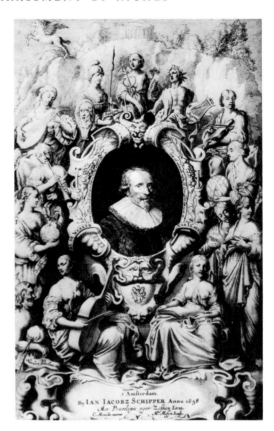

215. Engraved portrait of Jacob
Cats from title page of *Alle de Werken*
(Amsterdam, 1658). Houghton
Library, Harvard University

and pious family transplanted from Antwerp to Amsterdam, who corresponded
more suitably to his notion of the ideal wife — pious, learned, fair and rich.

While property could prevail over passion — at least in the *burgerij* — tender
sentiment was regarded as indispensable for a solid match. The conventions of
Renaissance courtship became popularized in bridal song books; exchange of
engraved gifts (sometimes baptismal spoons), embroidered cushions, and many
other tokens of affection announce the important part that feeling was meant
to play in conjugal courtship. And there was a standard program of socializing
through which the lovers were supposed to go that would allow their feeling
to blossom in ways not unlike modern custom. After an initial introduction or
encounter — often through the circle of family or neighborhood acquaintance —
a suitor would seek permission from a young woman's family to visit her at her
own home. Such visits would take place only under the watchful eye of senior
members of the family, though Dutch novels and poems in the later seventeenth and eighteenth centuries are full of mischief committed while only
a maid was acting as chaperone. After a decent time had elapsed, the couple

would "go public" in appropriately decorous ways: going to church together or walking on Sunday promenades along with the rest of the family. A formal betrothal, with exchange of medallions or other engraved keepsakes, would follow, sometimes with a "betrothal act" that could be notarized and, occasionally, signed in the lovers' blood! Once they were safely engaged, a great deal more freedom was allowed the couple, especially in burgher circles, on the understanding that passion ought not to be allowed too much rein before the marriage was solemnized by the magistrate.

Should such a disaster occur, or should one party break off the match for whatever reason, the injured could, in extremity, go to law to enforce the betrothal. Paternity suits, as we have seen, stood the best chance of success. But betrothal agreements, whether notarized or not, were not regarded as necessarily contractually binding, and magistrates seem to have been reluctant to enforce them without the drastic element of sexual violation intervening. It took a case like that of Zacharias Vatelet in Leiden, who had signed a notarized agreement, acknowledged a child to be his, sought consent of the girl's father and then, for capricious reasons, decided it was a bad idea after all—to make the magistrate insist.[142] In the twenty-two cases in Leiden that Haks cites between 1671 and 1795 where judgment was given, only seven were decided in favor of the marriage going ahead.[143] Given the much greater receptiveness of the law to paternity suits, it seems that there was no great eagerness to impose matches where the prospects for future connubial joy seemed bleak. That too, in its way, suggests that mutual affection was indeed thought to be indispensable for marital success.

Not that sentiment was supposed to guarantee a marriage would prosper. But without a generous helping of companionable warmth and love, commentators warned, the bed of roses could very easily turn into a bed of nails. And it would be a mistake to assume that male anxieties about the place of women in and out of the home faded with the onset of nuptial bliss. There remained the nagging suspicion, inherited from the rich stock of Renaissance misogyny, that the household might be too frail a vessel for the carnal heat that was known to lie simmering in the female body. Instead of the home being a haven from the cares of the world, it would reproduce and intensify them; in place of the domestic heaven, the unhappy marriage would be, in the words of one of its sharpest satirists, "a living hell." Along with a literature of happy endings, then, there also existed a prolific genre, both moral and fanciful, about miserable beginnings, a whole lore of marriages turned upside down. Particularly (though not exclusively) from the middle of the seventeenth century, popular writers like the versatile Hieronymus Sweerts, "Hippolytus de Vrye," turned their workaday talents to the topic of married woe. Their books were published cheaply in octavo, illustrated with simple copper engravings or

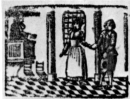 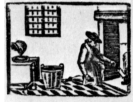 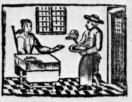 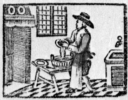 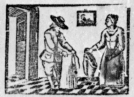 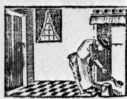 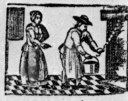

Door de hier beloofde Trouw, / Word Jan en Griet tot Man en Vrouw.

Nu ter Bruiloft, het word tyd, / Wyl den Disch reeds staat bereid.

Jan, wat doet gy? ruilt ge uw Broek / Voor uw Griet haar Schorteldoek?

Hier moet Jan al les ontfangen / Om het Eeten op te hangen.

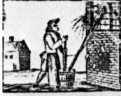 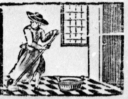 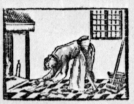 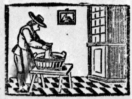

Nu het Eeten is bereid, / Jan een ander vuur aanleid.

't Eeten word door Jan gebragt, / Daar hem Griet reeds meê verwagt.

Na den Maaltyd Vaaten wasschen, / Dit toch zou uw Vrouw meer passen.

Ook 't opscheppen van de Asch, / Geeft de Vrouw veel beter pas.

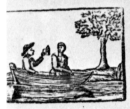 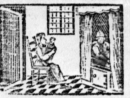 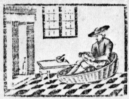 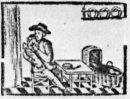

't Glaazen wasschen wil niet lukken, / Want hy spuit ze al in stukken.

't Schrobben schynt hem niet te vlyen, / Maar hy moet, om straf te myen.

Nu aan 't Veilen, om dat Griet / Straks uw werk volkomen ziet.

Door dit werk dat gy verrigt / Weet men ook uw eernaam ligt.

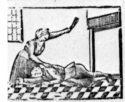 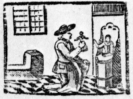 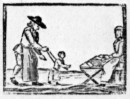 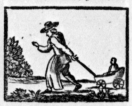

Griet en Jan met de Lantaaren, / Gaan ter Volewyk toe vaaren.

Jan in 't Kraambed, Griet met 't Kind! / Dit is 't klugtigst dat men vind.

Heeft hy 't Baakren nooit geleerd, / Griet dit toch van hem begeerd.

'... Schreijend jonggebooren bloed, / Word door Jan met Pap gevoed.

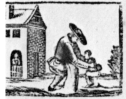 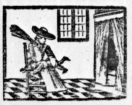 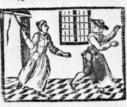 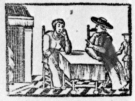

Hier gaat Griet haar Man kastyen / Daar hy 't Kind heeft laten schreijen.

Om zyn Griet en 't Kind te streelen, / Moet hy met het Popje speelen.

Hier zal Jan, daar hy 't leert loopen, / Snoepgoed voor zyn Kindje koopen.

Jan, vermoeid van 't Kind te draagen / Ryd het buiten in een Waagen.

...n die hond het jonge Wigt, / ...ot het zyn behoeft verrigt.

Om het kwaad van 't Kind te stuiten, / Doet het Jan tot straf besluiten.

Maar de Zweepflag is hier 't loon, / Voor het straffen van zyn Zoon.

Hier beraadflaagt men te zaam, / Waar toe 't Kind wel is bekwaam.

Gedrukt te Amsterdam, bij de Wed. C. KOK, geb. VAN KOLM, Tuinstraat.

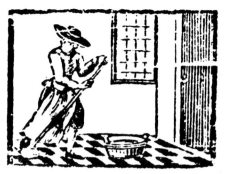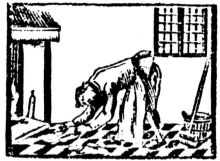

217. Detail from "The revised Jan de Wasscher"

216. Anon. woodcut, "The revised Jan de Wasscher." Atlas van Stolk, Rotterdam

woodcuts, and catered to the coarser end of the market — the same audience that still enjoyed the old-fashioned *kluchtspel* farces of domestic and peasant life when they could see them. And their contents were produced to formula, mixing recycled anecdotes with stock tales of gulled and cuckolded husbands, spendthrift wives who frittered away the family fortunes on whims and fashions. Cats had warned in *Vrouwe* that

> *Anything the husband acquires, the wife can squander,*
> *Anything the husband saves, the wife can exhaust,*
> *Anything the husband strives for with the sweat of his brow,*
> *Anything the husband produces, can be ruined by a prodigal wife.*[144]

The "promenading, spendthrift and modish women" who occupied the first pillar in *The Stock Exchange of Women* arrived in grand carriages dressed to the nines and with a large retinue of heavily liveried servants. Even their daughters, "aged eight or nine," dripped with jewelry and other unsuitable ornaments "so that one would think they were the greatest Lady."[145] Other domestic horrors included insatiable gluttons who ate their husbands out of house and home and slatterns who abandoned it altogether to sink in alcoholic stupor in the *kroeg* and spread calumny like poison around the neighborhood, and harpies who launched crockery across the parlor with tiresome regularity.

Many of these productions echoed ancient refrains in Renaissance and Reformation antifeminism. The battle of the trousers was one such genre that exposed male terror of role reversal, and it appears in almost all northern European popular literature in the sixteenth as well as the seventeenth century in one form or another.[146] But the partition of worlds was of such paramount importance within Dutch culture *and* gender roles so often threatened with a blurring ambiguity that it may have cut particularly deep notches on the collective psyche of Dutch men. At any rate the culture was adept at adapting old themes to modern domestic circumstances. The *Vernieuwde Jan de Wasscher* is essentially the battle of the breeches in contemporary dress but all the more telling for it. It relates the familiar story of a new husband quickly reduced to abject impotence by a domineering *broek-dragende* (breeches-toting) wife. No sooner do Jan and Griet return from the wedding than the husband meekly exchanges his breeches for the wifely apron. Suitably domesticated, he takes over all the household duties, laying the fire, cooking meals and waiting on his impatient wife. The real badge of inversion is his willingness to do the household ablutions, washing dishes, floors and windows, trembling all the while before Griet's punitive power. "He scrubs and shines with diligence/to escape Griet's punishments." But the role change also extends to child minding. Jan occupies the child bed, nurses and feeds the baby, plays with it and pulls its pram to buy it sweets. The full ignominy of the trouserless Jan is completed by an upset hierarchy of punishment. The baby cries and he is beaten for allowing it to howl. But when he smacks the child's bottom, his wife flogs him for his temerity.

In other satires, the wife moves by stages from submission through insubordination to usurpation. In *Biegt der Getroude* (The Marriage Trap) she gives notice of her willfulness by uncontrollable extravagance when shopping. Gradually the flag of insurrection is raised emblematically when the wife "sticks the broom out" by insisting on inviting as many of her friends around as often as she wishes and adds to her husband's ordeal by requiring his presence at the entertainments. So ensues what the writer calls "the war of chocolate against tobacco." But the role exchange is economic as well as social. As the husband loses the capacity either to resist or to earn enough to satisfy these demands, she demands to take over control of the family budget. Inexorably, he becomes sunk in resigned lethargy in the taverns and backgammon dens, fails to honor bills of exchange or make interest payments on debts, and the once spendthrift wife then becomes transformed into the prudent, diligent mistress of the house. While her man is sodden with drink and drabs, she runs the draper's shop. Inevitably, the inverted order is solemnized by the passing of the mandate of the trousers: *"de vrou heeft de broek aan."*[147]

Is it too much to see in these domestic nightmares the old terror of castration: Dulle Griet tutored by Judith? And in other examples, the masculine nightmare of men-women exposes inner frights with transparent clarity. The frontispiece to the *Beurs der Vrouwen*, which also features the female attributes of the serpent of guile and the ape of folly, has set in the statue's pedestal a frieze depicting a wrathful woman about to strike down a prostrate male. Van de Venne's engraving of *De Toneel der Vrouwelijcke Wraakgierigheid* (The Theater

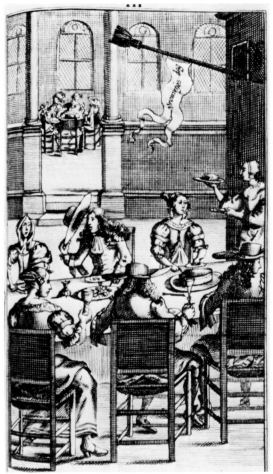

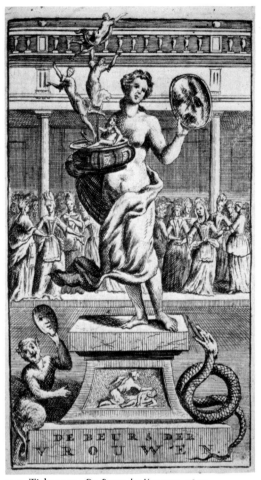

218. From [Jeroen Sweerts], *De Biegt der Getrouwde* (Amsterdam, 1679). Koninklijke Bibliotheek, The Hague

219. Title page, *De Beurs der Vrouwen*, 1690. Koninklijke Bibliotheek, The Hague

of Woman's Vindictiveness) was first included in one of Cats's cautionary tales against philandering. But it became popular enough to be issued as a narrative cartoon with the episodes told in small cartouches in the four corners of the main print. It tells the story of a cuckolded husband who, implored by his wife for forgiveness, forgoes his right to have her executed for her crime. When he is later caught out himself, his vengeful spouse not only has him decapitated but cheerfully wields the sword herself.

At a less hysterical level, the fear of being ensnared in marriage by a wily or unscrupulous woman runs through much of the phobic literature. Jan Mol's *Huwlijks Doolhof* (The Marriage Maze)[148] and the *Biegt der Getroude* (The Marriage Trap) were catalogues of the ruses, stratagems and duplicities of which courted and wedded women were capable. Both the frontispiece of Sweerts's little book (the sequel to the *Ten Entertainments of Marriage*) and van de Venne's profuse engraving the *Afbeeldinghe des Huwelyx onder der Gedaante van een Fuik* (The Sketch of Marriage in the Form of a Trap) use the image of a fish or lobster trap to exemplify the helplessness of the deluded lovers.[149] The Sweerts frontispiece also has a doleful male holding a mouse in a trap—another stock conceit—while the devil (seated on the trap) negotiates the courtship. Below right are the mixed blessings that await the marriage—masked deceit, tearful wailing and a houseful of children. Van de Venne's much earlier engraving was a visual anthology of the ills of wedded and unwedded love. A wedding procession at the center, accompanied by the musicians that were the traditional emblems of family harmony, walks towards the trap, already well stocked with families—from which one has been violently abducted by a

220. Theodor Matham after Adriaen van de Venne, *Toneel der Vrouwelijcke Wraakzierigheid*. Bodleian Library, Oxford

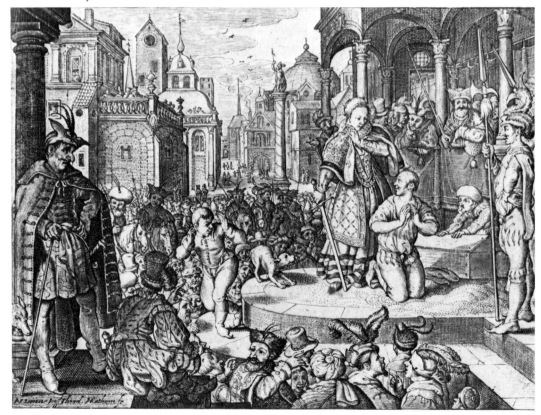

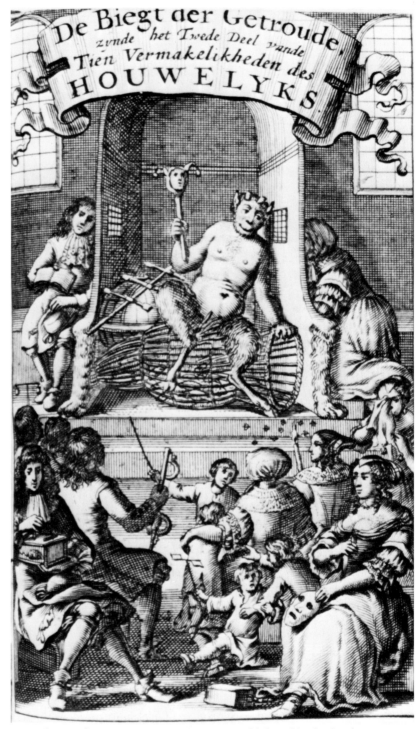

221. Title page from *De Biegt der Getrouwde*. Koninklijke Bibliotheek, The Hague

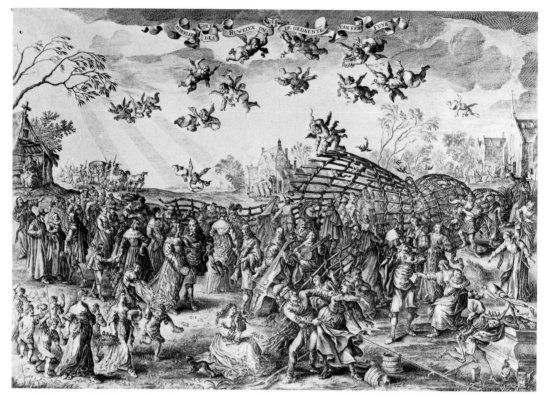

222. Adriaen van de Venne, *Afbeeldinghe des Huwelyx . . .* from *Complete Works,* 1658. Houghton Library, Harvard University

soldier. Significantly, outside the trap various kinds of extramarital complications take place, including the figure of a whore holding a lantern ("A beauteous whore is like a lantern without a light," ran the proverb) and an abandoned mother thrusting a betrothal writ on the delinquent father (bottom right). In the center foreground, a forlorn (and forsaken?) Venus, holding a sprig of myrtle, the lovers' totem, weeps while to her left putti and maidens strew rosebuds as they hold the flag of marriage with its symbol of two clasped hands. In the remote background one of Griet's minions thrashes her husband out of the house, while at bottom left, death claims the couple surrounded with the emblems of passing time—winged hourglass, smoke and wreath.

That image, left over from the darker shades of the northern Renaissance, is a reminder that both the older as well as the more modish attacks on conjugal sentimentality belonged to the tradition of the Follies, where perennial vices are exemplified in contemporary manners. But while the older satires made free use of allegorical devices in their didactic exercises, the art of the later works was to dwell on the business of everyday life. It was an evolution akin to that taking place in still life and genre painting in which, after 1660 or so, the material world gradually came to dominate the gently receding presence of moral symbolism. *De Tien Vermakelijkheden des Houwelijks* (The Ten Entertainments of Marriage) was particularly artful in the way in which it used the calendar of married life — in particular its celebratory feasts and parties — to indicate the successive stages of downfall. The finery of the wedding feast, the gorgeous apparel of the bride and the luxurious setting to which she had evidently been accustomed — Venetian mirrors, gilt-stamped leather hangings, ebony tables and silver dishes — are all taken as omens of the awful extravagance to come. After a period when the wife supposes herself to be infertile, and lets herself be duped by spurious "French" quacks, who fill the house with the reek of burning underthings soaked in urine (the standard "test" to ascertain pregnancy), she finally conceives and develops insatiable cravings for only the sweetest (and often most expensive) items: asparagus, pineapple, strawberries in wine and sugar, almond tarts and pasties, freshly made marzipan, white peaches and black cherries. When the baby finally appears the husband is called on to supply first the *kraamfeest,* caviar, oysters and sweet Rhine wine ("he saw that all of this was just wife-apery and extravagance but he was busy with birth-cakes and ox-tongues and smoked meats"[150]) and then later the *kindermaal* when it is breeched.

Although at the outset the author described marriage as "so crazy that one might as well don a cap and bells," the satire is relatively gentle throughout. The epilogue, however, takes a more solemn tone, commenting on "those many marriages which are so contrary and ill-assorted in humor that they are like light striving against darkness and become a living hell of curses, quarrels, even fighting and striking."[151] What could be responsible for such unhappy outcomes? They were not laid exclusively at the door of wives, for the stories also acknowledged that men could be "drunken beasts," "tyrants and monsters," without any provocation from their other half. And it urged intending wives to "detest gamblers like the plague, for even their winnings are losses; avoid idlers and loungers for they too are unworthy."[152] Nonetheless, it was when he came to list the more peculiarly female destructive traits that the writer really got into his stride. "Mostly," a bad marriage could be attributed to "the peevish, domineering, prodigal, selfish, haughty and wild nature of many of the female sex. . . . Many of them go about setting horns on their husband's head; many others forget themselves in brandywine and other strong drinks and go around all day thoroughly polluted" (the wonderful Dutch metaphor of *met een nat zeyl* — three sheets to the wind).[153]

If, according to these misogynist satires, all women were capable of doing mischief, some were more intent on it than others. All these tales and modern parables feature a subset of wicked women whose particular vocation in life is to inflict as much havoc as possible on the domestic order. And the worst of it was that they were very well placed to do so, for they provided necessary labor and services without which the household routine would not function at all. By virtue of their residence in the home, maidservants were the most subversive, but they were often supported by accomplices in knavery, whose visits at critical times in the domestic calendar gave them special opportunities for malice: in particular midwives and wet-nurses. Most such women—and especially maidservants—were hired from the lower orders, and the implication in the bourgeois satires was that home wrecking or abusing its trust was an oblique form of social rebellion, directed simultaneously and gratifyingly at men and at the propertied.

Midwives and wet-nurses feature as custodians of feminine secrets and the accomplices of their abuse. It was their intimacy with a world from which the male was, if not wholly excluded, then certainly at a distance, and their strategic position to commit dynastic fraud that made them automatically suspect. And in the *Beurs der Vrouwen,* pregnant women and their two kinds of accomplices share a "pillar" (for this is the stock exchange) where they form a kind of conspiratorial league against fathers and husbands. Midwives were often characterized as prime collaborators in plots to dupe husbands, or when an unmarried girl had slept with many suitors, selecting the most desirable as the putative father. They were equally suspected of exchanging children or covering for a wife's infidelity. (Quack physicians, too, as the enormous genre of *piskijken,* pee-gazing, pictures suggests, were suspected of colluding in a wife's amorous intrigue since they were the first to learn of its consequences.)[154] Midwives were also thought of as objectionably bossy, undermining the authority of the head of the household by demanding that expectant mothers eat all manner of odd foods, first in the interests of conceiving and then to ensure safe deliveries. Wet-nurses were a less "learned" and therefore less threatening group, and since doctors and divines alike were unanimous in urging breast-feeding on mothers, it is difficult to know whether they were a common feature of the middle-class household. But they were often typified as encouraging the young mother's lust for *snoeperij,* sweet things, enjoying them themselves while neglecting the baby. "They are so sluttish and slothful," said the author of the *Beurs*, "that they let everything lie around getting filthy and stinking."[155] It was their reputed habit of feeding the babe on impure paps or using strong liquor to make it drowsy that made them seem a threat to the health of the new generation. "Look for the wet-nurse," ran a popular saying, "and you will find her in the cellar." Horror stories of babies burned on the fire or drowned in a cask did the rounds, reinforcing their reputation for dereliction of duty.

All of this delinquency, however, paled in comparison with the crimes and misdemeanors of which maidservants were said to be capable. They were indisputably regarded as the most dangerous women of all, for they represented the presence of the footloose inside the home. Unmarried but nubile, entrusted with essential domestic work (but notoriously untrustworthy), they were thought of as a kind of surreptitious fifth column for worldliness, stationed in the heart of the conjugal home. There is no doubt, at any rate, that they marked a strong presence in Dutch urban society. According to Haks, servants made up around six percent of the whole population of Holland and between ten and twenty percent of all Dutch households had at least one servant in the middle and late seventeenth century.[156] Very often, however, the maidservant was the only servant. In the Zeeland town of Goes in 1642, seventy percent of households had just one maid; in Veere in 1682, the figure was eighty percent.[157] The great majority of these servants were women, and seem to have stayed in a single post on average between two and three years.[158] And the conditions of their hire were of such importance that in a number of towns, official ordinances (*dienstbode-reglementen*) were promulgated, setting up arbitration machinery to settle disputes between masters and servants. Surprisingly, these gave the servants at least some semblance of protection against arbitrary treatment. For if they had to have solid references from their last post to gain lawful employment, the employer was forbidden to fire a servant without due cause before the stated term of original hire — usually six months — was up. In Zeeland in the later seventeenth and early eighteenth centuries, there were eight cases in which the servant's side of a dispute was upheld by the magistrates.[159] None of this official intervention did much to calm the fretfulness about maidservants, for the anxiety about their being both unreliable yet indispensable marked the birth of an authentically bourgeois neurosis.

The literature of the sly, shiftless or insubordinate servant was not, of course, confined to the Dutch or indeed to the seventeenth century. It was one of the richest and earthiest of the comic genres of social mockery, and a variant of a still more ancient fool lore. In those highly stylized comedies, the fool is permitted to abuse and rail at his master the better to avoid, rather than provoke, a general and unlicensed attack on hierarchy. The fool takes on the master's own role of self-caviling while excluding outsiders from a more genuinely critical impertinence. When fools turned servants, though, the loyalty of their candor became more questionable and the line between salutary frankness and subversive insolence more ambiguous.

Dutch literature is full of maidservants who take obvious pleasure in speaking their mind before master and mistress. And their attitude in paintings of domestic life is anything but obsequious. It might perhaps have been expected of bourgeois households that they would seek to establish very firm lines of deference to masters by servants, the better to uphold their own social overlordship. And where the grandest patrician households boasted a staff of three to five servants, something of these common European conventions held good. But in the vast majority of family households, where one or two servants was the rule, boundaries concerning dress, eating habits or rooms were very feebly defined. The fact that in any number of family portraits it is difficult to distinguish the nursemaid from the mother, or even the fact that a servant was axiomatically included in the painting, gives the strongest possible sign of integration within the family circle. Older servants were as much intimates as employees of the family, and they inherited from traditional prototypes the expectation of a kind of homely rudeness but without the accompanying assumption that they were the chattels of their master. Servants who had passed the test of years and had advanced beyond the point where their

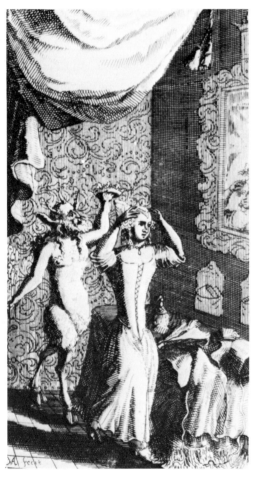
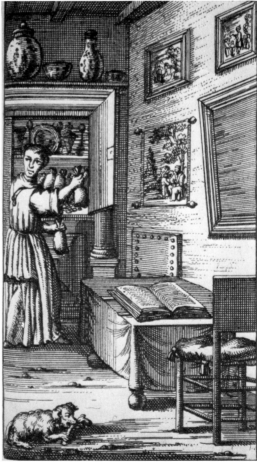

intimacy was fraught with dangers were, of course, the ideal. But younger women remained risky, their very integration within the residential family making it vulnerable to any betrayal of trust.

Household manuals pay great attention to the wife's responsibility for minimizing those risks by keeping a watchful eye on the maidservants. Never take one in your house without impeccable references, warned the *Ervarene en Verstandige Hollandsche Huyshoudster.*[160] Feed them decently, but avoid tea and coffee, which breed bad habits, in favor of the more healthful ale. If they insist "on the modern manner," then content them with a little coffee in the morning and a little dish of tea at noon. Make sure that they are not wasteful with the family's food by leaving hams or cheeses around to go moldy, butter to melt and bread to go stale. Pay them modestly (though not stingily) to begin with, and give them bonuses of a few guilders at the end of the year if

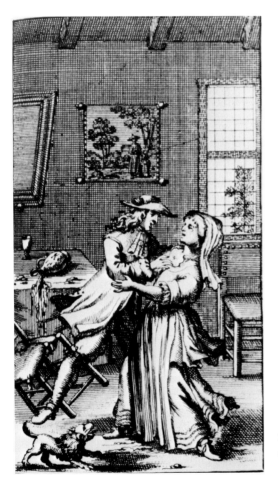

223–5. From [S. de Vries], *Seeven Duyvelen Regeerende Hedendaagsche Dienst-maghden,* 4th ed. (Amsterdam, 1682). Koninklijke Bibliotheek, The Hague

they are satisfactory. Always see that they have a detailed routine of domestic work and that they observe the proper times for the proper chores. Speak to them without gruffness, but discourage insolence as well as gossip, backbiting and toadying. Above all, forbid any undue familiarity between men and women servants, for in such intimacies lurk the seeds of domestic havoc.

The assumption underlying all this cautionary advice is that, if left unguarded, the naturally vicious instincts of the maidservant would assert themselves and turn the household upside down. The most graphic expression of that view was another misogynist satire of the 1680s, *The Seven Devils Ruling Present-Day Maidservants*.[161] An infuriated tract against the decadence of manners and the aping of French modes and fashions, it used the premise that the devil had conspired to destroy the Fatherland from within by insinuating demons into its homes, there to lure Dutch women to several and particular kinds of moral iniquity. And the devil's intimates and accomplices in this work were, of course, the maidservants. There then follows a typical catalogue of all the vices conventionally imputed to maids: their insubordination, laziness, garrulousness, insatiable appetite for food and drink. Some of the worst were even capable of "converting" otherwise dutiful and upright housewives to bad ways, egging them on, for example, to buy expensive clothes or finery for the house against the express wishes of their husbands. But the most pervasive and successful of the devils were the *diefachtige* and the *hoeraachtige*—theft and lust—in close alliance. The thieving maid had a whole repertoire of diabolical little tricks and ruses to cover her traces. Bottles that had been surreptitiously opened in the cellar might be carefully recorked and filled with water. Servants would themselves point out that a silver spoon was unaccountably missing and ask the mistress for money to replace it. They then would buy a cheap substitute at market and pocket the difference as well as the original spoon.[162] As agents of the devil of lust, though, maidservants were virtually unstoppable. They were, after all, nubile and very often "mansick" and could make themselves deliberately alluring, exposing their bosoms or their calves while pretending to work, wearing flimsy clothing or claiming in the middle of the night that they were frightened by thieves or ghosts and needed comforting. By such devilish ruses they could ensnare impressionable young sons, seduce husbands or trap new widowers into hasty second matches. In Zeeland, the Servants' Ordinance of 1673 provided for the nullification of any match between children of the house and servants and even banished the latter from the province if it could be proved that the children had "fallen prey" to the servants' wiles.[163] The syndrome of the besotted widower was, the author of *The Seven Devils* thought, especially common in Holland, and he delicately compared such follies to "a man shitting in his own hat and then setting it on his head."[164]

Despite the misogynist hysterics of this little book, it did reflect a somber reality in the connection between domestic service, petty crime and sexual misdemeanor. Maidservants were mostly victims rather than opportunists and, as the social inferiors of their employers, were often left defenseless against accusations of having trapped men into unlawful sexual acts. It needed *flagrante delicto* for the law to come to their aid, as in 1646 when neighbors heard the screams of Matthijs Pietersen's maid, Anneke, as he raped her in his warehouse cellar.[165] In 1622 the predikant Tobias Herkenius confessed that he had had sex with his maid (even while betrothed to another woman) and the Edam consistory obliged him to marry her. But that case would never have come to light had not the minister himself confessed — without any idea that he might be made to marry the girl![166] And for every one case that came before the courts, there must have been scores in which the maids were far too intimidated to seek the help of the law. More drastic means of concealment were sometimes attempted, for servants are often the unfortunates, like Barbara Jansdogter in 1659, who show up in the few cases of attempted infanticide.[167] Of the twenty-four trials for this crime brought before the Amsterdam magistrates between 1680 and 1811, twenty-two of the accused were maidservants.[168] Only very rarely did they have the means or the social confidence to pursue their seducers in paternity suits, for in doing so they risked the rebound that moral ignominy would fall on their, rather than the man's, shoulders. Not all such predicaments ended miserably. Some maidservants cohabited with their masters and either, as in Descartes' case, ended by marrying him, or as in Rembrandt's, with Hendrickje Stoffels remaining as concubine-consort, sharing the stewardship of the household and defying the imprecations of the church council's condemnation for fornication.

Whether or not there was a real social continuum between the maidservant fallen from grace (either for petty theft or pregnancy or both), cast out from the house and deprived of her testimonials, and the common prostitute, there was undoubtedly a cultural attitude that saw the effrontery of the whore barely concealed behind the mock-deference of the maid. (Lascivious maidservants were blamed, *inter alia,* for initiating young men into the kinds of vices that then launched them on a life of hardened whoring and boozing.) Occasionally, popular literature placed the blame the other way about, but even then the girl was portrayed as a willing partner in the illicit pleasure. Bredero's whore, "Pale An," who confesses to "running wild since my fourteenth year," speaks of "romping with masters' servants and their sons":

> *My master's eldest son was always pawing at my breasts*
> *I wasn't bothered. I let him do it*
> *You see, he loved me and I was green*

Oh, I'd grab him if he missed me
It happened once that while I made his bed
He caught me in his arms and threw me on the sheets
I can't begin to tell what fun the fellow had
Before he had his way . . .
'Twasn't bad at all — oh 'twas sweet.[169]

Whether victims or willing parties, there is no doubt at all that maidservants are prominently represented in the petty theft cases in the Amsterdam *Confessie Boeken,* and that many had connections with the underworld of fencing, whoring and procuring. Their entry might begin with a small lapse that could send them to the Spinhuis, where they would mingle with more seasoned offenders. In 1673, for example, Grietje Ijsbrandts, aged fourteen, was sentenced to two years' confinement for stealing three spoons.[170] And others convicted at about the same time were not much older: Neeltje Reynders, eighteen, committed for stealing her employer's coat; Lysbet Barent, for taking material from her master, an apothecary, in 1671. Some women might end their careers as they began. In July 1646, Barbara Jansdr., aged fifty-four, was convicted of stealing shirts, nightshirts and breeches from a Portuguese Jew even though she swore that she had bought them on the Nieuwmarkt.[171] Maidservants in The Hague specialized in another, more impressive skill: springing prisoners (often their brothers or lovers) from the Gevangepoort jail, for which a whole succession were sent to the Spinhuis or the flogging scaffold.[172]

Domestic service, then, was viewed as a kind of Trojan horse of worldliness effecting an illicit entry into the moral citadel of the burgher household. This is not to say, of course, that there were not maidservants who were regarded as loyal, trustworthy, diligent and pure. But there was no literature, popular or polite (and no art either), featuring the exemplary servant. More commonly they were shown as mischief makers, barrier breakers, tracking the outside world in and leading the inside world out into the street.

It is in the guise of imps of confusion that maidservants often appear in genre painting. They smirk in the background as *piskijken* physicians examine the urine of swooning young women for signs of lovesickness. They frolic with fiddlers or flirt in the cellar as the household order collapses around them. Nicolas Maes in particular enjoyed placing them in morally ambiguous situations. In both of these examples, maids are strategically placed at the turning point of a *levenstrap*, directly addressing the beholder and implicating us in the pleasures of temptation. In each case the choice is clearly presented: exalted or base; consecrated or profaned appetites; the world of the body (reinforced by globes and swords) or that of the soul lit by pure daylight. In each case

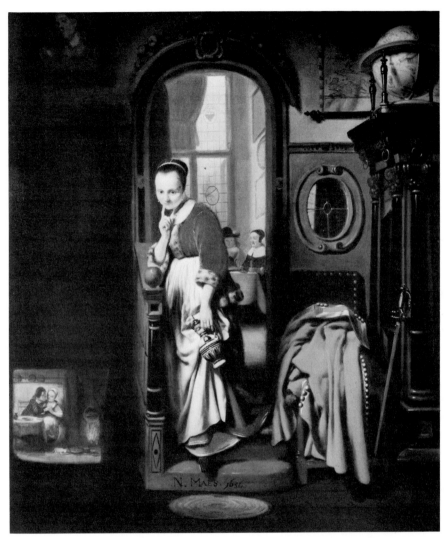

226. Nicolas Maes, *The Listening Maid*, 1656. By permission of the Trustees, Wallace Collection, London

a cat, symbol of wantonness, roots among the dishes as the domestic order falls apart.

These domestic upsets, the moralists argued, were all too easily achieved. For temptations lurked in the most unlikely place — in the heart of the home itself. The iconography of Dutch genre painting has detected erotic undertones in ostensibly humdrum objects like fire tongs, dead fowl or candlesticks. It is difficult to feel unequivocally certain that the symbolic weight carried by these workaday items was invariably transposed from emblem books to pictures. But although we are asked to see these symbols as blatant in their allusions to lust, *and* censorious in their visual commentary, this seems to force the business much further than it need go. The real forte of genre, especially for the "little masters" — Frans van Mieris the Elder, Metsu and Dou — was, as we have already noted, ambiguity, innuendo and temptation. And even where Steen's references are obviously bawdy, the mirth he solicits is often closer to the sly dig in the ribs than the unbuttoned guffaw. Eroticism, after all, feeds on possibilities rather than certainties — and both moralists and libertines had a common interest in lingering over the dangers (or delights) of sensual invitation. So it should not surprise us to see the baits of enticement painted with seductive exquisiteness over and again: glittering glasses of white wine held by the stem in a gesture of invitation; the opened shells of oysters, pink and wet; scarlet hose half rolled down an extended calf; a chemise opened over the swell of the breast.

It was the potential naughtiness of the innocuous — household dogs feature as symbols of both fidelity and mischief — that blurred the moral contours of the household. And when we are unsure whether we are looking at a picture of a home or a tavern, or whether what seems to be a tavern is actually a

227. Nicolas Maes, *The Eavesdropper.* Rijksbeeldende Kunst, The Hague

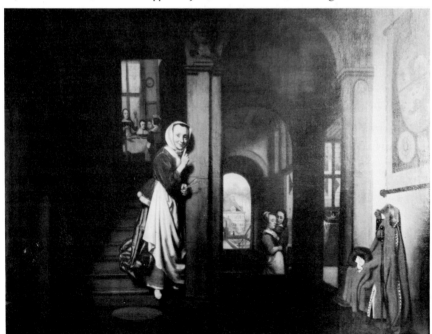

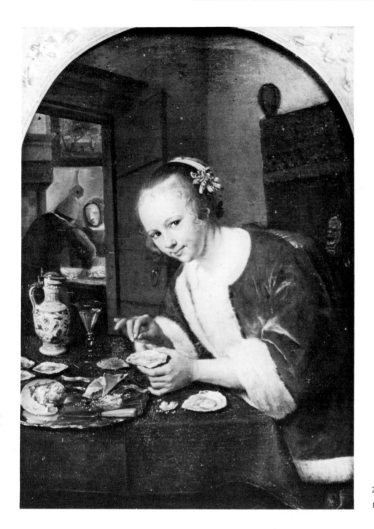

228. Jan Steen, *Girl with Oysters,*
1658–60. Mauritshuis, The Hague

brothel, it may not be because we lack hard-and-fast clues to the artist's unambiguous intention, but because he meant us to be unsure. Jan Steen's home, after all, *was* (at least for a while) a tavern. It would be futile to attempt to distinguish between scenes of good homely fun and public-house dissipation, because the figurative and actual territories were themselves deliberately mixed up. Where goings-on take place in the household or, conversely, children run around with gleeful worldliness in a tavern, there is a good chance that the picture is about the commingling of innocence and corruption.

The obscuring of moral boundaries occurred as much in the representation of "high" as of "low" life. The old Renaissance tradition of merry companies, gardens of love and *fêtes galantes,* both poetic and visual, had made fashion a

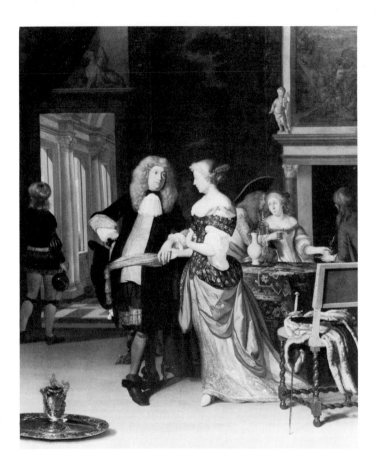

229. Eglon van de Neer, *Elegant Couple in an Interior,* c.1680. Private collection on loan to the Museum of Wales, Cardiff

perennial euphemism for amorous dalliance. Even when it appeared that the genre was exhausted, a new generation would rediscover the didactic useful-ness of ridiculing high manners in the name of homely virtues. In 1680, when ornate "French" fashions were said to be undermining plainer native style, Eglon van der Neer placed courting couples in balletic, *contrapposto* stances amid silverplate and baroque stone galleries while overlooked by the obliga-tory bawling cupid.[173] Other, similar studies by van der Neer were more obviously high-class brothel scenes, but this picture enjoys wandering freely in that indeterminate moral zone between refinement and decadence. Who-ever else they are, van der Neer's overdressed lounge lizards are obviously low types in high fashion.

The same moral slipperiness expressed itself in the venerable genre of courtesan literature. The *Spiegel der Vermaarde Courtisanen* (The Mirror of the Most Celebrated Courtesans), first published in 1630, was but one of a prolific

Renaissance genre that had exploited a peculiar kind of sexual snobbery by anthologizing the potted biographies and portraits of courtly kept women. Few of those portraits in either prose or line engraving were obviously salacious. Indeed, the line between proper and improper courtly life was made even more indistinct by the portraits' similarity, in most cases, to conventional engravings of duchesses and princesses. And where the origin of the courtesan was common (as in the case of Nell Gwyn), the descriptive verses not infrequently seem to celebrate rather than deplore the kind of social opportunism her career represented. The French verses were especially noncommittal. "La Belle Marotte de Nancy," for example, is made merely to recite her curriculum vitae—with a certain understated respect for aristocratic gallantry to boot:

> *Un beau prince de Dandemont*
> *Rempli d'ardeur et de courage*
> *Ravit ma fleur et pucellage*
> *Et m'emmena dans le piemont.*[174]

The Dutch verses, it need hardly be said, endeavor to clear up some of this moral shilly-shallying. "La Belle Angloise" is made to ruminate that *"Waar 't gout begint,/Is deugd maar wind"* (Where gold begins, / Virtue is but air). Yet of course the very publication of this evidently popular little book, and the many others like it, was a symptom of disingenuousness.

The moral limbo between fashionable kept women and common whores was filled, at least at the end of the seventeenth century, by the literature of the *zalet-juffers*. Best translated as "demi-mondaines," they featured in anthologies of stories or light bawdy comedies modeled on fashionable women of easy virtue from English Restoration libertine productions who came from, and pandered to, the immorality of the well-to-do. (Ariosto went through a burst of Dutch reprints at the end of the century.) In their Dutch incarnation, they were presented as a commentary on the evils of high living, loose morals and foreign fashions—especially French. In the cheery detail of the many ruses and stratagems by which the "salon princesses" duped and deceived men and exploited their gullibility, they were throwbacks to the older tradition of the artful mistress. And one book invented whole "guilds" and secret societies with codes of practices "that were more strictly observed than those of the Old and the New Testament.[175] At their conventicles each of the members would recite the chronicle of her latest triumphs over hapless imbecile males for the general entertainment of the company. Special commendation was reserved for the initiation efforts of promising novices, so that "Bonnatrice" was congratulated for breaking open her father's house safe and stealing fifteen

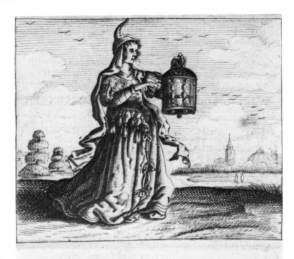

230. Adriaen van de Venne, "Though a whore may have a beauteous face, ' tis a lantern without a light," from Jacob Cats, *Spiegel van de Oude en de Nieuwe Tyt* (Rotterdam, 1627). Houghton Library, Harvard University

Al heeft een hoer een schoon gesicht/
'Tis een lanteerne sonder licht.

hundred guilders and then incriminating the innocent serving maid in the theft.[176] It was with devilish relish that she went on to describe the servant dragged off to prison by her hair. When the hoard was all used up, more could be had from short stays in a brothel or by cheating at cards or threatening to expose rich whorehouse clients to public notoriety.

The world represented in *The Life and Profession of Present-Day Zalet-Juffers* was not wholly fictitious. There was certainly a whole group of high-class whores who catered to a more expensive clientele and who, like their more tawdry sisters, were linked with fencing and all manner of petty larcenies. It is even not impossible that figures like the Machiavellian Artesia, whose sexual prodigies and criminal resourcefulness had made her the high priestess of the sisterhood, really were launched in their careers by the bankruptcy of a wealthy but prodigal father. And there may have been flamboyant figures like the mysterious "Duchess Emma," who spoke French, boasted fine carriages and liveried servants, and who was, in reality, "Mooy Agt" (Pretty Agt) the procuress. But many of the picaresque anecdotes relating the humiliation of hapless males at the hands of demonic and ruthless women had their source in ancient male paranoia about the succubic female rather than in any concern for social documentation. That women were out to drain men of their vital sap was the underlying view of writers like the author of *Venus Minsieke Gasthuis,* who reported a man tempted by two whores to ejaculate more than the allowed four times, and who, on the fifth, spent himself in his own blood.[177]

What both the Calvinist homilies and the misogynist satires document, however, is the Dutch male fixation — part fantasy, part reality — of lairs of vice lying in wait for the unsuspecting. The ever-vigilant Cats was little short of obsessed with this threat and in one of his works provided no fewer than five emblems, all dealing with the terror of sickness and disease dressed up in the guise of beauty. The beauty of courtesans and whores was "a lamp without a light," one that would burn and deform.[178] And those same obsessions and anxieties — and double standards — made themselves felt in literature that dealt with out-and-out common prostitutes. In some respects brothel lore like brothel painting was less complicated and less beguiling than closely related fancies on maidservants and *zalet-juffers*. Where the sly servant and her world represented the subversive *within* the home and so needed constant watching and patrolling/invigilating, the brothel was quite plainly an antihome, a counterhome, just as in this system of moral opposites the tavern was always thought of as a counterchurch. The procuresses were the antimothers: their wrinkles those of evil rather than piety, their prayers to Satan rather than God. And the girls themselves made up a kind of antifamily lodged in an antihome where they unlearned all the lessons which the bona fide home was organized to instill. (Until quite recently, the red-light establishments in Amsterdam struck tourists as quaintly cozy, travesties of the Dutch bourgeois household or the bric-a-brac bibelot shop, full of knickknackery, lace curtains, bibelots and potted plants, with their own gaudy version of *gezelligheid*.) In the seventeenth-century moralists' canon, the *musicos* and *speelhuizen* were schools of vice, just as home was the great school of virtue. On their premises, dirt, theft, squalor, deceit, drunkenness, immoderation inverted humanism's domestic norms: cleanliness, honesty, comfort, sobriety and moderation.

Only Bernard de Mandeville (transplanted to England) had the stunning insight that these two moral worlds, ostensibly at opposite poles, were in fact functionally related to each other. The moral salubrity of a seaport like Amsterdam, he argued in *A Modest Defence of Publick Stews* (in 1724), was actually dependent on the unofficial toleration of brothels, so that zones of purity and impurity were clearly marked, and honest housewives might go unmolested by what would otherwise be the uncontrollable licentiousness of the maritime population. "If courtesans and strumpets were to be prosecuted with as much rigor as some silly people would have it," he complained, "what locks and bars would be sufficient to preserve the honor of our wives and daughters? . . . Some men would grow outrageous, and ravishing would become a common crime."[179] By the same lights, though, the magistracy, which in reality condoned this convenience of civic hygiene (as well as the constabulary, who took payoffs from the houses), were obliged to hand down exemplary punishments, maintain a house of correction (the Spinhuis) for a few and patrol the district as though dedicated to its obliteration. "So by this means appearing unblameable," Mandeville reiterated in *The Fable of the Bees,* "the wary magistrates preserve themselves in the good opinion of the weaker sort of people who imagine that the government is always endeavoring, though unable, to suppress what it actually tolerates."[180] This deliberately imperfect invigilation, Mandeville argued, was in everyone's best interests and amounted to a kind of constructive civic hypocrisy that contrasted well with sanctimonious humanist utopianism. While its principles may have looked inconsistent, its practice actually upheld the normative code of the city without ever making it so absolute as to jeopardize prudent administration.

Mandeville's candor doubtless horrified the Dutch magistracy, as it certainly did the English. Yet he was absolutely correct in supposing that the world of virtue and vice lived in practice in a kind of symbiotic interdependence —at least in port cities like Amsterdam and Rotterdam. (The Hague, as one might expect, generated another kind of prostitution, around the demi-monde fringes of the court and what might be called its ancillary service industries— music houses, theaters and the like.) And there was a further, much more traditional aspect of the geography of venal sex that lent support to Mandeville's unsentimental notion of *de facto* official connivance. For the throngs of whores that plied their trade at fairs, "year-markets" and *kermisses* were extremely conspicuous and expected. In keeping with the implied notion of the moral exceptionality of these special occasions,[181] held, very often, on the outskirts of the large cities or in country market towns, jurisdiction over moral misdemeanors was correspondingly more relaxed. And there were some assemblies, like the Valkenburg horse fair, that were very well known for their whores, who descended, like sexual Gypsies, on the makeshift taverns and stalls in great troops. In 1611 one Willem Mouring went so far as to offer the bailiff of Wassenaar eighty guilders to be officially permitted to set up his platoon of Amsterdam girls at the horse fair and was initially turned down only because the sum seemed too paltry for so lucrative a license![182]

This benign disingenuousness was of a piece with other varieties of moral pluralism in which inconsistencies of principle were set aside (though not completely suppressed) for the sake of effective social management. To compare a whorehouse with a lottery, a *doelen* feast or the stock exchange (and there were some ministers of the church who did exactly that) is not to cast aspersions on the latter but to point up the many—but connecting—ways in which the Dutch managed to sustain a set of regulating ethics while living in the midst of an otherwise uncontrollable fleshly appetite–provoking world. For, as the anonymous author of *'t Amsterdamsch Hoerdom* succinctly put it, "the world cannot be governed Bible in hand."[183]

I suppose it served the Amsterdam magistracy right if their serpentine

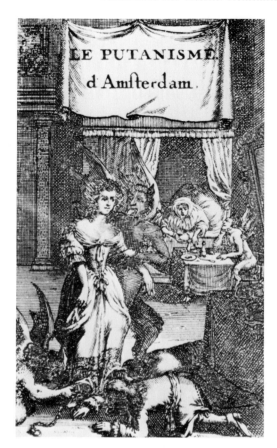

231. Anon. woodcut. Title page to French edition of *Amsterdam's Whoredom* ('s Gravenhage, 1694). Koninklijke Bibliotheek, The Hague

strategies for what might be called a prophylactic approach to civic morality was travestied or turned upside down for purposes that were entirely amoral. *'t Amsterdamsch Hoerdom,* the prototype of the popular eighteenth-century genre of whores' directories, was a little book that first appeared in Rotterdam in 1681 and subsequently enjoyed great popularity in several languages. It parodied official morality by purporting to be the "tour" of a Rotterdam police official of Amsterdam's low-life. Even the ancient literary device of an "invisible presence," which Vondel had used to transport Gijsbrecht van Amstel to the metropolis of the mid-seventeenth century, was borrowed for an altogether cruder production. From the didactic tone of the introduction (omitted in French editions!) one might imagine this to be an exemplary work of Erasmian humanism or Calvinist sermonizing: "The manifold disasters and misfortunes that now occur daily all have their origin in commerce with whores." And what follows is meant to "open the eyes of dumb and thoughtless youth" to the frightful consequences of frequenting *musicos* and gaming houses.[184]

Despite this unconvincing attempt to strike a proper tone, it becomes immediately apparent that the work is in effect not a tract but a punter's handbook, a detailed and evidently very knowledgeable gazetteer to Amsterdam prostitution. Its warnings were much more practical than moral, and more concerned with the safety of the customer's pocketbook than with the state of his soul. As a manual to sexual low-life, *'t Amsterdamsch Hoerdom* had much going for it. From its duodecimo size, its crude engravings and its mixture of obscene humor, chatty narrative and spurious documentary style, it was obviously catering to a popular readership — perhaps, like the pseudo-narrator, out-of-town provincials visiting the bad city and unsure whether they wanted their sex vicariously or direct. (There are many such latter-day introductions available at Amsterdam railway station bookstalls.) Surprisingly, perhaps, much of its description is corroborated by the details that can be gleaned of prostitutes' lives and practices from the judicial sources of the *Confessie Boeken*.

232. Map of prostitution in 17th-century Amsterdam

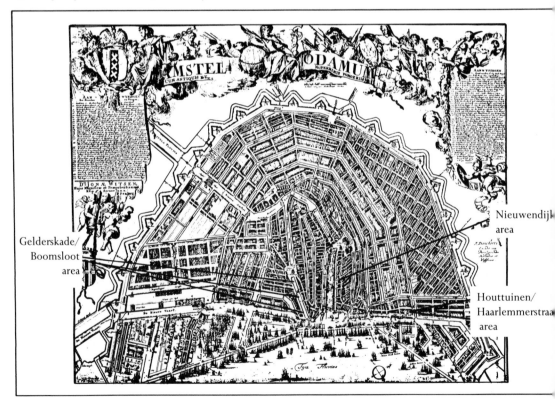

Gelderskade/
Boomsloot
area

Nieuwendijk
area

Houttuinen/
Haarlemmerstraa
area

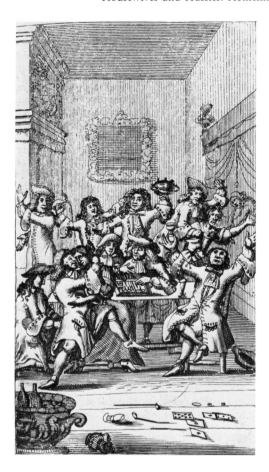

233. Anon woodcut, from
Amsterdam's Whoredom. Koninklijke
Bibliotheek, The Hague

The geography of prostitution, for example, in both the guide and the judicial declarations, corresponded (unsurprisingly) to the port areas of the city. So one of the first sights that would strike the incoming traveler, whether by barge from Haarlem or by ship at the docks, would be the troops of harlots who congregated around the dockside streets and alleys. Sir William Brereton, who arrived from the west in June 1634, had been warned about the perils of being summarily accosted, virtually at the city limits. "About nine hour we passed Harlemmer Port and came into a fair street, wherein of late swarmed the most impudent whores I have heard of who would if they saw a stranger come into the middle of the street unto him, pull him by the coat and invite him into their house."[185] He was spared this ordeal by a purge carried out three months earlier that seemed to have rid the area of its most blatant soliciting.

The change could only have been temporary, however, for the archives are full of girls giving their addresses as the Houttuinen, the Harlemmerdijk and the Harlemmerstraat—all on the western edge of the seventeenth-century city, close both the docks and the cart and barge entry routes. This was, in fact, one of three major axes of prostitution in Amsterdam. The other two were also closely connected with the maritime life of the city and its shifting, transient population of both girls and their clients. The areas also correspond strikingly with the red-light zone today, making prostitution one of the few Amsterdam trades remaining located in their seventeenth-century milieus. It may be some small satisfaction to those women subjected to the stern correction of the Spinhuis that its redundant and grimy facade remains besieged by the flourishing platoons of whores that still ply their trade along the Achterburgwal. One axis of the seventeenth-century zone ran down the Gelderskade at right angles to the eastern dock area of the IJ, with the Zeedijk, then as now, crowded with little drinking and smoking dens where fights broke out so regularly that the bailiff's men hardly bothered to patrol. This line went all the way down to the St. Antonie Breestraat, Rembrandt's street, where in a list of eighteen *musicos* and gaming houses of 1660, we hear of three of that address.[186] East of the Nieuwmarkt, around Bomsloot and the Montelbaan tower, there seems to have been another cluster, but the third major axis was the "central" zone between the Damrak and the Singel, along the Nieuwendijk, where in alleys like the Suikerbakkersteeg, Hasselaarsteeg and Haringpakkersteeg, some of the poorest "street whores" crowded the doorways of tiny unsavory hovels and slop joints. Finally, there were smaller constellations (probably of slightly less squalid establishments) right in the center of town, near the theater, the mint square, and right on the doorstep of the (male) house of correction, at the Heiligerswegpoort and the Nieuwe Spiegelstraat.

Few of these establishments were brothels in the modern sense of being places where customers came specifically for sex and completed the transaction on the premises. More commonly, client and prostitute would meet at a *musico* (or, in the Amsterdam slang, *Meniste bruiloft*, a Mennonite wedding!), a place of drinking and entertainment and dancing known for its girls, and run by a procuress-cum-hostess. Gaming—cards, backgammon or dice—was also an important part of the recreation, so that the hostess profited directly from liquor and gambling and indirectly from sex by charging the girls a rate for the use of her premises to make their contacts and for their out-lodgings (about twenty-five stuivers, or a higher rate of about four guilders if they actually boarded with her). Whether the girls lived in or out, though, they were very definitely the creatures of the procuress, usually an ex-whore herself who had saved enough to go into the entrepreneurial side of the trade. As in all the great metropolitan centers of Europe in the early modern period, this was almost exclusively a female-dominated profession. The exceptions seem only to have been men like Mouring, who were in the business of supplying traveling whores — mobile troops — for fairs and *kermisses* around the country and who followed in the train of quacks, peddlers, Gypsy fortune tellers, and acrobats. The urban procuresses flourished, in effect, through a diversified array of semicriminal activities: receiving stolen goods, smuggling — salt seems to have been a specialty — organized music and dance entertainment, drink and tobacco supplies and, of course, sexual procurement. The girls were indebted to the procuress, not just for food and board as well as their share of earnings from sex, but for the extravagant dress that was thought to be indispensable for the job. In some cases the procuress supplied needed shelter and security to girls who were a long way from their rural birthplaces or from towns in Germany or Danish Jutland. But in the majority of cases, the prostitutes came from localities in Holland itself, so that many may well have migrated to Amsterdam in search of a decent or indecent livelihood.[187]

Like their modern barstool counterparts, the "hostesses" were expected by their procuress to persuade their clients to drink as much as possible of the notoriously filthy liquor before doing any of their own sexual business. And *'t Amsterdamsch Hoerdom* attempted to alert prospective customers to the various ruses awaiting them in the *musicos*. Some of the "wine" was nothing other than candy syrup (at twelve stuivers the jug); sometimes it was adulterated and stretched. Beneath the long bench tables at which whores and men caroused would be the sand and sawdust bins into which the adroit whore would empty her glass, both to invite her "host" to buy her another and to avoid a drunken stupor of her own. Indeed, if the client became too drunk for sex, it was common for the prostitute to make good her loss of income by depriving him of his purse, or at least that part of it that would have paid for her services. And the most successful whores were also accomplished pickpockets who used sexual cunning to distract their customers from their second line of work. *'t Amsterdamsch Hoerdom* (in graphically obscene style) showed one whore at work, helping herself to the purse of a typical customer, a peasant or farmer who had come to town to market his produce and had stayed to drink off some of the proceeds before returning home.

"Come lovey," said the whore to the *boer* who was by her side. "Won't you feel me, and see if I do not have a fine mussel [vagina] on my belly?" The *boer* stuck his hand under her skirt and with two fingers felt inside her hole and said, "You are certainly well set up! In all my life I have never had a bigger *kwedio* [pussy] in my hand." "I can well believe it," said the whore, "that's why I'm called Beeletje [little picture] with the Great Cunt, and I can tell you that in all the city of Amsterdam there is no tart with so great a meat cleaver as me — for you know I can hide a pint can up it. . . ."

"What a devilish cunt is that," said the *boer.* "Let's feel it again" (he duly discovered it to be so). "Now what do you think of that" said the whore. "Come let me feel you now and see if you're as well equipped as me," and she stuck one hand in the front of his breeches and with the other removed his purse. That was so light, however, that he could scarcely have paid her. "You have a big boy in your pants there—we shall go well together." "That's fine with me," says the *boer.*[188]

The whore then disappears to relieve herself, and that was the last the *boer* saw either of her or of his purse.

A lot of this comic business comes straight from the rowdy *kluchtspel* farce tradition of the Amsterdam stage, in which bawds and procuresses were stock figures of low cunning and greed. And it also drew on the older conventions of "rogues and vagabonds" lore for good measure. But for all its lewd farce *'t Amsterdamsch Hoerdom* is not a work of fiction. Its account of the low-life entertainment provided in the *musicos* is evidently faithfully observed and described. The fancier establishments featured hurdy-gurdies, harmoniums or even small organs and competed for the services of Ashkenazi Polish Jewish fiddlers—who absented themselves on the Sabbath days of Friday and Saturday. These musicians worked hard—from four in the afternoon to eleven at night—without much rest, since the clientele, whether seamen or country folk, were eager to hear and dance to their favorite airs. The most requested songs in the late seventeenth century were "Bredas Biertje" (The Breda Small Beer), "The East Indies Rose Tree," "A Parsley Posey." The thumping, crashing dances that the boatmen and the German sailors especially loved included "The Hague Kermis" and "The Cabbage Salad."[189]

If the scene became too rowdy and drunken, if customers (as very often was the case) threatened the whores or the procuress, there were some men on hand to deal with them—though in more than one case it was evident that the lady of the house was more than capable of acting as her own bouncer. Pimps, the *pluggen,* were much rarer than in modern prostitution, and were more usually the protectors of the common street whores than of the girls of the *musicos,* but all gaming, drinking and whoring houses had some servants on hand to cope with trouble. Is it sentimental to see some element of solidarity in their shared occupational habits—and risks? (Honor among the dishonorable?) This precaution did not, of course, prevent the periodic brawls that erupted after a particularly juicy exchange of insults, or accusations of petty theft or client-stealing. "Your cunt must attract flies as well as other stuff," yelled one of the girls in *'t Amsterdamsch Hoerdom.* "I shit on you, Marie, and I stick my arse on your head."[190] She might as well have used the choice abuse of *mockegout* (she stinks), extracted from the ripe repertoire of private slang through which prostitutes, like other semicriminal types, safeguarded their sorority. The vocabulary might differ from place to place. In Amsterdam *migchelen* was to dance, *plug* was a pimp, *plugge-kit* was a brothel and *muyl-peeren* were the johns or tricks. Elsewhere, especially on the road and at fairs, thieves' cant supplied the slang, so that whores became *wederhaen* (chickens) or *glyden*, and the whorehouse a *glydebosch* or a *sonnenbosch*. Money was *bucht* or *monye* and the john was a *smalkage* or *hoerejager*. Passwords were used to help each other cheat the customers at cards or of their purses, and glasses of wine — red or white — were drunk or held in ways to tip each other off about an impending visit by the bailiffs.[191]

This clubbiness was a very small comfort in a grim and uncertain existence. While it would be a naive overstatement to see in the prostitutes' *stille huyzen* a kind of tatty counterfeit version of the *burgerlyke huis,* the *musico* was at least some sort of life raft for women who would otherwise have been without any means of survival. Uprooted, displaced, evicted even from their menial existence in the households of the propertied, unable to subsist on their paltry earnings from sewing or laundering — even if they had no child to support, as many did — they entered a peculiar world that catered specifically to the needs of the away-from-home. It was, as Mandeville surely understood, the Dutch domestic culture turned upside down.

To say as much is not to sentimentalize, in the hearts-of-gold vein, what was obviously a brutal and degrading life. Still less is it to indulge in the kind of wishful historical thinking that turns prostitution into an island of professional, female-run independence in an otherwise patriarchal culture.[192] The over-whelming impression given by the pathetic reports in the *Confessie Boeken* is of a makeshift, rootless, transient and terrifyingly insecure life. Those who survived the years of hard whoring between eighteen and thirty did so at the price of disfigurement from repeated doses of venereal disease, spells in the Spinhuis, repeated banishments and clandestine returns. Taartie Aerssens, who was arrested in 1649, was a twenty-nine-year-old and described as "a whore full of pockmarks and a thief, already banned from the city on pain of further punishment."[193] In all likelihood she was headed for a flogging or a spell on the pillory as well as a sentence in the Spinhuis. If, through some hard-headed knack for survival, prostitutes up in their turn as whorehouse keepers with a small sum to tide them over into old age (anything over fifty), they were still vulnerable to the same if not stiffer penalties of the law and the capricious favors of the *onderschout* (deputy sheriff) and his roughneck bailiffs, all of whom had to be kept sweet by handouts, free beer and girls pretty much on demand.

A few of the girls made an attempt to provide for their future by contracting marriages with those of their clients who offered some hope of security. An East India soldier or sailor, despite a notorious prodigality and addiction to *arrak,* was a prospect, and one of the girls in *'t Amsterdamsch Hoerdom* is said to have had a child by her sailor husband and become pregnant with a second while he was still away! The regularity of these alliances was in any case very dubious, since the lay authorities were highly unlikely to have registered them. Unlike regular members of a church congregation, an abandoned prostitute had no legal or moral compulsions available to summon her errant mate to his parental duties.

Is it possible to sketch a profile of the typical Amsterdam prostitute in mid- and late-seventeenth-century Amsterdam? The *Confessie Boeken* are so rich in biographical detail that they allow at least a kind of collective impression. Our average prostitute, then, would be between eighteen and thirty, though at one extreme there is a case of an eleven-year-old committed to the Spinhuis for whoring, and at the other, there were sad, ruined nightwalkers (*nagtlopers*, in the court term) of forty or even fifty who were apprehended.[194] While she would in all likelihood have come from a village or town in the province of Holland, would probably have known one of the many foreign-born girls who had come to Amsterdam to make a living. One reasonably typical group of six arrested in 1672 comprised a twenty-six-year-old from Zwartsluys and a twenty-four-year-old from Rotterdam, a thirty-four-year-old — probably their procuress — from Amsterdam, another twenty-four-year-old from the Friesland countryside, a twenty-six-year-old from Bruges in the Spanish Netherlands and a nineteen-year-old from Bremen.[195] And the geography of recruitment to prostitution extended further afield — very much along the lines of the Dutch-dominated trade routes — to Scandinavian ports like Bergen, Stavanger and Copenhagen; to the north German port towns of Kiel and Hamburg; and to a ring of neighboring Westphalian towns like Doesburg and Cologne, Lippstadt, Julich and Osnabruck.[196] Like the more distant immigrants, the great majority who came from Dutch towns and villages had come to Amsterdam hoping to make their way as seamstresses, knitters, lace workers or ribbon workers, and many gave those as their occupations (along with the other standby of laundressing) even when they were arrested for prostitution. And this may well have reflected the realities of their working life rather than being a spurious cover. Five prostitutes arrested in 1696, mostly in their teens and early twenties, were all identified as seamstresses as well as whores.[197] Some who set themselves up as brothel keepers retained their "straight" trade name as a moniker to distinguish their house. So that in one whores' directory of the early eighteenth century we find Tryn the Cupping Woman, Lys the Wafflewife, Catryn the Seamstress and Mary the Starcher along with Madame de la Touche and The Honorable Brechie.[198]

Others had fallen from grace as domestic servants in the manner of Bredero's Pale An and had taken to prostitution to support their small children. In one roundup in 1654, for example, one Norwegian girl was caught begging with her child, while another from Hamburg pleaded extenuation, having been abandoned by the young man from The Hague who had made her pregnant.[199] Many others had been caught thieving as well. Usually the items were fairly trifling, like spoons, a napkin or a sheet. Not many were so ambitious as the twenty-three-year-old Jannetje Lamberts from Haarlem, who was caught with a large diamond in her room.[200] Often it was women who had already fenced for them to whom they resorted when discharged from their spell in the Spinhuis or the banishment which many violated a few weeks (or even days) after its imposition. A few seem to have made good use of their knowledge of secret comings-and-goings into the city to profit from smuggling, especially in salt and beer.[201]

The key figures in the trade were the procuresses. Northern art had traditionally represented them as shriveled hags, the better to express their moral infirmity in outward vileness. The reality was rather different. The majority were only somewhat older, in their thirties or early forties, than the three to five whores whom they ran, and some were even younger. "Cathalyn," who went by several aliases and who was picked up with six women in 1634, had a fairly elderly ménage by the standards of the time. Forty-four herself, she kept three whores in their mid- or late twenties, one of whom was her personal maid; another, "Anna with the Jacket," was thirty-six, and the third was a still more veteran soul of fifty. More typical was "Rebecca Frans" of Delft, who was only twenty-five but who kept two other whores a few years younger than herself.

Introduced into a *musico* or *stille huis,* the new prostitute would probably have been given a working nickname, which sometimes marked her origins, like that of Catryn Davids of Copenhagen, who was called Northern Katie, and sometimes picturesque, like that of Annetje Hendricx, who was known as Anna in de Stal, and sometimes much cruder, like that of Krentecut (Currant Cunt) or that of the fifty-year-old procuress Catalyn Laurens, who had always been known as Soetecut (Sweetie Cunt).[202] Those names would stick to her just as long as she remained inside the endless cycle of banishments, violations, confinements and—if deemed truly incorrigible—more drastic and brutal punishments like branding and flogging. There are some extraordinary cases of recidivism that call into question the whole point of penalties for the prostitutes and their keepers, except by way of periodically advertising the city's official commitment to moral propriety. Jannetje Hendricx, alias Jeanne dans le Coin, was arrested when she was forty-three in 1673, exactly thirty years after her first arrest for petty theft. Like other young girls whom the magistrates hoped to reform before they were too inured to a life of vice and petty crime, she was sent to the Spinhuis—for three years, a stiff sentence—only to be banned a year later for malicious slander. She obviously broke her banishment pretty swiftly, for she was to be found back in the Spinhuis just a year later, in 1648. A year on, and already, at eighteen, a pretty hardened case, she was condemned to be flogged on the public pillory but was spared because of her pregnancy. She was instead banished for a long four-year sentence, after having stood in the pillory with a sign on her breast proclaiming her infamy. This was by no means the end of her record, however, which went on to a three-year banishment in 1656, floggings in 1659 and 1663, another banishment in June 1665, followed by a flogging (on a second arrest) in July of the same year, further floggings in 1668 and 1669 and finally another six-year stretch in the Spinhuis, by which time she must have come to know the place pretty well. When she was freed, early in 1672, she was banished; she immediately ignored the sentence and stole a basket from a woman in the Westerkerk, a crime that earned her yet another flogging and three more years back in the Spinhuis.[203]

Jeanne dans le Coin, it should be said, was exceptional in that she doggedly pursued a life of petty crime as well as whoring, and the entire repertoire of penalties seemed impotent to deter her, much less to reform her. Obviously she knew no other life or company and would have been helpless trying to set up as a seamstress or laundress in some small Holland town remote from the Amsterdam underworld that was literally her meat and drink. The same was true for Jannetje Jans, the knitter who followed a similar kind of career as whore and fence and who was arrested eleven times over a fifteen-year period between 1680 and 1695.[204] Soortie Torsens of Monnikendam, who was twenty-six when she was arrested in 1671, boasted *ten* prior convictions and a string of banishments and floggings.[205] It was not always easy to avoid trouble with the law. The best guesses of numbers have arrived at the (suspiciously round) figure of a thousand prostitutes in Amsterdam for the later seventeenth century.[206] And in 1680, the year in which 't Amsterdamsch Hoerdom was written, 125, or twelve percent, were arrested. This figure seems atypically high, and the arrest rate certainly varied considerably from year to year. Prostitutes who got by inside the *musicos* and *stille huyzen*, like the derisively named Hof van Holland (High Court of Holland[!]) or The Rats' Nest on the Binnen Amstel, selling their sex and avoiding either blatant crime or casual violence, stood a reasonable chance of escaping the sheriff's men, especially if their procuress took good care to oblige the men with the necessary sweeteners on regular demand. It was when they were remiss that roundups were organized, so that, for example, Tryntje Barents, described as a fifty-four-year-old whore and ribbon worker—but in fact a procuress—was arrested in 1673 along with one Clara (Claertje) Adriaans, a "laundress" who had done time in the Spinhuis ten years before and who had been dependent on her older colleague ever since. The same sort of roundup occurred in the spring of that year on the Bomsloot, where a *slaapvrouw* (landlady) called Mari Potters kept a house and her girls—a seventeen-year-old, an eighteen-year-old and a twenty-one-year-old—were all hustled off to the Spinhuis.[207] And tellingly, those arrests, as with Machtelt Harman, the forty-year-old procuress of the Boomstraat, picked up in 1668, often referred to the "great insolence and wantonness" of the accused. That usually indicated curses and filthy language used against the *schouts* men, who had pushed them a little too far.[208]

However prudent they were, it was not always easy to get out of the way of the casual violence that flowered in the hard-drink-swigging, knife-toting world of the Amsterdam whorehouses and gaming dens. The girls who were in the keeping of a well-established procuress stood better chances of self-

234. Detail, Hendrick Pot, *Brothel Scene.* Courtesy of the Trustees, National Gallery, London

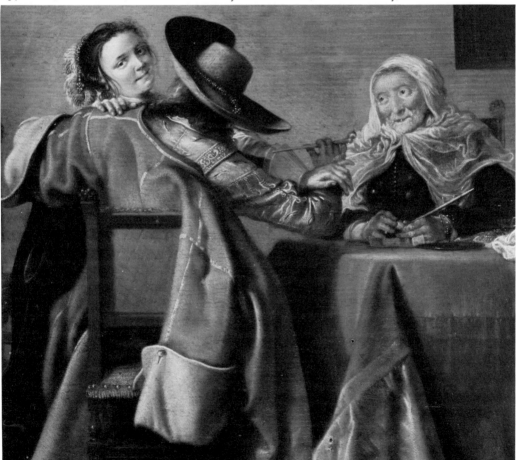

preservation than their back-alley sisters, who not infrequently did their business in the lane to avoid paying for bed and lodgings. And it was the thirty- to- forty-year-olds, riddled with the "Spanish pox," their bodies marked on the outside by flogging and branding and on the inside by mercilessly bad alcohol, women who were shunned by all but the most desperate and transient men—the dregs of a seventeenth-century seaport—that made up the most wretched casualties of a commercial culture.

Though the thought would have horrified the prim ministers who every Sunday summoned fire and brimstone to punish Amsterdam for its whores and whoremongers, the city's sexual entrepôt in some ways was a distorted mirror image of its more licit commerce. Just as its city district snaked round the docks, wharves, barge stations and warehouses, so its buyers and sellers of sexual services faithfully followed the geography of Amsterdam's trading network, with steady business coming from the Baltic trade and the hinter-land of the German river basins, punctuated by occasional bonanzas when the high-spending but notoriously unreliable East India fleets came home. In the moral economy of the Dutch Republic, the whorehouse, with its own family hierarchy, language and habits, was a kind of anti-home, one in which the control functions of domesticity had been turned on their head. Instead of home filtering out the dirt of the world, as all true burghers endeavored to guarantee, the *bordeel* was a place where the world (and its devil, said the predikants) made the comforts. And as much as orthodox wisdoms, humanist as well as Calvinist, insisted that the health and prosperity of the common-wealth required the absolute cleansing of such abomination, their less than diligent practice suggests the truth of Mandeville's perception. Virtue needed vice as a civic prophylactic, a sponge that could soak up all the loathsomeness that would otherwise seep into the purer body of their community. And virtue needed vice to mark off borders just because its own frontiers were so uncomfortably indefinite. Seen in the dim twilight of a guilty commercial conscience, it was all too possible for the wrinkles of pious reflection on a Bible-reading matron's face to transmogrify into the shriveled lines of the vicious hag.

CHAPTER SEVEN

IN THE REPUBLIC
OF CHILDREN

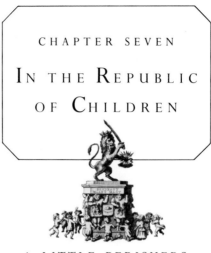

i LITTLE PERISHERS

Dutch art did not invent the image of the mortal child, but it was the first culture to make it impolite. Putti, by definition, cannot have dirty bottoms. At the same time that Rubens was festooning his history paintings with garlands of chubby pink infant sausage meat, Dou incorporated the all too earthy detail of a wiped behind in his witty and complicated genre painting of *The Quack*.[1] Not that this is any indication of hearty baby love, muck and all. For Dou — allegedly the most fanatically fastidious of painters[2] — may have been using the action distastefully among an array of images that connoted the fraud of the world, the baseness that lay behind the prettiness. He may in fact have been quoting the Zeeland Calvinist Johan de Brune's emblem of 1624, in which bottom-wiping is depicted in even more graphic detail. The *inscriptio* of the emblem, though, is the drastically gloomy "What is life/But stink and shit?"[3]

As with so many other emblems of this kind, though, the literally loving detail of the engraving subverts the distaste embedded in the motto. And the striking feature of this, not the only baby emblem in de Brune's book, is less the standard Calvinist expression of world contempt than the pungent homeliness of the image invoked to represent it. Nor is this the only place where the startling and earthy action appears. Jan Miense Molenaer, an artist who reveled in all manner of child painting, but none of it much prettified, used the theme again in his *Sense of Smell*, a Rabelaisian travesty of the familiar Renaissance series of the five senses.

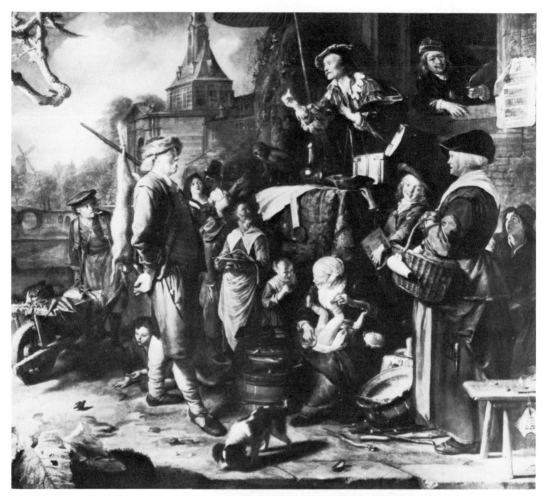

235. Detail from Gerard Dou, *The Quack*, 1652. Boymans-van Beuningen Museum, Rotterdam

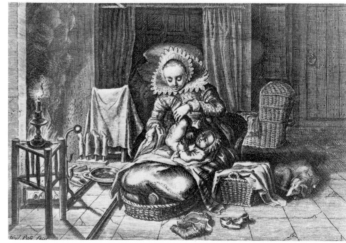

236. Emblem from Johan de Brune, *Emblemata* (Amsterdam, 1624). Houghton Library, Harvard University

Molenaer's scatological belly laugh, de Brune's ostensible severity and Dou's ambiguity all represent a nose-holding view of the baby child. But it is, nonetheless, a view of uncompromising earthiness. There are no cherubic wings, and the mischief here is done with more than cupid's darts. It speaks to us of a culture where babies came with unsavory smells and soiled linen — rather than with goldfinches, pomegranates and other attributes of the infant Jesus. When they suck at the breast, they do not stare with eschatalogically ordained determination at the beholder in the manner of the Christ-child, but bury themselves deep in the bosoms of their Dutch mothers. The depiction of small children in Dutch art, then, often broke out of the symbolic nursery of Christian and Renaissance polite conventions. It would be a mistake to suppose that they were thereby stripped of *any* symbolic frame of reference.[4] For just as the removal of Blessed Virgin Mary icons from images of the nursing mother did not betoken a purely secularized, dispassionately observed naturalism, so the view that Dutch culture had of their young came loaded with all kinds of moral preconceptions and prejudices.

That said, Dutch art nonetheless dumps us unceremoniously in the here-and-now world of little terrors. To walk in any art gallery from a room filled with Dutch landscapes into one where Jan Steen's hell raisers hold sway is to go from a world barely disturbed by the rustling of summer leaves straight into havoc. And in any war of Rubensian putti and Steen's tearaways, the former would be routed by the comprehensive arsenal of horrors that are unleashed in

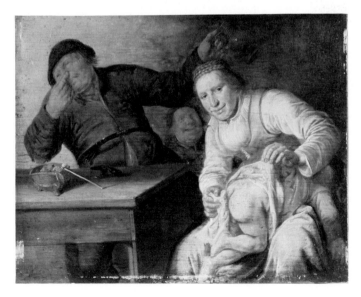

237. Jan Miense Molenaer, *The Sense of Smell,* 1637. Mauritshuis, The Hague

painting after painting. Their repertoire of naughtiness is all too real: not just face pulling, dish banging, cackling, yowling, howling, bellowing pandemonium, but gleeful pulls on pipes, swigging jars of ale and *roemers* of Rhenish. No pocket of a sleeping adult goes unpicked, no feebleness unmocked. Parlor floors are strewn with the predictable debris of smashed toys and broken eggs and trampled crockery. Yet the same children may be summoned by the same artist to grace and peace in moments of simple household routine.

That many of these pictures come loaded with messages about the follies of the world and that, in the many "as the old sing, so the young pipe" paintings, it is adult misconduct that leads children astray does not alter in the least the important fact that the *stock* of images of childhood from which such morals could be represented had changed in the most dramatic way. So the replacement of the putto by the little perisher is a moment of high significance not just in the history of art but in that of Western culture's view of its children. And the historian is bound to ask whether it in fact announces the "new world of children" that is said to have arisen a century later in England.[5] Was it the moment when children were emancipated from *both* their "medieval invisi-

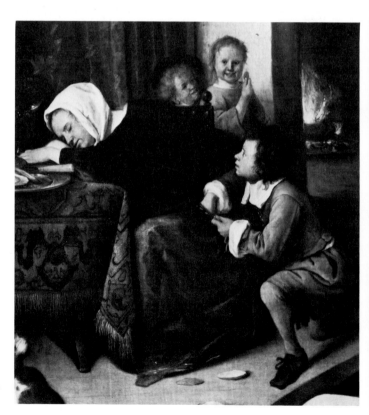

238. Detail from Jan Steen, *The Disorderly Household*, 1668. Wellington Museum, Apsley House, London

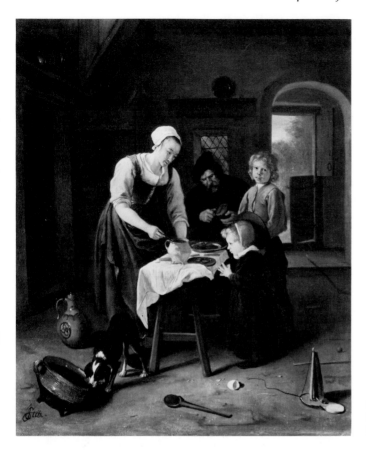

239. Jan Steen, *Saying Grace.*
Courtesy of the Trustees, National
Gallery, London

bility," as Philippe Ariès characterized it,[6] *and* from the patriarchal, evangelical
intimidation that seemed to be the price paid for Renaissance and Reformation visibility? Did it mean that children were now regarded neither as
miniature adults nor as vessels brimming with sin that needed emptying and
refilling with the milk of Christian humility and obedience? Were they now
seen and cherished for what they were, dirty diapers and all?

Travelers to the Republic were certainly surprised and disconcerted by the
softness with which children were treated. There was altogether too much
kissing and cuddling going on for the likes of Robinson and the pilgrims at
Amsterdam and Leiden. The prevailing custom of giving young children a
good-night kiss before settling them down was looked on by the sterner
Calvinists as a revolting habit, but even less doctrinaire souls, like William
Aglionby, thought that Dutch parents were far too indulgent towards their
young. Indeed, he claimed that they were punished for it "for many of them

rebel against their parents and at last go away to the Indies." And he was even more disturbed by their imperviousness to the notion of spoiling. "When any body tells them of their fondness to children, they presently say, 'Does anyone spoil their own face or cut off their nose?' "[7]

These are, of course, superficial and fragmentary impressions. Together with the ubiquitousness of children of all ages and conditions in their art, they tempt the conclusion that the Dutch were indeed fixated on their children to a degree and in a manner arrestingly unlike those of other European cultures. But it cannot be emphasized too strongly that fixation is not the same thing as benign liberation — and not, I think, the kind of affable mateyness attributed to the Hanoverian romper.[8] And though I do believe that the treatment of Dutch children went a long way towards rescuing them from some confining stereo-types, the way in which that happened presupposed that they were immediately saddled with many others. What we do *not* have is a brave new world of clearly defined zones of adults and children, with the former straining to comprehend the special needs and sensibilities of the latter. Our guide to the Dutch Republic of children had still better be Erasmus than Dr. Spock.

ii   BETWEEN THE WINDMILL AND THE WALKER

In the Kunsthistorisches Museum in Vienna there is a *Christ Carrying the Cross* by Hieronymus Bosch. Originally the panel formed the left wing of a triptych, which almost certainly had a *Crucifixion* and a *Lamentation* on its other wings.[9] It was an early treatment of a theme that Bosch painted many more times, and he set the style for later versions by crowding the panel with his alarming human zoo, on which expressions of idiocy, cruelty, obtuseness and spite were inscribed in every gesture and expression. The pressing of the pack onward to Calvary being so urgent and intimidating, it is all too easy to respond by moving on and away from the jostling terror. But there is a verso to the panel, which in its different way is quite as startling. In black tondo, set on a blood-red ground, it has a naked infant attempting its first steps, one hand on a walking frame, the other holding a toy windmill.

At first, it is the mysterious disconnection between solitary simplicity and overcrowded hysteria that is most striking. But the two sides of the panel are in fact united by theological symmetry. Christ's innocence and Christ's redemp-tive destiny are the essence of both, and they are joined by the pathetic indispensability of worldly experience for achieving that messianic end. For this is not any baby but the Christ Child at the very outset of His going into the world—the active incarnation that was the particular way in which redemption was to be realized, in flesh and blood. And in keeping with that "incarnational theology," as Leo Steinberg has so brilliantly disclosed,[10] the Christ Child's penis is shown along with the rest of his body, while (unlike other babies at toddling walk) his face bears the solemn expression of foreknowledge. For in his beginnings is written the end, and as in so many of these triptychs, the door is meant to intimate or announce the interior scripture. So that the Christ child's toys are not for carefree play. The toy windmill he carries in infancy is a presage of the cross he will carry, its light airiness a counterpoint

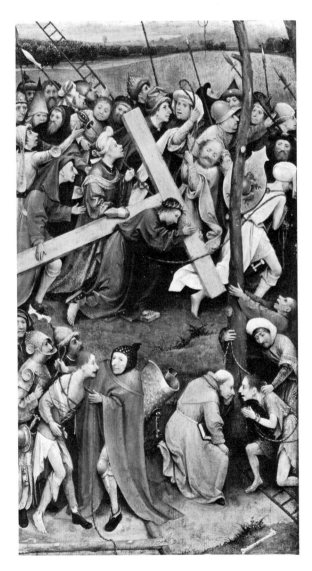

240. Hieronymus Bosch, *Carrying of the Cross.* Kunsthistorisches Museum, Vienna

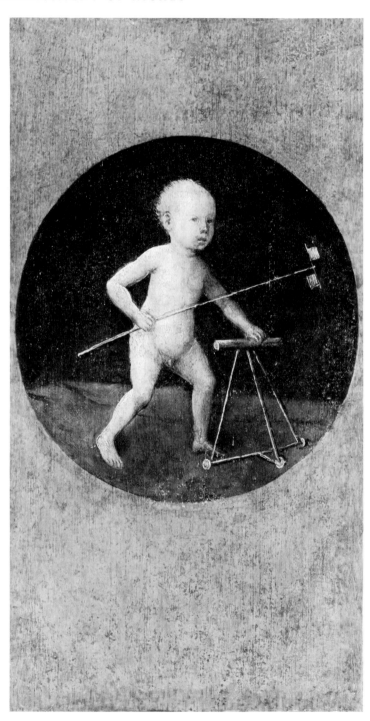

241. Hieronymus Bosch, *Christ Child with Whirligig.* Kunsthistorisches Museum, Vienna

to the heavy burden at the end. In a mid-sixteenth-century panel at Utrecht depicting the charitable offices of almsgiving and visiting the sick, a Christ child holds just such a pinwheel or whirligig as an attribute of his incarnation and destiny. In its landscape setting, the windmill had long been used by Netherlandish artists as a visual metaphor of the Cross. It appears, for example, in enormous prominence in Pieter Bruegel the Elder's *Crucifixion*. In its toy form, carried like a lance, children evidently used the pinwheel to stage mock tournaments, and Bruegel has two doing just that in his *Children's Games*. It is difficult not to think of it in that pseudo-knightly guise as the miniaturized attribute of the *miles Christianum*, the warrior for Christ, the creation of Erasmus's *Enchiridion* and the very epitome of militant godly humanism. Thus conflated, the windmill — like so many other contemporary symbols — does double duty as both a pathetic and a triumphant emblem, connected through the victory of the Passion.[11]

But what of the walker? The iconographical tradition is much less clear, but it may be the support that the Christ child, vulnerable to the pains of human flesh, had in the Father, at the beginning as well as at the end. Two centuries later, at any rate, the Pietist Jan Luiken supplied texts to his emblem of the walker that left nothing to speculation. The *inscriptio* at the head reads "Where frailty needs to lean/There God gives his support," and the *subscriptio* reads:

> *Thus must the babe learn to walk*
> *While on his little feet he cannot stand*
> *And so too the Lord supports us*
> *So that, as a weak frame*
> *We should not fall into Hell*
> *But learn the way to Heaven*[12]

The resort to everyday objects as attributes of the Christian life and their profuse insertion into scriptural representation was not only allowed but encouraged by the biases of Renaissance humanism. Not surprisingly, mercantile cultures such as those of Flanders and Venice seem to have been especially partial to investing a whole array of animate and inanimate objects with Christian purpose, that went well beyond the iconographic conventions supplied by medieval art. And this pleasure at extending the range of symbolic vocabulary away from the arcane and towards the familiar and the vernacular was not just casual or promiscuously sensuous. It also betokened the humanist determination to colonize the most mundane details of worldly life with the Christian ethos, so that it might become literally inescapable. In this way the Thomist separation of realms into an ineffable sacred mystery on high and a

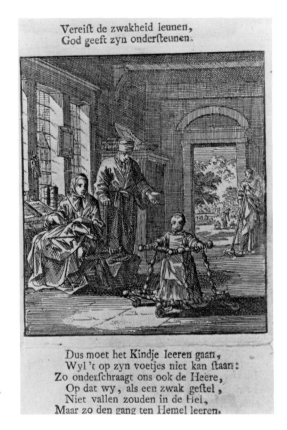

Vereift de zwakheid ieunen,
God geeft zyn onderfteunen.

Dus moet het Kindje leeren gaan,
Wyl 't op zyn voetjes niet kan ftaan:
Zo onderfchraagt ons ook de Heere,
Op dat wy, als een zwak geftel,
Niet vallen zouden in de Hei,
Maar zo den gang ten Hemel leeren.

242. Jan Luiken, *"De Loopwagen."*
Author's collection

knowable world below would be reincorporated into a seamless whole. Thus would be proclaimed the unity of God's creation with its Creator. And this reappropriation of the material world for a sacred purpose was at one with the view that held the appearance of Christ in human form to be the most sublime disclosure of God's faith in His created universe. Even had that not been so, however, the worldly experience of the Messiah would still have been strictly necessary for the program of expiation and redemption. And in a like manner the humanists, especially in the north, assumed the pathetic indispensability of worldly trials for their own redemption and that of their fellow Christians.

So that Christ as an infant, doing recognizably babyish things, is economically represented in the innocence of babyhood, announcing his commonalty with mortal flesh, yet at the same time separated from us by His foreknowledge of his destiny as crucified Messiah. And his attributes in the Bosch panel do this double service, both as expressions of playful discovery and as symbols of his eschatalogical captivity. As the Luiken reprise and variation of these themes suggests, this is a theme from which Christian cultures, and certainly the Netherlandish one, could not easily escape. Even though in the pious emblem the center of gravity of the message has undoubtedly been shifted from text to print, and so from didactic to ludic, it would be jejune to suppose that the moralizing mottos were inserted as perfunctory lip service to Protestant orthodoxy. Luiken himself certainly took them seriously — indeed almost obsessively — and even if many of his readers in this and other emblem books were more attracted by the detailed naturalism of his engravings and their anecdotal counsel, they could not have missed the morals that were tagged to them. At least half the point, if not the pleasure, of emblem books was puzzling through the cunning (or plodding) analogies between the representations of the exterior world and their meaning for the interior life of the spirit.

The balance, or tension, between play and instruction, innocence and comprehension, protection and free will that figures in both the Bosch panel and the Luiken emblem was not just a function of theological commands. Every parent understands the conflicting urges towards self-assertion and security, movement and safety, the whirligig and the walking frame that appear in infants from an astonishingly early stage. And they respond, in their turn, by being torn between encouraging the budding will to independence and feeling anxiety about the dangers that present themselves as a result. Many of Luiken's related emblems drew particular attention to such perils — especially in a world where the next street was filled with canal water — and to the protective role of earthly as well as celestial parents. In the print where a baby is about to totter into a canal, a swan protecting her cygnets swims past in one of Luiken's typically unsubtle secondary allusions to his main theme.[13] In a drawing, one of many done from life in the 1630s, when he himself had become a new father, Rembrandt captured with uncanny precision the instant when early steps are caught between eagerness and hesitation. While the baby, complete with bumper bonnet to safeguard it from spills, sails forward, the younger woman — perhaps the mother — urges it on, as the older — a grandmother or nurse — holds it back.

Though it was probably not Rembrandt's intention (unlike Luiken's) to use the behavior of babies and watchful parents to reflect on the human condition, the tug between safety and freedom (home and world) was indeed at the heart of things Dutch. Without belaboring the analogy, it is obvious that the dynamic urge to go into the world, to acquire and prosper, to explore and understand was deeply ingrained in the mentality of the young Republic. But just as obviously, that dynamism was mindful of its vulnerability, and it paid heed to the ministers who insisted that the only true safety lay with the God who had raised up the Republic and could as easily lay it low should His commandments be flouted. The parallel is not fanciful. More than one

243. Jan Luiken, emblem from *Des Menschen Begin, Midden en de Einde* . . . (Amsterdam, 1712). Houghton Library, Harvard University

historical tract liked to refer to the Dutch as the Nederkinderen in the manner of the Children of Israel, whose mantle they had assumed. This self-flattering metaphor of vigorous infancy was shared by other Protestant states that had repudiated the past—notably the Puritan Commonwealth—and was to become a cliché of both American and French revolutionaries. But in the seventeenth century it was not necessarily a republican self-image. Venice, for example, reveled in a kind of Methuselah complex and set greatest store by its antiquity and longevity and appropriately reserved greatest power for a closed caste of gerontocrats. It is also true that in its anxious beginnings, the child Republic had looked to a succession of fathers, *patri patriae,* William the Silent and Oldenbarneveld, to steady it in its gravest crises. Cats had rejoiced in his sobriquet of "Father" Pensionary and homilist. But by the mid-seventeenth century, the Pensionary de Witt was a young man in his thirties, and the Prince a mere child. And at least part of the tragic scenario that unfolded between them was of the revolt of pupil against tutor, and of the young Prince avenging

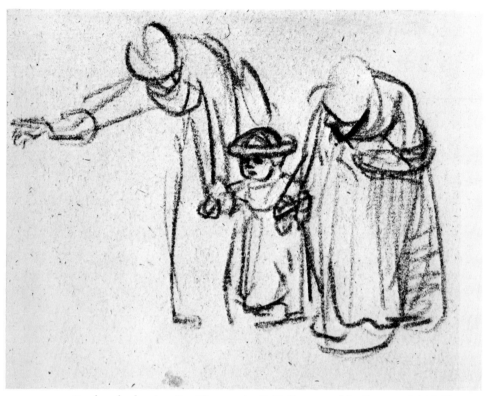

244. Rembrandt, drawing, *Two Women and a Child.* Courtesy of the Trustees, British Museum

the memory of his dead father, William II, upon his pseudo-stepfather, de Witt.

Both the special virtues and the frailties of the Republic, then, were tied up with its youthful self-awareness. According to the ministers of the church, it was born innocent of the sins of the past (even those of Protestant dynasts) and suspicious of the pretensions of states that argued from prescription. But unlike Peter Pan, neither the nation nor the individuals that comprised it could avoid growing up. And so the problem of acquiring worldly experience without forfeiting innocence was one that became common to the humanist program for the upbringing of children and the public business of the conduct of the state. The foreword of Luiken's book was dedicated to:

> *You young daughters and boys*
> *Simple and innocent lambkins*
> *Who set your feet on the world's racetrack*

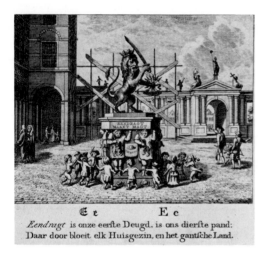

Eᵉ   E e

Eendragt is onze eerfte Deugd, is ons dierfte pand:
Daar door bloeit elk Huisgezin, en het gantfche Land.

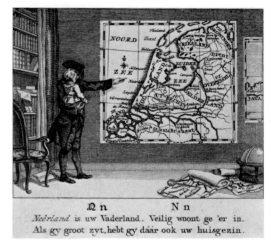

Nn   N n

Neêrland is uw Vaderland. Veilig woont ge 'er in.
Als gy groot zyt, hebt gy dáár ook uw huisgezin.

245. From J.H. Swildens, *Vaderlandsch AB Boek*
(Amsterdam, 1781). Houghton Library, Harvard
University

246. From J.H. Swildens, *Vaderlandsch AB Boek*.
Houghton Library, Harvard University

> *May you keep your simplicity*
> *Free from the bad ways of your elders.*[14]

The art of a good Dutch upbringing was somehow to preserve the distinction
between maturity and decadence. And whenever the infant virtue of the
Republic was said to be jeopardized by the decayed manners of adulthood —
a theme particularly dear to eighteenth-century Dutch moralists — the rejuvenation theme was given another airing. Conversely, instruction books designed for
children, like Swildens's alphabet book (1775), were conscientious in connecting
childish pursuits with civic duties. In *E* for *Eendracht* (Unity), for example, the
roundel dance of the children becomes an expression of the unity of the
several parts of the commonwealth. It is danced around the Dutch lion
rampant guarding the stockaded Republic and standing on a pedestal graven
with the hat of liberty. As it is children who will be the builders of republican
virtue, so a bricklayer's hod passes en route to an edifice surmounted with yet
another figure of the Maid of Liberty, accompanied by Religion and Prosperity.
And in an even more explicit attempt to associate the world of children with
their future as virtuous republican citizens, at the letter *N* for *Nederland*, a
father shows his baby the Fatherland (with colonies attached at right and on
the floor!) while offering the assuring message that "Nederland is your fatherland.
Safely [my emphasis] will you live therein/When you grow up, you too will
have your household there."[15]

Nor can it be accidental, or an artistic whim, that paintings of monuments and tombs of patriotic significance, like de Witte's picture of the tomb of William the Silent in the Oude Kerk at Delft, or Pieter de Hooch's picture of the Burgomasters' chamber in the Amsterdam Stadhuis, should invariably have included family groups in which children were highly conspicuous. They were, after all, the *spes patriae,* the hope of the Fatherland, and their presence before the grave of the father of the Fatherland was a kind of inter-generational learning exercise in the importance of historical legacy and future trust. For the Republic to survive and prosper, its children had to have drummed into them the lessons of the patriotic catechism. "Republics that set most store by their good citizens give most attention to the upbringing of their children," wrote van Beverwijck, and conversely, "the depravity of republics proceeds from the inattention and oversight of their good upbringing."[16]

Two important truths emerge from all these crisscrossing analogies, metaphors and symbolic concordances. First, that the boundaries between the concerns of the adult world and that of the children on whom they lavished so much time and attention were extremely weak. So that when we see children running riot or temporarily becalmed in some household chore, we are not merely glimpsing snapshots from the family album, but scenes from the interior of the Dutch mental world. Projecting onto children the anxieties and inner conflicts of their elders does not, of course, preclude the possibility that as a culture the Dutch were genuinely besotted with the children. And there is a good deal of evidence that parents (and nurses) were as likely to be accomplices in playfulness as mentors in instruction. But it does mean that when we notice the ubiquitousness of children in Dutch art — not as allegorizing putti, or as the infant Jesus — the phenomenon is more complicated than a sudden "coming into its own" of the world of the child.

The second conclusion is that the great dominating theme of the treatment of children — in art and in letters — was the polarity between the ludic and the didactic, between play and learning, between liberty and obedience, between independence and safety. And because that theme was rooted in adult concerns, it meant that the trials of growing up Dutch were perhaps more acute than those of growing up anywhere else. For it meant, in effect, that the adulthood (not to mention the Republic) into which one grew turned out to be exercised by the same quandaries as those alleged to be particular to childhood. To be Dutch at all, at least in the seventeenth century, was to be imprisoned in a state of becoming: a sort of perpetual political adolescence. Only the Dutch of the eighteenth century were released from that by the precocious decadence of their Republic, as though the commonwealth had gone from stripling vigor to feeble senescence without an interim period of maturity. It did not help matters that those who lamented that state of affairs in the 1780s in their turn called for a further dose of rejuvenation as the remedy, so that the revolution they inaugurated had all the plausibility of an old man in diapers.

What this does *not* mean, however, is that the extraordinary abundance of child picturing in the seventeenth-century Netherlands was a wholly bogus phenomenon; that these were invariably ciphers for that venerable humanist obsession — the mastery of folly by learning. Two chronologies are currently available along which historians of childhood have tracked its evolution from "invisibility" in the Middle Ages to affectionate conspicuousness in the eighteenth century. Philippe Ariès argued that children were extracted from their complete absorption in the medieval world only when they became an object of instructional obsession by the humanists or an object of amused manipulation by the aristocracy. The implication was that they were virtually better off invisible than visible, or at least that the price they paid for the emergence of childhood as a stage in its own right was heavier than the benefits. Lawrence Stone and others who have followed have de-sentimentalized the medieval period of "invisibility," claiming that it was in fact a self-protecting indifference in the face of dreadful infant mortality. Indifference was followed by the heavy vigilance of the "patriarchal" society before melting with the eighteenth century into the fond sentiment of the companionate family.

Both types of description suffer somewhat from undue attachment to a geological mode of classification in which the patriarchal culture is made to follow the age of invisibility and to be followed by that of affect much as the Silurian follows the Ordovician and is succeeded by the Devonian. For if we ask how children are represented in Netherlandish culture, and what this tells us about their importance to it, it is difficult to slot any answer into the available periodization. On the one hand it is undoubtedly true, as we have already seen, that adult concerns were projected onto the figures of children. That did not mean, however, that the world of Dutch children was swallowed up by the stereotypes of their parents. Suppose something like the exact opposite to be the case, namely, that adults shrank their own anxieties and pleasures to child size, rather like Anstey's Mr. Bultitude in the Edwardian moral fantasy *Vice Versa* — and it follows that child's play rather than fatherly admonition could in some circumstances dominate. And this is precisely what happened. While the intention in figuring grown-up matters in childhood guise was instructional, the solemnity of the exercise got lost in the translation. So that categories become marvelously confused. In more than one of Jan Steen's scenes of household havoc, it is the children who are worldly wise and wide awake and the adults who are fleeced, doped or slumped in unconsciousness. However forbidding the tutorial face of Christian humanism or Calvinism was when it frowned at the follies of the young, in its transcribed reality it beat a retreat before the raw vigor of play power.

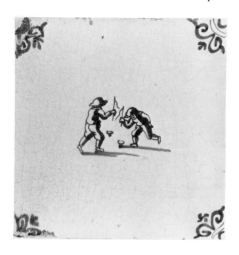

247. Delft blue and white tile from series
of children's games. Author's collection

iii EX NUGIS SERIA: CHILD'S PLAY?

Nothing illustrates the peculiar bias of Netherlandish culture towards children and their world more graphically than the compendia of children's games that they put into paint, print, and even wall tiles. It was a genre that seems to have been invented in the Netherlands, for although there are many instances of individual games being incorporated as anecdotal or allegorical detail in other medieval and Renaissance painting, nothing approached the Flemish and Dutch pictures in their systematically encyclopedic curiosity. Indeed, their eagerness to encode particular didactic meanings in each of the games and in their overall composition ought not to blind us to the sheer Rabelaisian pleasure in compilation—the collector's list fetish—that was so marked a trait of humanist cultures. The urge to catalogue and classify human behavior as well as flora and fauna, to order the richness and variety of natural phenomena, expressed itself visually in the "swarming" anthology pictures of Pieter Bruegel the Elder. But at a less dazzling level of virtuosity, the prints of Hieronymus Cock and Frans Hogenberg, both members of the Antwerp circle of humanist scholars and collectors in which Bruegel moved, testified to this preoccupation with profuseness in what was, after all, a very densely populated corner of the humanist universe.

But the *Children's Games* series was more than simply another item in the taxonomist's fascination with the *theatrum mundi* to put alongside the anthologies of festive practices in *The Battle Between Carnival and Lent* and that of native proverbs in *The Blue Cloak*. None of those subjects, after all, can sensibly be read as though it stands alone, innocent of any level of secondary meaning.

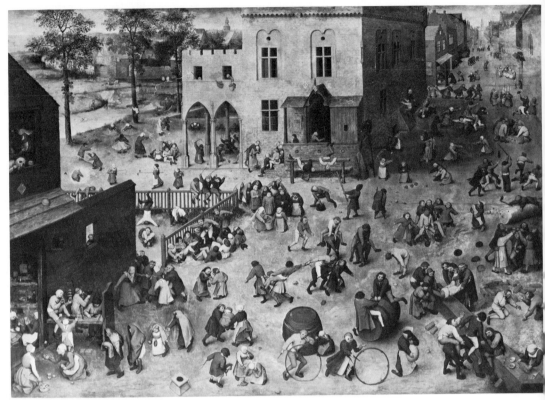

248. Pieter Bruegel the Elder, *Children's Games,* 1560. Kunsthistorisches Museum, Vienna

We are not yet in the (relatively) dispassionate world of Enlightenment classification of material phenomena. For the Renaissance collector, the business of ordering knowledge was inextricably tied with generating normative hierarchies and making distinctions between categories of virtue and vice, wisdom and folly, good and ill.

The *Kinderspelen* series of pictures being no exception to this general rule, they are dense with ambivalence towards their ostensible subject. Acutely observant about child's play, they also express more somber reflections on the world's folly. Recent art historical accounts have argued strenuously for either a moralizing or a ludic interpretation,[17] but there is no reason why the two manners should be mutually exclusive. Arguably it was the essence of northern Renaissance style to bring together wit and teaching. And Rabelais's own list of games in *Gargantua* combines precisely the humanist relish for the swarming phenomenon and his passion to subdue its spontaneity through classification.[18] Likewise the visual *Kinderspelen* embody the perennial conflicts between

diversion and instruction, between freedom and obedience, between exploration and safety that were at the heart of contemporary attitudes towards the
child. By situating the games not in some imaginary vacuum of time and
space but in topographically meaningful—and sometimes recognizable—
settings, nearly always with some public building, a town hall or guildhall, in
view, they evoke the civic and public virtues to which the correctly brought-up
child should be led. It is almost as though that civic architecture—the Abdij
at Middelburg or the Binnenhof at The Hague—performs the function of
didactic vigilance, a mute schoolmasterly presence watching, censoriously
surveying the spectacle of uninhibited folly. They are, however, an inanimate
presence, almost swamped (especially in the Bruegel) by all kinds of animation.
And on moving from emblematic prints to the more ambiguous realm of
paintings, it is impossible not to feel that gravity is not infrequently undone
by mischief and mirth. Not merely in the work of Steen, but in that of Jan
Miense Molenaer and his wife, Judith Leyster, there is a kind of roguish
ingratiation that levels down rather than up. So that the original Erasmian
program by which levity is meant to lead to gravity—*ex nugis seria*—rebounds
on its authors when adults are reduced to rompers. And into the tutor-pupil
relation that was both the humanist and the Calvinist ideal of family life,
there crept, unmistakably, the more companionable and relaxed tone of a
conversation piece.

   Any doubt that these crowded scenes were intended as more than visual
compilations should be dispelled by Jacob Cats's forthright text accompanying
his *Kinderspel*, which he used as a preface both for *Houwelijck* and for some
editions of *Silenus Alcibiadis.* "You may laugh," the poet says, "and think this is
but childish work . . . well laugh away . . ."

> *But while you with the children laugh*
> *So would I have you ponder*
> *That you are also in this very image*
> *As well as in the children's play*
> *And I know of no one that has ever lived*
> *That has not had his childish dolls*
> *That has not sometimes romped and sometimes fell.*
> *. . . This game though it seems without any sense*
> *has a little world therein*
> *[For] the world and its whole constitution*
> *Is but a children's game.*[19]

This is entirely faithful to the spirit (albeit a feeble echo) of Erasmian
intellectual cunning through which sober truths are wittily presented the

vision of their opposite: mirthful folly. And the mask (of tragedy rather than comedy, it should be noted) leaning from the upper story, left, in Bruegel's picture, as well as upside-down figures hanging from a form at the precise crossing point of the picture's diagonals, and very prominent in the head-stander, middle left—all supply just those kinds of oxymoronic visual clues that were a trademark of what might be called the Erasmian figurative style. It may be, of course, that it is anachronistic to use a seventeenth-century, self-consciously emblematic text to decode a sixteenth-century painting. But aside from the Bruegel's obvious standing as the prototype of all the many children's games prints that followed, it seems wildly improbable that humanist Antwerp would actually have been *less* attracted to the visual riddling and symbolic anthologies that remained popular for at least the first half of the following century.

It is not, in any case, any business of mine to offer yet another reading of Bruegel's painting and so add to a rapidly growing interpretative literature. It may or may not be a view of the seasons of man as well as the calendar year, or a comment on "the role of chance in man's life." When taken with the two Adriaen van de Venne prints for Cats's poem, the view of the Binnenhof at The Hague, probably by Jan van de Velde II, and other emblems and prints like those by Roemer Visscher and, much later, Luiken—what does the whole *topos* have to tell us about the Netherlandish view of children? First, although the Bruegel children, from their costume, are not literally miniaturized adults, the boundary between adult and childish behavior is made deliberately weak, to the point that some of the faces have been thought to be prematurely grown-up. That response may in itself be due to an unduly modern (or at least nineteenth-century) stereotype of the pretty infant, but in other studies of children, where their features are treated in large detail, the effect is of anything but unworldly juvenility. And this is not simply a matter of descriptive conventions. Jan Luiken's children in his prints are quite obviously the "innocent lambs" of his text and are correspondingly idealized. Dutch painters, especially perhaps Jacob Gerritszoon Cuyp, who had something of a specialty in wide-eyed babes, could, on commission, replicate the same reassuring image. But Molenaer's and Dirk Hals's and at least some of Jan Steen's children are ruddy-faced, wrinkle-eyed, gap-toothed and altogether too knowing for their own good (see fig. 253).

If it was Bruegel's intention to make the line between adulthood and child-hood visually ambiguous, that would only have been a way of reinforcing the morals that lay behind each of the games—just as his *Netherlandish Proverbs* were meant to show off adult follies in childish dress. In other words the miniaturization, or rather projection, was not literal but metaphorical. And while Bruegel's compendium of games is quite certainly the most exhaustive

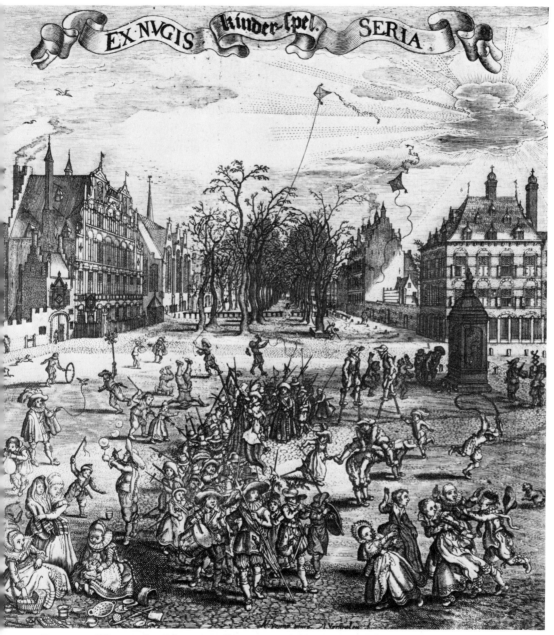

249. Experiens Silleman after Adriaen van de Venne, "Children's Games" from Jacob Cats, *Houwelijck* (Amsterdam, 1628). Bodleian Library, Oxford

before or since—ninety-one have been counted— those that feature prominently in the foreground are also those that were repeated over and over again in the prints, and that most easily lent themselves to repeated moralizing commentary. So that when Cats drew up his list of "instructive" games, he thinned out Bruegel's teeming tableau to those that would strike an immediate response: hoop bowling, stilt walking, bubble blowing, somersaulting, blindman's buff, hobbyhorse riding, windmill and whirligig playing, knucklebones and marbles, and tops, for both whipping and unraveling.[20] There was also mimic play, especially for girls—keeping house and playing with dolls—and in a version of the print by the sublimely named Experiens Silleman, a mock militia company parade. Cats also added one important pastime somehow missing from Bruegel's compendium—kite flying—which signified hubris and was reinforced in the later print by the "before and after" technique of showing both high flying and the consequential disaster of the snapped cord.

Characteristically, Cats left no one in any doubt at all about the emblematic significance of each of the games, and together his play-as-you-learn makes all counsel mirthless and sometimes bafflingly contradictory. The tops, for example, which needed whipping for their spin, signified the effort and pain that was

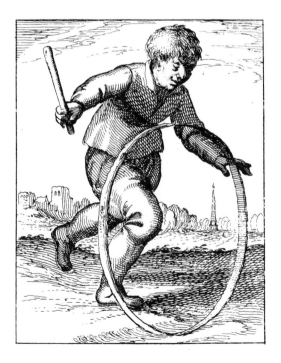

250. Emblem from Roemer Visscher, *Sinnepoppen*. Houghton Library, Harvard University

needed to get anywhere in life. On the other hand the toy windmill, the *molentje,* which goes hither and thither in search of a good wind, signified undesirable restlessness. Some games like stilts and hobbyhorse riding were too obviously associated with a particular moral — that of social climbing and pretentiousness — to allow any confusion. Balloons and bladder balls stood for the inflated emptiness of earthly affairs, and similarly bubbles had from time immemorial betokened the ephemerality of beauty and/or the fleeting character of childhood itself. But just as often, the moralists differed on the sense they assigned to some of the pastimes. Roemer Visscher's hoop pointed to the futility of life, while for Cats it was a symbol of eternal predictability and the revolution of the celestial bodies.

What do all these morals add up to? A striking number surely echo the theme that I have already suggested to be an abiding preoccupation of humanist and, for that matter, Calvinist instruction on childhood: the tension between play and learning and between free will and obedience. The kite flier who sees his "heaven-soarer" fall back to the dirt and become, in Cats's words, "just so much paper," the conceit and vanity of the stilt walker, the bravura of the leap frogger and the willfulness of the somersaulter or head-stander all indicate violations of the humanists' golden rule of moderation. To Calvinists they would have symbolized a perverse determination to fly in the face of divine decree, or, like the blindman's buff players, the folly of groping in the dark.

In their negative sense, then, the games attempt to instruct by pointing to their opposites, though there are also positive morals in games that are commended as models for correct behavior, those of discipline and perseverance like the top and the skipping rope. When Swildens came to repeat the theme yet again in his ABC book he even invited his child reader to distinguish — with some help from the engraver's needle — between those games that were "good for Netherlandish youth" and those that weren't.

To see that there is great ambiguity in the confusion of adult folly and childish distraction does not clear things up very much. There are, obviously, two quite distinct commentaries offered here, but their common symbolic vocabulary makes disentangling them very difficult. The first view makes childhood a preface to adulthood, albeit an indispensable and vital one, in which, if they are attended to properly, all the proper attributes of a virtuous citizen may be shaped and set. Accordingly, its tone is interventionist and didactic; games make up yet another pedagogic opportunity in the world's great moral classroom. In the second view, games are but the mirror of incorrigible adult folly. And that view is laconic, stoical and satirical, where its opposite is eager and activist. It is more preoccupied with vices than virtues and sees childhood not as the malleable opportunity but the inevitable colony of incorrigible human follies. "As the old sing, so the young pipe," that

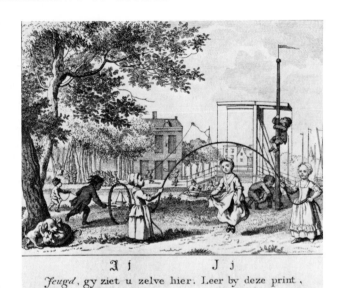

251. From J. H. Swildens, *Vaderlandsch AB Boek*

Jeugd, gy ziet u zelve hier. Leer by deze print ,
Welke fpelen 't nutfte zyn voor een Neêrlands kind.

most famous of Flemish proverbs, was brought to pictures over and over again and several times by just one artist, Jan Steen. Just as the first view looks forward with reforming optimism, the latter view looks back from adulthood with pessimistic acceptance.

These two different but not unrelated concerns with childhood correspond of course to the twin tempers that cohabited, like Heraclitus and Democritus, the mirthful and the doleful masks within northern humanism. Games as a form of improving instruction cleave to the Erasmus of *De civilitate morum puerilium libellus*. Games as a mirror of adult folly belong to the mood and style of *Encomium Moriae*. And just as both moods typified northern humanist thought and literature, both are also present in the games series of paintings and prints, at whatever cost to consistency and clarity. For both the tutorial and the satirical voices presuppose both the inevitability and the corrigibility of folly—"this is what children do, we did it ourselves"—and were it *never* done, there would be no countermodel from which to correct our behavior. The very sternest of the Renaissance moralists, even Calvin, were much given to relating the personal follies of their own youth, the better to shine the beacon on a purer path, to be sure, but with the implication that future generations are expected to repeat the mistakes of the past.

There is nothing in the seventeenth-century Dutch representation of children's games—either in painting or in print or even in the emblem book

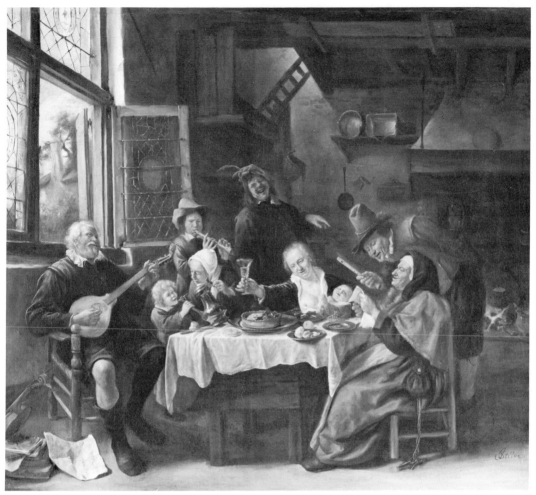

252. Jan Steen, *As the Old Sing, So the Young Pipe.* Philadelphia Museum of Art

texts — that clears up these inconsistencies, contradictions and ambiguities. It seems fruitless to search for, much less insist on, a *definitely* moral or ludic reading of those pictures, even where appearances seem to make a strong claim in one direction or the other. Take Dirk Hals's painting of two children playing cards. It seems on the face of it a classic *exemplum* of Visscher's emblematic little sermon in which card playing along with *dobbelsteen* (dice) functions as a sort of counterpedagogy.[21] Nor is there any doubt at all that cards and dice, quite aside from their connotations with a low-life milieu, lust for gold and violent contention, were thought peculiarly dangerous for the addictive way in which they dispossessed men of their will and reason, and so gave the devil, in the guise of Fortuna, sovereignty over the Christian way. Where that way is straight and plain, the way of Fortuna creeps like the crab, crookedly and sideways. And yet for all this, the observation of children's mischief in the picture is so winning and so without threat or malediction that its truthfulness rebounds moral responsibility back on the adult. So while its intention may have been tutorial, its effect is mischievously satirical.

Nor was it impossible even for the relentlessly didactic Cats to use toys in a wholly innocent celebration of childish pleasure. For a market stall crammed with every kind of toy, windmills and hobbyhorses, drums and dolls, illustrates one of his few emblems that actually commend rather than prohibit (fig. 255). And in this case, the moral, *"Schoon voordoen is half verkocht"* (Well set-out is half-sold), belongs to the world of primitive marketing rather than that of the mortified soul. For once the moral presumes the innocence rather than the guilt of childish gratification.[22]

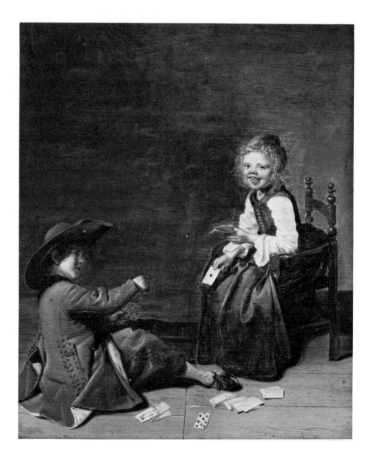

253. Dirk Hals, *Two Children Playing Cards*. Clark Institute of Art, Williamstown, Massachusetts

Leert het u kinderen niet.

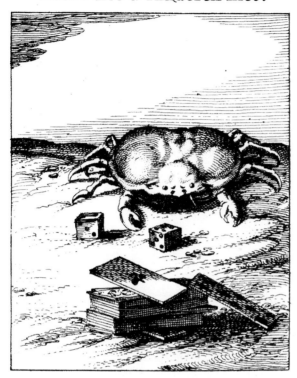

254. Emblem from Roemer
Visscher, *Sinnepoppen.* Houghton
Library, Harvard University

If there are ambiguities even in the emblem books, how much more uncertain is the weight of moral emphasis in the paintings. In many works of art that incorporate toys, intact or broken, their moral weight has been shaken loose in the playfulness of their execution. If instruction remains, its target has moved from children to adults. While the mischief of children's pranks is not altogether exonerated, it becomes more predictable and less culpable. It is the adult model of poor behavior that is implied in the extra awfulness of seeing it mimicked by children. And while scapegrace antics may be unavoidable in little ones, it proclaims, they are wholly reprehensible in you.

Nor is this simply a matter of private morality. For the public settings of the games create another deliberate counterpoint between child's play and the ostensible *gravitas* of the adult world. Bruegel's painting is thought to be set against some such archetypal guildhall, but there is no speculation necessary in the case of the prints. Indeed, Alma-Tadema, obviously a keen eye and memory, has inscribed in pencil, for the benefit of the unenlightened, on the Bodleian's folio copy, "This is Middelburg town hall," and made sure that he took the credit by signing the inscription! He is quite right, for the earlier

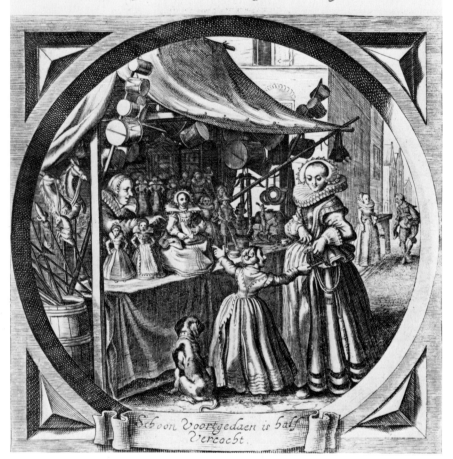

255. Emblem from Jacob Cats, *Spiegel van de Oude en de Nieuwe Tyt* (in *Complete Works,* 1659). Houghton Library, Harvard University

print is indeed set on the Abdijplein, where Cats and van de Venne spent their early years — in the heart of the Zeeland circles that nourished a particularly pious fusion of Calvinism and humanism. The Silleman (fig. 249) is set in The Hague — which, interestingly enough, would be Cats's destination as Grand Pensionary of Holland under Stadholder Frederick Henry. It looks down the tree-lined Voorhout from the Kneuterdijk, so that the most obviously imposing buildings of the Binnenhof, those associated with court and state, would have been off out of the picture frame on the right. By contrast, Jan van de Velde II's print, in the narrow format usually designed to go with city

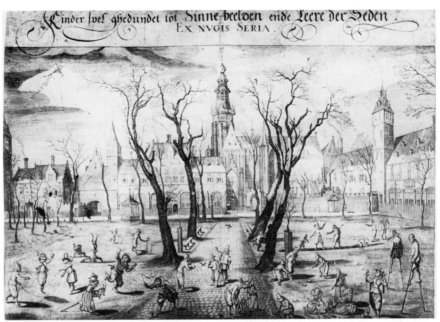

256. *Kinderspel* from Cats, *Alle de Werken* (*Complete Works*), Amsterdam, 1650. Bodleian Library, Oxford

descriptions and eulogies, looks directly out over the Vijver and to the Binnenhof itself (fig. 257).

Now, it could be, of course, that these are topographically accurate views. It is certainly true that games were indeed played in public places — on the Neude in Utrecht, for instance — and that church councils can occasionally be heard complaining of catch balls and wind balls that are kicked around in front of the church even while Sunday services are being held. But what must strike even the most hardened partisan of a naturalistic reading is the absence in the Cats engravings of any figures *other* than children from these places — unlike, for example, an Avercamp winterscape where children and adults, as well as all sorts of conditions and social types, are more or less realistically included in the same picture. Public spaces are made over to children precisely because their behavior, positive and negative, is being scrutinized in the light of their incipient citizenship in the commonwealth. In the Jan van de Velde print, adult figures such as riders and strolling couples do compete for space with the children. But they are given entry only as part of the didactic scheme. So that the most prominent horseman is placed suspiciously adjacent to a bubble-blowing boy and a lowly beggar addresses another boy on stilts, a symbol of vain ambition. Even more than little brides or little soldiers these are little

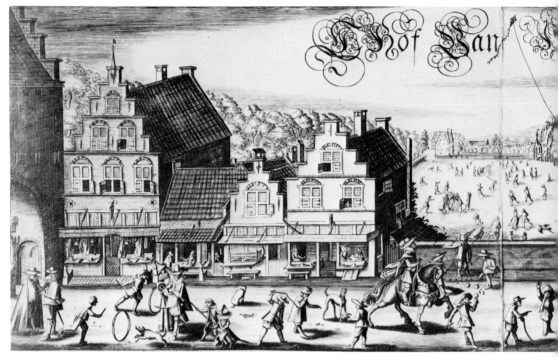

257. Jan van de Velde II (?), *Het Hof van Hollandt.* Bodleian Library, Oxford

258. Detail from *Kinderspel* (1628 ed.)

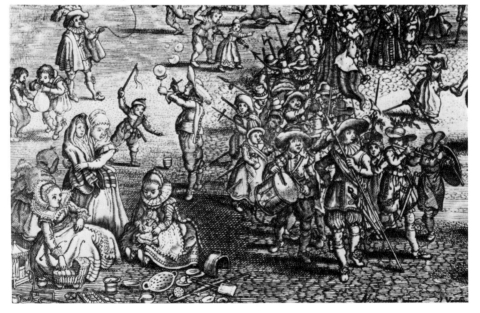

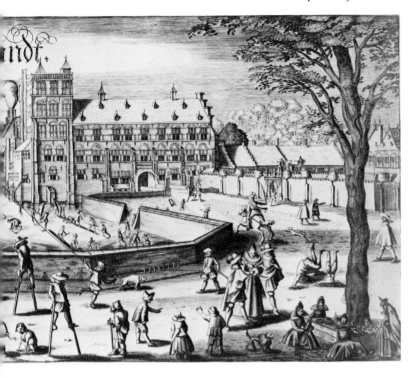

citizens, *burghers* in the most literal sense. Hence the central importance of the *schutter* parade in the plate (fig. 258) and the studiously preserved gender distinctions: "See how mankind reveals its true nature even in childhood."[23] The generational instruction of girls is conveyed by the simultaneous presence of a mother or nurse with a real baby and a young girl playing with a doll, a toy cradle, household utensils and other attributes of her inescapable destiny as one of Cats's heroic housewives. And that format of the separation of the sexes by virtue of their respective destinies became a stock type in family portraiture, especially in the more assertively Calvinist family groups. While the girls attend to their proper domain, though, the little men are made to understand their duties in defending the commonwealth.

> The girls play with dolls
> While boys show a braver spirit
> The girl goes to the crib
> While the boy lets the bugle sound
> The girl plays with little things
> That will serve in her kitchen

> *While the boy with a frail lance*
> *After the ways of rougher [rouwe] men*
> *Knows that all of Holland's blood*
> *With arms must defend the land.*[24]

These are, then, as much images of civic virtue as they are of private morality. What they are not are images of a notionally independent world of children, separated from the concerns of adults and provided now with their own autonomous "stage" of life. As Cats marshals them, they make a formidable case for the colonization of children's space and time by adult wishful thinking. But there were some games, more universal and perennial than those played with toy drums and kitchen utensils, that obstinately retained their ludic as well as their didactic symbolism. Indeed they retained them so successfully that by the time that western European culture came to see the special *virtue* of childhood as the *postponement* of responsible adulthood—in other words, its meaningless, carefree playfulness—their symbolism was available for use in exactly the opposite sense from that of Renaissance pedagogy.

It must be some sort of paradox that the most enduring of those images of innocent play was the soap bubble. Originally, the bubble had also done service as another icon of fickle transience and insubstantiality—*speculum fallax*—the bubble speculation, in which it was featured as an image of the world's deceit, in reality an empty and ephemeral orb, rather than the substantial sphere. Occasionally it appears alongside other evocations of the vanity of the world, as in Molenaer's bubble blower who accompanies the blond-tressed Dame World. And in this respect it was closely related in symbolic function as well as physical appearance to the balloon and inflatable bladder ball that also featured in the *Kinderspel* series. No image of feckless youth in the High Renaissance was without its bubble blower, in a mussel or more usually a scallop shell, so the bubble in its iridescent prettiness and airy evanescence came to be virtually an emblem for childhood itself.[25] Frans Hals used it in multiple variations and permutations on the theme as an attribute of his rosy-cheeked boys, sometimes shown blowing the bubble, sometimes enclosed within one and sometimes just suggesting it by the form of a tondo and the pointing finger to the spherical frame.[26] And in keeping with what we have seen over and over again to be the double-edged nature of that conception, the bubble invited not merely fascination with its beauty but a poignant foreknowledge of its abrupt end. As always, Cats had a particular knack for turning a poetic observation into a prosaic truism:

> *Attend to the child that blows bubbles*
> *And see how much he is amazed*

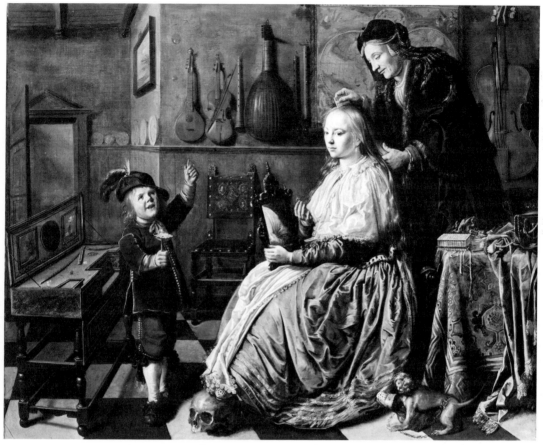

259. Jan Miense Molenaer, *Allegory of Vanity,* 1633. Toledo Museum of Art

> *That so much blown up froth and slobber*
> *Endures but so brief a phase.*[27]

Other moralists followed Erasmus's *Adages* in seeing the bubble as a symbol
less of childhood's brief excursion than of the transience of earthly life itself.
The Remonstrant divine Uytenbogaert referred to it somewhat daringly in a
sermon to the Stadholder's court, when he said, "Man is nothing other than a
bubble that children blow in a mussel shell, that glistens in the round . . . but
which in an instant disappears and is gone."[28] And this standard piety was
almost certainly what prompted the sitter for a Cornelis Ketel portrait of 1574
to have the verso done as a bubble blower.

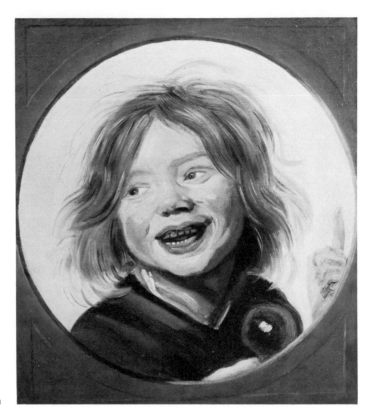

260. Frans Hals, *Boy Blowing Bubbles.* Whereabouts unknown

The bubble, then, was a perfect symbol for childhood as the Dutch saw it: an image that reflected both levity and gravity, that floated like childish reveries and popped as childhood itself had to end. It was a metaphor of both childhood and maturity, of play and of self-instruction. And its connotations must have been sufficiently familiar for Molenaer to have provided the youngest son in a family group with a scallop-shell bubble catcher (with features and pose very similar to that of the *Dame World*) without any further pictorial elaboration. In a picture devoted to recalling past as well as future generations, the image was very apt, if not particularly cheerful.

How much of this semantic cunning endured along with the persistent image is extremely difficult to gauge. The images that do persist, especially in the second half of the seventeenth century, seem to linger more innocently on the dreamy, leisured, playful aspects of bubbles, baubles and balloons, on air and shimmering iridescence, than on its more somber connotations. It may be that a Gerard Dou bubble blower is pondering the brevity of his own youth and beauty, but wistfulness seems held far off from the mood of the portrait. A similar study by Netscher adds the element in the boy's palette of a stock comment on the ephemerality of painted beauty, along with the cherubic beauty of his son, Constantijn. As unreserved pleasure in materials and textures came to dominate and finally to obliterate the moral reflections they had once triggered (both in still life painting and in genre portraits), so eighteenth-century bubble blowers were released from the morbid melancholy of their predecessors. In keeping with eighteenth-century sentimental notions of childhood as a state of unstained innocence, that period's bubblers take off, not from the emblem moralists but rather from Dirk de Bray's wonderfully airy and lighthearted woodcut. There, to the rapture of the children, bubbles drift off over an idyllic May-time landscape as an image of unconfined delight that almost seems to anticipate Victorian wishful thinking about the perpetuity of childhood.

By the time that the bubble floated on through the heady stratosphere of Victorian mawkishness, it had not only shed its Renaissance symbolism but actually reversed its sense. Instead of connoting childhood in terms of brevity, poignancy, and doomed grace, it became instead a symbol of its perpetuation, of a carefree Peter Pan–like idyll — the never-never land where no bubble pops. Jacobus Maris, the late-nineteenth-century Hague painter, varied the formula somewhat by representing in an aquarelle two young girls but with all intimations of mortality obliterated. For Millais, as for the Lever Brothers, soap manufacturers, who traded on the image, and the music hall singers who crooned "I'm forever blowing bubbles," the squeaky-clean little angel-children (for they had all but sprouted wings once more) were exactly the opposite of the sixteenth- and seventeenth-century Erasmian originals. Their bubbles had carried with them *contemptu mundi*: a knowledge of the vanity of the world, but equally, an example of the necessity of worldly knowledge to acquire the insight. The Victorian "Bubbles" — for now there was no distance between the child and his plaything — remained forever uncontaminated by the polluting world. And when soap altered its form from bubbles to snow-white flakes, its promoters had a ready-made tradition of the unstainable child to call on. "How blessed still to be a child," gushes the Lux advertisement. "Let the children romp to their hearts' content. Lux will make the dirtiest clothes magnificently bright again."

This apparently complete severance of idyllic childhood from worldly reality could not have been further from the seventeenth-century Dutch view. If their children were more cherished than in any other previous European culture, the regard was born of a certain obsessive self-regard in which they saw themselves in the guise of children attempting to make their way. But if the Dutch view was one which at least tried to come to grips with the painful problems of children set down in a hard world (rather than cloistered in a

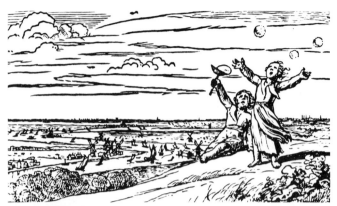

261. Dirk de Bray, *The Month of May,* woodcut after Jan de Bray, Almanach for 1666. Gemeentearchief, Haarlem

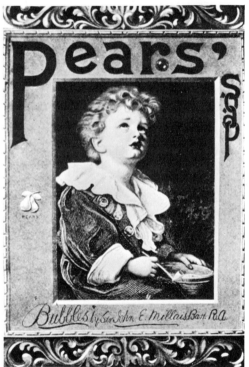

262. J.E. Millais's *Bubbles* as commercial emblem

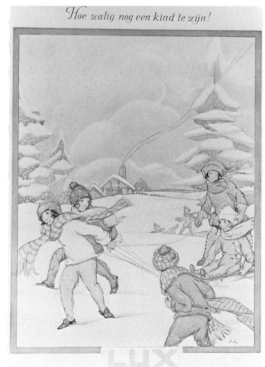

Hoe zalig nog een kind te zijn!

263. Lux Soap Advertisement, 1930s

nursery), its earnestness did not rule out sentiment and affection. And when they wanted to show babes in arms suckling at the breast or lovingly caressed and admired, Dutch artists had no need to invoke the Holy Family for their license. Plainly, it was an image of family tenderness in which the Dutch saw their most admirable qualities, and therein lies an important mystery of their family culture.

iv MAKING BABIES SAFE(LY);
THE DIARY OF A DUTCH MIDWIFE

What was the definition of a nightmare for a seventeenth-century Dutch family? A woodcut illustration from one of the simplest and most popular of the duo-decimo domestic health manuals, Heijman Jacobi's *Schat der Armen* (The Treasury of the Poor) supplies an answer. It shows the grim figure of death dragging off the swaddled figure of a newborn baby from its crib while its mother sleeps. Without actually dwelling on the content of the nightmare, the good doctor goes cheerfully on to discuss the various causes (rich and upsetting foods) of "heavy dreams" and appropriate remedies. But it is the print itself that is eloquent in its poignant simplicity. For in a tiny frame it speaks to us of a world of family feeling: of mothers who customarily slept with their babes by their bedside, of their most unquiet fears. The figure in the little print is a demon, an evil phantom, but in the conditions of early modern Europe, crib death was all too real.

It has been suggested, notably by Lawrence Stone, that crushingly high rates of infant mortality induced a kind of protective callousness in parents and siblings that expressed itself in stoical resignation or even indifference.[29] And that this self-denial of tenderness blocked off the route to more compan-

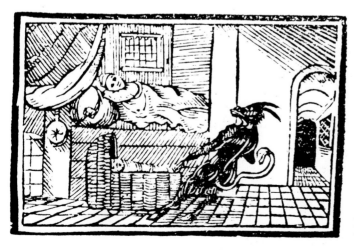

264. From Heijman Jacobi, *Schat der Armen*. Houghton Library, Harvard University

ionable family feeling between parents and children. It is undeniable that seventeenth-century Holland, like Puritan England, abounds in evidence of this sorrowing prostration before the inscrutable ways of the Almighty. When his wife's cousin seemed likely to lose their small daughter in 1660, Johan de Witt wrote to the parents that they should call on their "love, faith, and steadfastness" in accepting divine will, and understand that "it would be very unreasonable to prefer our own small pleasure in the enjoyment of children over the eternal joy which they come into when they leave us." When his own seven-year-old Catharina died in 1667, he wrote to kin that "it is permitted to us to accept willingly, the disposition of Almighty God in this."[30] But—and I think this is a large but—this kind of response was more a matter of Calvinist theology than demographic conditioning, and, more important, it did not in the least preclude a real outpouring of grief that occurred on the losses of these *onnozele schaapjes*, the little lambkins, as they were called over and again. De Witt's condolence to his relatives and his letters announcing the death of his own little daughter (*dochterken*) were formal expressions of fortitude and Christian obedience. But the *fact* of the sending and receiving of countless such grieving letters hardly suggests a general stoniness in the face of child mortality. Historians are overfond of inferring emotional content from variations of ceremonial form. And it is certainly true that the Calvinist Church enjoined the simplest possible funeral rites for the burial of an infant. In the engraving accompanying his discussion of funerals, le Francq van Berkhey shows a minimum of mourners with the small bier, in striking contrast to the grandeur and length of a patrician burial procession.[31] But this formal economy did not mean that the dead children were consigned to some therapeutic oblivion by the collective memory of the family. In some cases, steps were taken to memorialize them that seem distinctly pre-Romantic or sentimental in manner. Family group paintings—for example, by Maes and Mytens—commemorated the "lost souls" of deceased babies by having them fly over the living as angels in the heavens.[32] And in many other respects small children were accorded the same outward and intimate expressions of grief as those who had survived longer. Even in "companionable" genre scenes, like Netscher's *Maternal Instruction,* anxieties for the safety of children intrude, for on the back wall the artist has chosen to depict, not fortuitously, a *Massacre of the Innocents.*

Perhaps the most remarkable piece of evidence testifying to the anguish of parents at the death of their small children is literary. In 1632 and 1633, the great Dutch poet Vondel lost first a one-year-old son and then an eight-year-old daughter. On both occasions he wrote poems, as much therapy for himself and his wife as memorial pieces. Both are remarkable for their direct emotional poignancy and distress. But more surprisingly still (if one assumes that parents were steeling themselves to these losses with emotional indifference),

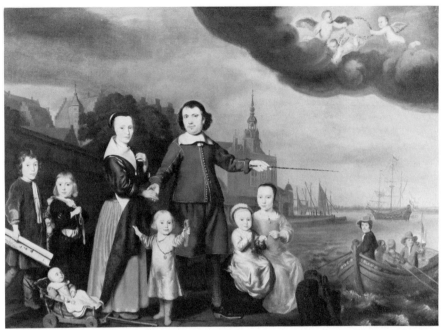

265. Nicolas Maes, *Captain Job Cuyter and Family,* 1659. North Carolina Museum of Art

both poems presuppose that the mother of the children is stricken with almost unbearable grief. The intention of the poems is consolatory, but both specifically mention the crying and keening of the mother and make no reference at all to stoicism in the face of inscrutable Divine intentions. The first poem, "Kinder-Lyck," a terrible play on *childish* and *child corpse*, spoke to the son, "little Constantijn, the blessed babe." More originally it had the babe himself speak to his grieving mother from his heavenly seat.

> *"Mother," says he, "why do you cry so*
> *Why do you keen over my bier*
> *Up here I live, up here I fly in the air*
> *A little angel in the heavens."*[33]

Modern sensibilities may gag at this sentimentality, but it is precisely the "modern" or "Victorian" quality of the sentimentality that is so arresting and so emphatically at odds with any notion of Christian fatalism in the death of infants. To be sure, Vondel was no Calvinist, and would become a Catholic, but his moral and emotional qualities were wholly representative of the

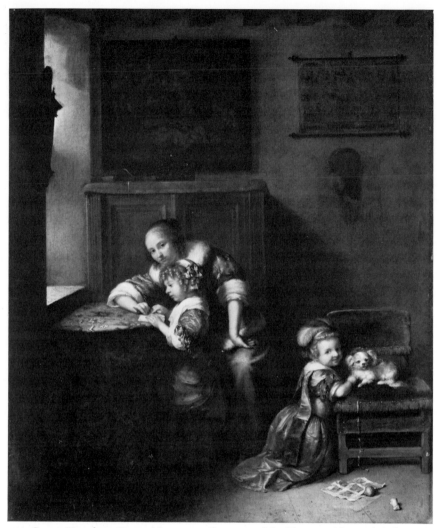

266. Caspar Netscher, *Maternal Instruction.* Courtesy of the Trustees, National Gallery, London

Dutch *burgerij* who commissioned paintings featuring their dead babies as cherubim in the sky.

The second Vondel poem, "Uitvaert van mijn dochterken" (The Funeral of My Little Daughter), is even more distressing. For far from repressing the recollection of his little girl's humanity and personality, the better to endure her loss, Vondel uses exactly the opposite emotional strategy: catharsis by total recall. The poem is, in large part, a faithful and realistic reminiscence of the child laughing, skipping and playing in the streets or playing with her dollies. Sentimentality aside, it is almost unbearably poignant to read, climaxing as it does with the vivid image of the wreath of green and gold leaves set on her dead brow. Whatever else, this was not a sensibility coping with death through sublimation.

Given the reasonable assumption that the demographic facts of life and death were quite as grim in the Dutch Republic as anywhere else in urban Europe, but prevailing attitudes towards infants, at least those recommended, were soft- rather than hardhearted, there seems reason to doubt that culture was conditioned by morbidity. In fact there is considerable evidence that the lives of small children, however vulnerable to sickness and plague, were held dear rather than cheap by the Dutch. With the birth of a child, the happy family entered a sort of state of civic grace. A *kraam kloppertje* made of paper and lace was posted on the door signifying sex, and the *kloppertjes* became yet another object of rich local ornamental variation: as elaborate and particularized as other domestic and civic fetishes, like the drinking horn or the bonnet pin. Moreover the posting of the *kloppertje,* along with the father's donning the paternity bonnet, announced a period when the household would be exempt from certain taxes and duties.[34] So the birth was very much a semipublic and neighborhood event, with innumerable parties and feasts marking the earliest calendar of the child.[35]

The local community, then, was not at all indifferent to the fate of its little treasures. Accidents, as we have seen from the Luiken prints, were as much a source of terror for parents as they are now. And the law could deal severely with carters or coachmen who hurt children even if it could be proved that the children ran into their path. In 1664, Joost Hendricksz., a coachman in The Hague, ran over a small boy and was given three days, bread and water in the city lockup but also ordered to pay a substantial sum for the boy's apprenticeship.[36] Infanticides—though rare events in the court records—were treated with horrified repugnance and, except in rare cases of mitigation, were routinely executed after humiliating public display.[37] Children's illnesses were not accepted with resignation. The physician and writer Stephanus Blankaart, for example, wrote a popular treatise specifically devoted to their diagnosis and treatment.[38] And all household management books came complete with advice on simples and "home medicines" (*huismiddelen*) that could be administered in the all too likely event of a child's falling sick or meeting with some sort of accident. *The Experienced Householder,* for instance, gave detailed advice on treating fevers with tinctures mixed from rose water and vinegar for the brow, chicory root and honey for belly pains, or as an alternative, a spoon of aniseed water or warm beer on a cloth while the navel is stroked with distilled cumin and wormwood oil. Convulsions were recognized then, as now, as crises that demanded professional attention from a physician, as did any suspicious outbreak of red spots, especially when combined with great thirst.

Physicians' concern, of course, does not necessarily indicate solicitousness on the part of the parents. Yet in genre painting — the type of art that not only speaks of the lives of ordinary burghers but was bought by them — the Dutch invented the poignant image of the sick child, most memorably in Gabriel Metsu's heartrending study in the Rijksmuseum.[39] Were there no other scrap of evidence available, the Metsu painting would stand all by itself as the most eloquent testimony imaginable to the tender pain felt by Dutch adult culture for its threatened *schaapjes*. Scrutinizing another kind of differential evidence, there does not seem to have been the same readiness to abandon children in public places among the poorest families in Holland as elsewhere in Europe. In Paris, for example, upwards of three hundred children were found abandoned in the 1670s, whereas the figure for Amsterdam, half as big a city, for 1700, was around twenty.[40] (And it was only towards the end of the eighteenth

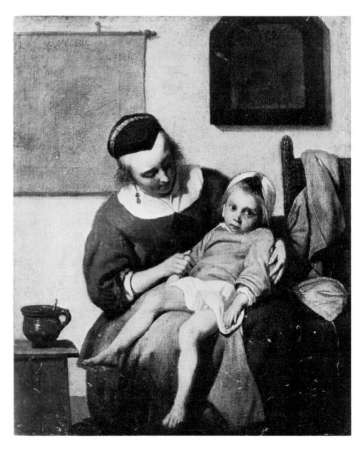

267. Gabriel Metsu, *The Sick Child.*
Rijksmuseum, Amsterdam

century that Amsterdam figures catch up with the general immiseration of the European scene elsewhere.[41]) The same pattern, moreover, seems to hold true for infanticide figures.[42] Both phenomena of relative benevolence may owe something to the more stable position of working families and their domestic budgets in the Republic, to the apparent ability—from celibacy or lower nuptial rates—of the Dutch population to stabilize its own growth and hold mean household size at the lowest in Western Europe. And the striking affluence and proliferation of orphanages and other institutions of charitable succor —even for children whose parents had belonged to no church congregation— obviously held down these unhappy statistics. Nonetheless, it seems equally likely that the disparity with other European urban experiences owed something to cultural aversion to child exposure and abandonment.

The protective instinct that I have suggested to be one of the controlling sentiments of family life was directed very intensely at offspring. A good deal of popular medical literature, for example, dealt with the optimal conditions under which children could be conceived, brought to term, and once safely delivered, nurtured through what was recognized as the dangerous period of early infancy. Cats, of course, had his own style of recommendation about selecting the kind of wife who would most likely bear fruit, and he meant it almost literally, since the frontispiece engraving to *Moeder* showed vines heavy with bursting grapes. And his specifications for the potentially fecund woman had a somewhat agricultural air about them. Such a wife should be:

> *Well made in limb and from a fleshy stock*
> *Of pleasing aspect and clean of teeth*
> *Born in the realm of our own Netherlands*
> *Not red of nose, nor otherwise unsound*
> *With no vile stink or rot in the mouth*
> *Not too scrawny nor too swollen up*
> *Not so familiar with carousing so as to . . . limbs*
> *Not in her first youth, nor all too much worn out*
> *And who before this time has borne a son already*

Especially desirable were those:

> *Whose nipples are rosy and sound; whose breasts are veined blue*
> *And made from solid stuff, and meet in one fine round*
> *Her milk of sweet flavor, neither too thin nor too fat.*[43]

The ideal age match, according to Cats, was a twenty-eight-year-old male with a twenty-one-year-old female. The author of *Venus Minsieke Gasthuis,* "I. V.

E., Medicinae Doctor" (probably the Rochelais physician and popular writer on sex, Nicolas Venette), knew that it was possible for a girl to conceive at the age of twelve or even ten, "if robust and strong," though eighteen to twenty was cited as the "normal" age of sexual maturity, with thirty-five as the outer date for fertility. In some rare cases, women had been known to give birth into their forties, but between forty-five and fifty was thought "unnatural" and over fifty nothing short of miraculous.[44] Many of the popular medical writers were prepared to endorse the usual remedies for sterility or impotence: truffles, asparagus, eggs, girolle mushrooms, oysters, ambered wine and the like. Van Beverwijck believed that conception simply depended on following his general prescriptions for a healthy life—clean air, plenty of fresh food and regular and moderate habits.[45] The most popular of all the reproductive and obstetric manuals, *Het Kleyn Vroetwyfs-boeck* (The Little Book of Midwifery), concerned itself in addition with the biological causes of male infertility. Passage of the seed from the testicles to the penis could be blocked, it was thought, and might be helped by massaging with eggs and oil, hanging the testicles in cold water or consuming copious quantities of fowl, meat and cow's milk—all thought excellent to give the testicles the energy they needed to transport fertile semen to the right place at the right time.[46]

The *Kleyn Vroetwyfs-boeck,* in its simple and inexpensive format with wonderful woodcut illustrations, was wholly traditional in its faithfulness to medieval and even classical reproductive biology. Pliny and Aristotle were cited along with Galen and Avicenna and the theory of the four humors. Since there was great interest in being able to determine the sex of a child before birth, popular works reiterated the old assumption that conception took place when warmer male seed generated heat in the cold, moist female seed. The degree of warmth in this ovarian combustion then determined the sex of the embryo, to the extent that girl fetuses would cool a pregnant woman while males would warm her.[47] While not much could be done after conception to affect this outcome, consuming hot and dry foods beforehand might tilt the odds towards producing a male. The same writer also claimed that if sexual activity was restricted to three or four times a month, the seed of both partners would be "better ripened, thicker and more dense with spirit" and so increase the chances of having a boy![48] Other works thought the phases of the moon to be crucial and there was no shortage of quacks offering miracle elixirs for the same purpose. De Witt scoffed at his wife Wendela's uncle, the great magnate Cornelis de Graeff, for putting his trust in one such superquack, Franciscus Joseph Borri, who claimed to be able to fix the sex of a fetus by the administration of a mysterious powder.[49]

Van Beverwijck, Blankaart and the *Kleyn Vroetwyfs-boeck* were concerned to provide advice on how to conduct life following conception so as to give the fetus the best chance of delivery at term. The *Kleyn Vroetwyfs-boeck* in its tenacious adherence to the obstetrics of the humors supposed that the uterus of older women (in their thirties) had dried out and therefore needed refreshment with warm and watery matter to soften it for nourishing the fetus. Young fat capons, goose fat, olive oil, wine and water, fat fish and above all, of course, large quantities of butter were recommended for this particular concern.[50] Van Beverwijck, as befitted a self-consciously more "modern" counselor, was somewhat better informed about nutrition, and advised that it would affect the size of the baby as well as the mother's health. Pregnant women were to eat sensibly, though not excessively, and try to ensure regular bowel movements. Stewed apples and prune juice in the mornings, or rhubarb with (inevitably) generously buttered food was recommended.[51] (The Dutch diet was in any case so heavily biased toward dairy foods that there was little chance of falling behind in lactic and calcium intake.) Above all, violent purges and enemas were to be avoided, as well as anything else that might shock the system unduly. That meant steering clear of powerful spices (even in the interests of a male heir) as well as noxious vapors given off by bad cheeses and eggs or the aroma from musk or civet. Dancing, "frisky jumping," riding and excessively vigorous exercise were also classified as harmful. Characteristically, *Venus Minsieke Gasthuis,* that compendium of sexual information, observed that the sexual as well as the gastric appetite of women was fiercer in pregnancy, and most authorities warned that overindulgence in sex could harm the developing fetus. "Who plows the field too much when the seeds are sown/Will spoil his own work and make it o'erthrown" was Cats's fustian way of putting it.[52]

Of course, mere determination to produce children under optimal circumstances does not in itself signify the budding of affectionate concern for infants, especially when the evidence is drawn exclusively from sexual health or popular medical manuals. But at least one contemporary witness to both the terror, and the euphoria of childbirth survives in a remarkable manuscript journal written over the space of fifty-two years by a midwife practicing in the small northern Friesland market town of Dokkum.[53] Like all such precious pieces of evidence, it stands as an island in a ocean of documentary silence, and the very fact of its conscientious recording might make it atypical. But that is not how it strikes the reader. On the contrary, it is the sheer ordinariness of the diary and its peculiar combination of account book and confessional journal that gives it the stamp of absolute credibility. It is, above all, a private document, so that there is no reason to suppose the writer held anything back for the sake of good taste. Indeed so harrowing are some of the details she records that it is impossible to imagine their being amended for posterity. More striking is her pious and eloquent acknowledgment of the tragedies of the birth bed. One would suppose that if a conventional attitude of stoical resignation or protective callousness would be registered anywhere, it would be in the record of one who witnessed obstetric calamity as a regular occurrence. Yet expectations to the contrary, the journal reveals an extraordinary degree of emotional and moral engagement in the business of birth, day after day, week in and week out, right to Vrouw Schrader's ninety-first year, in 1745, when she delivered her last baby, and her now trembling hand made the final record in her book.

The sensitivity working through these pages is all the more striking considering the poor reputation enjoyed by midwives in the seventeenth century. Doctors like van Beverwijck and Blankaart were suspicious of their notorious amateurism, their unregulated practice, their ignorance of anatomical detail and their reliance on folk remedies. In the informal medical hierarchy that placed academically trained doctors at the top and empirically practiced surgeons well below them, midwives were relegated to a still lower grade. There was an even more disreputable realm of semilicit and illicit medicine, practiced by quacks and cupping-women, barbers and bone setters, that flourished among the poor and working population.[54] And within that "medical underground"—fiercely opposed by both church authorities and surgeons' guilds—there was a further division of labor in which women predominated in certain specialized areas like cupping or blistering (an activity that also included soothsaying, white witchery and abortions), and clystering.[55] Midwives were certainly in a higher bracket of income, clientele and reputation, but they were nonetheless the target of the surgeons' jealousy against any infringement of their monopolistic control through guild regulation. The seventeenth century also saw the gradual accumulation of experimental obstetric knowledge startlingly witnessed by the *Anatomy Lesson* of Frederick Ruysch in which a dead infant is the object of the surgeon's dissection while the anatomist's own son, shown at right, ponders simultaneously the mysteries of mortal flesh and immortal science. One of his colleagues, Hendrik van Roonhuysen (1625–72), who had invented an obstetric "lever" in anticipation of forceps, became Amsterdam's official city obstetrician (*stadsvroemeester*) in 1648, and was a declared enemy of the assumed primitivism of "empirical" midwifery.[56] In Dordrecht, Van Beverwijck's own town, an edict had been issued permitting midwives to practice only when a licensed doctor was also present.[57] And he also noted that their original business in the village had been as much social as medical, centered on matchmaking and rough-and-ready examination of the couple's suitability for producing children. Their attendance at the childbed was simply in order to "receive" the infant and so discharge the final obligation that had begun with the match. They were, in a sense, expert witnesses, or obstetric notaries, to the propriety of marriages—to their settlement and successful consummation (for they were often called in

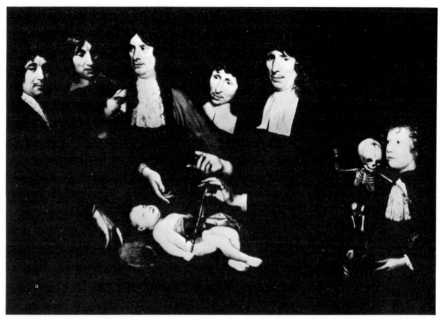

268. Jan van Neck, *The Anatomy Lesson of Dr. Frederick Ruysch,* 1683. Amsterdam Historical Museum

to determine if a wife was pregnant or not)—and to the proper delivery of the conjugal offspring. And their strategic position in all these critical events in the history of a marriage invited abuse—or at least a flourishing popular lore of fraud and deceit, of substitution of foundlings or the removal of "monsters."[58] Not that midwives were reputed to be wholly without special knowledge and craft. They were, of course, meant to be on hand in the event of complications and have some art—the *kunst* that was their key word—in correcting them. And they were responsible for immediate postnatal care: the cleaning and swaddling of the newborn.

Though Catharina Schrader herself was cut from a completely different cloth from these ancient stereotypes, she did share some of the physicians' mistrust of midwives who relied more on old lore than practical wisdom. And she often commented on the benighted superstitions with which the village people of Friesland surrounded the admittedly alarming business of childbirth. But she thought of the surgeons, if anything, as an even greater threat to the survival of both mother and child. Most midwives deferred to their authority, their being both male and passing as having a smattering of learning, but it surely helped Vrouw Schrader's confidence in occasionally contradicting their opinions to have had close knowledge of their practice from her surgeon husband. She took special exception to their combination of incompetence and dogmatism, especially in cases of premature diagnosis of fetal death. (Apart from unmistakable signs such as the early expulsion of placenta and cord, surgeons used very rough-and-ready techniques to determine this: a loss of umbilical pulse, the failure of a fetus to suck on an inserted finger.) In February 1711, for example, at the village of Nijkerk in the Oostdongeradeel district, the midwife was called to help a farmer's wife who had been in labor for three days and had been attended by another midwife and a *vroedmeester,* one van den Berg, who seems to have been both surgeon and male midwife. His opinion was that the child was already dead and that he would have to extract it to save the life of the mother. Its lodging in the birth passage was apparently so awkward that this would necessitate the amputation of its arms and legs *in utero* in order to free it. Any such surgical procedure would, of course, have hugely increased (if not guaranteed) the chances of fatality for the mother, quite apart from the distress, coming on top of the agonies of a pro-longed and apparently fruitless labor. At this point Vrouw Schrader appeared, dismissed midwife, surgeon and neighbors — for births, especially in the countryside, were still very much public events. The mother was laid in a freshly made warm bed and given a cup of mild broth as a fortifier. After an hour, labor duly recommenced and the mother was delivered of a baby daughter very much alive and kicking.

"And I said to the doctor — 'See, here is your dead child' — to his shame. He thought perhaps he would earn a hundred guilders! The friends and neighbors were very much amazed at this. Mother and child are well in heart."[59] On an earlier occasion, in 1706, the midwife and the doctor played the opposite roles (though still with the former triumphing over the latter). A delivery involving a *placenta previa* had a doctor in difficulties but still insisting that the baby was alive, whereas Vrouw Schrader took little time to show that it had been dead for some time and to concentrate her attention on the mother.[60]

It seems probable, then, that this boldness and skepticism about surgeons' monopoly on wisdom derived from personal experience. Her husband, Ernst Willem Cramer, came from Lingen across the River Ems and had set up practice in a remote area of Friesland facing the islands of the Waddenzee in a thinly populated countryside dotted with Mennonite settlements and villages of poor boatmen and fisherfolk. Before 1723 there was no medical college for the north of the province, nor even any guild of master surgeons to regulate the art. So that it seems possible that Cramer was himself something of an empirical rather than formally trained and licensed doctor. But if that was the case, there was nothing amateurish about his widow's work. It is not too much to say that she thought of herself as a mistress of a particular professional craft and that she strove to practice it with the highest standards of devotion and skill.

There was, however, nothing especially vocational about the way in which Catharina embarked on a career of midwifery. It was strictly a matter of family emergency that prompted her to find some means of supporting herself and her six children when their father died in 1692.[61] At the age of thirty-eight, she set up as traveling midwife serving the impoverished isolated hamlets of the coastal and island villages near Hallum. The physical conditions of her work—long distances to cover, rugged transportation and meager remuneration—must have been dispiriting. And her very first call was nearly her last. For on Twelfth Night, 1693, in the teeth of a biting snowstorm, she traveled for three hours on a sledge to the little village of Wyn to deliver a young woman in the throes of a brutal labor. When she arrived at last, she was half dead from the bitter cold. "I was carried into the house and my mouth broken open (it was iced over), brandy was poured into my mouth and there I found a hearty fire." After reviving she set to work with a will and after a hard and prolonged labor delivered her charge of a healthy daughter.

Brave and doughty though she showed herself in these early days, her inexperience made her somewhat defensive when working alone. And her diary entries for this time betray some signs of nervousness, calling on other, more senior midwives and deferring obediently to the surgeons who augmented the fees she charged directly to the family with an additional small sum. Both those fees were calculated on the length of the labor and the hours of her attendance, but an average two-day labor would come to about two guilders—something like the weekly wage of a skilled laborer. She received her fee, of course, irrespective of the outcome of the birth, which was not always happy. Her earnings over the most thriving years of her practice, between 1696 and 1712, varied from two to three hundred guilders, by no means a fortune, but a sufficient income—rather more than a schoolmaster's or a country predikant's but less than a prosperous shopkeeper's—to keep her family decently housed, fed and clothed. Her income, and perhaps her status, were about on a par with those of a custodian of a municipal orphanage or almshouse.[62] At any rate, by 1695 she had acquired enough experience, confidence and, presumably, savings to move to the market town of Dokkum, where she was to stay for the next fifty years.

In Dokkum, Vrouw Schrader seems to have established a formidable reputation very quickly, delivering eighty babies in her first year. The seasonality of births was very marked, with high periods occurring in July and August (nine months after the slaughtering of the family pig or ox). But throughout the year, the pace at which she worked was punishing and presupposes extraordinary reserves of stamina. In August 1696 alone she was at fourteen childbeds and in one rushed spell delivered on the 17th, 18th, 21st, 23rd, 25th, 27th and 28th of the month! By 1698 her rate had risen to 123 births, one of which was that of Kaat van Aylva, the wife of the *grietman* (the patrician sheriff) of Westdongeradeel, and for which she received the handsome fee of 66 guilders. The Aylvas were also the most powerful and influential noble family in the region, and from that time on, she had no need to seek out custom. In 1730, when she was evidently losing patients, the Aylvas remained faithful, for she delivered another son from a marriage between the family and another immensely powerful clan, the Burmania Rengers, and received 50 guilders this time for her services. In between she treated the wives of army officers, burgomasters, and advocates in Dokkum, but her clientele was by no means drawn exclusively from the elite. The Dokkum patriciate would hardly have stretched far enough to have made her a living even on the modest scale that sufficed for her needs. So that she ministered to the wives of tradesmen of the town, of Reformed Church predikants and Mennonite dominies, schoolmasters, skilled artisans like masons and carpenters, but also to the wives of poorer farm laborers, rope makers, weavers and boatmen of the coastal villages. In her busiest year, 1706, she attended at 137 deliveries and made three hundred guilders — no mean achievement for a widow in a country town. And it seems likely that she had become something of an institution in Dokkum itself, familiar with both the local notables and the common people, apparently inexhaustible and a pious worthy of the church.

At the height of her career, in 1713, at age fifty-eight, she was married again, this time to a local goldsmith and burgomaster of Dokkum, Thomas Higt. Whether to oblige him, or more likely to enjoy some sense of ease, she all but gave up her practice, though presumably kept her hand in, as her journal records fifty-six deliveries made between 1714 and 1722. This period of family stability also gave her the opportunity to make sound matches for her daughters, one marrying her second husband's nephew, and another daughter marrying a local predikant. Seven years after her remarriage, her second husband died and she resumed work, a hard business, when she was well into her sixties. She enjoyed another brief flourish of activity in the early 1730s when her income rose again to 260 guilders, and when she was seventy-eight she calculated, with some satisfaction, that she had to date received some 8,500 guilders for her lifetime's services. But despite this autumnal vigor — which included delivering her own grandchildren (including a grandson who arrived in 1726 as a stubborn breech baby and was named for Ernst Willem) — she never recovered the prime of her trade. In her old age she grumbled of local petty jealousies undercutting her custom and she may have been reluctant to use the forceps that were becoming accepted even in the Frisian backwaters. The truth behind her dwindling practice was of course that she was simply unable to sustain the grueling pace required in her kind of work, with draining two- or three-day labors coming perhaps twice a week. Yet she soldiered on indomitably, and even in 1741, at the age of 86, attended at twenty-eight births. In her late eighties, her entries become so spidery-frail that it seems astonishing that she managed to deliver twenty children in 1743 (at 88) or even the single births recorded, with no fee, in both 1744 and 1745. She died the following year, in 1746, with a faithfully kept account of four thousand babies to her credit.

Babies may have been Vrouw Schrader's livelihood for over fifty years, but they were more than just her stock-in-trade. For while her diary has routine entries when all goes well, there are unsparing, detailed descriptions of births that involve complications, and it is plain that she was emotionally as well as physically drained by these traumatic experiences. "Dear Lord preserve me from any such unfortunate births" is one of her standard responses to these calamities. And she was not thinking merely of her own susceptibilities either, for she not infrequently describes the labor pains endured by mothers as a "martyr's torment" or "torture"—and hated, above all, to see clumsy or unskilled midwives making that torment even worse.

There is no question that Vrouw Schrader drew great satisfaction from delivering babies in difficult and dangerous parturition. And it may have been her dexterity in these situations that produced what, by seventeenth-century standards, especially in rural areas, seems to have been a relatively low neonatal mortality rate. Or perhaps some revision of estimates—based on notoriously scanty data—may be in order.[63] Being a private document (and given its transparent conscientiousness of record), Vrouw Schrader showed no interest in disguising information. If anything, it draws attention to the more dramatic disasters in the longer and more graphic entries. But throughout Vrouw Schrader's career, the average rate of stillbirths—including babies that were dead before labor or died during delivery—ran at around one in thirteen or fourteen and rarely rose above fifteen percent. This compares with rates given by Flandrin for northern France around the same period of one in four, and in southern France, of one in eight, and by Lebrun for rural Anjou of one in three.[64] In 1696, her first year in Dokkum, she counted six stillbirths and one baby that died during delivery (as well as two harelips and three prema-ture infants, all of whom survived) out of a total of eighty-one deliveries. By modern standards, of course, this is nothing to boast about (nor did she), but with rudimentary equipment and practical rather than learned knowledge, it was something of an accomplishment.

Childbirth, for midwife and mother alike, was only too "natural" at the turn of the eighteenth century. Vrouw Schrader was, in effect, a transitional type between the most uninformed practices of the old midwifery, many of which appalled her, and the beginnings of an organized, formal obstetric pedagogy, the benefits of which she was too early a practitioner to enjoy. So that while she avoided some of the worst traditional practices—relentless purging of women while in labor, in the mistaken belief that it would accelerate contractions, or overfeeding followed by inducements to vomit— her standard equipment was rudimentary. She took with her by way of medical tools only shears for cutting the cord, hooks to help with turning infants in awkward presenting positions or to extract fetuses that had died *in utero,* and a catheter. There is no indication in her diaries of any familiarity with the relatively new Dutch appliances: Palfyn's head-manipulator or Hendrik van Roonhuysen's more advanced lever. And although forceps were gradually introduced in the early decades of the century, Vrouw Schrader seems to have been in no rush to accept them as an obvious improvement on her own hands. It also seems unlikely that she knew of, much less encouraged, the daring suggestion made by one book that mothers might go through labor more comfortably on their hands and knees.[65] The *Kleyn Vroetwyfs-boeck* happily remained loyal to the traditional *kraamstoel* (birthing chair) that allowed a sitting or squatting position, with its front cut away to allow the midwife to work, and curtains to protect the laboring mother's modesty.[66] It also allowed easy changes of position with pillows and cushions, much recommended by traditional obstetrics (and, of course, rediscovered by the "new" obstetrics of the twentieth century). Her medicines—*moederskruiden,* such as they were— were very much those of the "old" obstetrics, of Paracelsian vintage and older: tinctures of myrrh, aloe and aluwe, used as cataplasms and laves when, as very frequently happened, the perineum tore during the furious struggle to extract the fetus or in its final violent expulsion from the birth passage.[67] Saffron and aniseed waters were used as a mild sedative, and it seems likely that she followed "Doctor I.V.E.'s" recommendation to use warmed wine to soothe the inflamed and traumatized organs.[68] One traditional practice that probably was not a good idea was the use of food, albeit usually broths, to keep up the mother's strength during labor. And country midwives were even more liberal in their use of alcohol to accelerate, as they supposed, the progress of contractions. Vrouw Schrader occasionally prescribed alcohol—probably diluted eau-de-vie—to relax muscles during hard and prolonged labor,[69] and some- times melted butter as a lubricant to ease the emergence of the infant.[70] But she was dismayed by some of her sisters' ignorance about the excesses of drinking in labor. In 1708 she hastened to the bedside of a woman who had been laboring three days and was "desperate and burning," indeed who seemed plain drunk. By her side was an enormous flagon of beer. "I chastened the midwife who replied that she would have it so. . . . I said that if her child were born the bladder would burst in such a state. . . . she answered me that in a quarter of an hour she [the mother] had sunk a whole tankful."[71]

Catharina Schrader's most important tools, though, were her own hands, which seem to have been formidable instruments, at once pliant and immensely strong. She knew, from direct observation, that manipulation by brute force, seizing the fetus's ears or putting a hand in its mouth and lugging, could do horrifying damage and mutilation. If her own manipulative techniques were any more refined, it was, however, more through common sense than any formal instruction. She knew of ways to pull from under the fetal jaw, and how to turn fetuses carefully at the shoulder. She also appreciated how important the progressive dilation of the cervix was in gauging the progress and tempo of the labor, how easily the placenta could detach during a struggle to right a breech presentation, and how dangerous a prolapsed cord might be (nearly always fatal, whether through strangling or, more usually, infection). Most of her crises were of this kind, resulting from irregular or perilous presentations. In July 1696, for example, a rope worker's wife, Marijken, had twin girls, one presenting breech, the other transverse. She succeeded "through the art" (i.e., of manipulation) in delivering the breech feet first, but "with great difficulty," and thought that the placenta was bound to detach. Nonetheless both deliveries were brought off safely, and mother and children survived the ordeal unscathed.[72] She could do even better if the occasion called for it, delivering triplets, the first a breech, in September 1727, and in 1742, when she was eighty-seven, battling heroically for two hours to deliver a baby whose feet had been presented first. "In my forty-four years of work never have I seen so great violence," she wrote—yet both mother and child survived undamaged.[73]

Though the number of successful breech deliveries was impressive, they were always offset by the regularity of disasters. Torn and detached *placentae previae* during labor were almost always fatal; sometimes the infant smothered, sometimes it was strangled by the cord before it could be reached. And the battles to extract a fetus without tearing the mother to pieces—but while, of course, she must have been enduring excruciating agony—sometimes went on for days. Entries of births that lasted for three, four or five days appear at least once a month, and the sense of her comments is very often that the longer such labors went on, the less hope there was of saving both mother and child. Caesareans were very rare and never attempted on a live mother, but Vrouw Schrader could manage them on an already dead or expiring mother where there was indication of fetal life.[74] And quite often the midwife blamed herself for a tragedy even when there was little that could have been done. In 1701, after a long labor where arms were awkwardly born and the infant's head crammed against the pubic bone, the baby died in the passage, and she wrote that "after all that I made a good birth into a bad one."[75] There were other terrible occasions—as one in 1703, when the infant died before birth but it proved almost impossible to extract it except by using the hook and hauling it roughly down the passage. She was also well aware that even those successfully delivered might easily die in the days and weeks after birth, and she believed that if there were serious complications they would show within nine or ten days postpartum. These were almost always dysenteric or alimentary disorders and infections, and there was not much that the midwife or surgeon could do other than offer the simple kinds of tonics that Blankaart and similar writers described. Though no detailed notes were made on follow-up visits, many of those that recorded the well-being of mothers and children, especially after any kind of difficult delivery, were made after that critical period.

Birth deformities, of course, were distressingly common, and Vrouw Schrader's response to them varied a good deal according to the circumstances. Sometimes she took a detached, clinical interest, noting in February 1710 that she delivered a child (that survived for half an hour) with a gaping hole between its abdomen and its stomach "as big as a gold guilder" through which one could see into the body cavity and inspect the liver, heart and lungs.[76] At other times, she was more pious and emotional, thanking the Lord for carrying off a deformed child when it could only have given sorrow to its family. In January 1727 she wrote "God Almighty be thanked" that a hard cervix had killed off an infant who in any case would have been born without nose or mouth. "I can never marvel enough at Your miracles in these happenings, and the mother is doing well,"[77] she wrote, all in one rush of relief. She also knew that ignorant and superstitious villagers were capable of dreadful cruelty to any deformed creature that might survive. In November 1708, for example, at Oostzum, a farm laborer's wife had a posterior breech where the feet were born with difficulty but the head became firmly lodged at the cervix and could not be born. When the dead child was inspected, she wrote, "it was a pig's head, with no nose . . . very wretched. One hand had three fingers with one nail; the other the fingers had also grown into a single nail. The feet were the most terrible of all. O Lord, preserve us from such happenings."[78] What made this awful event even worse was the gossip of the villagers who on seeing the "monster" said that the mother had had so many pigs about her when she was pregnant that when she was at table one of them got up her skirts. Schrader was appalled by these kinds of "follies" (*zotterijen*) but never surprised.

While her compassion was always with the mothers in these dreadful circumstances, her piety could not but prompt her to judge some women who gave birth in morally suspicious circumstances. If all went well, she merely noted that there was no husband, sometimes adding the observation "Heer such-and-such's girl," with obvious implications. But at least once she felt that a sinner had been visited with terrible punishment. In the summer of 1709 the daughter of the gatekeeper of the Three Pipes Inn whom the midwife called "a disreputable young woman" was delivered of a child with deformed hands and feet and shriveled arms. Mercifully the child died within three weeks, but

Vrouw Schrader wrote that "The Lord punished her because she had herself sworn that she would not be a mother until she knew better."[79]

These were rare lapses of charity, though. For the most part, Catharina Schrader's journal is a document of rare sensitivity in the midst of circumstances that alternated between exhausted contentment and the most harrowing fear and sorrow. The midwife herself emerges as a woman of astonishing physical stamina, almost incredible calm and sangfroid in desperate situations, but one who never seemed to treat her patients as so much human livestock. And at the bottom of it all, with her six children and many grandchildren about her, there was obviously a passionate resolution to bring babies into the world without the terror, mutilation and grief that all too often accompanied their arrival. She seems, in short, as touched by the "sentiment" and "affect" towards mothers and infants as one could possibly imagine in any culture at any time. Yet she had, always, the feeling of a pious Dutch Calvinist that she bore a heavy responsibility before God and her fellow Christians. In 1706, the prayer with which she always began the entries of a new year declared:

> In my fiftieth year, as I descend in my years and climb up on the heavenly stairs towards my holy and blessed Jesus Christ, may the Lord my God in my dire need once more help your poor servant and give me strength and might, and keep me from bad and the wounds of calumny so that I might carry on with such heavy work with your help and through that your great and holy name will be thankfully praised. Amen.

It is difficult to discern anything either in the manual literature or in the record of immediate practical experience represented by the Schrader diary that suggests the sort of "protective callousness" that historians have associated with the high infant mortality rates of the seventeenth century. The Dutch did accept the loss of their babies and small children as the will of the Almighty, and consoled each other with that grim truth, as well as the standard cold comfort that little ones were better off in paradise than in the mortal world of tears. But these stock condolences ought in no sense to be taken as inconsistent with profound grief.

The impression of a culture in which passive resignation before the grim reaper and his predilection for small babies should at least be modified by one in which a safe delivery was treated as a matter of the most desperate importance. And by the same token, postpartum care and the welfare of the infant in its earliest weeks and months was also considered to be of the utmost importance in enhancing the prospect's of the baby's survival. Since it was common knowledge that this was the period when a child was most vulnerable to the innumerable lethal infections and contagions, medical writers placed great emphasis on family instruction in the basic needs of diet, hygiene and practical home medicine. The notion that infants were left to survive somehow in an environment of dirt, ignorance, malnutrition and periodically brutal handling assumes that the worst conceivable situation was in fact the norm— a misconception that would work equally well (or badly) for the twentieth century as for the seventeenth.

In fact, the advice in much of the early popular literature on infant care hardly differs from what are still the standard recommendations. Stephanus Blankaart's little book on child sicknesses, for example, was written in simple, intelligible Dutch rather than the Latin reserved for the profession, and was published in relatively cheap editions.[80] Like most popular medical manuals and treatises it enhanced its appeal with plates, some of them catering to the ghoulish taste for clinical freaks and deformities, illustrating the "scaly child," the "child born without an anus," the "child with intestine outside the body" and other such horrors. For the most part, though, it was concerned with wholly everyday matters of childrearing, and it was surprisingly comprehensive in its coverage. It not only dealt with the main ailments affecting babies and small children, but also gave advice on breast-feeding and other nutrition, physical handling of babies, tantrums and emotional difficulties, first aid, potty training and even early play and instruction. (Like many humanist doctors, Blankaart was hostile to regaling children with traditional ghost stories and frightening tales and rather solemnly proposed true histories or adventures instead.[81]) In other words, it anticipated almost exactly the standard advice of most child care literature available in the 1980s. Some of its specific recommendations—for example, on cord care: cleaning with spirit twice or three times a day followed by wipes with clean soft cloth—literally do not differ at all from the counsel given to new parents (myself and my wife) in "postpartum class" two years ago.[82] Van Beverwijck supplied a particular recipe for a potion made of syrup of violets and honied butter to cleanse out the meconium from a newborn's bowels.[83] The Kleyn Vroetwyfs-boeck insisted on caring for the infant's eyes with a clean linen or if possible silken cloth, and to avoid brilliant sunlight, which distresses babies (as indeed it does). And there are a good many tips in Blankaart's manual that will be immediately recognizable to modern parents: do not take your baby to bed with you, however tempting, as too many have been suffocated by parents rolling over on them; don't worry about cradle cap, but use a little oil (or butter) to moisten the scalp if need be; hiccups are nothing to be alarmed over and will pass without the infant's minding (though he could not resist repeating the story of an eleven-year-old boy who had hiccuped incessantly for over a year); don't leave babies dirty for too long or they will develop skin sores and rashes; don't let them go on crying for too long without seeing what the matter is.

Indeed washing the newborn—its whole body, as well as its ears, nose and eyes—was thought beneficial, rather than hazardous, for the baby's health, though afterwards it was greased with butter or almond oil or rose water. Teething pains were to be expected at six to eight months, and a teething ring made from ivory or an oblong hard biscuit should be offered to bring the baby some relief and help its little teeth grow strong. Remedies were simple and sensible. For prolonged hiccups, Blankaart prescribed tincture of saffron, mint or anise water; for excessive wind, a steadier feeding routine; for diarrhea, a tonic made with cinnamon, crocus and a little opium to settle the stomach. For older children's nightmares brought on by erratic feeding or teething, "sleep potions" from *Diascordium mithridatis,* anise and, more doubtfully, crabs' eyes, were offered, though Blankaart recommended gentle consolation by parents and a change of sleeping position as the best antidote. For common coughs and colds he suggested making sure the child was kept warm at night and so could sweat out the fever, and avoiding all kinds of sugary comforters often mistakenly given.[84] The ailments to take seriously and call a physician about were measles—recognized as potentially lethal—any sign of epilepsy, repeated and spontaneous nosebleeds, and severe thrush or aphtha.

Like van Beverwijck, though, Blankaart placed great emphasis on a proper and nutritious diet as the best means of maintaining good health and the infant's resistance to disease. He even knew, before European medicine had any understanding of vitamin deficiencies, that the best way to deal with rickets was to alter the child's diet in the direction of more fresh fruit and vegetables. And rose hip syrup was certainly recognized as a healthy cordial for small children. Like all contemporary (and indeed earlier) medical authorities, he insisted on maternal nursing as an indispensable element in the child's health. Once teeth appeared, however, he was concerned to distinguish between traditional baby foods and those that he thought most suitable for the infant's tender digestive system. Popular "paps" made of water, old white bread, sugar and wine were frowned on, as were those made from either sweet milk, biscuit and sugar, or beer, bread and syrup. All of this he thought too rich, too fatty or in other ways harmful and recommended instead a milder concoction of half water, half milk and old plain bread or biscuits. As for solid foods, when they came in, highly salted meats like ham, smoked bacon and pork (of course the standard meat for poorer farm families) should be avoided, as should fruit that was too acid or sour.

Recommendations on swaddling have been taken by historians of childhood as one of the signs of a premodern approach to infancy.[85] Swaddling has been thought to represent the kind of manipulative convenience that betrays parental indifference or self-centeredness rather than a more affectionate and benign attitude towards the child. And it is certainly true that objections to swaddling resulted in the gradual removal of the bands in the eighteenth and nineteenth centuries (though swaddling seems to have persisted in Russia, at any rate, until the early twentieth). But of course, there is swaddling and swaddling. Much depended on the tightness of the bands and the length of time that the infant was supposed to be swaddled. In the Dutch case, most authorities followed (and indeed quoted) Aristotle, Plato and Galen in recommending swaddling. But the classic reason given, to assist the sound growth of limbs, was often superseded by the need to protect the infant carefully from the cold and to help it sleep more soundly with the sense of protection that it needed in the period after birth. Nonetheless the packaging of the baby was undoubtedly overdone: bands of linen were wound carefully round its body from just below the neck to its feet, leaving it with little mobility. Yet modern authorities ought to hesitate before jumping to the conclusion that this was done essentially for the selfish convenience of parents, who were then free to ignore the baby or even hang the little parcel on a kitchen hook.[86] None of that callous indifference is at all apparent in Dutch child literature or painting. The swaddling of a baby twin being fed in an Esaias Boursse painting resembles exactly the tight blanket wrapping urged on modern parents to soothe very small babies by reproducing the snug fit of the womb. At this stage of their lives, security was of much greater importance than liberty, and there is equally no evidence that the swaddling bands remained on the infant after the first weeks, perhaps for two months at most. In the Thomas de Keyser picture of mother and child at the cradle, for example, it is quite apparent that the older baby — perhaps six or eight months of age — is no longer swaddled and is wearing shoes.

On the other stock criterion of "modern" infant care, there was no dissent. Maternal breast-feeding was urged by virtually every authority as imperative for the baby's health. Indeed Blankaart, Cats and Van Beverwijck all considered it to be *the* attribute of true mother love. "It can be no motherly heart that would, without [medical] reason let another suckle her children while her own breasts dried up," wrote Blankaart.[87] In *Moeder,* Cats composed a rapturous hymn in honor of the prolific splendor of the lactating breast:

> *Employ O young wife, your precious gifts*
> *Give the noble suck to refresh your little fruit*
> *There is nothing an upright man would rather see*
> *Than his dear wife bid the child to the teat*
> *This bosom that you carry, so swollen up with life*
> *So finely wrought, as if 't were ivory orbs*[88]

Neither "heavy beer" nor "rhenish wine" would do for the "fruit" but only "your pure milk can silence his cry." Beverwijck regaled his readers with all sorts of horror stories about wet nurses who fell asleep in front of fires while nursing, others who in a drunken stupor drowned their charges in tubs or deceitfully exchanged them for sickly infants. Wet nurses might be diseased or dry (and resort to polluted pap). "What mother would not rather suckle her child herself and so be a whole mother so as not to subject her innocent lamb to all these perils?"[89] Only if the mother was sick or diseased or dead should a wet nurse even be contemplated. And then care had to be taken that the nurse's milk was of a good color and texture: "neither brownish nor yellowish nor greenish, not bitter nor too salty but sweet, not too thick or bloody, not too fat nor greasy."[90]

But most of all it was well understood that the nourishment, both physical and moral, to be gained from breast-feeding was irreplaceable. "The reason for this is clear," wrote Blankaart, "since the child has already accustomed to nourishment within the mother," any change to another food source threatened that natural compatibility.[91] Much like a doctor today, he went on to prescribe a special regimen for the nursing mother. She should be warmly clothed, avoid strenuous activity (including sex, for it was thought that copulation affected the quality of the milk) and steer clear of wine and eau-de-vie. Beer, on the other hand, especially brown ale like Rotterdam or Weesper ale, was commended as nutritious. Buttermilk and whey, heavily salted or pickled foods and ripe game were all thought to pass on gas or else to sour the milk and were also disapproved of. Instead, fresh meat such as poultry, lamb and veal, fresh milk and stewed vegetables were approved of. Raw fruit and some vegetables, on the other hand, were thought to be full of "sourness" — especially salads, apples, cherries and pears and were best missed. If in spite of following this somewhat weak diet, flatulence occurred that could be passed on to the infant with the milk, aniseed or fennel-seed waters were thought to be an antidote. Nipples were to be treated with the utmost care, and if sore or cracked, gently rubbed with lanolin or oil of white lily. Should the opposite problem be the case and the infant be reluctant to suck, then some works counseled smearing the nipples with honey as an enticement.[92]

There is no doubt, then, about the ideal postnatal prescription: a healthy, loving mother nursing her own baby, and only gradually introducing any supplementary pap foods. But did Dutch mothers follow the doctors' advice? Wet nurses do seem to have been very rare in country or town and were generally called only in the case of maternal death or sickness. Moreover when a *min* was needed, it was a rule that she came to the home to nurse, where family and the *baker,* the dry nurse, could keep an eye on her, rather than the infant's being sent out. Even the *bakers,* who were a familiar feature of the burgher nursery until either the mother was churched or the infant weaned, came in on a daily basis rather than residing in the family home.[93] In that way most of the notorious abuses associated with nurses wet or dry could be avoided. The reluctance to use wet nurses unless medically necessary appears to have been true for all classes of the population, at least until well into the eighteenth century, when a few mothers among the regent elite took wet nurses to affect a certain status. Even this habit lasted but briefly before the rage for "natural" nursing, popularized by Tronchin, Rousseau and the sentimental Dutch women novelists, overtook aristocratic affectations. But most of the population did not need to be preached at by the eighteenth-century family moralists, for they had never lost the sense of maternal nursing as a basic family duty. We have only to look at one of the most basic items of traditional Dutch furniture, the simple, straw-woven *bakermat,* or nursing chaise — and find it included in many household inventories — to understand that maternal nursing was indeed the rule rather than the exception throughout Dutch society.

Perhaps it was even more than that. For it is as an expression of family love and devotion that mothers suckling their infants appear in innumerable Dutch genre paintings, drawings and prints. Before Dutch art made it a favorite theme, it had been confined to images of the Virgin nursing the Christ child. But there, as Leo Steinberg properly points out, theological symbolism necessarily took precedence over simple observation, so that in some pictures the child sucks while staring at the beholder or even in the act of walking.[94] In one of the most telling inversions of icons and objects in all of European religious art, the Dutch abolished images of the Madonna and Child from their churches, only to reinstate them surreptitiously as simple nursing mothers in paintings of church interiors. In many examples of the genre by Emmanuel de Witte and Gerard Houckgeest, Mariolatry has collapsed into mother-love. Even when nursing scenes are purely domestic, as in the great series by Pieter de Hooch, it should not surprise us to find them often placed immediately below sacred images. For maternal nursing was not just enforced; it was consecrated. Simple acts like that of lacing a bodice are lit by de Hooch with almost supernal purity. Thus, if the domestic setting was, for the Dutch, a personal church, the nursing mother was its primal communion.

Closely related to the nursing pictures are crib and cradle scenes in almost the same richness and number. Some of them show the child comfortably asleep — visually echoing the richness of seventeenth-century Dutch lullaby literature — "*Suja suja slaap.*"[95] Others have babies awake by their cribs. De Hooch's picture in this vein has become known as the *Moedervreugd,* and characteristically uses light raking across the faces of mother, child and crib to suggest a domestic paradise of repose and security. This, rather than any fantastic notion of sexual impropriety or the not much less farfetched notion

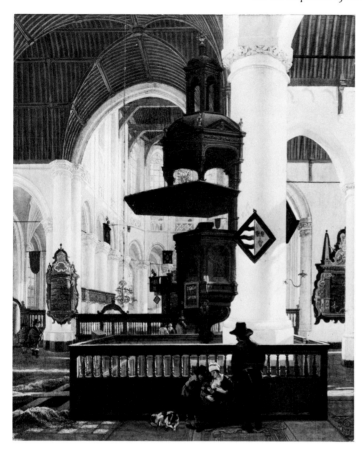

269. Gerard Houckgeest, *The St. Jacob's Kerk, The Hague*, 1651. Casualty, formerly Kunstmuseum, Dusseldorf

of manipulative parental indifference, is the true ethos of the Dutch burgher family home. It is the first *sustained* image of parental love that European art has to show us, and that, in itself, is a not unimportant moment in the history of the family (figs. 270–1).

Family harmony was not made from maternal affection alone. For another striking novelty of the family scenes is the domestication of the father and his absorption within the home circle. The donning of the paternity bonnet-crown was the outward sign of the father's pleasure in his offspring. More surprisingly, perhaps, fathers are occasionally shown participating in the work of caring for small children. Van Ostade has a peasant father spoon-feeding a child—an image he repeated many times—while the mother breast-feeds the baby. Willem van Mieris has a similar composite scene. And in a still more compelling image, an engraving for de Brune's *Emblemata* has a bonneted father walking his baby child in the night and crooning lullabies—a rich

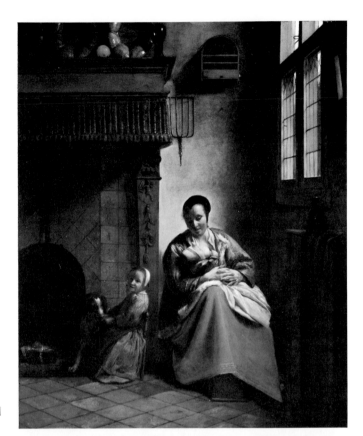

270. Pieter de Hooch, *Woman
Nursing an Infant, with a Child,*
1658–60. M.H. de Young Memorial
Museum, San Francisco

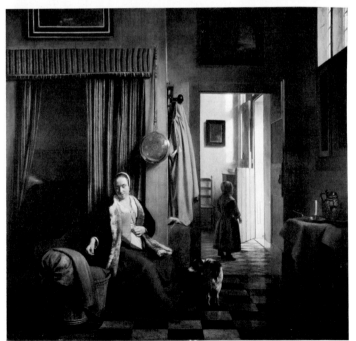

271. Pieter de Hooch, *A Woman
Lacing Her Bodice Beside a Cradle,*
1661–63. Gemäldegalerie, Berlin

Dutch genre—while his wife gets some needed sleep. This scene is so immediately familiar to modern households that its anticipation in this early-seventeenth-century print comes as an extraordinary shock. But the force of that surprise arises partly from stereotypical expectations of early modern paternity—the "patriarchal" family being governed by stern, remote and dynastically fixated fathers. It is possible that this impression may hold good for aristocratic households or even bourgeois homes in other cultures, but it is certainly misleading for the Dutch burgher society. It is, of course, true that the appealing de Brune print appears in the context of a text that evokes the help of God the *Father, "Schreeuw in nood, hemel's brood"* ("Cry in need, heavenly comfort"—literally, "bread"). And the *subscriptio* stresses the analogy between a baby's dependence on a father below and our frail dependence on our Father above, who likewise "soothes us with His words; takes us by the hand, sings us joyful songs . . . and brings about the death of all sorrows."[96] But the metaphor hardly dilutes the novelty of the image and its telling revelation of shared (though not interchangeable) domestic roles. For just as the childlike angel became the angelic child, the fatherly God became, without any suspicion of blasphemy, the godly *pater familias.* In so doing, the relation of signifying agent

272. Emblem from Johan de Brune, *Emblemata.* Houghton Library, Harvard University

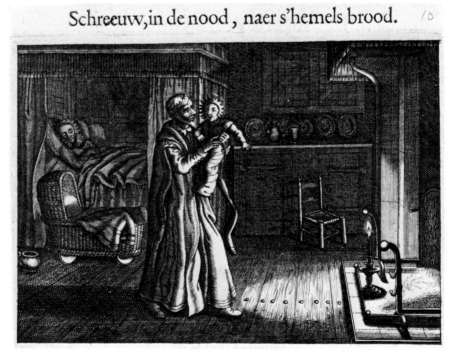

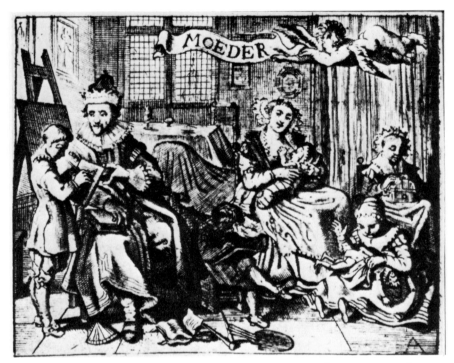

273. Adriaen van de Venne, *Moeder,* from Cats, *Houwelijck* (Amsterdam, 1632). Houghton Library, Harvard University

to the signified altered in a dramatic way from the business of other worlds to the business of this world.

While the domesticated father first appears in Dutch art, it would be anachronistic to cast him as the ancestor of the twentieth-century house-husband. The frontispiece print for Cats's *Moeder* is a perfect evocation of domestic harmony, with each member of the family content in his or her allotted role. But equally obviously the parental role models are separated by gender. So that it is the bonneted father who takes on the work of instructing his son according to classic humanist precepts, while the breast-feeding mother functions by example, as her daughter smacks the bottom of her doll. This is the ideal family regime according to the household gospel according to Cats. The active principle of instruction, the training for going into the world, is supplied by papa. The passive principle of training for reproducing and safeguarding the home (antiworld) is supplied by mama. Together they make a haven where those two key principles—liberty and protection, freedom and safety—are in precise equilibrium.

That, at any rate, was the idea. But children had an infuriating way of messing up great ideas, especially when coined by grown-ups for their benefit.

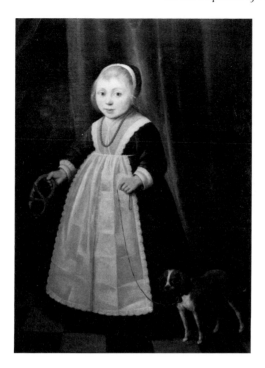

274. Jacob Gerritszoon Cuyp, *Portrait of a Child*. Collection of Sir John Plumb, Cambridge, England

v   THE PRETZEL AND THE PUPPY DOG

What is this little girl doing with the outsize pretzel?

It seems unlikely that she just happened to be toddling around with the monster cracker—along with her puppy dog—and that Jacob Cuyp thought the scene so fetching that he posed her just so, in the manner of Rembrandt's child drawings from life. Whimsical spontaneity may safely be ruled out. Cuyp was, among other things, a specialist in these dreamy, saucer-eyed, apple-cheeked kiddies, *"gras et joufflus* [fat and chubby-cheeked]," as Grosley was to typify them.[97] His winsome children were prettified versions of the moon-faced creatures that romp in Bruegel's "swarming" canvases. But they had been stripped of the problematic aspects of the child-personality—at once innocent and feckless, courting pleasure and moral disaster—that the sixteenth-century images personified. Such double-types do persist in Dutch representations. Both Dirk Hals and Jan Miense Molenaer created children whose play is made deliberately provocative, leering ragamuffins with rusty chins and knobbly noses. And thus begins the long tradition of countertypes that has endured throughout European culture. These "Haarlem" children are what adults fear: mischievous imps equipped with worldly knowledge, merciless instincts and inexhaustible energy. Their portraits talk back. To the truly fearful they seem to be literally little demons. Their opposites, then, must be what adults dream of: little angels. Cuyp's versions are so exquisite that they seem made of powder and rose water: the blond-tressed, snub-nosed types that, via the valley of pseudo-Renoir, made their relentless route march through the lower reaches of pastel-tinted bourgeois taste. They still stare with daunting cuteness from a million Mother's Day cards. Both the bad and the beautiful are emblematic types, of course, each as fantastic as the other, made to flesh out the contending traits that parents have seen in their small progeny.

So we should not expect Cuyp's little girl to be in the same blithe temper as her Victorian descendant: expressive only of the carefree poignancy of childhood, free to drift off to some gossamer paradise. Just as in the seventeenth century bubble-blowing was serious business, we should not be surprised to find signs of similar forebodings and anxieties about the fragility of

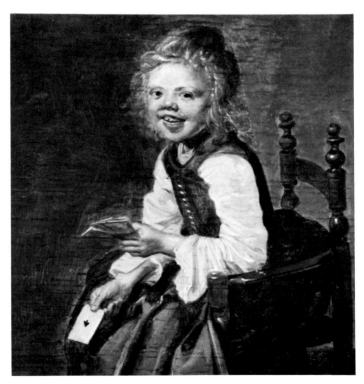

275. Detail from Dirk Hals, *Two Children*. Clark Institute, Williamstown, Mass.

infant innocence painted into the portrait. These items of symbolic baggage were not obligatory. It is not hard, especially in the later part of the century, when their gravity was making way for a lighter and more "conversational" image, to discover pictures of children unburdened by somber attributes. But in this case it is strictly inconceivable that Cuyp should have chosen so peculiar a set of props for their decorative effect or singular charm.

To make sense of the arrangement, we are bound to poke below the surface of pictorial description. And on closer inspection it turns out that nothing in the picture is the result of random record. What seem incidental details are symbolic couriers delivering messages about adult concerns over the fate of children's souls. The messages come wrapped in envelopes of outward appearances, but within lie texts of immaterial anxieties. Judging by some of the exterior clues it seems likely that the painting was done for a pious, if not Calvinist, family, since the coral necklace had long been a talisman to protect the wearer against evil and more particularly the incursion of demonic forces. The child's dress—as in other apparently pious family portraits like the Michiel Nouts in London—miniaturizes that of the exemplary God-fearing Calvinist mother, the safe haven of her sexual destiny.

The puppy symbolizes *leerzugtigheid,* Christian aptitude, and belongs to a tradition in which the instruction of children is reinforced by the visual analogue of training dogs in obedience. (Kittens, interestingly enough, seem in contrast to function as symbols of fecklessness or *unteachability,* so that when Steen paints children teaching a kitten to dance, we can assume that he has in mind a parody, not an exercise of true instruction.) The theme appears over and over again in Dutch art, in details that appear at first anecdotal but turn out on closer inspection to be important keys to understanding whole compositions. In Saenredam's *Interior of the Buurkerk at Utrecht,* for example, one of the two boys teaches a puppy in the aptitude posture and does so below a painting of Moses holding the Ten Commandments (fig. 276).

The instruction of puppies, moreover, was most often associated with girls. In the engraving for Cats's *Maagdewapen,* the maiden's coat of arms, the puppy dog is identified as *leerzugtigheid,* opposite the lamb, which represents *eenvoudigheid*, simplicity (fig. 277). Its most explicit transposition to painting was in the begging posture, seated on its hind legs, as it appears in the Ochtervelt of a predikant's family (fig. 278). (The prominently displayed top alludes to yet another stock emblem of pedagogical discipline, signifying perseverance.) But the leash in the Cuyp is surely meant to allude to the child's own early "leading bands," by which it was first taught the elements of worldly experience. Luiken's leading bands, of course, would make the parallel with godly instruction and obedience explicit. And the emblem *De Leiband* not surprisingly includes a dog in the background.

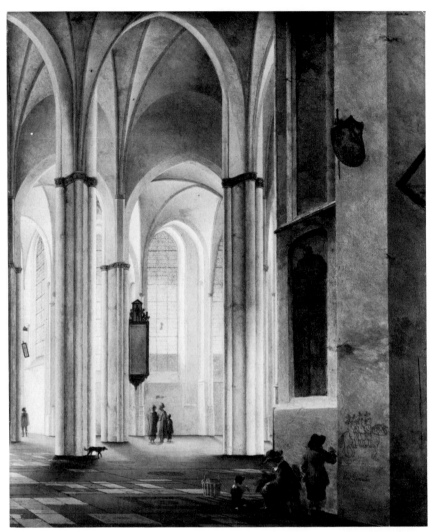

276. Pieter Saenredam,
*Interior of the Buurkerk,
Utrecht,* 1644. Courtesy of the
Trustees, National Gallery, London

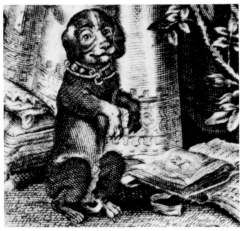

277. Detail from title page of Cats,
Houwelijck (Amsterdam, 1655)

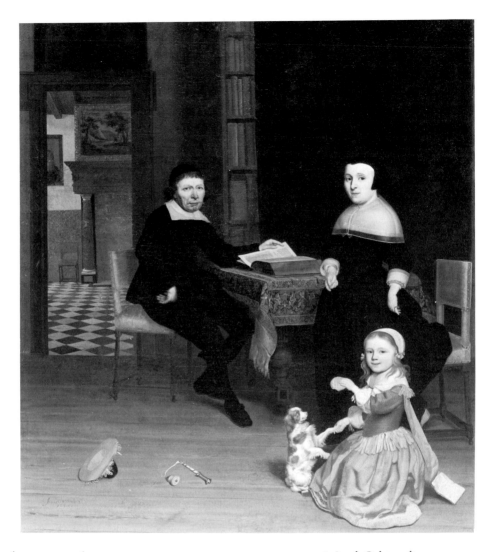

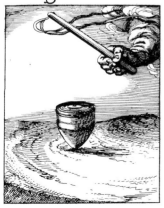

Soo langh de Roe wanckt.

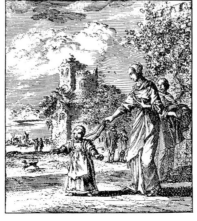

278. Jacob Ochtervelt,
Family Portrait, 1663. Fogg Museum
of Art, Harvard University

279. Emblem from Roemer
Visscher, *Sinnepoppen.* Houghton
Library, Harvard University

280. Jan Luiken, *"De leiband,"*
from *Des Menschen Begin, Midden
en de Einde.* Houghton Library,
Harvard University

So far, then, we have the two perennial motifs in the Dutch treatment of children—protection and instruction—included in the composition. But what of the most curious and extravagant attribute that Cuyp's child holds, the pretzel itself? As a form of baked confection, the shape is very old, perhaps of medieval Italian origins, though internationally familiar in the Middle Ages and appearing in illuminated manuscripts and Reformation woodcuts. A crudely functionalist folklore (to be found on the back of pretzel packets as well as more arcane sources) claims its origin in the dough ends which remained after monastic bakers had trimmed and decorated a loaf and which were looped and connected to form the device of hands in prayer. But pretzels also had particular associations with children. German sources tell us that they were worn as bracelets—*bretzelen*—on a child's arm at All Souls' Eve (Halloween) as amulets against the dark powers. So even in this connotation they would match well with the coral talisman, and with the ancient foreboding that the souls of children might be seized by the devil.

They also make appearances in Dutch iconography: with the children's train behind the forces of Lent in Bruegel's *Battle of Carnival and Lent* and in Jan Steen's Vienna *World Upside Down*. In the latter case, the biscuit is broken and along with other familiar debris—eggs especially—seems to belong to Steen's closet full of images of mischief. If we restore to the biscuit its Dutch name of *krakeling* (akin to the Old English *cracknel*), the connection between Bruegel and Steen, between contention and breakage, becomes clearer. The root of *krakeling* is *krakeel,* quarrel or fight, and when we know through antiquarian sources that small children pulled large *krakelingen* at each side in a little-finger tug-of-war similar to our practice with the wishbone of a chicken, a further piece of the mystery slots into place: the connection between playing and fighting. None of this would necessarily lead us to a particularly solemn conclusion, were it not for one more image of the *krakeling:* the engraving in the Calvinist de Brune's *Emblemata* that, as we have already seen, freely borrowed from the world of children to make rather dark and forbidding utterances on the dung-heap world. In this print, two pairs of hands clasp either side of the pretzel, like the hands of children in wishful play. But this is a didactic, not a ludic, image, for the text tells us that man's life is but struggle, and the struggle is predictably between the forces of good and evil, redemption and damnation.[98] In some other printed images the point is reinforced even more directly by the hands being those of God and the devil.

The iconographical jigsaw puzzle is now complete. And we can reasonably surmise that Cuyp painted his portrait for a pious family who wished to represent their little girl, as ministers constantly reminded them, as a theater of the contending powers of good and evil. The trophy for that tournament was her immortal soul. Innocent lamb, *onnozele schaapje,* that she was, her

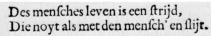

Des menfches leven is een ftrijd,
Die noyt als met den menfch' en flijt.

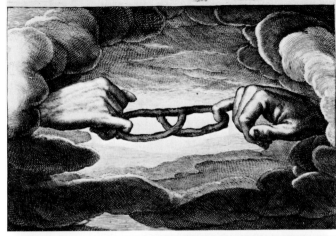

281. Emblem from Johan de Brune, *Emblemata,* 1624. Houghton Library, Harvard University

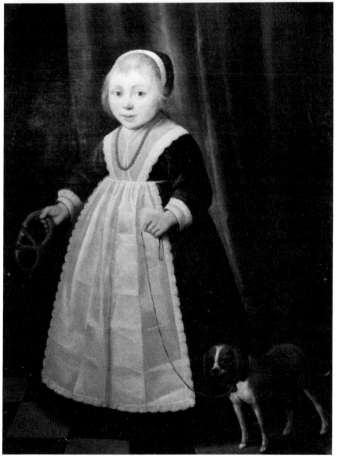

282. Jacob Gerritszoon Cuyp, *Portrait of a Child.* Collection of Sir John Plumb, Cambridge, England

frailty was symbolized in the frangible biscuit, compared in de Brune's *subscriptio* to the brittleness of men's spirit hard baked by the experience of the world. She would enjoy protection—the talismanic force of both pretzel and coral—but what was also needed was a more positive power: that of being led, through apt instruction, like the puppy, to a Christian life.

Like Cuyp's girl, children were perceived as being at risk in this way because they had within them from birth the seeds of both goodness and wickedness, a blessed or a cursed life. Choice or, more accurately, schooled choice was to play a vital role in the outcome of this moral contest. The Reformation had enhanced the importance of that trial by dissolving the stain of original sin. But Calvinism had replaced it with a doctrine of predestination that was just as heavy a moral burden on the shoulders of the child. But such was the enduring force of humanist educational ideas in the Netherlands, Erasmian teaching handed down in vernacular form through Valcoogh's *Rules for Schoolmasters*[99] that some room was made for the operation of free will in the instruction of the young. So that even though salvation no longer depended on such instruction, it was still thought essential to guide the child to proper distinctions between good and evil ways, between wholesomeness and naughtiness.

That children had more than their fair share of animal mischief ingrained in them was a common assumption. Another of the de Brune emblems shows a child in mid-tantrum with jettisoned toys strewn over the floor. The real engineer of all this angry chaos is shown in the form of a devil in the picture or mirror frame at the back. But pictures of childish devilment of the kind that needed thrashing out, according to the fiercest Puritan doctrine, are very rare. More often, the naughtiness of children is represented as either an aping of

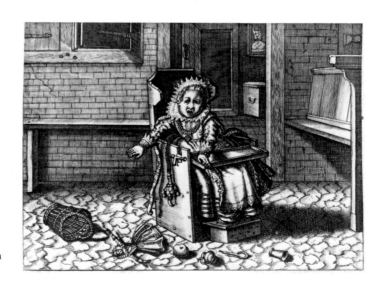

283. Emblem from Johan de Brune, *Emblemata.* Houghton Library, Harvard University

adult iniquities—as in the Steen scenes of "As the old pipe, so the young sing"—or else as gleeful teasing. Molenaer and his wife, Judith Leyster, produced between them a striking number of pictures of children, probably their own, caught in this characteristic half-mood between teasing and spite-

284. Judith Leyster, *Two Children with a Kitten and an Eel.* Courtesy of the Trustees, National Gallery, London

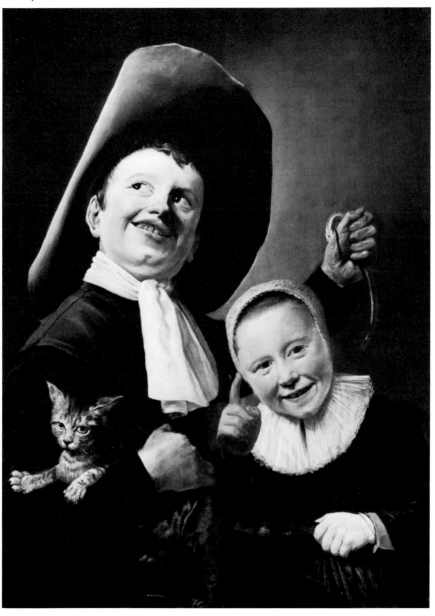

fulness. To take Leyster's double portrait with its kitten the emblem of playfulness, and the *paling,* eel (the slipperiness of life according to the proverb),
as another disquisition on the instinct against instruction, nature requiring
nurture, may be to emphasize "reading" over looking. For in keeping with
their roots in Hals's Haarlem bravura style, there is an undeniable comic strain,
with the little girl performing the "crazy" gesture at her brother that fatally
undermines any sort of solemn moralizing.

Hilarity, then, often unsettles gravity in these pictures of children at play.
While in prints that accompany emblem texts the comedy of the image can
finally be mastered by the seriousness of the text, in paintings the moral
location of levity is much more elusive. Take Molenaer's strange and disturbing painting of children and dwarves, almost a compendium of the ambiguities
surrounding the mutual behavior of children and adults. A narrowly "moral"
reading of the picture would produce a message of spitefulness punished, the
male dwarf turning on his persecutors. A "comic" reading would add to this

285. Jan Miense Molenaer, *Children with Dwarves,* 1646. Stedelijk van Abbemuseum,
Eindhoven

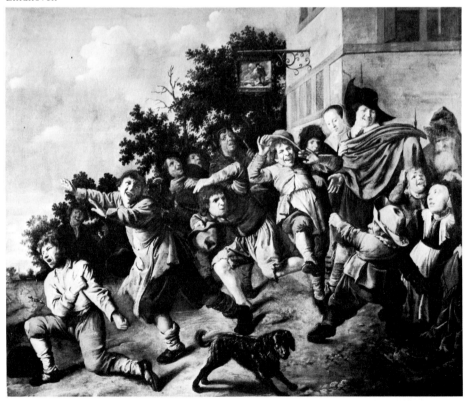

the joke that the children are being punished by an adult who is smaller than they, a play on the Bruegel *topos* of small people of indeterminate status, and that, as in many Steen comedies, the laughter comes not from the beholder outside the canvas but from an adult within it. His explicit amusement at the scene, especially when juxtaposed with the more ambiguous expression of the woman next to him, forces our own into subdued self-consciousness. An added complication is the figure of a bearded ancient—Januarius in summertime?—slouched against the wall and indifferent to the scene. The inn sign reads "The numbed peasant" and perhaps echoes his wintry stoicism. But who is stunned? The children who have been hit by the dwarf's rocks, the callous, very young adult—scarcely more grown than the children—who enjoys the spectacle, or the old man against the wall? Do we see the seasons of man along with his humors? At any rate the temper of the piece alters as these figures are surveyed from diversion to one of cruelty and pathos. The narrative in effect queues up three episodes of malice: that of children against dwarves; the dwarf's revenge; and adult indifference to both.

In these kinds of harsh comedies of childhood, wrongdoing gets its comeuppance almost by the laws of nature. But humanist pedagogy and family counsel urged more active intervention to tip the balance between naughtiness and goodness decisively in the right direction. On the other hand there were different views about how best to achieve this. The degree of severity to be applied to children's upbringing varied with the family's commitment to either a rigorous or a relaxed version of their faith.[100] Just as conjugal attitudes between husband and wife varied from the sternly patriarchal to the informal and affectionate, the same range of sentiment made itself felt within the culture. The Nouts and the Hals family portraits exemplify that range, with the one dominated by a literally black-and-white attitude to family relations, the other much more relaxed and informal both in composition and mood. In the Nouts (much as in the Cats engraving for *Moeder*), the father-son instruction proceeds from scripture and presupposes literate piety. Though there are pictures like Netscher's *Maternal Instruction,* where the mother teaches her daughter to read (see fig. 266), the stricter Nouts model of maternal domesticity imitated through a doll dressed in identical costume is more typical, at least, of "devout" households. In the Hals, family places are more cheerfully confused and the sexes are not so rigidly segregated. Even though there are perfunctory gestures towards moralizing symbolism in the rose that symbolizes the brevity of worldly beauty, the allusions are delicate rather than sententious. And other attributes—bunches of grapes held by the stem to signify maidenly chastity,[101] a peach signifying accord between heart and tongue (truth telling)—rarely overwhelm the intimacy and affability of these types of groups.

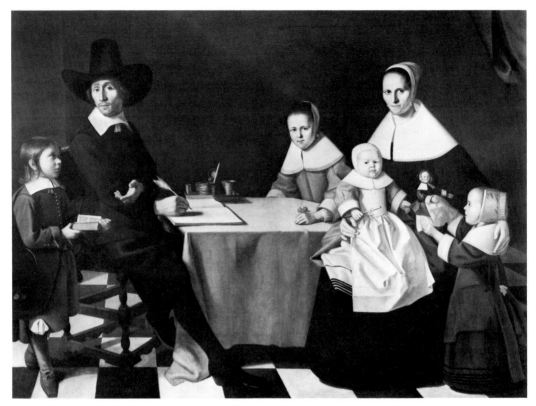

286. Attributed to Michiel Nouts, *Family Group*. Courtesy of the Trustees, National Gallery, London

Within the same faith, then, families might differ on the degree of indulgence to be shown to their children's playful instincts. Though some moralists recommended not sparing the rod to avoid spoiling the child, corporal punishment, as many travelers noted, was generally frowned on. Blankaart, who recognized that children could, at times, be little devils, opposed such punishment on the grounds that it made children grow up obdurate and stiff-necked. Instead, he said it was better "with a sweet admonition, to lead their thoughts to better ways." Van Beverwijck agreed that fear of the rod was better than its use since it was likely to harden the child into expectations of brutality and wickedness.[102] At the other extreme, it was thought foolish to allow children's willfulness to go unchecked and unpunished. But the humanist emphasis on giving some rein to the natural instincts of the child and cajoling it into learning was so strong that notions of "breaking the will," apparently strong in more intensely Puritan and evangelical cultures, were almost wholly absent in the Netherlands.

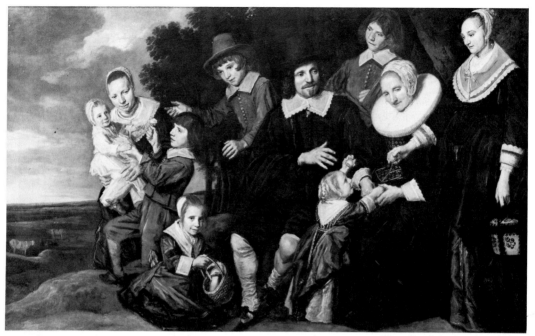

287. Frans Hals, *Family Group.* Courtesy of the Trustees, National Gallery, London

Even in those areas of human function that seemed to call for drastic intervention the orthodoxy was relatively gentle. On potty training, the seventeenth-century writers had nothing to learn from Dr. Spock. Don't take the infant to the *kakstoel* too early and don't frighten him into performing on cue was the general line. Turn the session into musical playtime by offering him toys like the rattle, a tambourine or a fife to toot on but try not to make the child too nervous.[103] Bed-wetting? Not to worry, they all go through it: *"pisse, pisse, kak, kakke/En eer men na haar siet, so is 't te laat"* ('Ere you see it, already too late). Doing it in his breeches at school at age seven or eight? Not a willful bladder but fear of being punished by his teacher, said Blankaart, adding the reassuring note that it would be much worse if he *couldn't* urinate.[104]

"In all this upbringing and education," wrote van Beverwijck, "children should not be kept on too tight a rein, but allowed to exercise their childishness, so that we do not burden their fragile nature with heavy things and sow untimely seed in the unprepared field of understanding. Let them freely play and let school use play for their maturing . . . otherwise they will be against learning before they know what learning is."[105] The ideal early education, then, for the preschooler (before seven) was to abolish the distinction between play and instruction and so to harness the child's natural vigor to the long-term ends of social virtue. From Christian Huygens downwards to much simpler advice manuals, the ideal of play-as-instruction, or ludic learning, was the conventional wisdom.

The proper place for such instruction was the family home. Only when children had been successfully weaned from mischief through the example of domestic virtue could formal schooling have the right effect. And in this respect it is not accidental that most genre paintings of schoolrooms, again following the example of Bruegel's engraving *The Ass at School,* are parodies of correct instruction. Steen's two pictures show, in the Erasmian manner, through foolish counterexample, the kind of instruction to avoid. The owl perched unnaturalistically on the wall at right, signifies folly rather than wisdom (see fig. 105), children mock their master instead of respecting him and the room is delivered to animal chaos instead of human obedience. And the only recourse the master has is to physical punishment. It is the world of

288. Jan Steen, *School for Boys and Girls.* National Gallery of Scotland, Edinburgh

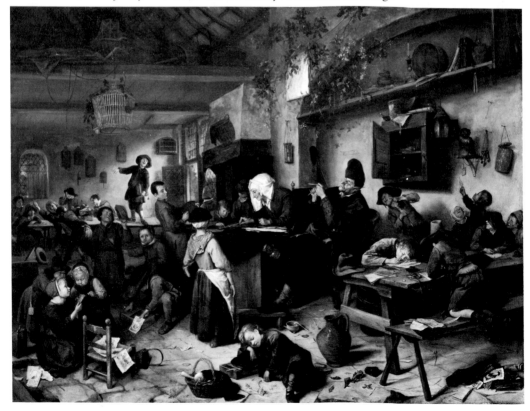

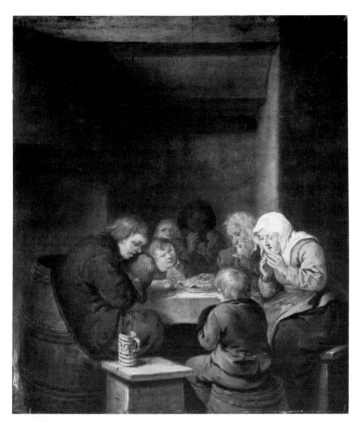

289. Jan Miense Molenaer, *Saying Grace*. Rijksmuseum, Amsterdam

education turned upside down, and one where play and instruction are not commingled but harmfully opposed.

Yet Jan Steen and Jan Molenaer were both equally capable of painting exactly the opposite kind of scene: children's wildness domesticated and subdued at home. Especially in the London Steen (see fig. 239), the playfulness of the child emphasized in the usual debris of toy wreckage on the floor has been mastered by the act of grace. Mealtimes were, again following Erasmus's commendations, occasions par excellence for lessons in the school of manners.[106] *Opvoeding,* the word for education, was, after all, etymologically rooted in the verb *voeden,* to nourish or feed, and if learning was supposed to nourish virtue, nourishment was supposed to be a form of learning itself. A later, anonymous print shows the same kind of instruction, probably at the *noen,* the midday meal, where, next to a significant puppy, a small child in a high chair is taught the rudiments of feeding. Equally, the preparation of food—peeling of vegetables like Maes's parsnips—could supply similar kinds of instruction in household virtue.

290. Nicolas Maes, *Maid Peeling Parsnips with Watching Child*, 1655. Courtesy of the Trustees, National Gallery, London

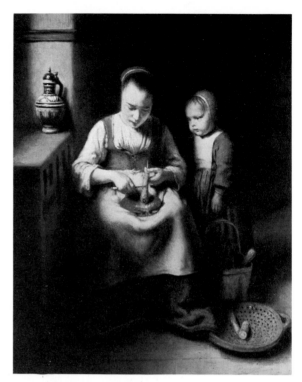

291. Jan Luiken, *De speelstoel* from *Des Menschen Begin, Midden en de Einde* (Amsterdam, 1712). Houghton Library, Harvard University

292. From Luiken, *Des Menschen . . .* Houghton Library, Harvard University

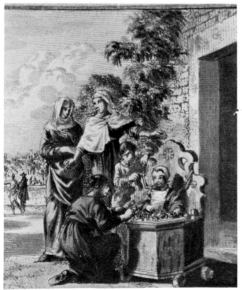

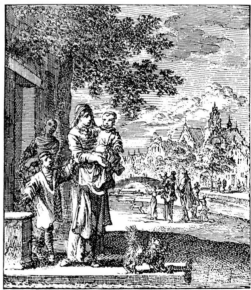

These were not the only ways to keep children out of mischief. Obedient observation had to be supplemented with more active encouragements to yoke nature and nurture together. Luiken's book emphasized this by showing in the prints the toys and playthings that would make best use of a child's

natural curiosity and energy. The *speelstoel* (play chair) was designed as a mobile playpen and is shown crowded with toys for the pretoddler. From the wonderful print done for Cats's *Spiegel van de Oude en de Nieuwe Tijd* (see fig. 255), it is possible to see that there were already stalls and shops specializing purely in toys and featuring the usual timeless stock of hobbyhorses, dolls, drums, tin whistles and the like. Luiken was hard put to it to draw positive morals from the bugle and drum and in fact used the din of the latter to make a general moral point about the credulousness of the populace.[107]

Occasionally, the bugle and drum were used, as in Cats's *Kinderspel,* as symbols of male adult patriotic responsibilities. And the doll house functioned in the same way for the girl, imbuing her, through emulation, with the domestic virtues that would lead her safely from childhood through the nubile years to marriage. The same was true for the miniature pots and pans that were used to "play house" as in the Luiken *poppegoed* print. Dollhouses were available in all sizes and styles in the Republic. And within them girls could reproduce by an endless kind of mimesis exactly the sort of idealized domestic regime to which, for better or worse, they were destined.

In addition to all its other functions and responsibilities, then, the Dutch family home was supposed to be an ideal school for the world. This was as much true of work as of play, and genre scenes set in humbler households such as those by van Ostade often show younger children carefully observing and older children participating in the work itself. This artisanal instruction through the family was in keeping with the notion of the home as superseding any other kind of workplace (including school) as a molding influence in the life of the young. Dutch families seem to have been much more reluctant than other contemporary cultures to relinquish their hold on the young. So that when boy children finally grew to the age of apprenticeship at fourteen, it was rare for them to go and reside with a master. Instead, they returned from work each night to the bosom of their family. In more patrician families, the moment of separation did not occur until their young women married or their young men went to the university.

That same potent grip exercised by the domestic hearth—literally the cradle of virtues—runs throughout Luiken's book, where the young man hardly achieves adulthood before he in his turn is putting on the paternity bonnet and beginning the cycle over again. For it is through that continuity that the art of growing up Dutch, retaining the innocence of the newborn with the wisdom of elders, could be safely accomplished. And just occasionally a note of resentment at this all-enveloping domestic coziness creeps into the relations between family members. For when Cornelis de Witt's wife wanted to criticize Johan, her brother-in-law, for exercising too much influence on her husband, she could think of nothing more fitting than to tell him that Johan "keeps you in diapers."[108]

Watersheds

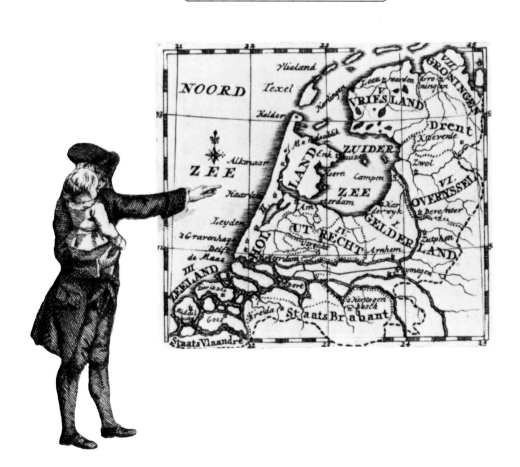

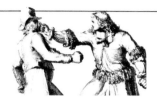

Can these bits and pieces of a culture be put together to make a coherent whole? Or are they so many odd specimens, so many randomly related attitudes, to be packed away in arbitrary clutter like the curios in a Dutch collector's cabinet? Perhaps this collection of common habits, sentiments and customs that I have tried to call a culture may, at least, be pictured. Emmanuel de Witte's interior of the Nieuwe Kerk at Delft with groups of burghers gathered around Hendrick de Keyser's tomb of William the Silent was, without straining for effect, just such a collage of native self-images. At its center, but well into the midground of the picture, is the historical reference point, the *Princeps Patriae* himself, Moses/David, forefather and martyr, in pious repose. But the groups of spectators balance quiet respect (the women at the left) with animated attention (the gesture of the well-dressed figure in the foreground). The tomb itself echoes that equipoise between the heroic and the ascetic, its late Renaissance flamboyance being set down amidst the whitewashed purity of the plain columns and pure light admitted through unstained glass. The same careful counterpoints are translated into color, so that the monochromatic domination of blacks, whites and grays sets off the vermilion splendor of the man's cape with added brilliance. There is, then, braggadocio and modesty, flamboyance and sobriety, family feeling and fatherly vigilance, the enjoyment of wealth and its contingent duties alluded to in the coin offered to the beggar boy's hat. It is the commonwealth in miniature, assembled about its *pater familias*.

De Witte's picture is, then, a vision of social patriotism, of common unforced loyalties. But was it more of a polite fiction, a consensual myth, than a reality? And if the cultural identity that I have tried to typify in these chapters was a bundle of shared beliefs, the skeptic is entitled to ask, shared by whom? Were

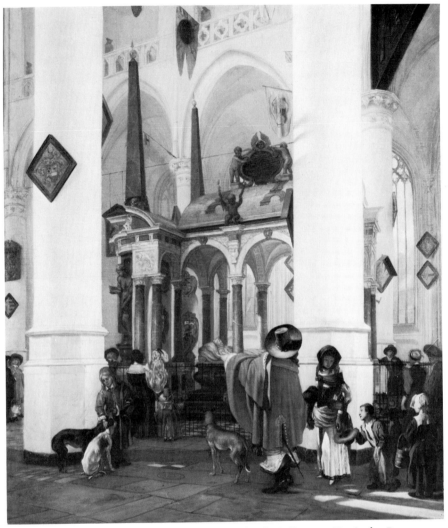

293. Emmanuel de Witte, *The Interior of the New Church, Delft,* 1656. Musée des Beaux-Arts, Lille

not those behavior patterns and collective self-images really the cultural property of an elite, and a small one at that, superimposed on the majority of the population? So what purports to be a consensus of *vaderlands gevoel,* patriotic sentiment, is in fact a device of social power? And are not the urchin and the *grande dame* in de Witte's painting joined by their mutual recognition of inequality, rather than fellow Christian feeling? To be embarrassed about riches presupposes their possession, to make a fetish of the household presupposes the ownership of a house.

In the sense that the collective ways of seeing themselves, and the world beyond, that I have classified as habitually Dutch were not a spontaneous generation but a conscious invention, and that the inventors belonged by and large to the educated, propertied nation, the objection is valid. Van Beverwijck, Cats, Grotius and many of the other projectors of the national imagination were not, by any account, men of the common herd. And it was they who gave shape, perspective and meaning to the rush of historical experience with which the Netherlanders were beset. They were, in a sense, the inventors of patriotic inevitability: the notion that a peculiar Dutch destiny lay immanent, locked in the crust of European history, waiting for some preordained eruption to blow it free of its ancient and unnatural containment. This was potent mythology, to be sure. But it would have been ephemeral, had it been just the self-serving fancy of a few humanist intellectuals and grandees. Its robustness, in fact, lay in the spell of self-recognition. To be free and to deserve godly succor, the Dutch were told, they had merely to be themselves and to remain true to themselves.

To a remarkable degree, for its time, Dutch culture was the property of all sorts and social conditions. An Avercamp winterscape with gentlefolk skating alongside rustics and sober burghers is an idyll, no doubt, but not so very far from the truth. It was certainly more than a conspiracy of false consciousness, a series of social fables devised to legitimate a monopoly of social power by the possessing classes. Of course it didn't do them any harm, either. But in the acid test of allegiance and sacrifice in a murderous and terrifying war, in the burden of heavy taxes, and in the perennial alarms and anxieties that hung around Dutch diplomacy, their belief in themselves as a common tribe held firm.

So I acknowledge a bias towards emphasizing those social and mental traits that tied Dutch men and women together rather than separated them. I don't believe it any more wicked than the alternative organizing concepts of "elite" and "popular" culture presupposing division along the lines of social differentiation. If my view is somewhat idealist, the opposite view is often unreflectingly materialist. How should Cats, whom all cultural historians agree to be a crucial figure, be so classified? A wealthy regent who occupied the most powerful office in the most powerful province of the Republic, he indisputably belongs to the elite. Yet his works were addressed to all Netherlanders and there is evidence that he found his mark. In terms of the number of editions, their variety and distribution, no seventeenth-century writer, not Vondel, not Bredero or Hooft could be said to be more popular. If he was indeed "Father" Cats, his audience ought perhaps to be thought of as an enlarged family.

Was Cats a "bourgeois"? Who was not? Beggars, prostitutes and courtiers at Honselaarsdijk were not, but that leaves a great many in between. Elsewhere in Europe, the term covers so few social types that its descriptive force can be quite sharp. In the Netherlands it is so inclusive as to be quite useless. The term, after all, belongs to the classifying vocabulary of nineteenth- and twentieth-century materialist social science that assumed systems of beliefs to be appendages of social power. Those frameworks of cultural analysis are notorious for their reductive insistence on a social continuum that extends from the division of labor to the destination of the soul. And so a lazy tautology has settled itself, like intellectual verdigris, on cultural descriptions that begin (and all too often, end, as well) by invoking the "bourgeois" ethos. Even so profound a historian as Huizinga yoked together "bourgeois" and "unheroic" as though that were an axiomatic partnership, when he seems to have meant the latter to denote "unfeudal."[1] What, after all, could be more obviously heroic than a flood culture? What could be more epic than the global bragging inlaid into the floor of the Amsterdam town hall's Burgerzaal, where the city is located, like the medieval Jerusalem, at the geographical, as well as the figurative, center of the universe. What could be more fantastical than the tulip mania, more epicurean than the *schutters* feasts, more flamboyant than the gables on the Huis Bartolotti, more orgiastic than a Steen kitchen *kermis?* And if I cite these obvious deviations from the platitudes of sobriety, aceticism, capitalist rationality that are supposed to typify Dutch "bourgeois" culture, I do so not out of mischievous countersuggestibility. Rather, I would hope to free the description of an early modern culture from its imprisonment in nineteenth-century terminology, especially that which planes down social paradox, contradiction and asymmetry to the smooth surface of an economic model. There were more mysteries of the flesh and the spirit at work in Rembrandt's Holland than are allowed for by sociological cliché.

So what will do instead? If "bourgeois" is translated into *burgerlijk,* more is altered than the linguistic form. "Proto-capitalist" becomes, instead, "civic." That seems altogether more appropriate. For the sensibility that joined Dutch men and women in a common feeling for family, nation, freedom and material comfort was civic in the classically republican sense, replenished through their own historical circumstances. But even this has its drawbacks as a descriptive term. For if "bourgeois" comes loaded with nineteenth-century assumptions, *burgerlijk* has perhaps too many eighteenth-century ones. It became, at any rate, one of the great rallying cries of the "patriot" movement of the 1780s and virtually a synonym for extended representation, a breakup of oligarchy.[2] Does any collective term make sense without twisting the mindset and language of contemporaries into anachronistic forms? What did they use to describe their *zeden en gewoonten,* their manners and mores? Scan pamphlets and manuals, letters and the "icons" of engraved goblets and one kind of term emerges rampant, like Zeeland's lion breasting the waves: *vaderlandse standvastigheid,* patriotic steadfastness.

Which brings us back to the beginning. For this sort of overarching sentiment of a common-wealth does seem to me to defy or, more properly, to transcend the actual divisions of property and even education. So that, in the spirit of Durkheim (rather than Weber), the culture is most helpfully thought of as a kind of social church — and a more elastic one than the formally predominant religious denomination. Though it may rankle with those who would prefer to see divergent social groups stripped of mystifying commonalties and restored to their "objective" antagonisms, such transcendent loyalties can be very potent. Like church membership or soccer following, they make a kind of visceral tribal allegiance, complete with totems and dependent on rich and intricately connected sets of symbolic expressions.

Which is to say that the socially superior members of the culture, its inventors, are not then its exclusive beneficiaries. Would it, after all, have been in some normative sense "better" for the skilled artisans of Dutch towns to have been in a state of constant rebellion against guild organization or if the *schutter* rank and file had marched on town halls to dismantle the oligarchical regencies — as they were urged to do in 1786 and 1787? The question is, in any event, *mal posée,* as the *Annales* would say. For, like the Venetian state, the Dutch Republic at its height was for the most part free from the kind of tumult and disorder that was chronic in other European societies. Recently, historians dissatisfied with this apparently successful consensus have pointed to food and tax riots in some of the Republic's major cities.[3] But with the one exception when the success of the Swedish armies in Pomerania in 1638 stopped the lifeline of the Baltic grain supply with riotous consequences in Leiden, in particular, it is difficult to see the seventeenth-century Republic as plagued with urban disorder of this kind, especially in comparison with French or Spanish popular violence. Nor is Leiden necessarily a typical case. Leiden, after all, was perhaps the most socially stratified of Holland towns, with a large underclass of textile workers living in crowded lodgings and terribly vulnerable to wage cutting as well as abruptly rising prices. What is striking about Rudolf Dekker's rich research on food and tax riots is how the tempo and frequency of these altered from a relatively placid and consensual "golden century" to a much more polarized and dangerous "age of the periwigs." In this respect, the traditional chronological distinctions seem to be reinforced, rather than subverted, by new research. Moreover, when urban crowds became angry and violent in the earlier period, it was not for endogenously generated social reasons. Far more often, as in 1672, the traumatic conditions of a war panic mobilized fear and hatred against that ruling group identified with the disaster. Nor was that mobilization unaffected or uncontrolled by an alternative ruling group that stood to be the benficiary of the political dislocation. So that the wrath of the crowd was in effect an instrument of intra-elite competition rather than a phenomenon making for far-reaching change. And its rallying cries and symbols were always those of imagined patriotic nostalgia: the cause of the Prince of Orange, the church militant, the defense of the Fatherland, the casting out of foreign demons from within the body politic. One of the misconceptions that was to make the generation of Batavian revolutionaries at the end of the eighteenth century so vulnerable was their notion that the culture and its social values were the target of popular anger, rather than their temporary political incarnations.

None of this is to say that Dutch culture in its prime was so successfully inclusive as to embrace all those who dwelled in the tents of Jacob, as its predikants liked to say. *Burgerlijk en vaderlyk* may have spread its net wide — from rural smallholders and fishermen at the base right up to the Trips and Bickers at the apex — but it did make some emphatic exclusions. And seeing what distinguished insiders from outsiders is one way of defining the limiting perimeter of the culture itself.

i DOORS

One such perimeter was the front door. In the 1660s, Jacob Ochtervelt painted a series of doorway and entrance hall studies that expressed with almost obsessive repetitiveness the delicate quality of that boundary.[4] The pictures all follow a single format: tradesmen or street musicians framed in the *voorhuis* (hall) doorway and being received by the well-dressed mistress of the house, sometimes with her maid or (significantly) girl child. Insiders and outsiders, then, are united within the picture frame but divided by the domestic threshold. And the degree of that separation varies from picture to picture. The Maurits-huis *Fish Seller* is just allowed into the hall while the poultry seller remains outside the door. An old woman selling cherries in an Antwerp picture has a benign shaft of light falling across her shoulders, but she remains without, though her cherries are admitted entry. And though Ochtervelt kept his 1665 street musicians outside, by 1670, in a Rijksmuseum picture, a similar group of mother, daughter and maid had actually allowed them to cross the threshold and play in the *voorhuis* itself.

In all these paintings, except perhaps the last and most relaxed, that distinction between home and world, between safety within and unknowns without, is sharply emphasized by the prominence of the door frame. But in all of them, too, the outside, represented in views of handsome streets or landmarks of the civic world such as churches, is not in the least threatening.

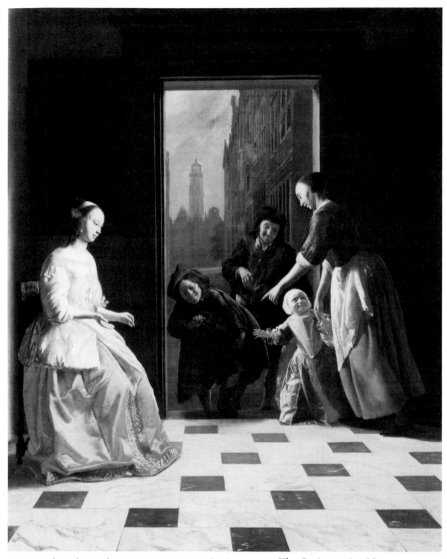

294. Jacob Ochtervelt, *Street Musicians at the Door*, 1665. The St. Louis Art Museum

And neither were the outsiders. For despite the strong contrast between elegant interiors and elegant clothes on the one hand, and the humble costumes of the visitors on the other, there is not the least doubt that the two groups are united by their acceptance of social hierarchy. The tradespeople and street musicians are deferential, the household responds with gracious coin. And implicit behind that transaction is the prior knowledge that those activities — selling or even street music — are licensed, in the literal sense, by the town, and in the figurative sense by the culture. So that it is no problem at all to fit this particular genre into Ochtervelt's more usual clientele of patrician subjects, for this is a settled and well-to-do version of outsiders. Or to put it another way, these are insiders' outsiders.

Some of these studies seem closer to supplication than a market transaction. They are far removed from the "market genre" established by Beuckelaer in the sixteenth century and refreshed by de Witte, with their brilliant still life detail and heroic treatment of the retailer. The front door scenes instead reduce the bravura of selling to a beck-and-call visitation. And in the inequal-ity of the encounter they seem closely related to another kind of genre topic: the meeting between rich and poor. Such confrontations would, in any event, spell out the barriers between supplicant and benefactor in the most direct fashion, tying together these social disparates only by a common understanding of their difference — what we might call the philanthropic oxymoron. That dif-ference is, essentially, residence. When orphans or leper children are brought in for the gracious inspection of the male and female regents of the institution,

295. Jacob Backer, *Regents of the Amsterdam City Orphanage,* 1633–34. Amsterdam Historical Museum

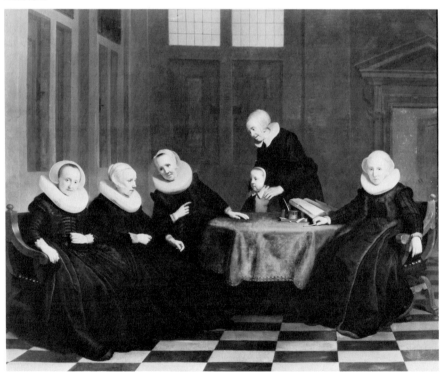

it is residence that is being conferred upon them, often symbolized in the homely dress that they have donned or are about to wear. So that when an abrupt encounter between donor and supplicant takes place on the very threshold of a residence, we might expect the natural inequality of social roles to be especially reinforced.

But such were the complications of the embarrassment of riches that these paintings end up as much undermining as reinforcing the mediating character of philanthropy. In Jan van der Heyden's brilliantly lit image of a grandiose Palladian estate, the artist has symbolized epicurean splendor of the most uninhibited kind. But at the estate gateway—the very boundary between aristocratic fantasy and common reality—a beggar woman stands in confronting accusation. But the reaction of the embarrassed patrician is to hesitate before two equally reprehensible actions: indifference before the claims of the poor, and their indiscriminate (as distinct from institutionalized) relief.

This dilemma is even more literally spelled out in Jan Steen's extremely beautiful painting known as *The Burgher of Delft and His Daughter*. Like the Ochtervelt doorway scenes, presumably the picture was commissioned to celebrate the philanthropy of the sitter. Yet the picture is riddled with disjunctions and uncertainties. Its three groups of figures—girl, man and beggars—

296. Jan van der Heyden, *An Architectural Fantasy*, c. 1670. National Gallery of Art, Washington, D.C.

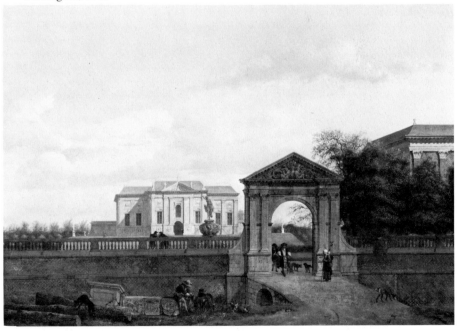

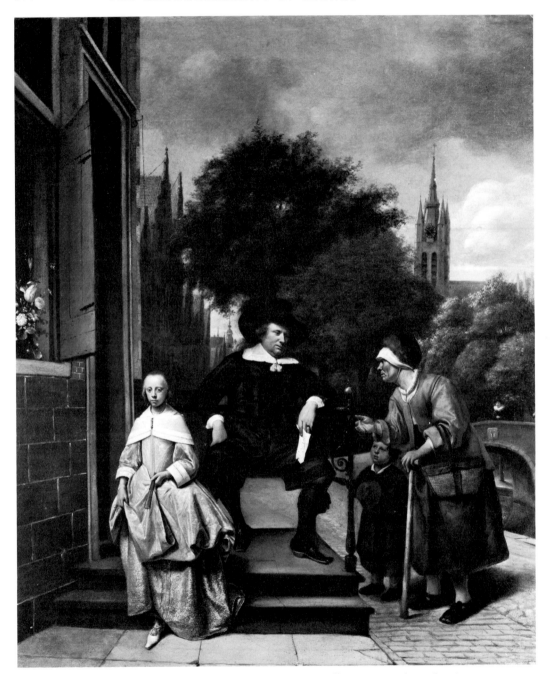

297. Jan Steen, *The Burgher of Delft and his Daughter,* 1655. "Private collection, United Kingdom."

are almost perversely disconnected from each other. Although the beggar woman directly addresses the burgher, he does not respond by returning her appeal or by any philanthropic gesture. In turn his "daughter" ignores both the remaining protagonists of the scene but directly commands the attention of the beholder. The very splendor of her apparel proclaims her less as some sort of relative of the central figure than the emblematic representation of worldly vanity, a quality characteristically re-emphasized by the full-blown flower arrangement didactically seated on the windowsill behind her. And the transience of that beauty is perhaps itself counterpointed by the world of imperishable values denoted in the architecture of the Oude Kerk seen across the Delft canal. Such conjunction of precise observation with symbolic connotation would, indeed, be exactly in keeping with the Delft manner of this time.

Everything points, then, somewhat overemphatically, to the requirement that the burgher should wish himself represented as the steward rather than the owner of riches, by giving some of it to the poor. But what is so striking about the painting is that he does not. Instead he hesitates while holding a paper that I think may be the license announcing the woman and child to be themselves *of residence,* that is to say, the woman is a local Delft indigent who has been given particular and special permission to solicit for charity. Indeed, the sympathetically observed relationship between mother and son (in startling contrast to the non-relationship between the well-to-do "father and daughter") would seem to support this. Our "burgher of Delft," then, responds to the embarrassment of his riches — of house, daughter, rich apparel — by being a judge in the sight (literally) of the church, an arbiter of the deserving poor, the figure for whom they may stand at the gate.

Similar themes and sentiments are reiterated in many other related pictures: Hendrick Sorgh's *Rich Family Visiting Poor People* or Adriaen Backer's *Regentesses of the Burger Orphanage of Amsterdam.* The contrast between the exquisite finery of the embroidered tablecloth and the curled coiffeurs of the regentesses and the pathetic condition of the children seems to us so shocking as to be tantamount to some sort of reproof. But again, that perception is modern, not contemporary. In all likelihood, the painting hung in the orphanage itself as an unabashed item of philanthropic self-congratulation.

These pictures, and the ethos they express, represent the incorporation of the poor and the miserable into the body of Dutch culture and its value system. It was a way of bringing outsiders inside — literally within the often handsome buildings of the almshouses and into a regime where we know from substantial evidence (see Chapter 3, pp. 174-75) they were amply fed and decently clothed. This widespread provision for the poor and sick in the Netherlands was much admired by visitors, even those who came from countries like England, where charitable institutions were well established.

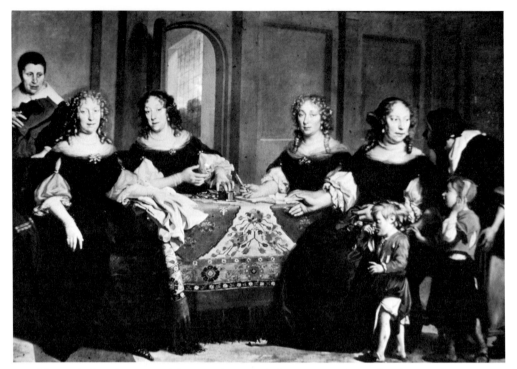

298. Adriaen Backer, *Regentesses of the Amsterdam City Orphanage,* 1683. Amsterdam Historical Museum

particular, the scale of endowment provoked envious comment. Parival, in 1662, noted that the Amsterdam hospital enjoyed eighty thousand livres of income and that "eighteen tonnes of gold" were set aside each year for the distribution of bread to the poor, "an immense sum that is afforded by the great riches of the city and the infinite number of merchants, the great affluence of the people, and which testifies to the charitable inclinations of the Dutch."[5]

The profusion and munificence of charitable institutions in the Netherlands, as elsewhere in baroque Europe, has been classified by modern historians as an exercise in "social control."[6] And there is no doubt that part of its momentum derived from prudential consideration. Where elites governed by suasion rather than coercion, philanthropic donation on a large and obligatory scale was a small price to pay for cushioning themselves against the threat of popular revolt. But this kind of manipulative explanation omits as much as it explains. In particular it pays little attention to the almost perfervid urge with which the Dutch were commanded to honor their good fortune by sharing some of it with the less well off. The Calvinist Reformed Church, of course, made it a strict duty of its members—and in 1675 Jacobus Hondius listed neglect of charity as one of the most heinous of his *Black Register of a Thousand Sins*.[7] But the commandment predated the Reformation as one of the most pressing concerns of Catholic humanism.[8] The justification of wealth through charity that Parival observed in Amsterdam had deep roots in Netherlandish culture and was quite different from any sort of renunciation ethic on Franciscan lines. It was rather a moral balancing act that permitted the retention, not the repudiation, of riches, on condition that they were yielded to communally determined ends. No wonder that Dives and Lazarus motifs turn up so often in both Catholic and Protestant culture—for instance, on the door relief of one of the Gouda Cathedral outhouses. And onto those ancient doctrines were grafted the more modern anxieties of the humanist social reformers about the moral and physical salubrity of their cities. And since the Reformed Church was never conceded a monopoly on charitable institutions, social welfare institutions proliferated from the 1580s onwards with the blessing of municipal as well as ecclesiastical authorities. Heilige Geest (Holy Ghost) institutions were created to provide specifically for the poor outside the Reformed Church

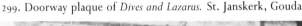

299. Doorway plaque of *Dives and Lazarus*. St. Janskerk, Gouda

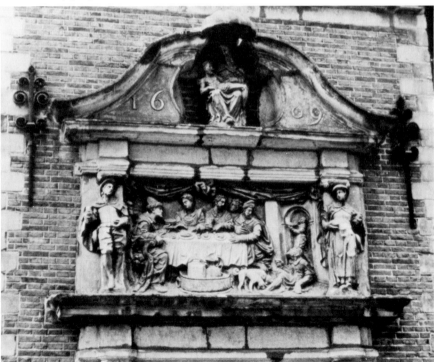

with no religious affiliation that would care for them—among which, of course, orphans loomed large. This curatorial enthusiasm, then, ought not to be identified exclusively with the church: it was at the heart of civic legitimacy.

From the sanctified distribution of bread celebrated in both prints and in Werner van der Valckert's extraordinary miscellany of cripples, urchins and simply hungry common people,[9] charitable obligations were extended to orphans, the sick, the mad and leprous, the aged and feeble. And correspondingly, opportunities to give to the poor became ubiquitous in Dutch society: in "Sunday boxes" passed around the church or brought to the house, in local excises on commodities like beer that were earmarked for an orphanage or a sick house, in lotteries expressly established to fund or endow a new

300. Werner van de Valckert, *Distribution of Bread by the Amsterdam Almoezeniershuis.* Amsterdam Historical Museum

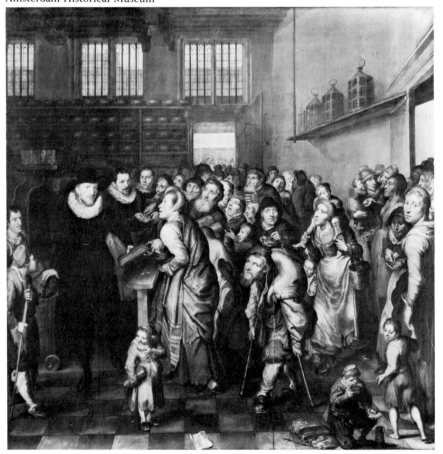

institution or improve an old one. Indeed it was virtually impossible to be a member of this society and not pay one's dues. So that rich or poor you were inevitably connected by this chain of charity, and the church constantly emphasized, "Give, for one day you may be needy as it pleaseth the Almighty."

There were, however, two conditions attached to the receipt of this charity. The first was, in effect, that the recipients acknowledge their gratitude to their benefactors by remaining within the bounds of *burgerlijk* culture: that is, by being pious, obedient and if at all possible joining the donor rather than the donee population as soon as circumstances allowed. But this meliorist optimism itself presupposed that they came from the community in the first place and had only temporarily fallen on difficult times — or that in sickness and old age they merited the charity of a community for which they had worked the rest of their lives. However poor, such people remained understood as burghers, and the relative wholesomeness of their living in almshouses confirmed that respectable status. They were dependent, to be sure, wards of the city or the church, but they became, by virtue of that, absorbed into its public ethos: symbols of the largesse of the city itself no less conspicuous than a public monument or the *schutters'* parades. Indeed they had their own ceremonies, like the procession of the lepers in Amsterdam on Printers' Monday, in which particular dignitaries of the guild and of the *leprozenhuis* participated to emphasize this unbroken *communitas*. In a similar sense, the children of the Amsterdam city orphanage (the *burgerweeshuis*) were accorded special seats on barges as wards of the city. So that if the poor and derelict plainly needed the charity of the rich, it is no less true, as both predikants and humanist magistrates emphasized, that the rich needed the poor for the quiet of their souls.

The philanthropic reinforcement of social dependence found odd echoes in the common people. The fishwives of the Amsterdam market, near the Dam, for instance, were notorious at recruiting young adolescent boys — many of them graduates of the orphanages — and supplying them with food, clothing and shelter in return for stolen goods. This, of course, was a travesty, rather than an imitation, of official charity, incorporating the needy into a criminal, rather than an improving institution. And authorities were also on the lookout for faked claims on their charity, whether from spurious indigence or through false address. In 1680, a woman from Bergen-op-Zoom married to a soldier garrisoned at Zwolle attempted to obtain charity from the Reformed Diaconie in Amsterdam by using papers written for her by a professional forger she had met at the Haarlemmerpoort. Found out, she was sentenced to a spell in the pillory with a notice pinned to her breast identifying the crime.[10]

It was a crime, then, for an outsider to pass herself off as an insider. There was, of course, nothing to stop the woman from seeking aid from her own community in Bergen-op-Zoom, but by attempting to crash the gates of another

community she had identified herself as suspiciously vagrant, a beggar pretending to be a burgher. As in every other early modern European society, the
enemies of a civic system of social regulation were the rootless, the shiftless
and the lawless. And Adriaen van de Venne drew their scarecrow features in a
series of wild and extravagant *grisailles* and listed forty-two types of rogues
and vagabonds in his picaresque poem "De Belacchende Wereld" (The Laugh-
able World). What van de Venne gives us, of course, are sketches from the
nightmares of the propertied, rather than any reliable social document. The
grotesque bundles of bones stuck into rags and tatters that stare threateningly
or cackle ominously from his pictures are social monstrosities. They emerged
from the depths of vagabond lore and were embellished by mannerist fascination with flamboyant deformity and demonic cunning. And they catered in
lingering detail to the respectable citizen's hunger to know about the fiendish
tricks, ruses and stratagems of the outcast. Especially sensational were their
resort to self-mutilation or bizarre eye salves to simulate blindness, so that
they might treated with more leniency as "infirm" rather than able-bodied
beggars.[11] Like all the criminal demonologies that followed[12] Van de Venne's
grotesques were really specimens in a bourgeois freak show. They were made

301. Adriaen van de Venne, from *Tafereel der belacchende werelt* ('s Gravenhage, 1635)

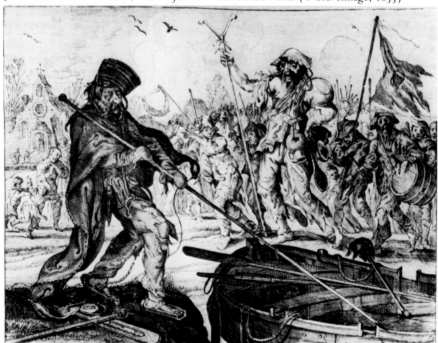

extreme to emphasize the barrier between burghers and outcasts, and they supplied a measured *frisson* of alarm without reducing a reassuringly immense
social distance.

What was the reality at the back of this fantastic terror? In the most
obsessively residential culture in Europe, vagrancy was, by definition, a social
threat. To be of no fixed abode constituted deviant behavior and was treated
as such. An important distinction has to be made between immigration and

302. Adriaen van de Venne, *'t zijn ellendige benen die Armoede moeten dragen* (It is miserable legs that must bear poverty). Grisaille. Museum Boymans-van Beuningen, Rotterdam

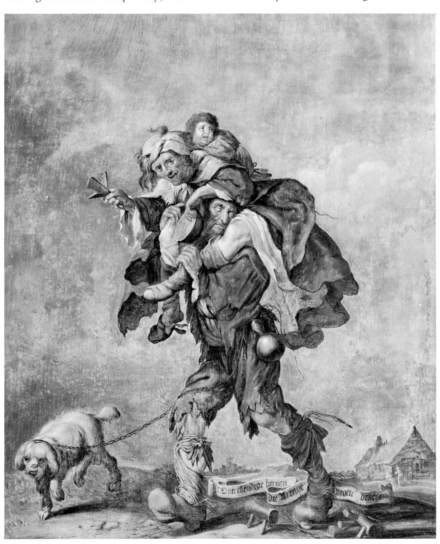

drifting, for the Republic was rightly famous for opening its doors to the persecuted of other countries, especially, of course, Protestants from the southern Netherlands and France, who wished to settle. But settlement was the operative word. A term of years, fifty guilders or marriage to a settled person would provide the *poorterschap* necessary to practice a trade and join a guild. So that immigrants could with relatively little difficulty join the ranks of the insiders, become, as they wished, Dutch. And while it is true that in the late seventeenth and eighteenth centuries a full twenty percent of those arrested in Amsterdam were of German origin (at a time when immigration to the city had increased), there is no evidence that they were being singled out for punitive attention on account of their foreign origin.[13]

Those marked as vagrants or vagabonds, by contrast, were deemed civically indigestible. Likewise beggars were a species of anti-workers, and the kind of cringing disingenuousness they cultivated was regarded by church and magistracy alike a kind of moral profanity. The Reformed Church, which in its local consistories and provincial synods was equally marked by a sense of religious residence, decreed begging a major sin. And the same social welfare regime instituted by the humanists that supplied the incorporating machinery of charity also invented institutions designed to deal with "professional" loiterers and ne'er-do-wells. The legislative basis for that treatment was the edict of 1595 enacted by the States of Holland. Under its provisions, able-bodied beggars were given a brief period (usually a month) in which to find employment, after which they were to be expelled. The infirm or aged were to be returned to their native town to receive alms there or else to beg with a valid three-month license. Violators of these terms were liable to be punished by flogging or, on further offenses, by branding.

The objective of this official action was to make the vagabond invisible, or at least to transform him into a settled person, preferably as a working man in his own native town. But temporary invisibility, pending this miraculous moral and social transformation, might be achieved through confinement. And where the residential "respectable" poor were incorporated, the vagrant, rootless tramp was incarcerated. Houses of correction, closely modeled on the Amsterdam *tuchthuis*, sprang up in Holland at the end of the sixteenth century, though by 1648 just four survived (an indication that the problem was well under control)—at Haarlem, Alkmaar and Gouda as well as Amsterdam.[14] At their most optimistic, the regime of hard labor of the houses was supposed to dissolve the stain of vagrancy, its dangerous and barefaced conspicuousness, by first inducing shame and then the urge for self-improvement, so that the corrected vagrant or petty felon would emerge a new man. Eager to work, he would have been transformed from outsider to insider. If by some mischance (as occurred, the magistrates soon appreciated, with the vast majority) this miraculous social alchemy failed, invisibility as far as the city was concerned could be achieved by banishment. And the standard sentence for vagabonds convicted of begging or petty theft or relatively minor affrays was banishment. Lest they return (as countless numbers did), they were occasionally subjected to branding or a mutilation that would be a visible sign that they ought to be dispatched back to invisibility.

There were even more drastic versions of civic invisibility than banishment. For a brief period at the end of the sixteenth and the beginning of the seventeenth centuries the Republic emulated the Venetians by operating two prison galleys to which "vagabonds and other unworthy persons" were sent from prison depots at Dordrecht and Vlaardingen. The red galley was captained by one Bartholomeus van Buren, whose ruthlessness and entrepreneurial energy in vagabond hunting anticipates the classic thief-takers of Hanoverian England. That the galleys, improbably rowed in the towering gale-tossed waves of the North Sea, were operated with merciless severity is suggested by the fact that, in 1601, in the red galley, where there was room for eighty-two rowers, some twenty-eight had died at their benches, and another eighteen to twenty were gravely sick.[15] But at least one of the galleys was still going in 1631 when Gillaum Bink was sentenced to a spell by the Hof van Holland for thieving in The Hague.[16]

Compared to other European cultures, the Dutch were more worried by the phantom of mass begging and vagrancy than by its reality, as evidenced by Van de Venne's scarecrow specters. Travelers repeatedly chorused their amazement at being able to walk the streets at night unmolested or with the sure knowledge that if they were set upon the felon would be quickly apprehended and dealt with.[17] They were equally astonished at the absence of the tribes of beggars that populated most European cities. The surprisingly low arrest rate, of both categories of delinquents, even in Amsterdam — the most crowded and criminal of Dutch towns — suggests that this was not just the imaginary optimism of tourists. That this should be the case, even with policing that was as rudimentary as anywhere else, is even more striking.

Where vagabonds were apprehended in criminal acts they were treated with a kind of punitive symmetry that reflected the nature of their misdeed. So that one was executed at Schoonhoven in 1589 for cutting off the hands and feet of the child of a farmer's wife who had refused him entry to her house.[18] And Brereton in 1634, before Haarlem, saw the standing remains of a vagabond who had been similarly refused hospitality. As he had burned down the house that was barred to him, he in his turn was burned.[19] Others who had been caught violating previous sentences of banishment might be flogged with rods up to fifty or sixty times, according to the English physician Edward Brown, who saw one such terrible beating at Haarlem in 1668.[20]

On the whole, though, the towns of the Dutch Republic seem to have been very much the models of good order their admirers claimed. But there were, within and between them, of course, places of peril. The harbor areas in Amsterdam, Sjoerd Faber tells us, were where a great many of the places of arrest were located, the Zeedijk, then as now being one of the most crime infested.[21] In The Hague, the taverns and slophouses around the Turfmarkt were similarly notorious. And in both cities, the very center, where well-practiced cutpurses might expect to pick off unwary and loaded travelers, was a place of frequent assault. The Dam and the Leidseplein were fruitful for theft in Amsterdam, and the Voorhout, not a stone's throw from the States General in the Binnenhof, was another dangerous milieu. In the summer of 1666, a lawyer named Roseboom was taking an early evening stroll on the Voorhout with his niece when they were set upon by two armed men. The lawyer was beaten up and robbed, while the girl was dragged along the ground by a rope around her neck.[22] And the same woods that made The Hague so ornamental a seat of government also made certain areas dangerous. In 1643 a decapitated head was found near the Huis ten Bosch, and in 1661 two daughters of a notary were assaulted by (it was emphasized) French house servants who first took them into the thick of the woods and then trapped them in a tavern before one of the women escaped through an open window and sounded the alarm at the Huis ten Bosch itself.[23]

"Citizen's arrest," the kind of spontaneous apprehension of malefactors for whom a hue and cry had gone up, was a common phenomenon in a society still largely unprotected by professional police. In fact the reputation of the *baljuwen,* the sheriff's constabulary, was so unsavory, and their demands for ransom fines, or *compositie-geld*, so notoriously capricious and greedy, that their visits were greeted with as much suspicion as relief. And the spirit of citizens' self-reliance was expressed even more graphically in a little book that must count as the first urban self-defense manual, the *Klare Onderrichtinge der Voortreffelijcke Worstel-Kunst* (Clear Tutorial in the Most Admirable Art of Wrestling). Published in 1674, its ostensible author was the professional wrestler Nicolaas Petter, who ran a fighting academy in Amsterdam. In fact it was put out by his pupil and successor, Robbert Cors, who showed as much entrepreneurial flair as formidable physical skill. With a perfect sense of a new market, Cors exploited citizens' anxieties, especially marked in Amsterdam, about their vulnerability to violent assault in cities and on highways. The subtitle of the book specifically proclaimed it to be "very useful and advantageous against all rough fighters and in defense against those who threaten or outrage by carrying knives." As if by way of assuring the respectable public to whom it was addressed, the book even carried a tariff of penalties that could be expected in Amsterdam for various kinds and degrees of assault: six weeks' bread and water in the lockup for toting a knife, double if anyone was wounded; a three-guilder fine for a fisticuffs attack; six months for throwing an iron projectile and hitting someone. Cors presumably hoped to trade on Petter's name and attract a different kind of clientele to his academy at the Gustavusburgh by the Prinsengracht. And his masterstroke in this effort at handbook self-advertisement was to commission Romeyn de Hooghe, whom he met, to produce the spectacular series of plates with which the basic arts of self-defense are graphically and carefully illustrated.

At one level, the book can be read as an early sports manual. But for some, it was also a document of republican ideology. The Harvard College copy, donated by the bibliophile Thomas Hollis, has Cors's radical commendation that "manly exercises cannot be too much encouraged by ingenuous, that is, free Nations," a sentiment that would later be given solemn endorsement by Rousseau. But it is obvious that Cors meant to seek a wider and more respectable audience than professional pugilists and wrestlers, who had traditionally entertained at court assemblies, and at fairs and *kermisses*. De Hooghe's brilliant engravings show well-dressed burghers, complete with wigs and ribboned hose, executing all manner of sharp moves against ominously represented low types coming at them with knives or fists. There is little from the modern canon of

303. and 304. Romeyn de Hooghe, engravings from N. Petter, *Klare Onderrichtinge der Voortreffelicke Worstel-Kunst* (Amsterdam, 1674). Houghton Library, Harvard University

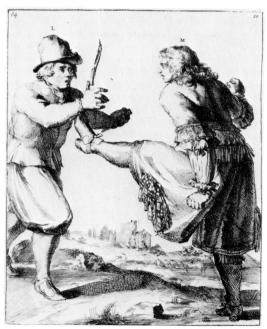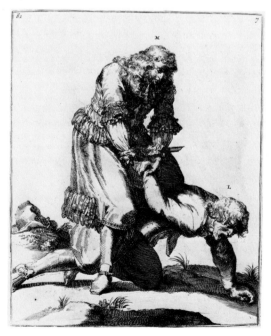

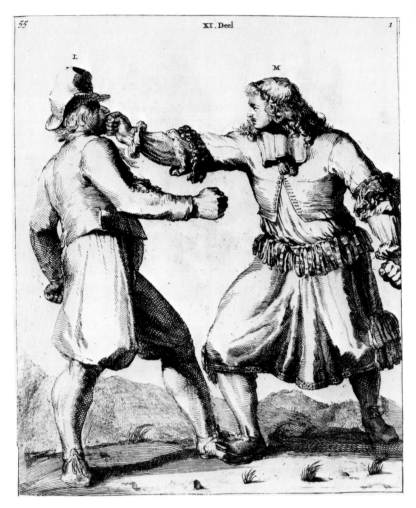

305. Romeyn de Hooghe,
engraving from N. Petter,
*Klare Onderrichtinge der
Voortreffelicke Worstel-Kunst*
(Amsterdam, 1674).
Houghton Library,
Harvard University

oriental martial arts—the drop kick, the straight right to the nose, the overshoulder throw—that is missing from Petter's book. He covers fist work, parries to the face and body, foot and leg fighting and every kind of two-handed defense and attack against knife attack. And the techniques are glossed in the text with the same mechanical seriousness and graphic detail devoted in comparable how-to manuals that deal with the crossbreeding of cattle, the diagnosis of gallstones or the classification of molluscs: "Insert foot (b) into groin (e)" is the general letter of the instruction. But its spirit is that of citizens' vigilance against outsiders who threaten from inside the heart of cities where they are up to no good. Its hero is that depressingly modern figure, the burgher as street fighter.

Criminals, beggars, vagabonds, men without occupation or abode then, were by definition outsiders against whom the community had to defend itself. But were there groups whose ethnic origins precluded full and authentic admission to the host culture? I have already argued that immigration itself was no bar at all to assimilation, and during the last quarter of the sixteenth century the northern Netherlands received as many as 150,000 refugees from the Spanish conquest of the south. As I have argued earlier, that great migration engendered serious friction in the host cities, where the perceived sin of the southerners was their immoderation—they were either too rich or too poor, too lawless or too fanatical in their Calvinism.[24] But their integration into the northern society—and, one should add, their enrichment of it, both materially and culturally—was only a matter of time. Mid-seventeenth-century Dutch history is full of powerful and influential figures of southern origins, just as the mid-eighteenth-century elites, despite their reputation for a more closed form of patriciate, opened enough fissures to let in wealthy Huguenot families. When migrants received rough treatment in Dutch towns, it was less because of their foreign origins than because of their indigence, or in the case of the Scandinavian and German seamen who keep showing up in tavern and street brawls in the *Confessie Boeken,* because of their natural habitat in disorderly areas of the city. And Sjoerd Faber has conclusively shown that there is no substance at all to the notion that *poorterschap* made any difference to the likelihood of obtaining bail pending trial in Amsterdam. Whether one was detained in the "Boeien" jail and interrogated or released on bail depended purely on the gravity of the crime committed.[25]

What of another immigrant group that added the complication of a different religion: the Jews?[26] Traditionally, the response of the Dutch to Jews in their midst has been thought the *locus classicus* of benign pluralism: an exceptional case of tolerance in a Christian Europe that either ejected or confined them in humiliating and degrading circumstances. There is much to support this optimistic scenario. There was no Amsterdam ghetto, no yellow badge, horned hat or lock-up curfew behind gates and walls. The costume of the Sephardim from the Iberian world in particular was indistinguishable from that of gentile Amsterdammers and, most significantly, the demonological exaggeration of physical features disappears from the depiction of Jews in their artistic rendering by Rembrandt and Lievens. Instead, the Semitism of their physiognomy was actually mobilized to enhance the narrative immediacy of scripture painting, so that Rembrandt gives us not only a David but a St. Matthew and a Jesus with the features of his Jewish neighbors on the Breestraat.

This was a radical departure from iconographic convention. But no less telling was the sheer matter-of-factness by which Jews became absorbed into

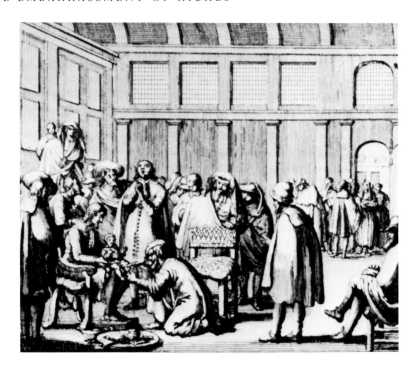

306. Jan Luiken, *Jewish Circumcision*, 1683. Houghton Library, Harvard University

the standard genres of Dutch culture. By the time that Johan Leusden and Jan Luiken came to engrave their series on the rites and manners of the Jews, scenes of circumcision, the baking of Passover matzoth or the funerary *shiva* could be shown without any sinister overtones of arcane practice. Luiken's *Jewish Circumcision* is exactly akin to other scenes from ethnographic works that had become popular in the second half of the century, and was now wholly divorced both from demonology and from the use of Jewish custom as a counterreference for the Christian mysteries.[27]

In the same way, the synagogue was no longer synonymous with "the false church." In prints, like Veenhuijzen's little engraving of the Sephardic synagogue on the Houtgracht for Tobias van Domselaar's *Description of Amsterdam,* it features as merely another notable sight of the city, like the stock exchange or the East India warehouse. And since the famous synagogue that replaced it in 1675 was built with many of the customary splendors of Christian church building — dark oak pews, handsome brass chandeliers and the like — Emmanuel de Witte, who specialized in church interiors, among other genres, painted it in exactly that way. In Melchior Fokkens's text, the guidebook prose is similarly unsensational. The author merely observes the fountain at which worshippers wash before entering the synagogue, the gallery in which women were seated, the twin doored ark in which the scrolls of the Law were kept "bedecked with rich ornaments" and the robes of the Rabbi Haham:

> Their Sabbath begins on Friday night when the Sun goes down, when they light their lamps in their houses and in their church that burn all through Saturday to the evening when their Sabbath is finished. . . . At some festivals that they have, candelabra and silver crowns are brought forth in their church which do make a great treasure and on the Sabbath day they clothe themselves in their finery and do not the least work.

The tone of such descriptions is that of curiosity (in the account of treasures and finery, even admiration) rather than fear and hatred. And it was this visibility without terror or humiliation that was so novel an experience for Jews in Christian society. Even in 1616 Rabbi Uziel was able to report to a correspondent, "At present, [our] people live peaceably in Amsterdam. The inhabitants of this city, mindful of the increase in population make laws and ordinances whereby the freedom of religions may be upheld. Each may follow his own belief but may not openly show that he is of a different faith from the inhabitants of the city." At a time when murderous riots were being unloosed against Jews in Frankfurt, this relative liberty represented a miraculous asylum.

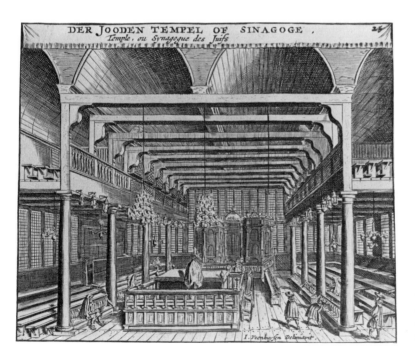

307. I. Veenhuijzen, *The Jewish Synagogue on the Houtgracht.* Author's collection

Not all of this toleration, impressive though it was, flowed from the milk of Christian charity, even in Amsterdam's very diluted form. If the Jewish presence was easily absorbed, it was not because it was so ubiquitous and indispensable to the metropolitan economy, but because it was so discreet and so marginal. In 1672, three years before the opening of the great synagogue, there were 7,500 Jews in a city of nearly 200,000, or just 3.75 percent of the population. It is true that they were disproportionately represented in sectors of the economy—constituting, for example, 13 percent of the depositors of the Amsterdam Bank. But they were still very much on the fringe of the great trading staples like Baltic grain, Muscovy furs or Swedish iron and copper. Even in the Levant trade, where their contacts with the Marrano-Hispanic world in the eastern Mediterranean might have been expected to force an entrée, their presence was relatively slight.

Nor was the guild-dominated structure of Amsterdam trades and crafts any more receptive. Flemish diamond polishers who had brought the craft from Antwerp mounted a campaign to restrict Jewish encroachment and largely succeeded in curtailing their share until the very end of the seventeenth century. Sugar refiners were similarly hostile, preventing the house of Pereira and Pina by legal intervention from directly marketing their product. Tobacco processing was the one area where the Jewish "Brazilian connection" (through Portuguese family ties) helped establish them in a profitable and secure economic niche.

Exclusion from guild membership was only gradually lifted and in some trades not at all. After 1668, when the guild exclusions were formalized, the only exception was the booksellers' guild, where their specialization in Hebrew printing as well as in Spanish, Ladino and Yiddish established a specialty that did not threaten native publishers. By midcentury they were admitted to the physicians' and apothecaries' guilds and were granted special licenses to trade within their own community. The brokers' and the surgeons' guilds admitted a few Jews, and, more inexplicably, the guild of fishmongers does not seem to have exercised any bar at all. These restrictions, though, did not preclude healthy diversification within the Jewish economy—always a sign of stable settlement. By the early eighteenth century, their economic base had broadened and diversified, and Jews could be found in haberdashery, kosher butchery, porcelain retailing, innkeeping, silver- and goldsmithing and even cheese making. But until the Batavian Republic's emancipation in 1796, they were the only group in the city for whom *poorterschap* did not at the same time qualify them for all manner of trades. Conversely Jews were thought to be disproportionately represented in high risk areas of the economy, in illicit speculation in commodity futures, or the infamous "trading in the wind" on doubtfully generated stock issues. The opprobrium ensuing from the collapse of these ventures, while not at all a recurrence of the medieval usury syndrome, could still rebound on the Jews and reinforce their reputation for dubious behavior. Jewish sterotypes, for example, feature all too prominently in one of Bernard Picart's most widely disseminated satirical prints on the *windhandel* of 1720. And in their more stereotypical role as diamond Shylocks they could be victimized by unscrupulous bullies like the bailiffs, always on the lookout for easy game. In 1674, for example, an Amsterdam Jewish jeweler received a summons to go to a house in The Hague to sell some diamonds to a well-born lady purchaser. Hardly had he arrived when the bailiff with his men entered the house, tore the jewels out of his hand and accused the Jew of wanting to sexually molest a married woman. Threatened with the scaffold and the *tuchthuis,* the Jew was offered his freedom for a *compositie* of six thousand guilders, more or less the supposed value of the diamonds that had been stolen from him![28]

There were other limits set on the absorption of the Jews into Dutch culture, most forcibly by the ministers of the Calvinist Church. Paradoxically, the church's predilection for describing its own flock as the reborn Hebrews did not dispose it to favor the real thing. In fact it gave an extra impetus to distinguish between mere gaberdined Semites who had somehow been carried over into the Christian era and the authentic children of the Covenant: themselves. And the more ordinary the Jews seemed — in dress, speech and manners — the more compelling this differentiation became. Sometimes the result was ugly rhetoric. In 1609 Abraham Costerus published his *History of the Jews,* in which many of the ancient libels about the "unclean race" were given a new gloss. While the more humanist and skeptical magistracy would never have translated these slanders into legislation, they were still concerned to spell out the conditions under which Jews could enjoy residence. These were classified in 1614 and 1615 under three headings. First, Jews might not in any way defame or slander the Christian religion and its Savior. Second, they were prohibited from any proselytizing activities, a gratuitous ban since the rabbinate was by tradition itself forbidden to seek converts and reluctant even to accept spontaneous apostates. And lest he even inadvertently ensnare Christians, Menasseh ben Israel received the assent in 1651 of the Amsterdam Church Council to publish only in languages other than Dutch! On the other hand, the church exerted untiring efforts to win converts, for if the Jews were to be tolerated it was in the eschatalogical hope that their conversion would herald the Last Days. So that in 1677, the Classis [Consistory] of Gouda, for example, appointed a preacher equipped to discourse on the Hebrew Talmud. Leiden University also had a professor whose particular brief it was to engage in pious disputations with the stiff-necked Hebrews.

The third and last restricting provision was that any sexual or conjugal liaison between a Jewish male and a Christian female was forbidden on pain of violent penalties (though, predictably, not the other way about). The Dutch, it seems, were not so released from medieval demons and terrors of blood pollution as to overcome anxieties about Christian serving maids' falling prey to the unscrupulous designs of Jewish employers on both their bodies and souls. Many cases are recorded in the judicial archives of Jews accused of forcing employees to convert, once they had ruined their innocence. As early as 1614, an ex-Baptist who had himself become a Jew in Constantinople and then had married and returned to the town of Hoorn in north Holland was tried for obliging an apprentice to convert. He was convicted and condemned to be burnt alive for the offense, his wife to be drowned. On this occasion, however, it was the lay authorities that were fanatical in their vindictiveness, and the church that successfully interceded for commutation of the sentence. A century later, however, at least one ultra-Calvinist tract was published defining sexual relations between Jew and Gentile (along with sodomy and bestiality) as an unnatural act.

Calvinist suspicions and anxieties did not, however, monopolize the cultural response to Jews and Judaica. Humanist scholars, many of whom were busy reviving Hebrew as one of the three indispensable classical languages, were capable of softening the divisions between one faith and another in the interests of scholarly community. And the most startling instance of what might be called cultural largesse was the preface to Menasseh ben Israel's *De Creatione Problemata* (1636) supplied by the Amsterdam orator, writer and professor of the Athenaeum Illustrae, Caspar Barlaeus. In this foreword he implied that Christians did not necessarily have a monopoly on piety and virtue, and that Jews and Christians might actually coexist as "friends before God." "Just as I am a son of Christ, so you are a son of Abraham" was the suggested parity that, predictably, brought down a storm of recriminations on Barlaeus's head.

Overtures of this degree of relativist benevolence were, however, very rare. Essentially the accommodation of Jews in the Republic—especially the more conspicuous, less prosperous and less educated Ashkenazim who started to flow in towards the end of the century—depended on passive rather than active advantages. Along with other minorities—including the nominally clandestine Catholics—the Jews were the residual beneficiaries of the highly federalized political institutions of the Republic. Theoretically, the States of Holland had the authority to intervene in matters concerning "aliens," but it was for a city to say who should or should not reside within its walls. In 1600, requests were made to the municipal authorities in Amsterdam by Christian traders anxious about Jewish competition to limit Jewish residence to specific quarters of the city. They were turned down, not so much on any active humanitarian grounds as because the regents thought it improper to abridge the right of any residents to live where they wished. The only exception, of course, was when a section of the population might be thought to be some sort of fifth column. And for a brief period the Iberian connections, language, names and customs of the Sephardic and Marrano Jews gave some cause for concern. In 1603 those suspicions resulted in the temporary arrest of their rabbi, Uri Halevi, at the house of prayer. But it was not long before the Jews' special knowledge of the Spanish enemy and their trading contacts in the Iberian imperial world became much more of an asset than a liability.[29] The same went for their equally intimate and important network of commercial contacts in the Ottoman Empire. So it was no surprise that in one important area the Jews acquired precisely the official identity of a Dutch *burger.* In 1657 the States General decreed that Dutch Jews living abroad or undertaking commercial ventures by land or sea were to be accorded the same rights of protection as any other citizens of the Republic.

It is less accurate, then, to speak of the Jews in Holland as wholly absorbed within domestic Dutch culture than of an independent Dutch Jewish world evolving over the course of the century. This social synthesis was not just the product of Dutch reticence and uncertainty, it was also the choice of Jews themselves, concerned not to be swallowed up by their host society. Even the grandees of the Amsterdam Sephardim, then, retained a sort of exotic and foreign aura. Some of them—like Moses Curiel (Jeronimo Nuñez da Costa), who laid the foundation stone of the great Sephardic synagogue, or Isaac Palache, the Sultan of Morocco's ambassador, who was buried in the Sephardic cemetery at Oudekerk, and the august Manuel, Baron de Belmonte, ambassador to the King of Spain, who resided in great splendor on the Herengracht— had in fact come to Holland as agents of foreign princes.

Immediately below this Sephardic aristocracy were families who put down roots in Amsterdam but who reverted unconditionally to Judaism while retaining their fluency in Spanish and Portuguese as well as the sensuous cultural style that was their particular heritage. In this group were the Pereira and Pinto families and Miguel Barrios, whose checkered career took him back and forth across religious and even national lines (he served for a while as a captain in the Spanish cavalry) before he settled down with a wife from the Pina family and went through a form of ritual penance in the synagogue. Gaspar Duarte, in this circle, originally from Antwerp, became a friend of Constantijn Huygens and was one of those approached by the Stadholder's court to raise funds for its dynastic politics. His daughter became a female member of Hooft's poetizing circle at Muiden Castle. Many of these Jews lived in the handsome houses built in the fashionable classical style and had engravings made of their residences by Romeyn de Hooghe. Their social habits were not far from those

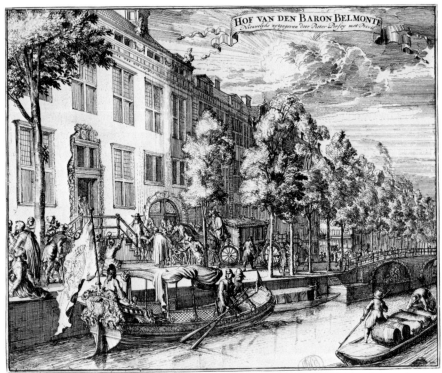

308. Romeyn de Hooghe, *House of the Baron Belmonte*. Rijksprentenkabinet, Amsterdam

of the wealthiest Christian patricians. They, too, entertained sumptuously, held music circles, bought pictures and fine oriental porcelain. They devised theatricals, dressed in expensive satins and spent much time designing matrimonial alliances, just as in the best *regenten* circles. When they died they went out in extravagant style, their tombstones at Oudekerk being covered with luxuriant carving. Those of the Texeira clan with their profusion of birds, harps and Bible scenes hark back directly to the lyrical flavor of Islamic Jewish Iberia.

By 1690, however, this delicate cultural balancing act was threatened by the arrival of Ashkenazi Jews in much greater numbers. Of the 7,500 Jews in Amsterdam at that time, 5,000 were immigrants from Germany, Poland, Bohemia and Lithuania. These newcomers duly built their own synagogue opposite the Sephardic temple, and created their own autonomous educational institutions, burial societies, dietary regulations and a Yiddish press. But their presence became much more conspicuously "alien" than that of the Sephardim. They settled thickly in streets like the Leprozenburgwal, the Nieuwe Kerkstraat and the Nieuwe Houtmarkt, which became known as the milieu of poor Jews, dressed strikingly differently from Dutch men and women and speaking a gabbling, incomprehensible tongue. And they turned to the menial "ghetto" trades disdained by the Sephardim like hawking, peddling, and old clothes dealing (much of it practiced without city licenses). There can be hardly any doubt that the Jewish fiddlers mentioned in *'t Amsterdamsch Hoerdom* as playing in the *musicos* were Ashkenazim of this generation of immigrants.

The influx of the Ashkenazim, then, in some ways re-marginalized the Jews within Dutch culture. Or rather it created, for a while, two sorts of Jews: those who were Jews first and Dutch second, and the smaller, older community of whom it might be fairly said the opposite was true. Yet in both cases, the degree of their acceptance and absorption was still a unique success in the otherwise miserable history of Jews and gentiles in early modern Europe. And just as in the host culture's addiction to the business of domesticity may be seen the particular color of its identity, so it is the reassuring mundaneness of Jewish life in Amsterdam — those prints of house cleaning before Passover, of burying the dead and teaching the young — that describe the synthesis of a Dutch Jewish world culture. It proved, against the odds, that at least in the porous polyglot world of Amsterdam, it was possible to be insider and outsider at the same time without suffering an acute attack of social schizophrenia or the periodic accusation of dual loyalties.

In Holland, for a while, the Jews stopped wandering — or at least they wandered no more and no less than the Dutch themselves. But there was one other group whose nomadism simultaneously defined their existence and disqualified them from any kind of residential place in Dutch society: the Gypsies.[30] And the edict of 1595 reinforced their separateness by making their treatment even harsher than that of other kinds of vagabonds. Unlike the brief respite offered to vagrants to find work before expulsion, or the return of infirm beggars to their native town, Gypsies — having neither the capacity to work nor a native town — were simply to be flogged and summarily banished, and if caught violating that penalty were to be branded as well as given a repeat dose of the chastisement. As Ivan Gaskell has pointed out, the emblem for poverty in Cesare Ripa's *Iconologia* was a Gypsy with a wagtail upside down, indicating that the bird without a nest was reduced to robbing those of others. So that the Gypsy was about as much of an enemy to a residential culture as one could possibly imagine. Accommodation being impossible, a state of almost military defense was the only prudent response.

If their habits proclaimed them antibodies in Dutch society, their beliefs made them anti-Christians. For if beggars were profane in church teaching, and Jews benighted, Gypsies were simply, as their name, *heiden*, announced, pagan.[31] The pseudo-Egyptian mumbo jumbo that flourished in fairground and popular lore only added more lurid color to their exotic and un-Christian nature. Being indifferent to belief, they would not scruple to abuse Christian teaching or practice. Church councils were particularly on the lookout for their habit of presenting children for baptism on arriving at a new district, in the hope of obtaining through non-Gypsy godparents some sort of local protection and patronage. Synods drew attention to the scandalous nature of the trick, offering infants who had already been baptized, children from families that were themselves unbaptized or had no intention of giving the child a Christian upbringing. In contrast with the eager welcome given to genuine Jewish converts to the church, approaches actually made by Gypsies for their absorption into the body of Dutch Christian society were derisively rejected.

While Gypsies seemed, outside of fairs and markets, to be a relatively minor phenomenon in the settled urban areas of the heartland of Holland Zeeland, the more wooded and wild areas of the land provinces, in Overijssel and Gelderland, were their more natural habitat. There the authorities were less well equipped for pursuit, and so it became almost customary to use the land provinces as a kind of dumping ground for the unwanted Romanies. In 1695, for example, we know of three hundred Gypsies bering chased into Gelderland. And as the threshold of hysteria about social undesirables descended during the eighteenth century, this kind of orchestrated brutality bore down on the Gypsy population with particular fierceness. So that while the Jews, who were being expelled from the Habsburg lands and harassed in Poland, were striking roots in Holland, the Gypsies were treated as a kind of social plague or enemy horde. In 1725 the States of Holland decreed that wherever Gypsies were spied, church bell tocsins were to be rung, summoning all able-bodied men over the age of sixteen to arm themselves.[32]

ii WORMS

The retaining membrane that held Dutch culture together for more than a century was a marvel of elasticity. Responding to appropriate external stimuli, it could expand or contract as the conditions of its survival altered. Under pressure, it could tighten to compress the Dutch into a sense of their indissoluble unity. In more expansive times it could relax and swell, allowing for internal differentiation and the absorption of a whole gamut of beliefs, faiths and even tongues. An omniscient kind of social filter swallowed up those foreign bodies and spat them out again as burghers: civically salubrious and residentially reliable. Under extreme attack, the culture could as a last resort defend itself by spontaneous rupture. But at some point or other, every historian concedes, this resilient bundle of connected cells became turgid. Just when this happened, however, is impossible, and almost certainly futile, to specify. It would be wonderful if historical processes all followed the scenario given to a movie actor in the 1950s who, as Michelangelo (who else?), triumphantly announced to the expectant crowd, "Men of Florence: the Renaissance is here." But there was no such helpful announcement of the end of the Golden Century or the dawn of the Age of the Periwigs that succeeded it. The distinctness of their separation is no more than a historiographical convenience, for one sort of culture evolved into another with almost imperceptible gradualness.

Yet, change it did. For although the boundaries of cultural time are more elusive than those of social space, they existed and the community of the Dutch crossed them at some point between the late seventeenth and the mid-eighteenth centuries. It was not, of course, some sort of great *trek* to the Age of Enlightenment or a picnic outing on that drowsy summer afternoon in which Huizinga pictured the Dutch eighteenth century languidly basking. Some social groups exited more conspicuously and faster than others. The most well-to-do patriciate, as their portraits attest, aspired to a more international style of dress, speech, diet, and architecture, dominated by French manners and English novels and journalism. At the other end of society, the differences that had favored Dutch artisans and workers over their foreign counterparts — their higher literacy, better real wages and diet — all faded as marginal advantages. For the first time the eighteenth century saw the emigration of skilled workers in some industries to countries as far apart as Spain and Russia, while those who remained behind, in traditional strongholds like shipbuilding and textiles, had to make do with contracting employment and a labor market made less favorable by the competition of rural labor and foreign migrants. At the top and the bottom of society, then, the Republic became less remarkable and more commonplace in Europe. Like oligarchies in Walpole's England or Regency France, its patriciate became less hospitable to arriving fortunes. Though it was not yet a society of alienated social blocks — the periwigs and paupers of the moralists' rhetoric — the great "family" of Dutch culture was in course of breaking down into poor kin and rich kin. Some commentators even wrote of a tacit conspiracy between the social extremes (as in the manipulation of drunken mobs by ambitious patricians) against the "broad middle" (*brede middenstand*).

Paradoxically, this estrangement took place in quiet, not bruising, times. The anxieties that had generated such fretful energy in the seventeenth century seemed to have been at least temporarily assuaged in the eighteenth. Prudence, pragmatism, moderation had all been on the minds of the great statesmen of the Golden Century, like de Witt, but they were the iron band within which the brilliants of imperial prosperity were set. The stewards of the eighteenth-century Republic, the legatees of nearly forty years of grinding warfare against France, operated in a more subdued temper. Simon van Slingelandt, the Pensionary of Holland, was brave enough in the 1720s to address the painful problem of the limits to Dutch power and did so with candor and intelligence. Given the fiscal exhaustion of the country and the disproportionate burden of taxation that Holland bore within the Republic, he could hardly avoid these gritty issues of means and ends. His task, and that of his successors, he thought, was to retrench from strength; to devise ways in which that minimum of force needed to secure the safety and prosperity of the state could be funded at least risk and expense. Its traditional goals, those set out by Pieter de la Court in the *Interest of Holland*—of trading in peace, of freedom from entangling continental alliances—were still maintained, but through a defensive rather than provocative posture. This was a tricky business. The ministers of the Republic knew that a *de facto* resignation from the status of a great power was tantamount to a kind of diplomatic suicide. So their calculus of decreasing risk produced instead what might be called the defense of prudential contingency: barrier forts that the troops of the Republic manned inside the Austrian Netherlands, reciprocal security agreements with the British government, a policy of "free ship, free goods" that allowed for nonbelligerent trading in wartime, instead of the grandly proclaimed universal precepts of the *mare liberum*. Mostly, the Pensionaries and patricians wished that by some miracle their immediate territories and seas would cease to be the major theater of conflict between the great powers. And insofar as France and Britain began to play for high stakes out in the Atlantic and to squabble like fighting vultures over the carcass of Mughal India, this respite was briefly granted.

These were the external markers of cultural alteration. Internally, perhaps, the culture of the Golden Age ended at the moment that it became the object of academic investigation. For there is a kind of elegiac antiquarianism to the works of the first generation of ethnographers like le Francq van Berkhey and Kornelis van Alkemade that began to appear in the middle of the eighteenth century. Half a century back, in the late seventeenth century, their predecessors had found an audience for descriptions of customs and habits of natives in remote and barbarous lands.[33] Though their main objective was the scientific compilation of data concerning the customs, diet, dress, speech and social manners of the Dutch—what might be called a kind of ecological encyclopedism—their work was touched with just a trace of historical wistfulness. Le Francq van Berkhey, the prodigious physician and scientific and literary virtuoso whose immense *Natural History of Holland* covered every conceivable organic phenomenon from shale deposits to the anatomy of the cow intestine to the rules of *katsbaan* (catch), was always delighted when he found rural or fishing communities still following old fashions of costume or diet. Around the south Holland delta villages of Goeree and Goedereede, for example, he discovered women still habitually wearing the old bonnets and heavy brass pins, but the manner of his recording suggested that it was already becoming something of a curiosity.[34] The same is true of his illustrations of the *kraamkloppertjes,* the cloth, lace and paper door plaques that announced the sex of a newborn, and of the resplendent engraved sheets of drinking horns, festive goblets and ceremonial standing salts that van Alkemade collected in *Nederlands Displegtigheid.*

Even for those who presented themselves as the guardians of an unbroken tradition of Dutch social mores, there was a defensive self-consciousness, even a preciosity, about the survival of "Fatherland spirit." The Amsterdam burgomaster who treated his guests to a banquet consisting of the "courses" of Dutch history — red herring and cheese (infancy), followed by plain puddings and roasts (prime), followed by French wines and delicacies (decadence) — was already playing on the appetite (as yet figurative rather than literal) for patriotic nostalgia.[35] The same was true of the "Spectatorial" journalism of the 1730s and 1740s and the sentimental novels of Aagje Deken and Betje Wolff that, in their diverse ways, appealed to traditional native virtues of simplicity, innocence, frugality and candor. They undermined their claims for a purely Netherlandish authenticity by their obvious borrowing from English novels of sensibility in the manner of Richardson. There was, in short, all the difference in the world between Bredero's celebration (in the preface to the *Spanish Brabander*) of his "simple rhyme . . . Amsterdam's own bud/A simple Netherlandish plant"[36] and the insecure strenuousness of the linguistic revivalists of the time of the periwigs. That they had something to resuscitate presupposes an elegiac quality to their concerns.

News of the death of traditional Dutch culture was, I am quite sure, greatly exaggerated. The great urban centers — congested and squalid Amsterdam, gin-soaked, bustling Rotterdam or the modish Hague — may have given cause for concern to these moralizing Spectators. And other centers — Leiden and Utrecht — university towns where many of the learned commentators were concentrated had lapsed into soporific decay. And many of the little towns of the Zaanstreek that had prospered on shipbuilding became ghostly backwaters, their skilled labor emptied into the slopping pail of Amsterdam. But habits of speech, dress, diet and the celebration of the family calendar in a peculiarly Dutch way were still very much in force in hamlets and towns throughout the Republic. Le Francq van Berkhey and van Alkemade may have gone around peering at these manners and mores as if they were so many of Leeuwenhoek's *animalculae,* but the objects of their scrutiny were blissfully ignorant of their curiosity. This was especially true of rural areas of the country, of traditional fishing communities, of the islands of the delta or of

the Zuider Zee, of towns like Deventer in the land provinces, or Enschede in
the east and Tilburg in the south that were beginning to prosper on the
ruralization of textiles. Such undisturbed continuities of habit of course
comforted those writers and preachers who feared the dilution of traditional
Dutch manners. But for the first time (though not at all the last) they were
described in terms of quaintness as though some happy historical accident had
preserved them as social fossils against the mutabilities and upheavals of
present time.

The eighteenth-century moralists did not doubt, then, that at the core of
the country the particular heritage of Dutch custom, language and even diet
persisted. But they were anxious whether that cultural heartland could survive
against the relentless encroachment of alien manners that seemed to them to
have colonized the upper and lower orders, especially in the towns. Their
nightmare was of outsiders swamping insiders so that the two became indistinguishable. A Republic that employed foreign mercenaries in its army,
foreign sailors in its navy, used French in its intellectual assemblies, aped
English manners of dress, clumsily adopted foreign norms of artistic refinement
(in painting, architecture and the theater), that even diluted its religion with
modish cosmopolitan libertinism, that aggravated this by exporting the flower
of their youth to the Indies, notorious for corrupting sound bodies and vulnerable souls—such a place was fast becoming indistinguishable from every other
dung heap of urban Europe. And since their sense of Dutch separateness was
bound up with their covenant with the Almighty—the armor of their freedom
—the loss of the one threatened to bring about the extinction of the other.

All this moral fretfulness simmered away in a pot of institutional continuity.
Stadholders came and went, "out" factions among the oligarchy replaced "ins"
to propitiate the rioting crowds without ever changing anything at all fundamental. But occasionally the lid of the pot blew right off, and the tremor
of fearfulness and hysteria that ran below the adamantine crust of the Dutch
augustan age erupted with spectacular force. The tempo of violent disorders in
the cities speeded up and their magistrates resorted to punitive counterviolence
with correspondingly greater regularity. The Amsterdam described in the
journals of the regent Jacob Bicker Raye is a grim townscape of gibbets and
platforms on which whores were flogged and wretched malefactors faced the
jeering crowds with proclamations of their misdeeds pinned to their breasts.
Bicker Raye's own predilection for the macabre and the prurient is itself a
register of an ugly but typical temper. But even allowing for his relentless
record of scandal and gruesome crime, it is evident that the informal,
unspoken consensus that had given Dutch culture its astonishing quality of
unforced cohesion was coming under serious strain. The third and fourth
decades of the century ended in 1748 with the towns of Holland in the grip of

a general insurrection against taxes and the governing patriciates that levied or farmed them out. For the first time since Grotius had argued without serious opposition that the "True Liberty" consisted in the delegation of sovereignty to ruling oligarchies, obedience to patrician authority (as distinct from particular groups) could not be taken for granted.[37]

The crisis of 1748, though, had been triggered, like that of 1672, by a war panic of sorts. But the troubles of periwig Holland were not all externally generated, for the years between 1730 and 1732 were also shaken by crises of other kinds that rose from deep within the flood tide of their collective conscience. With the social history of "marginal" groups now in fashion, historians have paid great attention to the most spectacular dislocation of the social consensus: a hysterical persecution of homosexuals in a culture that had virtually no history of witchhunts of any kind since the Anabaptists swung on the gallows two hundred years before. Historical geography being less popular, less attention has been paid to a more primal deluge: the massive collapse of the sea dikes along a broad stretch of coast in north Holland in the winter of 1731. (Indeed there was a series of catastrophic floods at this time — in 1726, 1728 and worst of all in 1740.) Yet in the minds and the sermons of the predikants, the two phenomena were intimately and causally connected, for the punishing flood had been sent (as it had been sent to Noah, and the fire to Sodom) as chastisement for the flood of iniquity that had swept the land. Water, as we have seen, was thought of in the rhetoric of the flood culture as purifying and differentiating. It could set apart the righteous from the wicked, wash away the filth and idolatry, and bring the stiff-necked to repentance. And once the waters had receded, the covenant that had been tarnished and broken could be renewed.

Both phenomena — of sin and of punishment — were marked by the invasion of aliens: by their burrowing intrusion into the body of the Republic's moral and physical fiber. The "Carolina" penal statutes of 1532 had made "unnatural vice" a capital crime, and further decrees, particularly in 1570, had been enacted by the States of Holland that expressed official abhorrence through elaborately comprehensive forms of execution: throttling, burning and drowning with a two-hundred-pound weight attached to the neck. During the seventeenth century there had been very occasional prosecutions recorded — at Breda in 1629, Utrecht in 1676 and Amsterdam in 1686, when a captain was charged with the corruption of his cabin boys.[38] And in 1702, the interrogation of one Gabriel de Berger, caught in an affray in the The Hague, had disclosed that the Vijverberg, literally a stone's throw from the High Court of Holland, the States and the government at the Binnenhof, was a place of casual homosexual soliciting. Nor was their world particularly clandestine. In special hearings that seemed to uncover a whole network of homosexual contacts in the city, de Berger confessed that two days before his arrest in a brawl with three men he claimed were going to force him to have sex, he had walked about *in transvestito* "out of pleasure."[39] Yet while these revelations were certainly news to The Hague magistracy, they were not so shocking as to push them into any draconian roundups of suspected "sodomites."

The events of 1730–32 were of a quite different character. For in both the numbers involved and the publicity given to the crimes, the rain of sermonizing literature and apocalyptic prophecies they called down, they rapidly assumed the proportions of a classic witchhunt. Beginning in the "core" cities of Utrecht and Amsterdam early in 1730, the cases brought to trial spread throughout the province, to The Hague, Leiden, Rotterdam, even to small towns like Vlaardingen. Other provinces were soon to unearth their own perpetrators of the *crimen nefandum*, especially in the northern fastnesses of the Republic, where Calvinist susceptibilities to denunciations were perhaps strongest. The most infamous proceedings of all took place in the Westerkwartier of Groningen, where the sheriff of Faan, Rudolph van Mepsche, and the local dominie of the nearby village of Oldekerk, Carel van Bijler, combined to terrorize the adolescent population of their local community with particular ferocity. After the confession under torture of eighteen youths and boys, some as young as fourteen were duly condemned and executed, while two deemed underage had their sentence commuted to a mere life incarceration in the house of correction.[40] There were other ugly proceedings centered on orphanages in Amsterdam and Utrecht. A servant at the Aalmoeseniersweeshuis municipal orphanage in Amsterdam was accused of corrupting boys, though it was not until 1740 that the boys themselves were dragged before the justices and terrified into confession. In Utrecht, a wine merchant, Blomsaed, was convicted on the testimony of five youths aged between fourteen and seventeen of having in effect sprung them from the orphanage at night to serve as prostitutes in return for watches and other trinkets.[41]

Except for the sadistic proceedings in Groningen orchestrated by van Mepsche, the rate of capital punishment was much less severe. While there were about two hundred and fifty cases tried in 1730 and 1731, with convictions brought in for all but a very few, the death sentence was carried out only in around ten percent of the judgments.[42] An edict of May 1730 by the States of Holland had repeated the ancient provisions of fire and water for the "abominable sin of sodomy" but in practice many sentences were commuted, and a combination of corporal chastisement, public humiliation and life banishment was the usual sentence. But there were enough actual executions to serve the theatrically exemplary purpose that the magistracy had in mind. In conformity with the draconian terms of the statute provision, the condemned were duly strangled, burned and drowned, though the century of Enlightenment ensured that their throttling was lethal before the other sentences were carried out. For those who were unable to witness these rites, popular prints like that of the fate of Anthony van Bywege in The Hague were available, and for those in a higher cultural bracket, the usual combination of allegory and documentary reportage on the fate of the modern Sodom and Gomorrah.

The net was cast wide socially as well as geographically. Though the majority of those convicted and sentenced came from the common people — couriers, apprentices, seamen, coachmen, house servants, house decorators, spice merchants, tanners, coopers, innkeepers, wine merchants, florists, weavers — members of the professional and even elite classes were not exempt. Surgeons, bookkeepers, the sheriff of Buren, a magistrate of Delft and even a burgomaster of Leiden were exposed as members of the fraternity, some of them practicing while apparently respectably married. The president of the Knightly Order of the States of Utrecht, Frederick Adriaen van Renswoude, one of the wealthiest and most powerful magnates of the province, was incriminated and escaped judgment only by remaining in permanent exile. Others were less fortunate.[43] A predikant in the east Holland town of Vianen, Emmanuel Valck, was convicted and committed suicide in his prison cell. This failed to exempt him from the rites of extirpation and purification, for his remains, like those of other felons, were put to the torch and then dumped, with the stipulated weights, into the river.

The social comprehensiveness of the homosexual world was not the only disconcerting feature to emerge from the spate of trials. There was also the matter of their visibility. An impression emerges that what most offended the governing classes (in addition to the moral revulsion of the pious) was the revelation that "unnatural practices" had been taking place, not in some hole-in-the-corner secret conventicle, but in the heart of Dutch towns, in the vicinity of their juridical or even spiritual centers. It was the sexton of the Dom Cathedral in Utrecht (where the tower provoked phallic jokes) who first brought homosexual scandals to the attention of the magistrates. His sons had witnessed scandalous acts taking place through a window opposite their own house. The alleys and streets around the cathedral had long been notorious for their boozy riot, but it took confessions of sodomy, and the disclosure of an entire network of homosexuals, complete with a gang of young male prostitutes who sold their services right in the center of the city in return for trinkets, for the shock of profane adjacency to register with full force.[44] The old cloister right by the Dom known as the academy, used as a promenading area, was identified by its habitués as a prime pickup site like the Vijverberg in The Hague. In Amsterdam it turned out that the undersides of particular bridges were the most concealed rendezvous of the homosexual community, but there, too, soliciting encounters went on around the town

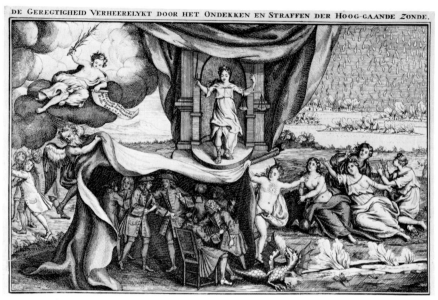

DE GEREGTIGHEID VERHEERELYKT DOOR HET ONDEKKEN EN STRAFFEN DER HOOG-GAANDE ZONDE.

309. Anon., *"Justice Triumphant,"* 1731. Rijksprentenkabinet, Amsterdam

hall itself. The fish market at the end of the Rokin, already known as a haunt of the receiving trade, was not only used for pickups, who could then go to the Serpent Inn for their sex, but according to the testimony of Maurits Schuring, acts of buggery had actually taken place just off the street by day as well as night.[45] Another suspect, Hendrik Voogd, confessed to having taking his breeches down at the fence of a garden in broad daylight in front of two men "and with his head against the fence, bent over so that the bigger man could abuse him from behind."[46]

The disclosure that homosexuals had been brazenly using the best-known public sites of Dutch towns for their commerce lent weight to the militant sodomite-hunters' contention that the Republic was being poisoned at its very heart by an invasion of alien filth. Their conspiratorial demonology was even reinforced by the further revelation that homosexuals from different towns knew each other, corresponded and even visited, and that they were connected in a sort of federation of sodomite conventicles. The key witness, who certainly had made a profession of interurban procuring, was one Zacharias Wilsma, who in a successful endeavor to prolong his own proceedings, appeared before judges in different towns to incriminate literally scores of unfortunates. As a casual mercenary soldier and servant with a company of horse, he had the perfect profession for making connections between groups of homosexuals "from Leeuwaarden to Breda, from Alkmaar to Maastricht," with The Hague as his particular headquarters.

It was not too difficult, then, to represent small groups of homosexuals dispersed throughout nearly every major town and province of the country as links in a chain of moral saboteurs: a sexual fifth column inside the republic of the righteous. They seemed, after all, to constitute a sort of satanic *imperium in imperio,* a travesty commonwealth, complete with its own underground vocabulary. Some of its terms seemed to parody their respectable origins, so that *nicht,* niece, for example, was the standard term for a homosexual among their own company. In the inflamed imagination of the detectives and judges they seemed to be almost a pastiche republic with its own social hierarchy, guilds, "academies" and conventicles. Was it purely fortuitous that they had infested places of public importance — promenades near churches, town halls? That they had penetrated innocent philanthropic institutions like the orphanages where God's work was meant to be done? As Wilsma's evidence made plain, even the army (and certainly the marines) was prey to their incursions, and safe places — the night watches and city walls — had been jeopardized by the *crimen nefandum.* In keeping with this theory of alien possession, it was even suggested that the origins of the epidemic — for such it began to seem — could be traced to the diplomatic negotiations in Utrecht that had eventually ended the wars against Louis XIV and had culminated in the Treaty of 1714. Those who took this view supposed that sexual corruption had been introduced into the Fatherland in the entourage of diplomats, notably the French, who — this being the heyday of the Regency — were thought of as irretrievably sunk in perversion and decadence. Through this insidious route, the Sun King had been on the verge of achieving posthumously what all his armies had been unable to bring about in forty years of warfare: the collapse of the godly commonwealth. And it was with some sense of exorcising foreign demons that the Utrecht court held its tribunal in the same building, the Huis van Hasenberg, that had housed the treaty negotiations seventeen years earlier.

The homosexual witchhunts of the 1730s, then, should best be thought of as a deviant variety of patriotism. Seen in this light, their occurring in peacetime rather than at a moment of critical panic like the trauma of 1672 becomes less mysterious. For as much as the Republic had long hungered after exactly the kind of peace it enjoyed in the early eighteenth century, it was not wholly liberated from ancient anxieties and insecurities. And without the self-evident allegiances that war imposed, there were time and space for the Dutch to brood over their own identity and the unsettling discrepancy between a heroic past and a prosaic future. The trials were a cathartic rite of passage, a largely self-imposed ordeal in which the integrity and solidarity of the national community were reaffirmed against a phantom enemy. It was an extreme instance of differentiating insiders and outsiders, the alien from the native, the authentic from the counterfeit, the godly from the diabolical and the natural from the perverse. For all the hysterical denunciations of the preachers, the proceedings themselves (except perhaps in Groningen) did not betray a loss of nerve by the ruling oligarchies. They resorted to torture to extract confessions, but that was nothing unusual in the Dutch Republic, for all its reputation for judicial civility. Their sentences attempted to distinguish between degrees of guilt, and there was even the occasional acquittal. If anything the control of the trials, as ugly and unjust as they were, within the regular institutions of justice—rather than a kind of messianic, clerically dominated tribunal—reinforced the legitimacy of the governing class.

This is not to say that the zealots of the Reformed Church were content to resign responsibility to the secular arm for weeding out the hosts of Satan. They saw the revelation of a homosexual commonwealth as merely the worst instance of a tide of depravity that had threatened to inundate the Republic. And they warned their flocks that punishment of the malefactors would in no way suffice to deflect the wrath of the Almighty. As Leonard Beels's explicit *Sodoms Zonde en Straffe* (Sodom's Sin and Punishment) made clear, what mercy could the new Sodom expect from an irate Jehovah?[47] And a print on the same subject that combined allegory, Old Testament analogy and contemporary

310. B. de Bakker, *"Timely Punishment,"* 1731–32. Rijksprentenkabinet, Amsterdam

TYDELYKE STRAFFE, VOORGESTELD TEN AFSCHRIK ALLER GODDELOZE EN DOEMWAARDIGE ZONDAREN.

reportage gave an even more vivid portent of terrors to come. While fire rained down on the offending city — which looked somewhat like a Dutch town — the Dead Sea rose over its debris. At left a ship sank into the deep. Fire and water would be the retribution, then — just as fire and water were prescribed in the sentence of the sodomites themselves, the cauterizing heat and the expiating flood.

The floods, at any rate, arrived pretty much on time, much to the satisfaction of their grim prophets. Indeed, with the simultaneous outbreak of a terrible cattle sickness that devastated herds in south Holland, and would spread to destroy the major part of the Friesland stock in the 1740s, a succession of plagues seemed to have been called down on the sinful. But it was the flood tide, of course, however familiar, that was immediately apprehended by the fearful as the rod of God. In the winter of 1731 a large portion of the dikes along the North Sea coast collapsed, leaving villages open to inundation.

Moreover, these floods were not like other floods. For when the remains of the destroyed sea dikes were examined, their timber piles were found to be honeycombed by gaping cavities. These had been created by a hitherto unknown teredine mollusk, now classified as the ship or pile worm, of formidable boring power and apparently insatiable appetite. What to the fascinated naturalists became *Teredo navalis* was to the population of the maritime provinces, and the predikants who saw this, an instrument of divine castigation. The worm had been, it was said by the authors of *The Worm a Warning to the Feckless and Sinful Netherlands* and *The Finger of God, Or Holland and Zeeland in Great Need from this Hitherto Unheard Plague of Worms,*[48] custom-made by the Almighty for the express purpose of punishing a stiff-necked people steeped in filth and sin. Lot, Noah and Jonah were all invoked and wonderfully confused in this rhetoric, but the message nonetheless was crystal clear. Just as the Lord had brought them up from the vasty deep, had delegated to them the power to distinguish between land and water, and had made them prosper and wax mighty by their lordship of the seas, so He could as easily return them to the consuming deluge. Popular prints of the worm catered to this sense of the oracular. And such was the feverishness of the response that it was some time before the learned classifiers dared reduce the whole phenomenon to the explicable proportions of a biological specimen. In the meantime special fast days were announced (one wit adding his hope that the worm might join the fast) and acts of public collective contrition like special donations for the poor. And whatever other punishment might be in store there was already the awful prospect of finding sufficient tax revenues to pay for the Norwegian stone that alone was thought strong enough to withstand any further depredations by the awesomely omnivorous worm.[49]

It was difficult to miss the apocalyptic symmetry of the two calamities. The alien worm had been sent to gnaw and bore its way into the very physical foundations of Dutch freedom and prosperity as a symbolic reproof of the abhorrent sin that had at its evil heart also the act of boring and gnawing. Nature had been sent to extirpate un-nature. But rather than wipe out Sodom with the fire or imprison the impenitent in a column of salt, the Lord had chosen that ordeal that would most emphatically and intuitively remind the Dutch of their special destiny in His Plan. And when the waters had receded, there was always the chance that the silt would redeem and the covenant be renewed.

311. Jan Ruyter, *Three pieces of wood from the piles on the sea-dikes showing how they were eaten through by the worms,* 1731. Rijksprentenkabinet, Amsterdam

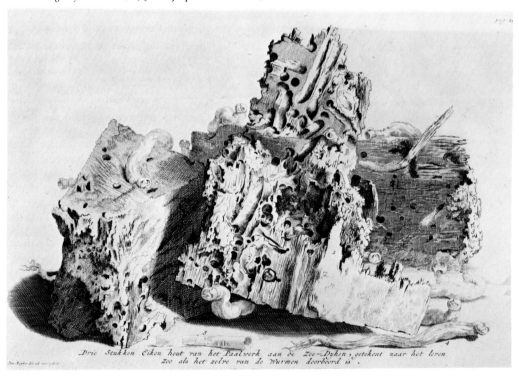

We end, then, where we began: in the moral geography of the Dutch mind, adrift between the fear of the deluge and the hope of moral salvage, in the tidal ebb and flow between worldliness and homeliness, between the gratification of appetite and its denial, between the conditional consecration of wealth and perdition in its surfeit. By the very nature of things, in a little land that had become, to its own surprise, the arbiter of the world, there could be no reconciliation of these dilemmas. No one, except those very few who dwelled entirely within the realms of either the sacred or the profane, ever imagined there would be. To be Dutch, as the indeterminate quality of the habitat always reminded them, was to live in a perpetual present participle, to cohabit with the unsettled. But while historical circumstances changed from generation to generation, the perennial resurrection of these dilemmas was itself some sign of continuity. To be Dutch still means coming to terms with the moral ambiguities of materialism in their own idiosyncratic but inescapable ways: through the daily living of it, in Sunday sermons on nuclear weapons and Monday rites of scrubbing the sidewalk.

Frontiers define. At the latest margin of their history, in the polders taken from the Ijsselmeer, where Frisian cows have replaced the herring busses of the Zuider Zee, two towns have been planted. But it is a *voortplanting,* a settlement that has brought forth different fruit. Lelystad, in the northeast, faces outward to the chill gray of the arrested sea. It is the progeny of one of the elements vigorously alive in Dutch culture: that which seems to master matter through economy; that which craves purity and simplicity. Lelystad is an example of physical and social engineering, the mathematics of space, and is fittingly named for the great hydraulic engineer Cornelis Lely, who, as a cabinet minister in the 1920s, created the immense scheme of endikement and reclamation in the Zuider Zee.[50] Lelystad was built in the 1960s as a dormitory town for Amsterdam and Utrecht, but it bears the mark of an earlier social aesthetic: that of de Stijl. Like Rietveld's chair or Mondriaan's paintings, Lelystad is a place of straight lines, of obedient geometry, of improving discomfort, of urban self-obliteration before the laws of horizontal nature. Where in older Dutch landscapes spires of churches and gables of little town halls and weigh houses pierce the horizon, in Lelystad the roofs are flat and the town is prone, as if preparing for the commuter sleep that was its raison d'être. Even the cows seem to lie lower than one would expect. Disorder, of course, is not so easily checked. The little boxes where commuters wait patiently for the buses that always arrive on time are covered with a palimpsest of graffiti that defy even the tireless detergency of the local guardians of purity. Motorbikes roar along the endless roads following the canals into foggy infinity, rending the anomie as they go. Lelystad lives, architecture notwithstanding.

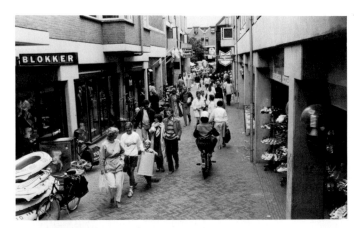

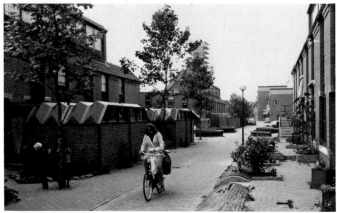

312. Houses and Shops, Almere

And then, for reluctant pioneers, there is Almere. At the southern tip of the Flevoland polder, and close enough to Amsterdam to catch its odd smells over the summer breezes of the Ijsselmeer, it was built in the late seventies on wholly different principles. Though its scale is even more ambitious than that of Lelystad, it represents, in effect, the other temper of Dutch culture: that of *gezelligheid,* coziness. Recently, in reaction against the vast anonymous compounds of high-rise buildings that comprise the urban overspills of the Randstad, there has been a turn back to neighborly intimacy. An English architect visiting the offices of the Centraal Beheer at Apeldoorn characterized them accurately as "a little collection of nesting boxes with open balconies looking down and up so you can talk to the people on the floor above you — like a chest of drawers with the drawers open."[51] And for a city that is supposed to house 200,000 people, Almere makes a decent effort to return to

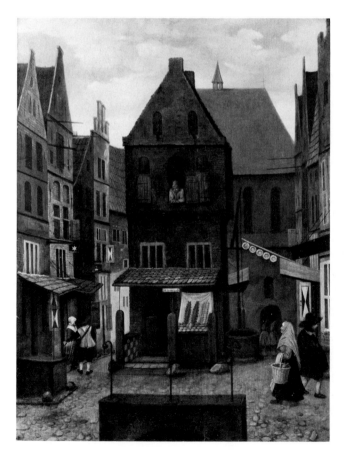

313. Jacobus Vrel, *Street Scene.*
Wadsworth Athenaeum,
Hartford, Conn.

the principle of the *buurt,* the neighborhood, by arranging its houses around courtyards. Inevitably these have a somewhat artificial look, so that from the air Almere looks more like a cantonment, as in Naarden, than a group of spontaneously clustered houses. But there is much brick and tile there, sloping roofs and little yards, and the people have responded with their own natural inclinations for the *gezellig.* Clogs hang from front doors; brass knockers are ritually burnished; windows are spotless; potted plants luxuriate in windows that frame interiors crammed with bric-a-brac; and in the surprisingly *gezellig* little shopping center, small faces bury themselves in cones of french fries dripping with mayonnaise.

That both Almere and Lelystad should testify to the perpetuation of peculiarly Dutch worlds is perhaps puzzling. But if there is one Dutch culture, there are many rooms within it. Like an Avercamp picture, it can swim with variety yet remain coherent unto itself. And such puzzles divert. They can even instruct. Or as the Master put it more grandiloquently: "All these elements of the general spectacle in this entertaining country at least give one's regular habits of thought the stimulus of a little confusion and make one feel that one is dealing with an original genius."[52]

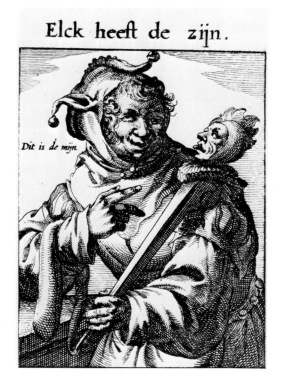

314. Concluding emblem, *"Everyone has his; this is mine,"* from Roemer Visscher, *Sinnepoppen.* Houghton Library, Harvard University

Appendices

Notes

Bibliography

List of Illustrations

Index

APPENDICES: THE PRICES OF CULTURE

I   THE LIBRARY OF A ZEELAND PATRICIAN
II   THE PAINTINGS OF TWO AMSTERDAM BURGHERS
III THE FIXTURES AND FITTINGS OF AN AMSTERDAM HOSTELRY
IV   THE INCOME OF A FRIESIAN MIDWIFE

Sources:

I Auction catalogue collection, *Bibliotheek Vereeniging ter Bervordering van de Belangen des Boekhandels,* Amsterdam.

II and III *Gemeentearchief, Amsterdam,* Archief van Desolate Boedels Kamer (Bankruptcy Chamber).

IV Bibliotheek, Universiteit van Amsterdam, *Dagboek van verlossingen van Catharina Geertruid Schrader* 1693–1745.

Prices given in guilders and stuivers.
(fl. 1 = 20 stuivers)

Some Comparative Prices	(mid-seventeenth century)
A tankard of ale:	½ stuiver
12 lb loaf of rye:	6–9 stuivers
weekly wage of	
skilled worker	fl. 2.8
small house in	
town	fl. 300
annual stipend of	
schoolmaster/predikant:	fl. 200

APPENDIX I: THE LIBRARY
OF A ZEELAND PATRICIAN

The earliest price catalogue in the archive of the Book Trade Society, 1658, reinforces the impression that the average price of learned works was fl. 3–5 and that pamphlets sold for 10 or 15 stuivers. In the library of Leonard Cats, a patrician of Middelburg, a Mercator Atlas sold for fl. 5, and de Brune's *Emblemata* for just fl. 2. On the whole, atlases were much more expensive than illustrated books.

The list below is a representative sample rather than the entire collection of books in the library. Typical of the culture it represents were an interest in Dutch and classical history, and accounts of world exploration and humanist political texts that were in no way inconsistent with the classic Calvinist (and Remonstrant) religious works.

The Library of D. Guilielmi, sold at Goes, Zeeland, 1687

		PRICE
Boxhorn	*Chroniek van Zeeland*	2.18
[Grotius]	*Deductie* (1654)	2.00
Scriverius	*Oude en Nieuwe Beschryving van Holland*	3.10
Carpentier	*Histoire génealogique des Pays Bas* (1664)	3.10
Grotius	*De antiquitate Respublica Batavae* (1610)	2.00
Aitzema	*Historie of verhaal van saken van staat en Oorlog* (1657, 17 vols.)	45.00
Tjassen	*Zeepolitie der vereenigde Nederlanden* (1652)	1.10
Valckenier	*'t Verwerde Europa* (1675)	5.00
[Domselaer]	*Het Ontroerde Europa* (1674, 2 vols.)	4.15
	Het Oude Goudse Chronijxen	2.00
Theodor de Bry	*Crudelitas Hispaniorum*	1.00
Sandys	*Voyages*	1.04
	Reisen van Ian Somer	3.00
	La Geographie de la France et de la Suisse	7.00
Hotman	*Francogallia*	1.00
Milton	*Pro Populo Anglicano defensio secunda* (1654)	1.18
Aubrey	*Mémoires*	1.16
van Mander	*Schilderboeck*	6.10
Vossius	*Ars Historica*	3.3
Boissardi	*Emblemata* (engr. de Bry)	1.18
Cats	*Alle de Werken* (1659, Schipper edn.)	7.15
	Trou-ring	.2
Vollenhoven	*Poésie* (1686)	2.0
Lipsius	*Werken* (Plantijn)	20.00
Grotius	*Bewijs van de Waare Godsdienst* (1648)	.12

Vondel	*Poezie* (1644, octavo)	.16
Heinsius	*Lofsangh van Iesus Christus* (1650)	.14
Ovid	*Metamorphose* (French edn)	.18
Bede	*Historia*	40.00
Josephus	*De Bello Judaeorum* (Scaliger's copy)	27.00
Dionysus Hali-		34.00
carnassus	*Concilia Generalia et Provincialia* (9 vols.)	69.00
Petrus Bor	*Nederlandse Oorlogen* (1621, 6 vols.)	33.00
[Commelijn]	*Leven en Bedrijf van Willem en Maurits,*	
	Prinsen van Oranje (1651)	8.00
	Leven en Bedryf van Frederik Hendrik	4.00
van Meteren	*Historien* (1614 folio)	4.00
Hooft	*Nederlandsche Historien* (1642)	4.00
Sully	*Mémoires*	8.05
Polydor Vergil	*Historia Anglica* (1570)	3.05
Buchanan	*Historia Scotica* (1581)	6.10
Garcilaso Inca	*Historia general del Perú* (1617)	6.19
Montanus	*Gedenkwaardige . . . der Oostindische*	
	Maatschappij aan de Keiser van Iapan	9.05
van Linschoten	*Schipvaart*	3.00
C. de Witt	*Lands Vloot* (1668)	1.00
	Plakaat-Boek van de Staten-Generaal	
	(1644–?)	3.00
Graswinckel	*Naspooring van de magt der Staten-*	
	Generaal in Holland (1667)	6.18
	Nederlandse Bybel (1637)	11.05
	La Bible de Genève (1588)	9.10
Calvin	*Institutes* (1654)	5.01
Melancthon	*Opera* (1567, 4 vols.)	6.15
Perkins	*Opera theologica* (2 vols.)	3.08
Uytenbogaert	*'van 't Ampt ende Authoriteyt eener*	
	Christelyke Overheyt (1610)	1.00
Cocceijus	*Ondersoek des Sabbaths*	1.00
van Beverwijck	*'t Begin van Holland in Dordrecht*	
Erasmus	*Adagia*	

APPENDIX II: THE PAINTINGS
OF TWO AMSTERDAM BURGHERS

i FROM THE ESTATE INVENTORY OF FRANÇOIS
VAN DER NOORDT'S BANKRUPTCY SALE
(February 8, 1681)

Some furniture has been included from the respective rooms for the sake of comparison. The obviously very grand bed of fl. 125 compares with fl. 30 for the most expensive of the landscapes in the same room. It is worth noting that the size of the painting and its frame were of great importance in determining its value, at least for the purposes of official assessment. There must have been many paintings worth less than the frame.

VOORHUIS (Lobby)	
2 chairs	5.00
Landscape	10.00
Landscape with Jacob and Rebecca	9.00
Sea-battle in gilt frame	20.00
Seascape showing a fire (at sea?)	4.00

SIDE-CHAMBER	
Mirror in black (ebony?) frame	2.10
Painting of a man, a child and little bird in gilt frame	25.00
Painting	15.00
Two landscapes	12.00
"Bruegelesque" landscape	30.00
Landscape	6.00
Bed	125.00
Painting of farm	10.00

ii SOME PAINTINGS AND FURNITURE FROM ANOTHER SALE
(March 27, 1682)

Landscape	3.00
Landscape	3.10
Winterscape	4.00
Still life with *roemer*	6.00
Still life	6.00
Larger still life	10.00
Two small landscapes	7.00
Mirror in black frame	10.00
Painting of *slagtyd* (Martinmas goose killing)	2.10
Brothel painting	1.10
Painting of a woman	
Painting of Gypsies	2.00
Picture of a young girl	6.00
Drawing	4.00
Painting of a Roman history	5.00
Painting of a castle	2.10
Painting of watermills	1.10

APPENDIX III: THE FIXTURES
AND FITTINGS OF AN AMSTERDAM HOSTELRY

From the bankruptcy estate assessment of Jan van Zoelen and Neeltje Zuykenaar, 1717. The entire estate fetched only fl. 971.13, so that this may be accounted a fairly modest household. The number of tables and chairs, napkins and tankards make it almost certain that their household was some sort of ale house or hostelry.

Table and two chairs and a bench	3.15
12 chairs	9.15
3 tables	9.05
6 chairs	3.10
Delftware	5.10
2 iron pots and some pewter	3.05
Assorted pots and pans	2.02
2 mirrors	7.00
3 dishes and 3 candlesticks	6.05
8 half-pint tankards	6.15
Another 8 half-pint tankards	6.15
Spoons, forks	9.15
Copper fire extinguisher bucket and kettle	11.00
2 candlesticks	5.00
Porcelain, some Delftware	6.05
2 tables with pipes	7.05
7 cushions	8.05
Curtains	2.15
Napkins and handkerchiefs	3.10
9 sheets	3.15
9 sheets	3.15
9 sheets	3.15
9 sheets	3.15
12 tablecloths	[not priced]
18 napkins	18.00
17 napkins	17.00
13 pieces of linen	[not priced]
7 curtains	[not priced]
Book with silver inlay binding and knife	9.15
Bed and pillows	16.10
Mattress	7.00
Peat and wood fuel	31.00
Cabinet	6.10

APPENDIX IV: THE INCOME
OF A FRIESIAN MIDWIFE, 1696–1745

Vrouw Schrader began work as a midwife in 1693 in the Frisian coastal countryside. But her systematic accounts date from 1696, when she established her practice in the market town of Dokkum. (See Chapter 7, pp. 525-35.)

YEAR	DELIVERIES	INCOME (GUILDERS)	YEAR	DELIVERIES	INCOME (GUILDERS)
1696	80	197 ±	24	35	122
97	?	204	25	59	157
98	123	310	26	57	148
99	109	225	27	73	188
1700	115	291	28	41	?
01	140	278	29	79	232
02	114	257	1730	74	260
03	117	230	31	99	260
04	130	260±	32	95	?
05	113	164	33	78	236
06	137	300	34–35	?	?
07	105	214	36	53	164
08	130	277	37	14	33
09	107	239	38–39	31	67
1710	122	267	1740	13	35
11	130	325	41	28	?
12	120	?	42	18	23
1714–22 (married years, gives up work)			43	20	?
1722	18	60	44	1	?
23	17	?	45	1	?

NOTES

Abbreviations

ARA   Algemeen Rijksarchief.
          The Hague

GA   Gemeente Archief.
          Amsterdam

KN   P. C. Knuttel,
          Catalogus van de Pamfletten verzameling
          berustende in de Koninklijke Bibliotheek

INTRODUCTION

1 Henry James, *Transatlantic Sketches* (Boston, 1875), 386.

2 In particular, A. Th. van Deursen, *Het kopergeld van de Gouden Eeuw,* 4 vols. (Assen, 1978–80); Herman W. Roodenburg, "The Autobiography of Isabella de Moerloose: Sex, Childrearing and Popular Belief in Seventeenth Century Holland," *Journal of Social History* (Spring 1985), 517–39; Rudolf Dekker, *Oproeren in Holland gezien door tijdgenoten* (Assen, 1979), *Holland in beroering, Oproeren in de 17de en 18de Eeuw* (Baarn, 1982).

3 Immanuel Wallerstein, *The Modern World System,* Vol. 2, *Mercantilism and the Consolidation of the European World Economy* 1600–1750 (New York, 1980), 65.

4 "Whether we fly high or low, we Dutchmen are all bourgeois—lawyer and poet, baron and labourer alike." J. H. Huizinga, "The Spirit of the Netherlands," in *Dutch Civilisation in the Seven-*

teenth Century, trans. Arno Pomerans (London, 1968), 112.

5 See, for example, Maurice Aymard, ed., *Dutch Capitalism and World Capitalism* (Cambridge, Eng., New York, Paris, 1982); Fernand Braudel, *The Perspective of the World* (New York, 1984).

6 Margaret Mann Phillips, *The "Adages" of Erasmus* (Cambridge, Eng., 1964), 211.

7 Comedie van de Rijcke-man (Haarlem, 1582), in *Het Roerspel en de Comedies van Coornhert,* P. van der Meulen, ed. (Leiden, 1955), 23–24.

8 Alexis de Tocqueville, *Democracy in America* (New York, 1840), vol. 2, Book 2, 147.

9 Kornelis van Alkemade, *Nederlands Displegtigheid,* 3 vols. (Rotterdam, 1732–35); see also his guide to funeral rituals and ceremonies, *Inleiding tot het Ceremonieel der Begravenissen* (Delft, 1723).

10 J. le Francq van Berkhey, *Naturlyke Historie van Holland,* 4 vols. in 7 books (Amsterdam, 1769–79).

11 Mary Douglas, *Cultural Bias* (London, 1978), 14.

12 Emile Durkheim, *The Division of Labour in Society,* trans. G. Simpson (London, 1933), 79–80.

13 William Bürger [Théophile Thoré], *Les Musées de la Hollande,* vol. 1 (Paris, 1858), 323.

14 Ibid., 37.

15 See Seymour Slive, *Jacob van Ruisdael* (New York, 1982), 67–77.

16 Paul Claudel, "L'oeil écoute," *Oeuvres Completes,* vol. 17 (Paris, 1960), 31–32.

17 Marcel Proust, "Sur la Lecture," preface to *Sesame et les Lys,* Jean Autret and William Burford, eds. (New York, 1971), 44–45.

CHAPTER ONE
MORAL GEOGRAPHY

1 See W. J. Brouwer-Ancker, "Het rasphuispoortje
   te Amsterdam en zijne geschiedenis," *De Navorscher*,
   44 (1894):565-70; A. W. Weissman, "Het tuchthuis
   en het Spinhuis te Amsterdam," *Oud Holland*, 26
   (1908):335-40.

2 Act 2, sc. 5, l. 35. See M. Boas, "De spreuk van
   de Rasphuispoort," *Jaarboek Amstelodamum* (1917),
   15:121-29.

3 The House of Correction in 1595 and the Spinhuis
   in 1597. For an excellent history of the two institutions see Thorsten Sellin, *Pioneering in Penology:
   The Amsterdam Houses of Correction in the Sixteenth
   and Seventeenth Centuries* (Philadelphia, 1944);
   A. Hallema, *Geschiedenis van het Gevangeniswezen
   Hoofzakelijk in Nederland* ('s Gravenhage, 1958),
   117-86.

4 For the philosophy and practice of this reform in
   another city, see Natalie Zemon Davis,
   "Humanism, Heresy and Poor Relief in Sixteenth
   Century Lyon" in *Society and Culture in Early Mod-
   ern France* (London, 1975); also A. Th. van Deursen,
   Het kopergeld van de Gouden Eeuw, vol. 1, *Het
   Dagelijks Brood* (Assen / Amsterdam, 1978), 71-89.

5 Cited in Sellin, 14.

6 Dirck Volkertsz. Coornhert, *Boeventucht ofte
   Middelen tot vermindering der schadelkye Ledighangers*
   (1573).

7 See A. Hallema, "Jan van Hout's Rapporten en
   Adviezen over den Amsterdam Tugthuis," *Bijdragen
   en Mededelingen van het Historisch Genootschap*, 48
   (1927):69-98.

8 Sellin, *Pioneering*, 43.

9 Hallema, *Geschiedenis*, 120, n.1.

10 Richard Carnac Temple, ed., *The Papers of Thomas
   Bowrey*, 1669-1713 (London, 1927); Hallema,
   Geschiedenis, 128.

11 Sellin, *Pioneering*, 58.

12 Ibid., 68.

13 J. de Parival, *Les Délices de la Hollande* (Leiden,
   1662), 96-97.

14 Martin Szombor, *Europa Varietas* (Kachau, 1620),
   cited in Rustem Vambery, "Das Amsterdammer
   Zuchthuis in ungarischer Beleuchtung," *Zeitschrift
   für die gesamte Strafwissenschaft*, 37 (1915-16):
   106-109.

15 Robert Davies, ed., *The Life of Marmaduke Rawdon
   of York* (London, 1863), 100; Edward Brown, *A Brief
   Account of Some Travels in Diverse Parts of Europe*
   (London, 1685), 70.

16 Robert Bargrave, *A Relation of Sundry Voyages and
   Journeys made by Robert Bargrave* (1652-53)
   (Rawlinson MSS. 79, Bodleian Library, Oxford);
   William Aglionby, *The Present State of the United
   Provinces of the Low Countries* (London, 1669), 270;
   Maximilien Misson, *A New Voyage to Italy*, 2 vols.
   (London, 1739, but a translation of The Hague
   edition of 1691), 29; William Montague, *The
   Delights of Holland, or a three months travel about that
   and other provinces* (London, 1696), 38; Thomas
   Nugent, *The Grand Tour; or A Journey through the
   Netherlands, Germany, Italy and France* (London,
   1738), 81; Joseph Marshall, *Travels Through
   Holland . . . in the Years 1768, 1769 and 1770*
   (London, 1772), 65.

17 Pieter Spierenburg, *Spectacle of Suffering: Executions and the Evolution of Repression from a Pre-Industrial
   Metropolis to the European Experience* (New York,
   1984). Jan Wagenaar, *Amsterdam in zyne opkomst,
   aanwas, geschiedenissen* etc. (Amsterdam, 1760),
   2:253. Wagenaar followed his dismissive remark
   by the comment: "en is er naar alle waarschijn-
   lykheid nimmer gewest " ("and *in all probability*
   [my emphasis] there never has been"), a choice
   of words that certainly leaves open some room for
   speculation.

18 Tobias Domselaer et al., *Beschrijving der Stat
   Amsterdam van Haar Eerste Beginselen oudtheydt
   vergrootingen en gebouwen en geschiedenis tot op den
   jaar 1666* (Amsterdam, 1665 [*sic*]), 102ff.

19 *Historie van de Wonderlijcke Mirakelen, die in menichte
   ghebeurt zijn, ende noch dagelijk ghebeuren, binnen de
   vermaerde Coop-stadt Aemstelredam: In een plaats
   ghenaempt het Tucht-huys, gheleghen op de Heylighe-
   wegh* (Amsterdam, 1612). There was also a French
   translation the same year, in Leiden. See
   A. Hallema, "Een merkwardig pamphlet
   betreffende het Amsterdam Tuchthuis in de 17de
   Eeuw," *Nieuwe Rotterdamsche Courant*, October
   27-28, 1931; also Robert von Hippel, *Die Entstehung
   der modernen Freiheitstrafe und des Erziehungs-
   Strafvollzugs* (Giessen, 1931); Sellin, *Pioneering*, 70.

20 Sir John Carr, *A Tour Through Holland . . . in the Sum-
   mer and Autumn of 1806* (London, 1807), 298-99;
   M. de Blainville, *Travels Through Holland, Germany,
   Switzerland*, 2 vols. (London, 1809), 1:36.

21 Sellin, *Pioneering*, 5.

22 For further details of this episode, see Chapter 8,
   pp. 603.

23 J. Lydius, *'t Verheerlikt Nederland* (1668), 28. "Doch

die Godt tot groote heerlijkheydt verheffen wil, besoeckt hy eerst met ghevaren ende uytterste onheylen. En waarlyck was 't gewelt van dese rampen soo groot, dat men licht afmeten kost dat het ons Hemel tot en beproeving opgheleydt was, willende dien onsterflicken Godt eens onderstaen of de deught en standvastigheydt van dit volck in sware saecken te lijden en uyt te voeren onkreuckbaer blijven soude."

24 Ibid., 49.

25 See, for example, Gerardus van Loon, *Beschrijving der Nederlandsche Historiepenningen*, 2 ('s Gravenhage, 1725): xx.

26 On this plan, and the inundations around Leiden, see G. 't Hart, "Rijnlands Bestuur en Waterstaat Rondom Het beleg en Ontzet van Leiden 1570–1580," *Leids Jaarboekje*, 66:13–33.

27 Jacob Duym, *Belegering der Stad Leyden* (1606); see also, for example, *Waarachtige Beschrijvinghe ende Levendighe Afbeeldinhe vande Meer dan Onmenschelijke ende Barbarische Tyrannije Bedreven by de Spaengiaerden in de Nederlanden* (Amsterdam, 1621), 155 ff.

28 J. J. Orlers, *Beschrijvinge der stadt Leyden* (Leiden, 1641), 520–22.

29 See Frederik Muller, *Populaire Prozaschrijvers der XVII en XVIIIe Eeuw* (Amsterdam, 1893); G. D. J. Schotel, *Vaderlandsche Volksboeken en Volkssprookjes van de Vroegste tijd en tot der einde der 18de eeuw*, 2 vols. (Haarlem, 1874), 2:154.

30 Muller, *Populaire Prozaschrijvers*, n.p.

31 *Ongeluckige Voyagie van 't Schip Batavia Nae de Oost-Indien Gebleven op de Abrolhos van Frederick Houtman . . .*(Amsterdam, 1647).

32 For English criticism, see Violet Barbour, "Dutch and English Merchant Shipping in the Seventeenth Century," *Economic History Review*, 1930, 261–90. On the price of seaworthiness and lower life-expectancy rates for Dutch ships see Richard W. Unger, *Dutch Shipbuilding to 1800* (Assen/Amsterdam, 1978), 44.

33 Willem Ysbrantsz. Bontekoe, *Journael ofte Gedenckwaerdige beschrijvinge vande Oost-Indische Reyse van Willem Ysbrandtsz. Bontekoe van Hoorn* (Hoorn, 1646) (citations from Spectrum edition, Utrecht/Antwerp, 1978), 43. See also the translation and introduction by C. B. Bodde-Hodgkinson and Pieter Geyl (London, 1929).

34 Ibid., 68.

35 For a translated edition and account of the Pelsaert voyage, see H. Drake-Brockman, *Voyage to Disaster: The Life of Francisco Pelsaert* (London, 1963).

36 Ibid., 40–41.

37 The proverbial expression and its explanation were from the Flemish historian Marcus van Vaernewijck, cited in Walter Gibson, *Pieter Bruegel* (London, 1977), 196.

38 Bontekoe, *Journael*, 36.

39 Ibid., 63.

40 Ibid., 42.

41 Ibid. (Geyl ed.), 3.

42 This was the thesis of Pieter Geyl, *Revolt of the Netherlands, 1555–1609* (London, 1958), 179. For a perceptive overview of the debate and a critical comment on Geyl's argument, see Geoffrey Parker, *The Dutch Revolt* (London, 1977).

43 This was also the view of Huizinga, *Dutch Civilization*, 16.

44 Quoted in Joh. van der Veen, *Dredge, Drain, Reclaim* (The Hague, 1948), 37.

45 For this view of land claims in early Zionism see Simon Schama, *Two Rothschilds and the Land of Israel* (London/ New York, 1979).

46 See Audrey Lambert, *The Making of the Dutch Landscape* (London/New York, 1971), 123 ff.; M. K. E. Gottschalk, *Stormvloeden en rivierstromingen* (Assen, 1974).

47 Sebastian Munster, *Cosmographia universalis*, Liber VI (Basel, 1552), 516. For the folk memory of the St. Elizabeth's Day flood, see H. van de Waal, *Drie Eeuwen Vaderlandsche Geschied-Uitbeelding*, 2 vols. ('s Gravenhage, 1952), 1:255–57; Lambert, *Landscape*, 123.

48 The earliest written account was by Chrysostom of Naples in his *De situ et de moribus Hollandiae* (1514), later incorporated by Petrus Scriverius in *Batavia Illustrata* (Leiden, 1614). See van de Waal, *Drie Eeuwen*, 256.

49 Lambert, *Landscape*, 215–16.

50 Pieter Corneliszoon Hooft, *Nederlandsche Historien* (Amsterdam, 1703 ed.), Book VI, 217.

51 Ibid., 218.

52 See J. de Vries, *The Dutch Rural Economy in the Golden Age* (New Haven, Conn./London, 1974); Lambert, *Landscape*, 216 f. For the history of land reclamation and the shaping of the landscape in this period, see the several excellent essays in *Het Land van Holland* (Amsterdam Historical Museum, 1978).

53 On the relationship between institutional power and the peculiarities of the Dutch landscape see H. van der Linden, "Iets over wording, ontwikkeling en landschappelijk spoor van de

Hollandse watertchappen," in *Het Land van Holland,*
101–13; S. J. Fockema Andreae, *Overzicht van de
Nederlandse waterschapsgeschiedenis* (Leiden, 1952);
Th. F. J. A. Dolk, *Geschiedenis van het
Hoogheemraadschap Delfland* ('s Gravenhage, 1939);
C. Dekker, "The Representation of the Freeholders
in Drainage Districts of Zeeland west of the
Scheldt during the Middle Ages," *Acta Historiae
Neerlandica,* 8 (1975), 1–30.

54 Andries Vierlingh, *Tractaet van Dyckagie,* eds. J. de
Hullu and A. G. Verhoeven, ('s Gravenhage, 1920),
22. In later passages Vierlingh berates men who
held dike-reeve offices as sinecures and "who have
never seen the tides or flood waters and know
nothing of the winds" (Ibid., 49). See also 218–19
and passim for comments in the same temper.

55 Van Veen, *Dredge,* 37–38.

56 Vierlingh, *Tractaet,* 396.

57 Ibid., 105.

58 Quoted in Van Veen, *Dredge,* 33.

59 Ibid., 36.

60 Ibid., 38.

61 Vierlingh, *Tractaet,* 22–23.

62 Ibid., 161.

63 [Owen Felltham], *A Brief Character of the Low Countries under the States. Being Three weeks observations of
the vices and vertues of the inhabitants* (London, 1660),
90–91.

64 *'t Verheerlijkt Nederland* (1668), i.

65 Petrus Cunaeus, *Of the Commonwealth of the Hebrews*
(London, 1653), A3–4 (Preface).

66 J. Hartog, *Geschiedenis van de Predikkunde en de
Evangelprediking in de Protestantsche kerk van Nederland*
(Amsterdam, 1865), 91.

67 [Jac. Lydius], *Wee-klage over den inbreuk van den
Alblasser-waard* (1658); see also *Generale Beschryvinge
van ons Tegenwoordige ingebroken Alblasser-waert in Zuyt
Hollandt* and the *Straf-predikaties* [punishment
sermons] of J. van Oudenhven on this event.

68 J. Krul, *Wereld-hatende Noodtsaeckelijcke* (Amsterdam,
1627), 49.

69 See Peter Sutton et al., *Masters of Seventeenth-Century
Dutch Genre Painting* (Philadelphia, 1984), 307–308.

70 Goethe, *Faust,* trans. and ed. Philip Wayne, Act
5, sc. 2, l. 269.

CHAPTER TWO
PATRIOTIC SCRIPTURE

1 Romeyn de Hooghe, *Spiegel van Staat der Vereenigde
Nederlands* (Amsterdam, 1706), 57. For an account

of de Hooghe's propaganda work see Harry T.
Wilson, "The Art of Romeyn de Hooghe" (Ph.D.
diss., Harvard University, 1974).

2 See, for example, the close relationship between
Spieghel der Spaansche Tyrannie (also published in
French) (Amsterdam, 1620) and [Abraham
Wicquevoort], *De Fransche Tyrannie* (Amsterdam,
1674). De Hooghe's own unsparingly graphic
engravings of French atrocities in his own
Schouwburg van Nederlandse Veranderinge (Amsterdam,
1674) undoubtedly owed a great deal to the earlier generation of anti-Spanish prints.

3 de Hooghe, *Spiegel,* 12.

4 Ibid., 5–6.

5 The degree to which eighteenth-century disturbances were a function of the tightening of the
oligarchy remains controversial. On the tax riots,
see Rudolf Dekker, *Holland in beroering. Oproeren
in de 17de en 18de eeuw* (Baarn, 1982).

6 On the "nostalgic" style of Patriot polemics see
Simon Schama, *Patriots and Liberators: Revolution in
the Netherlands 1780–1813* (London/New York,
1977), 21; ch.2.

7 de Hooghe, *Spiegel,* 4–6.

8 On the use of the ancient Batavians as a prototype for a national personality, see the brilliant
essay by I. Schöffer, "The Batavian Myth during
the Sixteenth and Seventeenth Centuries," in
P. A. M. Geurts and A. E. M. Janssen, eds.,
Geschiedschrijving in Nederland ('s Gravenhage, 1981),
84–109.

9 See S. Groeneveld, "Beeldvorming en realiteit.
Geschiedschrijving en achtergronden van de Neder-
landse Opstand tegen Filips II," in Geurts and
Janssen, *Geschiedschrijving,* 55–84. The same impres-
sion emerges strongly from the comprehensive
anthology of documents collected by E. H.
Kossman and A. F. Mellink, *Texts Concerning the
Revolt of the Netherlands* (Cambridge, Eng./New
York, 1974).

10 Amsterdam, however, was isolated on this issue
from all the Holland towns, with the exceptions
of Delft, and Rotterdam, which wanted a *longer*
period of truce. See Jonathan I. Israel, *The Dutch
Republic and the Hispanic World 1606–1661* (Oxford,
1982), 30–31.

11 Ibid., 62–64. It was part of the polemics against
Oldenbarneveld that he had been a tool of Spain
in concluding a truce allegedly so damaging to
Dutch interests.

12 See Herbert H. Rowen, *John de Witt, Grand Pension-*

ary of Holland (Princeton, N.J., 1978), 282-85, 474-76, Ch. 31.

13 Vermeer's widow conveyed the picture to her mother, who in 1677 seems to have objected to the attempts by her daughter's trustee to have it auctioned. See Albert Blankert, *Vermeer of Delft* (Oxford, 1978), 163.

14 On the map, see James A. Welu, "Vermeer: His cartographic sources," *Art Bulletin* 57 (1975): 529-47.

15 As early as 1920, Geyl attacked the autonomism of Belgian historicism (especially in Pirenne) by arguing that at the outset of the revolt against Spain there was a common Netherlandish culture, unified by language. See P. Geyl, *Holland and elgium: Their Common History and Their Relations* (Leiden, 1920). It was a position from which he never deviated throughout his career, reiterated as late as 1964 in *History of the Low Countries: Episodes and Problems* (London, 1964), 6. On the history of the Dutch language, see the classic work by J. te Winkel, *Geschiedenis van de Nederlandse Taal* (Culemborg, 1901).

16 Most obviously in *The Spanish Brabanter*. See the translation by H. David Brumble III (Binghamton, N.Y., 1982) and its famous preface where Dutch verse is characterized by Bredero as "A simple Netherlandish plant/ That gives forth no more sweetness than is looked for."

17 Kamer, "In Liefd Bloeyende" [H. L. Spieghel], *Tweespraack van de Nederduitsche Letterkunst* (Leiden, 1584), 103.

18 Ibid., 105.

19 J. van Vondel, *Aenleidinge ter Nederduitsche Dichtkunst* (Amsterdam, 1650), cited in te Winkel, *Geschiedenis*, 462.

20 D. Nauta, *Het Calvinisme in Nederland* (Franeker, 1949), 50-51.

21 G. Groenhuis, in his fine study of the Calvinist clergy, *De Predikanten* (Groningen, 1977), 37, gives an estimate of about 1,200 ministers for the whole Republic around the middle of the century.

22 On the image-breaking of 1566-67, see J. Scheerder, *De Beeldenstorm* (Bussum, 1974); A. J. M. Beenakker, *Breda in de eerste storm van de opstand. Van ketterij tot beeldenstorm 1545-1569* (Tilburg, 1971); A. C. Duke and D. H. A. Kolff, "The time of troubles in the county of Holland" in *Tijdschrift voor Geschiedenis* 89 (1976): 394-442.

23 This, at any rate, is the view of some recent writing on the Dutch revolt, notably by A. Th. van Deursen, that has begun to reemphasize, as it were, the qualitative importance of Calvinist allegiance in local emergencies.

24 See O. de Jong, "Unie en religie," in S. Groeneveld and H. L. Ph. Leeuwenberg, eds., *De Unie van Utrecht. Wording en werking van een verbond en een verbondsacte* (Den Haag, 1979), 155-81.

25 Groenhuis, *Predikanten,* 26ff.

26 *Paapsche stoutigheden* (Papist obstinacy) was one of the most recurrent items of complaint at the meetings of the provincial synods. At the Synod of Leiden in 1639, for example, there was a complaint about the widespread availability of Papist books and the establishment (in the seigneurial enclave at Culemborg) of a Jesuit seminary!; in Rotterdam in 1641, about their audacity in public burial rites; in Gorinchem in 1642, on the urgency of missionary preaching against Papist idolatry, etc., etc. See W. P. C. Knuttel, ed., *Acta der Particuliere Synoden van Zuid Holland, 1621-1700,* II, 1634-45 ('s Gravenhage, 1909), 216-18, 331, 376-77, and passim.

27 See J. J. Poelhekke, *Frederik Hendrik, Prins van Oranje* (Zutphen, 1978), 166.

28 Ibid., 164.

29 See J. G. van Dillen, "De Politieke en Kerkelijke Twisten te Amsterdam in de Jaren 1620 tot 1630," in idem, *Mensen en Achtergronden* (Groningen, 1964), 457-65.

30 Constantijn Huygens, *The Use and Non-use of the Organ in the Churches of the United Netherlands* (Gebruyck of Ongebruyck van't Orgel in de Kercken der Vereenigde Nederlanden), tr., Ericka E. Smit-Vanrotte (Brooklyn, N.Y., 1964). On the debate between Huygens and the militant Calvinists see H. A. Bruinsma, "The Organ Controversy in the Netherlands Reformation to 1640," *Journal of American Musicological Society,* 7 (1954): 205-12; A. J. Servaes van Royen, "Huygens contra Calckman en vice-versa," *Tijdschrift voor Nederlands Muziekgeschiedenis,* 9 (1914):170-73.

31 Johan Janszoon Calckman, *Antidotum Tegengift van't gebruyck of ongebruyck van 't orgel* ('s Gravenhage, 1641).

32 Calckman was not pleased by the decision of the synod, calling its members "airy plovers." It meant, of course, that the magnificent organs in the great churches of Amsterdam, Haarlem, Gouda, Delft and Utrecht were not merely decorative but were

put to full use in the devotional manner recommended by Huygens.

33 Groeneveld, *Beeldvorming,* 64. See also, idem, "Natie en nationaal gevoel in de sestiende-eeuwse Nederlanden," in *Scrinium et Scriptura. Opstellen betreffende de Nederlandse geschiedenis aangeboden aan J. L. van der Gouw* (Groningen, 1980), 372–87. See also E. H. Kossmann, "The Dutch Case: A National or Regional Culture?," *Transactions of the Royal Historical Society* (1929): 155–168.

34 In the preface to *The Rise of the Dutch Republic,* 3 vols. (London, 1889), Motley wrote that "The maintenance of the right, by the little provinces of Holland and Zeeland in the sixteenth century, by Holland and England united in the seventeenth century and by the United States of America in the eighteenth century forms but a single chapter in the great volume of human fate for the so-called revolutions of Holland, England and America are all links of one chain." On John Adams's identical view, set out in his "Memorial" to the States General, see Schama, *Patriots,* 60.

35 The phrase is taken from the superb introduction to E. H. Kossmann and A. F. Mellink, *Texts Concerning the Revolt of the Netherlands* (Cambridge, Eng., 1974), 40. See also Charles Wilson, *Elizabeth I and the Revolt of the Netherlands* (London, 1970).

36 Van Deursen characterizes the Union as the "fundamental law" of the Republic and, in contrast to other interpretations, emphasizes its unifying authority. But he correctly points out that its two essential aims—the common defense against the foreign enemy and the preservation of local privileges—were often hard to reconcile, at least in the short term. See A. Th. van Deursen, "Tussen eenheid en zelfstandigheid," in Groeneveld and Leeuwenberg, *Unie,* 136–54.

37 Article V of the Union of Utrecht, which dealt with revenue, did, in fact, refer to the kinds of indirect taxes and imposts it held to be appropriate—a long list extending from beer and salt to cattle and textiles—but that, it emphasized, should be raised "by common advice and approval." See Groeneveld, *Unie,* 32.

38 On Honselaersdijk, see D. P. Snoep, "Honselaersdijk: restauraties op papier," *Oud Holland,* 84 (1969):270–94. See Beatrijs Brenninkmeyer-de Rooij, "To Behold Is to Be Aware: History Painting in Public Buildings and the Residences of the Stadholders," in Albert Blankert et al., *Gods, Saints and Heroes: Dutch Painting in the Age of Rembrandt*

(Washington, D.C., 1980), 65–76.

39 Ibid.

40 Gerard van Loon, *Beschrijving der Nederlandsche Historiepenningen,* 3 vols. ('s Gravenhage, 1723–28).

41 Ibid., 1,172–73.

42 Ibid., 1,201.

43 For a full account of this important print see Egbert Haverkamp-Begemann, *Willem Buytewech* (Amsterdam, 1959), 170–71; Clifford S. Ackley, *Printmaking in the Age of Rembrandt* (Boston, 1980), 89–90.

44 van Loon, *Beschrijving,* 2, 55.

45 H. van de Waal, *Drie Eeuwen Vaderlandsche Geschied-Uitbeelding, 1500–1800* ('s Gravenhage, 1952), vol. 1: 62.

46 On the *Divisiekroniek* and other early history chronicles, see the indispensable account by H. Kampinga, *De Opvattingen over onze Oudere Vaderlandsche Geschiedenis* ('s Gravenhage, 1917); van de Waal, 1:127–56.

47 Ibid., xii.

48 [Wouter van Gouthoeven], *D'oude Chronijcke ende Historien van Holland* ('s Gravenhage, 1636).

49 G. D. J. Schotel, *Vaderlandsche Volksboeken en Volkssprookjes van de Vroegste Tijden tot het einde der 18de Eeuw,* 2 vols. (Haarlem, 1873), 2:19–21ff.

50 Petrus Scriverius [Pieter Schrijver], *Beschrijvinge van Out Batavien met de Antiquiteyten van dien Mitsgaders d'Afbeelding, Afkomst ende Historie der Edelen Hoogh-geboren graven van Hollant, Zeelant ende Vrieslant* (1636). This was the third edition of a work that had appeared first in 1612 and which was itself an extension of Scriverius's *Out Batavien* of 1606. See Kampinga, *Opvattingen,* 29; Schoffer, *Batavian Myth,* 97.

51 *D'oude Chronijcke,* 3.

52 Van de Waal, *Geschied-Uitbeelding,* 1:258–80; Brenninkmeyer de Rooij, 66; see also the 1657 version by Nicolaes van Galen, in *Gods, Saints and Heroes,* Catalogue no. 59, p. 220.

53 Scriverius, *Beschrijvinge,* A4, preface. Scriverius uses the marvelous noun *blaesbalcken,* literally a bladder-bellows, to suggest the airy folly of these tales.

54 Kampinga, *Opvattingen,* 25ff.

55 Vaenius (van Veen) began by editing a set of thirty-six etchings by Antonio Tempesta, with corresponding extracts from Tacitus's history, in 1612 and produced the series of paintings a year later. See van de Waal, *Geschied-uitbeelding,* 1:210–15; idem, "The iconographic background to Rembrandt's *Claudius Civilis* in *Steps Towards*

Rembrandt" (Amsterdam/London, 1974); see also Barbara Buchbinder-Green, "The Painted Decorations of the Town Hall of Amsterdam" (Ph.D. diss., Northwestern University, 1974), 188. I am also grateful to Margaret Carroll, who is currently preparing a monograph on the *Claudius Civilis* and its historical context, for much illumination on this subject.

56 Scriverius, *Beschrijving*, A5.

57 Hugo Grotius, *Liber de antiquitate reipublicae Batavicae* (Leiden, 1610). In the Dutch translation, *Tractaet vande oudheyt vande Batavische nu Hollandsche Republique* ('s Gravenhage, 1610), p. 13, Grotius emphasizes the "equality of rights" in the ancient "Batavian Republic" and insists that the "assemblies of the Bataves" were to be understood as characterizing a "free republic."

58 See, for example, Marcus Boxhorn, *Spiegeltjen, vertoonende 't lanck hayr ende hayrlocken, by de oude Hollanders ende Zeelanders gedragen* (Middelburg, 1644); Knuttel, *Acta der Synoden*, 5: 466–69; Borstius, *Predikatie tegen lang hayr* (Dordrecht, 1644); Florent Schuyl, *Raedt voor de Schier-siecke Hayr cloovers* ('s Hertogenbosch, 1644).

59 *D'oude Chronijcke*, 5–6.

60 It is important to note that references to *oudts ghebruyckelyk* (old usage) became standard in contemporary histories, so that the infamy of Spanish rule was precisely in its heedless violation of those customs. See, for example, Joh. Gijsius, *Oorsprong en Voortgang der Neder-Lantscher Beroerten ende Ellendicheden* (1616), 26.

61 Grotius, *Tractaet*, 24.

62 Ibid., 22–23.

63 On resistance theory see Quentin Skinner, *The Foundations of Modern Political Thought*, 2 vols. (Cambridge, Eng., 1978), 2:189–348.

64 Grotius, *Tractaet*, 25.

65 Ibid.

66 Gijsius, *Oorsprong*, 411.

67 [Willem Baudartius], *Waarachtighe Beschrijvinghe ende Levendighe Afbeeldinghe Vande Meer dan onmenschelijke ende Barbarische Tyrannije Bedreven by de Spaengiaerden in de Nederlanden* (Amsterdam, 1621), 276. Like many of the most vigorous propagandists of the Spanish "Black Legend," Baudart was a southerner who had left Leuven to escape Parma's advance.

68 [Jan Everhardt Cloppenburch], *Le Miroir de la Tyrannie Espagnole* (Amsterdam, 1620) incorporates particularly vivid and gruesome images of the Council of Blood and the Inquisition, captioned, significantly, in Dutch, and drawn from vernacular editions of the same work.

69 Pieter Cornelisz. Hooft, *Nederlandsche Historien* (Amsterdam, 1703 ed.), 473–74.

70 Ibid., 474.

71 Cited in Schotel, *Vaderlandsche Volksboeken*, 1:257.

72 On the Reformation, see Robert Scribner, *For the Sake of Simple Folk* (Cambridge, Eng., 1981).

73 Hooft, *Nederlandsche Historien*, 390.

74 Gijsius, *Ooorsprong*, 309–10; *Waarachtinghe Beschrijvinge*, 136–37.

75 Gijsius, *Oorsprong*, 309.

76 The fishing and coastal communities who were suffering badly from privateering and Flemish "armada" attacks in 1641–42 did not see it that way and wanted stepped-up protection and retaliation on Flemish fishing ports for their own losses. See Israel, *The Dutch Republic*, 325; also idem, "A Conflict of Empires: Spain and the Netherlands, 1614–48," *Past and Present* 76 (August 1977): 34–74.

77 Jacob Duym, *De Belegering der stad Leyden* (Leiden, 1600).

78 See the account of the "Netherlands-Israel" analogy in Groenhuis, *Predikanten*, 77–102. See also H. Smitskamp, *Calvinistisch nationaal besef in Nederland voor het midden der zeventiende eeuw* ('s Gravenhage, 1947). Like Groenhuis, I find extremely baffling E. H. Kossmann's contention (*In Praise of the Dutch Republic: Some seventeenth-century attitudes* [London, 1963], 12) that "for the seventeenth-century Calvinists their own country never did represent the new Israel, a nation elected by God." An overwhelming abundance of evidence, much of it cited by Groenhuis, contradicts this claim.

79 It was particularly important in England and New England. See Harold Fisch, *Jerusalem and Albion: The Hebraic Theme in Seventeenth Century Literature* (New York, 1964).

80 Cromwell had pragmatic reasons for the extraordinary proposal: the exclusion of the Prince of Orange from any future title to either the stadholderate or the English throne. See Rowen, *de Witt*, 49–50.

81 See Mark Kishlansky, *The Rise of the New Model Army* (Cambridge, Eng., 1979).

82 A. Valerius, *Neder-Lantsche Gedenck-Clanck* (Haarlem, 1626); the prayer was also published as *Nederlands Dank-Offer over de Behoudenis haarer Vryheid bij een plegtige Dank-dag gehouden* (Cat. Muller, 1432). On Valerius and the *Clanck*, see the essays by P. J. Meertens

and N. B. Tenhaeff in their facsimile edition (Amsterdam/Antwerp, 1947).

83 *Gedenck-Clanck* (Amsterdam, 1947 ed.), 275–77.

84 Everhard van Reyd, *Oorspronck ende Voortganck vande Nederlandsche Oorloghen* (Amsterdam, 1644), 122.

85 Jac. Lydius, *'t Verhogde Nederland* (1668), 1.

86 See Albert Blankert, *Kunst als Regeringzaak in Amsterdam in de 17de Eeuw* (Amsterdam, 1975), 43–46; *Gods, Saints and Heroes*, Cat. no. 39.

87 Joseph and Potiphar's wife was the engraved frontispiece and major theme of Jacob Cats's *Self-Stryt*; a central drama in Vondel's play, *Joseph in Egypten;* a poem by Jan Vos; as well as the subject of two paintings and a stunning etching by Rembrandt. Schotel, *Vaderlandsche Volksboeken*, II, 249, quotes a popular love song on the same subject. Jephthah was a more contentious subject, treated unsympathetically by Vondel in his 1614 poem, *Hymnus of Lofzangh van de Christelycke Ridder.*

88 See the catalogue entry by Susan Donahue Kuretsky, *Gods, Saints and Heroes*, 85:282.

89 Van Loon, *Beschrijving*, 1:192.

90 Vondel, *Hierusalem Verwoest* (Amsterdam, 1620), 2.

91 Van Loon, 1:241; see also van de Waal, 1:22; P. A. M. Geurts, *De Nederlandse Opstand in de pamfletten 1566–1584* (Utrecht, 1983), 289.

92 G. D. J. Schotel, *Het Oude Volkslied Wilhelmus van Nassouwen* (Leiden, 1880).

93 Schotel, *Vaderlandsche Volksboeken*, 2:251.

94 Michael Walzer, *Exodus and Revolution* (New York, 1985).

95 For the *Nieuw liedeken* see D. F. Scheurleer, *Van Varen en Vechten* ('s Gravenhage, 1914), 27. For the silver ewers, see Fredericks, *Dutch Silver from the Renaissance to the End of the Eighteenth Century* ('s Gravenhage, 1952–61), 4:29.

96 Joost van Vondel, *Passcha ofte De Verlossinge Israels uit Egypten* (1612), 57–58.

97 See Pieter van Thiel, "Late Dutch Mannerism," in *Gods, Saints and Heroes*, 79. I am grateful to Julie McGee of Bryn Mawr College, who is currently working on a monograph on Cornelis van Haarlem, for helpful discussion of his work in the Prinsenhof.

98 On Coornhert, see Ilja Veldman, *Maarten van Heemskerck and Dutch Humanism in the Sixteenth Century* (Maarssen, 1977), 55–93 and passim.

99 Walter Strauss, ed., *Hendrik Goltzius 1558–1617: The Complete Engravings and Woodcuts*, 2 vols. (New York, 1977), 1:222.

100 Ibid., 324ff.

101 Ibid., 282.

102 Ibid., 144–46.

103 It was based on Exodus 19:10,14, in which, following Moses's first descent from Sinai, the Children of Israel are sanctified by the washing of their clothes. See Franklin Robinson, *Seventeenth-Century Dutch Drawings from American Collections* (Washington, D.C., 1977), 5–6. I am grateful to Ronni Baer for confirmation about the theme of this drawing.

104 Geurts, *Pamfletten*, 289.

105 Vondel, *Pascha*, 58.

106 For a discussion of this issue, see Simon Schama, "A Different Jerusalem: The Jews in Rembrandt's Amsterdam," in *The Jews in the Age of Rembrandt* (Rockville, Md., 1981), 3–17.

107 Blankert, *Kunst als Regeringzaak*, 23. See also Buchbinder-Green, *Painted Decorations*, 153–56.

108 W. Kuyper, *Dutch Classicist Architecture* (Delft, 1980), 70; Katherine Fremantle, *The Baroque Town Hall of Amsterdam*, Chs. 1 and 2.

109 See J. J. Poelhekke, *Geen Blijder Maer in Tachtig Jaer* (Zutphen, 1983).

110 Joost van Vondel, *Poëzy*, 2 vols. (Franeker, 1682), 2:327; Blankert, *Kunst als Regeringzaak*, 35.

111 Jan Vos, *Alle de Gedichten* (Amsterdam, 1720), 1:395.

112 Geurts, *Pamfletten*, 289; Knuttel, *Catalogus*, 320.

113 [Jacobus Lydius], *'t Verheerlijckt Nederland* (1668) referred (p. 27) to the "bravery and steadfastness of the [ancient] Batavians" and quoted Cicero that the state was governed more through the help of the gods than the wisdom of men, but being a preacher, Lydius placed greatest emphasis on the providential nature of the ordeals that God had sent His people to test their fitness for election (p. 28).

114 In effect it relaxed the British Navigation Act sufficiently to allow the traditional Dutch claim of freedom of shipping on the high seas. See Rowen, *de Witt*, 632–33.

115 Pieter de la Court, *Het Interest van Holland ofte Grond van Hollands-welvaren* (Amsterdam, 1662).

CHAPTER THREE
FEASTING, FASTING
AND TIMELY ATONEMENT

1 H. Grotius, *The United States of the Netherlands* (ch), (*De Rebus Belgicus*), (London, 1681), 532–33. See also A. E. K., "Een beeld van warheid. Rond de stranding van een potvis," *Teylers Museum Magazijn*

(Spring 1984), 1–4. I am most grateful to Mr. Boyd Hill of the Kendall Whaling Museum for bringing this article to my attention as well as for much helpful information on Dutch whale prints.

2 Ibid.

3 E. van Meteren, *Belgische ofte Nederlandsch Historien van onsen tijden* (Delft, 1605), 356. Petrus Bor, *Oorsprongk, beginen venolgh der Nederlandsche Oorlogen beroerten en borgerlyke oneenigheden beginnende met de opdracht der selve landen, gedaen by Keyser Karel der Vijfden*, 4 vols. (Amsterdam, 1679–84), 3: 433.

4 There is some dispute about what exactly it was that was stranded and measured in Goltzius's engraving of 1594, Walter Strauss, *Goltzius*, 2:579, suggesting it was the "tuna washed ashore," and Linda A. Stone-Ferrier, *Dutch Prints of Daily Life* (Lawrence, Kan., 1983), 189–90, proposing a porpoise. In fact the animal is neither, being inconceivably large for a porpoise, and quite closely resembling a pilot whale, so that the title given in Frederik Muller, *Nederlandsche Historieplaten* (Amsterdam, 1863–70), vol. 1, no. 1033, of *Stranded Whale* should remain. See also M. V. and Dorothy Brewington, *Kendall Whaling Museum Prints* (Sharon, Mass., 1969), no. 529.

5 For the Matham print, ibid., no. 531. On the iconographic theme of stranded whales, see W. Timm, "Der gestrandete Wal, eine motivkundliche Studie," in *Forschung und Berichten Staatliche Museum Berlin* (1961), 76ff.

6 See the comments of E. Gombrich, *Art and Illusion* (London, 1960), 80–81. Versions of the engraving were reworked by Gillis van der Gouwen and later by Bernard Picart for the Dutch edition of Jean Leclerc, *Geschiedenissen der Vereenigde Nederlanden*, 2 vols. (Amsterdam, 1703), 1:233–34.

7 Bor, *Historie*, 433.

8 *Catalogue of all the Chiefest Rarities in the Publick Theater and Anatomy Hall* (Leiden, 1691), n.p. Matham's engraving of the 1598 whale was also displayed in the Leiden Anatomy Theater, evidently in the manner of a *memento mori*.

9 Ibid., n.p.

10 Ibid., *"groot getier en misbaar."*

11 Frederik Muller, *Beredeneerde beschrijvingen van Nederlandsche Historieplaten, zinneprenten, en historische kaarten*, 4 vols. (Amsterdam, 1863–82), 1, no. 1253a, *Prosopopeia*.

12 Grotius, *Nederlantsche Jaarboeken* (Amsterdam, 1681), 327.

13 *Walvisch van Berckhey*, Rijksmuseum voor Natuurlijke Historie, Leiden.

14 A. B. van Deinse, *Over de potvisschen in Nederland gestrand tusschen de jaren 1531–1788*, Zoologische Mededelingen (Leiden, 1918), 4:22–50; see also E. J. Slijper, *Whales* (tr. Arno Pomerans) (New York, 1961).

15 Pierre Belon, *De aquatilibus* (Paris, 1553); Guillaurme Rondelet, *Libri de piscibus marinis* (Lyon, 1554–55).

16 The full inscription reads: "Wanner ons 't Vierde Licht van 't nieuwe jaer quam groeten/Is hier dees wallevisch lang drie en zestig vieten/Bij Noordwijk op de See na Sandvoort weg gestrand/ *God Wende 't Quaed van ons en 't Lieve Vaderland*" (my emphasis).

17 *Letters From and To Sir Dudley Carleton Knight, during his Embassy in Holland from January 1615/6 to December 1620* (London, 1757), 89.

18 *Kendall Museum*, 535; Egbert Haverkamp-Begemann, *Willem Buytewech* (Amsterdam, 1959), 29–30; Clifford S. Ackley, *Printmaking in the Age of Rembrandt* (Boston, 1981), 97.

19 Haverkamp-Begemann, *Buytewech*, 30; see also *Willem Buytewech, 1591–1624* (Rotterdam/Paris, 1975), no. 124.

20 See Muller, *Historieplaten*, 1:1160; Ackley, *Printmaking*, 44–46; *Kendall Museum*, 533; Stone-Ferrier, *Dutch Prints*, 192–94.

21 Van de Waal, *Drie Eeuwen*, 1:20, 2:8. For a more fully informed elucidation see Arthur Eijffinger, "Zin en beeld bij twee historieprenten," *Oud Holland*, 93 (1979):251–69, which connects the image of the earth on wheels to the appearance of Stevin's sand-yacht at around the same time. Theodore Schrevelius's verse refers explicitly to the threatened "Batavian Fatherland and people" and asks for "forgiveness and peace" from the Almighty.

22 Above, p. 31.

23 Gibson, *Bruegel*, 197.

24 Haverkamp-Begemann; see also, J. Richard Judson in "Maarten de Vos" Representations of "Jonah cast over the Side." *Miscellanea I.Q. van Regteren Altena* (Amsterdam, 1969), 1:82–87.

25 See C. de Jong, *Geschiedenis van de oude Nederlandsche Walvisvaart* (1972).

26 "Stiers Wreedheydt," *Atlas van Stolk, Katalogus der Historie,-Spot, en -Zinneprenten betrekkelijk de Geschiedenis van Nederland* (Amsterdam, 1887), vol. 2, nos. 1938–40; see also Frederik Muller, *Historieplaten*, Supp., no. 1932a. J. Honig, Jr., "Stiers

Wreedheid," *De Navorscher,* 1869, 131–51.

27 *Aenmerckinge op de tegenwoordige staert-sterre* (Middelburg, 1618).

28 Schotel, *Vaderlandsche Volksboeken,* 124–25; for the persistence of the same kind of beliefs in England, see Keith Thomas, *Religion and the Decline of Magic* (London, 1971), 90–132.

29 KN. 8937, *Afbeeldinge en Beschrijving van de drie aenmerckenswaerdig wonderen in des Jaar 1664* (Amsterdam, 1664).

30 Schotel, *Vaderlandsche Volksboeken,* 1:121.

31 Ibid., 120.

32 See, for example, Atlas van Stolk, *Catalogue* 18 (82), "Luchtverschijnsel te Scheveningen en overstroming," etching from Bernardus Mourik, *Staatkundig historie van Holland* (Amsterdam, 1756–82).

33 Van de Waal, *Drie Eeuwen,* 1:19.

34 "Een Nieuw Lied van de Sterre met de Staart, die in Nederland is gezien in't jaar 1661" in *Het Tweede Deel van 't Maas-sluysche Hoekertje* (n.p.), 66–68.

35 See Arthur K. Wheelock in *Gods, Saints and Heroes,* 178, on the problematic nature of the de Gelder painting.

36 See also for the recurrence of the theme a 1625 pamphlet on the coming collapse of the Spanish empire, *Mene Mene Tekel Upharsin,* Atlas van Stolk, no. 1609. The scene also appeared in graphic art, notably in van de Venne's engravings for Cats's *Doodkist,* and on silver plaques and ewers by van den Hecken.

37 *Koddige en Ernstige Opschriften op Luyffens, Wagens, Glazen, Uythangborden enz.* (1682), 2:58.

38 Herman Melville, *Moby-Dick; or, The Whale,* Penguin English Library Edition (London, 1972), 557.

39 L. Burema, *De Voeding in Nederland van de Middeleeuwen tot de Twintigtste Eeuw* (Assen, 1953), 137–38.

40 Ray, *Observations,* 50.

41 "The people are universally great lovers of Money, very covetous and greedy of gain." Ibid., 53.

42 Marshall, *Travels,* 342.

43 See J. de Hartog, ed., *De Spectatoriale Schriften van 1741–1800* (Utrecht, 1872).

44 See Konrad Renger, "Fat and Thin Kitchens in Dutch Art," in Christopher Brown, ed., *Images of the World: Dutch Genre Painting in Its Historical Context* (on press).

45 Ronald Paulson, *Hogarth: His Life, Art and Times* (New York, 1971), 103.

46 On these ambiguities see Simon Schama, "The Unruly Realm: Appetite and Restraint in Holland in the Golden Age," *Daedalus,* 108:3, 103–23.

47 J. van Beverwijck, *Schat der Gesontheyt* (Dordrecht, 1656), a standard work, still very much based on traditional Galenic axioms of the humors, has chapters on Love, Envy, Jealousy as characteristic disturbances of their balance.

48 [Petrus Nijland], *De Verstandige Kok of Sorghvuldige Huyshouder* (Amsterdam, 1669). Wine-based reductions and sauces were particularly discouraged as much for their moral and alien nature as for any intrinsically culinary reasons. The domestic economy manual, *De Verstandige Huyshouder voorschrijvende de Alderwijste Wetten om profijtelijcke/gemackelijk en vermakkelijke te leven/so inde stadt als op 't Landt* (Amsterdam, 1661) was even more emphatic on linking the moral and material welfare of the household.

49 Jan Luiken, *Het Leerzaam Huisraad* (Amsterdam, 1711), 3.

50 Heijman Jacobi, *Schat der Armen* (Amsterdam, 1603), 15.

51 For the *banketjestukken* see N. R. A. Vroom, *De Schilders van het Monochrome Banketje* (Amsterdam, 1945); idem, *A Modest Message as Intimated by the Painters of the "Monochrome Banketje,"* 2 vols. (Schiedam, 1980). The standard work on still lifes remains Ingvar Bergstrom, *Dutch Still-Life Painting in the Seventeenth Century* (London, 1956).

52 On Kalf and van Beyeren and sumptuousness, see E. de Jongh in *Still-Life in the Age of Rembrandt* (Auckland, 1982), 79–82, 92–94. See also Lucius Grisebach, *Willem Kalf, 1619–1693* (Berlin, 1974).

53 Svetlana Alpers, *The Art of Describing* (Chicago, 1983), Chapter 3.

54 On Peeters and cheese paintings, see de Jongh, *Still-Life,* 65–69.

55 Jos. Lammers, "Fasten und Genuss," in *Stilleben in Europa* (Munster/Baden-Baden, 1979), 406–407.

56 Ibid., 411–12.

57 De Jongh, *Still-Life,* 67. For an important critical comment on the excesses of symbolic interpretation in still-life paintings, see idem., "The Interpretation of Still-Life Paintings: Possibilities and Limits."

58 Cats, "Self-stryt," in 1655 folio edition of *Alle de Werken,* 28. Roemer Visscher, in his *Sinnepoppen* (Amsterdam, 1614), no. 9, 131, also used the emblem of the butter churn to suggest a different moral — *"in de rommeling is de vet"* — that in

59 Johan de Brune, *Emblemata of zinne werck* (Amsterdam, 1624), 51–52. Among the other examples de Brune gives of fine things hiding rottenness are brothels packed with beautiful women (taken from Marcus Aurelius) and commercial sharp practice that hid fraud and deceit beneath a veneer of enterprise.

commerce, gain (*vet*) would come only from energy and the willingness to "stir things up."

60 For many of these emblematic references see *Tot Lering en Vermaak* (Amsterdam, 1976); on grapes, see E. de Jongh, "Grape Symbolism in paintings of the 16th and 17th centuries," *Simiolus* (1974), 166–91.

61 Cited in de Jongh, *Still Life*, 68.

62 Cited in *Stilleben in Europa*, 587, n. 11. See Jacob Westerbaen, *Gedichten* ('s Gravenhage, 1657), 538.

63 *Stilleben*; see also K. Jagow, *Kulturgeschichte des hareng*, 412–14.

64 J. H. Swildens, *Vaderlandsch AB Boek voor de Vaderlandsch Jeugd* (n.p., 1781).

65 See C. Salmasius, *Bericht von 1663 aus Paris: Uber den Zucker*, Manuskript-fragment aus dem nachlass des Claudius Salmasius (Berlin: Institut für Zuckerindustrie, 1977); for the daily use of sugar see also P. Zumthor, *La Vie Quotidienne en Hollande au Temps de Rembrandt* (Paris, 1959), 93.

66 Cited in R. B. Evenhuis, *Ook dat was Amsterdam*, 4 vols. (Amsterdam, 1967), 2:136.

67 James Gorman, "Sweet Toothlessness," *Discover* (October 1980), 50ff.

68 Vroom, *Schilders*, 126–88.

69 On the Spanish tradition, see William B. Jordan, *Spanish Still-Life in the Golden Age 1600–1650*, Kimbell Art Museum, Fort Worth, 1985.

70 The report of this dinner is given in a fragment of an English newspaper (unidentified), probably of the 1780s, preserved in the Kress Library, Harvard Business School. But the story had been circulating as a parable of patriotic revivalism for some time. I am grateful to Ruth Rogers for drawing the English report to my attention.

71 There were tax riots in different parts of the country in 1711, 1714, 1728, 1731, 1733, 1747, 1748, 1750, 1759 and 1763. There was also an authentic food riot in Rotterdam in the summer of 1740, following a winter of record cold. See Dekker, *Holland in Beroering*, 28, and, on 1748: 36. See also P. Geyl, *Revolutiedagen te Amsterdam* (Den Haag, 1936).

72 Dekker, *Beroering*, 28.

73 Jan de Vries, "Labor in the Dutch Golden Age" (Paper presented to American Historical Association, 1980), reprinted in a revised form as "An Inquiry into the Behavior of Wages in the Dutch Republic and the Southern Netherlands, 1580–1800," in Maurice Aymard (ed.), *Dutch Capitalism and World Capitalism* (Cambridge, Eng., Paris, 1982), 37–62.

74 Ibid., Table 5.

75 Ibid., 13. For much more approximately calculated wage rates in different occupations see Van Deursen, *Kopergeld*, vol. 1, *Het Dagelijks Brood*, 13–17, who comes to more pessimistic conclusions than de Vries.

76 De Vries, *Labor*, 12. For the riots of the 1690s, in particular the "Undertaker's Riot" of 1696, see Dekker, *Oproeren*, 37–117.

77 Van Deursen, 18–20.

78 See de Vries, *Rural Economy*; F. Snapper, *Oorlogsinvloeden op de overzee handel van Holland 1551–1719* (Amsterdam, 1959); A. M. van der Woude, *Het Noorderkwartier*, 2 vols. (Wageningen, 1972), 1:203. For fluctuations in grain prices, see the tables published in N. W. Posthumus, *Nederlandse Prijsgeschiedenis* (Leiden, 1964), 2:440–820. On the problems of the grain trade at the close of the seventeenth century see J. G. van Dillen, "Dreigende hongersnood in de Republiek in de laatste jaren der zeventiende eeuw," in *Mensen en Achtergronden* (Groningen, 1964), 193–226. For some careful statistical research that bears out this "optimistic" case, see J. A. Faber, "Dearth and Famine in Pre-Industrial Netherlands," *Low Countries Yearbook*, 13 (1980), 51–63.

79 A. M. van de Woude, "Variations in the size and structure of the household in the United Provinces of the Netherlands in the seventeenth and eighteenth centuries," in Peter Laslett and Richard Wall, eds., *Household and Family in Past Time* (Cambridge, Eng., 1974), 299–319.

80 These figures are based on Van Deursen, *Kopergeld*, 15.

81 Denis Diderot, "Voyage de Hollande," *Oeuvres complètes* (Paris, 1876), 17:420–21.

82 Nugent, *Grand Tour*, 115.

83 Ibid., 131.

84 For these prices see Burema, *Voeding*, 121. See also the price lists based on similar charitable institution records in Leiden, Utrecht and Amsterdam given in Posthumus, *Nederlandse Prijsgeschiedenis*, 2:440ff.

85 These prices are given by Michael Montias, _Artists and Artisans in Delft_ (Princeton, N.J., 1982), 112.

86 De Vries, _Rural Economy_, 155–64.

87 "Hippolytus de Vrye" [H. Sweerts], _de Tien Vermakelijkheden des Houwelijks_ (Amsterdam, 1678), 75.

88 G. D. J. Schotel, _Letterkundige bijdragen tot de geschiedenis van de tabak, koffij en thee_ ('s Gravenhage, 1848), 187; see also S. C. Blankaart, _Gebruik en misbruik van de Thee_ (Amsterdam, 1686).

89 Cornelis Bontekoe, _Tractaat van het Excellente Kruyd Thee_ (Amsterdam, 1678).

90 Ibid., 190.

91 Schotel, _Tabak_, 190–91.

92 Montesquieu, "Voyage en Hollande," in A. de Montesquieu, ed., _Oeuvres et Vie de Montesquieu_ (Bordeaux, 1896), 2:224.

93 J. Jonker, _De vrolijke bruidlofsgast, bestaande in boertige bruidlofsvertjes . . ._ (Amsterdam, n.d.), 423.

94 Burema, _Voeding_. Jan van Beverwijck, _Schat der Gezondheid_ (Dordrecht, 1652), 146.

95 _De Verstandige Huyshouder voorschrijvende de Alderwijste Wetten om profijtelijcke/gemackelijk en vermakkelijke te leven/so inde stadt als op 't Landt_ (Amsterdam, 1661), 18–30.

96 Burema, _Voeding_, 108–10.

97 Ibid., 99.

98 See J. P. Bruyn, "Men on Board 1700–1750," _Acta Historiae Neerlandica_, 1975.

99 Ibid.; see also Burema, _Voeding_, 109.

100 Van de Woude, _Noorderkwartier_, 505–507.

101 Kornelis van Alkemade and P. van der Schelling, _Nederlands Displegtigheden_ (Rotterdam, 1732), 17, n. 17.

102 See the rather extraordinary recipe for _olypodrigo_ in _De Volmaakte Hollandse Keukenmeid_ (Amsterdam, 1761), which calls for three sweetbreads and no fewer than ten coxcombs! The _Verstandige Kok_ gives, in addition to the basic recipe, a "Kostelijke" _olypodrigo_ that used chestnuts, asparagus, artichokes and marrowbones.

103 Burema, _Voeding_, 96.

104 Cited in A. C. J. Vrankrijker, _Het Maatschappelijk Leven in Nederland in de Gouden Eeuw_ (Amsterdam, 1937), 75.

105 Van Alkemade, _Nederlands Displegtigheden_, 2:10–15.

106 Aglionby, _Observations_, 227.

107 Frederiks, _Dutch Silver_, vol. iv (Den Haag, 1921–61); see also the splendid exhibition catalogue by A. L. den Blauwen, _Nederlands zilver_ ('s Gravenhage, 1979).

108 Schotel, _Maatschappelijk Leven;_ Zumthor, _Vie Quotidienne_, 193.

109 Ibid.

110 Alois Riegl, _Das Höllandische Gruppenporträt_, 2 vols. (Wien, 1931), 1:242ff; see also Seymour Slive, _Frans Hals_, 3 vols. (London, 1970), 1:39–49.

111 Van Alkemade, _Nederlands Displegtigheid_, 1:4, 125, 147; see also van de Waal, _Drie Eeuwen_, on the importance of open-air feasts and drinking rites to the historiography of Batavian ancestry. Drinking horns were also very important ceremonial treasures for the _schutter_ guilds.

112 See E. Haverkamp-Begemann, _Rembrandt: The Nightwatch_ (Princeton, N.J., 1982), 42.

113 Though (or possibly because) the Synod of Dordrecht had recommended them, sumptuary laws were not very common in the Netherlands. The most significant was passed in Amsterdam in 1655 restricting marriage feasts, and again in Amsterdam in November 1672, a more general ordinance against "unnecessary and sumptuous banquets." Both were enacted at times of crisis: 1655 being both a disastrous plague year and the time of a serious commercial depression due to the war with England; the latter, of course, caused a major military emergency. See Burema, _Voeding_, 104–105.

114 W. van der Poll, _Nederlandsche Volksfeesten_ (Leiden, n.d.); see also Schotel, _Maatschappelijk Leven_,

115 See Article 34, mentioned in Knuttel, _Acta_ ('s Gravenhage, 1910), 3:536.

116 See Evenhuis, _Ook dat was Amsterdam_, 2:119.

117 Ibid., 116–119.

118 Aglionby, _Observations_, 226.

119 For an exhaustive list of these celebrations see van Alkemade, _Nederlands Displegtigheden_, 1:192–350. The book cites the Huize van Warmond as an estate where a _jokmaal_ was held once a year with the heer and lady waiting on the servants.

120 [Sweerts], _Tien Vermakelijkheden_, 112ff. The account specifically mentions the _Verstandige Kok_ as providing for all these dishes.

121 See the recipe for "hypocras" given in _De Volmakte Hollandse Keuken Meid_, n.p.

122 See le Francq van Berkhey, _Natuurlijke Historie_, 3:1935.

123 Rowen, _de Witt_ (Princeton, 1978), 102.

124 Van Alkemade, _Nederlands Displegtigheden_, 1:193.

125 Burema, _Voeding_, 104–105; Resolution of Amsterdam _vroedschap_, 11 November 1672.

126 See D. Roorda, _Het Rampjaar: 1672_ (Bussum,

1971); H. Rowen, *John de Witt* (Princeton, 1978).

127 Schama, "Appetite and Restraint," 103–23.

128 For an excellent discussion of the officially organized campaign of Lenten suppression of traditional carnivalia, see Peter Burke, *Popular Culture in Early Modern Europe* (London, 1978).

129 Cited in Roelof Murris, *La Hollande et les Hollandais au XVII et XVIIème siècles, vus par les Français* (Paris, 1925), 256.

130 Ibid., 130.

131 On cuspidors, see Georg Brongers, *Pijpen en Tabak* (Bussum, 1964), 109ff.

132 Diderot, *Voyage,* 375.

133 Fynes Moryson, *An itinerary containing his ten yeeres travel,* 4 vols. (Glasgow, 1907–1908), 4:468–69.

134 Thomas Coryat, *Coryat's Crudities* (1905), 2:360. Peter Mundy, *Travels* (London, 1925), 78.

135 Brereton, *Travels,* 11–12.

136 Bargrave, *Relation of Sundry Voyages* (Bodleian Ms., Rawlinson Collection, 1652–53; 1655).

137 Cited in Jan Morris, *Oxford* (Oxford, 1978), 120.

138 A. Th. van Deursen, *Het kopergeld van de Gouden Eeuw* (Assen/Amsterdam, 1978), vol. 2, *Volkskultuur,* 40. Jacques van Loenen, *De Haarlemse Brouwindustrie voor 1600* (Amsterdam, 1950), 59. I am grateful to Richard Unger for this source and for much helpful information on Dutch brewing.

139 Brereton, *Travels,* 10.

140 H. Zeeman, *Drank en Drinkwinkels in Nederland van de Vroegste Tijden tot op heden* (Amsterdam, 1866), 10. For the earlier period see the outstanding monograph by Bernardus H. B. Hermesdorf, *De Herberg in Nederland: een blik in de beschavingsgeschiedenis* (Assen, 1957).

141 Ibid., 5–7; see also Schotel, *Het Oud-Hollandsch Huisgezin,* 305–307.

142 See Simon Schama, *Patriots and Liberators,* 40.

143 On clerical criticism see Schotel, *Maatschappelijke Leven,* 1:47. The major history, with much illumination on all aspects of tobacco production and consumption and on the debate over its use, is H. K. Roessingh, *Inlandse Tabak, Expansie en contractie van een handelgewas in de 17de en 18de eeuw* (Wageningen, 1976).

144 Ibid., 208.

145 Ibid., 413.

146 Ibid., 512.

147 Ibid., 200–201; for the Jewish role in the tobacco industry see H. I. Bloom, *The Economic Activity of the Jews of Amsterdam* (Williamsport, Pa., 1937), 60–64.

148 Brongers, *Pijpen en tabak,* 39ff.

149 For the most balanced and erudite comment on the problems of interpreting "smoking requisites" in still-life paintings see de Jongh, *Still-Life,* 101–105; *Tot Lering en Vermaak,* 54–57.

150 Cornelis Bontekoe, *Verhandeling wegens de deugden en kragten van de tabak* (Amsterdam, 1686); Blankaart, *Gebruik en misbruik;* see also van Beverwijck, *Schat der Gesontheyt,* 136.

151 Roessingh, 91.

152 Petrus Scriverius, *Saturnalia ofte Poetisch Vasten-Avond spel vervatende het gebruyk en misbruyk vanden Taback,* trans. Samuel Ampzing (Haarlem, 1630).

153 Visscher, *Sinnepoppen,* no. 10. For the Huygens poem, J. A. Worp, ed., *De gedichten van Constantijn Huygens* (Groningen, 1895), 5:298.

154 Cats, *Minne-en-Sinnebeelden,* in *Alle de Werken* (Amsterdam, 1700), 26.

155 *Acta der Particuliere Synoden van Zuid Holland,* 1:405–406.

156 Roessingh, *Inlandse Tabak,* 63.

157 Schotel, *Maatschappelijke Leven,* 1:37.

158 Ibid., 48–49.

159 *Verstandige Huyshouder.*

160 Schotel, *Maatschappelijke Leven.*

161 Evenhuis, *Ook dat was Amsterdam,* 2:98.

162 L. Knappert, "Het Huiselyk Leven," in H. Brugmans et al., *Het Huiselyk en Maatschappelyk Leven onzer Voorouders* (Amsterdam, 1931), 1:167.

163 Samuel Ampzing, *Beschryving ende lof der stad Haerlem in Holland* (Haarlem, 1628), 48.

164 Zeeman, *Drank en drinkwinkels,* 10, 25.

165 Evenhuis, *Ook dat was Amsterdam,* vol 2, 97.

166 Ibid., 96.

167 Knuttel, *Acta Particuliere der Synoden,* 6 vols. ('s Gravenhage, 1908, 1916), 1:507–508, 2:13.

168 H. C. Porter, *Reformation and Reaction in Tudor Cambridge* (Cambridge, Eng., 1958), 272.

169 See H. van de Waal, *Steps Towards Rembrandt* (London/Amsterdam, 1974), 28–43.

170 "John de Witt," *Fables Moral and Political with Large Explications* (London, 1703), fable 45.

171 See, for example, the woodcuts in André Thevet, *Les singularitez de la France Antarctique autrement nommee Amerique* (Paris, 1557).

172 Brongers, *Pijpen,* 35ff.

173 Steen's father was a brewer and he kept a tavern to supplement the income from his painting.

174 See, for example, the characteristic innuendo in Frans van Mieris's self-portrait. Otto Naumann, *Frans van Mieris the Elder 1635–1681* (Doornspijk,

1981), 2:24 (catalogue no. 21).

175 *Koddige en Ernstige Opschriften* (Amsterdam, 1685), 134.

176 Slobbe, 30.

177 E. de Jongh et al., *Tot Lering en Vermaak,* 246–49.

178 See Schama, *Daedalus,* 1979, 103–107.

179 "De Witt" [Pieter de la Court?], "The Drunkard and His Wife," in *Fables,* no. 45.

180 Gerard Knuttel, *Adriaen Brouwer: The Master and His Work* ('s Gravenhage, 1962), 26.

181 Roessingh, *Inlandse Tabak,* 85.

182 For these subjects, see especially the exhibition catalogue, *Ijdelheid der ijdelheiden. Hollandse vanitas-voorstellingen uit de zeventiende eeuw* (Leiden, Stedelijk Museum, de Lakenhal, 1970).

183 See, for example, the smoking pipe placed together with a skull, an hourglass and a scroll reading *quis evadet* in a drawing by David Bailly, reproduced in de Jongh et al., *Still-Life,* 191.

184 See E. Haverkamp-Begemann, *Willem Buytewech* 1591–1624 (Paris, 1975), 5–12.

185 See Ronald Paulson, *Hogarth's Graphic Works* (New Haven, Conn., 1970), 1:152.

186 [D. Pers?], *Bacchus Wonder Wrecken* [sic] *waer in Het Recht Gebruyck en Misbruyck des Wijns/daer verscheyden vermaeckelijcke en leerlijck historien wort afgebeelt en de lasteringe der Dronckenschap met levende verwen afgemaelt* (Amsterdam, 1628). On apes as symbols of lust and folly, see H. W. Janson, *Apes and Ape Lore in the Middle Ages and the Renaissance* (London, 1952).

187 See the biographical note in the exhibition catalogue *Willem Buytewech* 1591–1624, 3.

188 Bacchus, 91.

189 [Jac. Lydius], *Wee-klage over den inbreuk van den Alblasser-waard* (Dordrecht, 1658); see also *"straf-predicatie"* of Jacobus van Oudenhoven and others in *Generale Beschryvinge van der Tegenwoordige ingebroken Alblasser-Waard in Zuyt-Hollandt* (1658).

190 Cited in Evenhuis, *Ook dat was Amsterdam,* 2:39–40.

CHAPTER FOUR
THE IMPERTINENCE OF SURVIVAL

1 On Dutch public triumphs and ceremonies see D. P. Snoep, *Praal en propaganda. Triumfalia in de Noordelijke Nederlanden in de 16de en 17de eeuw* (Alphen aan de Rijn, 1975). There is now a considerable literature on civic and republican ritual festivity, most notably Edward Muir, *Civic Ritual*

in Renaissance Venice (Princeton, N.J., 1981), and for the French Revolution, Mona Ozouf, *La Fête révolutionnaire 1789–99* (Paris, 1976).

2 Rowen, *De Witt,* 582. The splendor of de Witt's and Christiaan Huygens's costumes, it should be said, prompted guffaws from Cornelis Tromp.

3 On the French republican personification see Maurice Agulhon, *Marianne au combat: l'imagerie et la symbolisme républicaine 1789 à 1880* (Paris, 1979).

4 On the sixteenth-century ceremonies see in particular Sheila Williams and J. Jacquot, *"Ommegangs anversois du temps de Bruegel et de van Heemskerck,"* in J. Jacquot, ed., *Les fêtes de la Renaissance* (Paris, 1960), vol. 2.

5 Snoep, *Praal en Propaganda:* Triumfalia in de Noordelijke Nederlanden in de 16de en 17de Eeuw, Alphen aan den Rijn, 1975.

6 Aglionby, *Present State,* A4.

7 For these population figures, see J. A. Faber et al., "Population changes and economic developments in the Netherlands" in *Afdeling Agrarische Geschiedenis Bijdragen,* 12 (1965), 47–113.

8 Cited in Douglas Coombs, *The Conduct of the Dutch: British Opinion and the Dutch Alliance during the War of Spanish Succession* (The Hague, 1958), 6.

9 On the European crises of the mid-seventeenth century, see Geoffrey Parker and Lesley M. Smith, eds., *The General Crisis of the Seventeenth Century* (London/Boston, 1978); Trevor Aston, ed., *Crisis in Europe 1560–1660* (New York, 1967). There was, of course, a midcentury crisis in the Republic as well in the form of William II's military campaign against Amsterdam, but even had the Stadholder not died prematurely, it seems unlikely it would have turned into civil war.

10 Rowen, *De Witt,* 280–81.

11 Elizabeth Onians is currently preparing a book dealing with this topic. See also Beatrijs Brenninkmeyer-de Rooij, "To Behold Is to Be Aware: History Paintings in Public Buildings," in *Gods, Saints and Heroes,* 65–76.

12 Katherine Fremantle, *The Baroque Town Hall of Amsterdam* (Utrecht, 1959), 30–56.

13 See Barlaeus [Kaspar van Baerle] *Marie de Médicis entrant dans Amsterdam ou Histoire de la Reception Faicte à la Reine Mère du Roy Tres Chrestien par les Bourgmaistres et Bourgeoisie de la Ville d'Amsterdam* (Amsterdam, 1638); also F. J. Dubiez, "Marie de Médicis, het bezoek aan Amsterdam in Augustus

1638," *Ons Amsterdam* (1958), 266–77; Snoep, *Praal,* P. Henrard, *Marie de Médicis dans les Pays Bas* (Paris, 1876).

14 The mid-seventeenth century was an important watershed in the history of state administrative building. Older palaces in the middle of cities like Whitehall, the Louvre and the Escorial suffered from their vulnerability to the urban uprisings that were a feature of the period. So that the move to more bucolic surroundings like Versailles, Kew or the Buen Retiro combined political prudence with the indulgence of royal court pleasures. Colbert, who had been an early enthusiast of Versailles, came to regret in the end his master's abandonment of the Louvre as a centralized seat of both court and government.

15 See, for example, the excellent discussion of the series of battle and surrender scenes in the Hall of the Realms at the Buen Retiro, Jonathan Brown and J. H. Elliott, *A Palace for a King* (New Haven, Conn., 1982).

16 See Rowen, *de Witt,* 413–16. De Witt's treatise was published as *Elementa Curvarum Linearum* (Amsterdam, 1659).

17 Quoted in Charles Wilson, *Profit and Power* (London, 1957), 107.

18 Ibid., 20; See G. Edmundson, *Anglo-Dutch Rivalry during the First Half of the Seventeenth Century* (Oxford, 1911).

19 Wilson, *Profit,* 12.

20 Hugo Grotius, *The Freedom of the Seas or the Right Which Belongs to the Dutch to Take Part in the East Indies Trade,* tr. and ed., R. van Dernan Magoffin (New York, 1916), 30, 36.

21 De Witt to van Beverningk, June 24, 1661; see also Wilson, *Profit,* 105.

22 See J. E. Farnell, "The Navigation Act of 1651, the first Dutch War and the London Merchant Community," *Economic History Review* (1964), 439–54.

23 A typical passage of Worsley's propaganda claimed that "our neighbors (after they had settled their Libertie and had been a while encouraged by Prosperitie) have, likewise for some years, aimed to laie a foundation to themselves for ingrossing the Universal Trade, not onely of Christendom, but indeed of the greater part of the known world." [Benjamin Worsley], *The Advocate; Or A Narrative of the State and Condition of Things between the English and Dutch Nations, in relation to Trade . . .*

(London, 1651).

24 On these changes of design see Unger, *Dutch Shipbuilding Before* 1800 (Assen/Amsterdam, 1978); see also Johan E. Elias, *De vlootbouw in Nederland in de eerste helft der 17de eeuw, 1596–1665* (Amsterdam, 1933), 88f.

25 Samuel Pepys, *Diary,* ed., Robert Latham and William Matthews, vol. 8 (1667), entry for 19th July (London, 1974).

26 Rowen, *de Witt,* 596.

27 Pepys, *Diary,* entry for August 23, 1667.

28 "Klinkdicht van de Heer Jacob Westerbaen; Holland aen Engelandt," in D. F. Scheurleer, *Van Varen en Vechten: Verzen van tijdgenooten op onze zeehelden en zees lager, lof en schimpdichten, mehozen, lieberen,* 2 vols. ('s Gravenhage 1914), 2:85–86.

29 Ibid., 62.

30 Jan de Mol, *Engels-Kuiper* (Middelburg, 1662); Knuttel, *Pamfletten,* no. 7330.

31 See Charles E. Hill, *The Danish Sound Dues and the Command of the Baltic* (Durham, N. C., 1926), 154–55; N. F. Noordam, *De Republiek en de Noordse Oorlog 1655–1660* (Assen, 1940), 88ff.

32 Owen Feltham, *A Brief Character of the Low Countries* (London, 1627).

33 *The Interest of England in the Present War with Holland* (1672), 13–14.

34 Jan Vos, "Vergrooting van Amsterdam," *Alle de gedichten,* 2:124; also published separately, Knuttel, *Pamfletten,* no. 8666, "De schatten vinden rust in de schaduw van de vrede."

35 Pieter de la Court, *The True Interests and Political Maxims of the Republick of Holland and West Friesland* (London, 1747, trans. of Amsterdam ed. of 1662), 206. He added, even more acutely, "If Holland, for fear of a war, shall begin a war it must, for fear of the smoke, leap into a fire."

36 Scheurleer, *Van Varen en Vechten,* 2:193. For the most vivid expression of these kinds of hurt feelings, see the propaganda poems written by Jacob Westerbaen, such as "Hollands Vloeck aen het Parlementsche Engeland," in *Gedichten* ('s Gravenhage, 1672), 1:328ff.

37 For the de Keyser tomb, see R. F. P. de Beaufort, *Het Mausoleum der Oranjes te Delft* (Delft, 1931).

38 B. Lossky, "La Bénédiction de la Paix, chef d'oeuvre rétrouvé de Hendrick Martensz. Sorgh," in *La Revue des Arts,* 1956, has argued that the kneeling figure is Maximilian of Bavaria, who, in 1641, saw an end to the Thirty Years' War, but

the evidence for this is very fragile. See also the catalogue entry in *Hollandse Schilderijen uit Franse musea* (Rijksmuseum, Amsterdam, 1971), 70.

39 See Jane Susannah Fishman, *Boerenverdriet: Violence between Peasants and Soldiers in Early Modern Netherlands Art* (Ann Arbor, Mich., 1983).

40 See Peter Sutton et al., *Masterpieces of Dutch Genre,* (Philadelphia, 1983), 189–90.

41 For a discussion of the representation of soldiers in Dutch art, see the contribution by J. W. Smit to Christopher Brown et al., *Images of the World* (London, 1986), forthcoming.

42 The commander of The Hague *schutterij*, initially anxious lest his men be incapable of restraining the violent mob, called on three companies of regular cavalry to be stationed before the prison in which the de Witts were being held. The cavalry officer in charge, de Tilly, was then summoned away to the perimeter bridges to "defend" The Hague against a nonexistent uprising of peasants but refused to move his men except on sight of a written order. When this was produced he moved his men off, and the Blue Banner company of the *schutters* actually incited the crowd to finish off the de Witts. See Rowen, *de Witt,* 878–79.

43 Pepys, *Diary,* entry for June 30, 1667, 309.

44 See the excellent account of the Medway raid in P. G. Rogers, *The Dutch in the Medway* (London/ New York, 1970).

45 See, for example, the splendid prints in Pieter Casteleyn's monthly journal, the *Hollantsche Mercurius,* published in Haarlem from 1651 onwards. Casteleyn was himself a painter and engraver, and well understood the importance of engraved illustrations to new reports.

46 [Lambertus van den Bosch], *Leven en Daden der Doorlugtige Zee-Helden* (n.p., 1683); see also the many poems collected by D. F. Scheurleer, *Van Varen en Vechten,* vol. 2.

47 [Van den Bosch], *Leven en Daden,* n.p.

48 Willem Usselincx, *Grondich Discours over desen aenstaenden Vrede-handel* (n.p., 1608).

49 Cited in Geoffrey Parker, "War and Economic Change: The Economic Costs of the Dutch Revolt," in J. M. Winter, ed., *War and Economic Development Essays in Memory of David Joslin* (Cambridge, Eng., 1975), 60.

50 See Israel, *The Dutch Republic and the Hispanic World,* 93–95, 149–52, 285–93; see also idem, "A Conflict of Empires: Spain and the Netherlands,

1618–48," *Past and Present* 76 (August 1977):37–74.

51 Ibid, 46–47.

52 Ibid.; see also Geoffrey Parker, "Why did the Dutch Revolt Last Eighty Years?" *Transactions of the Royal Historical Society,* 1976, 53–72.

53 See W. J. Hoboken, "The Dutch West India Company: The Political Background of Its Rise and Decline," in J. S. Bromley and E. H. Kossmann, eds., *Britain and the Netherlands* (The Hague, 1960), 1:41–61; Parker, "Economic Costs," 64.

54 Ibid., 58–59.

55 Immanuel Wallerstein, *The Modern World System,* vol. 2 (New York, 1980), 35–71.

56 *The Advocate,* 3.

57 De la Court, *Interest,* 207.

58 Ibid., 243.

59 Cited in Wilson, *Profit,* 12.

60 Quoted in Violet Barbour, "Anglo-Dutch Shipping . . ." *Economic History Review,* 1929, 290.

61 *The Dutch Storm, or It's an Ill Wind* (British Museum, Luttrell Collection), vol. 8, folio 87.

62 F. R. Harris, *The Life of Edward Montagu, Earl of Sandwich* (London, 1912), 2:4.

63 Pepys, *Diary,* entry for September 24, 1665.

64 Ibid, entry for November 16, 1665. For an account of the way in which some of the crew "did toss and tumble and spoil and break things in hold to a great loss and shame, to come at the fine goods," see *Diary,* entry for October 12, 1665; also Pepys, *Shorthand Letters,* 62–64.

65 Felltham, *Brief Character,* 2 [Charles Molloy], *De Jure Maritimo et Navali* (n.p., 1676), 4.

66 G. D. J. Schotel, *Het Oud-Hollandsch Huisgezin der Zeventiende Eeuw* (Leiden, n.d.), 56.

67 On these writers see the excellent discussion in Joyce Oldham Appleby, *Economic Thought and Ideology in Seventeenth-Century England* (Princeton, N.J., 1978), Ch. 4. Keymer's writings dated from the beginning of the century but had to wait until the 1660s for publication.

68 See, in particular, Josiah Child, *A Treatise Concerning the East India Trade* (London, 1681), 3, where Child began forthrightly, declaring, "I am of the opinion, the Dutch, Nationally Speaking, are the wisest people now extant for the contriving and carrying on their trade for the publick advantage of their Country."

69 Appleby, 77. See Roger Coke, *A Discourse of Trade* (London, 1670), 49–51.

70 Coombs, *Conduct of the Dutch,* 92.

71 Robert Ferguson, *Account of the Obligations the States of Holland Have to Great Britain* (London, 1711); Coombs, *Conduct,* 289.

72 *The Dutch Deputies, A Satyr;* see also Coombs, *Conduct,* 308. *The Bottomless Pit: Lawsuit of John Bull and Nicholas Frog against Lewis Baboon:* "Nick Frog was a cunning sly whoreson, quite the opposite of John [Bull] in many particulars: covetous, frugal . . . would pine his belly to save his pocket."

73 See, for example, *The Dutch Displayed,* one of many tracts dwelling on the Amboyna "massacre." "It is notorious to all the world that England gave birth to the independency of the States of Holland. . . . [And in return] . . . they insulted our coasts and by violence supported their fishermen," etc.; [Henry Stubbes], *A Justification of the Present War against the United Netherlands . . . the Obligations of the Dutch to England and their Continual Ingratitude* (London, 1672), 78: "How do they hold their freedom but by violence? Are these the principles of the Peace-Loving Hollanders? Do not these suggestions tend to the involving of all the world in Blood?"

74 See Alice Carter, *Neutrality or Commitment: The Evolution of Dutch Foreign Policy,* 1667–1795 (London, 1975).

75 Grotius, *De Iure Bello ac Pacis,* ed., Fr. Barbeyrac (Amsterdam, 1733), Book 2, Chs. 22–23: "De Causis Iniustis"; "De Causis Dubiis."

76 Cornelis de Witt was accused on trumped-up testimony of offering to remove a minor sentence from a barber-surgeon if he would assassinate the Prince of Orange. See Rowen, *de Witt,* 861ff.

77 *Observations concerning the present Affayres of Holland and the United Provinces* (n.p., 1622), 1.

78 *The English and Dutch Affairs Displayed to the Life* (London, 1664), 19.

79 Andrew Marvell, "The Character of Holland," in *Poetical Works* (Boston, 1857), 171–77.

80 Quoted in B. H. M. Vlekke, *The Evolution of the Dutch Nation* (New York, 1945), 1.

81 *The Dutch Deputies* (n.p.).

82 Pierre le Jolle, *Description de la Ville d'Amsterdam, en vers burlesque. Selon la visite de six jours d'une semaine* (Amsterdam, 1666), 317.

83 *The Dutch-mens Pedigree* (n.p., 1653).

84 *Catalogue of Prints and Drawings in the British Museum: Political and Personal Satires,* 1320–1689, no. 1028.

85 During the fourth Anglo-Dutch war of 1780–84, and even into the 1790s, graphic satirists and caricaturists like James Gillray still depicted the

Dutch as frogs for a dependable xenophobic ridicule. See, for example, M. D. George, *Catalogue of Political and Personal Satires Reserved in the Department of Prints and Drawings in the British Museum,* vol. 7, nos. 7181, 9414, 9421, etc.

86 *Observations,* 3.

87 Felltham, *Brief Character,* 2–3. Felltham's irresistibly abusive tract was first published under his name in 1652 but had already appeared in a pirated edition in 1648. It reappeared in 1659, 1676 and 1699 under his own name and many times in the eighteenth century under other titles such as *A Voyage to Holland or the Dutchman Described* (Dublin, 1746) or *A Trip to Holland* (London, 1786).

88 *Ibid.,* 2.

89 Wilson, *Profit,* 126.

90 [Stubbes], *Justification,* 5.

91 Felltham, *Brief Character,* 17.

92 I take the term from Keith Thomas's unpublished paper "The Vestimentiary Hierarchy in Early Modern England" (1978). Felltham, *Brief Character,* 30.

93 *Ibid.,* 48.

94 Marvell, "Character."

95 H. T. Colenbrander, *Bescheiden uit de Vreemde Archieven omtrent de groote Nederlandse Zeeoorlogen,* 1652–76, 2 vols. ('s Gravenhage, 1919), 1:217–19.

96 Coombs, *Conduct,* 324.

97 *Observations,* 4.

98 Marvell, "Character."

99 Felltham, *Brief Character,* 45.

100 Coombs, *Conduct.*

101 Ibid.

102 *The Dutch Won't Let Us Have Dunkirk* (1712). It continued in the same phobic vein: "There is not a Dutchman in that antimonarchical Commonwealth but has more venom in his heart and between his teeth against Majesty and Monarchy than there is venom under the teeth of a serpent."

103 Beresford, *Downing,* 183.

104 *Ibid.,* 89–90.

105 [Stubbes], *Justification,* 76.

106 *Ibid.,* 53.

107 See Charles Wilson, *Elizabeth I and the Revolt of the Netherlands* (London, 1970).

108 *An Exhortation to the Love of our Country.*

109 *The Interest of England in the Present War,* 25.

110 "Précis historique des campagnes de Louis XIV," in *Oeuvres,* ed. P. Mesnard (Paris, 1887), 5:244.

111 See, for example, Pierre Goubert, *Louis XIV and Twenty Million Frenchmen* (New York, 1970), 127.

112 See the persuasive argument of Paul Sonnino,

"Colbert and the Dutch War of 1672," *European Studies Review,* Jan. 1983, 1–11.

113 [Stubbes], *Justification,* 39.

114 [Henry Stubbes], *A Further Justification of the War with the United Provinces* (London, 1673), 3f.

115 John de Witt [Pieter de la Court], *The True Interests and Political Maxims of the Republic of Holland* (London, 1746).

116 Van Loon, *Beschryving,* III (1732), 17.

117 [Stubbes], *A Further Justification,* 10.

118 *Les Moyens de la France pour Ruiner le Commerce des Hollandois avec ses intérêts à l'égard des étrangers* (Brussels, 1671), 33.

119 See Pieter Geyl, *Oranje en Stuart* (Utrecht, 1939), passim.

120 See D. J. Roorda, *Her Rampjaar 1672* (Bussum, 1971).

121 See, for example, the Orangist propaganda in Knuttel, *Pamfletten 10199, Spiegel van State en Recht van Burghers* (n.p., 1672); see also *Toets-Steen voor de Herten der Bataven tot ouderscheydt van de Goede en de Quade* (1673).

122 Knuttel, *Pamfletten 10237, Beklagh over den Bedroefden Toestant in de Nederlantse Provintien* (Amsterdam, 1672).

123 See, for example, in this prophetic vein, Knuttel, *Pamfletten 9932, Eenige Prophetien en Revelatien Godst's Aengaende de Christen Werelt in dese Eeuw* (1672).

124 On the Van Beuningen "dream" see P. J. W. van Malssen, *"Louis XIV d'Après les Pamphlètes Répandus en Hollande"* (Amsterdam Diss., 1936), 77.

125 [Tobias van Domselaer], *Het Ontroerde Nederland* (Amsterdam, 1674); [A. de Wicquevort], *De Fransche Tyrannie . . .* (Amsterdam, 1674); *Advis Fidelle aux Véritables Hollandois* (The Hague, 1673); *Journael of dagelijksch verhael van de handel der Franschen* (Amsterdam, 1674); Lambertus van den Bosch, *Toneel des Oorlogs, Opgerecht in de Vereenigde Nederlanden,* 4 vols. (Amsterdam, 1675); Romeyn de Hooghe, *Schouwburg van Nederlandse Veranderinge* (Amsterdam, 1674).

126 [Wicquevort], *De Fransche Tyrannie,* 56.

127 Knuttel, *Pamfletten 13375;* van Malssen, *Louis XIV,* 53; de Hooghe, *Schouwburg,* 24.

128 On de Hooghe's engraved illustrations see John Landwehr, *Romeyn de Hooghe as Book Illustrator, A Bibliography* (Amsterdam, 1970); Harry T. Wilson, "The Art of Romeyn de Hooghe" (Ph.D. Diss., Harvard University, 1974).

129 Shaftesbury's famous speech was delivered in the House of Lords on the vote of one and quarter million pounds' supply for the war.

130 Bruyn, "Men on Board" *Acta Historiae Neerlandica,* vol. 7 (1974), 93–94.

131 See D. P. Snoep, "Classicism and History Painting in the Late Seventeenth Century," in *Gods, Saints and Heroes,* 237–39.

132 See Gérard de Lairesse, *Groot Schilderboeck* (Amsterdam, 1707).

133 On the cultural and political ramifications of the war of the League of Cambrai, see Felix Gilbert, "Venice in the Crisis of the League of Cambrai," in J. R. Hale, ed., *Renaissance Venice* (London, 1973), 274–92.

134 Joseph Addison, *Present State of the War and the Necessity of an Augmentation* (London, 1707); see also Coombs, *Conduct,* 185.

135 Coombs, *Conduct,* 307.

136 Ibid., 364–65.

137 "De Witt," *Fables Moral and Political,* no. 3.

138 Ibid., 12–13.

CHAPTER FIVE
THE EMBARRASSMENT OF RICHES

1 The most splendid celebration of the country house fashion, in verse and image, was Lukas Rotgans, *Zegepralende Vecht* (1719). But throughout the seventeenth century, the proud owners of such houses either wrote verses of praise to the country life in general and their estate in particular, or commissioned poems from others. Joan Huydecoper, merchant, rentier, patrician, diplomat and patron of Rembrandt, for example, commissioned such a eulogy for Goudestein from Jan Vos. The fashion for these verses of praise, like the villas themselves and the Georgic values they were supposed to express, was certainly much influenced by the Italian villas of the quinquecento. Nor was this purely a late-seventeenth-century fad. Huydecoper had bought the volume *Palazzi Antichi e Moderni* in 1627, though Philip Vingboons did not begin building at Goudestein until around 1639. Jacob Cats and Constantijn Huygens both indulged their open-air fancies in the first half of the century and wrote extremely long lyric verses celebrating the repose of nature. Even Jacob Westerbaen became "Heer van Brandwijk" and wrote the praises of his own house, Ockenburgh. See also his *Lands-Levens Lof* in *Alle de gedichten* ('s Gravenhage, 1672), 2:491.

2 Jean de Parival, *Les Délices de la Hollande* (Leiden, 1662), 81, wrote of Leiderdorp as the village where the magistrates and patricians of Leiden had made a retreat and where, as a consequence, there were *"plus de palais que de cabannes rustiques."*

3 On the building styles and some important examples, see Kuyper, *Dutch Classicist Architecture* (Delft, 1980), 153–64; also H. W. M. van der Wijck, "Country Houses in the Northern Netherlands," *Apollo* (November 1972).

4 Kuyper, *Classicism,* 160–61; See Cats, *Ouderdom, buyten-leven en hofgedachten op Sorghvliet* (Amsterdam, 1656).

5 Kuyper, 129–30; see also Lukas Rotgans, "Gezang op Goudestein," *Poezy van Verscheide Mengelstoffen* (Amsterdam, 1735), 253–64.

6 Aglionby, *Present State,* 266.

7 Ibid., 267.

8 Marshall, *Travels through Holland,* 347.

9 Josiah Child, *Brief Observations Concerning Trade* (London, 1668), 4. See also William Letwin, *Sir Josiah Child, Merchant Economist* (Cambridge, Mass., 1959).

10 Felltham, *Brief Account,* 62.

11 Temple noted that "there seems to have been growing on for these later years, a greater Vie of Luxury and Expence among many of the Merchants of the Town than was ever formerly known; Which was observed and complained of . . ." Sir William Temple, *Observations Upon the United Provinces of the Netherlands,* ed., Sir George Clark (Oxford, 1972) [Reprint], 124.

12 Thomas Coryate, *Coryate's Crudities, hashly gobled up in five months travells in France, Savoy, Italy, Rhetia commonly called the Grisons country, Helvetia alias Switzerland, some parts of High Germany and the Netherlands* (London, 1611), 639.

13 Barbon, for example, argued in 1690 that the nation "never thrives better than when riches are tost from hand to hand." On these writers see Appleby, *Economic Thought and Ideology in 17th Century England* (Princeton, N.J., 1978), 169ff.

14 Bernard de Mandeville, *The Fable of the Bees; or, Private Vices, Publick Benefits,* ed., D. Garman (London, 1934), 144.

15 Ibid., 148–49.

16 This, of course, is the classic argument made by Max Weber's *Protestant Ethic and the Spirit of Capitalism.* Attempts have been made to validate the "Weber thesis" on the basis of evidence drawn from the Netherlands, but none, in my view, have

been particularly convincing. See E. Beins, "Die Wirtschaftsethik der Calvinischen Kirche der Niederlande 1565–1650," *Nederlands Archief voor Kerkgeschiedenis* (1951), 24; and J. H. van Stuijvenberg, "The Weber Thesis: An Attempt at Interpretation," *Acta Historiae Neerlandica* (1975), 55–66; Nils M. Hansen, "Early Flemish Capitalism: The Medieval City, the Protestant Ethic and the Emergence of Economic Rationality," *Social Research* (1967), 226–48; Jelle C. Riemersma, *Religious Factors in Early Dutch Capitalism 1550–1650* (The Hague, 1967). Riemersma reviews some of the religious literature but comes to the surprising conclusion that "the general impression one retains from the utterances of Dutch ministers is that abuses in economic conduct did not greatly preoccupy them," and one certainly belied by much sermon and tract literature.

17 The best known was G. J. Saeghman's *Groot Comptoir Almanach,* published in Amsterdam from the 1650s and so famous that it appears in still-life paintings, in particular Gerrit Dou's stunning *Vanitas,* now in the Dresden Gemäldegalerie. On small-town almanacs see Schotel, *Vaderlandsche Volksboeken,* 1:31ff. On barge timetables, see Jan de Vries, *Dutch Rural Economy,* 205–209, and idem, "Barges and Capitalism: Passenger Transportation in the Dutch Economy, 1631–1839," in *AAG Bijdragen,* 21 (Wageningen, 1978):33–361.

18 Samuel Ampzing, *Beschryving ende Lof der Stad Haerlem in Holland* (Haarlem, 1628). This was a combination of verse, prose and superlative engravings and maps that was, in every sense, the first full Dutch *laudatio* worthy of the name, but with a characteristically Netherlandish dose of scriptural piety diluting the humanist panegyric. It was Ampzing who adapted Ovid in a wholly Calvinist style to coin the phrase here, the *"Vaderland der vromen"* (the Fatherland of the pious). The most important of the first generation of Amsterdam eulogies-cum-guidebooks was [Olfert Dapper and] Tobias van Domselaer, *Beschryving der Stat Amsterdan van haar Eerste Beginselen oudtheydt vergrootingen en gebouwen en geschiedenis tot op den 1665* (Amsterdam, 1665). For other eulogies-cum-guidebooks see Bibliography, pp. 664–65.

19 The medal, with Jan Vos's lines, was struck on the building of the new Amsterdam bourse in 1611; see van Loon, *Beschryving,* 1:81.

20 Casparus Barlaeus, *Marie de Médicis entrant dans Amsterdam, ou Histoire de la Réception faite à la Reyne*

mère du Roy très-Chrétien . . . par les Bourgmaistres et Bourgeoisie de la Ville d'Amsterdam (Amsterdam, 1638), Preface.

21 Melchior Fokkens, *Beschryvinge der Wijdt-Vermaerde Koop-Stadt Amstelredam . . .* 3rd edition (Amsterdam, 1664), 333.

22 "Van so veel Steens om hoog, op zo veel houts van onder," in Constantijn Huygens, *Koren-bloemen* (Amsterdam, 1672), 282.

23 Fokkens, *Beschryving,* 351.

24 See [Jeroen Sweerts], *Ernstige en Koddige opschriften op luyffels, waggens, glazen en uythangboorden* (Amsterdam, 1682–89). This was an annually published anthology of inscriptions, some bawdy, many comic, some serious, to be found on a variety of objects including signboards. For the history of signboards in the Netherlands, see J. van Lennep and J. ter Gouw, *Het boek der Opschriften* (Amsterdam, 1869).

25 Fokkens, *Beschryving,* 396.

26 Ibid., 395.

27 On the decorative arts industry in Delft, see the richly documented account in Michael Montias, *Artists and Artisans in Delft: A Socio-economic Study* (Princeton, 1982), esp. chapter 9; see also Peter Thornton, *Seventeenth-Century Interior Decoration in England, France and Holland* (New Haven, Conn./ London, 1978).

28 Peter Sutton, *Pieter de Hooch* (New York/Oxford, 1980), 92.

29 Karel van Mander, *Schilderboeck,* fol. 168; cited in Thornton, *Interior Decoration,* 340n.

30 Bodleian Library, Oxford, Douce Prints Portfolio, 136, no. 95.

31 G. A. Fokker, *Geschiedenis der Loterijen in Nederland* (Amsterdam, 1862), 76.

32 Ibid., 89–92.

33 Ibid., 30. Fokkens observes that the official prize catalogue for the Middelburg lottery ran to 83 pages!

34 Montias, *Artists and Artisans,* 192.

35 Gemeente Archief, Amsterdam, Desolate Boedels Kamer (hereafter GAA/DBK), July 1726. The blue damask houserobe was obviously of the most elaborate kind and was valued at fl. 95, an extraordinarily high price for any garment.

36 Sheila Williams and J. Jacquot, "Ommegangs anversois . . . " in *Les fêtes de la Renaissance* (Paris, 1969), vol. 2., 359–88.

37 On the expansion of Amsterdam and other Dutch urban centers in the seventeenth century and the

manner in which "planning" became a euphemism for chaotic commercial development, see the brilliant account by E. Taverne, *In 't land van belofte: in de nieuwe stadt; ideaal en werkelijkheid in de Republiek,* 1580–1680 (Maarssen, 1978); for detailed history of particular houses, see R. Meischke and H. J. Zantkuil, *Het Nederlandse Woonhuis van 1300–1800* (Haarlem, 1969).

38 Gustav Leonhardt, *Het Huis Bartolotti en zijn bewoners* (Amsterdam, 1979).

39 Ibid., 91–99; Meischke and Zantkuil, *Woonhuis,* 407–11.

40 Ibid., 409. This is an extraordinarily low price, and I have yet to read in any other inventory of a *painting* selling for less than a guilder, though many were priced at little more. Could the *schilderijen* mentioned in the Bartolotti inventory have included prints, which were indeed the "copper coin" of the art market?

41 For a preliminary report on Dutch probate sources see Johannes Faber, Thera Wijsen Beek and Anton Schurman in Ad van der Woude and Anton Schurman, eds., "Probate Inventories," *AAG Bijdragen* 23 (Wageningen, 1980):149–89.

42 See de Vries, "Wages."

43 GAA/DBK 2 March 1717.

44 GAA/DBK, 1717. Prices quoted are those fetched at auction.

45 In 1720, for example, a batch of ten chairs in the estate of Barent Meynders van Lee fetched three guilders ten stuivers while a single item described as "gown and skirt," albeit probably for best wear, made eight guilders at auction. GAA/DBK 17 September 1720. Twelve chairs, belonging to Jan van Zoelen and Neeltje Zuykenaar, together made less than ten guilders in 1717 and three tables cost just nine guilders together. On the evolution of Dutch furniture see K. Sluyterman, *Huisraad en Binnenhuis in Nederland in Vroegere Eeuwen* ('s Gravenhage, 1918).

46 On beds, see Thorton, 149–73.

47 On linen chests see G. T. van Ysselstein, *Van Linnen en Linnekasten* (Amsterdam, 1946). A single linen cabinet in the inventory of Hendrick ter Hoeven in 1717 made fl. 16.

48 See 23–24; Montias, *Artists and Artisans,* 312.

49 E. S. de Beer, ed., *The Diary of John Evelyn,* 2 vols. (Oxford, 1955), 2:39. *The Travels of Peter Mundy* (London, 1925), 4: 70–71; Jean de Parival, *Délices,* 25; Aglionby, *Present State,* 224–25.

50 MSS auction catalogues, Bibliotheek Vereeniging

ter Bevordering van de Belangen des Boekhandels, Amsterdam.

51 GAA/DBK 386, February 8, 1681, inventory of François van der Noordt.

52 Montias, *Artists and Artisans,* argues throughout his book from a great mass of archival evidence that there was a considerable range of status expectations and income within the artistic community from highly paid and high-status history painters like Michiel Miereveld to poor drudges like Evert van Aelst, who rented rooms from a tailor and died bankrupt. The prices Montias quotes (pp. 213–14) from the Delft dealer Abraham de Cooge in 1680 that range from a Tintoretto for fl. 250 and a *Crossing of the Dead* (sic, surely *Red?*) *Sea* by Schoonhoven for fl. 30, but which go no lower than fl. 20 for a Cuyp landscape, are quite untypical of the prices encountered in the Amsterdam bankruptcy auctions of the same period, prices that seem far lower and are indeed far more diverse in their range of genres.

53 GAA/DBK 386, 27 March 1682.

54 In Remmert Klundert's inventory (GAA/DBK, July 1726), 6 men's shirts went for fl. 8.15, 7 women's chemises for fl. 7.10 and 1 black damask gown for fl. 19.15.

55 B. E. de Muinck, *Een Regentenhuishouding omstreeks 1700* ('s Gravenhage, 1955), 342. The following account and the data are drawn from de Muinck's outstanding monograph.

56 Ibid., 180, 198.

57 This was the message of the *Beklagh over den Bedroefden Toestant in de Nederlandse Provintien* (KN 10237) and many similar *straf-predikaties* (punishment sermons) in the "disaster year" of 1672.

58 For the debate over "relative and absolute decline" see Joh. de Vries, *De economische achteruitgang der Republiek in de achttiende eeuw* (Amsterdam, 1958).

59 See Carter, *Neutrality or Commitment;* Schama, *Patriots,* 26–45.

60 Muinck, *Regentenhuishouding,* 312ff.

61 Montias, *Artists,* 263.

62 GAA, Familie Archief Backer, no. 75, Huwelijkse voorwaarden, en inventaris van huwelijksgoed van Cornelis Backer en Catharina Raye, 1660.

63 P. W. Klein, *De Trippen in de 17de Eeuw. Een studie over het ondernemersgedrag op de Hollandse stapelmarkt* (Assen, 1965), 176–80.

64 Tobias van Domselaer, *Beschryving der Stat Amsterdam,* 442, gives the figure of 16,727 deaths

for 1655, and 24,148 deaths for 1664 (compared with a "normal" median rate of around 4,500 in the mid-1620s. The year 1664 was one of the worst plague years in the city, but even its peak figure compares relatively favorably with the London figures for the summer of 1665. In Amsterdam in 1664 the worst week (the 36th) saw 1,041 burials, against the 6,000 to 7,000 burials in London, a city twice its size.

65 John Calvin *Commentaries and Letters* (tr. and ed.) J. Haroutanion and L. Pettibone Smith (Philadelphia, 1958), 350.

66 Aglionby, *Present State,* 291.

67 This was, of course, the theme of Erasmus's *Enchiridion* and was taken up by a number of Netherlands humanists, most notably Dirk Volkhertszoon Coornhert in *Zedekunst Dat is Wellevenskunst* (The Art of Morals, That Is, the Art of the Good Life). On the issue of "daily ordeals" in the life of public humanists, see the fine biographical study by Alistair Fox, *Thomas More: History and Providence* (New Haven, Conn., 1983).

68 Williams and Jacquot, "Ommegangs anversois," art. cit., 359–88.

69 On Heemskerck's engravings for the cycle, see Ilja Veldman, *Maarten van Heemskerck and Dutch Humanism in the Sixteenth Century* (Maarssen, 1977), 133–41.

70 Ibid., esp. Ch. 4, "Dirk Volkertsz. Coornhert and Heemskerck's Allegories," 55–93.

71 See P. van der Meulen, ed., *Het Roerspel en de Comedies van Coornhert* (Leiden, 1955), 81ff. Money also appears in the play as the agent of infamous and sinister practices.

72 Veldman, *Maarten van Heemskerck,* 93.

73 G. C. Udemans, *Geestelijk Roer van 't Coopmans Schip* (Dordrecht, 1640). The dedication (to the directors of the East and West India companies) mentions the "great afterthoughts and doubts of tender consciences" in the world of commerce and trade (p. 4).

74 Ibid., 5.

75 Ibid., fol. 19.

76 Ibid., fol. 15.

77 Simonides, *Vier Boecken van Godt's Ordeel* (Rotterdam, 1655).

78 Jacobus Lydius, "Een gelt-hont" in *Vrolycke Uren ofte der Wijse Vermaeck* (Dordrecht, 1650); *Wee-klagh,*

79 See Evenhuis, *Ook dat was Amsterdam,* 2:12, 15–17.

80 Ibid., 36–37.

81 *Gedachten op Geldt* (n.p., n.d.).

Om dat men Rycke vlegels eert
Is 't geldt by sotten meest begeert

Daerom is' t Geldt zoo hoogh in prys
't maeckt schelmen vroom en bussels wys.

82 On this theme, see Simon Schama, "The Sexual
   Economy of Genre Painting," in Christopher
   Brown, ed., *Images of the World: Dutch Genre Paint-
   ing in Its Historical Context* (London, forthcoming).

83 J. Krul, *Wereldt-hatende nootsaeckelijcke* (Amsterdam,
   1627), 91. The subtitle of the verse sermon was
   "How an abundance (*overvloed*) of riches weighs
   down the heart."

84 Evenhuis, *Ook dat was Amsterdam*, 2:80.

85 Jacobus Hondius, *Swart Register van Duysent Sonden*
   (Hoorn, 1675; Amsterdam, 1724).

86 Evenhuis, 2:84f.

87 On the church disciplinary action against le Maire
   see J. G. van Dillen, "Isaac le Maire et le Commerce de la Compagnie des Indes orientales,"
   Revue d'Histoire moderne 16 (1935):7-8.

88 Udemans, *Geestelijk Roer*

89 Evenhuis, 2:117-18.

90 Ibid., 2:156.

91 John Calvin, *Consilia, De usuri*, in G. Baum et al.
   (eds.). *Opera* (1863-1906), vol x.

92 Johannes Cloppenburgh, *De Foenore et Usuris brevis
   institutio* (Leiden, 1640).

93 On the church's view of interest rates see also
   Evenhuis, 2:156.

94 On le Maire's "ring" against the East India Company in 1609, see Van Dillen, "Isaac le Maire et
   le Commerce des Indes Orientales, " *Revue
   d'Histoire moderne*, 17 (1935):121-37.

95 Evenhuis, 2:158, 316-21.

96 On the West India Company see W. J. Hoboken,
   "The Dutch West India Company: the Political
   Background of Its Rise and Fall," in J. S. Bromley
   and E. H. Kossmann, eds., *Britain and the
   Netherlands*, vol. 1 (London, 1960).

97 Evenhuis, 2:157.

98 P. W. Klein, "The Trip Family in the 17th
   Century," in *Acta Historiae Neerlandica*, 208.

99 Idem, *De Trippen*, in *De 17de eeuw; een Studie over
   het ondernemersgedrag op de Hollandse Stapelmarkt*
   (Assen, 1965), 429.

100 See Katherine Fremantle, *The Baroque Town Hall
    of Amsterdam* (Utrecht, 1959), 73.

101 For a helpful guide to the bankruptcy procedures
    in Amsterdam, see the introduction to the
    archive of the Desolate Boedels Kamer,

Gemeente Archief, Amsterdam.

102 See J. G. van Dillen, "Oprichting en functie der
    Amsterdamse wisselbank in de zeventiende eeuw,"
    in *Mensen en Achtergronden*, 336-84.

103 Onslow Burrish, *Batavia Illustrata; or, A View of the
    Policy and Commerce of the United Provinces* (London,
    1728), 288.

104 Ibid., 292.

105 This is certainly the view of Udemans, *Geestelijk
    Roer*... (fol. 166), who is particularly interested
    in missionary work and gives details of the mis-
    sion schools on Amboina as an instance of a suc-
    cessful Christianizing policy in the Indies.

106 *Courante uyt Italien en Duytschland*, 27-28 June 1634.
    (The same courant, on July 23, 1633, mentions
    that an elephant and a tiger were among the cargo
    from the East Indies.)

107 Joseph de la Vega, *Confusion de Confusiones*, 1688,
    in *Portions Descriptive of the Amsterdam Stock Exchange*,
    ed., H. Kellenbenz (Boston, 1957).

108 Ibid., 21.

109 Ibid., 11.

110 The best accounts by far of the tulip mania are:
    E. H. Krelage, *Bloemenspeculatie in Nederland*
    (Amsterdam, 1942); N. W. Posthumus, "The Tulip
    Mania in Holland in the Years 1636 and 1637,"
    Journal of Economic and Business History 1:4 (August,
    1929):434-66.

111 Krelage, *Bloemenspeculatie*, 17ff.

112 Ibid., 31.

113 Roemer Visscher, *Sinnepoppen*, ed., L. Brummel
    ('s Gravenhage, 1949; Amsterdam, 1614), no. VC,
    5; Johan de Brune, *Emblemata* (Middelburg, 1624).

114 Krelage, *Bloemenspeculatie*, 42.

115 Ibid., 51.

116 Ibid., 64.

117 Ibid., 67.

118 Ibid., 66.

119 Ibid., 65.

120 [Pieter Jansz. van Campen], *Geschokerde Blom-
    Cap*... (Hoorn, 1637); see also, Krelage,
    Bloemenspeculatie, 65.

121 Posthumus, "Tulip Mania," 451 (extract from the
    first *Dialogue between Waermondt and Gaegoedt* on
    the rise and decline of Flora [*Samen-spraeck tusschen
    Waermondt ende Gaergoedt nopende de opkomste ende
    ondergangh van Flora*] [Haarlem, 1637]. The same
    dialogue gives the detailed account of the man-
    ner of sales in the tulip companies).

122 Ibid.

123 Posthumus, "Tulip Mania," 459; *Samen-spraeck tusschen Waermondt ende Gaergoedt . . .* (Haarlem, 1637).

124 Posthumus, "Tulip Mania," 452.

125 See A. Eijffinger, "Twee Historie-prenten . . . "

126 [Chrispijn van de Pas, Jr.?], *Floraas Mallewagen, behoordende bij de prent De Mallewagen alias het Valete der Bloemisten* (1637).

127 Krelage, *Bloemenspeculatie,* 142–96; *Flora's Bloem-Warande in Holland . . .* 3 vols. (Amsterdam, 1734–36).

128 See A. H. Cole, *The Great Mirror of Folly (Het Groote Tafereel der Dwaasheid): An Economic-Bibliographical Study* (Boston, 1949).

CHAPTER SIX
HOUSEWIVES AND HUSSIES;
HOMELINESS AND WORLDLINESS

1 *Schoon* is not the only Dutch word for clean. *Reyn* was used quite as frequently, especially when the sense of purity was intended. *Zindelijk* also carries the sense of cleanliness as a species of neatness or tidiness. Jacob Campo Weijerman, the witty eighteenth-century skeptic and freethinker, wrote a satire on the domestic obsession, *Hollands Zindelijkheid* (Amsterdam, 1717).

2 *The Present State of Holland; or, A Description of the United Provinces* (London, 1765), 211.

3 *The Dutch Drawn to Life* (1665).

4 Felltham, *Brief Character,* 27.

5 *De Ervarene en Verstandige Huyshouder,* 2d ed. (1743), 30ff.

6 Antoine de la Barre de la Beaumarchais, *Le Hollandois, ou Lettres sur la Hollande ancienne et moderne* (Frankfurt, 1738), 158.

7 [Aglionby], *Present State;* Parival, *Délices,* 29; de la Barre de la Beaumarchais, *Le Hollandois,* 274.

8 *The Works of Sir William Temple Bart,* 4 vols. (New York, 1815; New York, 1968), 2:472–73.

9 De Blainville, *Travels Through Holland . . . ,* 43.

10 Bargrave, *Sundry Relation,* 13.

11 Parival, *Délices,* 29; [Alexandre-Jean-Joseph de la Poupelinière], *Journal du voyage en hollande* (Paris, 1730), 88; de la Barre de la Beaumarchais, *Le Hollandois,* 274, wrote of *"l'attachement presque superstitieux"* of Dutch women to the cleanliness of their rooms and houses.

12 Samuel Paterson, *An Entertaining Journey to the Netherlands* (London, 1782), 150.

13 Joost van Damhouder, *Practycke in Crimineele Saecken* (Rotterdam, 1618), 334.

14 Pepys, *Diary,* entry for March 28, 1667.

15 Cited in Schotel, *Het Oud-Hollandsch Gezin,* 3.

16 Jan Luiken, *Het Leerzaam Huisraad* (Amsterdam, 1711), 78.

17 Mary Douglas, *Purity and Danger: An Analysis of the Concepts of Pollution and Taboo* (London, 1966), 7–57.

18 Ibid., "The Abominations of Leviticus," 41ff.

19 Ibid., 35.

20 Johan de Brune, *Emblemata,* 11.

21 Luiken, *Huisraad,* 74–75.

22 "Publius Felicius," *De Beurs der Vrouwen gesticht op Tien Pilaaren,* 4th ed. (1684), 272–74.

23 Luiken, *Huisraad,* 79.

24 See Chapter 3, pp. 158–63.

25 Jacob Cats, *Proteus ofte Minnebeelden* (Amsterdam, 1628), i–ii.

26 Ibid., "Huiselijke Zaken," 171.

27 Ibid., xxviii.

28 Cats, *Self-Stryt dat is Krachtige Beweeginge van Vleas en Geest,* 28–29.

29 Johan van Beverwijck, *Van De Wtnementheyt des Vrouwelicken Geslachts,* 2d ed. (Dordrecht, 1643), 206–12.

30 Ibid.; see also idem., *Schat der Gezondheid,* 192–93.

31 *De Ervarene en Verstandige Huyshouder,* xv.

32 On the organization of the *buurt,* see the contemporary account given by Aglionby in *Present State,* 226f.; see also Donald Haks, *Huwelijk en Gezin in Holland in de 17de en 18de eeuw* (Assen, 1982), 60–69.

33 See A. M. van de Woude, "De omvang en samenstelling van de huishouding in Nederland in het verleden," in P. A. M. Geurts and F. A. Messing, eds., *Economische ontwikkeling en social emancipatie, 18 opstellen over economische en sociale geschiedenis,* 2 vols. (The Hague, 1977). 1:200–239; see also Haks, *Huwelijk en Gezin,* 143–50.

34 A. M. Van der Woude, "Variations in the Size and Structure of Households in the United Provinces of the Netherlands in the Seventeenth and Eighteenth Centuries," in P. Laslett, ed., *Household and Family in Past Time* (Cambridge, Eng., 1972), 315.

35 Luiken, *Huisraad,* 75.

36 C. H. Boxer, *The Dutch Seaborne Empire* (London/ New York, 1965), 70–73.

37 Van Beverwijck, *Wtnementheyt,* 206; Cats, *Christelyke Huyswijf,* 366; Visscher, *Sinnepoppen,* 98.

38 See Tirtsah Levie and H. Zantkuil, *Wonen in Amsterdam* (Amsterdam, 1984).

39 Swildens, *Vaderlandsch ABC*, Emblem "2."

40 See Schama, "Unruly Realm"; Peter Sutton, "The Life and Art of Jan Steen," in *Jan Steen: Comedy and Admonition*, Bulletin of Philadelphia Museum of Art, vol. 78, no. 337-38, pp. 3-7.

41 De Brune, *Emblemata*, 231.

42 Visscher, *Sinnepoppen*, 9. The emblem of the comb, it should also be noted, was used here by Visscher to denote a purification of the Republic itself!

43 Cats, *Alle de Werken* (Amsterdam/Utrecht, 1700), 1:284, "Vrouwen Voordicht toegeeygent alle ware Huys-moeders." *Houwelijck* was published separately in 1628 with engravings by Adriaen van de Venne and remained the most popular and influential of all his homilies. In the preface to the 1655 edition, the publisher, Schipper, claimed that it had sold fifty thousand copies—an enormous number by seventeenth-century standards. Replete with the usual combination of aphorisms, didactic dialogues and exemplary tales, it divided the female odyssey through life into "Childhood," "Maidenhood," "Bride," "Wife" and "Mother," though van de Venne's frontispiece of the "Ladder of Life" also showed the matron and the widow, who were so prominent a feature of Dutch life.

44 Ibid., *Christelyke Huyswijf*, 323.

45 *Houwliijx-Spiegel aen de Nieuw Getroude* (Haarlem, 1686).

46 Johan van Beverwijck, *Schat der Gesontheyt* (Dordrecht, 1652), 160.

47 Cats, *Vrouwe*, 317.

48 See Jan Grauls, *Volkstaal en volksleven in het werk van Pieter Bruegel* (Antwerp/Amsterdam, 1957), 19-76.

49 Ray, *Observations*, 55.

50 Nugent, *Grand Tour*, 81.

51 Ray, *Observations*, 55.

52 Cited in Murris, *La Hollande*, 82.

53 On *kweesten* in Holland, see P. Neijn, *Lust-Hof der Houwelyken* (Amsterdam, 1697); Le Francq van Berkhey, *Natuurlijke Historie*, 3:933; Schotel, *Oud-Hollandsch Huisgezin*, 216-17 (who also mentions the comparable practice of *winterneven* in north Brabant); Haks, *Huwelijk en Gezin*, 111-12.

54 Aglionby, *Present State*, 32.

55 Moryson, *Shakespeare's Europe*, 385.

56 Joseph Shaw, *Letters to a Nobleman from a Gentleman Travelling through Flanders and France* (London, 1709), 43-44.

57 Diderot, *Voyage de Hollande*, in *Oeuvres* (Paris, 1819), vol. 7, 41.

58 Shaw, *Letters to a Nobleman*, 46.

59 Ibid., 39. Stories of the indifference of simple folk, especially the old, to money abound in the travel literature—alongside the equally indelible clichés about the Dutch avidity for gain. Sir William Temple, *Observations*, 88, visited an old sailors' home at Enkhuyzen, where he offered a crown to an old salt who declined asking "what he should do with money? for all that they ever wanted was provided for them at their House."

60 Shaw, *Letters to a Nobleman*, xii.

61 The classic equation of the rise of "affect" with the modernization of family life is Lawrence Stone, *Sex, the Family and Marriage in England 1500-1800* (London, 1977), esp. Ch. 3, 93-116, Chs. 6 and 8.

62 For an illuminating account of the legal rights of Dutch noblewomen, see Sherrin Marshall Wyntjes, "Survivors and Status: Widowhood and Family in the Early Modern Netherlands," *Journal of Family History* (Winter 1982):396-405.

63 My own reading of Dutch contemporary literature and informal primary sources accords generally with the German and Swiss evidence set out in Steven Ozment, *When Fathers Ruled: Family Life in Reformation Europe* (Cambridge, Mass., 1983), though our conclusions vary somewhat in emphasis.

64 GA. Familie-Archief Backer 75.

65 GA. Familie-Archief Bicker 79.

66 See L. J. Apeldoorn, *Geschiedenis van Nederlandse Huwelijksrecht voor de invoering van de Fransche wetgeving* (Amsterdam, 1925).

67 Haks, *Huwelijk en Gezin*, 88ff.

68 Ibid., 94.

69 Ibid., 89-90. The Zeeland marriage law of 1673 specifically mentioned serving maids who led sons on to "unchastity . . . in the hope of making a favorable marriage." See the excellent article by Marlies Jongejaan, "Dienstboden in de Zeeuwse Steden 1650-1800," *Spiegel Historiael* (May 1984): 214-21.

70 Ibid., 87.

71 Ibid., 94.

72 See tables in ibid., 185, 188-89, 192.

73 Shaw, *Letters to a Nobleman*, 46.

74 [H. Sweerts?], *De Biegt der Getroude*, vol. 2 of *De Tien Vermakelijkheden der Houweliks* (Amsterdam,

1679), 53ff.

75 Catharina Geertruid Schrader, Dagboek van de verlossingen 1693-1745, Amsterdam University Library.

76 Knappert, "Huiselijk Leven," 155; Evenhuis, *Ook dat was Amsterdam,* 2: vol. 3 (1971), 38.

77 For the full text, which I have very freely translated in the interests of reproducing the social manner of the verses, see the introduction by C. W. de Kruyter to *Letter-Juweel,* facs. ed. (Amsterdam, 1971), 12, and poem no. 1.

78 C168 in Pieter JJ. van Thiel et al., *All the Paintings of the Rijksmuseum in Amsterdam* (Amsterdam/Maarssen, 1976), 331.

79 Anna Maria Schurman, *The Learned Maid* (London, 1659), 2.

80 Ibid., 5.

81 Ibid., 8, 15.

82 For the iconography of genre, see in particular E. de Jongh, *Zinne- en minnebeelden in de schilderkunst van de zeventiende eeuw* (Amsterdam, 1967); also Christopher Brown, *Dutch Genre Painting.* A different view is taken by Svetlana Alpers, *The Art of Describing,* 229-33 and passim. For an account of the debate, see Linda A. Stone-Ferrier, "Pretty Ornaments and Clever Images: Interpretations of Dutch Art," in idem, *Dutch Prints of Daily Life* (Lawrence, Kan.), 3-35.

83 See Seymour Slive, "Notes on the Relationship of Protestantism to Seventeenth Century Dutch Painting," *Art Quarterly* (1956), xix.

84 Frima Fox Hofrichter, "Judith Leyster's *Proposition* — Between Virtue and Vice," in Norma Broude and Mary D. Garrard, *Feminism and Art History: Questioning the Litany* (New York, 1982), 173-81. On proposition pictures, see also Simon Schama, "The Sexual Economy of Genre Painting," in Christopher Brown, ed., *Images of the World: Dutch Genre Painting in Its Historical Context* (London, forthcoming).

85 Letter to van Beverwijck, published in Schuuman, *The Learned Maid,* 37-40.

86 Van Beverwijck, *Wtnementheyt,* 21.

87 Ibid., 211.

88 Ibid., 161.

89 [I. H. Glazemaker], *Deughdelijcke Vrou* (Amsterdam, 1642), 5, 49, 136.

90 Aglionby, *Present State,* 229.

91 For comparison of attitudes, see Alice Clare Carter, "Marriage Counselling in Seventeenth-Century England and Holland," in J. van Dorsten, ed., *Ten Studies in Anglo-Dutch Relations* (Leiden, 1974).

92 Petrus Wittewrongel, *Oeconomia Christiana ofte Christelicke Huyhoudinge* (Amsterdam, 1655), 13, 127, 137-39.

93 Cats, *Vrouwe,* 315.

94 Ibid., *Houwelyck,* 51-52.

95 Cited in Apeldoorn, *Huwelijksrecht,* 8.

96 Wittewrongel, *Oeconomia,* 179, 280-81.

97 *Houwlijx-Spiegel aen de Nieuw Getroude* (Haarlem, 1686).

98 Murris, *Hollande,* 105.

99 "Het Klein Hollands Goud-Vinkje."

100 *De Ervarene en Verstandige Hollandsche Huyshoudster,* 2d ed. (Amsterdam, 1743), 3, 8-9. *De Verstandige Huyshouder* (Amsterdam, 1661), 2, took a more stringent line, insisting that "the [domestic] economy is a Monarchy, and in such a government only one person may rule, namely the House-father."

101 Ibid., 10ff.

102 Ibid., x.

103 Ibid., 7.

104 Cats, *Vrouwe,* 367.

105 "I.V.E." [Nicolas Venette], *Venus Minsieke Gasthuis* (Amsterdam, 1687), 261.

106 De Brune, *Emblemata,* 9.

107 Van Beverwijck, *Schat der Gesontheyt,* 168.

108 *Venus Minsieke Gasthuis,* 213.

109 Ibid., 21.

110 Stone, *Family,* passim. Even in his pioneering and very perceptive work, Donald Haks finds it necessary to situate his research within the terms of reference of this "Whig" history of the family.

111 E. de Jongh, "Grape symbolism in paintings of the 16th and 17th centuries," *Simiolus* 7 (1974): 166-91.

112 David R. Smith, *Masks of Wedlock: Seventeenth-Century Dutch Marriage Portraiture* (Ann Arbor, Mich., 1982), Chs. 3 and 4.

113 For the theme of the interrupted husband see ibid., 126ff.

114 For a more densely emblematic interpretation see E. de Jongh, "Frans Hals als voorzetter van een emblematische traditie," *Oud Holland* 78 (1961).

115 On the contrast between these two proposition pictures see Schama, "Sexual Economy."

116 Haks, *Huwelijk en Genin,* 128-29.

117 Cats, *Sinne- en Minnebeelden,* 93.

118 Ibid., 21.

119 Idem, *Spiegel van de Oude en Nieuwe Tyt* (Rotterdam,

1627), 22–23.

120 Idem, *Maegdeplicht*.

121 Idem, *Spiegel van de Oude en Nieuwe Tyt,* 42, in *Alle de Werken,* 3–4; tr. Richard Pigot, from Cats and Robert Farlie, *Moral Emblems* (London, 1865).

122 Haks, 102.

123 Ibid., 97; D. J. Noordam, "Ongehuwde moeders en onwettige kinderen in Maassluis," *Holland* 9 (1977):165–78.

124 Pieter Neyn, *Lust-Hof der Houwelyken* (Amsterdam, 1697), 155.

125 Schotel, *Oud-Hollandsch Huisgezin,* 226–28.

126 Le Francq van Berkhey, 3:856.

127 Knuttel, *Acta der Synoden,* 3:300, "Lichtveerdich wechloopen der jonge luyden."

128 C. A. van Sypesteyn, "Johan de Witt in zijne betrekking tot den veldmaaarschalk Brederode, tot de freule Margaretha van Nassau en tot "l'Union de la Joye (1653–55)," *Vaderlandsche Letteroefeningen — Historie en Binnenlandsche Bibliografie* 109 (1869):419–38, 483–96.

129 Knuttel, *Acta der Synoden,* 3:237.

130 Ibid., 2:469.

131 See Apeldoorn, *Huweliksrecht,* 151f.

132 ARA, Hof van Holland, Index van Crimineele Sententien, 21 December 1646; April 1653; May 1664.

133 Haks, *Huwelijk en Gezin,* 127.

134 ARA Hof van Holland, Index van Crimineele Sententien, 13 March 1626.

135 For a full account of the Welhoeck affair, see G. Renier, *The Dutch Nation* (London, 1944), 161–80.

136 ARA Hof van Holland 5270-8.

137 KN 9197 (3 March 1665).

138 See Evenhuis, *Ook dat was Amsterdam,* 2:101.

139 See Apeldoorn, *Huwelijksrecht,* 165. It should be said that while the church took strong exception to "mixed" marriages within the Christian family it did not consider it a ground for invalidating a marriage.

140 Haks, *Huwelijk en Gezin,* 132.

141 Cats, *Twee-en Tachtigh jarigh leven,* in *Gedachten op Flapeloose Nachten* (Amsterdam, 1700), 43. See also G. Derudder, *Étude sur la vie et les Oeuvres de Cats* (Calais, 1898), 45–48.

142 Haks, *Huwelijk en Gezin,* 124.

143 Ibid.

144 Cats, *Houwelijck,* 317.

145 "Publius Felicius" [Joh. Strander?], *De Beurs der Vrouwen* (1690), 87–88.

146 David Kunzle, *The Early Comic Strip* (Berkeley, Cal.,

1973), 245–49; see also Natalie Zemon Davis, "Women on Top," in *Society and Culture in Early Modern France* (London, 1975), 124–51.

147 [H. Sweerts?] *De Biegt der Getroude zynde het tweede deel van de Tien Vermakelijkheden des Houwelyks* (Amsterdam, 1679), 88 (6de Vermak).

148 Jan de Mol, *Huwlijks Doolhof* (n.p., 1634).

149 Atlas van Stolk, Supplement 1600–1650.

150 "Hippolytus de Vrye" [Hieronymus Sweerts], *De Tien Vermakelijkheden des Houwelyks* (Amsterdam, 1684), 118.

151 Ibid., 156.

152 Ibid., 85–88.

153 Ibid., 156.

154 See J. B. Bedaux, "Minnekoorts-, zwangerschaps-en doodverschijnselen op zeventiende-eeuwse schilderijen," *Antiek* 10: i (1975):17–42; on collusion in deceit, see *De Listigheid der Kraamvrouwen* (Amsterdam, 1709); *De Verreezene Hippolytus* (1711), 34.

155 *Beurs der Vrouwen* (1690), 103: "Zwangere vrouwen, vroemoers en bakers."

156 Haks, *Huwelijk en Gezin,* 167–68.

157 Marlies Jongejaan, "Dienstboden in de Zeeuwse steden 1650–1800," *Spiegel Historiael* (May 1984), 210.

158 Haks, *Huwelijk en Gezin,* 171.

159 Jongejaan, "Dienstboden," 220.

160 *Ervarene en Verstandige Hollandse Huyshoudster,* 17.

161 [S. de Vries], *Seeven Duyvelen Regeerende de Hedendaagsche Dienst-Maeghden,* 4th ed. (Amsterdam, 1682).

162 Ibid., 71.

163 Jongejaan, "Dienstboden," 221.

164 *Seeven Duyvelen,* 177.

165 GA/Rechterlijke Archief, *Confessie Boeken,* 1646.

166 Van Deursen, *Kopergeld,* II, *Volkskultur,* 24.

167 ARA, Hof van Holland, Index van Crimineele Sententien, 21 February, 1659.

168 Sjoerd Faber, "Kindermoord, in het bijzonder in de achttiende eeuw te Amsterdam," *Bijdragen en mededelingen betreffende de geschiedenis der Nederlanden,* 73 (1978):224–40. See also Haks, *Huwelijk en Gezin,* 84.

169 G. A. Bredero, *The Spanish Brabanter,* ed. and tr. H. David Brumble III (Binghamton, N.Y., 1982), 71.

170 GA/RA 588.

171 GA/RA *Confessie Boeken* 370 (1671).

172 ARA, Hof van Holland, Index van Crim. Sent. See, for example, the cases of Catharina van der

Dussen and Maria Gerrits in 1646, Agneta Barteldr. 1660, Judith Niemand (sic) 1668, etc., etc.

173 See *Masterpieces of Seventeenth-Century Dutch Genre*, cat. no. 82, 270.

174 *Spiegel der Vermaardste Courtisanen*, 3d ed. (Amsterdam, 1710), 60. These works and versions of Aretino had evidently become popular in Holland towards the end of the century; see also the translation of Aretino, *Het Leven en Listen der Geriefelycke Courtisanen te Romen* (1680).

175 *Het Leven en Bedrijf van de hedendaagsche Haagsche en Amsterdamsche Zalet-Juffers* (Amsterdam, 1696), 224.

176 Ibid., 226.

177 *Venus Minsieke Gasthuis* (Amsterdam, 1687), 214.

178 Cats, *Spiegel van de Oude en de nieuwe tyt*, in *Alle de Werken*, 539; see also 540, 542.

179 Bernard de Mandeville, *A Modest Defence of Publick Stews* (London, 1724); see also Richard I. Cook, "The Great Leviathan of Lechery: Mandeville's *Modest Defence of Publick Stews*," in Irwin Primer, ed., *Mandeville Studies* (The Hague, 1975), 95–96.

180 Idem, *The Fable of the Bees*, 83–85.

181 See van Deursen, *Het kopergeld*, vol. 2, *Volkskultuur*, 34–38.

182 Ibid., 36.

183 *'t Amsterdamsch Hoerdom behelsende de listen en streecken, daar sich de Hoeren en Hoere-wardinnen van dienen; beneven der selver maniere leven, dwaaze bygeloovigheden en in 't algemeen 't geen by dese Juffers in gebruyk is* ('s Gravenhage, 1694). There is a French edition in the Bibliothèque nationale, Paris, *Le Putanisme d'Amsterdam* (Brussels, 1883), 114.

184 Ibid., 2.

185 Sir William Brereton, *Travels in Holland... 1634–35* (London, 1844), 55.

186 The list is given in J. F. van Slobbe, *Bijdrage tot de Geschiedenis en de Bestrijding der Prostitutie te Amsterdam* (Amsterdam, 1937), 31.

187 See Lotte van de Pol, "Vrouwencriminaliteit in de Gouden Eeuw," *Ons Amsterdam* (November 1982), 266–68. Ms. van de Pol pointed out my erroneous generalization in Schama, "Wives and Wantons," that many of the prostitutes came from foreign ports and rural areas just beyond the Republic. While there were such women identified in the *Confessie Boeken*, her correction, that most of the girls came from Dutch villages and towns, and many from nearby areas in Holland, is absolutely right. I am very grateful for her generous criticism.

188 *'t Amsterdamsch Hoerdom*, 157.

189 Ibid., 21.

190 Ibid., 144–45.

191 For underworld slang and cant, see *Historie ofte Practijke der Dieven Bestaende in ongehoorde wreeten en schelmerijen* (n.d., but almost certainly 1680–90); *'t Amsterdamsch Hoerdom*, 137.

192 This is the surprising conclusion of Lotte van de Poll's research in the *Confessie Boeken*.

193 GA/Rechterlijke Archief 581. *'t Amsterdamsch Hoerdom*, 18, spoke of a whore who had "been burned four times by the Spanish pox" but who still had a great trade, with four or five men a night.

194 Lysbet Jacobs of Delft, for example, nineteen years old, and Laentje Huysberg of Harderwijk (twenty-three), arrested in 1673, were described specifically as *nagtlopers* (*infame nagtloper* in the first woman's case), while Tryntje Henderick of Hamburg, seventeen years old, arrested at the same time, was described as frequenting taverns and whorehouses. GA/RA 371.

195 GA/RA 370.

196 For Hamburg see GA/RA 318 (1669), Anna Maria Rechters, pickpocket and whore; Lippstadt: RA 326 (1679) Annetje Tymons, twenty-three, *musico* girl; Copenhagen: Mary Pieters and Catryn Davids 1681 (RA 326); Cologne: Grietje Henrix (25) in an Agterburgwal whorehouse, 1673 (RA 588); Kiel: Anna Mayers, nineteen, stocking knitter and whore, one child, pregnant with a second, 1696; Julich: Maria Smits, twenty-eight, seamstress and whore; Stavanger: Barbara Roelofs; "Norway": Margriet Gover, twenty-five, begging with a child and whore, both 1654 (RA 310). These are a random but surely representative sample.

197 Aged: 17, 17, 20, 21, and (almost certainly the procuress) 28. GA/RA 599.

198 See van Slobbe, *Bijdrage*, 12.

199 GA/RA CB 310.

200 GA/RA CB 326 (1679).

201 GA/RA CB 320 (1671).

202 GA/RA CB 320 (June 1672). Sweetie Cunt had been banished twice from Amsterdam as a procuress, the last time in 1665, so had managed to stay clear of trouble for seven years.

203 GA/RA 588 (1673), fo. 119.

204 GA/RA 599 (1697).

205 GA/RA CB 320 (1671).

206 Sjoerd Faber, *Strafrechtspleging en Criminaliteit te Amsterdam 1680–1811. De nieuwe menslievendheid*

(Arnhem, 1983), 78. In fact Faber's figures are higher, as in this same year of 1680, thirty-one pimps and procuresses were also arrested. But the arrest rate fell off sharply in the eighteenth century.

207 GA/RA 588 (April 1673). This was a house on the Bomsloot where three whores, Margriet Aarse, seventeen, Lysbet Antonissen, eighteen, and another twenty-one-year-old, were lodged with their *slaapvrouw* (landlady).

208 GA/RA CB 318 (1669).

CHAPTER SEVEN
IN THE REPUBLIC OF CHILDREN

1 De Jongh et al., *Tot Lering en Vermaak,* 86–87; Ivan Gaskell, "Gerrit Dou, His Patrons and the Art of Painting," *Oxford Art Journal* 5:1 (1982):18, offers an interesting reading of the painting in which the central significance is said to be a comment on the art of painting itself, suggested by Dou's self-portrait in the background. Viewed this way, the "dirt" of the baby's bottom "suggests the excremental nature of the quack's endeavors," and so becomes another derogatory comment on the "baseness" of artistic deception. I am not altogether persuaded by the reading, but the blasted tree and a whole array of other details certainly suggest some sort of moral commentary on the quack's business.

2 It was the German artist Joachim von Sandrart, *L'academia Tedesca . . . oder Teutsche Academie der edlen Bau-, Bild- und Mahlerey-Kunste* (Nuremberg, 1675), who described Dou's almost obsessive concern for finish (it was indeed this famous quality that led to his work's being so highly prized) and his anxiety to prevent any dust from settling on his pigments, brushes or paintings, even to the extent of raising a Chinese parasol (probably the one shown in *The Quack*) over them. See also W. Martin, *Gerard Dou* (London, 1902), 85.

3 De Brune, *Emblemata,* 17, "*Dit lijf wat ist, als stanck en mist?*"

4 In the famous case of Rembrandt's urinating *Ganymede,* it has been pointed out by Margarita Russell in "The Iconography of Rembrandt's *Rape of Ganymede,*" *Simiolus,* (1977):5–18, that an image that has been assumed to be "shocking" or earthily realistic was drawn from conventional classical and iconographic sources. Accordingly, the peeing baby is supposed to represent not the dirt but the purity

of infancy as well as Aquarius the water-bringer. That may well be (though I have my doubts), but it remains important to see that Rembrandt could well draw on an unorthodox image (for the *Ganymede* is certainly that) to lend his visual narrative an intensity and directness missing from more conventional versions.

5 See J. H. Plumb, "The New World of Children in 18th-Century England," *Past and Present* 65 (May 1975):64–95.

6 Philippe Ariès, *Centuries of Childhood,* tr. Robert Baldick (London, 1962), Chs. 1 and 2.

7 Aglionby, *Present State,* 230.

8 See Plumb, "New World"; see also Philip Greven, *The Protestant Temperament: Patterns of Child Rearing, Religious Experience and the Self in Early America* (New York, 1977), who divides up child-rearing attitudes into strict (evangelical-Calvinist), moderate (civic humanist) and tolerant (eighteenth-century affectionate).

9 See Walter Gibson, "Bosch's Boy with a Whirligig: Some Iconographical Speculations," *Simiolus* 8(1975–76):9–15. For a different view, see Mary Frances Durantini, *The Child in Seventeenth-Century Dutch Painting* (Ann Arbor, Mich., 1983), 245–49.

10 Leo Steinberg, *The Sexuality of Christ in Renaissance Art and in Modern Oblivion* (New York, 1983).

11 Frances Durantini, *The Child,* 233–45, has argued against identifying the whirligig or pinwheel with windmills and, by extension, with any reference to the incarnation and Crucifixion of Christ. She resists any such identification in the Bosch panel. The claim is based on the mistakenly literalist argument that since toy pinwheels need effort to turn and windmills need none the two could not possibly be conflated. She also claims that the Bosch is the only instance in which a child that might be the Christ is shown with such a whirligig. This is not the case. A mid-sixteenth-century triptych of panels in the Centraal Museum at Utrecht depicting *The Works of Mercy* plainly shows the Christ child holding the toy windmill or pinwheel while blessing the office of visiting the sick and giving alms. In this case it was evidently not intended there as an emblem of folly.

12 Jan Luiken, *'s Menschen Begin, Midden en de Einde vertoonde het Kinderlyk Bedryf en Aanwas* (Amsterdam, 1712), 13, "Het Loopwagen." The book was dedicated to his son Caspar for the instruction of his grandson.

13 Ibid., 17, "De Valhoed."

14 Luiken, 's Menschen Begin, foreword.

15 Swildens, Vaderlandsche AB boek, n.p.

16 Van Beverwijck, Schat der Gezondheid, 2:192.

17 See, in particular, the contributions of Sandra Hindman, "Pieter Bruegel's Children's Games: Folly and Chance," Art Bulletin (September 1981), 448–75; and the self-consciously "anti-iconographic" approach of Edward Snow: "Bruegel's Children's Games: The Limits of Iconographic Interpretation," Representations, 2 (1983): 25–53. On the Netherlandish context of the Bruegel painting see H. F. M. Peeters, Kind en jeugdige in het begin van de moderne tijd 1500–1650 (Amsterdam, 1975), 92–126; Johanna Drost, Het Nederlandsch Kinderspel voor de zeventiende eeuw ('s Gravenhage, 1914). On the significance of games in the history of childhood, see Aries, Centuries of Childhood, 60–97. For an exhaustive survey of the theme of play see Durantini, The Child, 177–296. The usefulness of Durantini's compendium of games is somewhat marred by an indiscriminate and theoretically chaotic approach to interpretation. I myself don't find the emblematic themes of death and the passage of time quite so ubiquitous in paintings of children. At least as often they are mediated by the opposite and more benign view of childish innocence, enthusiasm and robust vitality.

18 François Rabelais, Gargantua and Pantagruel, Ch. 25.

19 Cats, Houwelijck, 234.

20 "Kinderspel," in Cats, Houwelijck.

21 Visscher, Sinnepoppen, 40.

22 Cats, Spiegel van de Oude en de Nieuwe Tijt, in Alle de Werken, 496.

23 Cats, Houwelijck, 235.

24 Ibid.

25 See the excellent catalogue note by Peter Sutton, Masterpieces of Dutch Genre, 262–63; also Tot Lering en Vermaak, 177–79, and on the homo bulla theme more generally, Tot Lering, 45–47; Durantini, The Child, 91–204.

26 See John Knipping, Iconography of the Counter-Reformation in the Netherlands, vol. 1 (Nieuwkoop, 1974), 86–89.

27 Cats, Houwelijck, 235–36.

28 Cited in Durantini, The Child, 192.

29 Stone, The Family, Sex and Marriage, 70.

30 Rowen, De Witt, 496–97.

31 Le Francq van Berkhey, Natuurlyke Historie van Holland, vol. 3, 1958–64.

32 Robinson, "Family Portraits of the Golden Age," Apollo (December 1979), 490–97.

33 Vondel, Poëzie, II, 40.

34 On the kraamkloppertjes, see Le Francq van Berkhey, Natuurlijke Historie, vol. 3 (Leiden, n.d.), 1244ff.; Schotel, Oud-Hollandsch Huisgezin, 35–38.

35 Ibid., 41–50; for kraam- en kindermaalen, see Alkemade, Nederlands Displegtigheden, 1:243–49.

36 ARA, Hof van Holland, Index van Crimineele Sententien (May–June 1664).

37 Sjoerd Faber, "Kindermoord, in het bijzonder in de achttiende eeuw te Amsterdam," Bijdragen en Mededelingen betreffende de Geschiedenis der Nederland 98(1978):224–40; see also Lily E. van Rijswijk-Clerkx, Moeders, kinderen en kinderopvang... (Nijmegen, 1981), 30. (I am most grateful to Frances Gouda for this reference.)

38 S. Blankaart, Verhandeling van de ziekten der kinderen (Amsterdam, 1684).

39 See Franklin Robinson, Gabriel Metsu, 1629–1667: A Study of His Place in Dutch Genre Painting of the Golden Age (New York, 1974), 62.

40 Van Rijswijk-Clerkx, Moeders, 30; H. ter Schegget, Het kind van de rekening. Schetsen uit ve voorgeschiedenis van de kinderbescherming (Alphen aan den Rijn, 1976), 19, gives the figure of twenty-nine found-lings in Amsterdam in 1700 and seventeen for 1714—but the figure rises spectacularly at the very end of the century to four hundred in 1795!

41 On abandonment figures in France, see Claude Delasselle, "Abandoned Children in Eighteenth-Century Paris," in R. Forster and Orest Ranum, eds., The Deviant and the Abandoned in French Society: Selections from the Annales, vol. 4 (Baltimore, Md./London, 1978), 47–82.

42 Faber, "Kindermoord, in Het Bijzonder in de Achttiende eeuw te Amsterdam," in Bijdragen... Geschiedenis der Nederlanden (1978), 224–40.

43 Cats, Houwelijck ("Moeder"), 165–66. This famous passage was also quoted at length approvingly by van Beverwijck, Schat der Gezondheid.

44 [Nicolas Venette], Venus Minsieke Gasthuis (Amsterdam, 1687), 118.

45 Van Beverwijck, Schat der Gezondheid, 173–75.

46 Het kleyn Vroetwyfs-boeck of vermeerden Rosengaert van de bevruchte Vrouwen/ende hare Secreeten Ontfanginge Baring/Vrouwen ende Mannen raedt te gheven (1645), Bijvoegsel (Appendix), 9.

47 Ibid., 3–8.

48 [Nicolas Venette], Venus Minsieke Gasthuis, 472.

49 Rowen, De Witt, 508.

50 Kleyn Vroetwyfs-boeck, 9.

51 Van Beverwijck, *Schat,* Bk. 2, 164–75.

52 *Venus Minsieke Gasthuis,* 132; Cats verses cited in van Beverwijck, *Schat,* Bk. 2, 164.

53 Catharina Geertruida Schrader, "Dagboek van verlossingen 1693–1745" (Universiteits Bibliotheek, Amsterdam).

54 See the fascinating material researched by Florence W. J. Koorn en H. Roodenburg, "Kopsters: Vrouwen in de Marge van de Gezondheidszorg," *Spiegel Historiael* (March 1984), 125–29.

55 Ibid., 125. There are at least two representations of *kopsters* at work but ministering to very different clienteles: Quirijn Brekelenkam's elegant painting of 1650 in the Mauritshuis, which suggests a relatively respectable custom for the women, and Coernelis Dusart's print of 1695 in the Bruegelesque tradition of the human follies. For a discussion of the Dusart, see Linda Stone-Ferrier, *Dutch Prints of Daily Life* (Lawrence, Kan., 1983), 92–94.

56 See Hendrik van Roonhuysen, *Heelkomstige aanmerkingen betreffende de gebreken der vrouwen* (Amsterdam, 1663). On the conflicts between "official" and "empirical medicine," see M. A. van Andel, *Chirurgijns, Vrije Meesters, Beunhazen en Kwakzalvers. De chirurgijnsgilden en de praktijk der heelkunde 1400–1800* ('s Gravenhage, 1981).

57 Van Beverwijck, *Schat der Gezondheid,* 181.

58 See, for example, *De Listigheid der Kraamvrouwen* (Amsterdam, 1709).

59 Schrader, "Dagboek," 10 February 1711.

60 Ibid., 1 August 1706.

61 For these biographical details, see the "Levenschets" bound in with the "Dagboek."

62 See Appendix IV, p. 622.

63 There is still a great deal of uncertainty about infant mortality rates at delivery or in the first few days postpartum. There is no question that mortality rates in the first year varied from 15 to 30 percent, but much of that was certainly due to environmental circumstances—malnutrition, dysenteric and gastric diseases—rather than to obstetric malpractice. At any rate, the assumption that the stillborn rate in preindustrial Europe was higher than for industrial Europe should certainly not be taken for granted.

64 Jean Flandrin, *Familles.* See also François Lebrun, *Les Hommes et la Mort en Anjou au XVIIe et XVIIIe siècles* (Paris/The Hague, 1971), 182.

65 *Venus Minsieke Gasthuis,* 265.

66 *Kleyn Vroetwyfs-boeck,* 9.

67 See, for example, the case of 14 June 1711, and her note on *modereskruiden* on 1 August 1709. The medicines used by Vrouw Schrader corresponded closely to the pharmacopoeia represented in the standard obstetric and midwifery manuals of Rueff and Roesslin.

68 *Venus Minsieke Gasthuis,* 75.

69 Schrader, "Dagboek," 10 July 1697.

70 Ibid., 3 January 1727.

71 Ibid., 19 July 1708.

72 Ibid., 7 August 1696.

73 Ibid., 26 April 1742.

74 Ibid., "year account" 1703.

75 Ibid., 2 July 1701.

76 Ibid., 5 February 1710.

77 Ibid., 3 January 1727.

78 Ibid., 15 November 1708.

79 Ibid., 9 June 1709.

80 Blankaart, *Verhandelinge van de Ziekten der Kinderen* (Amsterdam, 1684).

81 Ibid., 32. Blankaart also advised against explaining the facts of life to children until they were mature enough to comprehend sexual biology responsibly—though he was, like all adults then and now, not altogether certain when that time would come about.

82 Ibid., 22–23.

83 Van Beverwijck, *Schat der Gezondheid,* 2, 183.

84 Blankaart, *Verhandeling,* 173ff.

85 For example, Stone, *The Family,* 424–26.

86 Ibid., 425. In fairness, Stone is here citing an eighteenth-century child care authority, William Cadogan. He is correct in assuming that England led the way in abandoning swaddling during the century, though it is less clear that *tight* swaddling was followed so rigorously in the rest of Europe, excepting Russia. On Dutch eighteenth-century attitudes, see le Francq van Berkhey, *Natuurlijk Historie,* 2:1219.

87 Blankaart, *Verhandeling,* 3.

88 Cats, *Moeder, Houwelijck,* 391.

89 Van Beverwijck, *Schat der Gezondheid,* 2:187.

90 Ibid., 188.

91 Blankaart, *Verhandeling,* 2–3.

92 Ibid., 6–8.

93 Schotel, *Het Oudhollandsch Huisgezin,* 27; Knappert, "Het Huiselijk Leven," 125.

94 Steinberg, *Sexuality of Christ,* 5–6.

95 Schotel, *Vaderlandsche Volksboeken,* 2:261.

96 De Brune, *Emblemata,* 75.

97 Murris, *La Hollande,* 110.

98 For a brief discussion of the emblematic role of the *krakeling,* see E. de Jongh et al., *Tot Lering en Varmaak* (Amsterdam, 1976), 69–71.

99 Dirck Adriaensz. Valcoogh, *Regel der Duytsche Schoolmeesters,* ed. G. D. J. Schotel (1875).

100 For a useful typology of "relaxed" and "severe" Protestant attitudes towards early education see Philip Greven, *The Protestant Temperament* (New York, 1977).

101 On grape symbolism, see de Jongh, "Grape Symbolism," 1974.

102 Blankaart,*Verhandeling,* 30–32;VanBeverwijck,*Schat der Gezondheid,* 190.

103 Blankaart, *Verhandeling,* 28.

104 Ibid., 135–38.

105 Van Beverwijck, *Schat der Gezondheid,* 2:192–93.

106 See Norbert Elias, *The Civilizing Process* (New York, 1978).

107 Luiken, *'s Menschen Begin.*

108 Rowen de Witt, 506.

CHAPTER EIGHT
INSIDE, OUTSIDE

1 Huizinga, *Dutch Civilization in the Seventeenth Century,* tr. Arno Pomerans (London/New York, 1968), 112–13.

2 Schama, *Patriots,* 50–51, 74–88.

3 Rudolf Dekker, *Holland in beroering, oproeren in de 17de en 18de eeuw* (Baarn, 1982), Chs. 1, 2.

4 See Susan Kuretsky, *The Paintings of Jacob Ochtervelt, 1634–1682* (Montclair, N.J., 1979), 34–39.

5 Parival, *Les Délices de la Hollande* (Leiden, 1662), 98.

6 For example, in Catharina Lis and Hugo Soly, *Poverty and Capitalism in Pre-Industrial Europe* (Atlantic Highlands, N.J., 1979), 93.

7 Jacobus Hondius, *Swart Register van Duysent Sonden* (Amsterdam, 1724), 1.

8 See W. P. Blockmans and W. Prevenier, "Armoede in de Nederlanden van de 14de tot het midden van de 16de eeuw: bronnen en problemen," *Tijdschrift voor Geschiedenis* 88 (1975):501–38; for an excellent concise survey of both the philosophy and practice of Dutch poor relief, see Van Deursen, *Kopergeld,* vol. 1, *Dagelijks Brood,* 90–103; see also the exhibition catalogue *Arm in de Gouden eeuw* (Amsterdam Historisch Museum, 1966).

9 The representation of charitable works and of the poorhouse regents has been admirably treated in Sheila D. Muller, *Charity in the Dutch Republic: Pictures of Rich and Poor for Charitable Institutions* (Ann Arbor, Mich., 1985). Muller's fine book, a model synthesis of social history and art history, appeared too late for me to absorb its interesting conclusions into my discussion.

10 Cited in Sjoerd Faber, *Strafrechtspleging en Criminaliteit te Amsterdam, 1680–1811* (Arnhem, 1983), 258.

11 Adriaen van de Venne, *Tafereel van de Belacchende Werelt* ('s Gravenhage, 1635).

12 See, for example, Louis Chevalier, *Laboring Classes and Dangerous Classes in Paris During the First Half of the 19th Century,* tr. F. Jellinek (London, 1973), 359–72.

13 Faber, *Strafrechtspleging,* 258.

14 Van Deursen, *Kopergeld,* vol. 1, *Dagelijks Brood,* 84.

15 See A. Hallema, "Vlaardingen en Dordrecht als oudste galeidepots," *Tijdschrift voor Geschiedenis* (1955):69–94.

16 ARA, Hof van Holland, Index van Crimineele Sententien (1631).

17 A. Boussingault, *La Guide universelle de tous les Pays-Bas . . .* (Paris, n.d. [c. 1660]), 43, for example, noted that one could travel "freely, by land or water, day or night without any fear of being molested or meeting ill company for the States take care that the highways are safe for all traffic." It must be said that the safety of some areas frequented by foreigners, especially in the center of The Hague, was deteriorating rapidly around the turn of the century. For some of the cases of attack and affray by the Vijver see R. C. Bakhuizen van den Brink, L. van den Bergh and J. K. J. de Jonge, "De Baljuwen," *Het Nederlands Rijksarchief* (1857): 235–303.

18 Van Deursen, *Kopergeld,* vol. 1, *Dagelijks Brood,* 74.

19 Brereton, *Travels,* 49.

20 Edward Brown, *A Brief Account of Some Travels in Divers Parts of Europe* (London, 1685), 95.

21 Faber, *Strafrechtspleging,* 232.

22 Bakhuizen van de Brink et al., "De Baljuwen," 244.

23 Ibid., 243–44.

24 See the excellent discussion in Van Deursen, *Kopergeld,* vol. 1, *Dagelijks Brood,* 53ff.

25 Faber, *Strafrechtspleging,* 263.

26 For a fuller discussion see M. Gans, *Memorbook: The History of Dutch Jews from the Renaissance to 1940* (Baarn, 1977); Simon Schama, "A Different Jerusalem: The Jews in Rembrandt's Amsterdam," in *The Jews in the Age of Rembrandt* (Rockville, Md., 1981), 3–17.

27 On circumcision in Christian iconology, see Leo Steinberg, *Sexuality of Christ,* 49–65.

28 Bakhuizen van den Brink et al., "De Baljuwen,"
    255–56.

29 Jonathan Israel, "Spain and the Dutch Sephardim,
    1600–1660," *Studia Rosenthaliana* 12 (1978), 1–61;
    idem, "The Changing Role of the Dutch
    Sephardim in International Trade, 1595–1715," in
    Jozeph Michman and Tirrsah Levie (eds.), *Dutch
    Jewish History. Proceedings of the Symposium in the His-
    tory of the Jews in the Netherlands* (Jerusalem, 1984).

30 I owe much of what follows to the careful research
    and rich insights of Ivan Gaskell, who was kind
    enough to let me read his unpublished paper on
    Gypsies in Dutch art. See also Ivan Gaskell, "Trans-
    formations of Cervantes's 'La Gitanilla' in Dutch
    Art," *Journal of the Warburg and Courtauld Institutes*
    45 (1982):263–70. The standard work on Dutch
    Gypsies is O. van Kappen, *Geschiedenis der Zigeuners
    in Nederland* (Assen, 1965).

31 See the discussion by Voetius in *Disputatio de
    Gentilissimo et de Vocatione Gentium,* in *Selectarum
    Disputationum Theologicarum,* vol. 2 (Utrecht, 1665),
    652–59.

32 Van Kappen, *Zigeuners,* 419.

33 For example, Pieter Neijn's *Lusthof des Houwelycks*
    (much despised and corrected by le Francq van
    Berkhey, *Natuurlijke Historie*), 1131.

34 Le Francq van Berkhey, *Natuurlijke Historie,* II,
    745–767.

35 I owe a reference in the English press to the feast
    to the kindness of Ruth Rogers, librarian of the
    Kress Library, Harvard Business School. It was
    attached to a print of the 1780s and would, of
    course, have been appropriate propaganda for the
    Patriot movement of that period. But I have seen
    much earlier references to the culinary allegory
    and suspect that it became part of a repertoire of
    stories about patriotic regrets circulating in
    Amsterdam throughout the middle and later parts
    of the century.

36 Bredero, *Spanish Brabanter,* tr. David H. Brumble
    (Binghamton, N.Y., 1982), 43. I have altered his
    translation from *herb* to *plant.*

37 On the challenge to the Grotian definition of the
    "True Liberty," see the excellent discussion in I.
    Leonard Leeb, *The Ideological Origins of the Batavian
    Revolution: History and Politics in the Dutch Republic
    1747–1800* (The Hague, 1973), 29–39.

38 A. H. Huussen, Jr., "Strafrechtelijke vervolging
    van 'sodomie' in de Republiek," *Spiegel Historiael*
    (November 1982), 547–52. This number of the
    periodical was devoted to the history of homo-

sexuality in the Netherlands and has a helpful
bibliography. Much the most important contribution to the history of homosexual prosecutions
in Amsterdam is the excellent work of Theo van
der Meer, *De Wesentlijke Sonde van Sodomie en Andere
Vuyligheden. Sodomietenvervolgingen in Amsterdam
1730-1811* (Amsterdam, 1984). See also L. J. Boon,
"De grote sodomietvervolging in het gewest Holland 1730–31," *Holland* 8 (1976):140–52; M. A. de
Vrijer, "De storm over *crimen nefandum* in de jaren
1730-32," *Nederlands Archief voor Kerkgeschiedenis* 25
(1932):193–238. I am extremely grateful to Kent
Gerard of the University of California, Berkeley,
for many very helpful bibliographic and intellectual comments on this phenomenon.

39 Huussen, "Strafrechtelijke," 549.

40 See G. M. Tervaert Cohen, *De grietman Rudolf de
    Mepsche. Historische beschouwingen over een reeks
    crimineele processen* ('s Gravenhage, 1921); C. Kooy,
    "Rudolf de Mepsche en de Faanse processen,"
    Spiegel Historiael 6 (1979): 358–64.

41 Huussen, "Strafrechtelijke," 557–58.

42 Ibid., 550. For a complete list of the sentences in
    all Amsterdam cases, see van der Meer, *Wesentlijke
    Sonde,* Appendix I, 201–209.

43 On Renswoude, see the fine article by L. J. Boon,
    'Utrechtenaren': de sodomieprocessen in Utrecht,
    1730-32," *Spiegel Historiael* (November 1982),
    553–58.

44 Ibid., 554–55.

45 GA Rechterlijke Archief, *Secreet Confessie Boek,* May
    1730.

46 Ibid.

47 Leonard Beels, *Sodoms Zonde en Straffe of Streng
    Wraakrecht over Vervloekte Boosheidt en Loths Vrouw
    Verandert in Een Zoutpilaar* (Amsterdam, 1730).

48 Knuttel 16857; Louis D. Petit, *Bibliotheek van Neder-
    landsche Pamfletten* 6087.

49 Alice Carter, "Amsterdam and the 'Een Onbekende
    Soort van Worm' in 1730," *Jaarboek Amstelodamum*
    (1978), 239–49.

50 For a comparison of Lelystad and Almere as town
    planning concepts, see the splendidly illustrated
    number of *Abitare* devoted to Holland, 236 (July-
    August 1985): 31–38.

51 Quoted in "Focus on Business Property," *Highlife
    Magazine* (March 1985), 37.

52 Henry James, *Transatlantic Sketches,* 384.

A BIBLIOGRAPHIC GUIDE TO THE
HISTORY OF DUTCH "*MENTALITÉ*"

A conventional, alphabetically arranged bibliography of all the works consulted for this book would be prohibitively long and of little help to anyone interested in pursuing research in the diverse aspects of the Dutch "mentality" treated in this book. Instead I have selected those primary and secondary sources that may be of most help to students and scholars of Dutch cultural and social history. Following lists of introductory guides (sections i–v), the titles are arranged for the most part in groups that correspond to my chapters.

i HISTORIES OF DUTCH CULTURE IN ENGLISH

At present there are only two works specifically devoted to this topic to consult, the magisterial essay of Huizinga, Johan, *Dutch Civilisation in the 17th Century*, London/New York, 1968; and the admirable survey by Price, J. L., *Culture and Society in the Dutch Republic During the 17th Century*, London, 1974. Aspects of Dutch culture are treated in two introductory histories, both excellent: Haley, K. H. D., *The Dutch in the Seventeenth Century*, London, 1972; and Wilson, Charles, *The Dutch Republic*, London/New York, 1968. Burke, Peter, *Venice and Amsterdam: A Study in 17th Century Elites*, London, 1974, is essentially a social comparison but has much to say on the education and mental world of the Amsterdam patriciate. More recently, Regin, Deric, *Traders, Artists, Burghers: A Cultural History of Amsterdam in the 17th Century*, Assen, 1976, is in many respects a very perceptive and sensitive account of its subject and has the virtue of not drawing formal lines between "society" and "culture" too severely. The argument of the book, however, is depressingly dominated by unexamined assumptions about what makes a "bourgeois society."

In many respects the most satisfactory guide to Dutch culture in English is the magnificent survey of Dutch painting in the seventeenth century by Haak, Bob, *The Golden Age: Dutch Painters of the Seventeenth Century*, New York, 1984. And many aspects of political and social history are treated as an integral part of the latest (and best) study on Rembrandt: Schwartz, Gary, *Rembrandt: His Life, His Paintings*, New York, 1985.

ii BIBLIOGRAPHIC GUIDES TO THE HISTORY
OF "*MENTALITÉ*" IN THE DUTCH REPUBLIC

Dronckers, Emma, ed. *Verzameling F. G. Waller: Catalogus van Nederlandsche en Vlaamsche Populaire Boeken*. 's Gravenhage, 1936. (This is one of the most important collections of popular literature in the Koninklijke Bibliotheek in The Hague.)

De la Fontaine Verwey, Herman. *Copy and Print in the Netherlands: An Atlas of Historical Bibliography.* Amsterdam, 1962.

Knuttel, P. C. *Catalogus van de pamflettenverzameling berustende in de Koninklijke Bibliotheek.* 9 vols. 's Gravenhage, 1888–1920.

Landwehr, John. *De Nederlander Uit en Thuis. Spiegel van het dagelijkse leven uit bijzondere zeventiende eeuwse boeken.* Alphen aan den Rijn, 1981.

Muller, Frederik. *Populaire Prozaschrijvers der XVIIe en XVIIe Eeuw.* Amsterdam, 1893.

Schotel, G. D. J. *Vaderlandsche Volksboeken en Volkssprookjes van de Vroegste tijden tot het einde der 18de Eeuw.* 2 vols. Haarlem, 1873–74.

iii ART HISTORICAL SOURCES AND POPULAR IMAGERY

Dutch art history has become such a lively and prolific field lately that is in this discipline that much of the most important analytical and interpretative work (much of it in English) on Dutch culture and society has been accomplished. I list here only the major works of importance for historical research. Many others on specific topics and artists are cited in the notes.

The Rijksbureau voor Kunsthistorische Documentatie (The Bureau for Art Historical Documentation) in The Hague has produced the indispensable guide for historical research in Dutch art: the *Decimal Index to the Art of the Low Countries* (D.I.A.L.) to themes and subjects in Dutch art. This should be the first resource for any historian investigating social motifs in Dutch culture.

PRINTS

There are two great print collections in the Netherlands of fundamental importance for the history of Dutch culture, society and politics. Their catalogues are, respectively:

Atlas, van Stolk, *Katalogus der Historie- Spot En Zinneprenten betrekkelijk De Geschiedenis van Nederland.* 2 vols. Amsterdam, 1887.

Muller, Frederik. *Beredeneerde beschrijving van Nederlandsche Historieplaten, zinneprenten en historische kaarten.* 3 vols. Amsterdam, 1863–82. (Collection to be found in the Rijksprentenkabinet, Amsterdam.)

Two further collections of prints are rich in materials relating to the social and cultural history of the Dutch:

The collection of the Koninklijke Genootschap voor Oudheidkunde, also kept at the Rijksprentenkabinet, Amsterdam.

The Douce Collection, Bodleian Library, Oxford.

The seminal work on Dutch prints and other imagery as a source for the history of mentality is van de Waal, H., *Drie Eeuwen Vaderlandsche Geschied-Uitbeelding,* 2 vols., 's Gravenhage, 1952, which has a splendid 60-page English summary. On popular imagery see van Heurck, E. M., and Boekenoogen, G. J., *Imagerie Populaire des Pays-Bas,* Paris, 1930.

Ackley, Clifford S., *Printmaking in the Age of Rembrandt,* Boston/New York, 1981, is a magnificent exhibition catalogue with an important essay by William Robinson on collecting and connoisseurship and a comprehensive bibliography.

Stone-Ferrier, Linda, *Dutch Prints of Daily Life: Mirrors of Life or Masks of Morals?,* Lawrence, Kans., Spencer Museum of Art, 1983, has a stimulating essay by the author on the present debate on interpreting Dutch art and much of interest to the cultural historian.

ILLUSTRATED BOOKS

It is generally recognized by scholars that Dutch illustrated books form an immensely rich repertoire of literature that makes nonsense of any formal division between "popular" and "polite" culture. Although there is a great deal of erudite bibliographic history concerning these books there is, surprisingly, nothing like a serious critical history. Nor are there serious monographic studies on any of the greatest of the illustrators: van de Venne, Crispijn van de Pas, Jan Claesz. Visscher, and (later in the century) Jan Luiken and Bernard Picart. Romeyn de Hooghe is somewhat summarily treated in Landwehr, John, *Romeyn de Hooghe (1645-1708) as Book Illustrator,* Amsterdam/New York, 1970. See also Langedijk, G., *Aesopus in Europa. Bemerkungen zur politisch-satirischen Graphik des Romeyn de Hooghe* (1645-1708); Ph.D. diss., Wilhelms-Universitat, 1972; Wilson, Harry T., "The Art of Romeyn de Hooghe," Ph.D. diss., Harvard University, 1974.

For some basic guidance on illustrated books see:

Benesch, Otto. *Artistic and Intellectual Trends from Rubens to Daumier as Shown in Book Illustration.* Cambridge, Mass., 1943. See pages 20-39.

Bol, L. J. "Adriaen van de Venne as an Illustrator." *Tableau* 56 (1984). (English summary of longer article in Dutch in the same periodical.)

De la Fontaine Verwey, Herman. "De gouden Eeuw van Nederlandse boekillustratie, 1600-1635." In idem. *Uit het wereld van het boek.* vol. 2. *Drukkers, liefhebbers en piraten in de zeventiende eeuw.* Amsterdam, 1976. See pages 49-76.

EMBLEM BOOKS

Emblem books have been shown to have been crucial in shaping both the visual and verbal culture of the seventeenth-century Dutch and many are very striking for the ways in which the most celebrated (Cats, de Brune and Visscher) depart radically in form and visual allusion from the standard repertoire of Renaissance humanism enshrined in Alciati. (Other books like that by Daniel Heinsius and Otto Vaenius remained much closer to the classical norm.) As a tool for recovering the meaning in some witty and some grave genre paintings they are essential but must be used with great discretion and care. Wise words on this subject may be found in:

De Jongh, E. "The Possibilities and Limits of Interpreting Genre Paintings." In Brown, Christopher, ed., *Images of the World: Dutch Genre Paintings in Their Historical Context,* London, forthcoming.

See also:

Landwehr, John. *Dutch Emblem Books: A Bibliography.* Utrecht, 1962.

Praz, Mario. *Studies in Seventeenth-Century Imagery.* Rome, 1964.

De Vries, A. G. C. *De Nederlandsche Emblemata.* 's Gravenhage, 1889.

Zijderveld, A. "Cesare Ripa's *Iconologia* in ons Land." *Oud Holland* 64 (1949):117-18.

The major emblem books used extensively in this study are:

De Brune, Johan. *Emblemata ofte Sinnewerck.* Amsterdam, 1624.

Cats, Jacob. *Alle de Werken.* Amsterdam, 1659.

Heyns, Zacharias. *Emblemata.* Rotterdam, 1625.

Luiken, Jan. *Het Leerzaam Huisraad.* Amsterdam, 1711.

———. *Spieghel van 't menschelyk bedryf.* Amsterdam, 1694.

———. *Des Menschen Begin, Midden en de Einde . . .* Amsterdam, 1712.

Visscher, Roemer. *Sinnepoppen.* Amsterdam, 1614.

PAINTINGS

Three major exhibitions in the past ten years have fundamentally altered the character of scholarship and of interpretation in the field of Dutch art. They have also produced catalogues of the first importance to the cultural historian, each with comprehensive bibliographies.

Rijksmuseum. *Tot Lering en Vermak.* E. de Jongh. Amsterdam, 1976.

National Gallery of Art. *Gods, Saints and Heroes: Dutch Painting in the Age of Rembrandt.* A. Blankert et al. Washington, D.C., 1980.

Philadelphia Museum of Art. *Masters of Seventeenth Century Dutch Genre Painting.* Peter Sutton. 1984. On this all-important subject see also Brown, Christopher, *Dutch Genre Painting,*

London, 1984. E. de Jongh, *Portretten van echt en trouw Huwelijk en gezin in de Nederlandse kunst van de zevertierde eeuw* (Haarlem, 1986), is a magnificent catalogue of the Hals museum exhibition devoted to family and marriage portraits. The introductory essay is of great importance to historians and art historians alike. Unfortunately this work appeared too late for me to incorporate its rich insights into this book.

Mention should also be made of two important catalogues on Dutch still life painting:

Stilleben in Europa, Münster/Baden-Baden, 1979, much of which deals with Dutch still lifes, but which exceeds plausibility in its relentlessly symbolic approach to these paintings.

Dutch Still-Life Painting, E. de Jongh et al., Auckland, New Zealand, 1983, provides important corrective essays.

Finally, although I find myself in disagreement with some of the argument of her book, Alpers, Svetlana, *The Art of Describing: Dutch Art in the Seventeenth Century,* Chicago, 1983, is of the first importance for any serious student of both Dutch art and Dutch history.

OTHER VISUAL SOURCES

Signboards and inscriptions

Van Lennep, J., and J. ter Gouw. *Het Boek der Opschriften.* Amsterdam, 1869.

Sweerts, Jeroen. *Koddige en Ernstige opschriften op luyffels, waggens, glazen, uythangborden.* Amsterdam, 1682–89.

Medals and medallions

Bizot, P. *Medallische historie der Republyk van Holland.* Amsterdam, 1690.

Van Loon, Gerard. *Beschryving der Nederlandsche Historiepenningen.* 2 vols. 's Gravenhage, 1723–28.

Roovers, O. N. "De noord-nederlandsche triumfpenningen." *Jaarboek van het Koninklijke Nederlandsch Genootschap voor Munt en Penningkunde* (1953):1–49.

Ephemeral architecture and triumphal entries

Barlaeus, C. *Marie de Médicis entrant dans Amsterdam, ou Histoire de la Réception faicte à la Reyne Mère du Roy très-Chréstien par les Bourgmaistres et Bourgeoisie de la Ville d'Amsterdam.* Amsterdam, 1638.

Dubiez, F. J. "Maria de Medicis, het bezoek aan Amsterdam in Augustus 1638." *Ons Amsterdam* (1958):266–77.

Snoep, D. P. *Praal en Propaganda Triumfalia in de Noordelijke Nederlanden in de 16de en 17de eeuw.* Alphen aan den Rijn, 1975.

Incised and chased silver

Frederiks, J. W. *Dutch Silver,* 4 vols. (The Hague, 1961), especially volume 4, *Embossed Ecclesiastical and Secular Plates from the Renaissance to the End of the 18th Century.*

Gans, M. H., and Th. M. Duyvenede Wit-Klinkhamer. *Dutch Silver.* London, 1961.

Glass

Van der Boom, A. *Monumentale Glasschilderkunst in Nederland.* 's Gravenhage, 1940.

Van Regteren Altena, J. Q., et al. *De Goudsche Glazes, 1555–1603.* 's Gravenhage, 1938.

Rijksen, A. A. J. *Gespiegeld in Kerkeglas.* Lochem, 1947.

References to other art historical works may be found below in connection with specific topics.

iv TRAVELERS' AND FOREIGN VISITORS' REPORTS

This is a valuable and prolific source for the history of the Republic, although caution needs to be exercised in taking many of these accounts at face value, or even assuming that items (especially in English) purporting to be "A Trip to Holland" are in fact any such thing. The vigorous industry of Hollandophobia in both England and France ensured many reprints, piracies and formulaic reworkings of tracts produced between 1650 and 1670 (see Chapter 6). Many more well-disposed accounts, moreover, depended on hearsay and standard texts rather than personal witness. Obviously much needs to be known about authorship before assessing the reliability of these accounts. Their sheer number, however, is astonishing.

The most helpful guides to this vast literature are:

Jacobson Jensen, J. N. *Reizigers te Amsterdam Beschrijvende lijst van reizen in Nederland door vreemdelingen voor* 1850. Amsterdam, 1919.

Murris, Roelof. *La Hollande et les Hollandais au XVIIe et XVIIIe Siècles Vus par les Français.* Paris, 1925.

v   MANNERS AND MORES BOOKS

The best guide in English remains Zumthor, Paul, *Daily Life in Rembrandt's Holland,* London, 1962, which, though heavily indebted to Murris's compilation on French travelers' reports, is still richly detailed and highly perceptive.

The great eighteenth-century work on manners (as well as physical and economic geography) is le Francq van Berkhey, J., *Natuurlyke Historie van Holland,* 4 vols., Amsterdam, 1769–79.

The nineteenth and early twentieth centuries added their own anthologies of *"zeden en gewoonten,"* the most interesting of which are:

Brugmans, H., ed. *Het Huiseljk en Maatschappelijk Leven Onzer Voorouders.* Amsterdam, 1931. In particular the contribution of Knappert, L., "Het Huiselijk Leven," pp. 100–210.

Schotel, G. D. J. *Het Oud-Hollandsch huisgezin der zeventiende eeuw.* Arnhem, 1903.

———. *Het maatschappelijk leven onzer vaderen in de zeventiende eeuw.* Arnhem, 1905.

Vrankrijker, A. C. J. *Het maatschappelijk leven in Nederland in de Gouden Eeuw.* Amsterdam, 1937.

vi   MORAL (AND PHYSICAL) GEOGRAPHY

For reports of the "drowning cell" and of the Amsterdam Tugthuis more generally see Sellin, Thorsten, *Pioneering in Penology: The Amsterdam Houses of Correction in the Sixteenth and Seventeenth Centuries,* Philadelphia, 1944. See also Hallema, A., *Geschiedenis van het Gevangeniswezen Hoofdzakelijk in Nederland,* 's Gravenhage, 1958.

The Bontekoe shipwreck ordeal is given in Bontekoe, Willem Ysbrantsz, *Memorable Description of the East Indian Voyage* 1618–25, translated and edited by C. B. Bodde-Hodgkinson and Pieter Geyl, London, 1929; another important disaster account is Pelsaert, Francisco, *Ongeluckige Voyagie van't Schip Batavia,* Amsterdam, 1648, translated in an English edition by Drake-Brockman, H., as *Voyage to Disaster: The Life of Francisco Pelsaert,* London, 1963. Many more such accounts are listed in Muller, *Populaire Prozaschrijvers,* and Schotel, *Vaderlandsche Volksboeken.* One of the most popular (and prototypical) was the *Kort Verhael van d'Avontuerlijcke Voyagien en Reysen van Paulus Olofsz. Rotman,* Amsterdam, 1657.

For flood and reclamation, see Lambert, Audrey, *The Making of the Dutch Landscape,* London/New York, 1971. See also the excellent essay by Borger, G. J., "Vorming en Verandering van het Hollandse landschap." In *Het Land van Holland: Ontwikkelingen in het Noord en Zuidhollandse landschap,* Amsterdam, 1978. The most comprehensive account of flooding in the medieval and Renaissance period is Gottschalk, M. K. Elizabeth, *Stormvloeden en rivierstromingen in Nederland,* Assen, 1974. The major account of the "waterschap" institutions in Holland is Fockema Andreae, S. J., *Overzicht van de Nederlandse waterschapsgeschiedenis,* Leiden, 1952. For the consequences of reclamation for Dutch agriculture, see de Vries, Jan, *The Dutch Rural Economy in the*

Golden Age, New Haven, Conn./London, 1974.

On myths and legends of the St. Elizabeth's Day Flood and of floating cats and cribs, see van de Waal, *Drie Eeuwen.* Andries Vierlingh's treatise has been published by de Hullu, J., and A. G. Verhoeven, eds., *Tractaet van Dyckagie,* 's Gravenhage, 1920.

vii   PATRIOTIC SCRIPTURE
(Early histories, Hebraism and national self-consciousness)
CONTEMPORARY HISTORIES
AND CHRONICLES

[Baudartius, W.] *Waarachtighe Beschrijvinghe ende Levendighe Afbeeldinghe vande Meer dan onmen-schelijke ende Barbarische Tyrannije bedreven by de Spaengiaerden in de Nederlanden.* Amsterdam, 1621.

Bor, Pieter. *Morgen-wecker der Vrije Nederlantscher Provintien.*

Van Goudhoeven, Wouter. *D'oude chronijke ende historien van Holland.* 's Gravenhage, 1636. A continuation of *Chronycke van Holland.*

Grotius, Hugo. *Verhandeling van de Oudheyt der Batavische nu Hollandtsche Republique.* 's Gravenhage, 1610.

———. *Nederlantsche Jaarboeken. en historien sedert het jaer MDLV tot het jaer MDCIX.*

Gijsius, Joh. *Ooorsprong en Voortgang der Neder-Lantsche Beroerten ende Ellendicheden.* Leiden? 1616.

Hooft, P. C. *Nederlandse Historien.* Amsterdam, 1642.

de Hooghe, Romeyn. *Spiegel van Staat der Vereenigde Nederlanden.* Amsterdam, 1706.

Van Meteren, E. *Belgische ofte Nederlantsche Historien van Onse Tijden.* Delft, 1605.

———. *Historie der Nederlantscher Oorlogen* ('s Gravenhage 1614)

Schrijver, Pieter [P. Scriverius]. *Beschrijving van Out Batavien met de Antiquiteyten vandien Mitsgaders D'afbeelding, Afcomst ende Histrie der Edelen Hoogh-geboren graven van Hollant, Zeelant en Vrieslant.* Amsterdam, 1636.

———. *Batavia Illustrata.* Leiden, 1609.

———. *Corte historische beschryvinghe der nederlantsche oorloghen.* Amsterdam, 1636.

Spiegel der Jeucht ofte Spaense Tyrannie. Dordrecht, 1614.

Wachtendorp, Casparus. *Oude Hollandsche Geschiedenissen.* 1645.

The indispensable work on early Dutch history writing is Kampinga, H. *De opvattingen van onze oudere vaderlandsche geschiedenis bij Hollandsche historici der XVIe en XVIIe eeuw.* 's Gravenhage, 1917. Van de Waal, H., *Drie Eeuwen,* is also of fundamental importance in any discussion of the emergence of a Dutch national self-consciousness. On the Batavian theme, see the fine essay by Schöffer, I. "The Batavian Myth during the Sixteenth and Seventeenth Centuries." In *Geschiedschrijving in Nederland,* edited by P. A. M. Geurts and A. E. M. Janssen, vol. 2, 's Gravenhage, 1981, 85–108. On popular histories, see Breen, Joh. C. "Gereformeerde populaire historiographie in de 17de en 18de eeuw." *Tijdschrift voor Geschiedenis* 37 (1922). On the Calvinist polemics of Baudartius see Broek Roelofs, O. C. "W. Baudartius." Ph.D. diss., Univ. of Amsterdam, 1947. On the representation of the Batavian theme in the Amsterdam town hall, see Buchbinder-Green, Barbara. "The Painted Decorations of the Town Hall of Amsterdam." Ph.D. diss., Northwestern University, 1975. For an account of the political background to Bol's *Moses* in the town hall, see Blankert, Albert. *Kunst als regeringzaak in de 17de eeuw: rondom schilderijen van Ferdinand Bol.* Lochem, 1975.

For a skeptical view of the role of early nationalism in the Dutch revolt, see Groeneveld, S. "Natie, en nationaal gevoel in de zestiende eeuwse Nederlanden." In *Scrinium et Scriptura: Opstellen betreffende de Nederlandse geschiedenis aangeboden aan J. L. van der Gouw.* Groningen, 1980, 372–87. On propaganda pamphlets during the revolt, see the comprehensive study by Geurts, P. A. M. *De Nederlandse Opstand in de pamfletten* (1566–1584). Nijmegen, 1956.

On the role of Calvinism in shaping patriotic self-consciousness, see Smitskamp, H. *Calvinistische nationaal besef in Nederland voor het midden der zeventiende eeuw.* 's Gravenhage, 1947. On the predikants as a social group and the church's concept of a new Israel, see the outstanding monograph by Groenhuis, G. *De Predikanten.* Groningen, 1977. For Vondel's comparison of the Dutch and Hebraic epics, see his play *Passcha ofte de Verlossinge Israels uit Egypten.* Amsterdam, 1612. For patriotic anthems, see Valerius, Adriaen. *Nederlantsche Gedenck-Clanck.* Edited by P. J. Meertens, N. B. TenHaeff and A. Komter-Kuipers. Amsterdam/Antwerp, 1947. Reprint. Also reprinted as *Nederlands Dank-offer over de behoudenis haarer Vrijheid.* Haarlem, 1626. See also van Alphen, H. *Nederlandsche Gezangen.* Amsterdam, 1779.

viii BEACHED WHALES AND OTHER PORTENTS

Afbeeldinge en Beschryving van de drie aenmerckens-waerdige wonderen in den Jare 1661 't Amsterdam. Knuttel Pamphlet 8937. Amsterdam, 1665.

Van Deinse, A. B. *Over de potvischen in Nederland gestrand tusschen de jaren 1531-1788, Zoologische Mededeelingen.* Leiden, 1918, 22-50.

Eijffinger, Arthur. "Zin en Beeld: Eenige Kanttekeningen bij twee historieprenten." *Oud Holland* 93(1979).

Hill, Boyd. *Old World Marine Prints in the Kendall Whaling Museum, 1520-1785.* Sharon, 1986.

De Jong, C. *Geschiedenis van de oude Nederlandse walvisvaart.* 3 vols. Johannesburg, 1979.

Kraynenga, André. "Een beeld van waarheid; rond de stranding van een potvis." *Teylers Museum Magazijn* (Spring 1984), 1-4.

Niemeyer, J. W. "Een gestrande potvis." *Bulletin Rijksmuseum* 12 (1964):20-25.

Timm, W. "Der gestrandete Wal, eine motivkundliche Studie." *Forschung und Staatsmuseum Berlin.* 1961.

Twist, Pieter Jansz. *Comeet-boeckxen.* Hoorn, 1624. Further editions until 1681.

De Vries, Simon. *Wonderen soo aen als in, en-Wonder-Gevallen Soo op als omtrent De Zeen, Rivieren, Meiren Poelen en Fonteynen.* Amsterdam, 1687.

Zorgdrager, C. G. *Bloeyende opkomst der aloude en hedendaagsche Groenlandsche visschery.* Amsterdam, 1720.

See also the notes to Goltzius, Buytewech and Saenredam prints in Ackley, Clifford, *Printmaking in the Age of Rembrandt,* and Stone-Ferrier, Linda A., *Dutch Prints of Daily Life.*

ix FOOD, DRINK, TOBACCO

COOKBOOKS

van Eeghen, I. "Oude Kookboeken." *Maandblad Amstelodamum* 61(1974):91-93.

De Nieuw wel-ervarene Nederlands Keuken-Meyd. Amsterdam, 1775.

[Nijland, Petrus.] *De Verstandige Kok of Sorghvuldige Huyshoudster.* Amsterdam, 1668. And fifteen editions until 1800!

Sels, Hilda L. F. C. "Zuidnederlandse Kookboeken na de Middeleeuwen." *Spiegel Historiael* 20.

Van 't Veer, A. *Oud Hollands Kookboeken.* Utrecht, 1966.

De Volmaakte Hollandse Keukenmeid. Amsterdam, 1761.

FOOD AND DIET HISTORY

Blankaart, S. *Gebruik en misbruik van de thee.* Amsterdam, 1686.

Bruyn, J. "Men on Board, 1700-1750," *Acta Historiae Nederlandica* (1975).

Burema, L. *De Voeding in Nederland van de Middeleeuwen tot de twintigste Eeuw.* Assen, 1953.

Van Deursen, A. Th. *Het kopergeld van de Gouden Eeuw.* Vol. 1, *Het dagelijks brood.* Assen/ Amsterdam, 1978.

Nannings, J. H. *Brood en Gebakvormen en hunne Beteekenis in de Folklore.* Scheveningen, n.d.

Pluim, T., and J. N. van Hesteren. *Schetsen uit onze Beschavingsgeschiedenis.* Purmerend, 1898.

Scholte-Hoek, C. H. A. *Het gastmaal en de tafel in de loop van tijden.* Amsterdam, 1965.

Schotel, G. D. J. *Letterkundige bijdragen tot de geschiedenis van den tabak, de koffij en de thee.* 's Gravenhage, 1848.

ON DRINK AND DRINKING CEREMONIES

Van Alkemade, K., and P. van der Schelling. *Nederlands Displegtigheden.* 2 vols. Rotterdam, 1732.

Van Deursen. *Het kopergeld van de Gouden Eeuw.* Vol. 2, *Volkskultuur.* Amsterdam/Assen, 1978.

[Pers, D.] *Bacchus Wonder-Wrecken* [sic] *waar in het recht Gebruyck en misbruyck der Wijns door verscheyden vermaeckelijcke eerlijcke en leerlijck historien wort afgebeeld.* Amsterdam, 1628. Engravings by Gillis Scheyndel.

Zeeman, H. *Drank en Drinkwinkels in Nederland van de Vroegste Tijden tot op Heden.* Amsterdam, 1866.

TOBACCO

Brongers, G. A. *Nicotiana tabacum: The History of Tobacco and Tobacco Smoking in the Netherlands.* Amsterdam, 1964.

——. *Pijpen en tabak.* Bussum, 1964.

Brooks, Jerome E. *Tobacco, Its History Illustrated by the Books, Manuscripts and Engravings in the Collection of George Arents, Jr.* 5 vols. New York, 1937–52.

Everaerts, Gillis. *Panacea or the Universal Medicine.* London, 1659.

Roessingh, H. K. *Inlandse Tabak. Expansie en contractie van een handelsgewas in de 17de en 18e eeuw in Nederland.* Wageningen, 1976.

Schotel, G. D. J. *Den tabak, koffij en thee.* Amsterdam, 1848.

Schrijver, Pieter [Petrus Scriverius]. *Saturnalia ofte Poëtisch Vasten-Avondspel* . . . Translated by Samuel Ampzing. Haarlem, 1630.

STILL LIFES, VANITAS AND "SMOKER" PAINTINGS

Bergstrom, Ingvar. *Dutch Still-Life Painting in the Seventeenth Century.* London, 1956.

Ijdelheid der ijdelheden Hollands vanitas-voorstellingen der zeventiende eeuw. Exhibition catalogue. Stedelijk Museum De Lakenhal. Leiden, 1970.

Knuttel, Gerard. *Adriaen Brouwer: The Master and His Work.* Den Haag, 1962.

Schmidt-Degener, F. *Adriaen Brouwer et son évolution artistique.* Brussels, 1908.

Still-Life in the Age of Rembrandt. Exhibition catalogue. Auckland, New Zealand, 1982.

Stilleben in Europa. Exhibition catalogue. Munster/Baden-Baden, 1979–80.

Vroom, N. R. A. *A Modest Message as Intimated by the Painters of the "Monochrome Banketje."* 2 vols. Schiedam, 1980.

x STEREOTYPES AND SELF-IMAGES IN WAR AND PEACE

A typical popular pamphlet discussion of the virtues of peace is *Den Ongeveveynsden Nederlandschen Patriot,* Alkmaar, 1647; and many similar items may be found at appropriate dates in Knuttel, *Pamfletten.* The States Party view of the Republic's place in the world and its economic and political foundations was classically expressed in [de la Court, Pieter], *Interest van Holland, ofte gronden van Hollands-Welvaren,* Amsterdam, 1662. On de la Court, see the helpful article by van Tijn, Th., "Pieter de la Court. Zijn leven en economische denkbeeld," *Tijdschrift voor Geschiedenis* 69(1956):304–70. For the part de Witt may have played in the work see Fruin, R., "Het aandeel van den Raadpensionaris de Witt aan het Interest van Holland van Pieter de la Court," *Verspreide*

Geschriften 8:42–53. On de Witt's own views of the security of the Republic, see the definitive biography by Rowen, H., *John de Witt, Grand Pensionary of Holland, 1625–1672,* Princeton, N.J., 1978. A typical specimen of States Party justification of their defensive attitude to war is *Den Hollandschen Verre-Kyker,* 1671, which attempted to forestall the prospects of imminent military conflict. On the theoretical disputes over the nature of the Dutch state, see the lucid and perceptive account by Kossmann, E. H., *Politieke theorie in het zeventiende-eeuwse Nederland,* Amsterdam, 1980.

The anti-States Party (or "dynastic") view of the place of the army is discussed in Geyl, P., *Orange and Stuart,* and the crisis of 1650 by Poelhekke, J. J. On the prolonged military engagement of the Republic in the first half of the century, see Israel, J. I., *The Dutch Republic and the Hispanic World,* Oxford, 1984, and Poelhekke, J. J., *Frederik Hendrik Prins van Oranje. Eeen biographisch drieluik,* Zutphen, 1978.

On the reporting of naval warfare, and the political implications of the publicity, see the interesting study of Haije, Chr. F., *De Oprechte Haarlemsche Courant en Michiel Adriaansz. de Ruyter,* Haarlem, 1908; and on the early press more generally, Sautijn Kluit, W. P., *De Haarlemsche Courant,* Amsterdam, 1871. For the celebration of naval heroes see Bosch, Lambertus van den [Sylvius], *Leven en Daden der Doorlugtige Zee-Helden en Ontdeckers,* Amsterdam 1676; and for a modern anthology of poetry dealing with public events, see Scheuleer, D. F., *Van Varen en Vechten,* 's Gravenhage, 1914. For patriotic songs and anthems, see the splendid collection by van Vloten, J., *Nederlandse Geschiedzangen,* Amsterdam, 1864. There is as yet no work dealing systematically with the image of war in Dutch graphic art, or even of soldiers in *kortegarde* genre paintings. For a treatment of one aspect of the conflict between soldiers and civilians in art, see Fishman, Jane Susannah, *Boerenverdriet: Violence between Peasants and Soldiers in Early Modern Netherlands Art,* Ann Arbor, Mich., 1983. The visual aspects of Dutch public self-celebration are best treated through the medallic history of events, especially Van Loon, *Beschryving,* and Nicolas Chevalier, *Histoire de Guillaume III,* Amsterdam, 1692.

For the Dutch economy as cynosure, see Appleby, Joyce Oldham, *Economic Thought and Ideology in Seventeenth-Century England,* Princeton, N.J., 1978; and contemporary accounts by Burrish, Onslow, *Batavia Illustrata or a View of the Policy and Commerce of the United Provinces,* London, 1731, and Child, Josiah, *A Treatise Concerning the East India Trade,* London, 1681. For the perennial conflicts that arose from some of these perceptions and misperceptions see Barbour, Violet, "Dutch and English Shipping in the Seventeenth Century," *Economic History Review* (1930) 261–90; Farnell, J. E., "The Navigation Act of 1651, the First Dutch War and the London Merchant Community," *Economic History Review,* 439–54; Wilson, Charles, *Profit and Power,* London, 1957; ——, "Cloth Production and International Competition in the 17th Century." Non-Netherlands source material for the Anglo-Dutch wars is to be found in Colenbrander, H. T., ed., *Bescheiden uit vreemde archieven omtrent de groote Nederlandsche zeevorlogen, 1652–1676,* 's Gravenhage, 1919.

Hollandophobia as a peculiar feature of seventeenth-century political culture in England and France has yet to receive proper treatment. By far the best account remains Coombs, Douglas, *The Conduct of the Dutch,* The Hague/Achimota, 1958, which deals principally with early-eighteenth-century literature. The primary source materials are very rich, especially in English, and some of the most notable works in the genre are:

[Carew, George.] *Fraud and Oppression Detected and Arraigned.* 1676.

Observations Concerning the present Affayres of Holland and the United Provinces. 1622.

[Felltham, Owen.] *A Brief Character of the Low Countries under the States Being Three Weeks' Observation of the Vices and Vertues of the Inhabitants.* London, 1652.

The Dutch-mens Pedigree, Or, A Relation Shewing How They Were First Bred and Descended from a Horse-Turd Which Was Enclosed in a Butter-Box. 1653.

The English and Dutch Affairs Displayed to the Life. London, 1664.

The Dutch Displayed. London, 1666.

Marvell, Andrew. "The Character of Holland"; "Instructions to a Painter about the Dutch Wars." *Poems.*

[Stubbes, Henry.] *A Justification of the Present War Against the United Netherlands.* 1672.

——. *A Further Justification.* 1673.

The Interest of England in the Present War with Holland. 1672.

Several Remarckable Passages Concerning the Hollanders. London, 1673.

The Dutch Won't Let Us Have Dunkirk. 1712.

A Search After Dutch Honesty. 1712.

The Fable of the Cods' Heads. 1712.

The military and political crisis of 1672 and its polemics are dealt with in the fine work of Roorda, D., *Het Rampjaar: 1672*, Bussum, 1971; as well as in Rowen, H., *John de Witt.* The causes of the war are freshly debated in Sonnino, Paul, "Hugues de Lionne and the Origins of the Dutch War," *Proceedings of the Third Meeting of the Western Society for French History*, 68–78; and ——, "Colbert and the Dutch War," *European Studies Review*, 3–9, and "Louis XIV and the Dutch War," in *Louis XIV and Europe*, edited by R. Hatton, Columbus, Ohio, 1976. The war is more traditionally dealt with by Elzinga, Simon, *Het Voorspel van den Oorlog van 1672*, Haarlem, 1926. See also, Ekberg, Carl J., *The Failure of Louis XIV's Dutch War*, Chapel Hill, N.C., 1979.

Dutch counterpropaganda is reviewed in van Malssen, P. J. W., "Louis XIV d'après les Pamphlets Repandus en Hollande," Ph.D. diss., Univ. of Amsterdam, 1936. The most powerful texts, visually as well as textually, were:

Van den Bosch, Lambert. *Tooneel des Oorlogs in de Vereenigde Nederlanden* . . . Amsterdam, 1675.

Van Domselaer, Tobias. *Het Ontroerde Nederlandt* . . . Amsterdam, 1674.

De Hooghe, Romeyn. *Schouwburg van Nederlandse Veranderinge Geopent in Ses Toneelen.* Amsterdam, 1674.

Journael of daghelijcksche verhael van de handel der Franschen in de Steden Utrecht en Woerden. Amsterdam, 1674.

Korte verhaal rakende de oprechte Hollanders . . . 's Gravenhage, 1674.

Toets-Steen voor de Herten der Batavieren tot onderschedt van de Goede en de Quade. 1673.

Valkenier, Petrus. *'t Verwerd Europa, ofte Politijke en Historische Beschryvinge.* Amsterdam, 1675.

[de Wicquevort, A.] *De Fransche Tyrannie.* 2 vols. Amsterdam, 1674.

[de Wicquevort, A.] *Advis Fidelle aux Véritables Hollandois* . . . The Hague, 1673.

For French imagery of the war of 1672, see the superb *Collection Hennin* in the Bibliothèque Nationale, Paris (*Inventaire de la Collection d'Estampes relatives à l'histoire de France*), especially almanac frontispieces:

4598   *La France florissante*

4613   *La réjouissance des soldats françaises sur la déclaration de la guerre contre les Hollandois*

4615   *Les merveilleux progrès du roy*

4618   *Rhin passée à la nage par les Français*

There are many Calvinist sermons preached at the height of the crisis in 1672–73 contained in the pamphlet collection at the Koninklijke Biblitheek, The Hague (see the Knuttel *Catalogus*). Typically apocalyptic were, for example:

KN 10237   *Beklagh over den Bedroefden Toestant in de Nederlantse Provintien.* Amsterdam, 1672.

KN 9932   *Eenige Prophetien en Revelatien Godts Aengaende de Christen Werelt in dese Eeuw.* Amsterdam, 1672.

xi   THE CULTURE OF ABUNDANCE

CIVIC EULOGIES AND GUIDEBOOKS

Amsterdam

Barlaeus C. (van Baerle). *Marie de Médicis entrant dans Amsterdam, ou Histoire de la Réception faicte à la Reyne Mère* . . . *par les Bourgmaistres et Bourgeoisie de la Ville d'Amsterdam.* Amsterdam, 1638.

Dapper, Olfert. *Historische beschryving der stadt Amsterdam.* Amsterdam, 1663.

Van Domselaer, Tobias. *Beschryving der Stat Amsterdam van haar eerste beginselen oudtheydt vergrootingen en gebouwen ... tot op den jare 1665.* Amsterdam, 1665.

Fokkens, Melchior. *Beschryvinge der Wijdt-vermaarde Koop-Stadt Amsterdam.* Amsterdam, 1664.

Van Vondel, J. "Bouwzang" (On the Town Hall), *Poëzy* 1 (Franeker 1716):374; "Amstelredam," 2:297.

Vos, Jan. "Vergrooting van Amsterdam." *Alle de gedichten.* Vol. I, 123ff. Amsterdam, 1726. (Also published as a pamphlet, KN 8666.)

Von Zesen, Philips. *Beschreibung der Stadt Amsterdam.* Amsterdam, 1664.

On the town hall as civic apotheosis see:

Buchbinder-Green, Ruth. "The Painted Decorations of the Town Hall of Amsterdam." Ph.D. diss., Northwestern University, 1974.

A Description of the City House of Amsterdam. Amsterdam, 1751.

Fremantle, Katherine. *The Baroque Town Hall of Amsterdam.* Utrecht, 1959.

Delft

Van Bleiswijk, Dirck. *Beschryvinge der Stadt Delft.* Delft, 1667.

Haarlem

Ampzing, Samuel. *Beschryving ende Lof der Stad Haarlem in Holland.* Haarlem, 1628.

Leiden

Van Hout, Jan. *Der stadt Leiden dienst-bou.* Leiden, 1602.

Orlers, Jan Jansz. *Beschriving der Stadt Leyden.* Leiden, 1641.

For the realities of town planning behind the ostensible commitment to "planning," see the brilliant study by Taverne, Ed, *In het land van 't belofte: in de nieuwe stadt ideaal en werkelijkheid van stadsuitleg in de Republiek, 1580-1640.* Maarssen, 1978.

Dordrecht

Balen, D. *Beschrivinge der stadt Dordrecht.* Dordrecht, 1677.

THE HOUSE AS POSSESSION

The best sources for reconstructing the furniture and possessions of Dutch households are in probate records and bankruptcy inventories. For details of those used in my account see notes under Chapter 5. For a helpful report on systematic work in progress in these sources, see Faber, Johannes A., "Inhabitants of Amsterdam and Their Possessions, 1701-1710," in *Probate Inventories: A New Source for the Historical Study of Wealth, Material Culture and Agricultural Development,* edited by Ad van de Woude and Anton Schuurman, A.A.G. Bijdragen 23, Wageningen, 1980, 149-55. Profiles of the wealth of patrician families may also be recovered from marriage settlement inventories contained in the family papers of dynasties such as the Bickers, Backers, de Graeffs, Schaeps, etc. (See respective inventories published by van Eeghen, I. H., Gemeentelijke Archief Amsterdam.)

The inventory of furniture of the Stadholder's Residence in The Hague has been published by Drossaen, S. W. A., with additional note by C. Hofstede de Groot, and C. H. de Jonge, eds., "Inventaris van de Meubelen," *Oud Holland,* 1930, 193-236.

For secondary sources on burgher material culture see:

Kuyper, W. *Dutch Classicist Architecture.* Delft, 1980.

Leonhardt, Gustav M. *Het Huis Bartolotti en zijn bewoners.* Amsterdam, 1979.

Levie, T., and H. J. Zantkuil. *Wonen in Amsterdam.* Amsterdam, 1983.

Meischke, R., and H. J. Zantkuil. *Het Nederlandse Woonhuis van 1300-1800.* Haarlem, 1969.

Schotel, G. D. J. *Het Oud-Hollandsch Huisgezin der Zeventiende Eeuw.* Leiden, n.d.

Sluyterman, K. *Huisraad en Binnenhuis in Nederland in Vroegere Eeuwen.* 's Gravenhage, 1918.

Staring, A. *De Hollanders Thuis. Gezelschapstukken uit drie eeuwen.* 's Gravenhage, 1956.

Thornton, Peter. *Seventeenth-Century Interior Decoration in England, France and Holland.* New Haven, Conn./London, 1978.

CALVINISM AND THE EMBARRASSMENT OF RICHES

A great deal has been written on this topic, but inevitably with the object of either validating or invalidating the Weber thesis. See, for example:

Hyma, Albert. "Calvinism and Capitalism in the Netherlands, 1555–1700." *Journal of Modern History,* 1938.

Riemersma, Jelle C. *Religious Factors in Early Dutch Capitalism* 1550–1650. The Hague, 1967.

Van Stuijvenberg, J. H. "The Weber Thesis: An Attempt at Interpretation." *Acta Historiae Neerlandica* (1975): 50–66.

A less programmatic approach would be to return directly to the source materials of Calvinist preaching and tract writing on commercial and pecuniary subjects. See in particular:

Cloppenburgh, Johannes. *Christclycke onderwijsinge van woeker, interesseo, coop van renten ende allerleye winste van gelt met gelt.* Amsterdam, 1637.

Hondius, Jacobus. *Swart Register van duysent Sonden.* Hoorn, 1675.

Krul, J. *Wereldt-hatende Noodtsaeckelijke.* Amsterdam, 1627.

't Samen-spraeck voorgestelt van vier personen . . . KN 10022. 1672.

Saumaise, Claude. *Dissertatio de Foenore Trapezitico.* Leiden, 1640.

Trigland, J. *Opuscula, dat is verscheyden boeken en tractaten.* 2 vols. Amsterdam, 1639–40.

Udemans, Cornelis. *Geestelijk Roer van 't Coopmans Schip.* Dordrecht, 1640.

For the criticism by church synods of bankers ("lombards"), Sunday trading, usurious practice, etc., see Reitsma, J., and S. D. van Veen, *Acta der Provinciale en Particuliere Synoden gehouden in de Noordelijk Nederlanden Gedurende de jaaren,* 1572–1620; 's Gravenhage, 1892; and Knuttel, W. P. C., *Acta der Particuliere Synoden van Zuid-Holland,* 1621–1700, 3 vols. 's Gravenhage, 1907–10.

For church attitudes in general to wealth, usury and money, see the superb general survey of the Amsterdam church by Evenhuis, R. B., *Ook dat was Amsterdam,* vols. 2 and 3, Amsterdam, 1965, 1971. And for the theme's treatment in Dutch art, the thought-provoking article by de Jongh, E., "Austerity and Extravagance in the Golden Age," *Apollo* (July 1967):16–25. The Kress Library, Harvard University, has a number of Dutch Calvinist polemics against wealth, many of them with engravings in the manner of Heemskerck, Jacques de Gheyn and Karel van Mander.

SPECULATION: LOTTERIES, THE TULIP MANIA

Catalogus der Tentoonstelling, van Teekeningen, Schilderijen, Boeken, Pamfletten betreffende de Geschiedenis van de Bloembollencultuur en de Bloembollenhandel. Haarlem, 1935.

Cole, Arthur H. *The Great Mirror of Folly* [*Het Groote Tafereel der Dwaasheid*]*, An Economic-Bibliographic Study.* Boston, 1949.

Fokker, G. A. *Geschiedenis der Loterijen in de Nederlanden.* Amsterdam, 1862.

Krelage, E. H. *Bloemenspeculatie in Nederland.* Amsterdam, 1942.

Chrispijn de Pas(se). *Hortus Floridus* [*Den Bloemhof*]*.* Utrecht, 1614.

Posthumus, N. W. "The Tulip Mania in Holland in the Years 1636 and 1637." *Journal of Economic History* 1(1929):435–65.

Smith, M. F. J. *Tijd-affaires in effecten aan de Amsterdamsche beurs.* 's Gravenhage, 1919.

De la Vega, Joseph. *Confusion de Confusiones, 1688: Portions descriptive of the Amsterdam Stock Exchange.* Selected and translated with an introduction by Herman Kellenbenz. Boston, 1957.

xii HOUSEHOLD AND FAMILY LIFE:
WOMAN AND RELATIONS BETWEEN THE SEXES

While there has been considerable emphasis in Dutch historiography on quantitative and demographic aspects of the household, there is as yet only a sparse literature on the culture of the Dutch family. (For household size, see van der Woude, A. M., "Variations in the Size and Structure of the Household in the United Provinces of the Netherlands in the Seventeenth and Eighteenth Centuries," in *Household and Family in Past Time,* edited by Peter Laslett and Richard Wall, Cambridge, Eng., 1972, 299–318. The pioneering work in many respects is Haks, Donald, *Huwelijk en Gezin in Holland in de 17de en 18de Eeuw,* Assen, 1982. Much may be learned of property relations between husbands and wives from the notarial records in Holland (subject-indexed in Amsterdam for the years 1700–10) and from marriage settlement documents preserved in family archives. (Those of the de Graeff, Bicker and Backer families in Amsterdam have been catalogued and published by the Gemeente Archief.)

CONTEMPORARY MARRIAGE AND HOUSEHOLD MANUALS

Van Beverwijck, J. *Van de Wtnementheyt des Vrouwelicken Geslachts.* Dordrecht, 1643.

Cats, Jacob. *Houwelijck.* In *Alle de Werken.*

De Deughdelijcke Vrou. Amsterdam, 1642.

De Ervarene en Verstandige Hollandsche Huyshoudster. N.d., probably early eighteenth century.

Heyns, Zacharias. *Deuchden-Schole ofte Spieghel der jonghe-dochteren.* Rotterdam, 1625.

Lof des Houwlijcks. Alkmaar, 1610.

Houwlijx-Spiegel aen de Nieuw Getroude. Haarlem, 1686.

Wittewrongel, Petrus. *Oeconomia Christiana ofte Christelicke Huyshoudinge.* Amsterdam, 1655.

De Verstandige Huyshouder voorschryvende de Alderwijste wetten om profijtelijcke, gemackeliijk en vermakkelijk te leven, so in de stadt als op 't landt. Amsterdam, 1661.

On some of this literature see Carter, Alice Clare, "Marriage Counselling in the Early Seventeenth Century: England and the Netherlands Compared," in *Ten Studies in Anglo-Dutch Relations,* edited by J. van Dorsten, Leiden, 1974, 94–127. For the legal aspects of marriage during and after the Reformation see the important work by van Apeldoorn, L. J., *Geschiedenis van het Nederlandsche Huwelijksrecht voor de invoering van de Fransche wetgeving,* Amsterdam, 1925. See also de Blecourt, A. S., *Kort begrip van het oud Vaderlands Burgerlijk recht,* Groningen, 1967, especially pages 72–88. On abortion, see de Bruyn, J., *Geschiedenis van abortus in Nederland,* 1979.

Some of the most stimulating work on the culture of the Dutch household has been done by art historians in connection with the interpretation of genre painting. See, for example:

Durantini, Mary Frances. *Studies in the Role and Function of the Child in Seventeenth-Century Dutch Painting.* Ann Arbor, Mich., 1982.

Hofrichter, Frima Fox. "Judith Leyster's *Proposition* — Between Virtue and Vice." In *Feminism and Art History: Questioning the Litany.* Edited by Norma Broude and Mary D. Garrard. New York, 1982, 173–82.

Rietsma, E. Snoep. "Chardin and the Bourgeois Ideals of His Time." *Nederlands Kunsthistorischejaarboek* 24 (1973):147–69.

Robinson, William W. "Family Portraits of the Golden Age." *Apollo* (December 1979): 490–97.

Schama, Simon. "Wives and Wantons: Versions of Womanhood in 17th Century Dutch Art." *Oxford Art Journal* (April 1980):5–13.

——. "The Sexual Economy of Genre Painting." In *Images of the World: Dutch Genre Painting in Its Historical Context.* Edited by Christopher Brown. London, forthcoming.

——. "Rembrandt and Women." *Bulletin of the American Academy of Arts and Sciences* 38 (April 1985): 21–47.

Smith, David R. *Masks of Wedlock: Seventeenth-Century Dutch Marriage Portraiture* (Ann Arbor, Mich., 1982).

Staring, A. *De Hollanders Thuis. Gezelschappen uit drie eeuwen.* 's Gravenhage, 1956.

The history of childhood in the Netherlands remains surprisingly sparsely covered and invariably much influenced by Ariès, Philippe, *Centuries of Childhood,* London, 1962. See, for example, Peeters, H. F. M., *Kind en Jeugdige in het begin van de moderne tijd,* Meppel, 1975. Van de Louw, G., "Enfant et société: l'example des Provinces Unies," *Revue de Nord* (1976): 185–208, does not live up to its ambitious title. Infanticide is statistically treated in Faber, S., "Kindermoord in her bijzonder in de achttiende eeuw te Amsterdam," *Bijdragen en mededelingen betreffende de geschiedenis der Nederlanden* 93(1978):224–40. For a brief treatment of the early history of parents and children, see van Rijswijk-Clerkx, Lily E., *Moeders, kinders en kinderopvoeding. Verandering in de kinderopvoeding in Nederland,* Nijmegen, 1981. On children's games, see Drost, Johanna, *Het Nederlandsch Kinderspel voor de 17de eeuw,* 's Gravenhage, 1914.

On children's literature, see the excellent account given in Kunzle, David, *The Early Comic Strip,* Berkeley, Cal., 1973, which also deals interestingly with popular stories about the Battle of the Trousers. Some of the finest of the early children's books are preserved in the Atlas van Stolk, Rotterdam, but the earliest extant ABC book to my knowledge is Boddink, N., *Stichtigh ABC Tot Nut den Jeuchd* (1639?), preserved in the Stadsbibliotheek, Haarlem.

PROSTITUTION

The basic primary sources for the study of prostitution in Amsterdam are the *Confessie Boeken* of the Rechterlijk Archief in the Gemeente Archief. The other major contemporary source is *'t Amsterdamsch Hoerdom,* 's Gravenhage, 1694, reprinted Amsterdam, 1681, also translated as *Le Putanisme d'Amsterdam,* Brussels, 1883. The book is very rare, but copies survive in the Bodleian Library, Oxford, the Bibliothèque Nationale, Paris, and the Koninklijke Bibliotheek, The Hague. Other contemporary works on "high-life" harlots are:

[Aretino, Pietro] *Het Leven en Listen der Geriefelycke Courtisanen.* 1680.

Het Leven en Bedryf van de hedendaagsche Haagsche en Amsterdamsche Zalet-Juffers. Amsterdam, 1696.

Spieghel der Alderschoonste Courtisanen deses Tyt. Amsterdam, 1630.

For modern accounts see van Slobbe, J. F., *Bijdrage tot de Geschiedenis en de Bestrijding der Prostitutie te Amsterdam,* Amsterdam, 1937; and the much richer, archivally based publications of van de Pol, Lotte, in particular, *Vrouwencriminaliteit en prostitutie in de tweede helft der 17e eeuw in Amsterdam,* and "Vrouwencriminaliteit in de Gouden Eeuw," *Ons Amsterdam* (November 1982):266–68.

MISOGYNIST SATIRE

This appears to have been a very important genre in virtually all western European cultures at the end of the seventeenth century and early in the eighteenth century. Just why this period saw a flowering of these biting antifeminine comedies remains mysterious and merits serious investigation. The Dutch genre, printed with crude engravings in octavo format, was extremely popular. See, in particular:

Felicius, Publius [Joh. Strander?]. *De Beurs der Vrouwen gesticht op Tien Pilaaren.* 1690.

Jonktijs, Daniel. *Heden-daagse Venus en Minerve.* Dordrecht, 1641.

———. *Toneel der Jalouzien.* Amsterdam, 1666.

De Mol, Jan. *Huwlijks Doolhof.* Amsterdam, 1634.

De Listigheid der Kraamvrouwen. Amsterdam, 1709.

De Vereezene Hippolytus. 1711.

Venus en Cupido. n.d. (late seventeenth century). An attack on décolletage.

Sweerts, H. *De Biegt der Getrouwde.* Amsterdam, 1679.

De Tien Vermakelijkheden des Houwelyks. Amsterdam, 1684.

[De Vries. S.] *Seeven Duyvelen Regerende de Hedendaagsche Dienst-Maaghden.* 4th ed. Amsterdam, 1682.

MEDICAL, SEXUAL, OBSTETRIC AND MIDWIFERY LITERATURE

Apart from the extraordinary witness provided by Catharina Schrader's journal (see Chapter 7), the archive of the Amsterdam Collegium Obstetricum (1668–1798) is preserved in the Gemeente Archief.

Van Beverwijck, J. *Schat der Gesontheyt.* Dordrecht, 1636.

——. *Schat der Ongesontheyt.* Dordrecht, 1647.

Blankaart, S. *Verhandeling van de opvoeding en Ziekten der Kinderen.* Amsterdam, 1684.

——. *Venus Belegert en Ontset oft Verhandeling van de Pokken.* Amsterdam, 1685.

Van Helmont, J. B. *Dageraad ofte Nieuwe opkomst der Geneeskonst.* 1659.

Het Kleyn Vroetwyfs-boeck of vermeerde Rosengaert der bevruchte Vrouwen. 1645.

Manuale Operatien zijnde een Nieuwe Ligt voor Vroed-meesters en Vroed Vrouwen. Amsterdam, 1701.

Van Roonhuysen, Hendrik. *Heelkomstige aanmerkingen betreffende de gebreken der vrouwen.* Amsterdam, 1663.

Roesslin, H. *Den rhosegaert van de bevruchte vrouwen.* Amsterdam, 1616.

Rueff, J. *'t Boek van de Vroet-wijf.* Translated by Martyn Everaart as *De Conceptu et Generatione homini* (Amsterdam, 1645).

[Venette, Nicolas] *Venus Minsieke Gasthuis.* Amsterdam, 1687. Seven editions by 1715.
A translation of the French physician's *Tableau de l'Amour Considéré dans l'Estat de Mariage,* originally published in French with a false imprimatur of Parma. Its real place of publication in many languages was Amsterdam.

xiii CULTURAL BOUNDARIES

VAGRANCY AND CRIMINALITY

There is a rapidly growing modern literature on the subject of crime and punishment in the Netherlands, particularly for the eighteenth century, where the evidence is abundant. Especially notable are two very important works:

Faber, Sjoerd. *Strafrechtspleging en Criminaliteit te Amsterdam, 1680–1811. De nieuwe menselievendheid.* Arnhem, 1983.

Spierenburg, Pieter. *The Spectacle of Suffering.* Cambridge, Eng., 1984.

For contemporary views of "rogues and vagabonds," see the picaresque poem by van de Venne, Adriaen, *Tafereel van de belacchende werelt en deselfs geluckige Eeuwe...,* 's Gravenhage, 1635. A fascinating dictionary of thieving cant and abuse has survived: *Historie ofte Practijke der Dieven Bestaende in aengehoorde wreeten en schelmerijen...* n.d. For contemporary criteria of crime and punishment, see the handbook by van Damhouder, Joost, *Practijcke in Crimineele Saecken,* Rotterdam, 1618. And for Dutch treatment of the vagrant and "delinquent," see Spierenburg, Pieter, "The Sociogenesis of Confinement and Its Development in Early Modern Europe," in *The Emergence of Carceral Institutions: Prisons, Galleys and Lunatic Asylums, 1550–1900,* edited by Spierenburg et al., Centrum voor Maatschappij Geschiedenis, Erasmus Universiteit, Rotterdam, 1984, 9–77. I am very grateful to Dr. Spierenburg for bringing this important collection of essays to my attention.

On the philanthropic response to poverty, see the exhibition catalogue, *Arm in de Gouden Eeuw.* Amsterdams Historisch Museum, 1965. There is an excellent discussion of the pictorial representation of charity: Muller, Sheila D., *Charity in the Dutch Republic: Pictures of Rich and Poor for Charitable Institutions,* Ann Arbor, Mich., 1985.

On other aspects of the marginalization of the poor see:

Blockmans, W. P., and W. Prevenier, "Armoede in de Nederlanden van de 14de tot het midden van de 16de eeuw: bronnen en problemen," *Tijdschrift voor Geschiedenis* 88(1975): 501–38.

Van Deursen, A. Th. *Het kopergeld van de Gouden Eeuw.* Vol. 1, *Het dagelijks brood.* Assen, 1978.

Lenna Jansen, H. J. "The Dutch Burgher and the Poor: a cultural history of the welfare system in Holland." Ph. diss., University of Chicago, 1979.

De Bosch Kemper, J. *Geschiedkundig onderzoek naar de armoede in ons vaderland . . .* Haarlem, 1851.

Mentink, G. J. "Armenzorg en armoede in de archivalische bronnen in de Noordelijke Nederlanden, 1531–1854." *Tijdschrift voor Geschiedenis* 88(1975):551–61.

Oldewelt, W. F. H. "Het aantaal Bedelaars, Vondelingen en Gevangenen te Amsterdam in Tijden van Welvaart en Crisis." *Jaarboek Amstelodamum* 39(1942):21–34.

GYPSIES AND JEWS

Van Dillen, J. G. "De economische Positie en Betekenis der Joden in de Republiek en in de Nederlandsche Koloniale Wereld." In *Geschiedenis der Joden in Nederland.* Edited by H. Brugmans and A. Frank. Amsterdam, 1940, 561–615.

Dirks, J. *Geschiedkundige onderzoekingen aangaande het verblijf der Heidens of Egyptiers in de Noordelijk Nederlanden.* Utrecht, 1850.

Gans, M. H. *Memorboek: The History of Dutch Jews from the Renaissance to 1940.* Baarn, 1977.

Israel, J. I. "Spain and the Dutch Sephardim, 1609–1660." *Studia Rosenthaliana* 12(1978):1–61.

van Kappen, O. *Geschiedenis de Zigeuners in Nederland. De ontwikkeling van de rechtspositie der Heidens of Egypetnaern in de noordelijke Nederland, 1420–1750.* Assen, 1965.

Michman, Jozeph, and Tirtsah Levie. *Dutch Jewish History, Proceedings of the Symposium on the History of the Jews in the Netherlands.* Jerusalem, 1984.

Morgenstein, Susan W., and Ruth S. Levine. *The Jews in the Age of Rembrandt.* Rockville, Md., 1982.

THE SODOMY TRIALS OF 1730–32

A special number of the popular Dutch historical magazine *Spiegel Historiael,* November 1982, was devoted to the history of homosexuality in the Netherlands. It contains a number of pioneering articles on this subject, many dealing in particular with the events of 1730–32, by Boon, L. J.; Huussen, A. H. Jr.; Schenk, J. On the history of homosexual trials in Amsterdam throughout the eighteenth century, see van de Meer, Theo, *De Wesentlijke Sonde van Sodomie en Andere Vuyligheden. Sodomieten vervolgingen in Amsterdam, 1730–1811,* Amsterdam, 1984. For Leiden see Noordam, D. J., "Homosexualiteit en sodomie in Leiden, 1533–1811," *Leids Jaarboek* 75(1983). For Holland generally, see Boon, L. J., "De grote sodomietvervolging in het gewest Holland, 1730–31, *Holland* (June 1976):140–52. An important earlier contribution was de Vrijer, M. J. A., "De storm van her crimen nefandum in de jaren 1730–32," *Nederlandsch Archief voor Kerkgeschiedenis* 25/26(1933):193–238. On the Groningen trials see Tervaert, G. Cohen, *De grietman Rudolf de Mepsche. Historische-juridische beschouwingen over een reeks crimineele processen,* 's Gravenhage, 1921.

The two most widely known tracts against "sodomy" were:

Beels, L. *Sodoms zonde en straffe of strengwraakrecht over vervloekte boosheidt, en Loths vrouw verandert in een zoutpilaar.* Amsterdam, 1730.

Van Byler, H. C. *Helsche Boosheit of grouwelyke sonde van Sodomie.* Groningen. 1731.

THE PILE WORM

Carter, Alice Clare. "Amsterdam and the 'Onbekende Soort van Zee Worm' in 1730." *Jaarboek Amstelodamum* (1978):239–49.

LIST OF ILLUSTRATIONS

permission of Houghton Library, Harvard University

PHOTOGRAPHIC ACKNOWLEDGMENTS (other than
for museum photographs indicated in credit lines)

Jörg P. Anders, Berlin: 57, 188, 271
Dingjan, The Hague: 7, 93
John R. Freeman, London: 95, 127
Giraudon, Paris: 211, 212
Laboratoire et Studio Gerondial, Lille: 293
John Mills, Liverpool: 297
Ginny Papaioannou: 110, 125, 138, 147, 164, 165, 166, 167,
168, 243, 247, 263, 274, 282
Polyvisie, Hilversum: 37
Robert Slotover, London: 3
W. Smieder, Amsterdam: 148
J. Willemin, Paris: 205

INDEX

Underscored numbers indicate pages with illustrations

A NOTE ON THE TYPE

The text of this book was set in Percepta, a film version of Perpetua, designed by the British artist Eric Gill (1882–1940) and cut by The Monotype Corporation, London, in 1928–1930. In this contemporary typeface of original design, without any direct historical antecedents, the shapes of the roman letters derive from stonecutting, a form of lettering in which Gill was eminent. The italic is essentially an inclined roman. The general effect of the typeface in reading sizes is one of lightness and grace. The larger display sizes of the type are extremely elegant and form what is probably the most distinguished series of inscriptional letters cut in the present century.

Composed by Superior Type, Champaign, Illinois
Printed and bound by Halliday Lithographers, West Hanover, Massachusetts
Designed by Iris Weinstein and Julie Duquet